Advanced Cyber Security Techniques for Data, Blockchain, IoT, and Network Protection

Nirbhay Kumar Chaubey
Ganpat University, India

Neha Chaubey
Imperial College, London, UK

IGI Global
Publishing Tomorrow's Research Today

Published in the United States of America by
    IGI Global
    701 E. Chocolate Avenue
    Hershey PA, USA 17033
    Tel: 717-533-8845
    Fax: 717-533-8661
    E-mail: cust@igi-global.com
    Web site: https://www.igi-global.com

Library of Congress Cataloging-in-Publication Data

CIP PENDING

ISBN13: 9798369392256
Isbn13Softcover: 9798369392263
EISBN13: 9798369392270

Vice President of Editorial: Melissa Wagner
Managing Editor of Acquisitions: Mikaela Felty
Managing Editor of Book Development: Jocelynn Hessler
Production Manager: Mike Brehm
Cover Design: Phillip Shickler

British Cataloguing in Publication Data
A Cataloguing in Publication record for this book is available from the British Library.

All work contributed to this book is new, previously-unpublished material.
The views expressed in this book are those of the authors, but not necessarily of the publisher.

This book is affectionately dedicated to my father Shri Shyam Kishor Chaubey who is a lighthouse for us and my mother, the late Mrs. Subhraji Chaubey, who inspired me to live with purpose and meaning, always focus on giving back to the society, their love, courage, devotion have been the strength of my striving.

Nirbhay S. Chaubey

Ganpat University, Gujarat, India

This book is dedicated to my parents, Neelam Chaubey and Nirbhay Chaubey, both are role model for me, taught me to practice truth and honesty in life and inspired to be a good human being with values. My Sister Medha Chaubey and my brother Om Chaubey, both are very special to me for their constant support., thanks to my maternal grandfather Shri Hiramani Shukla and maternal grandmother Smt. Shubhadra Shukla, family members, teachers and friends who always encourage me in whatever I do.

Neha N. Chaubey

Imperial College, London, United Kingdom

Editorial Advisory Board

Table of Contents

Foreword xx

Preface xxi

Acknowledgment xxv

Chapter 1
A Comprehensive Review of Ontologies in Cybersecurity 1
    Vatsal Hasmukhbhai Shah, BVM Engineering College, India
    Rahil Maniar, BVM Engineering College, India

Chapter 2
Big Data Cyber Security Analytics 21
    Prerna Agrawal, GLS University, India
    Savita Gandhi, GLS University, India

Chapter 3
Blockchain in Cybersecurity 49
    Akhil John Mampilly, Lincoln University College, Malaysia
    Vijaya Kittu Manda, PBMEIT, India
    Chithirai Pon Selvan Muthu Perumal, Curtin University, Dubai, UAE

Chapter 4
Dynamic and Scalable Privacy-Preserving Group Data Sharing in Secure
Cloud Computing 89
    Astitva Bhardwaj, Sharda School of Engineering and Technology,
        Sharda University, India
    Akshita Sharma, Sharda School of Engineering and Technology, Sharda
        University, India
    Dharm Raj, Sharda School of Engineering & Technology, Sharda
        University, India
    Danish Ather, Amity University, Tashkent, Uzbekistan
    Anil Kumar Sagar, Sharda School of Engineering and Technology,
        Sharda University, India
    Vishal Jain, Sharda School of Engineering and Technology, Sharda
        University, India

Chapter 5

Cyber Security Techniques for 5G Networks 123

    Himadri Sekhar Das, Haldia Institute of Technology, India

    Sandipan Samanta, CGI, Bangalore, India

    Rajrupa Metia, Haldia Institute of Technology, India

    Debasish Samanta, IBM Kolkata, India

    Banibrata Bag, Haldia Institute of Technology, India

Chapter 6

Harnessing AI and Machine Learning for Effective Phishing Email Detection 147

    Ritesh Joshi, Prestige Institute of Engineering Management and
        Research, Indore, India

    Nirbhay Kumar Chaubey, A.M. Patel Institute of Computer Studies,
        Ganpat University, India

    Swati Patel, A.M. Patel Institute of Computer Studies, Ganpat
        University, India

    Md Danish Imtiaz, A.M. Patel Institute of Computer Studies, Ganpat
        University, India

    Ankit Kumar, A.M. Patel Institute of Computer Studies, Ganpat
        University, India

Chapter 7

Network Intrusion Detection System Using Machine Learning 173

    R. Gunasundari, Puducherry Technological University, India

    Ra Srinethe, Puducherry Technological University, India

    V. Thilagavathianu, Puducherry Technological University, India

Chapter 8

Secure Collaboration for Storing and Processing of Criminal Records Using
Blockchain Technology 205

    Hima Bindu, QIS College of Engineering and Technology, India

    Sanjana Muvvala, QIS College of Engineering and Technology, India

Chapter 9

The Role of Wireshark in Packet Inspection and Password Sniffing for
Network Security 225

    Manvi Mishra, SRMSCET&R Bareilly, India

    Md Shadab Hussain, SRMSCET&R Bareilly, India

    Nirbhay Chaubey, Ganpat University, India

    Prabhakar Gupta, SRMSCET, Bareilly, India

Chapter 10
The Silent Threat: Safeguarding Against PDF-Based Malware With
Intelligent Detection.. 245
    Ravi Kirtivadan Sheth, Rashtriya Raksha University, India
    Chandresh D. Parekha, Rashtriya Raksha University, India

Chapter 11
To Enhance Cyber Security for IoT 271
    Anubha Gauba, Department of Computer Science and Engineering, IKG
        Punjab Technical University, India
    Ravneet Preet Singh Bedi, IKG Punjab Technical University, India

Chapter 12
Unlocking the Power of Software-Defined Networking (SDN) in
Revolutionizing Network Management 309
    Manasa Kulkarni, Christ University, India
    Bhargavi Goswami, Queesnland University, Australia
    Joy Paulose, Christ University, India
    Lavanya Malakalapalli, IIT Dharwad, India

Chapter 13
Neptune Security: A Novel Approach Big Data Privacy Protection 337
    Vruddhi K Shah, L.J. University, India
    Jignesh Doshi, L.J. University, India

Chapter 14
Security Challenges in Internet of Things 355
    Purva Joshi, Institute for Communications and Navigations, Deutsches
        Zentrum für Luft- und Raumfahrt e.V. (DLR), Germany
    Seema Joshi, Gujarat Technological University, India

Chapter 15
An Implementation of Decentralized Secured Tweeting Platform: Security of
a Tweeting App 393
> *Sumathi Pawar, Information Science & Engineering, NMAMIT, Nitte,*
> *India*
> *K. Suma, Mangalore Institute of Technology and Management,*
> *Moodabidri, India*
> *Ankitha P., Information Science & Engineering, NMAMIT, Nitte, India*
> *Vandana B. S., Information Science & Engineering, NMAMIT, Nitte,*
> *India*
> *RajaLakshmi Samaga, Information Science & Engineering, NMAMIT,*
> *Nitte, India*

Chapter 16
Intrusion Detection in Networks Using Adversarial Networks and Weighted
Encoder Components 413
> *Nirbhay Kumar Chaubey, Ganpat University, India*
> *Ruby Dahiya, Galgotias University, India*
> *R. Venkateswaran, University of Technology and Applied Sciences,*
> *Oman*
> *Praveen R. V. S., LTIMindtree, India*
> *U. Hemavathi, Vel Tech Rangarajan Dr. Sagunthala R&D Institute of*
> *Science and Technology, India*
> *Sangeetha Subramaniam, Kongunadu College of Engineering and*
> *Technology, India*

Compilation of References 435

About the Contributors 483

Index 493

Detailed Table of Contents

Foreword xx

Preface xxi

Acknowledgment xxv

Chapter 1
A Comprehensive Review of Ontologies in Cybersecurity 1
Vatsal Hasmukhbhai Shah, BVM Engineering College, India
Rahil Maniar, BVM Engineering College, India

With the evolution of Semantic Web architecture and advancements in Generative AI, the demand for a universally accepted ontology in cybersecurity has significantly increased. This paper reviews five notable ontological frameworks: STIX, STUCCO, UCO, CTIM, and WAVED. It evaluates their strengths and limitations, providing a comparative analysis. The study offers recommendations for developing an optimal ontology, aimed at enhancing interoperability, security, and automation in cybersecurity systems, thereby addressing current gaps and promoting a more cohesive cybersecurity landscape.

Chapter 2
Big Data Cyber Security Analytics 21
Prerna Agrawal, GLS University, India
Savita Gandhi, GLS University, India

The prevalence of social media usage is rapidly escalating. In January 2024, India alone recorded a total of 462 million social media users. The rise in online users has led to a corresponding surge in cybersecurity frauds. Cybersecurity experts can utilize big data analytic tools to identify, prevent, and mitigate cyber assaults, as these technologies are capable of handling the enormous amounts of data collected from diverse sources. This chapter examines cybercrimes that can be identified using Big Data Analytics (BDA). The primary aim of this chapter is to offer readers a comprehensive understanding of how Big Data Analytics (BDA) is applied in the field of cybersecurity. It also aims to enlighten readers about current advancements in the application of BDA in cybersecurity and the challenges that are encountered in this domain.

Chapter 3

Blockchain in Cybersecurity 49

Akhil John Mampilly, Lincoln University College, Malaysia
Vijaya Kittu Manda, PBMEIT, India
Chithirai Pon Selvan Muthu Perumal, Curtin University, Dubai, UAE

Blockchain is a promising technology that can help organizations improve their cybersecurity. Blockchain has many inherent features that can help enhance data security, improve threat detection and response, strengthen authentication and authorization, and enhance cyber threat intelligence sharing. This is possible because of the innovative approach that Blockchain uses, such as immutable ledgers to store transactions, monitor assets, and build trust by providing access only to authorized participants. The chapter discusses cybersecurity best practices related to smart contracts, key management, network security, user education and awareness, incident reporting, privacy challenges, software updates, and decentralization. Key regulatory compliance aspects, such as GDPR and HIPPA, are discussed. The increasing interactions of Artificial Intelligence (AI), Machine Learning (ML), and the Internet of Things (IoT) with Blockchain can further provide improved cybersecurity services and hence form the discussion of the trends and potential future research section of this chapter.

Chapter 4
Dynamic and Scalable Privacy-Preserving Group Data Sharing in Secure
Cloud Computing 89

    Astitva Bhardwaj, Sharda School of Engineering and Technology,
       Sharda University, India
    Akshita Sharma, Sharda School of Engineering and Technology, Sharda
       University, India
    Dharm Raj, Sharda School of Engineering & Technology, Sharda
       University, India
    Danish Ather, Amity University, Tashkent, Uzbekistan
    Anil Kumar Sagar, Sharda School of Engineering and Technology,
       Sharda University, India
    Vishal Jain, Sharda School of Engineering and Technology, Sharda
       University, India

Cloud computing, a concept that is already extensively adopted and is expected to grow significantly, represents the information age of the future. The basic idea was created in the 1950s as big firms and organizations looked into remote data and application storage, despite utilizing modern terminology. The phrases Platform as a Service (PAAS), Infrastructure as a Service (IAAS), and Software as a Service (SAAS) lead in cloud computing in sharing of data and accessibility, it is economical, and it can bring a revolution in society. Therefore, this chapter explores some of the security problems relating to cloud computing witnessed in the past up to date in which a complete system for interchanging data securely is required. Further, the work outlined security issues inherent in the cloud environment, and a suitable mechanism for secure communication needs to be put in place. Finally, the chapter analyses the way that companies can gain additional market share through an understanding of their weaknesses and what the industry is currently doing, with the help of cloud computing.

Chapter 5

Cyber Security Techniques for 5G Networks 123

Himadri Sekhar Das, Haldia Institute of Technology, India
Sandipan Samanta, CGI, Bangalore, India
Rajrupa Metia, Haldia Institute of Technology, India
Debasish Samanta, IBM Kolkata, India
Banibrata Bag, Haldia Institute of Technology, India

The rapid deployment of 5G networks introduces new cybersecurity challenges due to their enhanced speed, low latency, and massive connectivity. To safeguard these networks, advanced techniques are essential, including network slicing for isolating threats, artificial intelligence and machine learning for real-time threat detection, and blockchain for securing transactions. Additionally, Zero Trust architectures ensure that every access request is authenticated, regardless of origin. These strategies, combined with robust encryption and anomaly detection mechanisms, are critical in addressing the diverse and evolving threats in the 5G ecosystem, ensuring secure and reliable communication for users and industries alike.

Chapter 6

Harnessing AI and Machine Learning for Effective Phishing Email Detection 147

Ritesh Joshi, Prestige Institute of Engineering Management and
*   Research, Indore, India*
Nirbhay Kumar Chaubey, A.M. Patel Institute of Computer Studies,
*   Ganpat University, India*
Swati Patel, A.M. Patel Institute of Computer Studies, Ganpat
*   University, India*
Md Danish Imtiaz, A.M. Patel Institute of Computer Studies, Ganpat
*   University, India*
Ankit Kumar, A.M. Patel Institute of Computer Studies, Ganpat
*   University, India*

Phishing attacks targeting email users pose a major cybersecurity threat, causing financial losses and data breaches. This research project aims to develop an advanced phishing detection tool using artificial intelligence (AI) to identify and mitigate email phishing attempts. At its core, the tool will feature a sophisticated AI model to analyze and classify emails as phishing or legitimate. The approach combines machine learning algorithms and natural language processing techniques to enhance detection accuracy. The proposed solution will be integrated into a web application, allowing users to input suspicious emails for real-time analysis. The AI model will examine various features of the email, including the content, sender information, and embedded links, to determine the likelihood of phishing. By leveraging supervised learning methods, our model will be trained on a diverse dataset comprising both phishing and legitimate emails, ensuring robust performance across different scenarios.

Chapter 7

Network Intrusion Detection System Using Machine Learning 173

   R. Gunasundari, Puducherry Technological University, India
   Ra Srinethe, Puducherry Technological University, India
   V. Thilagavathianu, Puducherry Technological University, India

Network intrusion detection systems help identify the type of attack a network faces. Cybersecurity professionals use this information to take the necessary steps to protect valuable information that otherwise could have been compromised. Traditional network intrusion detection systems are characterized by signature-based detection. This often leaves networks vulnerable to threats. The proposed idea uses a machine learning-based model that helps to promptly identify threats thereby fortifying security. The existing Machine-learning based models suffer from increased number of false alarms and the inability to handle huge data due to a lack of feature selection. This idea proposes using particle swarm optimization techniques for feature selection along with data balancing to decrease the false alarms and improve the model's overall performance. Further, hyper tuning and assembling the best-performing models have been done to improve the robustness of the model. This has been tested by evaluating the performance of the model in the presence of random noise and through stability score.

Chapter 8

Secure Collaboration for Storing and Processing of Criminal Records Using
Blockchain Technology 205

   Hima Bindu, QIS College of Engineering and Technology, India
   Sanjana Muvvala, QIS College of Engineering and Technology, India

Blockchain technology has sparked transformative changes across industries, offering secure ledgers for shared, tamper-proof transaction records. Its decentralization prevents data manipulation by requiring consensus from multiple participants. Applications span medicine, education, fintech, accounting, banking, and government, addressing issues like fraud, corruption, and identity theft. Introducing a new application, this chapter explores using blockchain for securely storing criminal records in police stations. This approach ensures long-term data preservation, reduces storage space, and maintains the integrity of critical evidence. By enabling secure collaboration between police and judiciary, it enhances evidence collection and strengthens governance, fostering a trustworthy law enforcement system.

Chapter 9
The Role of Wireshark in Packet Inspection and Password Sniffing for
Network Security 225

Manvi Mishra, SRMSCET&R Bareilly, India
Md Shadab Hussain, SRMSCET&R Bareilly, India
Nirbhay Chaubey, Ganpat University, India
Prabhakar Gupta, SRMSCET, Bareilly, India

In today's interconnected digital landscape, network integrity, efficiency, and security are paramount for business, institutional, and personal interactions. This chapter focuses on delving into the functionalities of Wireshark, offering an extensive exploration of packet inspection methodologies and effective strategies to mitigate the risks associated with password sniffing attacks. It involves capturing and analyzing network traffic, examining key protocols like HTTP, DNS, SMTP, and more, and demonstrating data transmission across the network Through practical demonstrations readers are guided through the process of deploying Wireshark to capture and analyze network packets in real-time. Focused on thwarting password sniffing—a common tactic used by adversaries to intercept and decrypt sensitive data, including login credentials. Wireshark enables readers to identify and counter common password-sniffing techniques. The chapter also covers proactive steps like adopting secure protocols, encryption algorithms, and best password management practices.

Chapter 10
The Silent Threat: Safeguarding Against PDF-Based Malware With
Intelligent Detection... 245

Ravi Kirtivadan Sheth, Rashtriya Raksha University, India
Chandresh D. Parekha, Rashtriya Raksha University, India

Given the fact that today's world is inundated with PDF files in personals and business relationships, the danger of bad-intentioned activity within these what look-like innocent documents has risen drastically. A threat that has been significant to internet security for the past years is the known PDF malware. PDF malware presents a big problem because it can hide within the complicated makeup of PDF files. These files can contain many types of content, including text, images, text, and hidden objects. These complications give hackers more opportunities to hide their malicious code that bypasses traditional antivirus software. The objective of this chapter was to develop a classification-based machine learning algorithm for detecting PDF malware and it get succeeded with an impressive overall accuracy of 99.3% by using a random forest classifier This important achievement and the ability of machine learning algorithms to detect and neutralize threat-based PDFs is also highlighted in this chapter.

Chapter 11

To Enhance Cyber Security for IoT 271

Anubha Gauba, Department of Computer Science and Engineering, IKG
Punjab Technical University, India
Ravneet Preet Singh Bedi, IKG Punjab Technical University, India

This is a fascinating and important subject that is becoming increasingly relevant in today's digital world. The rapid proliferation of IoT devices has revolutionizing several impacts of our daily lives. From smart homes and wearable systems to industrial sensors and autonomous vehicles, IoT technology has ushered in a latest era of connectivity and convenience. Moreover, with this connectivity comes an increased cyber security risk. This paper outlines a strategic approach to enhance cyber security for IoT deployments, ensuring the protection of data, devices, and networks.

Chapter 12

Unlocking the Power of Software-Defined Networking (SDN) in
Revolutionizing Network Management 309

Manasa Kulkarni, Christ University, India
Bhargavi Goswami, Queesnland University, Australia
Joy Paulose, Christ University, India
Lavanya Malakalapalli, IIT Dharwad, India

This chapter delves into the transformative impact of SDN on modern network management. By decoupling the control and data planes and centralizing network intelligence, SDN enables unprecedented flexibility, programmability, and efficiency in managing network infrastructures. The chapter examines various use cases, including data center network management, WAN optimization, and network security. These use cases demonstrate SDN's ability to dynamically allocate resources, optimize traffic flows, enforce security policies, and automate network provisioning. Despite challenges related to scalability, reliability, and security, SDN's benefits in providing a comprehensive, real-time view of the network, enabling adaptive adjustments, and fostering innovation are emphasized. Overall, this chapter underscores SDN's role in revolutionizing network management, paving the way for more agile, efficient, and secure networks that can meet the ever-evolving demands of today's digital landscape.

Chapter 13
Neptune Security: A Novel Approach Big Data Privacy Protection 337
Vruddhi K Shah, L.J. University, India
Jignesh Doshi, L.J. University, India

With the inclusion of various data such as structure, semi-structure and unstructured data, protecting one's online privacy is crucial in the fast-paced technological age we live in, and Neptune Security stands out as a major player in this space. The analysis emphasizes the crucial part that Neptune Security plays in managing rising privacy issues, especially in India's changing digital landscape. The impact of big data on privacy is an essential aspect of this study. Big data has completely transformed how data is analysed and decisions are made. It can be recognized by its immense scale and complexity. However, privacy is naturally challenged by the amount of data. In this scenario, Neptune Security plays a crucial role by using cutting-edge encryption techniques and adaptive access controls to quickly neutralize such threats. This study explores the complex relationship between privacy and big data to offer an in-depth analysis of the changing risks associated with the digital era.

Chapter 14
Security Challenges in Internet of Things 355
Purva Joshi, Institute for Communications and Navigations, Deutsches Zentrum für Luft- und Raumfahrt e.V. (DLR), Germany
Seema Joshi, Gujarat Technological University, India

Industrial and domestic appliances are IoT-connected. Sensors, phones, and security are examples. The benefits of device communication are various. Monitor IoT security risks. Simple methods and technology may secure devices and detect attackers. Security challenges in IoT include authentication and authorization, encryption, firmware and software vulnerabilities, insecure connections, and device patching and updates. Threats from IoT vulnerabilities Worse passwords allow IoT device theft. Used IoT devices can join larger networks. Low-encryption IoT devices may leak and misuse consumer data. IoT user mistrust, identity theft, and financial fraud may arise. Weak IoT devices can be hijacked by malicious networks to launch massive DDoS attacks on services and infrastructure. Damage, disruption, and death can result from industrial and critical infrastructure IoT devices. Hackers could break into IoT networks and access more systems and data. The chapter explains IoT security risks. Examine case studies last. Technology and industry cannot apply all attack avoidance measures.

Chapter 15

An Implementation of Decentralized Secured Tweeting Platform: Security of
a Tweeting App 393

> Sumathi Pawar, Information Science & Engineering, NMAMIT, Nitte,
> India
>
> K. Suma, Mangalore Institute of Technology and Management,
> Moodabidri, India
>
> Ankitha P., Information Science & Engineering, NMAMIT, Nitte, India
>
> Vandana B. S., Information Science & Engineering, NMAMIT, Nitte,
> India
>
> RajaLakshmi Samaga, Information Science & Engineering, NMAMIT,
> Nitte, India

A decentralized secured tweeting platform utilizes blockchain technology to distribute control and data across a network of participants, challenging the centralized model. It provides enhanced privacy, reduced content manipulation, and resistance to centralized control of user content. This system represents a decentralized tweeting social media platform with the objective of furnishing users with a communication environment that's both secure and characterized by transparency. Through the integration of smart contracts, users can transact directly and securely without the need for intermediaries. ReactJS empowers a responsive and user-friendly interface, fostering real-time interaction among users to create a decentralized social media platform, enhancing security and transparency to unprecedented levels. Blockchain technology confirms that data is securely stored, immutable and transparent. The proposed system enables users to post tweets, follow other users, like and comment on posts and engage in real-time messaging. This article also presents the implementation of the system.

Chapter 16

Intrusion Detection in Networks Using Adversarial Networks and Weighted
Encoder Components 413

Nirbhay Kumar Chaubey, Ganpat University, India
Ruby Dahiya, Galgotias University, India
R. Venkateswaran, University of Technology and Applied Sciences,
Oman
Praveen R. V. S., LTIMindtree, India
U. Hemavathi, Vel Tech Rangarajan Dr. Sagunthala R&D Institute of
Science and Technology, India
Sangeetha Subramaniam, Kongunadu College of Engineering and
Technology, India

This study introduces an innovative approach to network intrusion detection by harnessing the capabilities of adversarial networks and underscoring the importance of encoder components. Conventional intrusion detection systems frequently grapple with the real-time identification of intricate and evolving threats, rendering them susceptible to both false positives and negatives. Our proposed method aims to confront these inherent challenges. The proposed strategy, referred to as ID-ANWE, entails the integration of adversarial networks into the system. This augmentation enhances the system's ability to differentiate between typical network behavior and irregular, potentially malicious activities. Through a training process, these adversarial networks become proficient in distinguishing between legitimate network traffic and potential intrusion attempts, contributing to the establishment of a dynamic and adaptable security framework.

Compilation of References 435

About the Contributors 483

Index 493

Foreword

I am delighted to write the Foreword for this significant new book - "Advanced Cyber Security Techniques for Data, Blockchain, IoT, and Network Protection", edited by Professor (Dr.) Nirbhay Kumar Chaubey and Ms. Neha Chaubey. This comprehensive 16-chapter volume navigates the intersection of traditional and quantum cryptography methods, offering expert perspectives on cybersecurity's most pressing concerns and opportunities in cyber defense, showcasing cutting-edge techniques for securing complex systems, blockchain, IoT, and network infrastructures. Congratulations to the editors and authors on this remarkable achievement, poised to enlighten researchers, practitioners, and students seeking advanced cybersecurity knowledge. This book is a collaborative achievement, leveraging the expertise of accomplished authors, editors, reviewers, and advisory board members, renowned for their academic excellence in computer science, cybersecurity, networking, and communication engineering. The outcome is a definitive research handbook.

I highly recommend this book as an indispensable resource for academics, researchers, and university students, as well as business professionals and industry experts seeking to grasp the intricacies of Advanced Cyber Security Techniques.

Akshai Aggarwal
Gujarat Technological University (GTU), India

Preface

The digital revolution, driven by IoT, blockchain, and cyber-physical systems, has transformed global interactions and commerce. However, this increased connectivity also heightens cybersecurity vulnerabilities, necessitating innovative and resilient security measures to combat the rising tide of cyber threats, including data breaches, APTs, and emerging quantum-based attacks.

The limitations of classical cryptography, which once served as the backbone of secure communications, are becoming apparent. As quantum computing advances and surpasses the computational capabilities of today's systems, the traditional cryptographic methods are at risk of obsolescence. The vulnerabilities that arise from the increasing power of computers and the imminent breakthroughs in quantum computing necessitate a paradigm shift in the approach to securing digital infrastructures. The emergence of quantum cryptography offers an exciting and promising avenue for bolstering cybersecurity. Its inherent ability to provide theoretically unbreakable encryption makes it a game-changer for sectors that rely on secure data transmission and protection.

In this book, *Advanced Cyber Security Techniques for Data, Blockchain, IoT, and Network Protection*, we explore the current and future landscape of cybersecurity, focusing on the convergence of traditional security methods and quantum cryptography. The contributions in this volume bring together the expertise of researchers, practitioners, and thought leaders in the fields of cybersecurity, cryptography, blockchain, IoT, and network protection. By presenting a range of case studies, theoretical insights, and practical applications, this book serves as a comprehensive resource for understanding the current challenges and opportunities in cyber defense.

Chapter 1: This chapter delves into the evolving landscape of cybersecurity ontologies amidst advancements in the Semantic Web and Generative AI. It provides a comprehensive review of five leading ontological frameworks—STIX, STUCCO, UCO, CTIM, and WAVED—offering a detailed comparative analysis of their strengths and limitations. The study suggests a roadmap for developing an optimal, universally accepted ontology to improve interoperability, security, and automation across cybersecurity systems, addressing critical gaps in the current infrastructure.

Chapter 2: With the rise of social media users globally, cybersecurity threats have intensified. This chapter explores how Big Data Analytics (BDA) tools can be leveraged to detect and mitigate cybercrimes. It focuses on the rapid expansion of social media usage and the corresponding increase in fraud, offering readers insight into current advancements and challenges in applying BDA to protect cyberspace from malicious activities, particularly on platforms with massive data flows

Chapter 3: Blockchain is a game-changer for cybersecurity, with its immutable ledger and decentralized nature. This chapter explores the role of blockchain in enhancing cybersecurity practices, including threat detection, authentication, and authorization. It also covers best practices for smart contracts, key management, user awareness, and regulatory compliance, while exploring future trends and research opportunities through the intersection of AI, ML, IoT, and blockchain technologies.

Chapter 4: As cloud computing continues to expand, so do its associated security challenges. This chapter examines past and present security vulnerabilities in cloud systems, exploring mechanisms for secure communication and data interchange. It offers valuable insights into how businesses can leverage cloud computing securely to gain a competitive edge, emphasizing the importance of understanding cloud vulnerabilities and developing robust strategies to mitigate risks.

Chapter 5: 5G networks bring speed, low latency, and connectivity improvements, but also introduce new cybersecurity challenges. This chapter discusses advanced techniques like network slicing, AI-driven threat detection, and blockchain for safeguarding 5G networks. It also addresses the importance of Zero Trust architectures, encryption, and anomaly detection to mitigate the diverse and evolving threats in 5G environments.

Chapter 6: Phishing attacks continue to pose significant threats to organizations and individuals. This chapter presents an AI-based phishing detection tool designed to analyze and classify emails, distinguishing between legitimate and malicious content. By combining machine learning algorithms with natural language processing, the chapter highlights how advanced AI models can improve phishing detection accuracy and provide real-time solutions for securing email communications.

Chapter 7: Traditional network intrusion detection systems often fall short in handling large-scale data and minimizing false alarms. This chapter introduces a machine learning-based model combined with particle swarm optimization for enhanced feature selection. It highlights how hyper-tuning and assembling the best-performing models can improve the robustness and efficiency of intrusion detection, offering new solutions for fortifying network security in high-risk environments.

Chapter 8: Blockchain's potential extends beyond finance into critical sectors like law enforcement. This chapter explores the use of blockchain to securely store and share criminal records, ensuring the integrity and immutability of sensitive data. By enabling transparent collaboration between police and judicial systems, blockchain can enhance governance and trust in the legal system while addressing storage challenges and ensuring long-term data preservation.

Chapter 9: Password sniffing remains a significant threat in today's digital landscape. This chapter focuses on using Wireshark for real-time network packet analysis, guiding readers through capturing and inspecting traffic to mitigate password-sniffing attacks. The chapter emphasizes practical steps for employing secure protocols, encryption algorithms, and best practices to safeguard sensitive data and prevent unauthorized access.

Chapter 10: PDF files are a common vector for cyberattacks due to their complex structure. This chapter presents a machine learning-based classification model for detecting malware hidden within PDF files, achieving an impressive accuracy rate of 99.3%. The chapter demonstrates how such advanced models can enhance malware detection capabilities, helping organizations and individuals safeguard against malicious PDF threats.

Chapter 11: As IoT devices proliferate in homes, industries, and critical infrastructure, the associated cybersecurity risks have escalated. This chapter outlines strategies for securing IoT deployments, addressing issues like authentication, encryption, firmware vulnerabilities, and data protection. Through case studies, the chapter highlights the importance of securing IoT systems to prevent data leaks, identity theft, and large-scale cyberattacks.

Chapter 12: Software-Defined Networking (SDN) transforms network management by centralizing control and enabling dynamic resource allocation. This chapter explores SDN's role in improving network security, WAN optimization, and data center management. Despite its challenges, SDN's ability to adaptively enforce security policies and automate provisioning is critical for building secure, efficient, and innovative network infrastructures.

Chapter 13: Big Data's scale and complexity have introduced significant privacy concerns. This chapter examines Neptune Security's approach to managing privacy risks, particularly in India's evolving digital landscape. The chapter discusses the interplay between big data and privacy, emphasizing the need for cutting-edge encryption and access control techniques to protect sensitive information in an increasingly interconnected world.

Chapter 14: IoT security vulnerabilities pose risks to both consumer and industrial systems. This chapter explores the threats posed by weak authentication, encryption, and firmware in IoT devices. It highlights the need for robust security strategies to prevent data leaks, financial fraud, and DDoS attacks, offering case studies that demonstrate the real-world impact of compromised IoT systems.

Chapter 15: Blockchain technology is reshaping social media platforms by decentralizing control and enhancing user privacy. This chapter introduces a decentralized tweeting platform powered by blockchain, allowing users to securely post, interact, and communicate without relying on centralized authorities. By leveraging smart contracts and secure data storage, this platform promises unprecedented levels of transparency and user autonomy.

Chapter 16: Traditional intrusion detection systems struggle with evolving cyber threats. This chapter proposes the use of adversarial networks and encoder components to enhance intrusion detection capabilities. The innovative ID-ANWE system trains adversarial networks to distinguish between normal and malicious network traffic, providing a more dynamic and adaptable security framework for detecting sophisticated cyberattacks.

The book also highlights cutting-edge cybersecurity techniques designed to secure complex systems, including 5G networks, cloud computing environments, large-scale storage systems, and IoT devices. Moreover, it explores the role of emerging technologies like blockchain and distributed ledger technology (DLT) in enhancing data security, alongside examining the possibilities of quantum cryptography as a defense against the growing threats posed by quantum computing.

We believe that this book will offer readers an in-depth view of the crucial topics that define the future of cybersecurity. Whether you are an academic, a cybersecurity professional, a researcher, or a policymaker, the insights contained herein will equip you with the knowledge to address pressing issues and capitalize on emerging opportunities in this rapidly evolving field.

Our sincere gratitude goes to the contributors whose expertise and dedication have made this book possible. It is our hope that *Advanced Cyber Security Techniques for Data, Blockchain, IoT, and Network Protection* will inspire further research and innovation, helping to create a safer, more secure digital future for all.

Nirbhay S. Chaubey
Ganpat University, Gujarat, India

Neha N. Chaubey
Imperial College, London, United Kingdom

Acknowledgment

The editors would like to express their gratitude to everyone involved in this project, especially the authors. Without their contributions and support, this book would not have come to fruition. We extend our sincere thanks to each author for their valuable input. We also wish to acknowledge the significant contributions of the reviewers and editorial board members, whose insights helped improve the quality, coherence, and presentation of the chapters. Additionally, we greatly appreciate the authors who took on the extra responsibility of serving as referees.

We would like to express our sincere gratitude to Dr. Savita Gandhi, Dean of Computer Science at GLS University, Ahmedabad, India, for her encouragement and support in writing this book. Her ongoing assistance and excellent guidance have been our greatest motivation in shaping this work. We are also deeply appreciative of Dr. Akshai Aggarwal, former Vice Chancellor of Gujarat Technological University (GTU), Ahmedabad, India, for the invaluable insights and guidance he provided throughout the execution of this book project. Additionally, we want to acknowledge the support and patience of our family members, who have been instrumental throughout the entire process of this book project.

The editors would like to express their heartfelt gratitude to IGI Global, the publishers, who have continuously supported and guided us throughout the entire process of publishing our book.

Chapter 1
A Comprehensive Review of Ontologies in Cybersecurity

Vatsal Hasmukhbhai Shah

BVM Engineering College, India

Rahil Maniar
https://orcid.org/0009-0000-7321-9415
BVM Engineering College, India

ABSTRACT

With the evolution of Semantic Web architecture and advancements in Generative AI, the demand for a universally accepted ontology in cybersecurity has significantly increased. This paper reviews five notable ontological frameworks: STIX, STUCCO, UCO, CTIM, and WAVED. It evaluates their strengths and limitations, providing a comparative analysis. The study offers recommendations for developing an optimal ontology, aimed at enhancing interoperability, security, and automation in cybersecurity systems, thereby addressing current gaps and promoting a more cohesive cybersecurity landscape.

1. INTRODUCTION

The domain of cybersecurity has been in a long-standing feud regarding the development of a unified ontology. Several Ontologies have been proposed as a general solution to this problem but so far none of them have reached a collective consensus as being accepted the universal, definitive ontology. The acceptance of a universal ontology would benefit the practitioners of cybersecurity and would also

DOI: 10.4018/979-8-3693-9225-6.ch001

significantly decrease the vulnerability of upcoming systems to various malicious threats.

To illustrate, given below is a list of a few prominent cybersecurity ontologies.
STIX (Structured Threat Information Expression)
CybOX (Cyber Observable eXpression)
MAEC (Malware Attribute Enumeration and Characterization)
CAPEC (Common Attack Pattern Enumeration and Classification)
CWE (Common Weakness Enumeration)
ATT&CK (Adversarial Tactics, Techniques, and Common Knowledge)
OpenIOC (Open Indicators of Compromise)
VERIS (Vocabulary for Event Recording and Incident Sharing)
MISP (Malware Information Sharing Platform & Threat Sharing)
CIM (Common Information Model)
MITRE CAR (Cyber Analytics Repository)
MAR (Malware Analysis Repository)

Collecting information from all of these sources and integrating them with existing systems after filtering, eliminating redundancy, preprocessing and amending would hamper the organizations intending to utilize them effectively. Besides, in the foreseeable future, efficiency and use of automated systems is expected to rise significantly and with the current trend of Gen AI, fully automated AI based systems could propel the domain further. In this paper, five distinctive approaches proposing their ontologies have been examined and various insights regarding their approximate utility and how well they fare in the current scenario have been provided. The structure of this paper is as follows. Section 2 would briefly describe the methodology we opted for, while section 3 contains the examination of relevant ontologies in each sub section. Each sub section contains two further sub sections, representing their merits and demerits, respectively. Section 4 contains the conclusion and scope for future work. The paper has been written with an emphasis towards the work done in order to develop universal ontological approaches and their thorough summarization, in order to aid researches working on the domain. The conclusion and future work section provides further insights on the same.

2. METHODOLOGY

A thorough analysis of every paper in which the original ontology was published has been conducted. A brief description of each ontological framework along with added ontology architecture diagrams, directly from the source, has been provided for enhanced readability. The source paper and existing review papers have been examined to extract the merits and demerits, primarily aiding and impeding the ontology respectively. A concise representation table entails the section reviewing the last ontology, containing the merits and demerits for each ontology.

3. EXAMINATION OF ONTOLOGIES

3.1 Ontology for Vulnerability Management (OVM)

The first ontology we examine is the ontology for vulnerability management (OVM), published by Wang & Guo (2009). It contains all existing vulnerabilities in NVD (Booth et al., 2013). Issues like reasoning about vulnerabilities, vulnerability characterization and their impact analysis are primarily handled by it. It is constructed by following the DL knowledge engineering methodology. Design criterions proposed by Fenz et al. (2008) namely ontology clarity, coherence, extendibility, minimal encoding bias and minimal ontological commitment are followed. It is built on the result of CVE (Common Vulnerabilities and Exposures) and its related protocols and standards like CWE(Common Weakness Enumeration), CPE(Common Platform Enumeration), and CAPEC(Common Attack Pattern Enumeration and Classification). Essential vulnerability characterization expressions are expressed as high-level concepts of OVM architecture. It contains twelve top level concepts: Vulnerability, Introduction Phase, Active Location, IT Product, IT Vendor, Product Category, Attack, Attack Intent, Attack Method, Attacker, Consequence, and Countermeasure. Each of these concepts contains a subsystem hierarchy containing different sub classes and key concepts. OVM also provides utilities and a centralized repository that can be used for sharing and communication between all the participants in system security.

Figure 1. The conceptual model of the vulnerability ontology

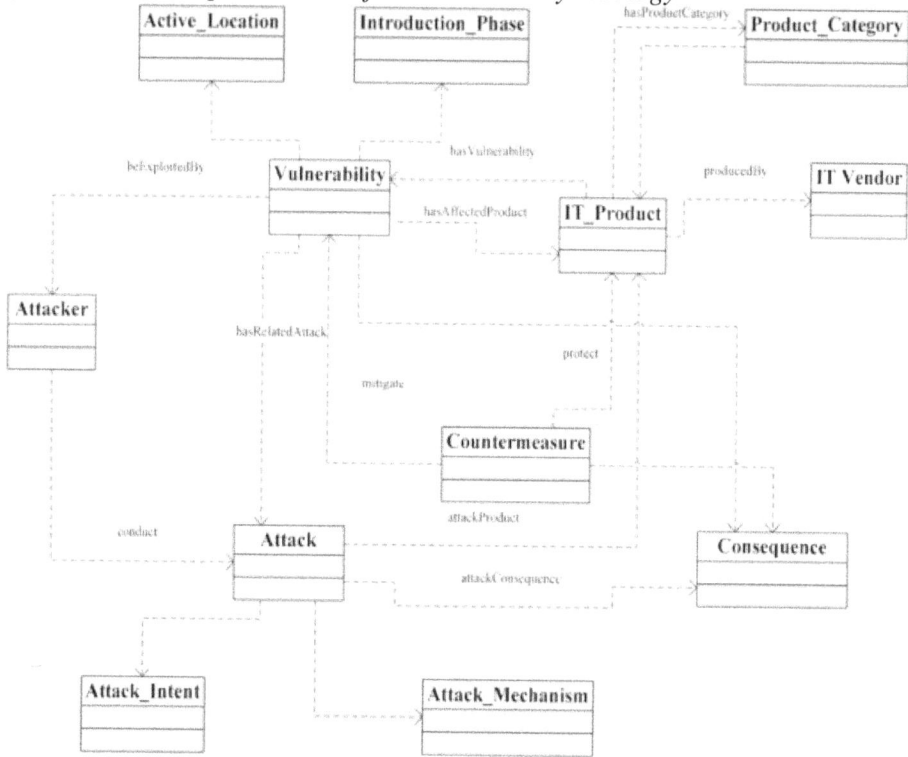

(Wang & Guo, 2009)

It supports limited automation and querying. It is one of the first ontologies published on the vulnerability domain, and was published under Information Security Automation Program (ISAP). Overall, it can be classified as a domain specific ontology.

3.1.1 Merits of OVM

- High interoperability and better exchange between parties
- Well-structured architecture
- Easy incorporation in existing concepts
- Enhanced automation

3.1.2 Demerits of OVM

- Limited reasoning and querying
- Difficult incorporation of nonexistent concepts

- Limited scope for General purpose
- Higher complexity (Wang & Cui, 2019)

3.2 Structured Threat Information Expression (STIX)

The second ontological approach analyzed is the STIX standard. Although not an ontology by textbook definition, STIX, despite resembling a language or a standard, follows a systematic approach and represents data in a structural manner. Thus, for the scope of this paper, it has been treated as an ontology. It is crucial to note that throughout this paper, when STIX is referred, it is a reference to the ontology published in the paper by Barnum (2012) and the one under MITRE corporation. STIX stands out from the rest as it focuses more on an approach that being community driven rather than establishing a rigid structure in which new information has to be incorporated. It focuses more on flexibility, expressivity, extensibility, automatability and readability. It provides a common mechanism and unifying architecture for cyber threat information. It consists of a core set of required guiding principles namely Expressivity, Integrability, Flexibility, Extensibility, Automatability, Readability and Architecture. The STIX structure consists of Observables, Indicators, Incidents, Tactics Techniques and Procedures (TTPs), Campaigns, Threat Actors, Exploit Targets, and Course of Action (COA). Due to its flexible approach, it boasts more use cases than other ontologies, as well as a prolonged life. It is most commonly used with Trusted Automated eXchange of Intelligence Information (TAXII). Even though both of them are entirely independent, they produce the best results when working in coalition.

Figure 2. Structured threat information expression (STIX) architecture v0.3

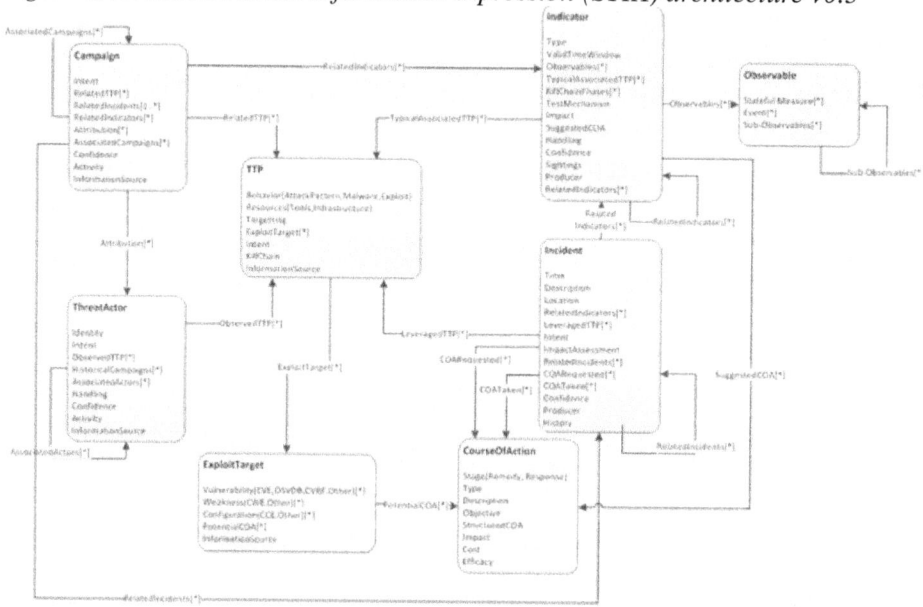

(Barnum, 2012)

Figure 3. STIX key construct and key inter-relationships

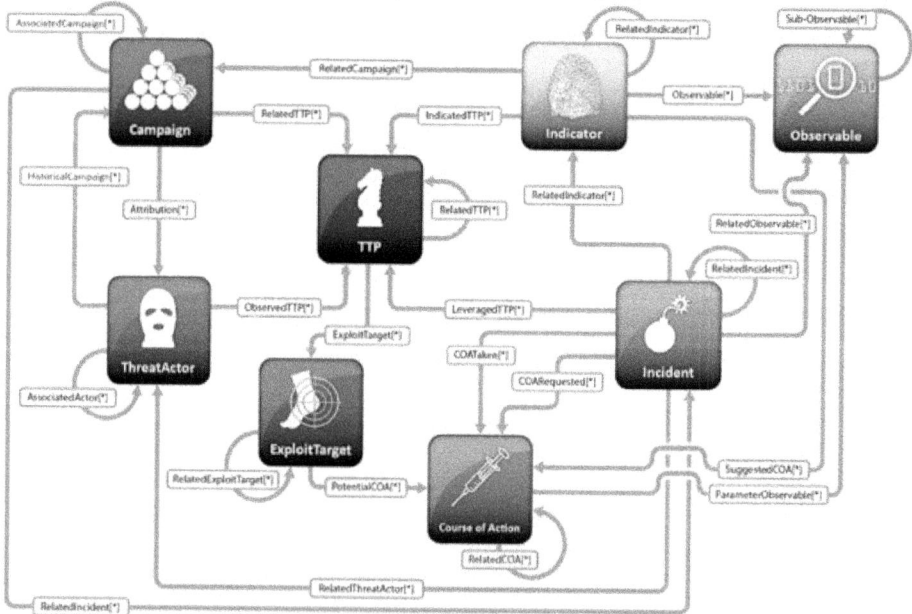

(STIX project https://stixproject.github.io/about/)

3.2.1 Merits of STIX

- Flexibility and extensibility
- Automatability
- Partial implementation
- Varied use cases

3.2.2 Demerits of STIX

- Complexity and computing overhead
- Interoperability and integration issues
- Anonymity and privacy concerns

3.3 Security Toolbox: Attacks and Countermeasures Ontology (STAC)

The third ontology examined is the STAC ontology developed by Gyrard et al. (2013) in proceedings of the 22nd International conference on the World Wide Web. With an intention to make an ontology for non-security experts, to help them design secure applications and be aware of the security concepts and risks in several domains, STAC has incorporated the concepts of Application, Requirement, Domain, Attack, Countermeasures, Feature, SecurityProperty, and the OSI model. The relationship between these concepts along with their structure are well defined in STAC. Besides these primary concepts, it also contains sub concepts, methods and properties. It is represented in the OWL (Web Ontology Language) framework. Its UI utilizes the following technologies: Java, REST Web Services (Jersey), Google Application Engine (GAE), Jena framework, SPARSQL language, HTML5, CSS3, Javascript and AJAX. STAC supports use cases such as domain specific querying for attack and countermeasures, additional information retrieval such as merits, drawbacks and security properties satisfied by countermeasures and searching for attacks and countermeasures for a specific OSI model layer.

Figure 4. Top level part of the STAC ontology

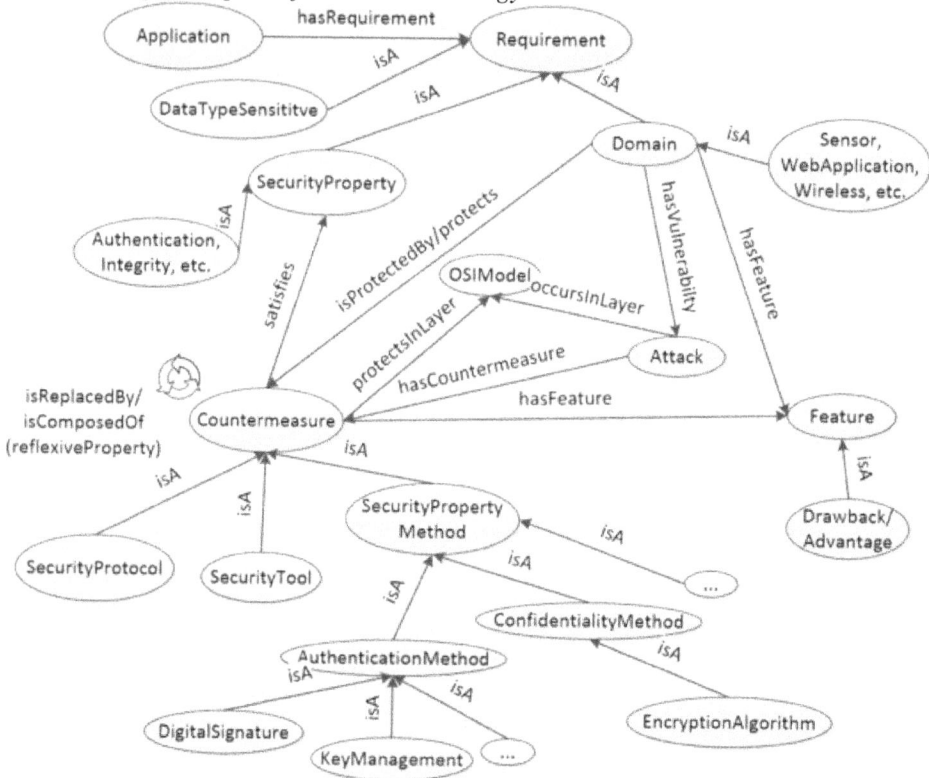

(Gyrard et al., 2013)

It incorporates information from various sources. STAC is constructed in a way that it is difficult to be amended by a third party, which makes it slightly unsuitable for instantly adding information about novel cybersecurity concepts, attacks and countermeasures. It has the specific purpose of aiding novice software developers develop secure software in a more robust and reliable manner.

3.3.1 Merits of STAC

- Highly interoperable outside domain
- Open-source framework utilization
- Support for domain specific retrieval

3.3.2 Demerits of STAC

- Difficult ad hoc updating process

- Specific scope
- Limited use case for domain intensive tasks
- Complex implementation (Gong & Tian, 2020)

3.4 Situation and Threat Understanding by Correlating Contextual Observations (STUCCO) Ontology

The fourth ontology examined is the STUCCO ontology (Iannacone et al., 2015). Developed by researchers at the National Laboratory and Standford University, the ontology has held up quite well throughout the years and is generally well revered among cybersecurity professionals. This ontology was made with a primary focus to assert interoperability of humans as well as automated systems. A relatively concise ontology which aptly classifies the key concepts of cybersecurity and defines their relationship with other related concepts. It uses JSON Schema to define the ontology, and querying is done using the GraphSON format. This conscious choice of departing from the ubiquitous frameworks (RDF or OWL) and using JSON has its own benefits and tradeoffs. It does suffer problems regarding ambiguously defined or incorrectly assigned terminology in existing literature. It also lacks potentially insightful information from unstructured data sources owing to its inherent limitation. On the contrary, STUCCO is highly interpretable for humans, making it easy to work with. Due to its more general nature, Lie et al. classifies it as a Unified Security Ontology. Overall, STUCCO is made more like a Wikipedia page that needs to be updated or manipulated time and time again, rather than a panacea to the cybersecurity world. This can be appropriately assessed seeing the number of Ontologies that chose to incorporate STUCCO as a data source. Most Ontologies thereafter were, in part, influenced by it.

Figure 5. Entities and relations in STUCCO ontology

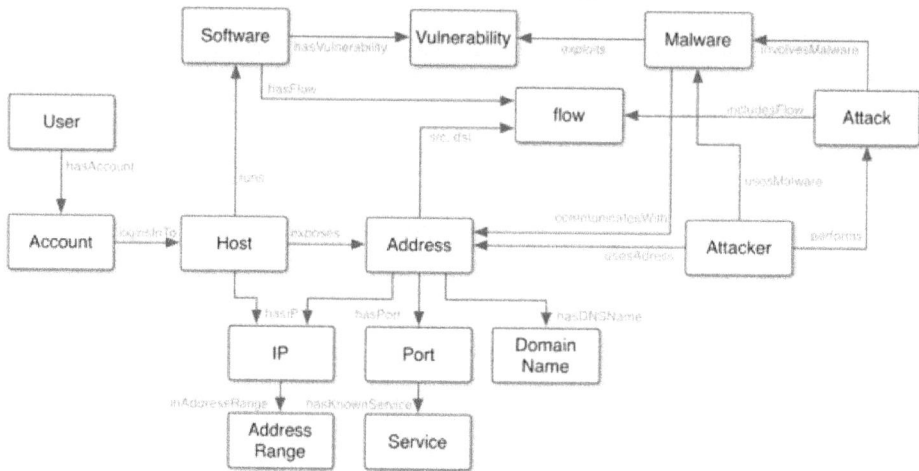

(Iannacone et al., 2015)

3.4.1 Merits of STUCCO

- High human interpretability
- Easy validation and schema definition
- Incorporation of metadata for inferences

3.4.2 Demerits of STUCCO

- Inability to use OWL-DL
- Lack of sources
- Limited use cases
- Inability to incorporate unstructured, potentially useful data

3.5 Unified Cybersecurity Ontology (UCO)

The fifth ontology that assessed is one developed by researchers at the University of Maryland (Syed et al., 2016), known as Unified Cybersecurity Ontology or UCO, concisely. This ontology tries to incorporate information from various sources of structured as well as unstructured data and attempts to design a general-purpose ontology as an extension to Intrusion Detection System Ontology (IDS) (Pinkston et al., 2003). It supports inferences, reasoning and specialized knowledge capturing. The framework for representation is OWL. It has a collection of classes which may or may not have sub-classes and their relationship with other classes. UCO is diverse and can support a variety of use cases as showcased in its research paper, can be mapped to general world ontologies and can be extended to add new information.

Figure 6. Mappings between UCO and general world ontologies in Linked Open Data Cloud

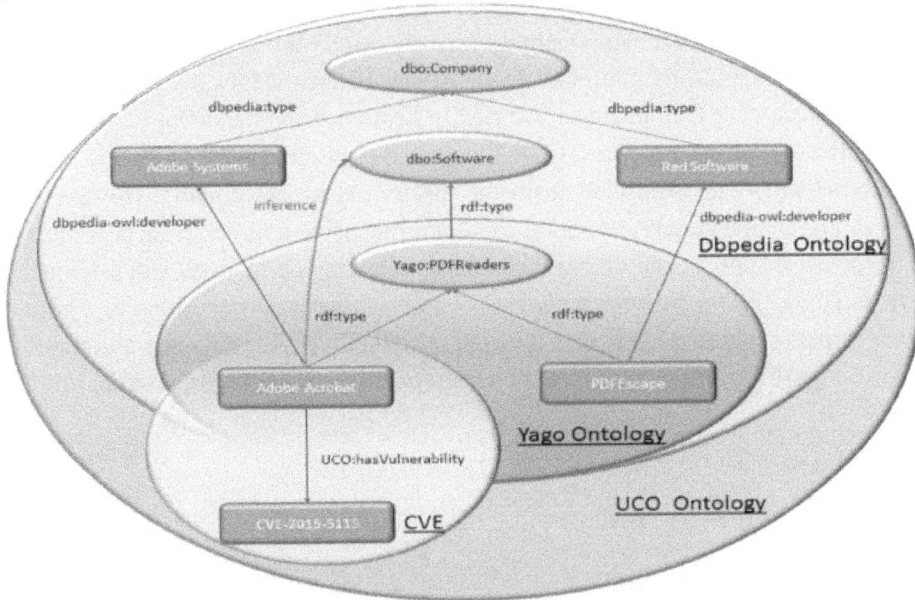

(Syed et al., 2016)

3.5.1 Merits of UCO

- Use of a semantic framework (OWL) instead of a syntactic one(XML).
- Supports reasoning/querying
- Extendable
- Vast/general scope

3.5.2 Demerits of UCO

- Limited use cases
- Difficult to integrate new concepts
- Inconvenient to implement partially
- Reliance on manual work

3.6 Cyber-Threat Intelligence Model (CTIM)

The penultimate ontology evaluated is CTIM, developed by Mavroeidis and Bromander (2017) - researchers at the University of Oslo, Norway. The primary objective of CTIM is to deal with cyber threats, and better equip organizations to handle their detection and prevention. It builds on top of the Threat model developed by Stillions (2014) and integrates the DML model to build the CTIM. It comprises of thirteen elements namely Identity, Motivation, Goals, Strategy, Tactics Techniques and procedures (TTPs), Attack Pattern, Malware, Infrastructure, Tools, Indicators of Compromise, Atomic Indicators, Target and Course of Action. Unlike the previous ontologies, CTIM tackles the specific issue of threats, hence, it automatically excludes itself from the discussion of universality. However, its representational accuracy, provided the comprehensive sources it incorporates is noteworthy. It supports automated reasoning, allowing deductions and inferences. Roy & Dutta (2022) has established a couple of germane criterions to evaluate cyber threat ontologies. Overall, CTIM fares well at tackling the issue it sets out to solve, i.e. enabling organizations to better prepare and defend against cyber threats.

Figure 7. Modified Detection Maturity Level (DML) Model

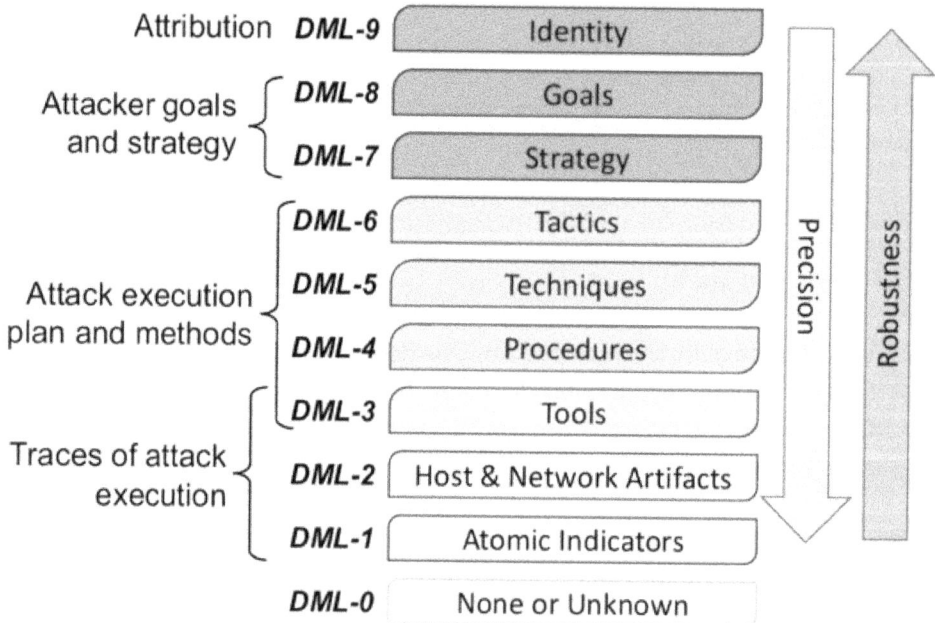

Attribution	**DML-9**	Identity
Attacker goals and strategy	**DML-8**	Goals
	DML-7	Strategy
Attack execution plan and methods	**DML-6**	Tactics
	DML-5	Techniques
	DML-4	Procedures
Traces of attack execution	**DML-3**	Tools
	DML-2	Host & Network Artifacts
	DML-1	Atomic Indicators
	DML-0	None or Unknown

Precision — Robustness

(Mavroeidis & Bromander, 2017)

Figure 8. Cyber-Threat Intelligence Model

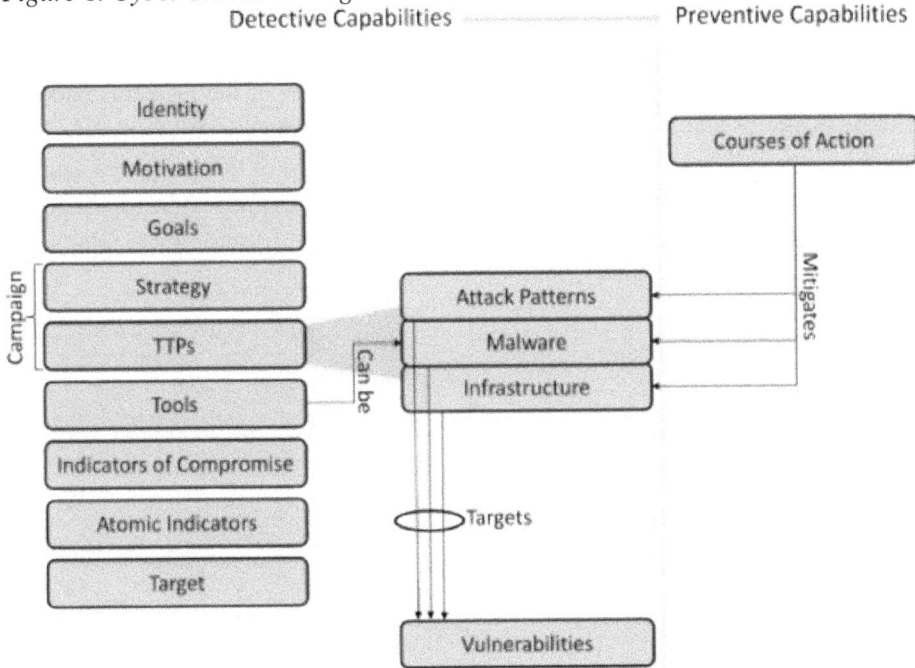

(CTIM Mavroeidis & Bromander, 2017)

3.6.1 Merits of CTIM

- Supports reasoning/querying
- Well defined structure
- High interoperability

3.6.2 Demerits of CTIM

- Limited scope/domain
- Ambiguity in representation
- Inextensibility

3.7 WAVED: Unified Ontology

The final ontology is contributed by the researchers at University of Texas with assistance from people at National Institute of Standards and technology. The acronym WAVED stands for Weakness, Attack, Vulnerability, Engage, D3fend. It builds upon the work done by Akbar et al., incorporating more frameworks and committing other progressive changes (Akbar et al., 2023a, 2023b). The primary use case of the ontology is to detect and mitigate Advanced Persistent Threat Campaigns(APT). Overall, being a relatively new ontology as of the time this paper is written, WAVED takes care of most campaign (issues that a universal ontology should leaving little room for inspection. It considers most of the renowned sources and makes incorporating new information easy but not entirely automated. Apart from mentioned gaps and inconsistencies in the paper, this ontology tackles most of the primary use cases fairly well.

Figure 9. Conceptual representation of WAVED ontology

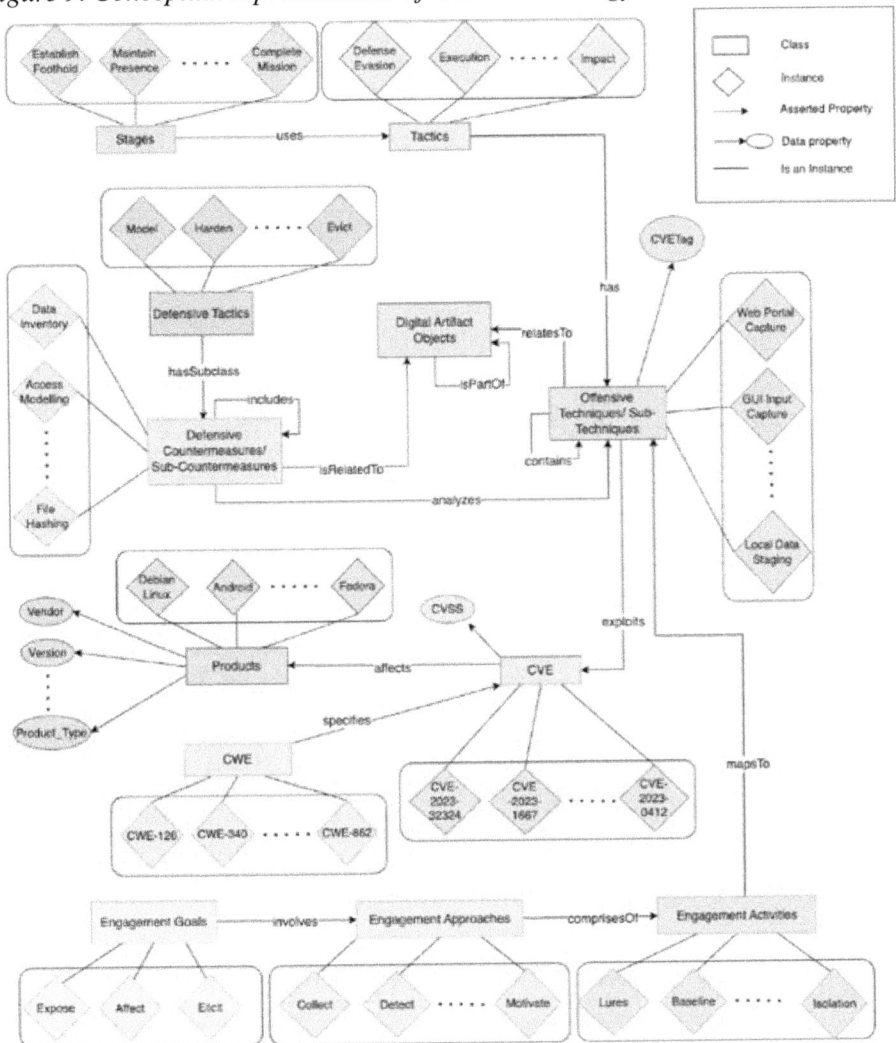

(Akbar et al., 2023b)

3.5.1 Merits of WAVED

- SPARSQL support
- Partial implementation possible
- Bidirectional nature
- Easy integration of new data
- Varied use cases

3.5.2 Demerits of WAVED

- Limited scope
- Difficult association
- Lack of test cases

Table 1. Tabular Summary of merits and demerits of each ontology

OVM	1.High Interoperability and better exchange between parties 2.Well Structured Architecture 3.Easy incorporation in existing concepts 4.Enhanced Automation	1.Limited Reasoning and querying 2.Difficult incorporation of non existent concepts 3.Limited Scope for General purpose 4.Higher Complexity (Wang and Cui, 2019)
STIX	1.Flexibility and Extensibility 2.Automateability 3.Partial Implementation and Use Cases	1.Complexity and Cognitive Overhead 2.Interoperability and Integration Issues 3.Anonymization and Privacy Concerns
STAX	1.Highly interoperable outside domain 2.Open source framework utilization 3.Support for domain specific retrieval	1.Difficult ad hoc updating process 2.Specific scope 3.Limited use case for domain intensive tasks 4.Complex Implementation (Gong and Tian, 2020)
STUCCO	1.High Human Interpretability 2.Easy Validation and Schema Definition 3.Incorporation of Metadata for Inferences	1.Inability to Use OWL/DL 2.Lack of Sources 3.Limited Use Cases 4.Inability to Incorporate Unstructured/ Potentially Useful Data
UCO	1.Use of a Semantic Framework (OWL) Instead of a Syntactic One (XML) 2.Supports Reasoning/ Querying 3.Extensible 4.Wide (General) Scope	1.Limited Use Cases 2.Difficult to Integrate New Sources 3.Inconvenient for Reasoning about Partially Anonymized/ Normal Work
CTIM	1.Supports Reasoning/ Querying 2.Well Defined Structure 3.High Interoperability	1.Limited Scope/Domain 2.Ambiguity in Representation 3.Limited Use Cases
WAVED	1.SPARQL Support 2.Partial Implementation 3.Flexible Relational/ Natural Structure 4.Easy Integration of New Data 5.Wide Use Cases	1.Limited Scope 2.Difficult to Associate Relations 3.Lack of Test Cases

4. CONCLUSION AND FUTURE WORK

As the cybersecurity community provides disparate approaches to solve the universal ontology problem, it is important to keep analyzing them and evaluating them on the basis of various parameters. Much work is due in implementing the best aspects of successful ontologies and remove their shortcomings. Most standard ontologies fare well if they have an equilibrium between managing complexity, adaptability and evolvability. There has been a recent trend of using NLP for extracting information from textual sources. The early results, including WAVED, have been promising. Semantic Web technologies combined with this approach have changed the landscape of the domain entirely. This paper has been published in hope that this examination has been helpful for people currently in the process of developing ontology and will aid them in determining what features should they implement to make their ontology optimal.

REFERENCES

Akbar, K. A., Rahman, F. I., Singhal, A., Khan, L., & Thuraisingham, B. (2023a, December). The Design and Application of a Unified Ontology for Cyber Security. In *International Conference on Information Systems Security* (pp. 23-41). Cham: Springer Nature Switzerland. DOI: 10.1007/978-3-031-49099-6_2

Barnum, S. (2012). Standardizing cyber threat intelligence information with the structured threat information expression (stix). *Mitre Corporation*, 11, 1–22.

Booth, H., Rike, D., & Witte, G. A. (2013). *The national vulnerability database (nvd)*. Overview.

Fenz, S., Ekelhart, A., & Weippl, E. (2008, March). Fortification of IT security by automatic security advisory processing. In *22nd International Conference on Advanced Information Networking and Applications (aina 2008)* (pp. 575-582). IEEE. DOI: 10.1109/AINA.2008.69

Gong, L., & Tian, Y. (2020). Threat modeling for cyber range: an ontology-based approach. In *Communications, Signal Processing, and Systems:Proceedings of the 2018 CSPS* Volume III*: Systems 7th* (pp. 1055-1062). Springer Singapore. DOI: 10.1007/978-981-13-6508-9_128

Gyrard, A., Bonnet, C., & Boudaoud, K. (2013, May). The stac (security toolbox: attacks & countermeasures) ontology. In *Proceedings of the 22nd International Conference on World Wide Web* (pp. 165-166). DOI: 10.1145/2487788.2487869

Iannacone, M., Bohn, S., Nakamura, G., Gerth, J., Huffer, K., Bridges, R., & Goodall, J. (2015, April). Developing an ontology for cyber security knowledge graphs. In *Proceedings of the 10th annual cyber and information security research conference* (pp. 1-4). DOI: 10.1145/2746266.2746278

Liu, K., Wang, F., Ding, Z., Liang, S., Yu, Z., & Zhou, Y. (2022). A review of knowledge graph application scenarios in cyber security. *arXiv preprint arXiv:2204.04769*.

Pinkston, J., Joshi, A., & Finin, T. (2003, July). A target-centric ontology for intrusion detection. In Workshop on Ontologies in Distributed Systems, held at The 18th International Joint Conference on Artificial Intelligence. Mavroeidis, V., & Bromander, S. (2017, September). Cyber threat intelligence model: an evaluation of taxonomies, sharing standards, and ontologies within cyber threat intelligence. In *2017 European Intelligence and Security Informatics Conference (EISIC)* (pp. 91-98). IEEE.

Roy, D., & Dutta, M. (2022). A systematic review and research perspective on recommender systems. *Journal of Big Data*, 9(1), 59. DOI: 10.1186/s40537-022-00592-5

Stillions, R. (2014). The DML model. *Retrieved Jan, 29*, 2022.

Syed, Z., Padia, A., Finin, T., Mathews, L., & Joshi, A. (2016, March). UCO: A unified cybersecurity ontology. In *Workshops at the thirtieth AAAI conference on artificial intelligence*.

Wang, B., & Cui, B. (2019). Ontology-based services for software vulnerability detection: A survey. *Service Oriented Computing and Applications*, 13(4), 333–339. DOI: 10.1007/s11761-019-00276-8

Wang, J. A., & Guo, M. (2009, April). OVM: an ontology for vulnerability management. In *Proceedings of the 5th Annual Workshop on Cyber Security and Information Intelligence Research: Cyber Security and Information Intelligence Challenges and Strategies* (pp. 1-4).

Chapter 2
Big Data Cyber Security Analytics

Prerna Agrawal
https://orcid.org/0000-0003-3097-639X
GLS University, India

Savita Gandhi
https://orcid.org/0000-0002-6581-2814
GLS University, India

ABSTRACT

The prevalence of social media usage is rapidly escalating. In January 2024, India alone recorded a total of 462 million social media users. The rise in online users has led to a corresponding surge in cybersecurity frauds. Cybersecurity experts can utilize big data analytic tools to identify, prevent, and mitigate cyber assaults, as these technologies are capable of handling the enormous amounts of data collected from diverse sources. This chapter examines cybercrimes that can be identified using Big Data Analytics (BDA). The primary aim of this chapter is to offer readers a comprehensive understanding of how Big Data Analytics (BDA) is applied in the field of cybersecurity. It also aims to enlighten readers about current advancements in the application of BDA in cybersecurity and the challenges that are encountered in this domain.

INTRODUCTION

The critical discipline of cybersecurity is dedicated to the prevention of unauthorized access, disruption, damage, and larceny of electronic devices, interconnections, and records (Mahmood & Afzal, 2013). Cybersecurity is crucial in the

DOI: 10.4018/979-8-3693-9225-6.ch002

interconnected digital world of the twenty-first century to safeguard individuals, organizations, and governments against a variety of threats (Apurva, 2017; Alpana, 2021). Online, information is continuously stored and exchanged. Cybersecurity is primarily concerned with maintaining confidentiality, integrity, availability, authenticity, and non-repudiation.

The term big data refers to extremely large and intricate compilations of information that are beyond the capabilities of conventional data processing systems to analyze and effectively manage. Big Data is defined by the three Vs: velocity, volume, and variety (Mahmood, 2013; Apurva, 2017; Rajsekhar, 2018; Alpana, 2021; Srivastava, 2019; Suraj, 2018). Large quantities of data, often ranging from terabytes to petabytes, are encompassed within the domain of big data. The information may originate from sensor data, social media interactions, business transactions, and other sources. Velocity, which pertains to the rapid emergence of big data, necessitates prompt management in order to extract valuable insights in a timely manner. Real-time or near-real-time processing is required for the following data sources: sensor data, social media streams, and website visit streams. These sources are able to rapidly generate data. Big data can be encountered in a multitude of formats, including unstructured, semi-structured, and structured data. Unstructured data, like images, videos, and text documents, does not adhere to a predefined data model; structured data, like databases, is well-organized and easy to search. Big Data is present in all sectors, including finance, smart cities, health care, business and marketing, and supply chain management (Mahmood & Afzal, 2013). The average person uses 6.7 different social networks each month, and 5.17 billion people throughout the world will be using social media by the end of 2024 (West, 2024). By 2028, mobile ads will have contributed $255.8 billion to the projected $219.8 billion in social media advertising expenditure in 2024 (West, 2024). With 52.4% of the population online as of the start of 2024, 751.5 million people in India were online. In January of 2024, there were 462 million social media users in India (Kemp, 2024).

The Big Data Cybersecurity Analytics is dedicated to enhancing cybersecurity operations through the implementation of advanced analytics techniques and big data technologies (Mahmood & Afzal, 2013). Conquering and minimizing intricate cyber attacks has proven to be exceedingly difficult for conventional cybersecurity measures on account of the proliferation in quantity, speed, and diversity of cyber threats. Big data cybersecurity analytics provides a solution to this issue by allowing organizations to collect, process, and assess enormous quantities of security-related data from multiple sources in real-time or nearly real-time (Mahmood, 2013; Apurva, 2017; Rajsekhar, 2018; Alpana, 2021; Srivastava, 2019; Suraj, 2018).

The primary objectives of this chapter are to determine the applications of BDA within the domain of cybersecurity, to underscore the various cyber-crimes that can be remedied with the assistance of these analytics, to educate readers on the application of BDA in the cybersecurity domain, and to propagate knowledge regarding the societal importance of BDA in cybersecurity.

PRESENT SCENARIO OF INDIAN CYBER CRIME

Cyber fraud is the practice of fooling people, organizations, or governments in order to obtain money or carry out other nefarious goals. It includes the use of digital devices, computers, and the internet. A broad variety of fraudulent schemes and tactics are included in the term "cyber fraud," which frequently takes advantage of flaws in human nature, organizational procedures, or technology (Mahmood, 2013; Apurva, 2017; Alpana, 2021). The sources of cybercrimes originate from the massive data that is generated through business, financial transactions, location-based data, social media, etc. (Apurva et al., 2017).

The National Crime Records Bureau (NCRB) report for 2023 shows that there were 1128265 complaints filed for cyber fraud overall across all Indian States (Cases of Cyber Frauds, 2024).

Figure 1. Cyber frauds in the states of India

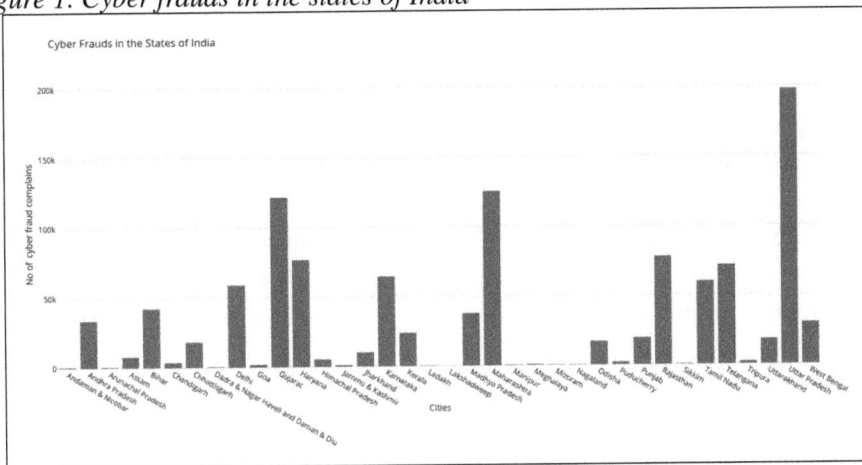

Figure 1 shows the total cyber fraud complaints filed state-wise across India. Cyber crimes will rise in tandem with the growth of online data, necessitating the development of robust cyber security systems that can detect trends in data, prevent cyber attacks, and protect data. The commencement of BDA in cyber security aids in enhancing detection, which lowers the incidence of cybercrime.

Need for Cyber Security in the Current Era

Due to the proliferation of an enormous volume of data online, there is a massive threat to the data. So there is a need for cybersecurity in the current era due to the following reasons (Mahmood & Afzal, 2013):

- **Growing Cyberthreats:** As technology develops, so do cybercriminals tools. Cyberthreats are becoming more and more varied, encompassing ransomware, malware, phishing scams, and increasingly advanced hacking methods.
- **Data Safety:** As a result of data digitization, both individuals and enterprises now keep enormous volumes of private information online. Cybersecurity means ensuring that this data is shielded from theft, tampering, and unwanted access.
- **Privacy Worries:** In the digital age, people's privacy is vulnerable. Cybersecurity measures assist in preventing nefarious actors from using people's personal information.
- **Protection of Critical Infrastructure:** Interconnected computer systems play a major role in the provision of essential services like electricity, transportation, healthcare, and banking. In order to shield these systems from cyber assaults that could hinder regular business operations or unleash general mayhem, cybersecurity is essential.
- **Monetary Effect:** Cyber assaults can have severe financial consequences for corporations and governments. Investing in cybersecurity helps to lessen the financial losses caused by data breaches, system unavailability, and reputational harm.
- **Compliance Requirements:** Many industries have guidelines for data protection and cybersecurity. Adherence to these laws not only assures legal compliance, but it also leads to the maintenance of consumer and partner trust.
- **Emerging Technologies:** As cutting-edge technologies such as the IoT, AI, and cloud computing progress, the vulnerability of cyber threats expands. The implementation of resilient cybersecurity protocols is crucial in mitigating the risks linked to these technologies.

Types of Cyber Crimes

Cybercrime comprises illicit activities executed through the utilization of computers or the internet. Theft and distribution of corporate data, requesting payment to prevent the data loss, installing vulnerabilities on a targeted computer, and intrusion into corporate or government computers are all examples of cybercrime (Mahmood,

2013; Apurva, 2017; Rajsekhar, 2018; Alpana, 2021; Srivastava, 2019; Suraj, 2018; Rawat, 2021; Alani, 2017). The following are prevalent forms of cybercrime:

- **Malware:** An abbreviation for malicious software, comprises a diverse array of software applications that are specifically engineered to cause harm, disturbance, or illicit entry into computer systems. Malware consists of spyware, adware, viruses, worms, and Trojans, among others.
- **Phishing:** Phishing is classified as a type of cybercrime in which individuals manipulate victims into divulging sensitive information, including financial details, login credentials, or confidential data, via fraudulent websites, emails, or messages. To deceive victims, phishing attacks frequently pose as legitimate organizations, such as government agencies or institutions.
- **Identity Theft:** In order to commit fraud or impersonate another individual, identity theft involves obtaining their confidential information, such as their name, (SSN) Social Security number, or credit card details. To obtain these records, cybercriminals may employ a variety of approaches, including phishing, data breaches, and social engineering.
- **Data Breakdowns:** Data breaches transpire when malevolent actors obtain illicit entry into the systems of an organization or company and pilfer confidential data, comprising but not restricted to financial records, customer information, or intellectual property. The affected organization may incur reputational harm, financial losses, and legal liabilities as a result of data theft.
- **Ransomware:** A kind of malicious software that immobilizes a target's computer system or encodes its data and files, subsequently asking payment in cryptocurrency in swap for the decryption key or to restore the entryway to the system. Conspiracy involving ransomware can cripple organizations, interrupt vital services, and extort money from victims.
- **Cyber Extortion:** In the absence of a ransom, cyber extortion entails threatening harm to organizations or individuals, including data breaches, DDoS assaults, or reputational harm. Unless their demands are complied with, cyberextortionists may threaten to disclose sensitive information or disrupt services.
- **Cyberbullying and Online Harassment:** Cyberbullying and online harassment involve intimidating, threatening, or harassing individuals through digital venues, including online discussion groups, social media, and messaging applications. Without consent, this may involve sending abusive messages, disseminating falsehoods, or disclosing private information.
- **Financial Fraud:** Credit card fraud, investment hoaxes, identity theft, phishing schemes, and other forms of financial fraud may be perpetrated by cyber-

criminals with the intention of obtaining money or victims' sensitive financial information.

- **Cyber Espionage:** For political, economic, or military objectives, cyber espionage entails using cyber attacks to obtain illicit access to sensitive information or intellectual property. Government agencies, corporations, and organizations may be the targets of cyber espionage attempting to acquire classified information or trade secrets.
- **Distributed Denial of Service Attacks (DDoS):** DDoS attacks disable legitimate users by inundating an intended network or system with an excessive amount of traffic or requests. DDoS attacks have the potential to cause significant disruptions to online services, websites, or networks, thereby subjecting the victim to financial losses and reputational harm.

Types of Cyber Attacks

Cyber attacks are malevolent endeavors executed by groups or individuals with the intention of damaging computer systems, networks, or devices through the usage of digital technology. Below are the frequent varieties of cyber attacks (Mahmood, 2013; Apurva, 2017; Rajsekhar, 2018; Alpana, 2021; Srivastava, 2019; Suraj, 2018; Rawat, 2021; Alani, 2017):

- **Viruses:** Malicious software that infiltrates legitimate programs or files through file attachments; propagates upon execution of said files.
- **Worms:** Self-replicating malware that spreads throughout systems and networks, frequently capitalizing on weaknesses to infect additional devices.
- **Trojans:** Malicious software masquerading as authentic software, designed to infiltrate a system without authorization or take sensitive information.
- **Ransomware:** Malicious software that locks computer systems or encrypts files, requiring a ransom in cryptocurrency in exchange for decryption or restoration.
- **Email Phishing:** In an effort to trick receivers into disclosing critical data, including passwords or financial details, cybercriminals employ deceptive email tactics by posing as legitimate entities.
- **Spear Phishing:** It refers to a form of phishing that is designed to deceive particular organizations or individuals by utilizing personalized information in an attempt to increase the probability of success.
- **Phishing:** Phishing attacks are commonly executed via voice communication channels, including phone calls and voice messages. These attacks manipulate victims by using social engineering techniques.

- **Denial of Service (DoS) Attacks:** Make an identifiable system or network unavailable to authorized users by flooding it with requests or traffic.
- **DDoS Attacks:** Complicate the operation of botnets, which are networks of compromised devices, in order to deluge the target with traffic, thereby depleting its resources and resulting in a total disruption.
- **Interception:** Without the victims knowledge, attackers intercept and eavesdrop on communication between two parties in order to manipulate data or take sensitive information.
- **Spoofing:** One type of malicious activity is spoofing, in which perpetrators assume the identity of reputable organizations or network devices in order to trick users or obtain illicit entry to systems.
- **SQL Injection Attacks:** Vulnerabilities in web applications or databases are exploited to implement malevolent SQL queries, enabling malicious actors to circumvent authentication procedures, gain unauthorized access to sensitive data, or alter the contents of the database.
- **Cross-Site Scripting (XSS) Attacks:** Install harmful code into online apps, which, when run in the browsers of unwary users, let attackers steal session cookies, lead visitors to harmful websites, or carry out other unlawful activities.
- **Zero-Day Exploits:** Exploit software or hardware vulnerabilities that are undisclosed to the vendor or have not been corrected, thereby enabling malicious actors to take advantage of the weaknesses prior to the release of security updates or remedies.
- **Insider Threats:** Insider threats encompass malicious activities or data breaches executed by personnel, contractors, or business associates within an organization. These individuals exploit their authorized access privileges to pilfer data, sabotage systems, or inflict additional damage.
- **Social Engineering:** Social engineering attacks involve the manipulation of human psychology or the exploitation of trust in order to trick individuals into divulging sensitive data, including passwords or access credentials, or into carrying out actions that are advantageous to the assailant.
- **Advanced Persistent Threats (APTs):** sophisticated and targeted cyber assaults executed by organized and well-funded adversaries, frequently with financial gain, sabotage, or espionage as their primary motivations; typically characterized by persistent infiltration of target networks and the execution of multiple stages.

THE WORTH OF BIG DATA

Big Data applies to the processing, analysis, and storage of massive amounts of data from several sources. When more conventional means of data processing, storage, and analysis are insufficient, big data approaches and solutions become essential. Big Data is all on fast discovering hidden information, analyzing massive volumes of unstructured data, and integrating unrelated data sets. Big Data settings collect data from various sources, including internal applications, sensors, and external sources. Big Data solutions can analyze data for enterprise applications or enrich current data in data warehouses (Erl et al. 2015). Here are key reasons below with which the worth of the big data is clearly shown (Mahmood, 2013; Apurva, 2017; Rajsekhar, 2018; Alpana, 2021; Srivastava, 2019; Suraj, 2018; Erl, 2015):

- **Knowledge-Driven Decision Making:** Organizations can utilize big data analytics in order to make educated judgments based on facts rather than guesswork or gut feelings. Organizations can enhance their comprehension of consumer behavior, market trends, and operational inefficiencies through the analysis of vast quantities of data originating from diverse sources.
- **Enhanced Performance and Productivity:** By identifying inefficiencies in processes and operations, big data analytics enable organizations to optimize workflows, allocate resources more effectively, and streamline operations. This leads to increased productivity, cost savings, and efficiency.
- **Enhanced Customer Knowledge:** The utilization of big data analytics empowers organizations to obtain comprehensive understandings of the preferences, behaviors, and needs of their customers. Enterprises have the ability to enhance customer satisfaction and loyalty, customize marketing initiatives, and tailor products and services through the analysis of client data derived from diverse channels, such as social media engagements, website transactions, and purchase records.
- **Innovation and Emerging Business Prospects:** The abundance of information contained in big data has the potential to stimulate innovation and generate new business opportunities. By analyzing emerging technologies, market trends, and consumer behavior, organizations can identify unfulfilled needs, create novel products and services, and enter fresh markets.
- **Risk Management and Fraud Prevention:** The utilization of big data analytics has the potential to assist organizations in more effectively identifying and reducing risks. Organizations that conduct real-time analysis of vast data sets are capable of detecting anomalies, identifying potential security threats, and averting fraud before it takes place. This is particularly crucial in industries such as insurance, finance, and cybersecurity.

- **Innovations in Healthcare and Life Studies:** The utilization of BDA in healthcare and life sciences holds the capacity to revolutionize patient care, pharmaceutical research, and disease control. Researchers can accelerate the discovery of novel medications and therapies, identify malady patterns, and develop individualized treatment regimens by analyzing enormous data sets, including clinical trials, genomics data, and patient records.

Big Data Life Cycle

The functional requirements for big data are taken into consideration by the Big Data Life cycle. An explanation of the Big Data Life Cycle is provided in Figure 2, which demonstrates that data must first be obtained, then organized, and lastly integrated. Following a successful implementation of this phase, the data may be examined in order to remedy the issue that has been found. It is now time for management to take action based on the findings of the analysis (Arya & Dayanand, 2017).

Figure 2. Big Data Life Cycle

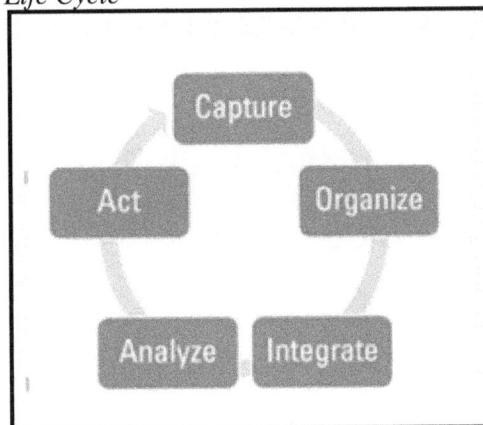

Source: (Hurwitz et al., 2013)

For instance, Amazon.com may suggest a book to a customer based on a past purchase, or it might provide a voucher for a discount on a product that is connected to the one that the customer has already purchased. Despite their apparent simplicity, the complexities of these functions may be intricate and difficult to understand. When combining several sources of data, it is essential to verify that the outputs are logically consistent. It is essential to implement suitable security and governance procedures for certain data sources in order to safeguard sensitive information.

Ecosystem of Big Data

Big data is described as significant volumes of both organized and unstructured information that are either too large or too variable for a normal relational database to handle. This ecosystem encompasses immense amounts of both types of data. This ecosystem is used to collect, handle, and analyze data with as little delay as possible. A breakdown of the various stages of the Big Data Ecosystem is shown in Figure 3. Among its components are data sources, data ingestion, data storage, data processing, and data visualization (Judith, 2013).

Figure 3. Big Data Ecosystem

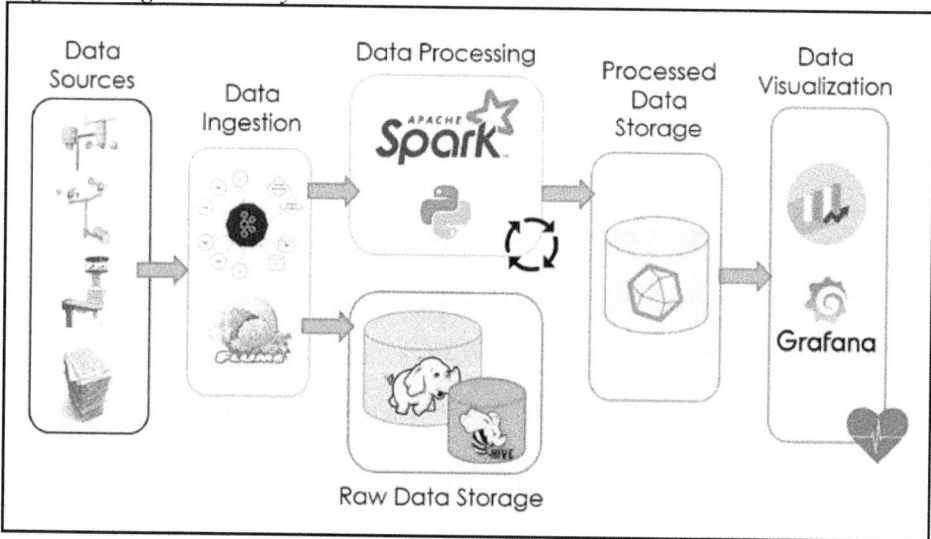

Source: (Hurwitz et al., 2013)

- **Sources of Data:** The first thing that has to be done is to collect records from a broad variety of sources, such as sensors, databases, IoT devices, social media, and many more. The data could be organized, semi-structured, or un-structured, depending on the situation.
- **Ingestion of Data:** It is vital to preserve the data in a system when collection is complete that is either a storage or processing apparatus. In this step, the data is transferred from its original source to a platform that stores information or data. Examples of such platforms include a warehouse, a data lake, or a distributed file system (DFS). During the phase known as "data storage," the information that was acquired is preserved in a storage system that is appropriate for the purpose. It is possible that this will incorporate a distrib-

uted file system such as a NoSQL database, HDFS, which stands for Hadoop Distributed File System, a cloud-based storage service, a data warehouse, Amazon S3, or Google Cloud Storage.

- **Processing of Data:** Once the data has been stored, it is processed in order to get insights and information that is helpful. At this step, a broad variety of data processing methods are used, such as the modification of data, the purification of data, the augmentation of data, the grouping of data, and the uniformity of data. Information may be processed in real time, in batches, or in streaming mode, depending on the requirements of the situation.
- **Data Visualization:** Data analysis results are frequently displayed with graphs, dashboards, charts, and other tools. This stage includes presenting the data.

Sources for Big Data

Big data may be gathered from a broad range of sources, including traditional organized databases as well as unstructured sources like feeds from social media platforms and sensor monitoring data. These sources can be used to acquire big data. The following is a list of some of the often used sources of enormous amounts of data (Mahmood, 2013; Apurva, 2017; Rajsekhar, 2018; Alpana, 2021; Srivastava, 2019; Suraj, 2018):

- **Transactional Data:** Data created via company transactions, such as sales records, invoices, and contacts with customers, are examples of what are referred to as transactional sources of information. Databases that are relational or data warehouses are often used to store it.
- **Social Media:** Facebook, Twitter, Instagram, and Linked-In are examples of social media platforms that create a significant quantity of data in the form of posts, comments, likes, shares, and other similar activities. These data have the potential to give insights into the sentiment, behavior, and trends of customers.
- **Information from Machines and Sensors:** Internet of Things devices, sensors, and machines provide vast amounts of data relating to temperature, pressure, movement, and other related topics. This data is used for activities such as predictive maintenance, monitoring, and optimization in a variety of industries, including manufacturing, healthcare, and transportation.
- **Information from the Web and Text:** Web pages, blogs, forums, and news stories all include a lot of information that may be retrieved and analyzed for a variety of reasons, including sentiment analysis, trend tracking, and content suggestions.

- **Logging Data:** The server logs, application logs, and network logs are the types of log data that record the actions and events that occur inside the systems and networks. The analysis of log data may assist in the detection of abnormalities, the resolution of problems, and the enhancement of system performance.
- **Geospatial Data:** Geographical positioning system (GPS) data, satellite images, and location-based services all contribute to the generation of geospatial data, which may be used for logistics optimization, urban planning, and location-based marketing.
- **Government Data:** Information that is useful for investment research, risk management, and the identification of fraudulent activity may be found in financial data, which includes information about the stock market, banking transactions, and financial statements.
- **Genomic Data:** In the domains of healthcare and life sciences, genomic data, which is derived from DNA sequencing and medical records, offers insights into genetic diseases, tailored medication, and the health of populations.
- **Government Data:** Datasets that are made accessible to the public and come from government agencies give information on a variety of topics, including climate, economy, and demography. These data sets are often used for research, the formulation of public policy, and applications related to public service.
- **Encounters with Customers:** Records of customer service encounters, such as call center transcripts, chat logs, and emails, provide significant insights into the preferences, problems, and levels of satisfaction of customers.
- **Audio and Video Data:** It is possible to get insights into speech patterns, face expressions, and customer preferences by analyzing audio and video data. This is especially useful in light of the growth of multimedia material.

These are only a few examples, and the sources of big data continue to grow as a result of developments in technology and shifts in the patterns of data collection.

OVERVIEW OF BIG DATA ANALYTICS

Big Data Analytics (BDA) is a field of research that focuses on extracting value from enormous data sets, especially major, previously implicit, undisclosed, and potentially useful insights. These findings have a direct impact on the formation or adjustment of the current company plan, and they serve as the drive for the project that is often referred to as via Data with Decision. It is hypothesized that large amounts of data include patterns of use, occurrences, or behaviors that may be identified individually. In an effort to apply mathematical models to these patterns, BDA and a wide variety of other data mining approaches, such as cluster analysis, prescriptive analytics, and association rule mining, are used. When these approaches are used, the findings that are achieved are often shown on interactive dashboards. These dashboards provide firms with assistance in maintaining their competitive edge, increasing revenues, and enhancing their customer relationship management (Mahmood, 2013; Apurva, 2017; Rajsekhar, 2018; Alpana, 2021; Srivastava, 2019; Suraj, 2018).

Figure 4. Big data analytics process

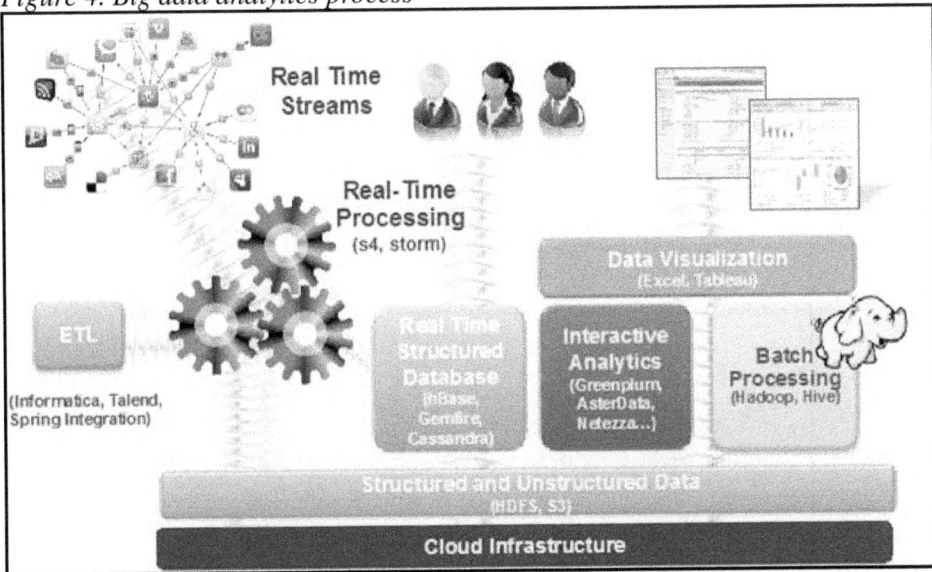

Source:(Mahmood & Afzal, 2013)

The basic phases of the BDA procedure are shown in Figure 4. To begin, analysis is based on pre-processed data that is chosen in real-time from massive data streams. Extract Transform Load (ETL) is a name for this tedious operation that may take up to 70–80% of the time spent on BDA. As part of its duties, it processes data that is inconsistent, incomplete, or missing values; normalizes, discretizes, or reduces data; uses cluster analysis, box plots, and normality testing to ensure the data is statistically sound; and uses descriptive statistics, such as correlations, histograms, and hypothesis testing, to help understand the data. Data cleansing is followed by storage in BDA databases (e.g., cloud, mobile, network servers, etc.), and analytics and Hadoop are used for further analysis if needed. After that, computer visualization tools are used to convey the results in interactive displays. BDA is an iterative process driven by input to any previous step that aims to improve results by fine-tuning analytical methodologies (Mahmood & Afzal, 2013).

Types of Analytics Approach

Big Data analytics provide empirical support for data-driven decision-making, eliminating the need for relying just on intuition or prior experience. Analytics may be arranged into 4 categories based on their results: descriptive, diagnostic, predictive, and prescriptive analytics (Erl et al. 2015). Figure 5 shows the value and complexity rise from descriptive to prescriptive analytics.

Figure 5. From descriptive to prescriptive analytics, value and complexity rise

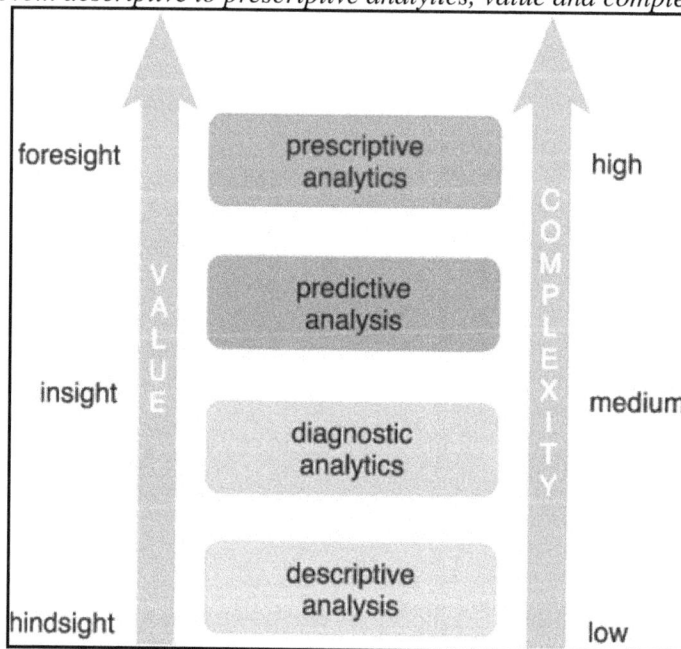

Source: (Erl et al. 2015)

Descriptive analytics are implemented in order to provide answers to inquiries pertaining to past events. Information is generated by contextualizing data using this type of analytics. Frequently, descriptive analytics are executed through the utilization of ad hoc reporting or dashboards. The reports predominantly consist of inert information presented in the form of data grids or graphics, which illustrate historical data. Enterprise-based queries are executed on operational data repositories.

The objective of diagnostic analytics is to ascertain the root cause of a past phenomenon through the use of inquiries that center on the event's rationale. Determining what information is pertinent to the phenomenon in order to provide answers to queries that seek to ascertain the cause of an occurrence is the objective of this type of analytics. While diagnostic analytics offer greater utility than descriptive analytics, they also demand a more sophisticated set of skills. Typically, diagnostic analytics necessitate the acquisition of data from various sources and its subsequent storage in a format that facilitates drill-down and roll-up analyses. The outcomes of diagnostic analytics are delivered to consumers via interactive visualization techniques that facilitate the detection of trends and patterns.

The implementation of predictive analytics is done with the objective of ascertaining the potential outcome of a future event. Predictive analytics augments information with significance. in order to produce knowledge that elucidates the interrelation of said information. On the premise of past events and the intensity and magnitude of the associations, predictive models are constructed to generate future outcomes. Predictive analytics endeavors to forecast the consequences of events by identifying patterns, trends, and anomalies in current and historical data. This may result in the recognition of potential opportunities as well as hazards.

Prescriptive analytics extend the insights gained via predictive analytics through the provision of actionable recommendations. The emphasis is placed not only on the optimal prescribed course of action, but also on the underlying rationale. Put simply, prescriptive analytics generate results that are defensible through reasoning, as they incorporate components of situational awareness. Consequently, one may use this form of analytics to obtain an advantage or reduce a risk. Prescriptive analytics are the most valuable form of analytics; therefore, they demand the most sophisticated set of skills, in addition to specialized software and tools.

Recent Big Data Analytics Tools and Technologies

To deal with the deluge of data produced by modern technology, BDA methods and technology have advanced substantially. A few tools and technologies are listed below (Srivastav, 2019; Arya, 2017; Rassam, 2017; Raju, 2016; Quinto, 2018):

- **Hadoop:** Hadoop, developed by Apache, is a free and open-source platform for storing and analyzing massive information in distributed computing environments. Its two primary parts are the Hadoop Distributed File System (HDFS) for preserving data and the Map Reduce programming approach for handling that data.
- **Spark:** Apache Spark offers in-memory data processing capabilities and is a general-purpose cluster computing system that is quick. Batch processing,

graph processing, machine learning, and real-time stream processing are just a few of the many applications it offers.

- **NoSQL Databases:** The massive amounts of semi-structured or unstructured data may be easily managed by NoSQL databases such as Cassandra, Couchbase, and MongoDB. They are very good for large data analytics applications because of their versatility and scalability.

- **Apache Kafka:** One popular tool for developing streaming apps and realistic time data pipelines is Apache Kafka, a distributed streaming platform. It makes it possible to analyze massive or huge amounts of data streams in real-time once they have been ingested.

- **Apache Flink:** With Apache Flink, a stream processing framework, continuous data streams may be processed with minimal latency and high throughput. Stateful computations, exactly-once semantics, and event-time processing are all supported.

- **Apache Hive:** Apache Hive is a Hadoop-based data warehousing engine that permits users to query and analyze massive data sets housed in the Hadoop Distributed File System (HDFS) using an interface similar to SQL.

- **Apache HBase:** Apache HBase is a NoSQL database based on Hadoop that is distributed, scalable, and consistent. With its random read/write access to HDFS data, it can manage massive tables with billions of rows with ease.

- **Apache Storm:** For processing and analyzing continuous streams of data, one may utilize Apache Storm, a distributed real-time stream processing system. It helps in processing data with minimal latency and is fault-tolerant.

- **Apache Drill:** Among the many data sources that Apache Drill facilitates interactive analysis of massive data sets are Hadoop, NoSQL databases, and cloud storage. Drill is a distributed SQL query engine.

- **Machine Learning Libraries:** Powerful tools for creating and deploying machine learning models on big data sets are provided by libraries like Tensor Flow, scikit-learn, and PyTorch. Spark and other big data (BD) systems are compatible with these libraries, allowing for distributed inference and training.

- **Data Visualization Tools:** Tableau, Power BI, and Apache Super Set are just a few examples of data visualization tools that allow users to build interactive dashboards and visualizations to discover and share insights in massive data sets.

The Need for Big Data Analytics in Cybersecurity

Adopting BDA makes sense for a broad spectrum of reasons, including the novel approaches it offers to enhance business analytics. Technologies used in security that are not completely secure and are unable to identify threats, fraud, or cybersecurity. Many big data analytics (BDA) frameworks and tools are currently available and may be used to identify patterns in immense amounts of data as anomalous activity. Finding connections in the big data is made easier by a broad spectrum of ML approaches, such as clustering, data visualization, and outlier detection (Mahmood, 2013; Apurva, 2017; Rajsekhar, 2018; Alpana, 2021; Srivastava, 2019; Suraj, 2018; Rawat,2021).

BDA has been actively investigated and applied to various business sectors, the strength of big data in cybersecurity is being felt as an outcome of the increasingly complex networks and increasingly advanced threats. Big data has a tendency to obscure the real threat picture, and cybersecurity is thought to be one of the particularly crucial, if not the crucial, critical domains in this regard.

Adoption of Big Data Analytics in Detecting Cyber Crime

Cybercrime detection and prevention rely heavily on BDA, which helps businesses collect, evaluate, and draw conclusions from massive amounts of data from various sources. Some examples of how cybercrime detection uses big data analytics are as follows (Mahmood, 2013; Apurva, 2017; Rajsekhar, 2018; Alpana, 2021; Srivastava, 2019; Suraj, 2018; Arya, 2017; Rassam, 2017; Rawat,2021; Alani,2021; Angin, 2019):

- **Anomaly Detection:** Network traffic, system logs, and user activity data may be analyzed by big data analytics algorithms to detect anomalies, which might be signs of a cyber assault. Security problems may be detected more rapidly if businesses establish baseline behavior patterns and monitor for variations from these patterns.

- **Cyberattack Trends and Pattern Recognition:** Machine learning, data mining (DM), and other big data analytics tools can identify trends and patterns in cyberattack strategies and tactics. Organizations may improve their ability to foresee and respond to cyber attacks by reviewing attack data from the past and looking for trends.

- **Behavioral Analysis:** With the usage of BDA, businesses may examine user actions and spot suspicious patterns, such as attempts at illegal access, data exfiltration, or privilege escalation. Company insider threats and compromised accounts may be detected by tracking user activity across many platforms and apps.

- **Integrating Threat Intelligence:** In order to discover new vulnerabilities and threats, BDA systems may take in and process data from a variety of sources, such as threat intelligence feeds and the dark web. Organizations may proactively protect and cover themselves against cyber assaults by comparing internal security data with external threat information in order to detect signs of penetration.
- **Event Correlation:** In order to discover possible security problems, big data analytics technologies may correlate security alerts and events from several sources, including firewalls, intrusion detection systems, and endpoint security solutions. Organizations may improve response effort prioritization and decrease false positives by combining and correlating data from several sources.
- **Forensic Investigation:** By examining massive amounts of log data, network traffic, and system artifacts, big data analytics allows enterprises to do forensic investigations of security occurrences. The best way for firms to prepare for investigations and legal actions is to recreate attack scenarios and determine what caused security breaches.
- **Real-Time Monitoring and Response:** Organizations may do identification and react to cyber threats in realistic time with the help of BDA systems real-time monitoring and analysis capabilities. To prevent the security issues from becoming worse, businesses might use stream processing and real-time analytics.
- **Predictive Analysis:** The application of BDA for predictive analytics allows for the exploitation of patterns and historical data to foretell future cyber dangers and vulnerabilities. Cyber threat mitigation measures may be prioritized and future attack scenarios can be predicted, allowing enterprises to take a proactive stance in defense.

The big data analytics is used for detecting various cyber attacks like malware infections, phishing attacks, DoS and DDoS attacks, insider threats, ransomware attacks, SQL injection attacks, brute force attacks, zero-day attacks, cryptojacking attacks, social engineering attacks, etc. Big data analytics allows enterprises to analyze massive volumes of data, spot trends and abnormalities, integrate threat information, do forensic analysis, and react to security issues in real-time, all of which contribute significantly to the detection of cybercrimes. Organizations may fortify their cybersecurity defenses and safeguard themselves from various cyber threats by using the power of big data analytics.

RELEVANT WORK

The real-time analysis of large-scale data for cyber security (CS) has always been a significant problem. Over the years, extensive research has been conducted on this issue. This section discusses different research that has been carried out until now on BDA.

The issues that the domain of cybersecurity is confronted with in the context of big data are emphasized in the paper (Mahmood & Afzal, 2013). They have demonstrated that security analytics, which involves the real-time extraction of valuable information gleaned from streams using big data analytics techniques, is becoming an increasingly important requirement for cybersecurity systems. This paper gives a thorough examination of the current state of security analytics, including its description, tools, technology, and trends. Thus, its purpose is to convince the reader that analytics will soon be used as a supreme cybersecurity solution. The paper (Apurva et al., 2017) delves into the architecture, cybercrime classifications, and big data analytics methods for investigating large data's salient features. Also covered, with relevant data, are the many kinds of analytics, the rise of big data analytics, and the algorithms that may prove to be the most useful in addressing cybercrime concerns via targeted analytics. Additionally, the growing difficulties of cyber security are addressed. It also delves into the process of utilizing data analytics and the specific key elements that should be considered when extracting potentially useful information from big data. This information has the potential to be of great assistance in the field of cyber security. The paper (Rajsekhar & Pawan, 2018) emphasizes the cutting-edge difficulties that the cybersecurity sector faces in the big data context. They have shown that security analytics, or the real-time extraction of actionable knowledge and insights from streams utilizing big data analytics methodologies, is becoming an increasingly crucial necessity for cybersecurity systems. This paper thoroughly examines the present status of security analytics, including its definition, technologies, trends, and tools. Its purpose is to convince the reader that analytics will soon be used as an outstanding cybersecurity solution. The paper (Alpana, 2021) highlights some of the usage of big data technology in cybersecurity in the digital age. It presents a theoretical framework based on the TAM model, recognizing that the deployment of big data technologies for cyber security is determined by their ease of use and utility. The paper then uses a qualitative research approach, evaluating material from credible sources. The paper (Srivastava & Umesh, 2019) examines the significance of big data, multiple definitions of big data security and privacy, the value of big data analytics with security, various obstacles in BDA, and privacy concerns in BDA. The paper (Suraj et al., 2018) examines many sorts of assaults on big data, its storage mechanisms, and realistic time analytics methods. This study also covers the various social network assaults. The paper (Arya & Dayanand,

2017) examines the importance of big data and cyber security, various big data technologies, and the usefulness of big data analytics in the field of cybersecurity. The paper (Rassam et al., 2017) examines the traditional systems/technology and (SIEMT) Security Information and Event Management tools and demonstrates their inadequacies in addressing advanced, sophisticated threats and vast data scales. The paper also delves into the prerequisites for the successful implementation of big data analytics in the cybersecurity landscape and cyber threat intelligence to address sophisticated threats and high data volumes. The paper also emphasizes the obstacles that have arisen as a consequence of this adoption and offers some suggestions for overcoming these obstacles in future research. The paper (He et al., 2019) discusses the usage of a third-party database for doing searches with regard to the subject of big data's cyber applications. Subsequently, using Citespace and other bibliometric methods, these papers are subjected to article co-citation analysis and co-word analysis. The investigation indicates that big data technology is extensively used in cyberspace, with its implementation expanding in both scope and complexity each year. The paper (Rawat et al.,2021) examines current research endeavors in the field of cybersecurity as it pertains to big data. It also emphasizes the measures taken to safeguard big data and its potential as a cybersecurity tool. The document provides a concise overview of current research findings, presenting them in the form of tables. It highlights emerging patterns, unresolved research questions, and issues that need more investigation. This paper aims to provide readers with a comprehensive comprehension of cybersecurity in the age of big data. It also covers the latest research trends and unresolved difficulties in this dynamic field of study. The paper (Alani, 2021) presents a comprehensive assessment of the use of BDA in developing, upgrading, or defying cybersecurity systems. The paper examines cutting-edge research in a variety of big data applications in cybersecurity. The paper divides applications into categories such as anomaly detection and intrusion, malware detection, spamming and spoofing detection, ransomware detection, cloud security, and code security, as well as another category that surveys alternative lines of study in big data and cybersecurity. The paper (Angin et al., 2019) explores the significance of big data and cybersecurity. Furthermore, it explores the significance of BDA in the field of cybersecurity. Furthermore, it asserts that the demand for the BDA is certain to increase in the future. The paper (Romil et al., 2023) shows that the ever-changing challenges and risks to big data security have rendered conventional approaches obsolete, calling for fresh, intelligent frameworks to address the issue. The authors conducted a comprehensive examination of the domains of literature review on large data protection in order to gain a better grasp of the present situation. Using ML approaches they proposed an outfit solution for massive data cryptography. The paper (Nwobodo, 2024) explores into the need for improved cybersecurity measures to protect sensitive data and guarantee the reliability of digital infrastructures in an age defined by massive data generation and advanced analytical methods. This paper also concludes that safeguarding vital digital assets and keeping faith in digital ecosystems requires better cybersecurity policies in the age of big data and complex analytics. To reduce cyber risks and make the most of big data for long-term growth and innovation, businesses should implement data governance frameworks and use state-of-the-art analytical tools. The paper (Tank & Chaubey, 2020) investigate cybersecurity risks and solutions in the context of cloud computing from a virtualization perspective. The authors also go over the process of creating their unique virtualized environment-based 'Flush+Flush' cache assault detection method. The paper (Jani & Chaubey, 2020) acquires a fundamental understanding of the Internet of Things (IoT), recognizes the several types of risks that could breach an IoT system, and takes steps to limit the effects of such attacks.

Table 1 presents a comparison of the use of BDA in the field of cybersecurity. The papers have been compared based on three factors given below:

- Purpose of the paper
- Challenges with BDA
- Future Score of Using BDA in Cyber Security

Table 1. Comparison of using BDA in cybersecurity

Paper	Purpose	Challenges with BDA	Future Scope of Using BDA in Cyber Security
(Rawat et al., 2021).	Exploration of current cybersecurity research with respect to big data. It was also discussed how big data is safeguarded and how it may be utilized as a cybersecurity tool.	1. Adopting Big Data as a Security Tool. 2. Big Data Regulations. 3. Decentralized and context-aware data storage. 4. Using artificial intelligence. 5. Scalability of Security Techniques in the Big Data Era.	More encryption methods and access controls may be included in the BDA to improve cybersecurity.
(Alani, 2021)	Provides a comprehensive assessment of how big data analytics may be used to develop, improve, or defy cybersecurity systems. It also reviews current research on big data applications in cybersecurity.		Future cybersecurity systems will rely significantly on analyzing vast volumes of data to identify and prevent unwanted behavior. Identification of potential research directions for exploiting big data in cybersecurity applications is detecting intrusions and anomalies, including malware and ransomware. Cybersecurity applications include code security, cloud security, spoofing, spamming, and phishing.
(Alpana, 2021)	Utilizing the TAM model, the study determines that the applicability of big data technologies to cyber security is contingent on their utility and case of use.	The TAM paradigm is restricted to contemporary cyber security applications of big data technologies.	The primary emphasis should be placed on the identification of forthcoming ramifications linked to the progressions in big data technologies.
(Srivastava & Umesh, 2019)	Big Data Analytics is designed to establish a secure environment to facilitate unauthorized access.	1. Originating Place of Data. 2. Big Data Security Stock 3. Foundational human-computer interaction. 4. Information security concerns associated with big data. 5. Secrecy.	

continued on following page

Table 1. Continued

Paper	Purpose	Challenges with BDA	Future Scope of Using BDA in Cyber Security
(Angin et al., 2019)	To quickly evaluate massive amounts of data from many sources in order to identify patterns of attacks and outliers, big data analytics is crucial for making systems more resilient and less susceptible to attacks.		The demand for BDA in cloud computing security grows in the future.
(He et al., 2019)	Searches a third-party database for studies on the big data application in cyberspace.		Along with cyber security, co-word analysis enables new frontier study fields such as BDA in energy management, edge computing, and big data analysis.
(Rajsekhar & Pawan, 2018)	This includes security analytics in addition to the issues facing the Cybersecurity sector in view of big data.		Analyzing datasets pertaining to networks using security analytics methods in order to lower the number of false positives in an unlawful transaction prediction model.
(Suraj et al., 2018)	The various cyber security assaults that target large data, its storage/saving mechanism, and realistic time analytics approaches were discussed.	Social network data is enormous and susceptible to graph-based threats.	Minimizing noise in the data reduces information loss.
(Apurva et al., 2017)	In order to combat cybercriminals and protect the welfare of innocent civilians, big data analytics will be utilized.	1. The solution is expensive. 2. Skilled workers are not readily available. 3. Data integration is a challenge. 4. Processing incoming data.	By effectively extracting potential big data information using BDA techniques, significant advancements can be made in the field of cyber security.

continued on following page

Table 1. Continued

Paper	Purpose	Challenges with BDA	Future Scope of Using BDA in Cyber Security
(Arya & Dayanand, 2017)	BDA for security aims to acquire intelligence that is immediately actionable.	1. Certain organizations might lack a data-driven approach. 2. Businesses might perceive BDA as a method to generate value from data. 3. Users and the analytics team collaborate throughout the analytics process, beginning with the definition of the scope and continuing through data extraction and recovery. 4. The management's confidence in the analytics result may be compromised.	1. Uncover concealed insights. 2. Better decision-making. 3. Implement business process automation.
(Rassam et al., 2017)	The implementation of big data analytics solutions has become imperative in mitigating the intricate risks associated with big data.	1. Managing unstructured data. 2. Analysis in real time. 3. Streaming Analysis of Data. 4. Data Protection. 5. Provenance of Data. 6. Visual Analytics. 7. Adaptability.	1. Big Data Security and Privacy. 2. Behavioral Analytics 3. Visualization 4. Internet of Things
(Mahmood & Afzal, 2013)	In addition to highlighting the cutting-edge challenges confronting the cybersecurity industry in light of big data, the paper showcased security analytics.		Implementation of security analytics methodologies on data sets pertaining to networks with the objective of reducing the occurrence of false positives in an illicit transaction prediction model.

CONCLUSION

As the number of social media users grows rapidly, so does the occurrence of cyber frauds. In order to stay ahead of cyber attackers, BDA technologies will play a crucial role in detecting, preventing, and mitigating cyber crimes. Various forms of Big Data Analytics (BDA) have proven to be effective in comprehending trends and uncovering novel vulnerabilities and threats. Despite the challenges that lie ahead in using Big Data Analytics (BDA) in cybersecurity, it has significant potential for future growth and development.

REFERENCES

Alani, M. M. (2021). Big Data in cybersecurity: A survey of applications and future trends. *Journal of Reliable Intelligent Environments*, 7(2), 85–114. DOI: 10.1007/s40860-020-00120-3

Alpana, S. (2021). Big Data Technologies for Cyber Security in the Digital Era. *Social Science Research Network*. DOI: 10.2139/ssrn.4629044

Angin, P., Bhargava, B., & Ranchal, R. (2019). Big Data Analytics for Cyber Security. *Security and Communication Networks*, 1–2, 1–2. Advance online publication. DOI: 10.1155/2019/4109836

Aviral Apurva, Pranshu Ranakoti, Yadav, S., Tomer, S., & Nihar Ranjan Roy. (2017). *Redefining cyber security with big data analytics*. DOI: 10.1109/IC3TSN.2017.8284476

Arya, D. (2017). Big data Analytics in Cyber Security. *International Journal of Engineering Research & Technology (Ahmedabad)*, 5(10).

Buyuaa, R., & Calheiros, R. N. (2016). *Big Data Principles and Paradigms* (1st ed.). Elsevier.

Cases of Cyber Frauds. (2024). Pib.gov.in. https://pib.gov.in/PressReleaseIframePage.aspx?PRID=2003158

Erl, T., Khattak, W., & Buhler, P. (2015). *Big data fundamentals: Concepts, drivers & techniques*. Prentice Hall.

He, J., Xian, M., & Liu, J. (2019). The Application of big Data in cyberspace: A Survey. In *International Conference on Communications, Information System and Computer Engineering e* (pp. 570–574). IEEE Xplore. DOI: 10.1109/CISCE.2019.00132

Hurwitz, J. Alan Nugent, & Dr. Fern Halper. (2013). Big Data For Dummies (1st ed.). Wiley.

Jani, K. A., & Chaubey, N. (2020). IoT and Cyber Security: Introduction, Attacks, and Preventive Steps. In Chaubey, N., & Prajapati, B. (Eds.), *Quantum Cryptography and the Future of Cyber Security* (pp. 203–235). IGI Global., DOI: 10.4018/978-1-7998-2253-0.ch010

Kemp, S. (2024, February 20). *Digital 2024: India — DataReportal – Global Digital Insights*. DataReportal – Global Digital Insights. https://datareportal.com/reports/digital-2024-india#:~:text=The%20state%20of%20digital%20in%20India%20in%202024&text=There%20were%20751.5%20million%20internet,percent%20of%20the%20total%20population

, M. V., Nikhil Kumar Singh, & Deepak Singh Tomar. (2018). Big data Analytics of cyber attacks: a review. *2018 IEEE International Conference on System, Computation, Automation and Networking (ICSCA)*. DOI: 10.1109/ICSCAN.2018.8541263

Mahmood, T., & Afzal, U. (2013). Security Analytics: Big Data Analytics for cybersecurity: A review of trends, techniques and tools. *2013 2nd National Conference on Information Assurance (NCIA)*. DOI: 10.1109/NCIA.2013.6725337

Nwobodo, N. L. K., Nwaimo, N. C. S., & Adegbola, N. E.Luther Kington Nwobodo-Chioma Susan NwaimoAyodeji Enoch Adegbola. (2024). Enhancing cybersecurity protocols in the era of big data and advanced analytics. *GSC Advanced Research and Reviews*, 19(3), 203–214. DOI: 10.30574/gscarr.2024.19.3.0211

Quinto, B. (2018, June 12). *Next-Generation Big Data*. Apress. http://books.google.ie/books?id=teZfDwAAQBAJ&printsec=frontcover&dq=Next-Generation+Big+Data&hl=&cd=1&source=gbs_api

Rao, N. R., & Pandey, P. K. (2018). Security Analytics:Big Data Analytics for CybersecurityA Review of Trends, Techniques and Tools. *IJCRT, 6*(1), 579-584. https://www.ijcrt.org/papers/IJCRT1802412.pdf

Rassam, & Maarof, Mohd. (2017). Big Data Analytics Adoption for Cybersecurity: A Review of Current Solutions, Requirements, Challenges and Trends. *Journal of Information Assurance and Security, 11*, 124–145. https://mirlabs.org/jias/secured/Volume12-Issue4/Paper14.pdf

Rawat, D. B., Doku, R., & Garuba, M. (2021). Cybersecurity in big data era: From securing big data to data-driven security. *IEEE Transactions on Services Computing*, 14(6), 2055–2072. DOI: 10.1109/TSC.2019.2907247

Rawat, R., Oki, O. A., Sankaran, K. S., Olasupo, O., Ebong, G. N., & Ajagbe, S. A. (2023). A new solution for cyber security in big data using machine learning approach. In *Lecture notes on data engineering and communications technologies* (pp. 495–505). DOI: 10.1007/978-981-99-0835-6_35

Srivastava, N., & Chandra Jaiswal, U. (2019). Big Data Analytics Technique in Cyber Security. *RE:view*, 579–585. Advance online publication. DOI: 10.1109/ICCMC.2019.8819634

Tank, D. M., Aggarwal, A., & Chaubey, N. K. (2020). Cyber Security Aspects of Virtualization in Cloud Computing Environments: Analyzing Virtualization-Specific Cyber Security Risks. In Chaubey, N., & Prajapati, B. (Eds.), *Quantum Cryptography and the Future of Cyber Security* (pp. 283–299). IGI Global., DOI: 10.4018/978-1-7998-2253-0.ch013

West, C., & West, C. (2024, April 26). *50+ Must-know social media marketing statistics for 2024*. Sprout Social. https://sproutsocial.com/insights/social-media-statistics/

https://towardsdatascience.com/do-you-really-need-to-implement-big-datatechnologies-in-your-ecosystem-ea840a3cf286

Chapter 3
Blockchain in Cybersecurity

Akhil John Mampilly
https://orcid.org/0009-0003-2626-0070
Lincoln University College, Malaysia

Vijaya Kittu Manda
https://orcid.org/0000-0002-1680-8210
PBMEIT, India

Chithirai Pon Selvan Muthu Perumal
https://orcid.org/0000-0001-9295-3340
Curtin University, Dubai, UAE

ABSTRACT

Blockchain is a promising technology that can help organizations improve their cybersecurity. Blockchain has many inherent features that can help enhance data security, improve threat detection and response, strengthen authentication and authorization, and enhance cyber threat intelligence sharing. This is possible because of the innovative approach that Blockchain uses, such as immutable ledgers to store transactions, monitor assets, and build trust by providing access only to authorized participants. The chapter discusses cybersecurity best practices related to smart contracts, key management, network security, user education and awareness, incident reporting, privacy challenges, software updates, and decentralization. Key regulatory compliance aspects, such as GDPR and HIPPA, are discussed. The increasing interactions of Artificial Intelligence (AI), Machine Learning (ML), and the Internet of Things (IoT) with Blockchain can further provide improved cybersecurity services and hence form the discussion of the trends and potential future research section of this chapter.

DOI: 10.4018/979-8-3693-9225-6.ch003

INTRODUCTION

Cybersecurity is becoming more critical now than before for several reasons. Increasing digitalization and internet connectivity, evolving cyber threat situations, excessive reliance on technology, growing value for data, Nation-State cyber attacks, Cybercrime becoming offered as a service, and lack of cyber security awareness could be the critical reasons for this. Considering these reasons, organizations, especially large-sized enterprises, are devoting substantial resources to protect their data, systems, and infrastructure to improve their cybersecurity measures. The global cybersecurity market is expected to experience significant growth, expanding from an estimated $190.4 billion in 2021 to a projected $298.5 billion by 2028, representing a compound annual growth rate (CAGR) of 9.4% over the forecast period (Markets & Markets, 2024). Individuals are also increasingly becoming cybersecurity aware and taking proactive steps to safeguard their data and devices.

New evolving technologies, such as Blockchain, offer revolutionary approaches to building a reliable and cybersafe infrastructure, helping organizations be resilient. Blockchain is renowned for its inherent features, providing a robust background for enhancing digital security. A Deloitte survey found that most respondents (58%) said cybersecurity is one of several issues affecting their overall blockchain- or digital assets–related strategy (Deloitte, 2020). Blockchain-based secure exchange of information is a top use case for 45% of respondents, as per another survey (Deloitte, 2021).

Chapter Outline

The "Introduction" section of the chapter sets the context and gives a background of the increasing importance of Blockchain in cybersecurity. Then, a brief "Literature Review" introduces the technology and explains how its built-in features offer security. Then, the "Blockchain Security for the Enterprise" section highlights the need for enterprises to embrace and adapt to technological advancements. Then, the section "Benefits of Blockchain in Cybersecurity" explains the advantages of technology in building and maintaining a safe cybersecurity infrastructure. This is followed by the "Cybersecurity Best Practices" section that explains some industry-tested best practices that are of practical importance. The "Blockchain Security Considerations" and "Regulatory Compliance" sections discuss various aspects to be considered in Blockchain implementations and the need for regulatory compliance from the perspective of leading regulatory aspects. Finally, the "Future Trends and Challenges" discusses trends and challenges that can be pointers for future research.

LITERATURE REVIEW

Blockchain-based digital services face challenges from regulations (GDPR), ransomware defense, supply chain attacks, and scalability issues related to data storage (Wylde et al., 2022).

Fundamental Concepts of Blockchain

Building robust cybersecurity complaint applications requires a fundamental knowledge of the underlying technologies, in this case, Blockchain technology. This section gives an in-depth overview of Blockchain's architecture, signifying decentralization, the need for cryptographic hashing, and the standards of Immutability and transparency that distinguish Blockchain as a revolutionary technology.

Blockchain Architecture and Core Principles

Decentralization is the core of the features offered by Blockchain. This feature helps store Data in Blocks. For optimization reasons, each Block waits for sufficient data and bundles sizeable data (such as by bundling multiple transactions) before the Block is completed and broadcast on the Blockchain network. This architecture differs from legacy centralized systems. As Figure 1 shows, a typical Blockchain Block contains a Block Header with a timestamp, the actual data to be stored (say, for example, a collection or bunch of transactions), and a Cryptographic Hash of the previous Block. Blocks are connected to form a chain. Network participants verify the blocks called nodes. The nodes ensure the data is immutable and cannot be altered (Tripathi et al., 2023).

Figure 1. Block structure in a Blockchain

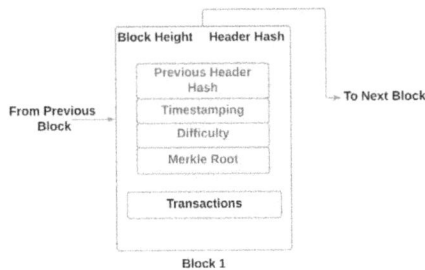

Source: (Tripathi et al., 2023)

Two types of cryptographic keys are commonly used for encryption - Public and Private. These keys help enable secure communication between nodes in the Blockchain network. Public keys are generally used for generating addresses, which are unique identifiers to send and receive funds. Private keys are used to ratify and digitally sign transactions.

For example, assume that Party A wants to send 1 Bitcoin (BTC) to Party B. Part A uses his private key to sign a transaction specifying the recipient's address and the amount of BTC he wishes to send. Once Party A signs the transaction, it is broadcast to the Bitcoin network. The network then verifies the transaction and adds it to the Blockchain ledger. Once added, it is considered permanent and cannot be reversed. So, when a person wants to create a cryptocurrency transaction, he uses his private key to sign the transaction. This proves that the owner of the funds has authorized the transaction, and that the transaction is to be distributed to all nodes across the network.

Miners, referred to as groups of network nodes, combine these transactions into a Block and timestamp it. This Block is then mined using a consensus mechanism and integrated into the network. Figure 2 shows the workflow of Blockchain.

Figure 2. Workflow of the blockchain network

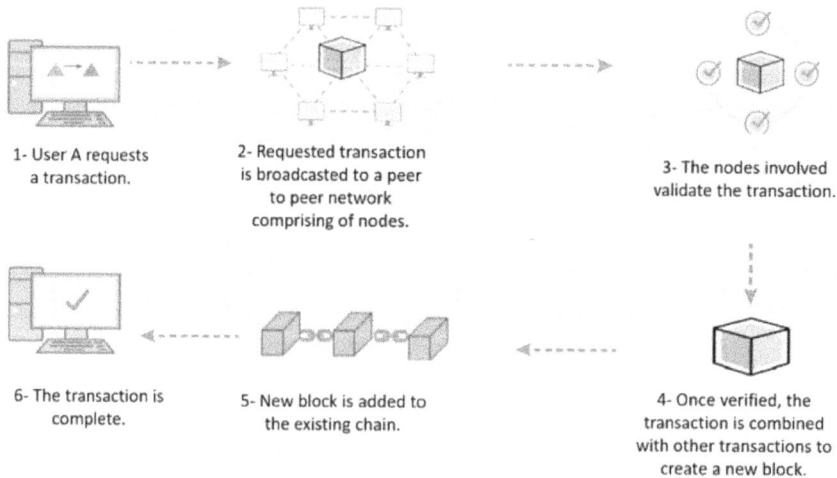

1- User A requests a transaction.

2- Requested transaction is broadcasted to a peer to peer network comprising of nodes.

3- The nodes involved validate the transaction.

6- The transaction is complete.

5- New block is added to the existing chain.

4- Once verified, the transaction is combined with other transactions to create a new block.

Source: (Sami Berkani et al., 2023)

Consensus Protocols

Consensus Protocols are algorithms that run in a distributed network. These algorithms help all the nodes to agree and reach a typical state or decision. This is vital for the decentralization process because of three reasons:

- Ensure data integrity and prevent double-spending, which is vital in cryptocurrency-related implementations.
- Maintain the consistency of distributed databases.
- Enable reliable communication and coordination among multiple nodes.

Nodes are a critical component for implementing the consensus protocols. Nodes can add new data to the Blockchain while keeping the previous data unaltered. Nodes provide the certainty that the Blockchain remains secure, encrypted, consistent, and up to date with provisions for further research. In addition, they validate the transactions, ensuring everything is in order (Kaur et al., 2021). Though about 58 consensus algorithms are in force (Singh et al., 2022), Table 1 gives an idea of famous consensus protocols and their node mechanisms. Table 2 shows the various roles that Nodes play. Studies have shown that consensus protocols are critical in maintaining Blockchain integrity and security. Old algorithm versions that have not been upgraded for a while or are not optimized will become a bottleneck, leading to high latency, as seen in public Blockchain networks. This deters applications from real-time environment deployments (Taylor et al., 2020). Several research studies (Xiao et al., 2020; Kaur & Gupta, 2021; Oyinloye et al., 2021; Singh et al., 2022; Xu et al., 2023) are devoted to consensus protocols, their optimizations, and the search for a suitable alternative.

Table 1. Consensus Protocols and their mechanisms

Name of Consensus Protocol	Mechanism of Nodes
Proof-of-Work (PoW)	Nodes contest with each other to solve complicated mathematical problems. The winning node will get the authority to authorize transactions and create new blocks in the Blockchain.
Proof-of-Stake (PoS)	Nodes are used to authenticate transactions and create fresh blocks as per requirement. However, this authority comes to them based on their cryptocurrency quantity.
Practical Byzantine Fault Tolerance (PBFT)	It uses a fixed number of nodes to reach an arrangement. The nodes are picked even if some nodes are found to be malicious or have failed.

continued on following page

Table 1. Continued

Name of Consensus Protocol	Mechanism of Nodes
Raft	A leaderless consensus protocol that uses a majority of nodes to achieve consensus.
Paxos	A consensus protocol designed for distributed systems where nodes may fail or experience delays.
Delegated Proof of Stake (DPoS)	Only a few nodes are selected by a voting process to be validators and have a higher chance of getting the authority to add nodes.
Proof of Authority (PoA)	Nodes/validators are typically pre-selected by the network creators. These validators are typically trusted community members like large businesses or organizations.

Table 2. Typical Node roles in achieving Consensus on a Blockchain

Role	Description
Proposer	Initiates the consensus process by proposing a new state or decision.
Acceptor	Evaluate the proposal and either accept or reject it.
Leader	Coordinates the consensus process and ensures all nodes agree on the proposed state or decision.
Follower	Participates in the consensus process by sending votes or messages to other nodes.
Validator	Verifies the validity of proposed states or decisions.

Blockchain systems build trust in the system with their transparency and traceability features. Transactional data stored in the Blocks can be traced using timestamps because of the ordered chain storage mechanisms. Hash, Digital Signature, the Distributed Consensus Protocol, and the Decentralized architecture help enhance security (Zheng et al., 2018). Digital signatures provide a secure way to authenticate the identity of the parties participating in the transaction. Distributed consensus protocols work to keep all nodes settled on the overall ledger's current state.

Decentralization and Cybersecurity

Decentralization Governance and Security: Decentralization, authenticity, consistency, and pseudonymity are core features of Blockchain (Schlatt et al., 2023). These features increase the security strength of an existing secure network. Data copies are distributed across the nodes due to the decentralized architecture. This makes data tampering significantly more challenging (or impossible) than existing solutions. Data stored with traditional mechanisms can be easily compromised as they depend on a single trusted authority for verification and storing encrypted data

(Taylor et al., 2020). This feature can help in the cybersecurity context of digital certificate management, thereby improving the security of online transactions and communications. However, despite these enhancements, it should be noted that these only partially substitute existing cybersecurity solutions.

Immunity to DDoS Attacks: Blockchain's decentralized nature and storage are primarily public and resistant to Distributed Denial of Service (DDoS) attacks. The nature of DDoS attacks is to disrupt the available services by flooding the Internet traffic. Traditional DDoS are challenging to control because they come from multiple sources. However, due to the distributed architecture, there will be no single point of failure, making the Blockchain network immune to a DDoS attack. (Rodrigues et al., 2017). Further, Blockchain transactions are verified by multiple nodes in the network. This makes it very difficult for attackers to flood the network with fake transactions and overwhelm the system.

The Ethereum network was under a DDoS attack in 2017. However, the attack was unsuccessful, and the network could continue functioning normally. This demonstrated the resilience of blockchain technology to DDoS attacks.

Data Manipulation and Fraud: Traditional centralized data storage behavior generates security issues and is prone to data tampering. However, Blockchain technology is tamper-proof as it uses cryptography in addition to its distributed architecture. (Zhang & Chen, 2019).

Addressing Cybersecurity Risks Through Decentralization: Blockchain technology eliminates the necessity for central control by distributing it among individual nodes. This increases transparency and traceability, thereby enhancing cybersecurity and preventing unauthorized manipulation and control of data.

Cryptographic Hashing

The fundamental concept of Blockchain technology is cryptographic hashing, which fortifies its strength, integrity, and trustworthiness along with other consensus mechanisms. Adding a block to the Blockchain automatically links to the previous Block and becomes resistant to tampering. Blockchain technology's Immutability is paramount because it prevents unauthorized data tampering and deters threat actors from attempting to alter the data (Adeghe et al., 2024). Digital signatures in Blockchain validate the genuineness of transactions and guarantee that the data is unaltered. (Uikey et al., 2024)

Advanced cryptographic algorithms used by Blockchain technology are energy-intensive, consuming significant processing power. Most existing consensus mechanisms are energy-intensive, leading to delays and increased costs (Adeghe et al., 2024).

Hashing algorithms like SHA-256 are used widely in Blockchain technology. They are tamper-resistant and shield against cryptographic attacks. Despite this, the ever-evolving cyber threats necessitate continuous research and development to develop dynamic countermeasures (Fernández-Caramés & Fraga-Lamas, 2020)

Ensuring Data Integrity with Immutability

Blockchain provides reliability and accuracy for data storage, making it the technology of choice in several fields where decision-making is done with precision. Immutable and its impossible-to-tamper features give a differentiating edge to Blockchain technology over others (S. Zhou et al., 2023). Consequently, the transparency features make it ideal for sharing and recording data, especially in collaborative environments. Blocks interlink with each other to form a chain. Each Block contains a unique cryptographic hash of its transactions and a hash of the previous Block. This strong chained interconnection implements Immutability. Data cannot be tampered with without breaking the chain. This feature makes Blockchain technology a secure and safe way to store data (L. Zhou et al., 2024)

Transparency and Trust

Blockchain technology is a pioneering cybersecurity force, fostering transparency, security, and trust. Public, private, and consortium Blockchains are currently popular types of Blockchains. In Public Blockchains, the visibility of the ledger is available to all members, as everyone can view the same ledger. Only the group members can view it in consortium and private Blockchains. Using a Blockchain ledger ensures that the data cannot be altered or tampered with at any cost. (Leteane & Ayalew, 2024). Blockchain technology deters cybersecurity attacks such as DDoS and DoS due to its tamper-proof, immutable, and decentralized nature. It inadvertently fosters trust among the network participants, securing data through consensus mechanisms. (Hasan et al., 2024)

BLOCKCHAIN SECURITY FOR THE ENTERPRISE

Strengthened Data Integrity with Blockchain

Data that includes sensitive information such as passwords, identities, and critical organizational data must be safeguarded at all times, whether at rest, in processing, or transit. It is imperative to shield this data from unauthorized alterations or tampering by threat actors across all phases. Consequently, maintaining data integrity is an essential and complex endeavor. Due to its immutable ledger and secure transactions, Blockchain technology is a comprehensive solution that upholds data integrity while strengthening security and privacy.

Blockchains allow only data to be added. Once added successfully, the data cannot be removed, deleted, or modified without the consensus of the participants. This is because each Block in a Blockchain contains a hash of the previous Block. So, the chain of blocks is all cryptographically linked. Attempting to modify a block will require modifying all subsequent blocks as well. This is computationally infeasible. This feature of Blockchain is called immutable and has applications where data integrity and security are essential. It helps organizations streamline decision-making and improve trust and transparency. The cryptographic features of Blockchain enhance data integrity. Their integration with further cybersecurity measures is pivotal for safeguarding information and ensuring adequate data governance (Salagrama et al., 2023).

Identity Governance and Validation

Identity and Access Management (IAM) became vital, considering that every person needs to have a digital identity to validate their identity, access resources, and claim benefits offered by authorities. A typical example is the unique identity systems such as the Social Security Number (SSN) in the USA, Government Gateway in the UK, SingPass in Singapore, and the Aadhaar Card in India. The system allows us to:

1. Prove the identity of the citizen
2. Authenticate digitally
3. Allow citizens to access various services

Studies show that current IAM systems do not have sufficient security measures. The currently available ones are generally inadequate for fighting imminent cyber threats. This raises concerns and makes them prone to identity theft and misuse of information. Sharing data with external service providers without the user's explicit consent raises doubts about the adequacy of existing consent mechanisms. Blockchain-based identity management systems' decentralized characteristics provide robust solutions to counter these challenges. Blockchain offers enhanced security, privacy, and user control, making it a promising alternative for managing digital identities securely and efficiently (Agarkar et al., 2024).

Immutability and Trustworthiness

The immutable characteristic is how Blockchain technology gains trust. The technology offers compelling features that make users willing to trust it to generate value. The data is decentralized and can be traced by all participants in the network. The data cannot be altered or transferred without collusion. This distinct cryptographic feature makes Blockchain technology trustworthy and differentiates it from other legacy computer systems. The Immutability and transparency of Blockchain augment confidence in the reliability and accuracy of data. Immutability, along with the tamper-proof nature of Blockchain technology, leads to improved and efficient data management (Ali et al., 2023). Above all, the system implements trust, which is superior to the traditional password-handled human-driven security systems. This attracts several practical implementations such as Vehicle Information Systems (Distefano et al., 2021), E-Governance (Ahmad et al., 2021), Blockchain-enabled exchanges, and marketing domains (Tan & Saraniemi, 2023), amongst others.

Security Challenges: Mitigation in Blockchain Deployment

A typical Blockchain is considered immutable and secure due to its decentralized capabilities. However, several challenges, such as privacy, interoperability, scalability, and full compliance with legal requirements, remain concerns for many enterprises. While Blockchain technology is transparent, it still requires mechanisms to ensure the privacy of certain transactions. Increased privacy in Blockchain is meant to stop illicit access and copying of sensitive information. The volume of Blockchain usage has considerably increased due to its trustworthiness and adoption by many enterprises. This rise in the number of transactions has led to delays. The scalability issue can be addressed by redesigning the Blockchain and optimizing storage (Joshi et al., 2018). Interoperability in Blockchain is paramount, but the knowledge to achieve it is limited. The seamless communication and data exchange between distinct Blockchain technologies are crucial for its sustenance. (Belchior et al., 2021).

BENEFITS OF BLOCKCHAIN IN CYBERSECURITY

Securing the Data

In traditional methods, data can be tampered with, altered, and deleted without much effort. The need for data protection led to the emergence of Blockchain technology, which is decentralized, immutable, and secure against vulnerabilities. Each Blockchain block contains the preceding Block's cryptographic hash, forming a chain resistant to tampering. Figure 3 depicts the Arrangement of Blocks in a Blockchain. Table 3 lists software tools and services that incorporate Blockchain in cybersecurity.

Figure 3. Arrangement of blocks in a Blockchain

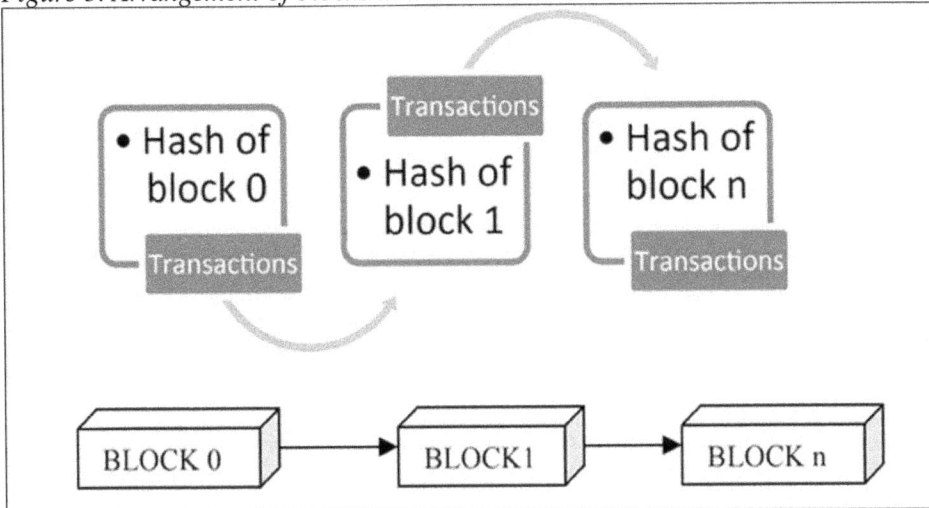

Source: (Fatima et al., 2022)

Table 3. Live software and services that implemented Blockchain in cybersecurity

Software	Area of Implementation	Brief Description
IBM Blockchain Transparent Supply	Data Provenance and authentication	Blockchain-based platform for tracking the provenance and authenticity of products throughout the supply chain.
Uport Microsoft Azure Active Directory (AAD)	Identity Verification and Management	These decentralized identity verification platforms use Blockchain to store and manage personal data.
Chainlink's Threat Intelligence IBM's Blockchain-based Threat Intelligence CyberSponse's Blockchain-based Threat Intelligence	Cybersecurity Threat Intelligence	Blockchain-based threat intelligence platform that provides real-time threat data.
Wire Signal Telegram's Blockchain-based Messaging	Secure Communication and Messaging	These are secure communication platforms that use Blockchain to provide end-to-end encryption.

continued on following page

Table 3. Continued

Software	Area of Implementation	Brief Description
Xage Security	Industrial IoT	Provides a blockchain-protected security fabric for industrial IoT.
REMME	Authentication	Implements blockchain-based authentication to replace password-based systems.
Guardtime KSI	Blockchain-base Time stamping	Uses Blockchain for data integrity verification and protection against insider threats.

Decentralization, Immutability, Cryptographic Methods (Fatima et al., 2022)., identity management (Liu et al., 2020), and Self-Sovereign Identity (Monrat et al., 2019) make the system robust.

Transparency and Trustworthiness

Blockchain technology operates on a trustless framework, yet it generates trust due to its immutable, transparent, decentralized records and transactions. Unlike legacy centralized systems, which cannot be trusted blindly, Blockchain's tamper-proof and transparency prevent fraudulent transactions, thereby gaining trust among users (Monrat et al., 2019).

Digital Signatures and Smart Contracts

Blockchain technology uses digital signatures to confirm the authenticity and verification of identities. On the other hand, smart contracts automatically verify signatures based on predefined conditions (Monrat et al., 2019).

Secure Platform Transactions

Blocks of transactions are stored in public records in Blockchain technology, allowing all network participants to verify and validate the blocks. While they can view all transactions, they cannot be tampered with or altered, thus making Blockchain technology secure and efficient (Monrat et al., 2019). Figure 4 explains transaction flow on a Blockchain.

Figure 4. Transaction Flow on Blockchain

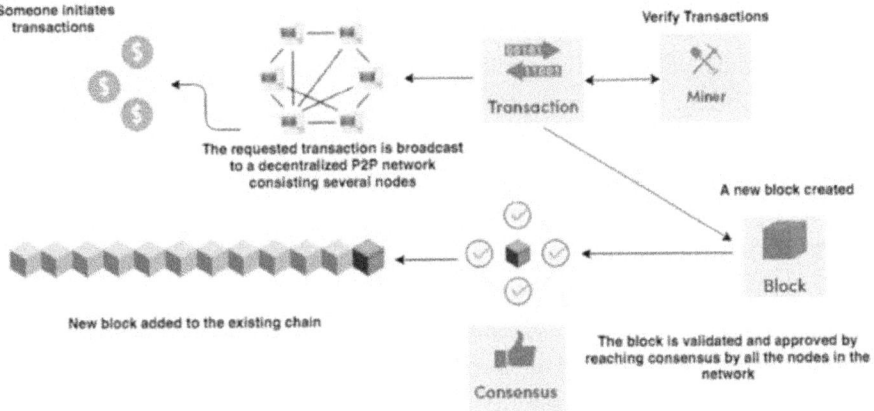

CYBERSECURITY BEST PRACTICES

Figure 5 lists critical areas of cybersecurity best practices for system integrations to consider in making the Blockchain network more robust.

Figure 5. Critical Areas of Cybersecurity Best Practices

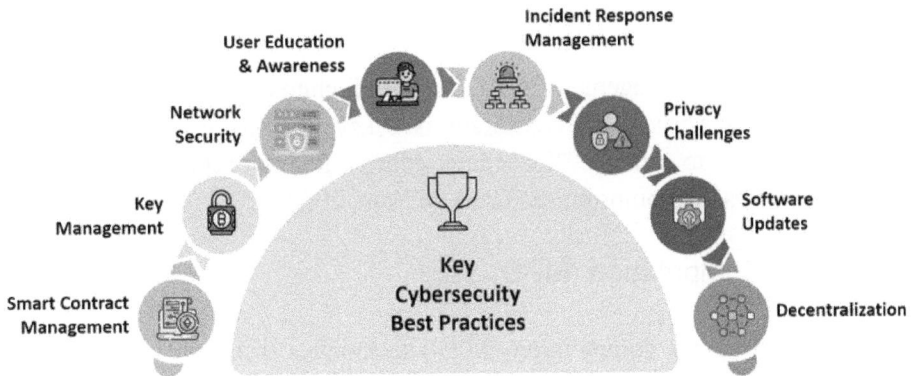

Smart Contract

A Smart Contract is a program that responds to various significant events. The direct involvement of two parties or intermediaries is unnecessary for its development **(John et al., 2023)**. Smart contracts enhance security and revolutionize business operations by automating processes, increasing efficiency, and optimizing costs (Guo & Yu, 2022).

Smart Coding Standards

With the ever-growing demand for application software development, developers are fast-tracking the production environment, which may compromise best practices for security and increase vulnerability risks. Implementing secure coding standards is crucial to reduce these vulnerabilities. Adopting standards and established industry guidelines can significantly improve code quality and security (Nath et al., 2023).

Key Management

Private Security Keys

The Blockchain technology uses Public Key Infrastructure (PKI) (Pal et al., 2021). Authorized network users use private keys to sign and verify digital transactions (Bhushan et al., 2021). In the cryptographic system, competent and secure key management is necessary (Pal et al., 2021).

Key Rotation

Rotational Key Management in Blockchain Technology can mitigate several security attacks. If a private key is compromised, key rotation is essential to generate a new pair of keys to enhance Blockchain security. Regular rotation of keys helps ensure security is not compromised (Park & Nam, 2022).

Multi-Party Computation (MPC)

Secure multi-party computation (MPC) techniques distribute the generation and management of keys among various parties to enhance privacy and build trust. Secure MPCs are difficult for threat actors to compromise (J. Zhou et al., 2021).

Network Security

Selection of Consensus Mechanism

The core job of consensus mechanisms is to verify data. However, selecting a suitable consensus mechanism goes beyond the core job. The decision impacts the security and scalability of the network. The selected consensus mechanism should resist attacks like double-spending and Sybil attacks. They are resilient mechanisms for authenticating ongoing transactions and maintaining agreements between network nodes. They guarantee the network's safety, operational continuity, and fault tolerance (Lashkari & Musilek, 2021).

Node Security

Blocks store transactional data. The blocks are interconnected to form a chain (Bhushan et al., 2021). Nodes in the Blockchain network must verify that no alterations or tampering to the data recorded within each Block. Securing each node within the Blockchain is essential for the data's safety, security, and integrity. Blockchain incorporates pseudonymous identities to guarantee the participant's security and confidentiality (Idrees et al., 2021).

User Education and Awareness

User education and awareness can go a long way to preventing Blockchain scams, enhancing Blockchain infrastructure, reducing cybersecurity risks, and improving incident reporting. Figure 6 shows the importance of user education and awareness of Blockchain and cybersecurity.

Figure 6. User education & awareness on blockchain and cybersecurity

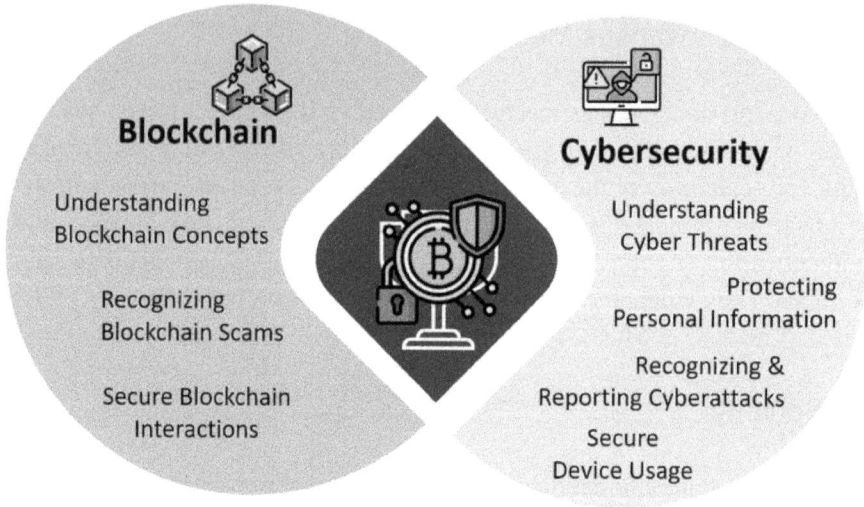

User Education

Blockchain is often mistaken for Digital Currency. Most people are unaware that Blockchain is a technological implementation behind various digital currencies such as Bitcoin. Blockchain has several applications beyond cryptocurrencies and is used as a technology in several platforms to perform various transactions. To attain user acceptance of Blockchain technology, user-friendly and easily accessible strategies and solutions should be adopted. People should be educated on how to use this application securely and conduct activities that promote awareness among them (Ravichandra et al., 2024).

Phishing and Social Engineering Awareness

Phishing attacks are a common cybersecurity threat that trick users into revealing their credentials through emails or websites. Humans often fall prey to phishing attacks through reconnaissance or social engineering. While there is no foolproof solution to counter such attacks, users must be educated and aware of preventive measures (Andryukhin, 2019).

Password Management

Blockchain technology must be secured by educating users to use strong passwords with a minimum of 14 characters and enabling multi-factor authentication (MFA) to enhance security (Andryukhin, 2019).

Periodic Security Evaluations

Privacy and security concerns in Blockchain technology are alarming and challenging for development. Organizations should conduct periodic assessments to discover possible security vulnerabilities and take steps to address these risks (Bhutta et al., 2021).

Regulatory Compliance

Organizations must follow laws and regulations regarding compliance issues, consistency in standards, disputes over rights issues, and rising IoT economic challenges (Bhutta et al., 2021).

Incident Response Management

Response Strategies

Security threats are proliferating due to the increased adoption of Blockchain technology. Blockchain engineering primarily focuses on developing applications, with scant attention to security threats. Blockchain's current system of reporting security incidents is centralized and needs more structure. Implementing a structured incident reporting and rapid response mechanism will limit the impact of damage and facilitate immediate response and recovery. Figure 7 depicts the reporting of security incidents and prompt response in six steps in a decentralized manner (Putz et al., 2022). Similarly, malware can be detected and prevented by tracking the spread of malicious software and identifying infected devices.

Figure 7. Six steps process for incident reporting

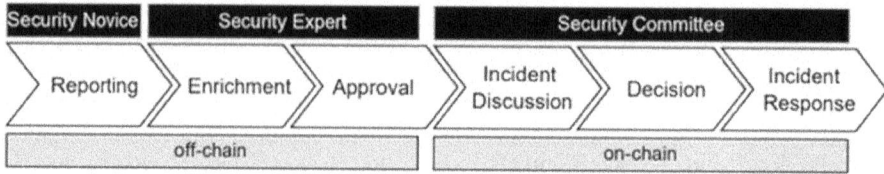

Source: (Putz et al., 2022)

Privacy Challenges and Solutions

Privacy Protection in Blockchain Adoption

Blockchain technology faces various scalability and privacy challenges, such as those posed by GDPR. Although several privacy protection solutions are available for implementation, organizations and individuals must be more open to adopting Blockchain technology due to concerns about compromising their privacy on public platforms. Self-Sovereign Identity (SSI), Zero-Knowledge Proofs (ZKPs), and ring signatures can hide users' identities and transactions. Sophisticated privacy procedures ensure the effectiveness of zero-knowledge methods in Blockchain technology (Bernabe et al., 2019).

Software Updates

Periodic Software Update

Timely updates of Blockchain technology software ensure that potential future security threats and vulnerabilities are countered and mitigated promptly (Lee, 2018).

Decentralization

Data Security

In Blockchain technology, data is decentralized and stored in blocks distributed across the network, minimizing the impact of data extortion. Blockchain data is tamper-proof and encrypted, making it impossible for threat actors to manipulate it (Ismail et al., 2024).

Collaborative Cybersecurity Initiatives

Blockchain technology users must share information regarding threat intelligence, jointly respond to threats, and mitigate them collectively. Collective cybersecurity helps eradicate threats and eliminate single points of failure (Miller & Pahl, 2024).

BLOCKCHAIN SECURITY CONSIDERATIONS

Despite Blockchain technology's decentralized, immutable, and tamper-proof nature, it is prone to certain security risks due to digitalization and increasing acceptance by organizations and individuals. Cyberattacks can cause significant losses to organizations, affecting their brand reputation, financial stability, and technological infrastructure (Ibarra et al., 2019).

Understanding Double-Spending and 51% Attacks

A 51% cyberattack compromises the Blockchain's integrity, making it a high-risk category. Threat actors can rewrite the Blockchain and create a new version to undertake malicious activities, known as a double-spending attack. Any authorized user or miner holding 51% of the mining hash rate can execute the attack maliciously, altering Blockchain credentials and transactions in the network. Some potential manipulations can be:

a. Reverse transactions, resulting in a double-spending attack
b. Tamper with or modify transactions
c. Interfere with other miners' operations
d. Prevent transaction confirmations (Apone-Novoa et al., 2021).

Notable examples of 51% attacks include (Y. Chen et al., 2022):

- On May 22, 2018, millions of anonymous coins (XVG tokens) were stolen from the Verge Blockchain.
- On May 16, 2018, threat actors illegally traded 12,239 gold bits on Bitcoin Gold (BTG).
- On January 5, 2019, Ethereum Classic (ETC) incurred a loss of $1.1 million.
- Vertcoin (2019), Grin (2020), Expanse (2020), Litecoin Cash (2020), and Firo (formerly Zcoin) (2021) too suffered from 51% attacks.

These attacks highlight the importance of implementing robust security measures to prevent 51% attacks. Some immediate steps that were to be taken include:

- Increasing the mining difficulty
- Implementing proof-of-stake (PoS) consensus
- Using a decentralized network spreading to multiple nodes located in multiple data centers
- Implementing robust security protocols
- Regularly updating and patching software

Mitigation Strategies

Penalty System: Threat actors must incur a heavy cost to perform the attack in the delayed block approach system. The attacker must mine a more significant number of blocks consecutively to join the genuine chain.

Delayed Proof of Work (DPoW): This system must follow the most extended chain rule, making it difficult for the attacker to gain control.

PirlGuard: Like Delayed Proof of Work (DPoW) and the Penalty System, PirlGuard imposes a heavy penalty on threat actors, thus minimizing risk.

ChainLocks: This process is speedy as only one block confirmation is required to execute the transaction.

Merged Mining: This process is costlier for the threat actor as it combines the hashing power of two cryptocurrencies (Sayeed & Marco-Gisbert, 2019). Figure 8 shows defense mechanisms in 51% attacks.

Figure 8. Defense Mechanisms on the 51% Attacks

	Advantage	Risk Elements	Vulnerability Identify	Cost	Functionality
Penalty System	The penalty makes the attack much more costly to perform. The delayed block approach sets the attacker to mine a large number of blocks in a sequence before joining the legit chain.	The introduced penalty may not be sufficient to mitigate the attack fully. Attackers targeting low hashing coins have a higher chance of success. Hence, the risk level is **Medium**.	Identifies the vulnerability before the genuine chain adopts it.	This technique is a research prototype. No implementation cost is introduced.	Proof of Work (PoW)
DPoW	Does not recognize the longest chain rule. Notarization provides extra defense. Flexible and greater security enhancement than Bitcoin blockchain.	An attacker with 51% hashing can execute the 51% attack within the 10-minute notarized period. However, extensive security makes the risk level **Low**.	Does not identify the vulnerability ahead. Coins with few seconds of confirmation time can be at risk.	Practically implemented on about 20 Blockchains. A cost is introduced to execute this security technique.	Any UTXO based Blockchain
PirlGuard	Follows a similar approach as Penalty System and dPoW. Therefore, introduces a penalty to adversaries.	Notarization involves master nodes. The master nodes intensify it as a centralized technique. However, the overall security policy makes the risk level **Low**.	Identifies the vulnerability ahead as soon as it is recognized.	Practical implementation. May incur a fee.	Ethash Algorithm
ChainLocks	Transactions are confirmed after a single block confirmation, making the process very fast.	1 block confirmation may lead to double-spending with just minimal hashing, such as 1 confirmation attack. Hence, the risk level is **High**.	Locks-in the very first block as a genuine block by discarding any other blocks or chain of blocks.	ChainLocks is released to 'testnet'. It does require an implementation cost.	Dash
Merged Mining	Merges the hashing power of 2 crypto-coins, making the attack more costly. The low reputed coins can benefit immensely from this process.	It is not a security policy; hence, an attacker in possession of the required hashing can carry out a 51% attack. Therefore, the risk level is **High**.	No security policy in place to identify the vulnerability in advance.	Practically implemented. Does not require a cost for implementation.	Auxiliary Proof of Work (PoW)

Source: (Sayeed & Marco-Gisbert, 2019)

Theft of Keys

Safeguarding Digital Assets

A private key is a form of digital identity in Blockchain technology that allows authorized users in the network to perform transactions. Blockchain technology promises privacy and anonymity; private keys are vital for safeguarding digital assets. However, if a threat actor steals the private key, assets will be lost and cannot be recovered (Efanov & Roschin, 2018).

Mitigation Strategies

Secure Storage Solutions

A cryptographic Hardware Security Module (HSM) safeguards data integrity and confidentiality by storing and managing keys and passwords. It is tamper-resistant, encrypted, and physically protects the device's security (Alrubei et al., 2022).

Blockchain-Based Multi-Factor Authentication (BMFA)

It provides secure authentication by combining multi-factor authentication (MFA) with the features of Blockchain. Such a combination is called a Blockchain-based MFA (BMFA). BMFA utilizes a decentralized and immutable ledger to store sensitive data, enhancing security by adding further protection against malicious actors (Almadani et al., 2023). MFA adds an extra layer of security by requiring users to provide multiple forms of identification before they can access a Blockchain system.

Key Rotation

The security keys should be rotated periodically to minimize security risks. For a threat actor to pose a significant security risk, they would need to compromise each user within a short time frame to gain the required number of users to make changes, which is extremely difficult. (Šimunić et al., 2021).

Code Exploits

Even though Blockchain technology is immutable, threat actors can exploit the code, resulting in irrecoverable losses. The 2016 DAO attack is a famous example where the threat actors exploited vulnerabilities and caused a loss of around $60 million in Ether (He et al., 2024).

Mitigation Strategies

Audits: Regular audits will be conducted to check for and review vulnerabilities, weaknesses, and potential attack vectors in Blockchain systems (Moubarak et al., 2018). Conducting regular audits is essential, especially before major updates or releases. There are several audits being undertaken, including Smart Contract Audits, Security Audits, Compliance Audits, Performance Audits, Infrastructure Audits, Governance Audits, and Code Audits and Vulnerability Scanning. It helps prevent attacks, ensures compliance, and builds trust among users.

Secure Code: Secure code standards are to be followed to stay protected from vulnerabilities (Bhardwaj et al., 2021)

Code Analysis Tools: Code analysis tools are generally used to examine the source code of software applications. The objective is to categorize potential vulnerabilities and security weaknesses. These tools help perform both manual and automated penetration testing. They simulate cyberattacks to identify exploitable vulnerabilities.

Penetration testing is a security assessment technique. It is used to identify weaknesses in the system or network. This is done by mimicking an attack on the network externally or internally. Penetration testers have a good arsenal of tools and techniques. Their job is to find vulnerabilities that malicious actors could potentially exploit. Several penetration testing frameworks are now available for Blockchain applications (K. Chen et al., 2024).

Lateral movement is another dimension of it. It refers to the ability of an attacker to progressively move deeper within a network after gaining initial access to a system. Their objective is to seek high-value assets. Attackers may use various techniques to move laterally, such as exploiting vulnerabilities in operating systems, applications, or network protocols (Smiliotopoulos et al., 2024).

Organizations conduct penetration testing and lateral movement testing periodically. These tests can be done manually or using automated tools. The objective of these tests is to identify weak spots and vulnerabilities that can laterally spread in the network (Bhardwaj et al., 2021)

Physical Security Measures

Physical security is vital in the process of securing Blockchain infrastructure. This is done by protecting the nodes from threat actors. Organizations must adopt tamper-proof detection and prevention solutions to protect the system from intruders (Alrubei et al., 2022).

Other Mitigation Strategies

Other mitigation strategies include:
- Bug Bounty Programs in which ethical hackers are incentivized to find and report vulnerabilities.
- Formal verification is where mathematical methods prove the correctness of smart contracts and protocols.
- Consensus Mechanism Improvements are implementing more secure consensus algorithms. Hybrid consensus mechanisms can also be considered to balance security and efficiency.
- Real-time monitoring systems, especially network monitoring, to detect unusual activities or potential attacks.
- Secure Key Management is done by implementing robust critical management practices, including hardware security modules (HSMs).
- Regular Updates and Patches are to be done to keep all blockchain software components up-to-date.

- Interoperability Standards can be developed and adhered to security standards for cross-chain interactions.
- Governance mechanisms can be formulated, including emergency response procedures for critical vulnerabilities.
- Education and Training for developers, operators, and users about blockchain security best practices. This can be done on an ongoing basis.

REGULATORY COMPLIANCE

Enterprises always keep an eye on regulations and compliance when deploying Blockchain solutions. Compliance with data protection laws and industry-specific regulations is necessary to dodge legal and reputational risks. Compliance with existing legal and regulatory frameworks is a prerequisite for any technology, old or new. The implementation of Blockchain technology in cybersecurity is no exception. Blockchain deployments should follow regulatory laws and standards. Professionals involved in integrating Blockchain technology into cybersecurity frameworks must thoroughly understand the legal and regulatory landscape. While privacy and regulatory compliance are not always complementary, privacy mechanisms are still necessary for certain transactions. Law enforcement authorities can access user transactions despite remaining private (Buterin et al., 2024). This section focuses on two crucial regulations – the General Data Protection Regulation (GDPR) and the Health Insurance Portability and Accountability Act (HIPAA).

General Data Protection Regulation (GDPR)

The General Data Protection Regulation (GDPR) is a critical framework enacted by the European Union (EU) in May 2018. It is a comprehensive personal data protection law. It became a role model for similar data protections enacted by various countries. It applies to any organization that deals with the personal data of EU residents, irrespective of its location. The GDPR expects organizations to apply suitable technical and organizational measures to ensure the security and confidentiality of personal data. Failure to comply with GDPR will be costly. The Cambridge Analytica Scandal (2018), Google, Facebook, and Uber GDPR fines (2019) are examples of the compliance costs involved. Figure 9 shows a list of key provisions of GDPR.

Figure 9. Key Provisions of GDPR

Several Blockchain Use Cases are now available to stay compliant with GDPR. Some of these include:

1. Ethereum's GDPR Compliance measures
2. IBM's Blockchain and GDPR platform
3. Blockchain-based Identity Verification via Self-Sovereign Identity (SSI)
4. Blockchain-based Data Storage via InterPlanetary File System (IPFS)

The decentralization and transparent record of data transactions provided by Blockchain technology can enhance data security and compliance with the GDPR by facilitating controllers and processors of data (Hristov & Dimitrov, 2018). However, the GDPR has some strict requirements for data controllers and processors. There is an obligation to notify data subjects of data breaches and provide them access to their data.

The EU Blockchain Observatory Report 2018 said there is no contradiction principle between GDPR and Blockchain technology because GDPR is not against technology. However, it is about how it is used (Patrick & Haie, 2018). There was also a discussion about whether certain Blockchains, such as Permissioned Blockchains, should be exempted from GDPR, considering the controls that users are given (Anisha, 2019). The debate led to two tendencies - purists and fundamentalists

(Poelman & Iqbal, 2021). The Decentralization feature raises concerns about data ownership and control that might conflict with the fundamental principles of GDPR (Zemler & Westner, 2019). Further, sharing personal data across multiple nodes is another issue. The Right to Erasure challenges Blockchain because the immutability feature makes deleting personal data difficult (or maybe impossible).

Organizations have devised alternatives to address this challenge, leading to a new wave of GDPR-complaint Blockchain networks (Haque et al., 2021). Techniques such as cryptographic obfuscation, zero-knowledge proofs, or off-chain storage help ensure GDPR compliance while preserving the benefits of Blockchain technology.

Health Insurance Portability and Accountability Act (HIPAA)

The Health Insurance Portability and Accountability Act (HIPAA) is a critical framework in the healthcare sector. It is a US federal law enacted in 1996. It focuses on ensuring the protection of patient data. HIPAA applies to healthcare organizations. Table 4 shows a partial list of stakeholders to whom HIPAA is applicable.

Table 4. HIPAA stakeholders and why it impacts them

Stakeholder	Impact
Healthcare providers	They electronically transmit health information concerning certain transactions, including claims, benefits, and referrals.
Health plans	These include physical and mental health, dental, vision, and prescription drug insurers, health maintenance organizations (HMOs), government healthcare providers and insurers, long-term and end-of-life care (nursing home) providers and insurers; employer-sponsored group health plans; church and religious health plans, and multi-employer plans. There are, of course, few exceptions.
Healthcare clearinghouse	These entities process nonstandard health information they receive from another entity into a specific standard format or data.
Business associates	These include persons or organizations, often third parties, using or disclosing individual PHI to perform or provide functions, activities, or services for a covered entity. Business associates include claims processors, data analysts, utilization reviewers, and billing service providers.

These entities are expected to employ proper technical and organizational measures to safeguard the security and confidentiality of patient data. The goal of HIPAA is to safeguard the confidentiality and security of protected health information (PHI). This is achieved through establishing nationwide guidelines regulating electronic sharing, privacy protections, and security of PHI. Figure 10 shows lists the key provisions.

Figure 10. Key provisions of HIPAA

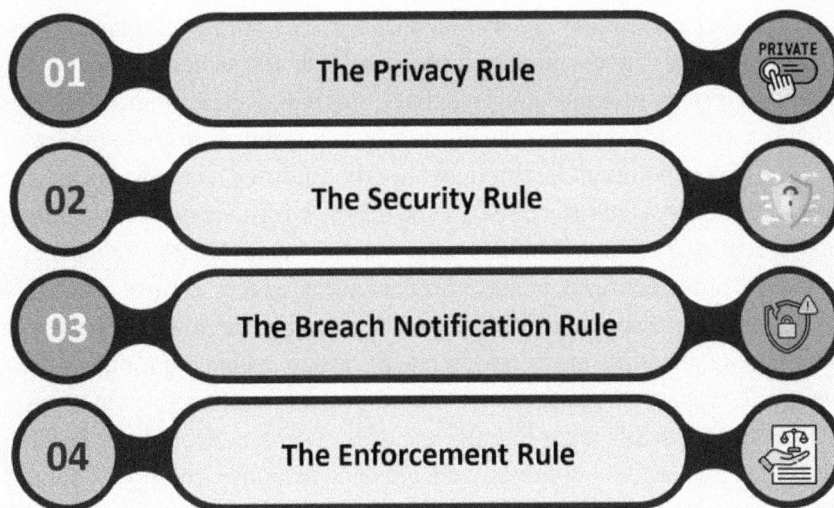

01	**The Privacy Rule**
02	**The Security Rule**
03	**The Breach Notification Rule**
04	**The Enforcement Rule**

Blockchain offers decentralization and transparent records of patient data transactions. This can enhance data security and compliance with HIPAA. HIPAA also imposes strict requirements for healthcare organizations. It puts us obligated to notify patients of data breaches and provide them access to their medical records. Blockchain technology poses unique challenges to HIPAA compliance. The Security Rule mandates that covered entities and associates employ administrative, physical, and technological protections to ensure electronic PHI's privacy, accuracy, and accessibility. Organizations must implement specific techniques to address this challenge. Some standard methods are encryption and access controls.

Other Regulations

Apart from those discussed above, several other relevant regulations apply to enterprises in various contexts. Here are a few mentions:
- Payment Card Industry Data Security Standard (PCI DSS)
- Gramm-Leach-Bliley Act (GLBA)
- The California Consumer Privacy Act (CCPA)
- The New York State Department of Financial Services (NYDFS) Cybersecurity Regulation
- The EU's Markets in Crypto-Assets (MiCA) regulation.

These regulations place requirements on entities that handle individuals' information, protect the security of sensitive information, and establish standards for using Blockchain technology in financial services. Organizations can ensure regulatory companies by conducting a thorough risk assessment. Periodic checks can be undertaken to identify any potential compliance gaps. Timely addressing identified security gaps and lapses using appropriate controls helps in the long run. The risk assessment points and techniques are to be modified, considering the unique characteristics of Blockchain technology and the evolving cybersecurity challenges.

Robust security measures should be employed to protect the Blockchain network and its data. These measures include implementing access control mechanisms, employing cryptographic algorithms, and conducting regular security audits. Additionally, organizations must have incident response plans to mitigate security breaches or data leaks. Organizations should prepare and impose clear policies, procedures, and protocols regarding the use of Blockchain technology. Guidelines for data protection, access controls, and incident response guidelines should be prepared. They have to be updated to ensure compliance with evolving regulatory requirements. Data encryption and anonymization techniques can safeguard sensitive data while maintaining the integrity of the Blockchain's records.

Organizations should consider engaging a legal counsel with technology expertise and regulatory compliance. The council is expected to provide guidance on specific regulatory requirements and to ensure compliance with those requirements. Legal counsel can also guide on the potential legal implications of Blockchain technology, including issues related to liability, intellectual property, and jurisdiction.

FUTURE TRENDS AND CHALLENGES

Several new challenges are being uncovered as technologies are adopted more frequently. Some of the challenges will be related to cybersecurity. This section will present global trends in adopting AI and other technologies with Blockchain and security. It focuses on using Quantum computing to enhance cyberattack defense, surpassing traditional approaches and revolutionizing cybersecurity.

1. **Trilemma**: The blockchain network suffers from a situation called Blockchain Trilemma. It says that a Blockchain network can achieve, at most, two desirable properties: Security, Scalability, and Decentralization. Cybersecurity strength gets weakened if a chosen security factor for Blockchain implementation is underweighted in a bid to achieve scalability and decentralization. This situation grossly inhibits IT practitioners from implementing a robust system (Vijaya

Kittu & Gupta, 2024). Some preliminary solutions in sharding and others are currently being researched and explored.

2. **Crypto Assets**: More research on crypto assets, such as cryptocurrencies and NFTs, is required, considering the challenges from the law enforcement and forensic dimensions, primarily because crypto assets are blamed for being the favorite mode of payment for terrorism finance. Issues in the cybersecurity area arise in the form of transaction tracing because of this. The pseudo-anonymous nature of many cryptocurrencies can make it challenging for law enforcement to trace illicit transactions.

3. **IoT**: Increased use of IoT devices will mean an increased need to secure them. Integrating IoT with Blockchain helps prevent unauthorized access and data breaches. However, IoT-Blockchainre-related cybersecurity issues can arise in the form of smart contract vulnerabilities, 51% attacks on Blockchain, and data breaches. More quantitative studies on fault tolerance, latency, and efficiency could require more attention going forward.

4. **AI for Blockchain Security:** AI and Blockchain have several applications in terms of data, algorithm, and computation power. Some of the applications, such as data sharing, privacy-preserving, trusted decisions, and decentralized intelligence, are related to data management with extensions to improving security (Wang et al., 2021).

   a. **Automating Threat Detection and Response**: Using Machine Learning (ML), a large quantum of data can be analyzed to detect and respond to potential threats and trigger automated responses to mitigate risks, often in real-time. This can vastly improve overall security (Manoharan & Sarker, 2024).

   b. **Detecting and Preventing Malicious Activities**: AI algorithms can be configured to continuously monitor networks (such as Blockchain networks) for suspicious activity and fraud (Varun Shah, 2022). This can substantially lower the time and effort required to detect and respond to cyberattacks. Machine learning models can be trained to detect and flag unusual transaction patterns. For example, unusually large or frequent transactions may indicate a security breach or an attempted attack.

   c. **Enhancing Transaction Verification**: They can help verify the genuineness of the transactional data even before it is committed to the Blockchain network.

   d. **Optimizing Consensus Mechanisms**: Generally speaking, consensus mechanisms are slow and resource-intensive, thereby becoming the topic of researcher interest. Optimizing algorithm parameters can make the Blockchain faster and more efficient; however, care should be taken not to disturb the balance of decentralization, security, and performance. For example, ML algorithms can predict the likelihood of a valid transaction. Transaction verification will be faster and reduce the need for resource-intensive consensus mechanisms. Similarly, newer algorithms, such as Parallel Proof of Work, were proposed and are in various stages of experimentation.

    e. **Counter AI-Powered Attacks**: AI can help enterprises develop and maintain a proactive security stance. This can be done by identifying and addressing potential weaknesses in their Blockchain systems. AI can help prepare for new challenges, including the potential for AI-powered attacks. They can address demands for AI model validation and explainability. For example, attackers may use ML algorithms to identify and exploit Blockchain network vulnerabilities or launch a social engineering attack. Hence, robust AI model validation and explainability mechanisms can be built to ensure transparency and accountability.

5. **AI and Smart Contract Security**: Smart Contracts are used to program new-generation decentralized applications such as Decentralized Finance (DeFi) (John et al., 2023). Because they are human-written code, they are vulnerable to attacks and bugs. Past experiences show that these bugs can lead to significant financial losses. AI can help analyze smart contract code and identify potential vulnerabilities and bugs. It can also help build more secure and reliable smart contracts.

6. **AI for Data Analytics**: Blockchain data can be used in data analytics with AI. Insights from transactional data can be drawn. Patterns and anomalies that may indicate malicious activity can be identified. Security analysts can use the inputs to prioritize threat investigation and find potential vulnerabilities. This can lower risks and fraudulent activities, especially in B2B networks.

7. **AI and Data Privacy**: Generative AI algorithms use Large Language Modules (LLMs). LLMs need access to large volumes of data for training and analysis. This causes concerns regarding data privacy and the potential misuse of personal information. A compromised information technology system can be a good source of training data because it is rich in transactional data sources. However, Blockchain systems are extremely tough to compromise because of decentralization.

8. **Breaking Existing Encryption**: Quantum computers have the potential to break existing encryption algorithms, such as RSA and ECC (Sharma et al., 2021). This poses a significant threat to Blockchain security because these are common and popular algorithms that many Blockchain systems run on. Organizations must brace for this possibility by exploring post-quantum cryptography and developing mitigation strategies.

9. **Quantum-resistant Cryptography**: Quantum computers can be used to develop new cryptographic algorithms that are resistant to traditional attacks (Chaubey & Prajapati, 2020). These can significantly enhance the security of Blockchain networks and the data stored on them. There are three ways in which this can be done:
    - Developing new digital signature algorithms
    - Creating more secure hash functions
    - Improving the security of smart contracts

Quantum-resistant cryptography is a promising emerging research branch (Allende et al., 2023). It is believed that the algorithms built using it are even more secure against quantum computers. Although quantum computers remain in the early phases of development, many researchers are making strides toward realizing their full potential. Keeping an eye on quantum-resistant cryptography at the development stages can help prepare for the future.

CONCLUSION

Enterprises can use the Blockchain to improve their cybersecurity systems. They can achieve enhanced data security, improved threat detection and response, strengthened authentication and authorization, and enhanced cyber threat intelligence sharing. Most of these capabilities originate from the fundamental characteristics of Blockchain. Features such as immutable ledgers can help secure transactional data storage. It also helps monitor assets and build trust by providing access only to authorized participants. Its decentralized and distributed ledger system presents a structure for improving digital security and addressing the evolving cyber threat environment.

However, integrating Blockchain technology with existing cybersecurity measures presents some challenges. The chapter brings in novelty by suggesting cybersecurity best practices. These help system integration experts address them to ensure a smooth and effective Blockchain-cybersecurity implementation. Enterprises should consider privacy concerns, scalability issues, the need for skilled professionals, and regulatory compliance. Organizations must re-evaluate their compliance with GDPR and HIPAA, depending on their applicability, when dealing with sensitive data. Despite the challenges, Blockchain technology for cybersecurity provides significant benefits. Using technology and its unique features, enterprises can improve their security levels and protect their critical data and assets from cyber threats.

The intersection of Blockchain and other technologies, such as AI, ML, and IoT, to improve cybersecurity is a trending research topic. This will advance the security levels of enterprises' cybersecurity infrastructure.

REFERENCES

Adeghe, E., Okolo, C., & Ojeyinka, O. (2024). *Evaluating the impact of blockchain technology in healthcare data management: A review of security, privacy, and patient outcomes.* Open Access Research Journal of Science and Technology., DOI: 10.53022/oarjst.2024.10.2.0044

Agarkar, A., Karyakarte, M., Chavhan, G., Milind, P., Talware, R., & Kulkarni, L. (2024). Blockchain aware decentralized identity management and access control system. *Elsevier, 31.* DOI: 10.1016/j.measen.2024.101032

Ahmad, D., Lutfiani, N., Rizki Ahmad, A. D. A., Rahardja, U., & Aini, Q. (2021). Blockchain Technology Immutability Framework Design in E-Government. *Jurnal Administrasi Publik : Public Administration Journal*, 11(1), 32–41. DOI: 10.31289/jap.v11i1.4310

Ali, V., Norman, A. A., & Azzuhri, S. R. B. (2023). Characteristics of Blockchain and Its Relationship With Trust. *IEEE Access : Practical Innovations, Open Solutions*, 11, 15364–15374. DOI: 10.1109/ACCESS.2023.3243700

Allende, M., León, D. L., Cerón, S., Pareja, A., Pacheco, E., Leal, A., Da Silva, M., Pardo, A., Jones, D., Worrall, D. J., Merriman, B., Gilmore, J., Kitchener, N., & Venegas-Andraca, S. E. (2023). Quantum-resistance in blockchain networks. *Scientific Reports*, 13(1), 5664. DOI: 10.1038/s41598-023-32701-6 PMID: 37024656

Almadani, M., Alotaibi, S., Alsobhi, H., & Hussain, O. (2023). Blockchain-based multi-factor authentication: A systematic literature review. *Elsevier, 23.* DOI: 10.1016/j.iot.2023.100844

Alrubei, S., Ball, E., & Rigelsford, J. (2022). Adding hardware security into IoT-blockchain platforms. *IEEE*, 1–6. DOI: 10.1109/LATINCOM56090.2022.10000585

Andryukhin, A. (2019). Phishing attacks and preventions in blockchain based projects. *IEEE*, 15–19. DOI: 10.1109/EnT.2019.00008

Anisha, M. (2019). The GDPR-Blockchain Paradox: Exempting Permissioned Blockchains from the GDPR. *Fordham Intell. Prop. Media & Ent. L.J., 29.* https://heinonline.org/HOL/LandingPage?handle=hein.journals/frdipm29&div=35

Apone-Novoa, F., Orozco, A., Villanueva-Polanco, R., & Wightman, P. (2021). The 51% attack on blockchains: A mining behavior study. *IEEE, 9*, 140549–140564. DOI: 10.1109/ACCESS.2021.3119291

Belchior, R., Vasconcelos, A., Guerreiro, S., & Correia, M. (2021). A survey on blockchain interoperability: Past, present, and future trends. *ACM Computing Surveys*, 54(8), 41. DOI: 10.1145/3471140

Bernabe, J., Cánovas, J., Hernández-Ramos, J., Moreno, R., & Skarmeta, A. (2019). Privacy-preserving solutions for blockchain: Review and challenges. *IEEE, 7*, 164908–164940. DOI: 10.1109/ACCESS.2019.2950872

Bhardwaj, A., Hussian Shah, S. B., Shankar, A., Alazab, M., & Kumar, M. (2021). Penetration testing framework for smart contract blockchain. *Springer, 14*, 2635–2650. DOI: 10.1007/s12083-020-00991-6

Bhushan, B., Sinha, P., Sagayam, K., & J, A. (2021). Untangling blockchain technology: A survey on state of the art, security threats, privacy services, applications and future research directions. *Elsevier, 90*. DOI: 10.1016/j.compeleceng.2020.106897

Bhutta, M. N. M., Khwaja, A. A., Nadeem, A., Ahmad, H. F., Khan, M. K., Hanif, M. A., Song, H., Alshamari, M., & Cao, Y. (2021). A Survey on Blockchain Technology: Evolution, Architecture and Security. *IEEE Access : Practical Innovations, Open Solutions*, 9, 61048–61073. DOI: 10.1109/ACCESS.2021.3072849

Chaubey, N. K., & Prajapati, B. B. (Eds.). (2020). *Quantum Cryptography and the Future of Cyber Security*. IGI Global., DOI: 10.4018/978-1-7998-2253-0

Chen, K., Zhang, M., Liang, R., Chen, J., Peng, J., & Huang, X. (2024). Research on the Application of Penetration Testing Frameworks in Blockchain Security. In Li, S. (Ed.), *Computational and Experimental Simulations in Engineering* (Vol. 146, pp. 307–330). Springer Nature Switzerland., DOI: 10.1007/978-3-031-44947-5_25

Chen, Y., Chen, H., Zhang, Y., Han, M., Siddula, M., & Cai, Z. (2022). A survey on blockchain systems: Attacks, defenses, and privacy preservation. *Elsevier, 2*(2). DOI: 10.1016/j.hcc.2021.100048

Deloitte. (2020). *Deloitte's 2020 Global Blockchain Survey: From promise to reality* (Deloitte Insights) [Industry / Business Report]. https://www2.deloitte.com/content/dam/Deloitte/tw/Documents/financial-services/2020-global-blockchain-survey.pdf

Deloitte. (2021). *Deloitte's 2021 Global Blockchain Survey: A new age of digital assets* (Deloitte Insights, p. 28) [Industry / Business Report]. https://www2.deloitte.com/content/dam/insights/articles/US144337_Blockchain-survey/DI_Blockchain-survey.pdf

Distefano, S., Giacomo, A. D., & Mazzara, M. (2021). Trustworthiness for Transportation Ecosystems: The Blockchain Vehicle Information System. *IEEE Transactions on Intelligent Transportation Systems*, 22(4), 2013–2022. DOI: 10.1109/TITS.2021.3054996

Efanov, D., & Roschin, P. (2018). The all-pervasiveness of the blockchain technology. *Elsevier, 123*, 116–121. DOI: 10.1016/j.procs.2018.01.019

Fatima, N., Agarwal, P., & Sohail, S. (2022). Security and privacy issues of blockchain technology in health care—A review. *Springer, 314*, 193–201. DOI: 10.1007/978-981-16-5655-2_18

Fernández-Caramés, T., & Fraga-Lamas, P. (2020). Towards post-quantum blockchain: A review on blockchain cryptography resistant to quantum computing attacks. *IEEE, 8*. DOI: 10.1109/ACCESS.2020.2968985

Guo, H., & Yu, X. (2022). A survey on blockchain technology and its security. *Elsevier, 3*(2). DOI: 10.1016/j.bcra.2022.100067

Haque, A. B., Islam, A. K. M. N., Hyrynsalmi, S., Naqvi, B., & Smolander, K. (2021). GDPR Compliant Blockchains–A Systematic Literature Review. *IEEE Access : Practical Innovations, Open Solutions*, 9, 50593–50606. DOI: 10.1109/ACCESS.2021.3069877

Hasan, K., Sajid, M., Lapina, M., & Shahid, M. (2024). Blockchain technology meets 6G wireless networks: A systematic survey. *Elsevier, 92*, 199–220. DOI: 10.1016/j.aej.2024.02.031

He, F., Li, F., & Liang, P. (2024). Enhancing smart contract security: Leveraging pre-trained language models for advanced vulnerability detection. *IET Blockchain*, ●●●, 1–12. DOI: 10.1049/blc2.12072

Hristov, P., & Dimitrov, W. (2018). *The blockchain as a backbone of GDPR compliant framework*. 8th International Multidisciplinary Symposium / SIMPRO 2018, Romania. https://www.researchgate.net/publication/328576742_The_blockchain_as_a_backbone_of_GDPR_compliant_frameworks

Ibarra, J., Jahankhani, H., & Kendzierskyj, S. (2019). *Cyber-physical attacks and the value of healthcare data: Facing an era of cyber extortion and organised crime*. Springer. https://link.springer.com/book/10.1007/978-3-030-11289-9

Idrees, S., Nowostawski, M., Jameel, R., & Mourya, A. (2021). Security aspects of blockchain technology intended for industrial applications. *Electronics (Basel)*, 10(8), 951. https:// kdoi.org/10.3390/electronics10080951. DOI: 10.3390/electronics10080951

Ismail, S., Nouman, M., Dawoud, D., & Reza, H. (2024). Towards a lightweight security framework using blockchain and machine learning. *ScienceDirect*, 5(1), 100174. Advance online publication. DOI: 10.1016/j.bcra.2023.100174

John, K., Kogan, L., & Saleh, F. (2023). Smart Contracts and Decentralized Finance. *Annual Review of Financial Economics*, 15(1), 523–542. DOI: 10.1146/annurev-financial-110921-022806

Joshi, A., Han, M., & Wang, Y. (2018). *A Survey on Security and Privacy Issues of Blockchain Technology* (2). *1*(2), Article 2. DOI: 10.3934/mfc.2018007

Kaur, M., Zubair khan, M., Gupta, S., Noorwali, A., Chakraborty, C., & Kumar Pani, S. (2021). MBCP: Performance analysis of large scale mainstream blockchain consensus protocols. *IEEE, 9*. DOI: 10.1109/ACCESS.2021.3085187

Kaur, M., & Gupta, S. (2021). Blockchain Consensus Protocols: State-of-the-art and Future Directions. *2021 International Conference on Technological Advancements and Innovations (ICTAI)*, 446–453. DOI: 10.1109/ICTAI53825.2021.9673260

Lashkari, B., & Musilek, P. (2021). A comprehensive review of blockchain consensus mechanisms. *IEEE Access : Practical Innovations, Open Solutions*, 9, 43620–43652. DOI: 10.1109/ACCESS.2021.3065880

Lee, J. (2018). Patch transporter: Incentivized, decentralized software patch system for WSN and IoT environments. *Sensors (Basel)*, 18(2), 574. Advance online publication. DOI: 10.3390/s18020574 PMID: 29438337

Leteane, O., & Ayalew, Y. (2024). Improving the trustworthiness of traceability data in food supply chain using blockchain and trust model. *The JBBA*, 7(1), 1–12. Advance online publication. DOI: 10.31585/jbba-7-1-(2)2024

Liu, Y., He, D., Obaidat, M. S., Kumar, N., Khan, M. K., & Raymond Choo, K.-K. (2020). Blockchain-based identity management systems: A review. *Journal of Network and Computer Applications*, 166, 102731. DOI: 10.1016/j.jnca.2020.102731

Manoharan, & Sarker, M. (2024). Revolutionizing Cybersecurity: Unleashing the Power of Artificial Intelligence and Machine Learning for Next-Generation Threat Detection. *International Research Journal of Modernization in Engineering Technology and Science*. Advance online publication. DOI: 10.56726/IRJMETS32644

Markets and Markets. (2024). *Cybersecurity Market* (TC 3485; p. 597). https://www.marketsandmarkets.com/Market-Reports/cyber-security-market-505.html

Miller, L., & Pahl, M.-O. (2024). Collaborative cybersecurity using blockchain: A survey. *arXiv, 1*(1), 35.

Monrat, A., Schelén, O., & Andersson, K. (2019). A survey of blockchain from the perspectives of applications, challenges, and opportunities. *IEEE, 7*. DOI: 10.1109/ACCESS.2019.2936094

Moubarak, J., Filiol, E., & Chamoun, M. (2018). On blockchain security and relevant attacks. *IEEE*, 1–6. DOI: 10.1109/MENACOMM.2018.8371010

Nath, P., Mushahary, J., Roy, U., Brahma, M., & Singh, P. (2023). AI and blockchain-based source code vulnerability detection and prevention system for multiparty software development. *Elsevier, 106*. DOI: 10.1016/j.compeleceng.2023.108607

Oyinloye, D. P., Teh, J. S., Jamil, N., & Alawida, M. (2021). Blockchain Consensus: An Overview of Alternative Protocols. *Symmetry*, 13(8), 1363. DOI: 10.3390/sym13081363

Pal, O., Alam, B., Thakur, V., & Singh, S. (2021). Key management for blockchain technology. *ScienceDirect*, 7(1), 76–80. DOI: 10.1016/j.icte.2019.08.002

Park, C.-S., & Nam, H.-M. (2022). A new approach to constructing decentralized identifier for secure and flexible key rotation. *IEEE Internet of Things Journal*, 9(13), 10610–10624. DOI: 10.1109/JIOT.2021.3121722

Patrick, V. E., & Haie, A.-G. (2018). *Blockchain and the GDPR: The EU Blockchain Observatory Report* (Practitioner's Corner 531). EDPL. https://heinonline.org/HOL/LandingPage?handle=hein.journals/edpl4&div=88

Poelman, M., & Iqbal, S. (2021). Investigating the Compliance of the GDPR: Processing Personal Data On A Blockchain. *2021 IEEE 5th International Conference on Cryptography, Security and Privacy (CSP)*, 38–44. DOI: 10.1109/CSP51677.2021.9357590

Putz, B., Vielberth, M., & Pernul, G. (2022). BISCUIT - Blockchain security incident reporting based on human observations. *ACM*, 1–6. DOI: 10.1145/3538969.3538984

Ravichandra, T., Madaan, Dr. V., Sharma, Dr. A., Deshmukh, Dr. S., Agrawal, Prof. Dr. R., Gumber, Dr. G., & Khan, Dr. M. (2024). A study on individual awareness and perception towards blockchain technology in India. *IJISAE, 12*(8), 239–250.

Rodrigues, B., Bocek, T., Lareida, A., Hausheer, D., Rafati, S., & Stiller, B. (2017). A blockchain-based architecture for collaborative DDoS mitigation with smart contracts. *Springer*. https://link.springer.com/content/pdf/10.1007/978-3-319-60774-0_2.pdf

Salagrama, S., Bibhu, V., & Rana, A. (2023). Blockchain based data integrity security management. *Elsevier, 215*, 331–339. DOI: 10.1016/j.procs.2022.12.035

Sami Berkani, A., Moumen, H., Benharzallah, S., Yahiaoui, S., & Bounceur, A. (2023). Blockchain use cases in the sports industry: A systematic review. *Springer.* DOI: 10.1007/s44227-024-00022-3

Sayeed, S., & Marco-Gisbert, H. (2019). Assessing blockchain consensus and security mechanisms against the 51% attack. *Applied Sciences (Basel, Switzerland), 9*(9), 1788. Advance online publication. DOI: 10.3390/app9091788

Schlatt, V., Guggenberger, T., Schmid, J., & Urbach, N. (2023). Attacking the trust machine: Developing an information systems research agenda for blockchain cybersecurity. *Elsevier, 68.* DOI: 10.1016/j.ijinfomgt.2022.102470

Sharma, M., Choudhary, V., Bhatia, R. S., Malik, S., Raina, A., & Khandelwal, H. (2021). Leveraging the power of quantum computing for breaking RSA encryption. *Cyber-Physical Systems, 7*(2), 73–92. DOI: 10.1080/23335777.2020.1811384

Šimunić, S., Bernaca, D., & Lenac, K. (2021). Verifiable computing applications in blockchain. *IEEE, 9,* 156729–156745. DOI: 10.1109/ACCESS.2021.3129314

Singh, A., Kumar, G., Saha, R., Conti, M., Alazab, M., & Thomas, R. (2022). A survey and taxonomy of consensus protocols for blockchains. *Journal of Systems Architecture, 127,* 102503. DOI: 10.1016/j.sysarc.2022.102503

Smiliotopoulos, C., Kambourakis, G., & Kolias, C. (2024). Detecting lateral movement: A systematic survey. *Heliyon, 10*(4), e26317. DOI: 10.1016/j.heliyon.2024. e26317 PMID: 38404775

Tan, T. M., & Saraniemi, S. (2023). Trust in blockchain-enabled exchanges: Future directions in blockchain marketing. *Journal of the Academy of Marketing Science, 51*(4), 914–939. DOI: 10.1007/s11747-022-00889-0

Taylor, P. J., Dargahi, T., Dehghantanha, A., Parizi, R. M., & Choo, K.-K. R. (2020). A systematic literature review of blockchain cyber security. *Digital Communications and Networks, 6*(2), 147–156. DOI: 10.1016/j.dcan.2019.01.005

Tripathi, G., Abdul Ahad, M., & Casalino, G. (2023). A comprehensive review of blockchain technology: Underlying principles and historical background with future challenges. *Elsevier, 9,* 1–6.

Uikey, D. Brarskar, Dr. R., & Ahirwar, Dr. M. (2024). A blockchain-based digital notary system provides reliable and tamper-proof timestamping and verification services for digital documents: A review. *International Journal for Multidisciplinary Research (IJFMR), 6*(2). https://www.ijfmr.com/papers/2024/2/17429.pdf

Varun Shah. (2022). *Machine Learning Algorithms for Cybersecurity: Detecting and Preventing Threats*. DOI: 10.5281/ZENODO.10779509

Vijaya Kittu, M., & Gupta, V. (2024). The Blockchain Trilemma of the IT Project Manager. In *Modern Management Challenges: A Case Compendium* (pp. 66–77). Excel India Publishers. https://zenodo.org/records/11910324

Wang, R., Luo, M., Wen, Y., Wang, L., Raymond Choo, K.-K., & He, D. (2021). The Applications of Blockchain in Artificial Intelligence. *Security and Communication Networks*, 2021, 1–16. DOI: 10.1155/2021/8690662

Wylde, V., Rawindaran, N., Lawrence, J., Balasubramanian, R., Prakash, E., Jayal, A., Khan, I., Hewage, C., & Platts, J. (2022). Cybersecurity, Data Privacy and Blockchain: A Review. *SN Computer Science*, 3(2), 127. DOI: 10.1007/s42979-022-01020-4 PMID: 35036930

Xiao, Y., Zhang, N., Lou, W., & Hou, Y. T. (2020). A Survey of Distributed Consensus Protocols for Blockchain Networks. *IEEE Communications Surveys and Tutorials*, 22(2), 1432–1465. DOI: 10.1109/COMST.2020.2969706

Xu, J., Wang, C., & Jia, X. (2023). A Survey of Blockchain Consensus Protocols. *ACM Computing Surveys*, 55(13s), 1–35. DOI: 10.1145/3579845

Zemler, F., & Westner, M. (2019). Blockchain and GDPR: Application Scenarios and Compliance Requirements. *2019 Portland International Conference on Management of Engineering and Technology (PICMET)*, 1–8. DOI: 10.23919/PICMET.2019.8893923

Zhang, X., & Chen, X. (2019). Data security sharing and storage based on a consortium blockchain in a vehicular ad-hoc network. *IEEE, 7*. DOI: 10.1109/ACCESS.2018.2890736

Zheng, Z., Xie, S., Dai, H.-N., Chen, X., & Wang, H. (2018). Blockchain challenges and opportunities. *International Journal of Web and Grid Services*, 14(4), 352. DOI: 10.1504/IJWGS.2018.095647

Zhou, J., Feng, Y., Wang, Z., & Guo, D. (2021). Using secure multi-party computation to protect privacy on a permissioned blockchain. *Sensors (Basel)*, 21(4), 1540. DOI: 10.3390/s21041540 PMID: 33672175

Zhou, L., Diro, A., Saini, A., Kaisar, S., & Hiep, P. (2024). Leveraging zero knowledge proofs for blockchain-based identity sharing: A survey of advancements, challenges and opportunities. *Elsevier, 80*. DOI: 10.1016/j.jisa.2023.103678

Zhou, S., Li, K., Xiao, L., Cai, J., Liang, W., & Castiglione, A. (2023). A Systematic Review of Consensus Mechanisms in Blockchain. *Mathematics*, 11(2248), 2248. Advance online publication. DOI: 10.3390/math11102248

KEY TERMS AND DEFINITIONS

Blockchain: A distributed and immutable ledger technology that records transactions and other data securely and transparently by storing data in multiple decentralized nodes depending on a central authority.

Cybersecurity: The technology, measure, or practice of protecting computer systems, networks, and data from unauthorized access, use, disclosure, disruption, modification, or destruction. It also includes steps to prevent or mitigate impact.

Decentralization: The process of distribution of control and decision-making among multiple participants in a system rather than a single central authority.

Decentralized Security: A security system that is not controlled by a single entity but rather by a network of nodes or participants or teams who are disperse.

Immutable Ledger: A digital record book (ledger) that cannot be altered, deleted, or tampered once a transaction has been recorded. It is immune to data corruption.

Incident Response Management: The process of responding to and recovering from cybersecurity incidents. It is a structured approach of dealing with incidents affecting information security and data.

Key Management: The process of creating (generating), storing, distributing, protecting, managing, and destroying cryptographic keys used for the encryption and decryption of data.

Network Security: The processes in protection of computer networks from unauthorized access, use, disclosure, disruption, modification, or destruction.

Regulatory Compliance: The necessity for organizations to be aware and follow the laws, policies, and regulations governing the use and protection of data.

Smart Contracts: Small self-executing contracts are automatically executed upon some conditions being met (triggered). The code will have the terms of the agreement.

Chapter 4
Dynamic and Scalable Privacy–Preserving Group Data Sharing in Secure Cloud Computing

Astitva Bhardwaj

https://orcid.org/0009-0005-2256
-9999

Sharda School of Engineering and Technology, Sharda University, India

Akshita Sharma

https://orcid.org/0009-0003-7589
-2517

Sharda School of Engineering and Technology, Sharda University, India

Dharm Raj

https://orcid.org/0000-0001-8363
-0515

Sharda School of Engineering & Technology, Sharda University, India

Danish Ather

https://orcid.org/0000-0003-1596
-5553

Amity University, Tashkent, Uzbekistan

Anil Kumar Sagar

Sharda School of Engineering and Technology, Sharda University, India

Vishal Jain

https://orcid.org/0000-0003-1126
-7424

Sharda School of Engineering and Technology, Sharda University, India

ABSTRACT

Cloud computing, a concept that is already extensively adopted and is expected to grow significantly, represents the information age of the future. The basic idea was created in the 1950s as big firms and organizations looked into remote data and application storage, despite utilizing modern terminology. The phrases Platform as a Service (PAAS), Infrastructure as a Service (IAAS), and Software as a Service

DOI: 10.4018/979-8-3693-9225-6.ch004

(SAAS) lead in cloud computing in sharing of data and accessibility, it is economical, and it can bring a revolution in society. Therefore, this chapter explores some of the security problems relating to cloud computing witnessed in the past up to date in which a complete system for interchanging data securely is required. Further, the work outlined security issues inherent in the cloud environment, and a suitable mechanism for secure communication needs to be put in place. Finally, the chapter analyses the way that companies can gain additional market share through an understanding of their weaknesses and what the industry is currently doing, with the help of cloud computing.

1. INTRODUCTION

Cloud computing (CC) is one of the biggest and most popular debatable topics today. It refers to a computing structure where applications run on virtual servers and are accessed through the internet, eliminating the need for data or programs to be stored on users' computers for offline retrieval. However, the concept behind CC is not new. In the 1950s, large enterprises, governmental agencies, and educational institutions set up huge mainframe computers that enabled multiple users to physically approach different terminals and share CPU time (Jadeja, Y., 2012). CC is a networked architecture in which information is hosted in the cloud instead of being stored locally on a device and is accessed over the internet. The notion behind "CC" may appear novel, but it already existed in the 1950s when large enterprises, governments, and schools constructed massive mainframes that multiple people could use simultaneously by connecting to a particular terminal (Ali, M., 2015). However, there are multiple service delivery models, with Platform as a Service (PaaS), Infrastructure as a Service (IaaS), and Software as a Service (SaaS) being the most popular. This is made possible through the infrastructure provided by a cloud service provider, which acts as a computing platform for the customer (Mell, P., 2009).

The sphere of cloud computing (CC) is transforming how companies operate, particularly in terms of sharing group data and leveraging its advantages. This approach enables individuals or organizations that share the same dataset kept in the cloud to access, share, and collaborate on it. For instance, group data sharing encompasses a wide range of applications, including team editing in MS Word and modification of Microsoft Excel (Simla Mercy, S., 2014). Another important aspect of cloud-based database systems is group data sharing across multiple tenants in a single environment, which is especially significant for SaaS applications. Researchers benefit from this by working together with large datasets, facilitating data analysis, and sharing information across different research groups and institutions. Sharing data with a group on a cloud offers many positives, such as remarkable accessibility that allows users to view and share almost anything from any location with internet access (De Capitani di Vimercati, S., 2015). This accessibility supports remote work and collaborative efforts worldwide, a crucial element in today's globally connected environment. Cost-effectiveness is another advantage, as it eliminates the need for physical storage and maintenance costs, with cloud providers handling the supporting infrastructure (Mahakalkar, N., 2017). Scalability is perhaps the most important component, as it ensures that group data sharing can expand, contract, and adapt as needed. Real-time updates are a unique feature of cloud-enabled collaborations, allowing individuals to see what their coworkers are doing in real-time, reducing version control issues, and enhancing production processes (Tchao, E. T., 2021).

A major concern about group data sharing in the context of cloud computing (CC) revolves around security issues. As involvement with cloud services increases, ensuring the protection of shared information's availability, confidentiality, and integrity becomes critical. This can be addressed through several important security measures. The first step involves data encryption, which is crucial for both data transmission and storage (Hendre, A., 2015). This ensures that despite security loopholes, important information remains secured from unauthorized access (Bharadwaj, D. R., 2018). Access control is another significant issue, where permissions are granted on a strictly need-to-know basis. Popular access control methods include access management systems and role-based access control. The risk of potential data loss can be mitigated through regular data backup and recovery approaches, which facilitate smooth data recovery after unforeseen incidents. Additionally, user awareness and education are vital for effectiveness (Sendi, A. S., 2014). It is crucial to inform users about the risks involved and ensure safety when using such services, as human error remains a significant threat despite technological advancements (Somani, G., 2017). Effective security for group data sharing with CC can be achieved through integrated technological solutions combined with training and educational programs (Joshi, A., 2022).

Cloud computing (CC) has been at the center of many hot debates and is set to represent the future of the information age. Originally developed around the 1950s, this technology involves storing software and information on separate external servers that can be accessed over the Internet (Lai, S.-T., 2015). The availability, affordability, ease of scaling up, and timeliness in updating information across multiple devices with group data sharing on the cloud are transforming collaboration. However, security remains a primary concern, highlighting the need to inform users about limitations, authentication, and data encryption (Kaur, R., 2015). A comprehensive strategy involving advanced technological tools and user education is essential for securing group data sharing in the cloud (Liu, W., 2012).

The major contribution of the paper is as follows:

- The paper provides an overview of CC, by exploring the background of CC and various types of security concerns in CC, and gives a brief introduction to the architecture.
- It explores various vulnerabilities in CC.
- It majorly emphasizes insider threats and external attacks.
- It highlights the recent advancements in CC

This paper's remaining sections are arranged as follows: Section 2, highlights the realm of CC, providing a comprehensive overview. Section 3 presents a deep dive into the vulnerabilities that plague CC. Section 4, pivots to recent advances in the CC industry. Section 5, concludes our paper by summarizing the key points discussed in the preceding sections.

2. OVERVIEW OF CLOUD COMPUTING

Customers are currently able to use computers such as servers, storage, and apps on demand with the assistance of the Internet. It offers flexibility, scalability, and a cheaper (affordable) alternative without maintaining physical infrastructure for businesses.

2.1 Background

In the past, a portion of the Internet with some infrastructure was commonly represented by the cloud. Today, online services are referred to as "cloud" services. Unlike earlier systems with limited transaction capacities, cloud computing (CC) now supports an enormous number of activities within seconds. This capability allows tasks such as event forecasting, analysis, and data pre-processing to be completed efficiently. To utilize cloud services, users must remain connected to their devices to access and operate these massively processing virtual machines located globally (Furht, B., 2010). Older systems that were in use before the advent of CC can be referenced to track its progress. In the context of CC, a provider delivering services over the Internet is called the "cloud," and "computing" involves using computers to process computations or resources. As John McCarthy suggested in 1961 at MIT, if these types of computers were promoted as the future of computing, it might eventually be categorized as a public utility, akin to the telephone system (Garfinkel, S., 1999). Salesforce was among the first to use the term "CC" when it was founded in the late 1990s, initially offering its SaaS and customer relationship management (CRM) services (Salesforce, 2023). The Salesforce model is a prominent

CC paradigm that provides users with development platforms such as Microsoft Azure (Microsoft, 2023) and Google's App Engine (Google, 2023), alongside PaaS. Another option is the IaaS model, introduced in 2006 by companies like Amazon Elastic Compute Cloud (EC2).

2.2 Security Concerns

Organizations must solve several security issues brought on by group data sharing in the cloud to safeguard their sensitive data and maintain data integrity. Strong security measures must be put in place when numerous users or groups cooperate and share data in a cloud environment.

2.2.1 Data Storage

Cloud architecture is determined by the services provided. With customer data now stored in the cloud, local access has been lost, necessitating a backup system to ensure the availability and integrity of data files on cloud servers. One major concern is the ability to detect any unauthorized modifications or data corruption as soon as possible, which is a longstanding aspect of data security service quality. While cloud computing (CC) introduces new and complex security risks, it also reveals that traditional cryptographic primitives are no longer sufficient. Since users do not directly manage their data security measures in CC, immediate application of security protocols is challenging. Therefore, it's crucial to ensure that credible information is uploaded into the cloud even when the exact content of the data is unknown. Furthermore, CC involves more than just third-party data warehousing; it includes updating dynamic data with storage accuracy (Amazon, 2023).

The ability of users to modify stored data in the cloud—such as inserting, deleting, amending, and adding new entries—requires maintaining storage accuracy during dynamic updates. This evolving nature necessitates new strategies, rendering outdated integrity assurance policies obsolete. Additionally, CC involves the concurrent, cooperative, and distributive management of data centers. To enhance data security, information from a specific user is stored in multiple physical locations, creating redundancy and reducing the risk of data compromise. Therefore, developing a realistic cloud data storage system with integrity in the real world will significantly benefit from distributed protocols for storage correctness verification (Wang, Q., 2009). Figure 1 illustrates a cloud data storage security pattern as depicted below.

- **Front End:** The front end is used by the client. The client-side APIs and applications required to access CC services are included. The front end consists of tablets, smartphones, thin and fat clients, and web servers (such as Internet Explorer, Firefox, Chrome, and others).
- **Back End:** The back end is used by the service provider. It is in charge of managing every resource required to provide CC services. Included are servers, virtual computers, traffic management systems, servers, security procedures, and a tonne of data storage.
- **Client Infrastructure:** The client infrastructure is one component of the front end. For cloud communication, it offers a GUI (Graphical User Interface).
- **Application:** A client's desire to use any program or platform can be considered an application.
- **Service:** A cloud service manages the services one can access based on the demands of the client.
- **SAAS:** An alternative title for it is cloud application services. Most SAAS programs don't require downloading or installation and operate rapidly in the web browser.
- **PAAS:** It obtains access to a platform that relieves you of the burden of worrying about the infrastructure and technical details by offering all the services and tools needed to develop, run, and manage software applications.
- **IAAS:** Cloud infrastructure services is another term for it. It oversees the administration of application data, runtime environments, and middleware.
- **Storage:** Storage is one of the main components of CC. It provides enough cloud storage capacity for data management and archiving.
- **Runtime Cloud:** Runtime Cloud provides virtual computers with access to the execution and runtime environments.
- **Infrastructure:** It provides hosts, networks, and application services. A few examples of the hardware and software components that make up cloud infrastructure that are necessary to implement the CC idea are servers, storage, network devices, and virtualization software.
- **Management:** Coordination between several components, such as runtime clouds, storage, infrastructure, and applications, is facilitated by backend management.
- **Security:** Security is one feature of the CC back end. A security mechanism is put in place at the back end.
- **Internet:** Communication can link the front and back ends of the internet.

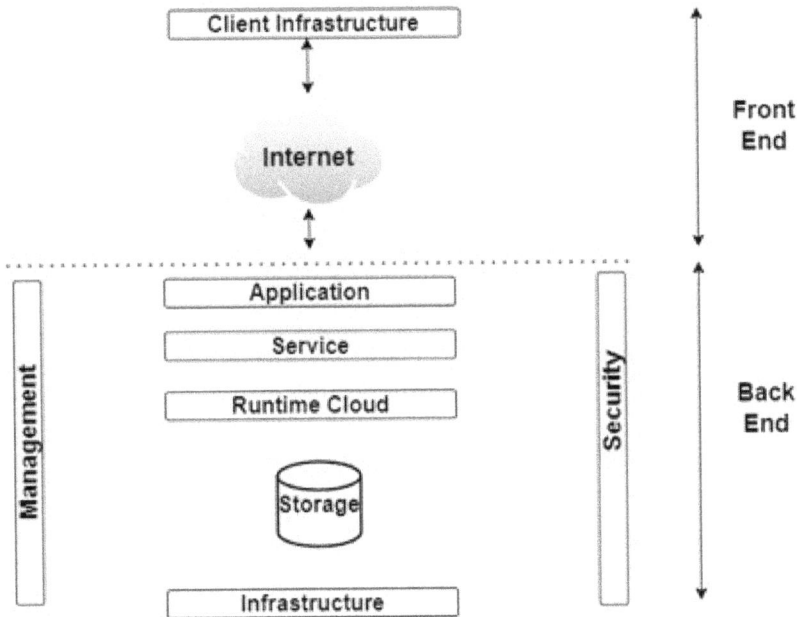

Figure 2. Architecture of Cloud Computing

3. ASSOCIATED VULNERABILITY

It speaks about a system's weak spot, a security flaw that an attacker could exploit. Several factors that lead to these weaknesses include wrong configurations, ineffective access controls, unsafe APIs, and software bugs.

3.1 Insider Threats

The worst-case scenario for suppliers and cloud consumers alike is a malicious system administrator employed by the cloud service. The insider has authorized user credentials that allow her to access critical data because of her business relationship with the cloud provider. An administrator responsible for routinely backing up the systems (virtual machines, data storage) hosting client resources, for example, could potentially take advantage of her access to backups and pilfer sensitive customer information. It might be challenging to locate such indirect data access. Depending on the insider's objectives, the results of an insider assault on a cloud infrastructure might range from data leakage to catastrophic damage to the impacted systems and data. Regardless, the supplier will be hit with harsh business repercussions. Insider attacks are a concern for all popular cloud types (IaaS, PaaS, and SaaS) if the insider has access to the data centers or cloud management systems (Bohn,R. B.,2011).

It may be argued that the consequences of the insider threat in the cloud, as previously mentioned, are similar to those of an insider in the conventional outsourcing paradigm. This is somewhat accurate because outsourcing may reveal private information to unapproved parties, but CC is different because it provides a full replacement for outsourcing via IaaS and PaaS. Consequently, the CC paradigm may be used to outsource a significant portion of the infrastructure rather than specific services like web hosting or application hosting (Bishop,M.,2008). Three types of cloud-related insider threats are discussed in the below section.

3.1.1 Rouge Administrator

Let's start by examining the type of insider to which Cloud Security Alliance (CSA) is alluding that is, a malicious administrator working for a cloud provider. In their job, researchers typically deal with this insider connected to the cloud. This insider often proposes attacks that compromise data integrity and confidentiality by stealing personal information. This danger raises the possibility that insiders may have been motivated by money, which is frequently the case in cases of fraud and theft of intellectual property. Another possibility is Information technology (IT) sabotage, which occurs when an employee attempts to undermine the IT system of their company. Because administrators in cloud systems work for providers rather than for the enterprises that use them, some individuals may discount this kind of criminal action (Alliance, C.S, 2010).

However, this cannot be completely ruled out. Even though it's unusual for an insider to harbor resentment toward the victim organization, this kind of hostility could be detrimental to both the victim organization and the reputation of the cloud provider. The insider was employed by a company that a victim business engaged to handle customer data processing for data mining as a system administrator. The insider had access to the victim organization's systems and data even though they weren't required for their employment. It was found that a password-free file on one of these servers contained encrypted password data.

The insider obtained access to the data of several clients of the target organization took millions of personal records, and brute-forced over 300 passwords. Luckily, the insider was never caught selling or giving away the information. This case study demonstrates a scenario involving a dependable business partner and a configuration that is a lot like CC. Even with the Computer Emergency Response Team (CERT) ongoing efforts to aggregate current insider threat events, this is one of the very few examples we have of a cloud-related problem. Nonetheless, there are numerous examples of trustworthy business partners' employees, independent contractors, and contract workers using their access to networks and data for identity theft. It is important to remember that the threat posed by different kinds of rogue administrators differs for cloud architectures from traditional business environments.

There are four administrative tiers in the cloud to consider:
- Hosting Company Administrators
- Virtual Image Administrators
- System Administrators
- Application Administrator

3.1.2 Cloud Weakness Exploits

Security professionals may overlook a different type of insider danger associated with cloud computing: an employee who uses cloud services to expose vulnerabilities in the company's data or systems to get unauthorized access. It is occasionally made possible by variations in access control or security policies between local and cloud-based systems. This can be done intentionally or inadvertently. The threat's intensity may also depend on how hard it is for an organization to quickly establish direct administrative control over systems and data. Insiders of this type are probably looking for ways to get access to sensitive information that they can either utilize for future employment opportunities (intellectual property theft) or sell (fraud). The cloud could offer the simplest and least likely method of evading security safeguards. Sabotage attacks, however, are not to be ignored. The cloud infrastructure itself is unlikely to be compromised by a local insider, given the services' robustness, reliability, and remote location. If an insider wants to damage the organization, it would be better to target a local system for sabotage rather than reveal sensitive or embarrassing company information.

A malevolent outsider deceived a staff member of the impacted company into opening a document that contained malware.

Eventually, the attacker used that vulnerability to gain access to the CC provider-hosted email service for the firm. The victim organization knew about the attack as it was occurring, but it was too late to halt email service and save crucial data from being lost. The organization's difficulties authenticating with the cloud provider's support staff added to the delay. The perpetrator of this accidental insider assault had no desire to cause harm to the company. Nevertheless, the external attacker was able to gain the internal administrator's login credentials and use them to initiate an assault. The absence of direct control over email services by the target organization was the exploited weakness that enabled this assault to succeed.

3.1.3 Cloud Malfeasance

The third kind of cloud insider is someone who exploits cloud services to hurt their organization. This insider is comparable to the previous kind that targets cloud-hosted data or systems. However, the third kind of insider attacks specific systems or data that aren't necessarily connected to cloud-based services by using the cloud. The following situations could lead to this kind of attack:

- An employee in financial distress uses cloud services to break passwords and get unfettered access to the company's bank accounts.
- Disgruntled insiders impede forensic analysis and incident investigation by mounting a distributed denial of service assault on their organization using many inexpensive, readily setup cloud services.
- An employee planning to leave the company gathers and steals sensitive information via cloud storage to take a job with a competitor.

On the other hand, CERT has numerous examples of third-party insiders using cloud-based services to steal information. Usually, these are instances of theft of intellectual property. Attackers commonly use file-sharing services like Dropbox or web-based email like Gmail, Hotmail, etc. to bypass security measures that filter and monitor business email attachments. (Moore,A.P,2011). Below is the combined summary of all the insider threats in Table 2.

Table 2. Summary of insider threats

Insider Threats	Description
Rogue Administrator (Alliance, C. S.,2010)	Untrustworthy insiders can tarnish the cloud company, steal data, disrupt access, and exploit admin levels.
Cloud Weakness Exploits (Lamport,L.,1982)	Insiders can exploit cloud vulnerabilities for illegal access, fraud, data theft, replication lag, and lack of control.
Cloud Malfeasance (Moore,A.P,2011)	Insiders exploit the cloud for attacks, data theft, DDoS, and external cloud for data theft.

3.2 External Attack

External attacks in CC are like digital break-ins, where cybercriminals attempt to infiltrate cloud systems from outside sources

3.2.1 Distributed Denial of Service (DDoS) Attack

DDoS overwhelms cloud services with traffic, blocking legitimate users from using them. Attackers use botnets or numerous hacked devices to organize this flood. Figure 3 outlines the architectural aspects of the DDoS attack (Deshmukh, R.V.,2015).

The major types of DDoS attacks are:

- Attacks from several sources, like brute force or Classic DDoS
- System exploit attack. (Attack target on a pointed system like feed streaming, image rendering, or content delivery)

There are various types of DDoS attacks such as DDoS attacks that can be made to utilize all of the network's resources, all of the bandwidth, or a mix of the two. The three forms of DDoS assaults are volumetric (Gbps), protocol (pps), and application layer (reps) (Somani,G.,2017). Attacks or floods that target the network's bandwidth can be initiated using botnets or amplification. Protocol assaults frequently operate at layers 3 and 4 of the OSI model on network devices like routers, where they target the CPU and memory of servers and intermediate devices. Depending on the vector and packet size, the majority of assaults can be classified, and the categories frequently overlap [33]. DDoS attack types are seen through the lens of CC. A variety of cloud components are attacked depending on the attacker's intention and potential vulnerability. The several cloud components that are vulnerable to DDoS assaults include Cloud Infrastructure (VMs, Hypervisor, and Cloud Scheduler), Cloud Services (SAAS and Web Services), and Cloud Customers (Cost Accountability Component).

Below we have discussed some of the defence strategies against DDoS attacks:

- **Prominent IDS:** The deployed intrusion detection system needs to be precise and current. The machine must be able to locate the backend traffic and provide an early alert based on the credentials and behavioural variables. It serves as the alarm for the Cloud Security Break-in (Yu,S.,2013).
- **Firewall Traffic Type Inspection Feature:** It will examine the origin and destination of incoming traffic as well as the traffic's nature, utilizing technologies like IDS. During the inspection, this function can arbitrate between good and bad traffic flow (Wahab,O.A.,2017).
- **Limiting the Source Rate:** One of the main problems with a DoS attack is that it should use all available bandwidth. Locating the attack's origin and blocking or restricting the associated IP address is important (Kautish,S.,2022).

Figure 3. Distributed Denial of Service (DDoS) Attack

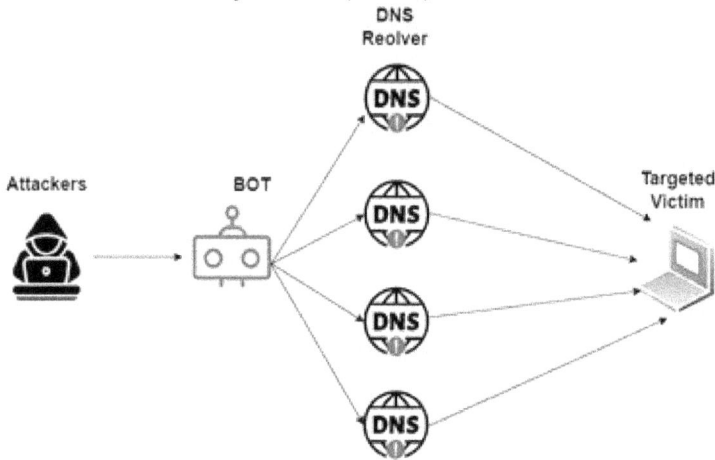

3.2.2 Malware Injection Attack

The growing adoption by businesses and individuals has made CC services that provide convenience as well as scalability beyond comparison. Nonetheless, with so many people relying on cloud-based services, hackers have sought innovative methods of exploiting vulnerabilities. One type of attack that could be used to penetrate cloud-based systems and steal confidential information is the cloud malware injection attack (Naval, S.,2015). This essay takes us into cloud malware injection attacks and how they can work, what could happen, and possible preventive measures. The attacker must change some of the cloud-executable code or services to make them malicious. The other forms of external attack are also referred to as metadata spoofing attacks. In this instance, an attacker gets the data from the internet and applies pressure on individuals to unwittingly upload hazardous material (Rhee, J.,2014). One of them includes this, being one of the major ways in which malware can be introduced into the cloud. Cloud-based assaults include the illegal injecting of malware into infrastructure and the system. The IAAS, PAAS, and SAAS layers of the cloud architecture could be subjected to these kinds of attacks (Musleh, A.S,2019). The focusing techniques of the attack are in Figure 4 as seen below.

The normal sequence of these attacks is as follows:
- **Injection Points:** Malware injection attacks frequently make use of holes in web applications, APIs, or improperly configured cloud services. These flaws might be anything from inadequate access controls and unsafe APIs to unclean inputs in online forms.

- **Malware Payload:** The malware that has been injected can be in the shape of viruses, trojans, ransomware, or spyware. Once inside the cloud environment, it can breach data security, steal confidential data, or interfere with cloud services.
- **Propagation:** Infected instances of malware in a cloud setting can spread across connected resources, potentially harming a large variety of users and data.

Below we have discussed some defence strategies against Malware Injection Attacks:

- **Regular Security Audits:** Conduct recurring security audits and vulnerability evaluations of your cloud applications and infrastructure. Recognize vulnerabilities as soon as possible and patch them to decrease attack surfaces.
- **Implement Strong Access Control:** Apply the least privilege and rigorous access control principles. Ensure that users only have the permissions required for their roles and responsibilities (Bi,J.,2022).
- **Web Application Firewall (WAF):** Use a WAF to block malicious requests and payloads that are directed at web apps and APIs, filter incoming traffic, and detect them.
- **Intrusion Detection and Prevention Systems (IDPS):** Use IDPS to monitor network traffic and identify any unusual activity that might indicate an attempt to infiltrate the system with malware.
- **Security Education and Training:** Inform staff members and cloud administrators about security best practices, social engineering risks, and how to spot and handle phishing scams.
- **Security Patching and Updates:** Maintain all cloud hardware and software up to date with the most recent security updates to reduce known vulnerabilities.
- **Cloud Security Solutions:** By making use of the cloud security services and solutions provided by your cloud service provider (CSP), you may strengthen the security of your cloud environment (Khan, H.A.,2019).

Figure 4. Cloud malware injection attack

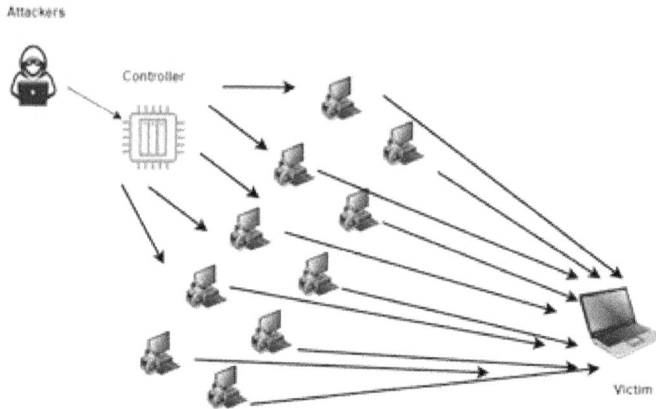

3.2.3 Flooding Attack

When a lot of traffic is started on a network or service, it can result in flooding, a sort of denial-of-service assault. It results in the server or host overusing the system's random-access memory (RAM). In these assaults, the primary aim is to block legitimate users from accessing the protected source by disrupting its provision (Kim, H.,2010). The architectural layout for the flooding attack is illustrated in Figure 5.

Flooding assaults can take several different forms in the context of CC:
- **Traditional DoS Attacks:** A single attacker or a small group of attackers flood a cloud service or server with traffic in a typical DoS assault, exhausting its resources and resulting in a brief or protracted outage (Nishanth, N.,2021).
- **DDoS Attacks:** The coordinated effort of numerous hacked devices or botnets to flood the target with traffic during a DDoS attack makes it much harder to mitigate and defend against (Wu, Z.,2023).
- **Application Layer Attacks:** Some flooding attacks target certain cloud-based services or apps, taking advantage of flaws or overtaxing their resources.

Below we have discussed some defence strategies against Flooding Attacks:
- **Traffic Filtering and Access Control:** Use firewalls and access control lists (ACLs) at the network level to filter incoming traffic. Deny traffic from known malicious IP addresses or regions and only let traffic from reliable sources. To filter traffic before it reaches your cloud resources, use cloud-based security services or on-premises security appliances.

- **Content Delivery Networks (CDNs):** Using CDNs will help you spread traffic and cache information closer to your customers. Your cloud infrastructure will work less hard because CDNs can handle traffic spikes and screen out harmful traffic.
- **Load Balancers:** To uniformly distribute incoming traffic among many cloud servers or instances, use load balancers. In the case of an assault, load balancers can help keep a single server from becoming overloaded. To dynamically alter the number of server instances based on traffic demand, use auto-scaling techniques (Wu, Z.,2023).
- **Rate Limiting and Traffic Shaping:** Use rate limitation to limit the number of requests or connections coming from a single client or IP address. By doing this, an attacker can't overwhelm your services with requests. Prioritize valid traffic and reduce the impact of DoS assaults by using traffic shaping.
- **Anomaly Detection Systems:** To keep an eye on network traffic, use specialised anomaly detection software or intrusion detection and prevention systems (IDPS) and find strange patterns or behaviors that might indicate an attack. Set up alerting systems to send administrators notifications or start automated defense mechanisms when an assault is discovered.
- **Content Security Solutions:** To analyze and filter traffic at the application layer, use web application firewalls (WAFs). WAFs allow normal traffic to get through while blocking malicious requests and payloads. To check for known risks in incoming and outgoing traffic, use anti-malware and anti-virus software.
- **Redundancy and Failover:** Redundancy should be considered when designing your cloud infrastructure. To ensure that traffic may be diverted to unaffected resources if one site is the target of an attack, use numerous data centers or availability zones. Implement failover systems that, in the event of an attack, swiftly redirect traffic to alternative servers or regions.
- **DDoS Mitigation Services:** Use DDoS mitigation services from third parties that are skilled in identifying and preventing large-scale attacks. Several cloud service providers also include DDoS protection services.
- **Incident Response Plan:** Create and test a flood attack-specific incident response strategy regularly. Make sure your team is prepared to act quickly and decisively in the event of an attack. Establish communication guidelines, such as how to alert pertinent parties and, if required, involve law police.

- **Continuous Monitoring and Analysis:** Keep an eye on network performance and traffic to spot any patterns or potential flaws that attackers might try to exploit. Analyse attack data and take lessons from past mistakes to strengthen your defenses (Aydeger, A.,2021).

Figure 5. Flooding attack

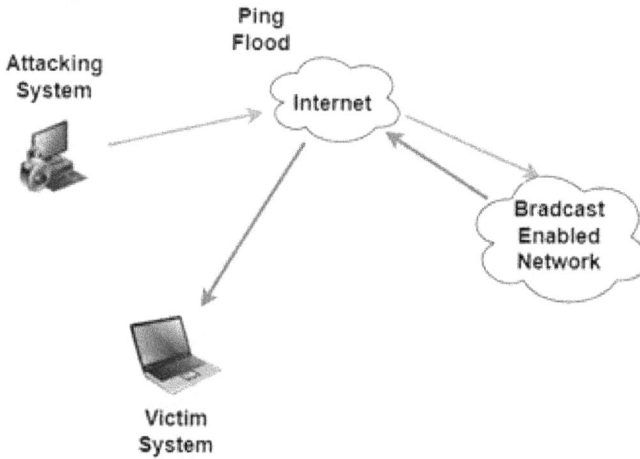

3.2.4 Side Channel Attack

An attack will be developed to position a malicious virtual machine near the target cloud server. It is a security vulnerability when carrying out cryptographic operation and deciphering the computer's cryptographic information while gathering data on the entire host machine (Miki, T.,2019). In contrast to previous security attacks, side-channel attacks impact both the software and hardware platforms. Instead of concentrating on how software vulnerability leads to coding errors or mismatched codes, it will have an impact on hardware specifications such as device operating systems (Sayyah Ensan, S.,2021). This type of attack can occur with any operating system whether it is Linux, windows, or any other one. Unlike previous security assaults that are only limited to either the software or hardware platform, a side channel attack has two dimensions, that is, the hardware and software. Rather than concentrating on what makes software vulnerability cause bad coding or mismatch some code bits, think about the impact that can be caused on hardware such as what type of OS device should have (Das,D.,2018). An example of such an attack applies to all OS: for example, Linux, Windows, etc. As shown in Figure 6, the side-channel attack structure is illustrated. Various types of side-channel attacks are:

- **Acoustic Cryptanalysis Attack:** When a person uses a computer, this component may keep an eye on the electronic circuits that are released into the environment. Additionally, it may gather data about the device's electrical usage and electromagnetic fields.
- **Cache Attack:** Cache attacks in a physical system context take advantage of when and how the cache is processed.
- **Fault Analysis Attack:** These attacks gather data from a system when a failure develops during system computing.
- **Timing Attack:** Attacks of this nature that monitor data transfer between the CPU and memory.

Below we have discussed the defense strategies against side-channel Attacks:

For security against side-channel attacks, the virtual firewall appliance is paired with randomly generated encryption decryption. Through this combination, the cloud computing architecture's front and back ends will both be secure (Liu, W.,2022). First and foremost, businesses should put a high priority on using secure cryptographic methods and defense against side-channel attacks. To stop cross-VM data leakage, it's essential to segregate and secure virtual machines and containers. Hardware selection and hypervisor security should both be carefully taken into account. Strict access control procedures and ongoing monitoring should be in place to catch abnormalities. Furthermore, incorporating noise and randomization into timing and power consumption channels can assist in thwarting attackers (Aljuffri, A.,2021). In Table 3 we have discussed the summary of all the previous external attacks.

Figure 6. Side Channel Attack

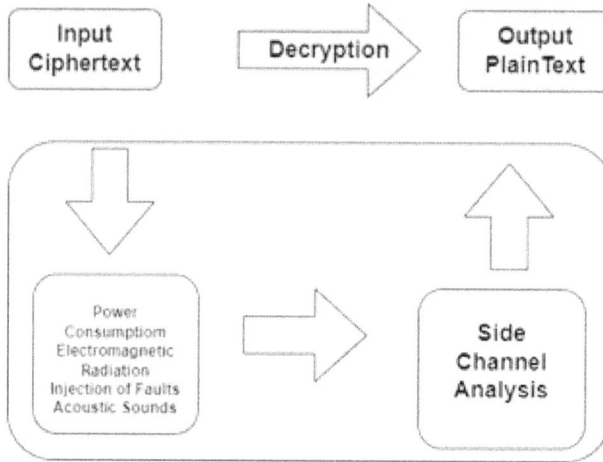

Table 3. Summary of Attacks

Attack	Type of Attack	Reason for Vulnerability	Security Violation	Consequences
Denial of Service(DoS)	External Attack	Storage Vulnerability Datacentre vulnerabilities	Visualization Level Security Issue	Software Interruption and modification
Malware Injection Attack	External Attack	Loss of power and environmental control	Physical Level Security issues	Hardware Modification and theft
Flooding Attack	External Attack	RREQ or data flooding vulnerability	Traffic low-level security issues as well as communication buffer overflow issue	Network Traffic congestion
Side Channel Attack	Passive / Active Attack	Operating System vulnerability	Using malicious Cross-VM to attack the cloud	It will affect both the software and hardware platform

4. RECENT ADVANCES

(Burra, M.S., 2023)proposed a distributed and decentralized cryptography method to boost the security of key generation for group members. (Raj, D.,2023) presented important facets of VANET research including applications, security measures, routing algorithms, and communication protocols. (Chaudhary, A.,2023) presented the structure of URL-based characteristics, we investigated their different detection methods and strategies. Next, the performance is analyzed based on different dataset combinations of URL properties. We conclude our research to stimulate the development of better URL-based phishing detection systems. (Ding, R.,2023) proposed that we should implement an effective integrity-checking system to achieve complete identity anonymity. The proposed approach can also make key management easier and minimize the responsibilities associated with certificate administration. (Hao, K.,2023) proposed the issue of safe data exchange in IBD. We introduced the hybrid chain method to carry out transactions for sharing data safely and effectively. They first suggest a unique idea called the Interoperable Consensus Group (ICG), which groups together several fundamental consensus nodes, each overseeing at least one local blockchain. (Ali, S.A, 2023)presented a collection of noteworthy studies that have predicted software defects using machine learning techniques. The most often used techniques are Support Vector Machine (SVM), Random Forest (RF), and NB (Nave Bayes). It has been discovered that Random Forest and Naive Bayes perform the best among them. (Sudarsa, D.,2023) presented a way to protect privacy when exchanging data over the cloud. (Ali, M.,2023) presented a design ready for cloud data storage and offered a practical solution to these issues with a novel service model known as Confidentiality-based Classification-as-a-Service (C2aaS), which performs data processing by handling data dynamically based on the data security level. (Abdullayeva, F.J,2023) presented a new cyber security reference model for CC consisting of components that comprise several CC tiers. To deliver CC's cybersecurity, the virtualization and service layers are crucial, and they are not fully captured by the current reference models. (Ameur, Y.,2023)presented unresolved problems and potential areas for improvement, they analyzed the multi-cloud security solutions that are currently available in this study using homomorphic encryption. (Anto Viji, A,2022) proposed that the Secure Aware Scheduling Model (SASM) presented in this research was created to manage scheduling and improve security in CC. The suggested model operates in two phases, including the optimum scheduling process and security enhancement. (Xiao, M.,2022) presented the pertinent theories and methods for deploying network security for CC and private cloud security platforms. (An, S.,2022)presented Cloud Safe, a cutting-edge cloud security evaluation and enforcement solution. To perform an automatic security assessment and implement the proper security measures for the cloud, Cloud Safe integrates several security tools. To demonstrate Cloud Safe's applicability and usefulness, they constructed it and carried out security evaluations in Amazon AWS. (Miao, Y.,2022) proposed to accomplish compact record ciphertext size, threshold decryption, and threshold multi-keyword search. They initially present a Threshold Multi-Keyword Search (TMS) technique (also known as the basic TMS scheme) for cloud-based group data sharing in this study. Then, to accomplish traceability and validation of threshold results, they further extend this basic TMS. (Huang, Q.,2021) proposed a multi-owner secure data group sharing and conditional dissemination scheme for CC, where the data disseminator can distribute the data to a new group of users if the attributes comply with the access policies in the ciphertext. (Nhlabatsi, A.,2021) proposed a threat-specific risk assessment methodology that considers a variety of cloud security attributes (e.g., vulnerability information, attack probability, and impact of each attack related to the identified threats) in addition to client-specific security requirements in the cloud. (Huynh, T.T.,2021) proposed schemas for data generation, storage, and exchange. After transforming valuable digital data from raw data supplied by a data owner, a group member produces a certificate based on the data's ciphertext. (Zhang, S.,2020) proposed a Group Key Management Protocol (GKMP) for file sharing on cloud storage. A mixed encryption technology-based group key generation strategy is suggested in response to network threats via the public channel. (Halabi, T.,2020) presented a federation creation method that dissuades CSPs from forming relatively insecure federations and joining a federation that lowers minimum security loss. They achieve higher security levels preserved within federations, and lower frequencies and severities of SLA Security breaches using our methodological approach according to experimental data. (Gan, C.,2020) presented the problem of spreading malware among the VMs under the IaaS architecture. First, a dynamical propagation model for examining vital elements associated with malware proliferation, and in particular, effects of installing antiviruses into VMs will be presented. (Kumari, A.2020) presented secure and effective elliptic curve cryptography (ECC) authentication schemes for cloud-supported SMS. The suggested methodology is divided into six stages: patient registration, healthcare center uploading, treatments, check-ups, emergency, and patient data uploading. (Zhao, W.,2020) presented the initiation of the study of the cloud-enhanced HNF computations and the proposal of an effective outsourcing scheme that renders the scarce client's ability to delegate the bulky task to a rich, though probably disloyal cloud servicer. (Zhang, Z.,2020) presented both the major abuse and key escrow issues of employing ABE in a cloud context. The secret key is generated on behalf of the user by two constructors [a KGC and an AA]. (Li, Z.,2020) presented a queueing theory-based mathematical model for measuring the resilience of container-based clouds against low-rate DDoS attacks. (Yang, Y.,2020) presented an EF-TANKS-VOD: an escrow-free traceable attribute-based multiple keywords subset search system with verifiable outsourced decryption. (Luo, J. -L,2020) presented that to minimize resource wastage in assigning virtual security functions, they assemble Service function chains(SFCs) into a security service function tree by combining them. (Tank, D. M., 2020) explored virtualization aspects of cybersecurity threats and solutions in the cloud computing environment.

Table 4.

Author	Year	Description
(Burra,M.S.,2023)	2023	Decentralized security with mobile members and anti-multi-threading efficiency.
(Raj,D.,2023)	2023	Important facets of VANET research include applications, security measures, routing algorithms, and communication protocols.
(Chaudhary,A.,2023)	2023	Using various URL properties, we analyze the performance of URL-based detection algorithms. Our study aims to support the advancement of phishing detection systems.
(Ding,R.,2023)	2023	Streamlining operations and reducing taxes through a simple predicate for authorized user data sharing.
(Hao,K.,2023)	2023	ICG enables secure data sharing through core consensus nodes with local blockchain support.
(Ali,S.A,2023)	2023	By reviewing several noteworthy studies on machine learning techniques for software defect prediction, we discovered that Naive Bayes outperforms Random Forest and SVM.
(Sudarsa,D.,2023)	2023	Cloud data privacy: 9 steps - setup, register, manage keys, handle files, encrypt.
(Ali,M.,2023)	2023	C2aaS adapts data processing for secure cloud storage.
(Abdullayeva,F.J,2023)	2023	The new cloud security strategy combines virtualization, services, social media, and IoT that will tackle cybercrimes.
(Ameur,Y.,2023)	2023	Check how secure the cloud is using homomorphic encryption.
(Anto Viji,A,2022)	2022	The SASM model is used to enhance security and task allocation of resources more efficiently.
(Xiao,M.,2022)	2022	It advises improving private cloud security to save on costs for organizations with data storage challenges.
(An,S.,2022)	2022	Cloud Safe simplifies security verifications within Amazon AWS, making everything function well.
(Miao,Y.,2022)	2022	A cloud protocol for secure data sharing with search, decryption, compression, and result tracking for trust.
(Huang,Q.,2021)	2021	Data is securely shared based on user attributes and access rules within encrypted files.
(Nhlabatsi,A.,2021)	2021	A tailored risk assessment method considers client needs, vulnerabilities, and attack likelihood in the cloud.
(Huynh,T.T.,2021)	2021	On IPFS: analog to digital, group signature verification, blockchain storage for user-verified access.

continued on following page

Table 4. Continued

Author	Year	Description
(Zhang,S.,2020)	2020	Efficient cloud file sharing: hybrid encryption, security against network threats, and verification to prevent collaborative attacks.
(Halabi,T.,2020)	2020	Promote collaboration security from disloyalty-prone cloud vendors as well as reduce SLA vulnerabilities.
(Gan,C.,2020)	2020	Curbs malware spread in IaaS by studying determinants and VM antivirus impact.
(Kumari,A.,2020)	2020	ECC-based SMS authentication model with 6 phases: registration, data submission, treatment, inspection, and emergency.
(Zhao,W.,2020)	2020	Explores secure and efficient cloud-based computation for resource-constrained clients trusting untrusted cloud servers.
(Zhang,Z.,2020)	2020	Involving a KGC and AA this research addresses the problems of ABE critical abuse and escrow in the cloud.
(Li,Z.,2020)	2020	Queueing theory evaluates the efficiency of a system to deny attackers based on its ability to track how requests or tasks are arranged.
(Yang,Y.,2020)	2020	Introduced EF-TANKS-VOD, eliminating the need for escrow in attribute-based keyword subset search.
(Luo, J. -L,2020)	2020	Service function chains (SFCs) link to create composite virtual clusters, reducing hardware resource load.
(Tank, D. M., 2020)	2020	The objective of this chapter is to explore virtualization aspects of cybersecurity threats and solutions in the cloud computing environment.

5. CONCLUSION

CC refers to virtual computers accessed via the Internet through which applications and data are hosted in remote servers rather than a user's computer. This work offers an overview of CC as a developing discipline that was seeded by the late 1950s. It investigates the idea of shared data in the cloud emphasizing the revolutionary power of groups. Group data sharing has revolutionized how businesses manage and deploy their data, providing unparalleled availability, affordability, flexibility, and up-to-date information. Nevertheless, security emerges as the major issue as CC progressively transforms the online world. The confidentiality and integrity of shared data can only be assured by access control and data encryption that enable its realization in all its forms. This paper further discusses the complicated CC security. It analyses the implications that surround CC, for example, data breaches, insider threats, and attacks outside. Organizations should be aware of these security problems and vulnerabilities to bolster their shield against possible hazards posed on the network. This research also implies that organizations and their counterparts should adopt CC with much caution, as it is still vulnerable to security concerns. In the age of information, it means that two strategies must be taken to fully leverage the benefits offered by cloud technology and at the same time to protect sensitive data and systems against constantly changing threats.

REFERENCES

Abdullayeva, F. J. (2023). Cyber resilience and cyber security issues of intelligent cloud computing systems. *Results in Control and Optimization*, 12, 100268. DOI: 10.1016/j.rico.2023.100268

Ali, M., Khan, S. U., & Vasilakos, A. V. (2015). Security in cloud computing: Opportunities and challenges. *Information Sciences*, 305, 357–383. DOI: 10.1016/j.ins.2015.01.025

Ali, M., Tang Jung, L., Hassan Sodhro, A., Ali Laghari, A., Birahim Belhaouari, S., & Gillani, Z. (2023). A confidentiality-based data classification-as-a-service (C2aaS) for cloud security. *Alexandria Engineering Journal*, 64, 749–760. DOI: 10.1016/j.aej.2022.10.056

Ali, S. A., Roy, N. R., & Raj, D. "Software Defect Prediction using Machine Learning", 2023, Proceedings of the 17th INDIACom; 10th International Conference on Computing for Sustainable Global Development, INDIACom 2023, PP: 639-642, Sudarsa, D., A, N. R., & AP, S. (2023). An effective and secured authentication and sharing of data with dynamic groups in cloud. *Data and Knowledge Engineering, 145*, 102125. DOI: 10.1016/j.datak.2022.102125

Aljuffri, A., Zwalua, M., Reinbrecht, C. R. W., Hamdioui, S., & Taouil, M. (2021, November). "Applying Thermal Side-Channel Attacks on Asymmetric Cryptography," in IEEE Transactions on Very Large Scale Integration (VLSI). *IEEE Transactions on Very Large Scale Integration (VLSI) Systems*, 29(11), 1930–1942. DOI: 10.1109/TVLSI.2021.3111407

Alliance, C. S. "Top threats to cloud computing, version 1.0," Cloud Security Alliance, Tech. Rep., March 2010. [Online]. Available: http://www.cloudsecurityalliance.org/ topthreats/csathreats.v1.0.pdf

Ameur, Y., Bouzefrane, S., & Vinh, T. L. (2023). Handling security issues by using homomorphic encryption in multi-cloud environment. *Procedia Computer Science*, 220, 390–397. DOI: 10.1016/j.procs.2023.03.050

An, S., Leung, A., Hong, J. B., Eom, T., & Park, J. S. (2022). Toward Automated Security Analysis and Enforcement for Cloud Computing Using Graphical Models for Security. *IEEE Access: Practical Innovations, Open Solutions*, 10, 75117–75134. DOI: 10.1109/ACCESS.2022.3190545

A. Aydeger, M. H. Manshaei, M. A. Rahman and K. Akkaya, "Strategic Defense Against Stealthy Link Flooding Attacks: A Signaling Game Approach," in IEEE Transactions on Network Science and Engineering, vol. 8, no. 1, pp. 751-764, 1 Jan.-March 2021, .DOI: 10.1109/TNSE.2021.3052090

Bharadwaj, D. R., Bhattacharya, A., & Chakkaravarthy, M. "Cloud Threat Defense – A Threat Protection and Security Compliance Solution," *2018 IEEE International Conference on Cloud Computing in Emerging Markets (CCEM)*, Bangalore, India, 2018, pp. 95-99, DOI: 10.1109/CCEM.2018.00024

Bi, J., Luo, F., He, S., Liang, G., Meng, W., & Sun, M. (2022, September). False Data Injection- and Propagation-Aware Game Theoretical Approach for Microgrids. *IEEE Transactions on Smart Grid*, 13(5), 3342–3353. DOI: 10.1109/TSG.2022.3174918

Bishop, M., & Gates, C. "Defining the Insider Threat", in *Proc. of the 4th Annual Workshop on Cyber Security and Information Intelligence Research*, Tennessee, Vol. 288, 2008.

Burra, M. S., & Maity, S. (2023). A Distributed and Decentralized Certificateless Framework for Reliable Shared Data Auditing for FOG-CPS Networks. *IEEE Access : Practical Innovations, Open Solutions*, 11, 42595–42618. DOI: 10.1109/ ACCESS.2023.3271605

Chaudhary A.; Krishna K.C.; Shadik M.; Raj D., "A review on malicious link detection techniques", 2023, Artificial Intelligence, Blockchain, Computing and Security: Volume 1, Volume-1, PP: 768-777, DOI: DOI: 10.1201/9781003393580-114

Das, D., Maity, S., Nasir, S. B., Ghosh, S., Raychowdhury, A., & Sen, S. (2018, October). ASNI: Attenuated Signature Noise Injection for Low-Overhead Power Side-Channel Attack Immunity. *IEEE Transactions on Circuits and Systems. I, Regular Papers*, 65(10), 3300–3311. DOI: 10.1109/TCSI.2018.2819499

Deshmukh, R. V., & Devadkar, K. K. (2015). Understanding DDoS attack & its effect in cloud environment. *Procedia Computer Science*, 49, 202–210. DOI: 10.1016/j. procs.2015.04.245

Furht, B., & Escalante, A. (2010). *Handbook of cloud computing* (Vol. 3). Springer. DOI: 10.1007/978-1-4419-6524-0

Gan, C., Feng, Q., Zhang, X., Zhang, Z., & Zhu, Q. (2020). Dynamical Propagation Model of Malware for Cloud Computing Security. *IEEE Access : Practical Innovations, Open Solutions*, 8, 20325–20333. DOI: 10.1109/ACCESS.2020.2968916

Garfinkel, S. (1999). *Architects of the information society: 35 years of the Laboratory for Computer Science at MIT*. MIT press. DOI: 10.7551/mitpress/1341.001.0001

Hao, K., Xin, J., Wang, Z., Yao, Z., & Wang, G. (2023, August 1). Efficient and Secure Data Sharing Scheme on Interoperable Blockchain Database. *IEEE Transactions on Big Data*, 9(4), 1171–1185. DOI: 10.1109/TBDATA.2023.3265178

Hendre, A., & Joshi, K. P. "A Semantic Approach to Cloud Security and Compliance," 2015 IEEE 8th International Conference on Cloud Computing, New York, NY, USA, 2015, pp. 1081-1084, DOI: 10.1109/CLOUD.2015.157

Huynh, T. T., Nguyen, T. D., Hoang, T., Tran, L., & Choi, D. (2021). A Reliability Guaranteed Solution for Data Storing and Sharing. *IEEE Access : Practical Innovations, Open Solutions*, 9, 108318–108328. DOI: 10.1109/ACCESS.2021.3100707

Jadeja, Y., & Modi, K. "Cloud computing - concepts, architecture and challenges", Computing, Electronics and ElectricalTechnologies (ICCEET), 2012 International Conference on, pp. 877-880, 2012. DOI: 10.1109/ICCEET.2012.6203873

Joshi, A., Raturi, A., Kumar, S., Dumka, A., & Singh, D. P. "Improved Security and Privacy in Cloud Data Security and Privacy: Measures and Attacks," *2022 International Conference on Fourth Industrial Revolution Based Technology and Practices (ICFIRTP)*, Uttarakhand, India, 2022, pp. 230-233, DOI: 10.1109/ICFIRTP56122.2022.10063186

Kaur, R., & Kaur, J. "Cloud computing security issues and its solution: A review," 2015 2nd International Conference on Computing for Sustainable Global Development (INDIACom), New Delhi, India, 2015, pp. 1198-1200.

Kautish, S., A, R., & Vidyarthi, A. (2022, September). R. A and A. Vidyarthi, "SDMTA: Attack Detection and Mitigation Mechanism for DDoS Vulnerabilities in Hybrid Cloud Environment,". *IEEE Transactions on Industrial Informatics*, 18(9), 6455–6463. DOI: 10.1109/TII.2022.3146290

H. A. Khan et al., "IDEA: Intrusion Detection through Electromagnetic-Signal Analysis for Critical Embedded and Cyber-Physical Systems," in IEEE Transactions on Dependable and Secure Computing, vol. 18, no. 3, pp. 1150-1163, 1 May-June 2021, .DOI: 10.1109/TDSC.2019.2932736

Kim, H., Chitti, R. B., & Song, J. (2010, May). Novel defense mechanism against data flooding attacks in wireless ad hoc networks. *IEEE Transactions on Consumer Electronics*, 56(2), 579–582. DOI: 10.1109/TCE.2010.5505973

Kumari, A., Kumar, V., Abbasi, M. Y., Kumari, S., Chaudhary, P., & Chen, C.-M. (2020). CSEF: Cloud-Based Secure and Efficient Framework for Smart Medical System Using ECC. *IEEE Access : Practical Innovations, Open Solutions*, 8, 107838–107852. DOI: 10.1109/ACCESS.2020.3001152

Lai, S.-T., & Leu, F.-Y. "A Security Threats Measurement Model for Reducing Cloud Computing Security Risk," 2015 9th International Conference on Innovative Mobile and Internet Services in Ubiquitous Computing, Santa Catarina, Brazil, 2015, pp. 414-419, DOI: 10.1109/IMIS.2015.64

Lamport, L., Shostak, R. E., & Pease, M. C. (1982). The Byzantine Generals problem. *ACM Transactions on Programming Languages and Systems*, 4(3), 382–401. DOI: 10.1145/357172.357176

Li, Z., Jin, H., Zou, D., & Yuan, B. (2020, March 1). Exploring New Opportunities to Defeat Low-Rate DDoS Attack in Container-Based Cloud Environment. *IEEE Transactions on Parallel and Distributed Systems*, 31(3), 695–706. DOI: 10.1109/TPDS.2019.2942591

Li, Z., Jin, H., Zou, D., & Yuan, B. (2020, March 1). Exploring New Opportunities to Defeat Low-Rate DDoS Attack in Container-Based Cloud Environment. *IEEE Transactions on Parallel and Distributed Systems*, 31(3), 695–706. DOI: 10.1109/TPDS.2019.2942591

Liu, W. "Research on cloud computing security problem and strategy," 2012 2nd International Conference on Consumer Electronics, Communications and Networks (CECNet), Yichang, China, 2012, pp. 1216-1219, DOI: 10.1109/CEC-Net.2012.6202020

Liu, W., Zhang, Y., Tang, Y., Wang, H., & Wei, Q. (2023). ALScA: A Framework for Using Auxiliary Learning Side-Channel Attacks to Model PUFs. *IEEE Transactions on Information Forensics and Security*, 18, 804–817. DOI: 10.1109/TIFS.2022.3227445

Luo, J.-L., Yu, S.-Z., & Peng, S.-J. (2020). SDN/NFV-Based Security Service Function Tree for Cloud. *IEEE Access : Practical Innovations, Open Solutions*, 8, 38538–38545. DOI: 10.1109/ACCESS.2020.2974569

Mell, P., & Grance, T. Version 15 The NIST definition of cloud computing October 7.National Institute of Standards and Technology; 2009 https://csrc.nist.gov/ groups/ SNS/cloud-computing

Miki, T., Miura, N., Sonoda, H., Mizuta, K., & Nagata, M. (2020, January). A Random Interrupt Dithering SAR Technique for Secure ADC Against Reference-Charge Side-Channel Attack. *IEEE Transactions on Circuits and Wystems. II, Express Briefs*, 67(1), 14–18. DOI: 10.1109/TCSII.2019.2901534

Moore, A. P., Capelli, D. M., Caron, T. C., Shaw, E., Spooner, D., & Trzeciak, R. F. (2011). A preliminary model of insider theft of intellectual property. *Journal of Wireless Mobile Networks, Ubiquitous Computing and Dependable Applications*, 2(1).

Musleh, A. S., Chen, G., & Dong, Z. Y. (2020, May). A Survey on the Detection Algorithms for False Data Injection Attacks in Smart Grids. *IEEE Transactions on Smart Grid*, 11(3), 2218–2234. DOI: 10.1109/TSG.2019.2949998

Naval, S., Laxmi, V., Rajarajan, M., Gaur, M. S., & Conti, M. (2015, December). Employing Program Semantics for Malware Detection. *IEEE Transactions on Information Forensics and Security*, 10(12), 2591–2604. DOI: 10.1109/TIFS.2015.2469253

A. Nhlabatsi et al., "Threat-Specific Security Risk Evaluation in the Cloud," in IEEE Transactions on Cloud Computing, vol. 9, no. 2, pp. 793-806, 1 April-June 2021, .DOI: 10.1109/TCC.2018.2883063

Nishanth, N., & Mujeeb, A. (2021, September). Modeling and Detection of Flooding-Based Denial of Service Attacks in Wireless Ad Hoc Networks Using Uncertain Reasoning. *IEEE Transactions on Cognitive Communications and Networking*, 7(3), 893–904. DOI: 10.1109/TCCN.2021.3055503

Pan, J.-S., Chen, S.-M., & Nguyen, N. T. (Eds.). "On cloud Computing Security Issues," ACIIDS 2012, Part II, LNAI 7197, pp. 560–569, 2012.

Q. Huang, Y. Yang, W. Yue and Y. He, "Secure Data Group Sharing and Conditional Dissemination with Multi-Owner in Cloud Computing," in IEEE Transactions on Cloud Computing, vol. 9, no. 4, pp. 1607-1618, 1 Oct.-Dec. 2021, .DOI: 10.1109/TCC.2019.2908163

[R. B. Bohn, J. Messina, F. Liu, J. Tong, and J. Mao, "NIST cloud computing reference architecture," in Proceedings - 2011 IEEE World Congress on Services, SERVICES 2011, 2011, no. July 2011, pp. 594–596.

R. Ding, Y. Xu, H. Zhong, J. Cui and G. Min, "An Efficient Integrity Checking Scheme With Full Identity Anonymity for Cloud Data Sharing," in IEEE Transactions on Cloud Computing, vol. 11, no. 3, pp. 2922-2935, 1 July-Sept. 2023, .DOI: 10.1109/TCC.2023.3242140

Raj D.; Sagar A.K., "Vehicular Ad-hoc Networks: A Review on Applications and Security", 2023, Communications in Computer and Information Science, Volume-1921 CCIS, PP: 241-255, DOI: DOI: 10.1007/978-3-031-45124-9_19

Rhee, J., Riley, R., Lin, Z., Jiang, X., & Xu, D. (2014, January). Data-Centric OS Kernel Malware Characterization. *IEEE Transactions on Information Forensics and Security*, 9(1), 72–87. DOI: 10.1109/TIFS.2013.2291964

Sabrina De Capitani di Vimercati. Sara Foresti, Stefano Paraboschi, Member, Gerardo Pelosi, and Pierangela Samarati, "Three server swapping for access confidentiality," IEEE Transaction on Cloud Computing, 2015. Neha Mahakalkar, Vaishali Sahare, "Implementation of re-encryption-based security mechanism to authenticate shared access in cloud computing," International Conference on 12 May 2017.

Salesforce, "Salesforce crm." https://www.salesforce.com/platform. [Online; accessed 25-Sep-2023]. Microsoft, "Windows azure." http://www.microsoft.com/azure. [Online; accessed 25-Sep-2023]. Google, "Google app engine." http://code.google.com/appengine. [Online; accessed 25-Sep-2023]. Amazon, "Amazon elastic computing cloud." https://aws.amazon.com/ ec2. [Online; accessed 26-Sep-2023] Q. Wang, C. Wang, J. Li, K. Ren, and W. Lou, "Enabling public verifiability and data dynamics for storage security in cloud computing," in Proc. of ESORICS'09, Saint Malo, France, Sep. 2009. P. Saripalli, and B. Walters, "QUIRC: A Quantitative Impact and Risk Assessment Framework for Cloud Security," 2010 IEEE 3rd Intl. Conf. on Cloud Computing; Miami, FL, July, 2010.

Sayyah Ensan, S., Nagarajan, K., Khan, M. N. I., & Ghosh, S. (2021, December). "SCARE: Side Channel Attack on In-Memory Computing for Reverse Engineering," in IEEE Transactions on Very Large Scale Integration (VLSI). *IEEE Transactions on Very Large Scale Integration (VLSI) Systems*, 29(12), 2040–2051. DOI: 10.1109/TVLSI.2021.3110744

Sendi, A. S., & Cheriet, M. "Cloud Computing: A Risk Assessment Model," *2014 IEEE International Conference on Cloud Engineering*, Boston, MA, USA, 2014, pp. 147-152, DOI: 10.1109/IC2E.2014.17

S. Simla Mercy, Dr. G. Umarani Srikanth, "An Efficient Data Security System for Group Data Sharing in Cloud System Environment," 2014.

Somani, G., Gaur, M. S., Sanghi, D., Conti, M., & Buyya, R. (2017). DDoS attacks in cloud computing: Issues, taxonomy, and future directions. *Computer Communications*, 107, 30–48. DOI: 10.1016/j.comcom.2017.03.010

G. Somani, M. S. Gaur, D. Sanghi, M. Conti and M. Rajarajan, "Scale Inside-Out: Rapid Mitigation of Cloud DDoS Attacks," in IEEE Transactions on Dependable and Secure Computing, vol. 15, no. 6, pp. 959-973, 1 Nov.-Dec. 2018, .DOI: 10.1109/TDSC.2017.2763160

T. Halabi and M. Bellaiche, "Towards Security-Based Formation of Cloud Federations: A Game Theoretical Approach," in IEEE Transactions on Cloud Computing, vol. 8, no. 3, pp. 928-942, 1 July-Sept. 2020, .DOI: 10.1109/TCC.2018.2820715

Tank, D. M., Aggarwal, A., & Chaubey, N. K. (2020). Cyber Security Aspects of Virtualization in Cloud Computing Environments: Analyzing Virtualization-Specific Cyber Security Risks. In Chaubey, N., & Prajapati, B. (Eds.), *Quantum Cryptography and the Future of Cyber Security* (pp. 283–299). IGI Global., DOI: 10.4018/978-1-7998-2253-0.ch013

Tchao, E. T., Quansah, D. A., Klogo, G. S., Boafo-Effah, F., Kotei, S., Nartey, C., & Ofosu, W. K. (2021b). On cloud-based systems and distributed platforms for smart grid integration: Challenges and prospects for Ghana's Grid Network. *Scientific African*, 12, e00796. DOI: 10.1016/j.sciaf.2021.e00796

Viji, A. A., Jasper, J., & Latha, T. (2022). Efficient secure aware scheduling model for enhancing security and workflow model in cloud computing. *Optik (Stuttgart)*, 170349, 170349. Advance online publication. DOI: 10.1016/j.ijleo.2022.170349

O. A. Wahab, J. Bentahar, H. Otrok and A. Mourad, "Optimal Load Distribution for the Detection of VM-Based DDoS Attacks in the Cloud," in IEEE Transactions on Services Computing, vol. 13, no. 1, pp. 114-129, 1 Jan.-Feb. 2020, .DOI: 10.1109/TSC.2017.2694426

Z. Wu, S. Peng, L. Liu and M. Yue, "Detection of Improved Collusive Interest Flooding Attacks Using BO-GBM Fusion Algorithm in NDN," in IEEE Transactions on Network Science and Engineering, vol. 10, no. 1, pp. 239-252, 1 Jan.-Feb. 2023, .DOI: 10.1109/TNSE.2022.3206581

Xiao, M., Guo, M., & Zhu, W. (2022). Research and implementation of network security deployment based on private cloud security platform. *Procedia Computer Science*, 208, 565–569. DOI: 10.1016/j.procs.2022.10.078

Y. Miao, R. H. Deng, K. -K. R. Choo, X. Liu and H. Li, "Threshold Multi-Keyword Search for Cloud-Based Group Data Sharing," in IEEE Transactions on Cloud Computing, vol. 10, no. 3, pp. 2146-2162, 1 July-Sept. 2022, .DOI: 10.1109/TCC.2020.2999775

Y. Yang, X. Liu, X. Zheng, C. Rong and W. Guo, "Efficient Traceable Authorization Search System for Secure Cloud Storage," in IEEE Transactions on Cloud Computing, vol. 8, no. 3, pp. 819-832, 1 July-Sept. 2020, .DOI: 10.1109/TCC.2018.2820714

Yu, S., Tian, Y., Guo, S., & Wu, D. O. (2014, September). Can We Beat DDoS Attacks in Clouds? *IEEE Transactions on Parallel and Distributed Systems*, 25(9), 2245–2254. DOI: 10.1109/TPDS.2013.181

Z. Wu, S. Peng, L. Liu and M. Yue, "Detection of Improved Collusive Interest Flooding Attacks Using BO-GBM Fusion Algorithm in NDN," in IEEE Transactions on Network Science and Engineering, vol. 10, no. 1, pp. 239-252, 1 Jan.-Feb. 2023, .DOI: 10.1109/TNSE.2022.3206581

Zhang, S., Han, S., Zheng, B., Han, K., & Pang, E. (2020). Group Key Management Protocol for File Sharing on Cloud Storage. *IEEE Access : Practical Innovations, Open Solutions*, 8, 123614–123622. DOI: 10.1109/ACCESS.2019.2963782

Zhang, Z., Zeng, P., Pan, B., & Choo, K.-K. R. (2020, October). Large-Universe Attribute-Based Encryption With Public Traceability for Cloud Storage. *IEEE Internet of Things Journal*, 7(10), 10314–10323. DOI: 10.1109/JIOT.2020.2986303

Zhao, W., Tian, C., Tian, W., & Zhang, Y. (2020). Securely and Efficiently Computing the Hermite Normal Form of Integer Matrices via Cloud Computing. *IEEE Access : Practical Innovations, Open Solutions*, 8, 137616–137630. DOI: 10.1109/ACCESS.2020.3011965

Zissis, D., & Lekkas, D. (2010). Addressing cloud computing security issues. *Future Generation Computer Systems*, ●●●, 1–10.

Chapter 5
Cyber Security Techniques for 5G Networks

Himadri Sekhar Das
https://orcid.org/0000-0002-3509-3388
Haldia Institute of Technology, India

Sandipan Samanta
CGI, Bangalore, India

Rajrupa Metia
Haldia Institute of Technology, India

Debasish Samanta
IBM Kolkata, India

Banibrata Bag
Haldia Institute of Technology, India

ABSTRACT

The rapid deployment of 5G networks introduces new cybersecurity challenges due to their enhanced speed, low latency, and massive connectivity. To safeguard these networks, advanced techniques are essential, including network slicing for isolating threats, artificial intelligence and machine learning for real-time threat detection, and blockchain for securing transactions. Additionally, Zero Trust architectures ensure that every access request is authenticated, regardless of origin. These strategies, combined with robust encryption and anomaly detection mechanisms, are critical in addressing the diverse and evolving threats in the 5G ecosystem, ensuring secure

DOI: 10.4018/979-8-3693-9225-6.ch005

and reliable communication for users and industries alike.

INTRODUCTION

5G, the fifth generation of mobile networks, shows a significant leap forward in telecommunications, promising transformational changes across businesses and common existence. Unlike its predecessors, 5G is designed to offer fastest data speeds massive connectivity, and highly reliable communication, making it the foundation for innovations such as the Internet of Things (IoT), smart cities, autonomous vehicles, and advanced healthcare applications (Huseien, F. G. & Shah, W. K., 2022). With the skill to support until a so many instruments per square kilometer, 5G networks proper to handle the explosive development of related instruments and duties, enabling new potential that were previously the dimension of science movie.

The architecture of 5G networks is built on several key technologies, including millimeter-wave spectrum, massive MIMO (Multiple Input, Multiple Output), network slicing, software-defined networking (SDN), and network function virtualization (NFV). These technologies work together to deliver unprecedented performance and flexibility, allowing network operators to tailor services to specific use cases and customer requirements (Lorincz et al., 2024). Network slicing, specifically, is a pioneering feature that allows the invention of diversified virtual networks inside a single physical network foundation, each advanced for different types of aids, to a degree high-speed movable broadband, depressed-latency uses, and large IoT connectedness. Figure.1 Different features of 5G Technology such as high capacity, faster response, wide range etc.

Figure 1. Different features of 5G Technology

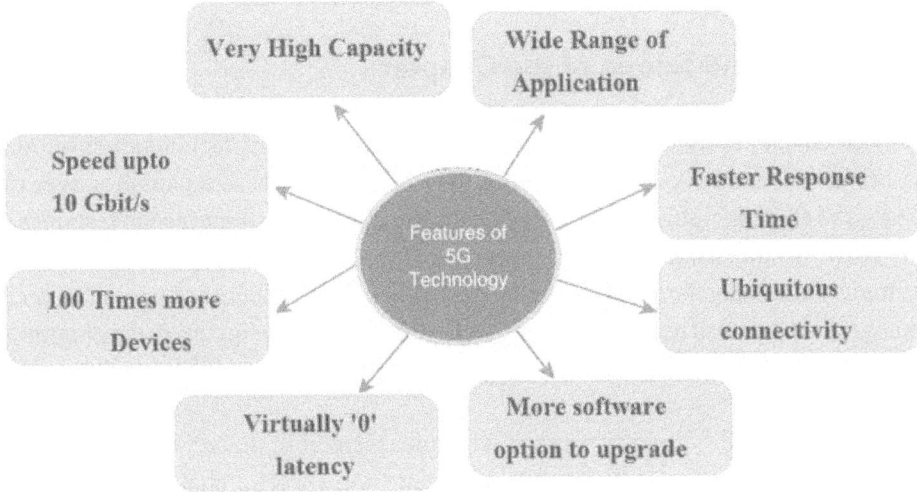

IMPORTANCE OF CYBERSECURITY IN 5G

As 5G networks enhance the determination of modern ideas foundation, their security is of principal significance. The raised connectivity and relation of tools and methods within a 5G network mean that safety rifts in one few the network can have tumbling belongings, potentially upsetting detracting aids and causing extensive harm (Georgiou et al., 2021). The stakes are specifically high in areas in the way that healthcare, conveyance, energy, and finance and availability of data are important.

One of the primary concerns with 5G is the expanded attack surface. The introduction of new technologies such as SDN, NFV, and edge computing, along with the vast number of IoT devices connected to 5G networks, creates numerous points of vulnerability. Cyber attackers can target not only the network infrastructure but also the devices, applications, and services running on it (Georgiou et al., 2021). Traditional security measures that were effective in earlier generations of mobile networks may no longer suffice, necessitating the development of new cybersecurity techniques specifically tailored to the unique challenges of 5G (Fakhouri, H. N., 2023).

Moreover, the potential for cyber-attacks on 5G networks to have geopolitical implications adds another layer of complexity to the security landscape. As nations compete to lead in 5G deployment, concerns about espionage, sabotage, and the use of 5G infrastructures for offensive cyber operations have come to the forefront.

Ensuring the security of 5G networks is therefore not just a technical challenge, but also a matter of national security and international relations.

Objectives and Scope of the Chapter

This chapter aims to give an overview of the cybersecurity techniques developed to protect 5G networks. By examining the evolution of these techniques over the years, the chapter highlights the adaptive strategies that have emerged in response to the growing and changing threat landscape. The discussion will cover a wide range of topics, including the security challenges unique to 5G, the role of upcoming technologies such as artificial intelligence (AI), blockchain, and quantum cryptography in enhancing 5G security, and the practical implementation of these techniques in real-world scenarios.

The scope of this chapter is broad, encompassing both theoretical and practical aspects of 5G cybersecurity. It will delve into the specific challenges posed by technologies like network slicing, SDN, and NFV, and explore how these challenges are being addressed through innovative security solutions. The chapter will also examine the implications of 5G security for critical infrastructure and IoT devices, offering insights into the best practices for securing these vital components of the 5G ecosystem.

Background and Motivation

The evolution of mobile networks from 1G to 5G reflects a dramatic progression in technology, capacity, and capability. The first generation (1G) introduced basic voice communication, relying on analog signals with limited security features. With the advent of 2G, digital signals were employed, enabling more secure communication through basic encryption and the introduction of SMS services. 3G networks marked the beginning of mobile data services, allowing internet access and multimedia messaging, while 4G revolutionized the mobile experience by providing high-speed internet, supporting video streaming, and enabling the rise of mobile apps. Each generation brought enhancements not only in speed and functionality but also in security, responding to the evolving threat landscape. However, none of these previous generations anticipated the level of connectivity, data generation, and dependency that 5G would introduce.

5G, with its promise of ultra-fast speeds, low latency, and the ability to connect billions of devices, represents a quantum leap over its predecessors. It is designed to support not just smart-phones but a vast array of connected devices, from autonomous vehicles to smart cities and industrial IoT applications. This exponential growth in connectivity and data flow, however, also brings unprecedented security challenges.

Key Security Challenges Unique to 5G

The construction and functional traits of 5G networks present various safety challenges that are unique to the former era. One of the basic challenges is the raised attack surface on account of the massive number of connected devices. The unification of IoT tools into 5G networks method that each device can conceivably symbolize an entrance point for cyber attacks (Banafaa, M et al., 2023). Many of these devices have restricted computational capacity and depository, making it troublesome to implement robust security measures.

Another detracting challenge is network slicing, that admits the concoction of diversified in essence networks inside a sole material foundation. While this is a key feature for optimizing resource use, it further raises concerns about the isolation between slices and the potential for cross-slice attacks.

The Need for Enhanced Security Frameworks

Given these challenges, there is a clear need for enhanced security frameworks tailored specifically to 5G networks. Traditional security measures that were sufficient for 4G and earlier networks are inadequate in addressing the complexities and risks posed by 5G. New security frameworks must be designed to protect the diverse and dynamic environment of 5G, ensuring that data integrity, confidentiality, and availability are maintained across all aspects of the network. These frameworks must incorporate advanced technologies such as artificial intelligence for threat detection, blockchain for secure transaction management, and quantum cryptography for future-proof encryption.

SECURITY CHALLENGES IN 5G NETWORKS

Increased Device Density and IoT Integration

One of ultimate meaningful protection challenges in 5G networks is the unprecedented increase in design bulk and the extensive unification of the Internet of Things (IoT). 5G networks are planned to support up to a million devices per square kilometer, a moving increase over previous generations (O'Connell et al., 2020). This extreme mass of related designs, varying from smart phones to sensors in smart cities, expands the attack surface, making it smooth for computerized attackers to aim exposures.

Many IoT tools have limited transformation capacity and storage, that confines their ability to implement strong freedom measures. These devices frequently run on outdated or insecure software, making them susceptible to attacks such as malware injections, distributed denial-of-service (DDoS) attacks, and unauthorized access. Furthermore, the boundless number of IoT designs affiliated to 5G networks way that even a narrow security gap can have pouring belongings, endangering the entire network. Figure.2 Different security challenges in 5G network such as network slicing and virtualization, new attack surface, edge cloud opens up new attack surface.

Figure 2. Different security challenges in 5G network

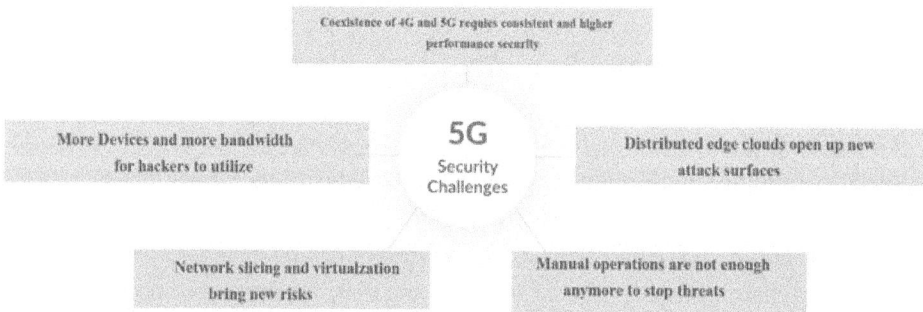

Heterogeneous Network Architectures: 5G networks are inherently heterogeneous, integrating a wide variety of technologies, protocols, and devices. This heterogeneity is a double-edged sword: while it enables 5G to support diverse applications and services, it also introduces complexity that makes security management more challenging (Pons, M. 2023). The combination of different radio access technologies (e.g., LTE, mm Wave, and Wi-Fi), multiple vendor equipment, and diverse user requirements creates a fragmented network environment where traditional security mechanisms may not be effective. The challenge lies in ensuring consistent and comprehensive security across this varied landscape. For instance, vulnerabilities in one component, such as a Wi-Fi access point, could potentially be exploited to compromise other parts of the network. The need for seamless interoperability between these different components also increases the risk of configuration errors and security loopholes that attackers could exploit.

Virtualization and Software-Defined Networking (SDN): The adoption of virtualization and Software-Defined Networking (SDN) in 5G networks offers numerous benefits, such as flexibility, scalability, and cost-efficiency. Virtualization decouples network functions from the underlying hardware, enabling the creation of virtual network functions (VNFs) that can be deployed and managed dynamically (Kim, J. 2023). SDN, on the other hand, allows centralized control of network traffic, providing greater agility in network management.

Network Slicing and its Security Implications

Network slicing is a key feature of 5G networks, admitting the creation of multiple in virtual networks, or "slices," inside a single material foundation. Each slice can be tailored to specific applications or services like improved mobile broadband, ultra-reliable reduced-abeyance communication, or large machine-type communication. While network slicing offers significant benefits in agreements of resource growth and service customization, it also presents unique security challenges.

One of the primary concerns is the isolation between slices. If isolation mechanisms fail, an attacker could potentially access multiple slices, leading to cross-slice attacks that compromise the security of different services. Additionally, the dynamic nature of slicing, where slices can be created, modified, or terminated on demand, complicates the task of ensuring consistent security policies across all slices. The need to manage security across multiple slices, each with different requirements and characteristics, further increases the complexity of securing 5G networks.

Privacy Concerns in 5G

Privacy is another critical issue in 5G networks, driven by the vast amount of personal and sensitive data generated and transmitted by connected devices. The granularity of data collected by 5G networks, including location data, usage patterns, and personal preferences, raises significant privacy concerns. Inadequate privacy protections could lead to unauthorized data collection, tracking, and profiling of users, potentially violating their privacy rights.

The integration of IoT devices into 5G networks exacerbates these concerns, as many IoT devices lack strong privacy protections. For example, smart home devices, wearables, and health monitors can collect detailed information about an individual's daily activities, health status, and more. If this data is intercepted or misused, it could lead to severe privacy breaches (Popoola, O. 2024). Additionally, the use of technologies like edge computing, where data processing occurs closer to the data source, introduces new privacy risks as sensitive data is distributed across various locations, potentially outside the control of the user.

Addressing these privacy concerns requires the implementation of robust data protection mechanisms, including encryption, anonymization, and user consent management, as well as the development of regulatory frameworks to govern data collection and usage in 5G networks.

EVOLUTION OF CYBERSECURITY TECHNIQUES

During the initial stages of 5G development, researchers and industry stakeholders began exploring the foundational security frameworks necessary to support this next-generation network. The focus act understanding the unique necessities of 5G, containing its capability to support massive device connectivity, ultra-reliable low-latency ideas, and enhanced mobile broadband. Early research identified the need for robust security mechanisms that could address the anticipated challenges, such as increased attack surfaces and the complexity of network management.Figure.3. shows the different tools and techniques of cyber security such as network security, operational security, information security, application security eta.

Figure 3. Different tools and techniques in cyber security

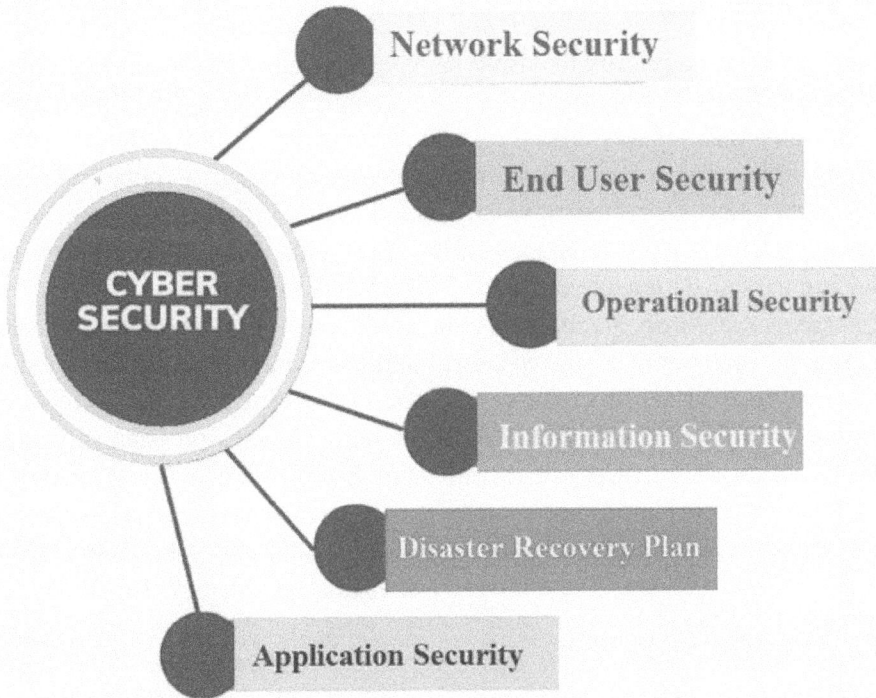

Importance of Cybersecurity Tools and Techniques

SDN and NFV as Enablers for 5G Security: Software-Defined Networking (SDN) and Network Function Virtualization (NFV) emerged as critical enablers for 5G security during this period. SDN's centralized control plane offered enhanced visibility and control over network traffic, enabling more effective monitoring and response to security threats. NFV allowed network functions to be virtualized and managed more flexibly, making it possible to deploy security measures dynamically across the network. These technologies were seen as essential for the scalability and adaptability required in 5G networks, laying the groundwork for more advanced security architectures.

Blockchain as a Potential Security Solution: Blockchain technology began gaining attention as a potential solution for enhancing security in 5G networks. Its decentralized nature and ability to provide immutable, transparent records made it an attractive option for securing transactions, managing identities, and ensuring data integrity in distributed networks. Early research explored the feasibility of integrating blockchain into 5G to address challenges such as secure authentication, privacy protection, and the management of decentralized IoT networks.

Standardization Efforts by 3GPP and ITU: As 5G technology advanced, standardization became a priority to ensure the interoperability and security of global 5G networks. The 3G Partnership Project (3GPP) and the International Telecommunication Union (ITU) played crucial roles in defining the security architectures for 5G. These efforts focused on developing comprehensive security frameworks that addressed the unique characteristics of 5G, including network slicing, virtualization, and the integration of IoT (Morgado, A.2018). The standards established during this period laid the foundation for secure 5G deployments worldwide.

Emergence of Network Slicing and Associated Security Concerns: Network slicing, a salient feature of 5G, became a focal point of security research. The ability to create multiple virtual networks, each tailored to specific use cases, introduced new security challenges, particularly in maintaining isolation between slices and ensuring consistent security policies across them (Zhang, L. Chen, Y. and Zhang, Q. 2017). Researchers explored various techniques to secure network slices, including the use of dedicated security protocols, encryption, and access controls to prevent cross-slice attacks and ensure the integrity of each slice (Xiao, Y. He, X. Hu, L. and Huang, D. 2018).

AI and Machine Learning for Real-Time Threat Detection: The potential of artificial intelligence (AI) and machine learning (ML) to enhance 5G security became increasingly evident during this period. AI and ML were recognized for their ability to analyze amounts of data in real-time, identifying patterns and anomalies that could indicate security threats. Early implementations of AI-driven security solutions focused on intrusion detection, anomaly detection, and predictive analytics, offering a proactive approach to threat management in 5G networks.

Zero-Trust Architectures and End-to-End Encryption: The concept of zero-trust architecture gained prominence as a critical approach to securing 5G networks. In a zero-trust model, no user or device is trusted by default, regardless of whether they are inside or outside the network perimeter. This approach emphasized the importance of continuous verification, least-privilege access, and end-to-end encryption to protect data as it moves across the network (Chen, S. 2019). The adoption of zero-trust principles was seen as essential for defending against increasingly sophisticated cyber threats in the 5G environment.

AI-Driven Anomaly Detection: Building on earlier research, AI-driven anomaly detection systems became more sophisticated, leveraging advanced machine learning algorithms to identify and respond to security threats in real-time. These systems were capable of detecting subtle deviations from normal network behavior, allowing for the early detection of potential attacks. AI's ability to adapt and learn from new data made it an invaluable tool for maintaining the security of dynamic and complex 5G networks.

Quantum Cryptography for Future-Proof Security: Quantum cryptography emerged as a promising solution for future-proofing 5G security. With the potential advent of quantum computing, traditional encryption methods were at risk of becoming obsolete. Quantum key distribution (QKD) offered a way to secure communications by leveraging the principles of quantum mechanics, making it theoretically impossible for attackers to intercept and decode encrypted data. Research during this period focused on integrating quantum cryptography into 5G networks to ensure long-term data security (Abbas, R. Jan, S. and Ali, F. 2020).

Collaborative Threat Intelligence Sharing: Recognizing the importance of collaboration in combating cyber threats, 5G security strategies began to emphasize the sharing of threat intelligence among stakeholders. Collaborative platforms were developed to enable the real-time exchange of information about emerging threats, vulnerabilities, and attack vectors. This collective approach enhanced the ability to detect, analyze, and respond to threats more effectively, creating a more resilient security environment for 5G networks (Mahbub, M. 2021).

Adaptive Security Models: As the complexity of 5G networks increased, adaptive security models became essential for maintaining robust protection. These models were designed to dynamically adjust security measures based on the current threat landscape, network conditions, and user behavior. Adaptive security systems leveraged AI and machine learning to continuously evaluate risks and implement appropriate countermeasures, ensuring that 5G networks remained secure in the face of evolving threats.

Lightweight Cryptography for IoT Devices: The integration of IoT devices into 5G networks required the development of lightweight cryptography solutions tailored to the limited computational resources of these devices. Research focused on creating efficient encryption algorithms that could provide strong security without compromising performance. Lightweight cryptography became a critical component of securing IoT ecosystems within 5G networks, protecting sensitive data and ensuring the integrity of device communications (Sikder, S. 2022).

Homomorphic Encryption and Secure Multi-Party Computation: As data privacy and security became increasingly important, homomorphic encryption and secure multi-party computation emerged as cutting-edge techniques for protecting sensitive information in 5G networks. Homomorphic encryption allowed data to be processed while still encrypted, ensuring that sensitive information remained secure even during computation (Zhang, X. 2023). Secure multi-party computation enabled multiple parties to jointly compute a function without revealing their individual inputs, providing robust privacy protection in collaborative environments.

Blockchain for Decentralized Security Management: Blockchain technology continued to gain traction as a decentralized approach to security management in 5G networks. Its ability to provide tamper-proof records and secure identity management made it an ideal solution for managing trust in distributed environments. Blockchain was increasingly used to secure transactions, authenticate devices, and manage access controls in 5G networks, offering a resilient and transparent security framework.

Resilient Security Architectures for Critical Infrastructure: As 5G networks became integral to critical infrastructure sectors such as energy, transportation, and healthcare, the need for resilient security architectures became paramount. Research focused on developing security frameworks that could withstand attacks, ensure the continuity of essential services, and quickly recover from disruptions. These architectures incorporated advanced threat detection, redundancy, and failover mechanisms to protect critical infrastructure from cyber threats and ensure the reliability of 5G-enabled services (Wang, J. 2024).

This year-wise evolution of cybersecurity techniques for 5G networks illustrates the ongoing efforts to address the unique challenges posed by this transformative technology. Each stage of development has brought new innovations and strategies, reflecting the dynamic nature of the 5G security landscape.

Cutting-Edge Technologies in 5G Cybersecurity

Role in Threat Detection and Response: Artificial Intelligence (AI) and Machine Learning (ML) are performing more and more crucial acts in reinforcing cybersecurity inside 5G networks. These technologies are employed to resolve vast amounts of data generated by 5G networks, recognizing patterns and oddities that can indicate potential warnings. AI-compelled warning discovery systems can monitor network carry as unauthorized access, quickly recognizing and diminishing risks to a degree illegitimate access, malware, and Distributed Denial of Service (DDoS) attacks. The talent of AI to suit and learn from new data create it a strong tool for coming back to the active and developing danger landscape in 5G environment.

AI for Predictive Security Modeling: In addition to real time threat discovery, AI and ML are more and more used for predicting security shaping in 5G networks. By resolving historical data and identifying currents, AI can think potential freedom occurrence before they occur. Predictive models can expect exposures, forecast attack patterns, and support insights into ultimate likely future thrats, permissive full of enthusiasm security measures. This capacity is specifically valuable in 5G networks, place the sheer scale and complexity of related tools demand a progressive approach to maintain security (Bibri, E. S. 2023).

Blockchain Technology

Decentralized Security Management: Blockchain technology offers a decentralized approach to security management in 5G networks, addressing some of the inherent challenges associated with centralized security frameworks. By leveraging the immutability and transparency of blockchain, 5G networks can achieve secure identity management, authentication, and access control across a distributed environment. Each transaction or event recorded on the blockchain is cryptographically secured, making it nearly impossible to alter or tamper with the data. This decentralized approach enhances trust and accountability, especially in scenarios involving multiple stakeholders or distributed devices (Hasan, B. K. 2024).

Quantum Cryptography: Quantum Key Distribution (QKD): Quantum Cryptography, specifically Quantum Key Distribution (QKD), is arising as a contemporary solution for securing 5G networks against future threats. QKD influences the standard of branch of quantum physics to securely deliver encryption answers between parties.Any attempt to intercept or measure the quantum keys alters their state, immediately alerting the parties to a potential eavesdropping attempt. This inherent property of quantum cryptography makes it an ideal solution for securing sensitive communications in 5G networks, ensuring that encryption keys remain confidential and unaltered (Adnan, M. H. 2022).

Future Applications in 5G Security: While QKD is now ultimate prominent request of quantum cryptography in 5G, future applications are likely to extend beyond key distribution. As quantum computing advances, traditional encryption plans concede possibility enhance vulnerable to quantity attacks. To counter this, scientists are investigating post-quantum cryptographic algorithms that can resist such specific attacks. In the future, quantum cryptography can be joined into broader 5G protection foundations, safeguarding not just key exchanges but also the completeness and secrecy of all data transmitted across the network.

Homomorphic Encryption: Ensuring Data Privacy in 5G: Homomorphic encryption is a hopeful technology for guaranteeing data privacy in 5G networks. Unlike usual encryption systems, homomorphic encryption allows data expected processed in its encrypted form, meaning that delicate facts can be resolved or manipulated without always being decrypted. This capability is specifically valuable in 5G surroundings where data solitude is paramount, to a degree in healthcare and smart city uses. Homomorphic encryption enables secure data giving and processing, guaranteeing that private and sensitive facts remains protected even during computation (Shi, S. 2020).

Potential Use Cases and Challenges: The potential use cases for homomorphic encryption in 5G are vast, including secure data analytics, privacy-preserving machine learning, and encrypted cloud computing. For example, in healthcare, homomorphic encryption could allow medical data to be analyzed by third-party service providers without exposing the raw data, preserving patient confidentiality. However, there are also significant challenges associated with the widespread adoption of homomorphic encryption in 5G networks. One of the primary challenges is the computational overhead, as homomorphic encryption is currently more resource-intensive than traditional encryption methods. Additionally, ensuring compatibility with existing systems and standards will be critical for the successful integration of homomorphic encryption into 5G cybersecurity frameworks.

These cutting-edge technologies are poised to revolutionize the cybersecurity landscape in 5G networks, offering advanced solutions to address the unique challenges posed by this next-generation technology. Each technology brings its own set of benefits and challenges, and their successful implementation will be key to securing the future of 5G.

Cybersecurity in 5G Network Slicing

Overview of Network Slicing: Network slicing is a important feature of 5G science that enables the concoction of diversified in virtual networks, or "slices," on a distinct physical network foundation. Each slice is tailor-made to meet distinguishing efficiency, capacity, and aid necessities, making it attainable to give diverse types of duties over the same network. For example, individual slice might be improved for high speed mobile broadband, while another can be dedicated to extreme low latency communications for responsibility-detracting uses.

The idea of network slicing admits network manipulators to efficiently accomplish and assign possessions established the needs of various applications and consumers. This virtualized approach supports the flexibility to offer personalized duties and boost overall network efficiency. Each slice run alone, accompanying its own set of network functions and resources, this authorizes the support of various use cases such as autonomous vehicles, smart cities, and industrial IoT.

Security Challenges in Sliced Networks: Network slicing introduces several unique security challenges that can be addressed to ensure the overall integrity and safety of 5G networks:

Isolation and Segregation: One of the primary security concerns is ensuring effective isolation between slices. Since each slice operates independently but shares the same physical infrastructure, a security breach in one slice could potentially impact others. Ensuring that data and functions in one slice do not interfere with or compromise those in another is critical for maintaining overall network security.

Dynamic Nature of Slices: The dynamic creation, modification, and termination of network slices add complexity to security management. The ability to rapidly deploy and scale slices means that security policies and configurations must be adaptable and consistently enforced across the network. This dynamic nature makes it challenging to monitor and manage security effectively.

Resource Allocation and Management: Network slices share physical resources, such as computing power and storage. Ensuring that resources are allocated securely and efficiently without creating vulnerabilities or resource contention is crucial. An attacker could exploit resource sharing to launch attacks or degrade the performance of other slices.

Complexity of Management: The management of multiple slices, each with different security requirements and policies, increases the complexity of maintaining a secure network environment. Coordinating security measures across various slices and ensuring compliance with different security policies can be a significant challenge.

Techniques for Isolating and Securing Slices

Several techniques and strategies are employed to address the security challenges associated with network slicing:

Virtualization-Based Isolation: Virtualization technologies are used to create isolated environments for each network slice. This isolation is achieved through the use of virtual machines or containers, which ensure that each slice operates independently and cannot directly access or interfere with the resources of other slices. Techniques such as virtual private networks (VPNs) and firewalls are used to enforce security boundaries between slices.

Access Control and Authentication: Strong approach control devices are achieved to ensure that only approved individuals can approach or modify network slices. This contains robust confirmation agreements and role-based access controls (RBAC) that restrict approach established the user's duty and right. Additionally, slice-distinguishing credentials and permission checks help assert the integrity and security of each slice.

Encryption and Data Protection: End-to-end encryption is used to protect data transmitted within and between network slices. This guarantees that sensitive facts debris secret and secure from illegal access. Data protection measures also include encryption of stored data and secure key management practices to safeguard against data breaches.

Monitoring and Threat Detection: Continuous monitoring and real-time threat detection are essential for identifying and mitigating security threats in network slices. Advanced monitoring tools and intrusion discovery systems (IDS) are employed to discover divergent behaviour, unlawful approach attempts, and potential attacks. Machine learning and AI-driven analytics of logical analysis reinforce the talent to identify and put oneself in the place of another threats effectively.

Policy Management and Automation: Automated policy management tools are used to enforce security policies consistently across network slices. This contains the use of safety industrialization frameworks that can dynamically regulate procedures established current network environments and threats levels. Automation helps streamline freedom administration and guarantees that tactics are applied evenly across all slices.

CASE STUDIES AND PRACTICAL IMPLEMENTATIONS

Case Study: Secure Network Slicing for Smart Cities

In an arrangement for a smart city, network slicing was used to devise loyal slices for various smart city applications, such as traffic management, public security, and preservation of natural resources. To secure these slices, virtualization-located seclusion was implemented to guarantee that data and functions in each slice remained separate. Access controls and encryption were working to care for sensitive data, and continuous monitoring was used to discover and put oneself in the place of another potential security incidents. The arrangement showed how network slicing commit specify tailor-made duties while upholding powerful security measures.

Case Study: Industrial IoT with Network Slicing

A large industrial facility utilized network slicing to support its industrial IoT (IIoT) applications, including real-time monitoring and automation. Each IIoT application was allocated its own network slice to meet specific performance and security requirements. Techniques such as encryption, access control, and policy management were used to protect the integrity and confidentiality of industrial data. The implementation highlighted the importance of adaptive security measures in managing complex and dynamic industrial environments.

Practical Implementation: 5G Network Slicing for Healthcare

In a healthcare setting, network slicing was used to create secure, low-latency slices for telemedicine, electronic health records (EHRs), and medical device communication. Security measures included encryption of medical data, access controls for healthcare providers, and monitoring for potential security threats. The implementation demonstrated how network slicing could be tailored to meet the stringent security and performance requirements of critical healthcare applications (Gao, S. 2024).

These case studies and practical implementations illustrate the effectiveness of various techniques in addressing the security challenges associated with network slicing. They provide valuable insights into how network slicing can be deployed securely in different contexts, ensuring that the benefits of 5G technology are realized while maintaining robust security and privacy.

IOT SECURITY IN 5G NETWORKS

Unique Challenges Posed by IoT in 5G

The integration of the Internet of Things (IoT) into 5G networks introduces several unique security challenges due to the large number and diversity of connected devices. These challenges include:

Device Heterogeneity and Scalability: IoT tools change widely in conditions of fittings capabilities, operating systems, and ideas obligations. This variety confuses the exercise of uniform security measures. Moreover, the sheer scale of IoT designs in 5G networks (conceivably until a heap tools per square kilometer) presents challenges in directing and securing specific a big and different array of endpoints (Allioui, H. & Mourdi, Y., 2023).

Resource Constraints: Few IoT devices have limitations on processing power, memory and battery life. These constraints make it difficult to deploy traditional, resource-intensive security solutions. Lightweight security mechanisms that can operate efficiently on constrained devices are essential but challenging to implement effectively.

Insecure Device Design: Some IoT devices are designed with minimum security features, potentially leaving them vulnerable to attacks. Common issues include hard-coded credentials, lack of encryption, and inadequate software update mechanisms. Exploiting these vulnerabilities can lead to unauthorized access, data breaches, and manipulation of device behaviour (D. M. et al, 2020).

Inter-Device Communication: IoT devices often correspond to accompanying each other and accompanying principal systems over differing networks. Securing these ideas channels is critical for fear that unjustified data approach, tampering, or eavesdropping. Ensuring secure ideas obligations across diverse and conceivably untrusted networks adjoins complexity to IoT safety.

Data Privacy and Integrity: IoT ploys generate and send abundant volumes of delicate data, containing individual, health, and functional information. Ensuring the solitude and integrity concerning this data is crucial, exceptionally in applications like healthcare and smart centers place data breaches take care of have significant results.

Lightweight Cryptography and Secure Firmware Updates

Lightweight Cryptography: Lightweight cryptography is designed to provide robust security while accommodating the limited resources of many IoT devices. Key aspects of lightweight cryptography include:

Efficient Algorithms: Lightweight cryptographic algorithms are optimized for low-power and low-memory environments. Examples include lightweight block ciphers like PRESENT and SPECK, and lightweight hash functions such as SHA-3 variants specifically designed for constrained devices.

Ensuring End-to-End Security in IoT Ecosystems

Comprehensive Security Framework: Ensuring end-to-end security in IoT ecosystems requires a comprehensive approach that addresses security at every layer of the network. Key components of an end-to-end security framework include:

Device Security: Ensuring that IoT devices are securely designed and configured, with robust access controls, encryption, and secure firmware update mechanisms. This includes implementing secure boot processes and protecting device credentials.

Network Security: Securing the ideas channels between IoT tools and network foundation through encryption, secure contracts, and network separation. Implementing interruption detection and prevention systems (IDPS) can help monitor and keep against network-located attacks.

Data Security: Protecting data at rest and along the way utilizing encryption and data purity means. Ensuring that sensitive data is anonymized and securely stored for fear of an unauthorized approach and breaches.

Access Control and Identity Management: Implementing strong authentication and authorization mechanisms to control access to IoT devices and data. This includes using multi-factor authentication (MFA) and role-based access controls (RBAC) to ensure that only authorized users and devices can interact with the IoT ecosystem.

Monitoring and Incident Response: Continuously monitoring IoT networks for security threats and anomalies. Developing and maintaining an incident response plan to quickly address and mitigate security incidents when they occur (Jani, K. A. et al., 2020).

Collaboration and Standards: Collaboration between industry stakeholders, standardization bodies, and regulatory authorities is essential for establishing best practices and standards for IoT security. Adhering to established security standards and guidelines helps ensure that IoT devices and networks are protected against known threats and vulnerabilities.

FUTURE DIRECTIONS IN 5G CYBERSECURITY

Anticipated Threats and Emerging Challenges

As 5G networks continue to evolve and expand, several anticipated threats and emerging challenges are likely to impact their cybersecurity landscape:

Advanced Persistent Threats (APTs): APTs, from extended and targeted high-tech-attacks, proper to become more advanced and frequent. Attackers can influence 5G's high-speed, reduced-abeyance proficiencies to conduct complex attacks that can persist unfound for comprehensive periods.

Increased Attack Surface: The unification of a broad number of IoT designs and the growth of network slicing build a more extensive attack surface. Each new instrument and network slice presents potential exposures that maybe used by hateful performers.

Supply Chain Vulnerabilities: The complexity of 5G infrastructure, with its reliance on a global supply chain, increases the risk of supply chain attacks. Ensuring the integrity of hardware and software components throughout the supply chain will be critical to preventing these types of attacks.

Quantum Computing Threats: The arrival of quantum computing poses a potential warning to current cryptographic arrangements. Quantum computing take care of potentially break widely-used encryption algorithms, making it owned by evolve and implement quantity-resistant cryptographic methods (Chaubey, N. et al, 2020).

AI-Powered Attacks: As AI and machine learning technologies become more advanced, they may be used by attackers to automate and enhance their attack strategies. Defending against AI-driven threats will require sophisticated and adaptive security measures.

6G and its Security Implications

The transition from 5G to 6G is expected to introduce new technologies and capabilities that will have significant implications for security:

Ultra-High-Speed and Low-Latency Communications: 6G will promise even faster speeds and lower abeyance than 5G, permissive new applications in the way that augmented reality (AR) and virtual reality (VR) with greater fidelity. However, these progresses concede possibility also bring about new attack headings and challenges in acquiring extreme-fast communication channels.

Advanced AI Integration: 6G networks are likely to integrate more advanced AI technologies for network management and optimization. While AI can enhance security, it also introduces new risks related to AI system vulnerabilities and adversarial attacks on machine learning models.

Enhanced Connectivity and Automation: 6G will further enhance connectivity and automation across various sectors, including smart cities, autonomous vehicles, and industrial automation. Ensuring the security of these interconnected systems will be critical to preventing disruptions and maintaining safety.

New Radio Technologies: 6G is expected to introduce new radio technologies and spectrum bands, which will require novel security approaches to protect against potential threats specific to these technologies.

Privacy and Data Protection: With the increased data collection and sharing capabilities of 6G, protecting user privacy and ensuring data protection will become even more crucial. New privacy-preserving technologies and regulations will be needed to address these concerns.

CONCLUSION

The cybersecurity landscape for 5G networks is marked by evolving threats and challenges, including increased device density, advanced persistent threats, and the potential impacts of quantum computing. Addressing these issues requires innovative approaches, such as lightweight cryptography, AI-driven threat detection, and secure firmware updates. The transition to 6G will introduce new technologies and security implications, necessitating future-proofing strategies and robust policy frameworks. Continuous innovation and collaboration among industry stakeholders, researchers, and regulators are crucial for advancing security measures. Securing the future of 5G demands proactive and adaptive solutions to safeguard against emerging risks and ensure network integrity.

The chapter on Cybersecurity Techniques for 5G Networks offers a novel contribution by presenting a comprehensive, year-wise analysis of the evolution of security measures tailored to the unique challenges posed by 5G technology. Unlike previous reviews that primarily focus on individual aspects or static overviews, this chapter highlights the dynamic progression of security strategies, showcasing how they have adapted to address emerging threats and technological advancements over time. It uniquely integrates discussions on cutting-edge techniques such as AI-driven threat detection, homomorphic encryption, and blockchain-based decentralized security, providing a forward-looking perspective on how these innovations are shaping the future of 5G security. Additionally, the chapter emphasizes the practical implications of these techniques for critical infrastructure and IoT devices within 5G networks, making it a valuable resource for both academic researchers and industry practitioners seeking to understand and mitigate the complex security challenges of next-generation networks.

The chapter concludes that cybersecurity in 5G networks is a rapidly evolving field, driven by the complex challenges and opportunities introduced by this transformative technology. Over the years, security strategies have advanced from basic conceptual frameworks to sophisticated, multi-layered approaches that leverage cutting-edge technologies such as AI, blockchain, and homomorphic encryption. These innovations are crucial in addressing the diverse and dynamic threats faced by 5G networks, particularly in protecting critical infrastructure and IoT ecosystems. The ongoing research and development efforts signal a trend towards more resilient, adaptive, and decentralized security architectures, which will be essential as 5G continues to expand globally. Looking forward, the chapter underscores the importance of continuous collaboration between academia, industry, and standardization bodies to ensure that 5G networks are secure and reliable for all users.

REFERENCES

Adnan, M. H., Ahmad Zukarnain, Z., & Harun, N. Z. (2022). Quantum Key Distribution for 5G Networks: A Review, State of Art and Future Directions. *Future Internet*, 14(3), 73. DOI: 10.3390/fi14030073

Allioui, H., & Mourdi, Y. (2023). *Exploring the Full Potentials of IoT for Better Financial Growth and Stability: A Comprehensive* Survey. *Sensors (Basel)*, 23(19), 8015. DOI: 10.3390/s23198015 PMID: 37836845

Banafaa, M., Shayea, I., Din, J., Azmi, H. M., Alashbi, A., Daradkeh, I. Y., & Alhammadi, A. (2023). *6G Mobile Communication Technology: Requirements, Targets, Applications, Challenges, Advantages, and Opportunities,* Alexandria Engineering Journal, 64, 245-274, ISSN 1110-0168, DOI: 10.1016/j.aej.2022.08.017

Bibri, E. S., Krogstie, J., Kaboli, A., & Alahi, A. (2023). *Smarter eco-cities and their leading-edge artificial intelligence of things solutions for environmental sustainability: A comprehensive systematic review, Environmental Science and Ecotechnology,* 19, 100330, ISSN 2666-4984, DOI: 10.1016/j.ese.2023.100330

Chaubey, N.. (2020). *Quantum Cryptography and the Future of Cyber Security*. IGI Global., DOI: 10.4018/978-1-7998-2253-0

Chen, S., Liu, Y., & Cui, S. (2019). *Security in 5G networks:* A survey," *IEEE Access*, vol. 7, pp. 30474-30488. Abbas, R. Jan, S. and Ali, F. (2020). Security and privacy in 5G: A survey of emerging challenges and future directions. *IEEE Access : Practical Innovations, Open Solutions*, 8, 211657–211691.

Fakhouri, H. N., Alawadi, S., Awaysheh, F. M., Hani, I. B., Alkhalaileh, M., & Hamad, F. (2023). A Comprehensive Study on the Role of Machine Learning in 5G Security: Challenges, Technologies, and Solutions. *Electronics (Basel)*, 12(22), 4604. DOI: 10.3390/electronics12224604

Gao, S., Lin, R., Fu, Y., Li, H., & Cao, J. (2024). Security Threats, Requirements and Recommendations on Creating 5G Network Slicing System: A Survey. *Electronics (Basel)*, 13(10), 1860. DOI: 10.3390/electronics13101860

Georgiou, K. E., Georgiou, E., & Satava, R. M. (2021). 5G Use in Healthcare: The Future is Present. *JSLS : Journal of the Society of Laparoendoscopic Surgeons*, 25(4), 00064. DOI: 10.4293/JSLS.2021.00064 PMID: 35087266

Hasan, B. K. Sajid, M. Lapina, M. Shahid, M. Kotecha, K. (2024). *Blockchain technology meets 6 G wireless networks: A systematic survey,* Alexandria Engineering Journal, 92, 199-220, ISSN 1110-0168, DOI: 10.1016/j.aej.2024.02.031

Huseien, F. G., & Shah, W. K. (2022). *A review on 5G technology for smart energy management and smart buildings in Singapore*, Energy and AI, 7,2022,100116,ISSN 2666-5468,DOI: 10.1016/j.egyai.2021.100116

Jani, K. A.. (2020). IoT and Cyber Security: Introduction, Attacks, and Preventive Steps. In Chaubey, N., & Prajapati, B. (Eds.), *Quantum Cryptography and the Future of Cyber Security* (pp. 203–235). IGI Global., DOI: 10.4018/978-1-7998-2253-0.ch010

Kim, J., Kim, Y., Yegneswaran, V., Porras, P., Shin, S., & Park, T. (2023). *Extended data plane architecture for in-network security services in software-defined networks*,Computers & Security,124,102976,ISSN 0167-4048,DOI: 10.1016/j.cose.2022.102976

Lorincz, J., Kukuruzović, A., & Blažević, Z. (2024). A Comprehensive Overview of Network Slicing for Improving the Energy Efficiency of Fifth-Generation Networks. *Sensors (Basel)*, 24(10), 3242. DOI: 10.3390/s24103242 PMID: 38794095

Mahbub, M. Shami, S. and Alam, S. M. (2021). *Adaptive security in 5G networks Challenges and solutions,"* IEEE Communications Magazine*, 59, no. 4, pp. 20-26. Sikder, S. Rahmati, A. and Saxena,N. (2022). *Lightweight security mechanisms for 5G IoT devices," IEEE Transactions on Mobile Computing*, l. 21, no. 1, pp. 27-39.

Morgado, A., Mohammed, K., Huq, S., Mumtaz, S., & Rodriguez, J. (2018). *A survey of 5G technologies: regulatory, standardization and industrial perspectives, Digital Communications and Networks*,4,2,2018,87-97,ISSN 2352-8648, https://doi .org/DOI: 10.1016/j.dcan.2017.09.010

O'Connell, E., Moore, D., & Newe, T. (2020). Challenges Associated with Implementing 5G in Manufacturing. *Telecom*, 1(1), 48–67. DOI: 10.3390/telecom1010005

Pons, M., Valenzuela, E., Rodríguez, B., Nolazco-Flores, J. A., & Del-Valle-Soto, C. (2023). Utilization of 5G Technologies in IoT Applications: Current Limitations by Interference and Network Optimization Difficulties-A Review. *Sensors (Basel)*, 23(8), 3876. DOI: 10.3390/s23083876 PMID: 37112216

Popoola, O. Rodrigues, M. Marchang, J. Shenfield, A. Ikpehai, A. Popoola, J.(2024). *A critical literature review of security and privacy in smart home healthcare schemes adopting IoT & blockchain: Problems, challenges and solutions, Blockchain: Research and Applications*,5, 2,2024,100178,ISSN 2096-7209,DOI: 10.1016/j.bcra.2023.100178

Shi, S., He, D., Li, L., Kumar, N., Khan, M. K., & Choo, K. R. (2020). Applications of blockchain in ensuring the security and privacy of electronic health record systems: A survey. *Computers & Security*, 97, 101966. DOI: 10.1016/j.cose.2020.101966 PMID: 32834254

Tank, D. M.. (2020). Cyber Security Aspects of Virtualization in Cloud Computing Environments: Analyzing Virtualization-Specific Cyber Security Risks. In Chaubey, N., & Prajapati, B. (Eds.), *Quantum Cryptography and the Future of Cyber Security* (pp. 283–299). IGI Global., DOI: 10.4018/978-1-7998-2253-0.ch013

Zhang, L., Chen, Y., & Zhang, Q. (2017). *Network slicing for 5G: Challenges and opportunities,*" *IEEE Internet Computing*, vol. 21, no. 5, pp. 20-27. Xiao, Y. He, X. Hu, L. and Huang, D. (2018). *AI-enhanced security in 5G network slicing. IEEE Wireless Communications*, 25(5), 119–125.

Zhang, X., Zhang, J., & Zheng, L. (2023). *Towards privacy-preserving 5G networks Homomorphic encryption and blockchain," IEEE Transactions on Information Forensics and Security*, 18, 378-390. Wang, J. Li, Y. and Wang, Z. (2024). *Resilient security architectures for 5G and beyond: A survey. IEEE Network*, 38(3), 47–55.

Chapter 6
Harnessing AI and Machine Learning for Effective Phishing Email Detection

Ritesh Joshi

https://orcid.org/0000-0002-0138-8786

Prestige Institute of Engineering Management and Research, Indore, India

Nirbhay Kumar Chaubey

A.M. Patel Institute of Computer Studies, Ganpat University, India

Swati Patel

A.M. Patel Institute of Computer Studies, Ganpat University, India

Md Danish Imtiaz

https://orcid.org/0009-0003-7341-5506

A.M. Patel Institute of Computer Studies, Ganpat University, India

Ankit Kumar

A.M. Patel Institute of Computer Studies, Ganpat University, India

ABSTRACT

Phishing attacks targeting email users pose a major cybersecurity threat, causing financial losses and data breaches. This research project aims to develop an advanced phishing detection tool using artificial intelligence (AI) to identify and mitigate email phishing attempts. At its core, the tool will feature a sophisticated AI model to analyze and classify emails as phishing or legitimate. The approach combines machine learning algorithms and natural language processing techniques

DOI: 10.4018/979-8-3693-9225-6.ch006

to enhance detection accuracy. The proposed solution will be integrated into a web application, allowing users to input suspicious emails for real-time analysis. The AI model will examine various features of the email, including the content, sender information, and embedded links, to determine the likelihood of phishing. By leveraging supervised learning methods, our model will be trained on a diverse dataset comprising both phishing and legitimate emails, ensuring robust performance across different scenarios.

1 INTRODUCTION

In the digital age, phishing is one of the most common and harmful kinds of cyberattacks. In order to trick people into disclosing sensitive information, such as passwords, credit card details, and other personal information, criminal actors pose as reliable organizations. Usually, email is used for these attacks, in which the attacker creates emails that look to be from reputable sources, such as banks, social networking platforms, or businesses. Luring recipients to open malicious links, download malicious attachments, or directly provide sensitive information is the aim (Yasin & Abuhasan 2016).

Phishing has evolved significantly over the years, becoming more sophisticated and harder to detect. Early phishing attempts were often easy to spot due to poor spelling, grammar, and obviously fake links. However, modern phishing attacks use advanced techniques such as social engineering, personalization, and even artificial intelligence to craft highly convincing emails. Phishing attacks can have serious consequences. They can include identity theft, money loss, and widespread data breaches that threaten an organization's security.

The rise in the frequency and sophistication of phishing attacks highlights the critical need for effective detection mechanisms. Because phishing attacks are dynamic, traditional methods like rule-based systems and blacklists have not proven to be effective enough (Zareapoor & Seeja, 2015). Blacklists can only protect against known threats and need constant updating, while rule-based systems can be bypassed by attackers who continually adapt their tactics.

Effective phishing detection is crucial for several reasons:
- **Financial Security:** Phishing attacks have the potential to cause large financial losses for both people and businesses. Detecting and blocking these attacks can prevent unauthorized access to bank accounts, credit card fraud, and other financial crimes.
- **Data Protection:** Phishing often targets sensitive personal and corporate data. Preventing these attacks helps protect personal information

and intellectual property, reducing the risk of data breaches and maintaining privacy.

- **Reputation Management:** Phishing assaults can cause serious harm to an organization's reputation. Consumers and clients may come to doubt a company's capacity to secure their data, which could result in a decline in business and legal issues.
- **Regulatory Compliance:** Strict data protection laws, including the GDPR in Europe and HIPAA in the US, apply to a wide range of sectors. Effective phishing detection helps organizations comply with these regulations and avoid costly fines.

The Evolution of Phishing Detection

Over the years, phishing detection has evolved from basic keyword-based approaches to more advanced techniques involving artificial intelligence (AI) and machine learning (ML) (Salloum et al., 2021). Traditional methods included:

- **Blacklists:** These are lists of known phishing URLs, email addresses, and domains. While useful, they are reactive rather than proactive and require continuous updates to remain effective.
- **Rule-Based Systems:** These systems use predefined rules to identify phishing emails based on certain characteristics, such as suspicious links or certain phrases. However, they struggle with false positives and cannot easily adapt to new phishing strategies.
- **Heuristic Methods:** These involve manually crafted rules and patterns to detect phishing. Although more flexible than blacklists, they still lack the adaptability and accuracy needed to handle sophisticated phishing attacks.

Introduction to AI and Machine Learning

Artificial intelligence and machine learning have transformed the cybersecurity industry, offering powerful tools to detect and mitigate phishing attacks (Atawneh & Aljehani, 2023). Artificial intellect (AI) is the simulation of human intellect in machines with thought and learning programs. As a branch of artificial intelligence, machine learning uses statistical models and algorithms to help computers learn from experience and data to execute tasks more effectively.

Objectives of the Chapter

In this chapter, we explore the use of artificial intelligence and machine learning techniques to develop robust phishing email detection systems. We utilized two publicly available datasets to train and evaluate the performance of various algorithms.

The rest of the paper is organized as: Section 2 contains the related work covering work carried out on phishing email detection using various approaches. Section 3 presents the methodology to be carried out in proposed research work, covering data collection, data pre-processing, feature extraction, model implementation and model training. Performance evaluation is carried out in section 4. Section 5 highlights the rationale behind the results obtained and its significance. Section 6 presents the conclusion and at last section 7 future direction of work.

2 RELATED WORKS

Phishing is a common cyberthreat that uses clever tricks to fool people into disclosing private information like credit card numbers, passwords, or personal information. Attackers impersonate trusted entities like banks, government agencies, or well-known companies through fraudulent emails, messages, or websites designed to appear legitimate. These communications often employ urgency, fear, or offers of rewards to prompt recipients into taking immediate action, like opening dangerous attachments or clicking on doubtful links.

The ultimate goal of phishing attacks is to exploit human trust and vulnerabilities for financial gain, identity theft, or unauthorized access to sensitive data. Sophisticated phishing campaigns may use sophisticated social engineering techniques to increase their credibility and likelihood of success. For instance, attackers may create convincing replicas of official logos, email templates, or login pages to deceive victims.

Phishing attacks continue to evolve, adapting to circumvent traditional cybersecurity defenses. These global threats can result in monetary losses, harm to one's reputation, and legal implications for people, companies, and organizations. Detecting and mitigating phishing threats requires a combination of robust cybersecurity measures, user education on identifying phishing attempts, and proactive monitoring of digital communications. By staying vigilant and implementing effective security practices, individuals and organizations can better protect themselves against the pervasive threat of phishing.

Traditional phishing detection methods typically rely on heuristic-based rules, blacklist databases, and manual inspection to identify and block phishing attempts. Heuristic rules analyze email content for suspicious keywords, patterns, or formatting consistent with phishing tactics. Blacklists maintain a database of known phishing

URLs or domains, blocking access to these sites. While these methods offer basic protection, they are limited by their reliance on predefined rules and static databases, which struggle to keep pace with evolving phishing techniques and zero-day attacks. Additionally, manual inspection is labour-intensive and prone to human error, making it less effective for large-scale detection.

In contrast, AI and ML-based phishing detection methods leverage advanced algorithms to examine large volumes of data and detect subtle patterns indicative of phishing behaviour. Machine learning models can automatically learn from labelled datasets to identify characteristics such as unusual sender behaviour, deceptive content, or suspicious URLs. Techniques such as natural language processing (NLP) extract meaning from text, while anomaly detecting algorithms flag deviations from normal email behaviour. Moreover, deep learning models like convolutional neural networks (CNNs) and recurrent neural networks (RNNs) excel at processing complex, unstructured data to uncover hidden threats.

Altwaijry et al. (2024) discovered that deep learning models particularly hybrid CNNs and LSTMs are more reliable and accurate than conventional techniques. The significance of feature engineering and NLP techniques was highlighted in their work. Strong solutions for real-world detection are offered by these algorithms, which successfully captured intricate patterns in phishing emails. Sanchez & Duan (2012) discovered that SVM and ensemble approaches performed exceptionally well in phishing detection, emphasizing the significance of strong algorithms in improving accuracy and robustness. A hybrid spam filter was suggested by Atawneh & Aljehani (2023) that merged a deep multilayer perceptron neural network with rectified linear units and an N-gram tf-idf feature selection with an integrated distribution-based balancing technique. In the benchmark datasets for SpamAssassin and Enron, this filter correctly identified spam emails. Furthermore, Rawal et al. (2017) emphasized the significance of feature selection in enhancing model performance by using machine learning approaches to create an effective phishing detection system.

The usefulness of NLP approaches in conjunction with machine learning was highlighted in a thorough study on phishing detection strategies conducted by Salloum et al. (2021). Khonji et al. (2013) conducted a thorough study in which they compared machine learning classifiers for phishing email detection, including Decision Trees, Random Forests, and Support Vector Machines (SVM). Their research showed that the best detection accuracy is provided by ensemble approaches, especially Random Forest. Yasin & Abuhasan (2016) presented an intelligent categorization model that shows how machine learning methods may greatly increase the detection accuracy of phishing emails. Harikrishnan, Vinayakumar, & Soman (2018) investigated several machine learning techniques for phishing email detection and showed how different classifiers could improve detection robustness and accuracy. This further supported the trend toward machine learning.

Using the J48 decision tree as the base classifier, Zareapoor and Seeja's comparative study from 2015 examined feature extraction and selection strategies for phishing email detection. It found that careful selection feature selection greatly improves machine learning model performance. In their 2020 study, Li et al. (2020) investigated the use of deep learning approaches for phishing email detection and discovered that, in contrast to conventional machine learning techniques, Long Short-Term Memory (LSTM) networks greatly increased detection accuracy and decreased false positives. Feature engineering has been shown to play a crucial role in enhancing detection accuracy. Domain-specific features and careful feature selection are important, as Yang et al. (2019) shown in their work, which demonstrated the superior performance of SVM and ensemble approaches over other classifiers. PhishNet-NLP is a natural language processing-based system designed by Verma, Shashidhar, & Hossain (2012) to identify phishing emails by utilizing characteristics found in the emails' headers, links, and body. This approach uses context to improve accuracy when distinguishing "actionable" and "informational" emails, outperforming previous methods with a 97% detection rate.

Hassanpour et al. (2018) used character-level convolutional neural networks (NN) to show how effective fine-grained pattern recognition is in phishing detection, attaining excellent accuracy and resilience to obfuscation tactics. In order to increase detection rates Bountakas & Xenakis (2023) and Al-Daeef et al. (2014) underlined the significance of mixing various feature types. Extensive reviews and comparison studies were carried out by Unnithan et al. (2018) and Alhogail & Alsabih (2021), which emphasized the necessity for adaptive models to address developing phishing strategies and the resilience of ensemble methods. Neural networks were used by Zhang & Yuan (2012) for phishing detection, and they showed excellent accuracy. Their model made use of a multilayer feedforward neural network that was constructed in Java using the Encog Java Core package. MATLAB packages were utilized to carry out the other algorithms.

In order to improve detection accuracy in real-time online environments, Smadi, Aslam, & Zhang (2018) provide a novel framework for phishing detection that blends neural networks with reinforcement learning. To overcome the drawbacks of static datasets, the system automatically grows the training dataset and dynamically adjusts to novel phishing activities. In managing zero-day phishing assaults, this strategy outperforms previous solutions significantly with its high accuracy and low false positive rates.

In summary, the results underscore the importance of machine learning and deep learning for phishing detection. Further research is needed on ensemble methods like Random Forest, XGBoost, KNN, and SVM. Combining domain-specific feature engineering with NLP enhances detection accuracy, providing strong defence against evolving phishing tactics. Future studies will likely focus on developing real-time, adaptive detection systems to counter advanced cybercriminal strategies.

3 METHODOLOGY

The development of our phishing email detection system involved integrating advanced machine learning algorithms with two carefully curated datasets: the Spam/Ham Email Classification Dataset and the Phishing Emails Dataset. These datasets were chosen for their diverse representations of email content, encompassing both legitimate communications and various forms of phishing attempts. The Spam/Ham dataset provided a balanced foundation for training models on typical email patterns, while the Phishing dataset enriched our models with real-world phishing tactics.

Data pre-processing ensured dataset quality and uniformity, involving tasks like text normalization, HTML tag removal, tokenization, and removing stop words and punctuation. This preparation standardized text formats, eliminated irrelevant content, and structured text into meaningful tokens, enhancing the models' ability to detect phishing patterns accurately.

Feature extraction further refined the dataset by incorporating TF-IDF and indicators specific to phishing detection, such as urgency threats, money mentions, and random string identification. These both features combined and provided contextual insights crucial for distinguishing between legitimate and malicious emails, boosting detection accuracy.

Models were trained and evaluated using advanced algorithms like Random Forest, Logistic Regression, XGBoost, and K-Nearest Neighbors (KNN). They were assessed using metrics such as accuracy, precision, recall, and F1-score to gauge their effectiveness in identifying phishing attempts while minimizing false positives.

This methodology exemplifies a comprehensive approach to phishing email detection, combining robust data pre-processing, sophisticated feature engineering, and rigorous model evaluation. By leveraging machine learning and diverse datasets, our study aimed to develop a resilient detection system capable of safeguarding users against evolving phishing threats in real-world email environments.

3.1 Data Collection

Data collection refers to the methodical process of gathering, organizing, and preparing raw information from numerous sources to build datasets for analysis, modelling, and decision-making purposes. In the context of developing AI models, data collection involves identifying relevant sources of data, extracting pertinent information, and ensuring the data's quality and completeness. This process is essential for creating datasets that accurately represent the problem domain and enable machine learning algorithms to learn patterns, make predictions, or perform other tasks effectively. Data collection may include techniques such as web scraping, database querying, sensor data acquisition, or manual data entry, depending on the nature of the data and its availability. Properly executed data collection ensures that AI models are trained on representative and diverse datasets, enhancing their ability to generalize and perform well in real-world applications.

For this study, we utilized two comprehensive and publicly available datasets from Kaggle to train and evaluate machine learning models specifically for phishing email detection, each contributing unique characteristics essential for comprehensive analysis.

3.1.1 Spam/ Ham Email Classification Dataset

- **Source:** https://www.kaggle.com/datasets/yashpaloswal/spamham-email-classification-nlp
- **Description:** This dataset includes a mixture of emails marked as phishing or legitimate. It is useful for NLP-based feature extraction methods like TF-IDF since it contains a variety of features that were taken from the email content, metadata, and supplementary context. The primary content for text analysis is provided by the 'Text' column, while the 'Label' column designates whether the email is phishing (spam) 1 or legitimate (ham) 0. This dataset provides a fair sample of both phishing and legitimate emails, providing a strong basis for model training.

3.1.2 Phishing Emails Dataset

- **Source:** https://www.kaggle.com/datasets/subhajournal/phishingemails
- **Description:** This dataset offers comprehensive samples of emails that have been detected as phishing attempts and focuses exclusively on phishing emails. The primary text of the email is provided for analysis in the 'Email' column, while the 'Label' column designates whether or not the email is phishing (1) or not (0). This dataset is essential for comprehending the particular traits and trends that are frequently observed in phishing emails. This dataset's independent analysis provides the study with new perspectives on the distinctive elements and methods of phishing assaults.

By utilizing these datasets separately, our approach ensured:

- **Focused Model Training:** Each dataset was used independently to train machine learning models, optimizing their ability to identify specific characteristics of spam or phishing emails without mixing contexts.
- **Precise Evaluation:** Models were evaluated separately on their performance with each dataset, allowing for tailored adjustments and improvements based on the distinct challenges posed by spam and phishing emails.
- **Realistic Scenario Simulation:** Testing against separate datasets simulated varied real-world scenarios, providing insights into the models' adaptability to different types of email threats.

These datasets served as crucial resources in developing robust phishing detection methodologies, contributing to the advancement of cybersecurity practices aimed at mitigating the risks associated with phishing attacks in diverse digital environments.

3.2 Data Pre-Processing

Data pre-processing is the initial step in data analysis where raw data is cleaned, transformed, and organized for further analysis or modeling. This process ensures that the data is accurate, complete, and relevant. It involves tasks such as data cleaning (handling missing values, correcting errors), data transformation (normalization, standardization), and feature extraction (creating new features from existing data). The goal is to enhance data quality, making it suitable for machine learning algorithms and other analytical techniques. Properly pre-processed data leads to more accurate modeling, better performance of algorithms, and meaningful insights. Here, we elaborate on each step involved in the pre-processing of the dataset.

Loading the Data: Initially, datasets were loaded and structured using Pandas, a versatile Python library for data manipulation. Pandas allowed seamless import of data from various sources and organized it into data frames for easy exploration and manipulation. It streamlined data cleaning and transformation, handling missing values, correcting data types, and performing essential manipulations like filtering and aggregation. This established a solid foundation for further pre-processing steps, ensuring data quality and integrity before tasks like normalization, tokenization, and feature extraction, thereby facilitating an efficient workflow for analytical and machine learning tasks.

Text Normalization: To ensure consistency and alleviate issues related to case sensitivity, all text within the emails underwent conversion to lowercase. This crucial normalization process standardized the representation of words regardless of their original capitalization. By converting all text to lowercase, variations such as "Email" and "email" were treated uniformly across the entire dataset. This approach ensured that the machine learning algorithms and text processing techniques applied thereafter would interpret and analyze text consistently. Standardizing the case of words helped in avoiding discrepancies that could arise from different capitalizations, thus enhancing the accuracy and reliability of subsequent analyses. Moreover, this normalization step simplified comparisons and computations involving text data, facilitating more effective and efficient data processing and modelling tasks.

HTML Tag Removal: To increase the quality of the email content for analysis, regular expressions were used to eliminate HTML tags present in the emails. HTML tags, while useful for rendering emails in browsers or email clients, do not contribute meaningful information for the content analysis required in machine learning models. These tags include elements like `<div>`, `<span>`, `<p>`, and others that structure the presentation of the email but add no value to understanding its textual content. By employing regular expressions, a powerful tool for pattern matching, all HTML tags were effectively stripped from the email bodies. This process ensured that the remaining text was purely informative, free from the clutter of formatting codes. Removing these tags was essential as their presence could potentially skew the results, leading to inaccuracies in feature extraction and model training. By eliminating non-informative HTML elements, the dataset became cleaner and more representative of the actual language used in the emails, thereby enhancing the reliability of the subsequent analytical processes and improving the overall performance of the phishing detection system.

Tokenization: The next step involved tokenizing the text using NLTK's word tokenize function. Tokenization breaks down text into individual tokens, like words or punctuation marks. For example, the sentence "The quick brown fox" is split into ["The", "quick", "brown", "fox"]. This process allows for finer-grained analysis, aiding in better feature extraction and more accurate modeling. Tokenizing is essential for identifying and handling individual words, facilitating tasks like removing stop words and stemming. This step laid the groundwork for further refinement, enhancing the model's ability to detect phishing attempts.

Stop words and Punctuation Removal: The data pre-processing phase also included the crucial step of removing common stopwords and punctuation marks from the text. Stopwords are words that occur frequently in the language but carry little meaningful information in the context of distinguishing between phishing and legitimate emails. Examples of such stopwords include "and", "the", "is", "in", and "at". These words, while essential for the grammatical structure of sentences, do not significantly contribute to the analytical goals of identifying phishing content. By eliminating these stopwords, the text became more focused on the words that are more likely to be indicative of phishing attempts. Simultaneously, punctuation marks were stripped away from the text. Punctuation, although important for the readability and structure of sentences, does not add value to the analysis aimed at identifying phishing characteristics. Removing punctuation marks further refined the text, ensuring that only the words themselves were analyzed. This step was crucial for reducing noise in the data and enhancing the signal-to-noise ratio, making it easier for the machine learning algorithms to detect patterns and features relevant to phishing. Together, the removal of stopwords and punctuation marks streamlined the textual data, focusing the analysis on meaningful words. This pre-processing step significantly enhanced the accuracy of subsequent analyses, such as feature extraction and model training, by ensuring that the data fed into the algorithms was cleaner and more informative. Consequently, this refinement process contributed to building a more effective and precise phishing detection system.

3.3 Feature Extraction

Feature extraction transformed pre-processed text data into a structured format for machine learning algorithms by converting raw data into measurable characteristics or features. The main method was Term Frequency-Inverse Document Frequency (TF-IDF) vectorization, which evaluates the importance of a word in a document relative to a collection of documents, highlighting unique words that might indicate phishing. Additionally, keyword identification and syntactic pattern recognition were used to extract specific terms and structural patterns associated with phishing emails. This combination of techniques improved the accuracy and robustness of the phishing detection model.

TF-IDF, or Term Frequency-Inverse Document Frequency, is a statistical measure that evaluates the importance of words in a document relative to a collection of documents, known as the corpus. The TF component measures how frequently a term appears in a document, while the IDF component measures how important a term is within the entire corpus by considering its rarity across documents. By combining these metrics, TF-IDF assigns higher weights to terms that are significant within individual documents but less common across the corpus. This prioritization helps identify unique and meaningful words that often indicate phishing attempts, enhancing the model's accuracy in distinguishing between phishing and legitimate emails.

To improve the model's detection of phishing attempts, a few unique features were manually extracted in addition to TF-IDF vectorization. Among these attributes were:

Urgency Keywords: Phishing emails often include urgent language such as "urgent", "immediately", and "action required". This urgency aims to elicit swift and often impulsive responses from recipients by creating a sense of immediate importance. These tactics exploit human tendencies to prioritize urgent matters, increasing the likelihood of recipients bypassing normal cautionary steps. For instance, emails threatening account suspension or promising unexpected rewards prompt recipients to click on malicious links or disclose sensitive information hastily. Recognizing these urgency keywords is crucial in distinguishing phishing emails from legitimate ones, which typically do not rely on such coercive tactics. This feature extraction process enhances detection accuracy by identifying and flagging emails that exploit urgency to manipulate recipients.

Monetary Mentions: References to money, including specific Rupee or dollar amounts, are common in phishing emails and serve various deceptive purposes. Phishing attempts often promise financial rewards, such as claiming lottery winnings or inheritance amounts, to lure recipients into divulging personal information. Alternatively, these emails may use fear tactics, threatening penalties or account suspension unless immediate payments are made. Such references exploit recipients' desires for gain or fears of loss, triggering emotional responses that can override rational judgment. For instance, an email might promise a 10,00,000 prize for clicking a link or provide a bank notice demanding a 500 payment to avoid account freezing. Identifying and flagging these monetary references during feature extraction is critical for phishing detection systems. It enables machine learning models to better distinguish between legitimate emails and those attempting fraud through financial manipulation.

Random Strings: Phishing emails often use random strings of characters to evade spam filters and detection algorithms. These strings disrupt text parsing and obscure malicious content. For example, phishers might use excessive special characters or deliberate misspellings like "pa$$w0rd" instead of "password," or disguise URLs as "hxxp://example[dot]com." These tactics exploit filters' limitations and can evade even sophisticated analyses if not flagged. Effective phishing detection systems identify and interpret these anomalies to distinguish normal language variations from deceptive tactics, bolstering email security.

These features were extracted from email text using regular expressions and logical conditions. Initially, the text was vectorized using TF-IDF, transforming it into a numerical matrix where each entry indicated the significance of a term in the email. Subsequently, manually extracted features were incorporated into this matrix, creating a comprehensive feature set that captured both the semantic content of the emails and specific indicators related to phishing.

By combining TF-IDF vectorization with targeted feature extraction, the resulting feature set provided a robust foundation for training the machine learning models. This approach ensured that the models could leverage both the subtle textual patterns and explicit phishing markers, significantly enhancing their ability to accurately discriminate phishing emails from legitimate ones. The integration of these diverse features was crucial for building a sophisticated and effective phishing detection system.

3.4 Model Implementation

The model implementation phase was a critical step in developing a reliable phishing email detection system. It refers to the process of integrating the chosen algorithms into a functional system capable of making predictions based on input data. This stage encompasses various tasks, including selecting appropriate models, configuring them for optimal performance, and ensuring their seamless operation within the broader data processing pipeline. Careful model selection tailored to the specific problem is essential, followed by rigorous testing and validation to fine-tune the models, ensuring they can accurately predict outcomes and handle real-world data variations effectively. Proper implementation also involves setting up mechanisms for continuous monitoring and updating of the models to maintain their effectiveness over time. Selecting the appropriate machine learning algorithms was a pivotal part of the implementation process. Four different algorithms were chosen for their distinct strengths and complementary capabilities in handling classification tasks.

3.4.1 Random Forest

Random Forest is a versatile ensemble learning method well-suited for handling large feature sets typical in text classification tasks. It works by constructing numerous decision trees during training and aggregating their predictions. Each tree is trained on a random subset of data, and at each split, a random subset of features is considered. This diversity among trees helps prevent overfitting and improves the model's ability to generalize to new data.

One of Random Forest's strengths is its robustness. By combining predictions from multiple trees, it mitigates the risk of individual trees overfitting the training data. This makes it reliable for generating stable and accurate predictions, particularly in tasks involving large datasets and high-dimensional feature spaces like text data.

Random Forest excels in managing high-dimensional data by focusing on informative features at each split. This capability is crucial in text classification, where each word or token can be treated as a separate feature. Moreover, the model provides a measure of feature importance, aiding in understanding data patterns and guiding feature selection.

In summary, Random Forest was chosen for its robustness, effectiveness in handling complex feature spaces, and ability to produce reliable predictions in text classification tasks. Its ensemble approach ensures balanced performance across diverse datasets and enhances resilience against overfitting, making it a powerful tool for detecting phishing emails.

3.4.2 Logistic Regression

Logistic Regression is a fundamental linear model widely used in machine learning and statistics for binary classification tasks. It extends to multiclass problems through methods like one-vs-rest. The model predicts the probability of an input belonging to a specific class using a logistic (sigmoid) function, which maps real numbers to a range of 0 to 1, ideal for probability estimation.

During training, Logistic Regression optimizes parameters to maximize the likelihood of observing the data, establishing a linear relationship between input features and the log-odds of the target variable. Its simplicity allows efficient training on large datasets, and the coefficients reveal feature impact, ensuring interpretability.

Logistic Regression's strengths lie in its role as a straightforward baseline model, offering insights into data relationships crucial for interpretability in fields like healthcare and finance. It's computationally efficient for real-time and large-scale applications, suitable for linearly separable data, and serves as a robust foundation for complex models. While it may not capture intricate patterns like advanced algorithms, its interpretability, ease of implementation, and reliability make it invaluable in machine learning applications.

3.4.3 XGBoost

XGBoost (eXtreme Gradient Boosting) is a robust implementation of gradient boosting that excels in classification tasks due to its efficiency and performance. It builds decision trees sequentially, each correcting errors made by the previous models to progressively improve accuracy. A notable feature is its utilization of second-order gradients (Hessian) in the loss function, which enhances update precision and speeds up convergence.

This method is adept at handling sparse and missing data through a sparsity-aware algorithm, making it suitable for real-world datasets where data completeness varies. XGBoost also incorporates regularization techniques (L1 and L2), which mitigate overfitting by penalizing complex models, ensuring robust and generalizable performance.

Another advantage of XGBoost is its efficient use of parallel processing, leveraging multi-core processors to accelerate training times significantly. It employs optimized tree pruning techniques that reduce computational complexity while maintaining predictive power, making it scalable for large-scale datasets.

XGBoost's strength lies in its ability to capture intricate relationships and dependencies in data, crucial for tasks such as phishing email detection where identifying subtle patterns is key to distinguishing between legitimate and malicious emails. Overall, XGBoost's advanced features and optimization strategies make it a powerful choice for developing accurate and efficient machine learning models in diverse classification scenarios.

3.4.4 K-Nearest Neighbors (KNN)

K-Nearest Neighbors (KNN) is a non-parametric machine learning algorithm widely used for classification tasks, such as phishing email detection. It operates on instance-based learning principles, making decisions by comparing new data points with their nearest neighbors in the feature space. This method is ideal for scenarios with irregular decision boundaries or complex data relationships.

To classify a new data point, KNN computes distances (typically Euclidean) between the point and all training data. It then identifies the 'k' nearest neighbors based on these distances. The parameter 'k' influences performance and can be adjusted based on dataset characteristics. KNN assigns the class label by majority voting among the nearest neighbors.

KNN's popularity stems from its simplicity and intuitive nature, making it accessible for beginners in machine learning. It doesn't assume data distribution and handles non-linear relationships well, adapting dynamically to changes and noise in data. Its versatility extends to both binary and multiclass classification tasks without modification, making it adaptable for evolving datasets and immediate classification needs.

In phishing email detection, KNN's instance-based approach compares incoming emails to known phishing examples, identifying suspicious patterns based on proximity in the feature space. Its capability to handle non-linear boundaries effectively enhances the accuracy of distinguishing between legitimate and malicious emails, bolstering the reliability of phishing detection systems.

3.5 Model Training

Model training in machine learning involves teaching algorithms to recognize patterns and make predictions from input data. Initially, pre-processed data is split into training and validation/test sets. Algorithms like random forest, logistic regression, XGBoost, and K-Nearest Neighbors (KNN) are chosen based on data characteristics and the problem at hand. The training process adjusts model parameters through optimization methods such as gradient descent, aiming to minimize differences between predicted and actual outcomes in the training data. Hyperparameters like learning rate or regularization strength are tuned to optimize performance and prevent overfitting. Evaluation metrics assess the model's ability to generalize to new data, often using techniques like cross-validation for validation. The goal is to develop a predictive model that reliably makes accurate predictions on new data, solving practical problems in fields such as healthcare, finance, and cybersecurity.

3.5.1 Data Splitting

The initial step in model implementation involved dividing the pre-processed datasets into separate training and testing sets to evaluate the model's performance on unseen data, thereby reducing the risk of overfitting. An 80-20 split ratio was applied, with 80% of the data allocated for training and the remaining 20% reserved for testing. To ensure that the distribution of phishing and legitimate emails was consistent across both sets, stratified splitting was utilized. This technique preserved the proportional representation of each class within the datasets, ensuring balanced and accurate reflection of the overall data distribution. By maintaining this balance, the model was better equipped to generalize its learning to new data, enhancing its robustness and reliability in detecting phishing emails.

3.5.2 Training

The model training phase was crucial for developing a robust phishing email detection system. Machine learning models like Random Forest, Logistic Regression, XGBoost, and K-Nearest Neighbors (KNN) were trained on pre-processed datasets to learn patterns distinguishing phishing emails from legitimate ones. For instance, models analyzed features such as urgent language and mentions of money.

Hyperparameter tuning, akin to adjusting oven settings for optimal baking, was performed to enhance model performance using cross-validation. This comprehensive training and tuning approach ensured the models could accurately differentiate between legitimate and malicious emails.

By the end of the training phase, the models were well-equipped to identify phishing attempts with high accuracy, providing a robust defence against cyber threats.

3.5.3 Cross-Validation

Cross-validation is a key technique in machine learning for evaluating model performance by dividing data into multiple subsets or folds. Instead of a single train-test split, it iteratively trains and tests the model on different subsets.

Here's how it works: the dataset is split into k folds. In each iteration, one-fold is the validation set, and the remaining k-1 folds are for training. This process repeats k times, and evaluation metrics like accuracy or F1-score are averaged across all iterations for a reliable performance estimate.

The advantage of cross-validation is that it provides a more robust estimate of the model's generalization to unseen data, reducing overfitting or underfitting risks. It also aids in hyperparameter tuning by testing different hyperparameter sets in each iteration, ensuring optimal performance without overfitting to a specific data subset.

In summary, cross-validation enhances model reliability and generalizability, providing comprehensive evaluation and optimization for better performance across various datasets.

4 PERFORMANCE EVALUATION

Performance evaluation in phishing detection involves testing how well a machine learning model differentiates between legitimate and phishing emails. After training the model on labelled data, its performance is gauged using an unseen test set, such as 1,000 emails labelled as phishing or legitimate. Key metrics include accuracy, precision, recall, and the F1-score.

Two evaluation methods were used: the test dataset approach and 10-fold cross-validation. The test dataset method calculates metrics on a separate test set to check generalization. In 10-fold cross-validation, the dataset is split into 10 parts; the model is trained on 9 parts and validated on the remaining part, repeated 10 times. This method provides a comprehensive performance measure and reduces overfitting risk.

These evaluations reveal the model's strengths and weaknesses, informing decisions on its deployment or further refinement, ensuring reliable performance across varied scenarios. The key steps and metrics involved in the performance evaluation process are outlined below:

4.1 Accuracy

A key performance indicator for machine learning models, particularly those intended for the identification of phishing emails, is accuracy. Accuracy in the context of phishing detection refers to the percentage of emails correctly classified (phishing and legitimate) out of all emails the model has analyzed.

To illustrate with a simple example, suppose you have a dataset of 100 emails, out of which 80 are legitimate and 20 are phishing attempts. After training your model and applying it to this dataset, the model correctly identifies 70 legitimate emails and 15 phishing emails. In this case:

- True Positives (TP): The model correctly identifies 15 phishing emails.
- True Negatives (TN): The model correctly identifies 70 legitimate emails.
- False Positives (FP): The model incorrectly identifies 10 legitimate emails as phishing.
- False Negatives (FN): The model incorrectly identifies 5 phishing emails as legitimate.

To calculate accuracy, you sum up the correctly classified emails (TP + TN) and divide it by the total number of emails:

$$Accuracy = \frac{TP + TN}{Total\ number\ of\ emails} = \frac{15 + 70}{100} = 0.85$$

So, the accuracy of the model in this example is 85%.

Accuracy provides a straightforward measure of how often the model's predictions match the actual labels. However, in imbalanced datasets (e.g., more legitimate emails than phishing emails), accuracy alone may be misleading. In such cases, precision, recall, and F1-score offer a more nuanced evaluation, highlighting the model's ability to correctly identify phishing emails and avoid false positives.

4.2 Precision

Precision is a crucial metric used to assess the performance of machine learning models, particularly in tasks like phishing email detection. In this context, precision measures the fraction of accurately identified phishing emails among all those predicted as phishing by the model.

To elaborate with an example: Imagine a scenario where a phishing detection model predicts 100 emails as phishing. Out of these predictions, 80 are genuinely phishing emails (True Positives), while 20 are legitimate emails that were wrongly classed as phishing (False Positives). The precision in this example would be determined as follows:

$$Precision = \frac{True\ Positives}{True\ Positives + False\ positives} = \frac{80}{80 + 20} = 0.8$$

As a result, the model's accuracy is 80%. This indicates that 80% of the time the model is accurate when it identifies an email as phishing.

Precision is crucial when false positives (legitimate emails misclassified as phishing) have significant consequences, such as in cybersecurity, where minimizing false positives is essential to avoid blocking legitimate communications. However, it should be interpreted together with recall and F1-score for a complete evaluation of the model's performance.

4.3 Recall

Recall, also known as sensitivity or true positive rate, is a fundamental metric used to evaluate the performance of machine learning models, particularly in tasks like phishing email detection. Recall measures the proportion of genuine phishing emails that are correctly identified by the model out of all the phishing emails present in the dataset.

To explain recall with an example: Let's consider a dataset of 100 phishing emails. After applying a phishing detection model, the model correctly identifies 70 of these phishing emails (True Positives). However, it misses 30 phishing emails, incorrectly classifying them as legitimate (False Negatives).

The recall is calculated as:

$$Recall = \frac{True\ Positives}{True\ Positives + False\ Negatives} = \frac{70}{70 + 30} = 0.7$$

Thus, the recall of the model is 70%. This specifies that the model can correctly identify 70% of all phishing emails present in the dataset.

Recall is especially important in scenarios where missing a phishing email (false negative) can have severe consequences, such as security breaches or financial losses. A high recall means that the model is effective at capturing most of the actual phishing attempts, reducing the risk of such harmful incidents.

4.4 F1-Score

The F1 score is a metric that provides a balanced assessment of a model's performance by combining precision and recall into a single value, especially in tasks like phishing email detection where both false positives and false negatives are critical.

The F1 score is calculated using the harmonic mean of precision and recall, offering a balanced assessment of the model's performance:

$$F1\ score\ =\ 2*\frac{Precision*Recall}{Precision + Recall}$$

Here's why the harmonic mean is used: It gives additional weight to lower values. If either precision or recall is low, the F1 score will also be low, promoting models that have both high precision and high recall.

For example, if a phishing detection model achieves a precision of 0.75 (75%) and a recall of 0.80 (80%), the F1 score would be:

$$F1\ score\ =\ 2*\frac{0.75*0.80}{0.75 + 0.80}\ =\ 2*\frac{0.6}{1.55}\ =\ 0.77$$

In this instance, precision and recall performed in a balanced manner, as indicated by the F1 score of 0.77.

A high F1 score in phishing detection means that the model can correctly identify phishing emails while minimizing false positives and false negatives. It is a valuable indicator for assessing the model's overall efficacy across different thresholds and datasets, offering a thorough evaluation of its predictive skills.

4.5 10-Fold Cross-Validation

10-fold cross-validation is a widely used technique in machine learning to assess model performance robustly. It divides the dataset into 10 equal parts, using nine for training and one for validation, repeated 10 times so each part is used for validation once. This method provides a more accurate estimate of model generalization to new data compared to a single train-test split. By averaging performance metrics across iterations, it reduces the risk of skewed results due to a particular data split, helping to detect issues like overfitting and ensuring consistent model performance. This comprehensive approach maximizes data utilization and enhances confidence in the model's predictive accuracy on unseen data.

Performance Metrics for Datasets

The following tables summarize the performance metrics (accuracy, precision, recall, and F1-score) for both datasets, evaluated on a single train-test split. Table 1 and Table 2 summarises classification accuracy on Spam/Ham Email Dataset and Phishing Emails Dataset respectively.

Table 1. Classification Performance on Spam/Ham Email Dataset

MODEL	ACCURACY	PRECISION	RECALL	F1-SCORE
Random Forest	0.981675	0.968641	0.958620	0.963604
Logistic Regression	0.979057	0.985401	0.931034	0.957446
XGBoost	0.979057	0.971631	0.944827	0.958041
KNN	0.965968	0.940350	0.924137	0.932173

Table 2. Classification Performance on Phishing Emails Dataset

MODEL	ACCURACY	PRECISION	RECALL	F1-SCORE
Random Forest	0.955071	0.926308	0.964333	0.944939
Logistic Regression	0.951304	0.927308	0.952893	0.939926
XGBoost	0.953188	0.916772	0.971063	0.943137
KNN	0.729351	0.600671	0.963660	0.740051

The following tables summarize the performance metrics (accuracy, precision, recall, and F1-score) for both datasets. Table 3 and Table 4 summarises classification accuracy on Spam/Ham Email Dataset and Phishing Emails Dataset respectively using 10-fold cross validation.

Table 3. Classification Performance using cross validation on Spam/Ham Email Dataset

MODEL	ACCURACY	PRECISION	RECALL	F1-SCORE
Random Forest	0.983932	0.965354	0.967840	0.966433
Logistic Regression	0.981490	0.969743	0.952490	0.960887
XGBoost	0.983407	0.958436	0.972944	0.965556
KNN	0.962628	0.929164	0.913761	0.921237

Table 4. Classification Performance using cross validation on Phishing Emails Dataset

MODEL	ACCURACY	PRECISION	RECALL	F1-SCORE
Random Forest	0.958030	0.929573	0.966633	0.947722
Logistic Regression	0.955554	0.930931	0.958293	0.944362
XGBoost	0.957922	0.923634	0.973609	0.947948
KNN	0.749420	0.617360	0.956377	0.750290

By using these evaluation methods, the study ensures that the models are not only accurate but also robust and reliable in real-world scenarios where phishing emails vary widely in their characteristics. This thorough evaluation process confirms the models' practical applicability and effectiveness in detecting phishing emails.

5 JUSTIFICATION

Phishing attacks pose a major cybersecurity threat, exploiting human vulnerabilities through deceptive tactics. This chapter delves into developing and evaluating machine learning models for phishing email detection. It begins by explaining phishing and its impact, then outlines methodologies such as data pre-processing, feature extraction, and model implementation.

The chapter reviews machine learning algorithms like Logistic Regression, Random Forest, XGBoost, and K-Nearest Neighbors (KNN) for their effectiveness in detecting phishing. It details evaluation metrics like accuracy, precision, recall, and F1-score, emphasizing the importance of using test datasets and 10-fold cross-validation for robust performance assessment.

Two Kaggle datasets, the Spam/Ham Email Classification and Phishing Emails datasets, were used for training and evaluation. Most models showed high accuracy on the initial dataset, with Random Forest at 98%, Logistic Regression and XGBoost at 97%, and KNN at 96%. On the second dataset, Random Forest, Logistic Regression, and XGBoost maintained 95% accuracy, while KNN dropped to 72%.

This chapter provides a structured approach to phishing email detection, highlighting the importance of proactive cybersecurity measures and ongoing research. It serves as a valuable resource for professionals and researchers aiming to implement and optimize machine learning-based phishing detection systems.

6 CONCLUSION

In conclusion, this study explored phishing email detection using machine learning, highlighting the need for strong cybersecurity measures against sophisticated threats. Phishing attacks exploit human trust and urgency to steal sensitive information, posing significant risks to individuals and organizations. The study demonstrated the effectiveness of machine learning in enhancing defences against these threats, covering data pre-processing, model implementation, and evaluation.

The chapter began by explaining phishing tactics and their psychological manipulation. It then detailed the construction of phishing detection systems, including text normalization, HTML tag removal, and feature extraction. Key machine learning algorithms like Logistic Regression, Random Forest, XGBoost, and K-Nearest Neighbors were assessed for their ability to identify phishing emails, each showing strengths in different aspects.

Evaluation metrics such as accuracy, precision, recall, and F1-score measured model performance, confirming their effectiveness. While most models achieved high accuracy on the initial dataset, K-Nearest Neighbors showed a performance drop on a second dataset, underscoring the need for adaptable and robust detection strategies.

7 FUTURE WORK

Moving forward, this study highlights several promising directions for improving phishing email detection systems. Enhancing feature engineering with more sophisticated lexical, syntactic, and semantic features, and exploring deep learning approaches like RNNs and transformer models such as BERT, could significantly boost performance. Addressing adversarial attacks and implementing real-time detection systems to analyze emails upon receipt are crucial. Combining content analysis with behavioural analysis could provide a more comprehensive defense. Diversifying datasets to cover a broader range of phishing tactics and fostering collaborative threat intelligence sharing among organizations are also essential. These advancements will strengthen cybersecurity defenses against evolving phishing threats.

REFERENCES

Al-Daeef, M. M., Basir, N., & Saudi, M. M. (2014). A method to measure the efficiency of phishing emails detection features. In *2014 International Conference on Information Science & Applications (ICISA)* (pp. 1-5). IEEE. DOI: 10.1109/ICISA.2014.6847332

Alhogail, A., & Alsabih, A. (2021). Applying machine learning and natural language processing to detect phishing email. *Computers & Security*, 110, 102414. DOI: 10.1016/j.cose.2021.102414

Altwaijry, N., Elnagar, N., Alshurideh, M., & Shaalan, K. (2024). Advancing phishing email detection: A comparative study of deep learning models. *Sensors (Basel)*, 24(7), 2077. DOI: 10.3390/s24072077 PMID: 38610289

Atawneh, S., & Aljehani, H. (2023). Phishing email detection model using deep learning. *Electronics (Basel)*, 12(4261), 4261. DOI: 10.3390/electronics12204261

Bountakas, P., & Xenakis, C. (2023). Helphed: Hybrid ensemble learning phishing email detection. *Journal of Network and Computer Applications*, 210, 103545. DOI: 10.1016/j.jnca.2022.103545

Harikrishnan, N. B., Vinayakumar, R., & Soman, K. P. (2018). A machine learning approach towards phishing email detection. In *Proceedings of the anti-phishing pilot at ACM international workshop on security and privacy analytics (IWSPA AP)* (Vol. 2013, pp. 1-6).

Hassanpour, R., Dogdu, E., Choupani, R., Goker, O., & Nazli, N. (2018, March). Phishing e-mail detection by using deep learning algorithms. In *ACM Southeast Regional Conference* (pp. 45-1). DOI: 10.1145/3190645.3190719

Khonji, M., Iraqi, Y., & Jones, A. (2013). Phishing detection: A literature survey. *IEEE Communications Surveys and Tutorials*, 15(4), 2091–2121. DOI: 10.1109/SURV.2013.032213.00009

Li, Q., Liu, W., Wu, H., Xie, C., & Yang, W. (2020). LSTM based phishing detection for big email data. *IEEE Transactions on Big Data*, 8(1), 278–288. DOI: 10.1109/TBDATA.2020.2978915

Rawal, S., Sharma, A., Kumar, S., & Pandey, H. (2017). Phishing detection in e-mails using machine learning. *International Journal of Applied Information Systems*, 12(7), 21–24. DOI: 10.5120/ijais2017451713

Salloum, S., Alshurideh, M., Elnagar, N., & Shaalan, K. (2021). Phishing email detection using natural language processing techniques: A literature survey. *Procedia Computer Science*, 189, 19–28. DOI: 10.1016/j.procs.2021.05.077

Salloum, S., Alshurideh, M., Elnagar, N., & Shaalan, K. (2022). A systematic literature review on phishing email detection using natural language processing techniques. *IEEE Access: Practical Innovations, Open Solutions*, 10, 65703–65727. DOI: 10.1109/ACCESS.2022.3183083

Sanchez, F., & Duan, Z. (2012). *A sender-centric approach to detecting phishing emails. In 2012 international conference on cyber security*. IEEE.

Smadi, S., Aslam, N., & Zhang, L. (2018). Detection of online phishing email using dynamic evolving neural network based on reinforcement learning. *Decision Support Systems*, 107, 88–102. DOI: 10.1016/j.dss.2018.01.001

Unnithan, N. A., ... (2018). Machine learning based phishing e-mail detection. In *Proceedings of Security-CEN@ Amrita* (pp. 65-69). https://doi.org/DOI: 10.1145/3190645.3190652

Verma, R., Shashidhar, N., & Hossain, N. (2012). Detecting phishing emails the natural language way. In *Computer Security–ESORICS 2012:17th European Symposium on Research in Computer Security, Pisa, Italy, September 10-12, 2012. Proceedings 17* (pp. 824-841). Springer Berlin Heidelberg. DOI: 10.1007/978-3-642-33167-1_47

Yang, Z., Chen, Z., Xiao, W., Liu, Q., & Zhang, Y. (2019). Phishing email detection based on hybrid features. [). IOP Publishing.]. *IOP Conference Series. Earth and Environmental Science*, 252(4), 042039. DOI: 10.1088/1755-1315/252/4/042051

Yasin, A., & Abuhasan, A. (2016). An intelligent classification model for phishing email detection. *arXiv preprint arXiv:1608.02196*.

Zareapoor, M., & Seeja, K. R. (2015). Feature extraction or feature selection for text classification: A case study on phishing email detection. *International Journal of Information Engineering and Electronic Business*, 7(2), 60. DOI: 10.5815/ijieeb.2015.02.08

. Zhang, N., & Yuan, Y. (2012). Phishing detection using neural network. *CS229 Lecture Notes*, 301. https://doi.org/DOI: 10.1145/3180445.3180464

Chapter 7
Network Intrusion Detection System Using Machine Learning

R. Gunasundari
Puducherry Technological University, India

Ra Srinethe
Puducherry Technological University, India

V. Thilagavathianu
Puducherry Technological University, India

ABSTRACT

Network intrusion detection systems help identify the type of attack a network faces. Cybersecurity professionals use this information to take the necessary steps to protect valuable information that otherwise could have been compromised. Traditional network intrusion detection systems are characterized by signature-based detection. This often leaves networks vulnerable to threats. The proposed idea uses a machine learning-based model that helps to promptly identify threats thereby fortifying security. The existing Machine-learning based models suffer from increased number of false alarms and the inability to handle huge data due to a lack of feature selection. This idea proposes using particle swarm optimization techniques for feature selection along with data balancing to decrease the false alarms and improve the model's overall performance. Further, hyper tuning and assembling the best-performing models have been done to improve the robustness of the model. This has been tested by evaluating the performance of the model in the presence of random noise and through stability score.

DOI: 10.4018/979-8-3693-9225-6.ch007

INTRODUCTION

In the rapidly evolving landscape of cybersecurity, network intrusion detection systems play an important role in protecting the networks from unauthorized access, threats and anomalies. A network intrusion detection system monitors the incoming network traffic or system activities and checks for malicious activities or policy violations and reports it to the network administrators (Vanin et al., 2022).

Traditional intrusion detection systems can be broadly classified into two types. Signature based network intrusion detection system and anomaly-based network intrusion detection system (Singh & Singh, 2014). Signature based intrusion detection systems (Kumar & Sangwan, 2012) involve the usage of a database to identify potential threats. The NIDS monitors the traffic pattern and compares it with the traffic pattern present in the database. If the pattern matches, then an alarm is raised. This helps in reducing the number of false positive cases where an alarm is raised for normal traffic. However, this also allows for a potential breach wherein an attacker might change the traffic pattern for the attack. It also is not efficient in the case of zero-day attacks and unknown threats. Also, the database has to be frequently updated. This is practically impossible in the current scenarios, where the threats to networks are exponentially increasing. This calls for the need for a NIDS that is capable of identifying unknown threats.

An anomaly-based network intrusion detection system detects deviations in the network pattern in order to identify potential threats. It initially monitors normal network traffic to determine the baseline and then uses that as the basis (instead of a database) for identification of deviations. This helps in detecting new and unknown threats. However, it poses disadvantages such as increased number of false positives and struggles with baseline establishment. It also is resource intensive and requires computational resources for continuous monitoring and analysis of the network traffic.

Leveraging the advantages while mitigating the limitations of traditional network intrusion detection systems is extremely crucial for the development of a robust network intrusion detection system. Machine learning is the tool that helps us achieve this. Since machine learning algorithms are trained on a large dataset that contains both normal and malicious traffic, it has improved pattern recognition capability and thus helps in reducing false positives. Also, feature engineering techniques (Venkatesan, 2023) can be used to improve the accuracy of detection. Since machine learning models can continuously learn, they can adapt to new patterns and thus can establish a dynamic and adaptive baseline for anomaly detection. Machine learning algorithms are designed to deal with large datasets.They can also pre-process and analyse data more efficiently and can be parallelly processed thus reducing the computational overhead and improving the resource efficiency.

The existing machine learning based network intrusion faces issues with very high volumes of data and this affects the accuracy of detection and the detection rate. This can be mitigated by making use of feature selection techniques (Pudjihartono et al., 2022) instead of using all the features present in the data. This would reduce the computational overload, as well as reduce the detection time, reduce the number of false positive and helps in the overall improvement in the performance of the network intrusion detection system. Further, hyper tuning (Kusumaputri & Arifin, 2022) the different machine learning algorithms employed for the purpose, helps in identifying which algorithms are optimal. This also helps in selecting the best performing algorithms and to ensemble them. Ensemble- is a method that helps in leveraging the advantages posed by the different hyper tuned machine learning algorithms. This helps in building a network intrusion detection system that is robust- that is, a system that works in different scenarios.

In order to implement the proposed idea CICIDS-2017 (Panigrahi & Borah, 2018) dataset was used. This dataset contains normal and malicious network patterns observed for seven days and thus has a large volume. Various machine learning algorithms like Random Forest, Decision Tree etc. (discussed further) were used for pattern recognition. Optuna was used for hyper tuning. Finally, the model was ensembled and tested.

The following presents the overall structure of the chapter:

The chapter discusses the literature review done prior to implementing the proposed idea. This involves the study of similar systems proposed by different authors and their limitations.

It also discusses the methodology and outlines the approach taken for the development of the proposed idea, the preprocessing techniques, feature selection and model selection.

The implementation section of the chapter provides the system architecture, algorithms used and the testing environment.

The results and discussion section presents the results obtained and the analysis and inference drawn from the results

The chapter concludes with the conclusion and the future scope of the proposed system.

The key terms and definitions are given in the appendix.

LITERATURE REVIEW

The proposed model focuses on feature selection techniques to improve the accuracy of predictions enabling the detection of unseen attacks. The model is trained with CIC IDS 2017 dataset. Exploratory Data Analysis is performed to observe trends in the dataset, then the data is preprocessed following which Feature selection technique Particle Swarm Optimization is employed, then the dataset is balanced using RUS and ADASYN sampling algorithms Machine learning algorithms such as K-Nearest Neighbours, Random Forest, Decision tree, Gaussian Naïve Bayes, XGBoost, Catboost, LightGBM, Adaboost and Logistic regression. These individual models are hypertuned using Optuna and ensembled in order to ensure robustness and stability in the presence of external noise. The performance of the trained ensemble model was evaluated in three ways, and the stability of the model was verified using the stability score by varying the size of the perturbations. The robustness of the model was verified by adding random noise. Finally, 5 fold cross validation was performed to check for overfitting.

In their study titled "Machine and Deep Learning Based Comparative Analysis Using Hybrid Approaches for Intrusion Detection System,".A. Rashid, M. J. Siddique and S. M. Ahmed presented their idea wherein the core idea of the paper is based on a Comprehensive comparative analysis of ML algorithms on NSL-KDD and CIDDS-001 datasets; promotion of hybrid feature selection methods for improved classifier performance. The paper presents a comparative analysis of intrusion detection systems using machine and deep learning approaches on the NSL-KDD and CIDDS-001 dataset. Limitations of the paper include not addressing all existing network security problems; need for future research on more progressive Deep Learning approaches and up-to-date datasets.

After the exploration of the above paper, the Datasets mentioned in the paper were studied and the advantages and disadvantages of the datasets were analyzed and important observations were noted, decision was taken to proceed with the Machine learning approach for the proposed model and the limitations of the above paper was carefully noted and aimed to be fixed in the proposed model. This paper was helpful in comparing and contrasting machine learning and deep learning models.

In 2024, Ramu, C., Rao, T.S. & Rao, E.U.S. in their paper titled "Attack Classification in Network Intrusion Detection System Based on Optimization Strategy and Deep Learning Methodology" propose an innovative meta-heuristic optimization and deep learning-based methodology to enhance the performance of Network Intrusion Detection Systems, achieving superior results compared to existing models. The methodology involves the Conversion of symbolic features to Boolean, normalization using z-score, and data balancing using SMOTE and RUS, Feature selection process using extended Pelican Optimization algorithm (Ex-Pel) to select the optimal set of features, Classification is done using Self-Attention Assisted Weighted Auto Encoder (SAttn_WAE) model for attack detection, The proposed model considerably outperformed alternative methods on the UNSW-NB15 dataset. Limitations include the fact that the study does not address the potential limitations of the proposed model in real-world implementation.

This paper was studied in detail and important conclusions regarding the proposed model were derived, Data balancing and feature selection techniques that proved to give best results in the above model was also utilized in the proposed model. The UNSW-NB15 dataset was studied thoroughly and advantages and disadvantages were considered in the selection of the dataset for the proposed model.

In February 2023, Srinath Venkatesan in the paper titled "Design an Intrusion Detection System based on Feature Selection Using ML Algorithms" proposes development of a model for intrusion detection using ML algorithms; The paper presents a comparative study of machine learning algorithms, including Decision Tree, Random Forest, and SVM, to build an efficient intrusion detection system, and concludes that the Random Forest algorithm performs the best with the selected features. Limitations include the Presence of duplicate records leading to potential false positive results;, need for further research using different ML algorithms and feature selection techniques.

The response and predictions of different classifier algorithms like Decision tree, Random forest and Support Vector Machine after the feature selection process was noted. This paper was helpful to analyze the various machine learning classifier algorithms individually and the advantages of the feature selection method in the paper was further studied.

In their paper titled "An Explainable Machine Learning Framework for Intrusion Detection Systems," M. Wang, K. Zheng, Y. Yang & X. Wang (2020) propose a framework using SHAP for providing explanations for IDSs; first application of SHAP method to improve transparency of IDSs. The proposed framework provides local and global explanations to improve the interpretability of any intrusion detection system (IDS).

The framework helps cybersecurity experts better understand the predictions made by the IDS and the characteristics of different cyber attacks and allows cybersecurity experts to optimize the structure of the IDS based on the differences in explanations between different classifiers. exploration of SHAP method on more sophisticated attacks like APTs Furthermore, the different interpretations between different kinds of classifiers can also help security experts better design the structures of the IDSs. The Limitation of the paper is that SHAP method not possible to work in real-time; need for experimentation on more datasets.

This paper focuses largely on the transparency of the Intrusion Detection System which makes the model more understandable, and the model was applied to sophisticated attacks and the interpretations from the model are detailed and helpful in designing better IDSs. The Limitations were noted

In 2020, Kunhare, N., Tiwari, R. & Dhar, J. in their paper titled "Particle Swarm Optimization and Feature Selection for Intrusion Detection System" propose a methodology involving a comparative study of different classifiers for NIDS metrics, using

RF for feature selection and PSO for optimization, inspired by swarm intelligence. The method of using particle swarm optimization with feature selection achieved better accuracy and performance compared to other machine learning algorithms on the NSL-KDD dataset. This outperformed other existing algorithms that used feature selection on the same NSL-KDD dataset, while only using 10 features.

The feature selection method – Particle Swarm Optimization was used in this paper and is employed in the proposed model, the technique was extensively studied and researched in detail. The NSL-KDD dataset used in the paper was studied and merits and drawbacks were carefully observed and noted for further reference. This paper is one of the core papers of the proposed model.

Important conclusions were made after the review of the literature, the datasets like NSL-KDD, UNSW-NB15 used in various papers and other available datasets like KDD-Cup 99 and CIC IDS datasets were thoroughly researched and CIC IDS 2017 dataset was decided to be used. It is a recent dataset with real-world network traffic data, it offers detailed labeling compared to KDD-Cup 99 and NSL KDD. It comprises 2830743 records capturing various types of network activities associated with cyber attacks. The class imbalance of the CIC IDS 2017 dataset was tackled using data balancing techniques like ADASYN and RUS sampling methods.

After a thorough study of various models from the literature and considering their advantages and limitations, the workflow of the proposed model was decided. Exploratory Data Analysis was performed in order to derive important insights and elaborate visualizations and statistical summary from the dataset this was performed as Univariate analysis, Bivariate analysis and multivariate analysis in three steps then preprocessing techniques like One Hot Encoding for categorical variables and Log transformation was done before Particle Swarm Optimization following which different classifier algorithms were applied. Data balancing was done to prevent the bias towards a particular class, after this process different classifier algorithms were applied, then the individual models were hyper tuned using Optuna, ensembled using soft voting and tested using testing methods like Stability score and Cross validated.

METHODOLOGY

The proposed model is implemented with a series of steps with an emphasis on feature selection with an aim to improve the accuracy of the network intrusion detection system and the identification of unseen attack types. In addition, our model is structured based on an ensemble of several hyper tuned models, making it robust and stable even in the presence of external noise. The steps involved in the process are Collection of Dataset, Exploratory Data Analysis, One Hot Encoding,

Feature Selection, Data Balancing, Classification, Hypertuning, Ensemble, and Model Approbation. This section focuses in detail on each carried out in this model.

A Dataset is a collection of data structured in rows and columns, where rows represent a sample or an instance and columns represent features or attributes. Datasets are used for machine learning model training, in supervised learning dataset contains both features and labels, which facilitates model training and predictions. Features can contain numerical or categorical values.

The dataset used in the proposed model is CICIDS2017 which is a recent dataset with detailed labelling and real-world network traffic. It contains cyberattacks such as Denial of Service (DoS), Distributed Denial of Service (DDoS), brute-force attacks, port scans, bot, web attack XXS, FTP-Patator, infiltration, heartbleed, web attack SQL injection, and SSH Patator.

Exploratory Data Analysis aims at gaining important insights and patterns and understanding the relationship between attributes, their statistical trends, and characteristics in the dataset. It includes a combination of methods like statistical summary, data visualization, and dimensionality reduction. In the proposed model Univariate, Bivariate, and Multivariate analyses were carried out. In Univariate analysis, distribution a variable is observed in isolation. Bivariate analysis shows how two variables are related to one another and how one influences the other. The multivariate analysis considers multiple variables to understand complex relationships, and patterns within a dataset.

One-hot encoding is a data preprocessing technique that is used to convert categorical variables into numerical variables suitable for machine learning algorithms to process. This approach allows the use of categorical variables in models requiring numerical inputs and avoids the problem of ordinality. In One Hot Encoding, the categorical parameters will create individual columns for each of the labels and the column corresponding to the correct label is represented by 1 and the values of other columns are 0. The steps involved include the identification of categorical variables, creating dummy variables for each category, assigning binary values to represent the presence or absence of each category, and combining the dummy variables to form the one-hot encoded representation (Karthiga et al., 2021).

Feature selection focuses on the identification of selection of the most relevant features that belong to the original dataset. It is a technique to eliminate the curse of dimensionality, which improves the model performance and reduces overfitting (Venkatesan, 2023). The various types of feature selection techniques include Filter methods that evaluate the features based on the statistical measures, Wrapper methods that form feature subsets by iteratively training models on the different combinations of features, and Embedded methods that select features based on their contribution to the prediction of the model (Pudjihartono et al., 2022).

Particle Swarm Optimization (PSO) is the machine learning algorithm that draws inspiration from the collective dynamics noted in fish schools or flock of birds. Its use is extensive and spans many different fields, most notably in solving optimization issues such as the complex feature selection task in machine learning (Gad, 2022). The PSO process progresses through a sequence of iterative stages. It begins with the Initialization phase, where a set of particles is generated, each representing a potential solution by capturing a subset of features. Following this, in the Fitness Evaluation phase, each particle's effectiveness is measured using a fitness function, typically involving training a machine learning model with the chosen features and evaluating its performance using logistic regression in the model.

As optimization advances, the Velocity Update phase adjusts each particle's speed based on its current position, local best position, and global best position, guiding them toward promising areas within the search space. Subsequently, the Position Update step occurs, where particles move through the search space based on their updated velocities, mimicking collective flow seen in natural collective behaviors.

Finally, the Termination criterion marks the conclusion of the PSO algorithm, activated when reaching a predefined threshold like a maximum number of iterations or achieving a satisfactory fitness level. This structured series of steps allows PSO to effectively explore and exploit the search space, ultimately converging towards optimal or nearly optimal solutions for complex optimization challenges.

Data balancing is a machine learning technique that is used to correct class imbalance encountered in datasets. It addresses the issue of model becoming biased towards one class (Mooijman et al., 2023). In the proposed model two techniques are used for data balancing: Random Under Sampling (RUS) (Ramu et al., 2024) and Adaptive Synthetic Sampling (ADASYN) (He et al., 2008).

Random Undersampling (RUS) is a technique used to balance data by reducing the number of instances in the majority class. The process involves identifying the majority class and then randomly removing instances from it until balance with the minority class is achieved.

RUS has several benefits, including its straightforward implementation and computational efficiency, especially with large datasets, as it decreases the size of the majority class. However, RUS also presents challenges, such as the potential loss of important information from the majority class, which can affect the overall representativeness of the dataset.

Adaptive Synthetic Sampling (ADASYN) is a machine learning technique designed to balance data by generating synthetic samples for the minority class. The ADASYN process includes several steps: identification, synthetic sample generation, and adaptation. Initially, the minority class with fewer instances is identified. Next, synthetic samples are generated with higher density in sparser regions of the minority class distribution. Finally, synthetic samples are adaptively generated, focusing on difficult-to-learn regions based on the local class distribution. ADASYN has several advantages. It dynamically adjusts to challenging data regions, enhancing classifier learning by being adaptive. Additionally, it reduces information loss by generating synthetic samples in underrepresented areas of the minority class.

Detection using classifier algorithm involves machine learning models to categorize data samples into different classes, In the proposed classifier algorithms are used to find the type of cyber attacks. K-Nearest Neighbors (KNN), Random Forest (RF), Decision Tree(DT), Gaussian Naïve Bayes, Logistic Regression, XGBoost (Extreme Gradient Boosting), Catboost, Adaboost(Adaptive boosting), LightGBM are the classifier algorithms used in the model.

Hyperparameter tuning, also known as hyper tuning, involves adjusting the hyperparameters of a machine-learning model to enhance its performance. In machine learning, hyperparameters are configuration settings that are not learned from the data but rather set before the learning process begins. Hyperparameter tuning involves systematically searching through a predefined space of hyperparameters to find the combination that results in the best performance, typically measured using a metric such as accuracy, precision, recall, or F1 score, depending on the problem at hand. In the proposed model Optuna, an open source hyperparameter optimization framework was used.

Optuna is a versatile hyperparameter optimization framework designed to streamline the exploration of search spaces through automated configuration of ranges, distributions, and constraints. Optuna supports various optimization algorithms such as Tree-structured Parzen Estimator (TPE), Bayesian Optimization, and Genetic Algorithms, ensuring robust exploration for optimal hyperparameters

The workflow with Optuna begins with defining an objective function that evaluates performance metrics based on hyperparameter inputs. Through iterative evaluation and adaptive search strategies, Optuna refines hyperparameter configurations to maximize model performance. At completion, the framework provides the best configuration identified during the search, enhancing the efficiency of model training.

Ensemble methods are techniques in machine learning algorithms in which different models are combined to improve the overall efficiency of the model making it more stable and robust, since different models capture different aspects of the dataset. Soft voting ensemble is used in the proposed model.

Soft voting is a technique used in the classification process that involves many individual classifiers. The final prediction is the average of predicted label probabilities among all classifiers. The class that achieves the highest is the final prediction. Soft voting helps in the generalization of the model to unseen attacks.

Model testing is the process in which the performance of trained machine learning model is evaluated, in order to assess its generalization, stability, and accuracy. In the proposed model Stability score, Noise accuracy, and Cross-validation are used for model testing.

Stability scores, noise accuracy, and cross-validation are commonly combined to provide a thorough assessment of model reliability and performance.

Stability scores shows the consistency of predictions, indicating how much they fluctuate with variations in input data, quantifying robustness, the higher the score, the more reliable the model.

Noise accuracy measures the model's ability to maintain accuracy when exposed to noisy or corrupted data, revealing its resilience in adverse conditions. By simulating noisy conditions or introducing perturbations to the dataset, noise accuracy offers insights into the model's ability to withstand adverse conditions.

Cross-validation offers a structured method to estimate how well the model generalizes across diverse data samples, mitigating the risk of overfitting. The process involves partitioning of data into subsets, training the model on a subset. The proposed model used 5 fold cross validation.

Integrating these techniques offers a comprehensive view of the model's capabilities and limitations, empowering practitioners to make informed decisions during model selection and deployment. By leveraging stability scores, noise accuracy, and cross-validation in tandem, stakeholders gain deeper insights into the model's strengths and weaknesses, facilitating robust evaluation and optimization processes in machine learning applications.

IMPLEMENTATION

The workflow of the implemented idea can be given using the following block diagram:

Figure 1. Block Diagram

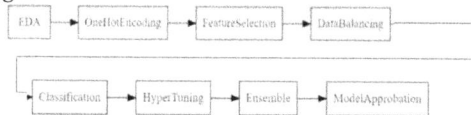

CIC IDS 2017 dataset was used for carrying out the implementation of the proposed idea. The dataset contains 2830743 entries out of which the null entries were dropped. The number of entries after dropping the null values was 2827876 (Panigrahi & Borah, 2018).

The first step in the implementation of the proposed idea was exploratory data analysis (Oyelakin et al., 2023). This was done to get more insight into the data and the relationship between different features and how this affected accurate prediction of the attack types. Univariate, bivariate, and multivariate analyses were carried out for the above purpose. Univariate analysis involved the plotting of the incidences of different outcomes in the given dataset. This was visualized by making use of a count plot. This helped us identify the nature of the dataset and the proportion of different outcomes in the dataset. This served as the factor due to which data balancing step was carried out. Bivariate analysis involved finding the correlation between the different features present in the dataset. Multivariate analysis involved finding the correlation between all the features which was then visualized with the help of a heatmap. As mentioned before, feature selection and dimensionality reduction are the main goals behind the proposed idea. So, in order to get insight on the importance of different features, this process was done (Tukey, 1977).

The dataset contains 79 features out of which 1 is the output. The target variables which are the attack names are categorical. For ease of computation and to enable the use of different algorithms, one-hot encoding was carried out. This converted the categorical variables into numerical values (Karthiga et al., 2021).

Further, feature selection was carried out by using particle swarm optimization algorithm (Kunhare et al., 2020). PSO is highly efficient in high-dimensional spaces where traditional feature selection methods struggle. Also, it has global optimization capability. Thus, in this method, the position and the velocity of each particle are updated based on the number of generations initialized. The local best is identified and gradually the global best is identified. This collaborative approach involving inertia, social components, and the cognitive component ensures a better selection of feature subsets to be used in the model. It is also simple to implement. Unlike several other feature selection methods that involve complex mathematical computations, particle swarm optimization—a technique that is based on the behavior of birds and fish—is simpler . Thus, it is simpler to implement and integrate into workflows. Also, it is extremely adaptable and can be used to implement various objective functions such as in the case of the proposed idea, whose objective function is to decrease the number of features while also improving accuracy. PSO is also good at handling feature interactions. Feature interactions refer to the effect produced by different features together (which were earlier studied in the exploratory data analysis) which is different from the individual effects of the features. Since the dataset contains different features that interact with each other, PSO was adopted for feature selection. Initially, 10 generations were initialized considering the huge volume of the dataset. This categorized the features into different feature subsets. Each feature subset was then tested by a fitness function. Logistic regression was used as the fitness function in the implemented idea. The accuracy of each feature subset was obtained. Further, this was continued for all the ten generations and the global best accuracy was determined. The feature subset that returned the global best accuracy was taken and the rest of the features were discarded for further processing.

From the exploratory data analysis, in univariate analysis, it was observed that the dataset was highly imbalanced. The number of normal patterns exceeded the attack patterns by a huge margin. A few attacks like Heartbleed had very few counts. A dataset like this would not produce accurate results, as it would lead to biasing towards the majority class. Thus, data balancing (Mooijman et al., 2023) was carried out to balance the dataset. An approach with both oversampling and under sampling was carried out to ensure that the data is perfectly balanced. The under sampling process was carried out on the majority class by means of random under sampling. The minority classes were oversampled by making use of adaptive synthetic over-sampling technique (He et al., 2008). This resulted in a balanced dataset, and the dataset was finally ready to be classified with various machine learning algorithms and to observe the accuracy.

Nine different classifier algorithms were used for the classification of the dataset. The algorithms include random forest, K-nearest neighbor, Logistic regression, decision tree, LightGBM, and boosting algorithms like Adaboost, Catboost, XGBoost, and Gradient boost. The evaluation metrics for each of these algorithms were: the accuracy of prediction, precision, F1 score, recall, the time taken to train the model, and the time taken to test the model. These models were then subjected to hypertuning by using Optuna (Kusumaputri & Arifin, 2022)—a hyperparameter optimization framework. The feature space was defined and the hyperparameters to be tuned (keeping the improvement of accuracy, to be the objective function) were specified for each of the above-mentioned machine learning algorithms. Parallel processing was done in order to speed up the computation and to reduce the computational overhead. The accuracy, precision, F1 score, and recall were observed for each of the algorithms. The best-performing algorithms based on the above four evaluation metrics were selected and were subjected to hypertuning .

The ML algorithms that were ensembled include XGBoost, Catboost, Random Forest, and LightGBM. XGBoost is well known for its efficiency and effectiveness. It has high speed and built-in regularization to check for overfitting. It can also handle missing values. Catboost can handle categorical variables without having to preprocess the data separately. It automatically handles missing data and is robust to overfitting. Random forest is an ensembled model of several decision trees that has the capability of handling large datasets and is also robust against overfitting. LightGBM is a gradient boost algorithm that is designed to handle large datasets. It is high speed and is highly memory efficient. Based on the aforementioned reasons and also due to their high performance based on the established evaluation metrics set during classification and hypertuning, the above models were selected for ensemble. The ensemble was done using soft voting and the final ensemble model was obtained (Dietterich, 2000).

The obtained ensemble model was then tested using different methods. Initially, the stability score of the model was computed by varying the perturbation level. Then, the dataset was subjected to synthetic noise and the ensemble model was used to classify the dataset. Finally, a five-fold cross-validation was done in order to ensure the absence of overfitting. Thus, the robustness of the model was checked. The detailed explanation regarding the various intermediate and final results obtained and their inferences is elaborated in the results and discussions section of this chapter.

RESULTS AND DISCUSSION

EDA

Statistical Summary- a summary of the results of different statistical analysis carried out in the dataset.

Figure 2. Statistical Summary

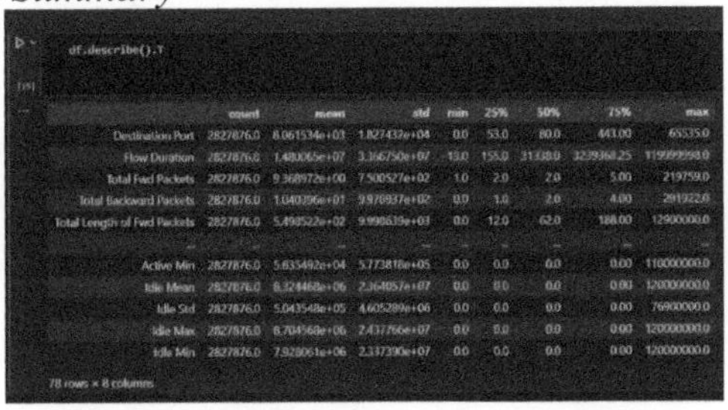

```
df.describe().T
```

	count	mean	std	min	25%	50%	75%	max
Destination Port	2827876.0	8.061534e+03	1.827432e+04	0.0	53.0	80.0	443.00	65535.0
Flow Duration	2827876.0	1.480065e+07	3.366750e+07	13.0	155.0	31308.0	3239368.25	119999998.0
Total Fwd Packets	2827876.0	9.368972e+00	7.500527e+02	1.0	2.0	2.0	5.00	219759.0
Total Backward Packets	2827876.0	1.040396e+01	9.978937e+02	0.0	1.0	2.0	4.00	291922.0
Total Length of Fwd Packets	2827876.0	5.498522e+02	9.998639e+03	0.0	12.0	62.0	188.00	12900000.0
...	...	...	...	...	...	...	...	...
Active Min	2827876.0	5.635492e+04	5.773818e+05	0.0	0.0	0.0	0.00	110000000.0
Idle Mean	2827876.0	8.324468e+06	2.364057e+07	0.0	0.0	0.0	0.00	120000000.0
Idle Std	2827876.0	5.043548e+05	4.605289e+06	0.0	0.0	0.0	0.00	76900000.0
Idle Max	2827876.0	8.704568e+06	2.437766e+07	0.0	0.0	0.0	0.00	120000000.0
Idle Min	2827876.0	7.928061e+06	2.337390e+07	0.0	0.0	0.0	0.00	120000000.0

78 rows × 8 columns

Inferences

The inferences derived from the above statistical summary are as follows:

1. The large difference between the mean and the median values of a few features indicates the potential skewness.

Ex: Flow duration and total length of backward packets

2. The large gap between the 75th percentile and the maximum value in a few features such as Flow duration and total length of backward packets indicates the presence of outliers.
3. Features related to packet lengths and flow, show high variability and a wide range of values. These features might hold potential importance.
4. However, flag count features show low mean values and low standard deviations. This indicates that they are not frequently observed in the dataset and might not hold much importance.

Ex: FIN Flag count, SYN Flag count, RST Flag count etc.

Histograms and Boxplots

Figure 3. Flow Duration: Time duration between receiving the first and last packets in the flow.

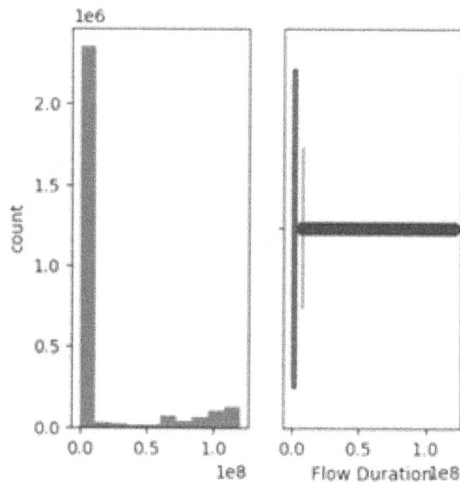

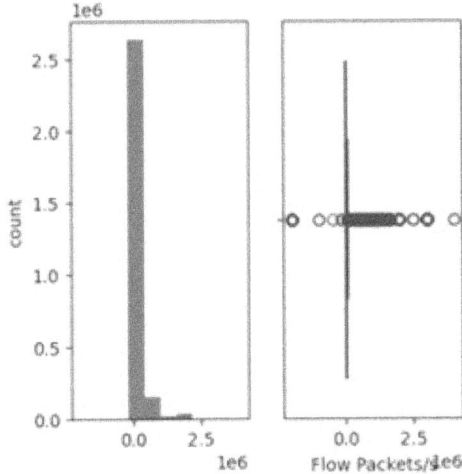

Figure 4. Flow Packets: Number of packets per second in the network flow

For the purpose of univariate analysis histograms and boxplots were plotted for all the 78 features. Histograms are the graphical representation of numerical data in the form of rectangles. Boxplots are used to depict groups of numeric data using boxes and lines. Figures 3 and 4 show two such histograms and boxplots plotted for the features Flow Duration (Fig 3) and Flow packets/s (Fig 4) respectively.

The histogram (Fig 3) displays the distribution of flow durations. It shows how frequently each flow duration range (shown on the x-axis) occurs in the data.

The histogram (Fig 4) shows the distribution of the number of flow packets received per second in the data.

The x-axis (flow packets/s) represents the range of packet rates observed and the y-axis (count) represents the number of times a specific packet rate (shown on the x-axis) was observed in the data.

The boxplots (Fig 3 and Fig 4) summarizes the distribution of flow durations with key statistics:

The center line (horizontal line inside the box) in Fig 3 represents the median flow duration around 1.25 ms. This is the 50th percentile, indicating that half of the flows lasted less than or equal to this duration, and the other half lasted longer than or equal to this duration. In Fig 4 this represents the median packet rate of $1.4*10^6$ packets/s. This is the 50th percentile, indicating that half of the time the observed packet rate was less than or equal to this value, and the other half of the time it was greater than or equal to this value.

The box represents the interquartile range (IQR). This shows the range that contains the middle 50% of the flow durations and flow packets/s. The box extends from the first quartile (Q1, 25th percentile) to the third quartile (Q3, 75th percentile).

The whiskers extend from the box and may indicate potential outliers. These are data points with flow durations that fall outside the range of 1.5 times the IQR below the first quartile or above the third quartile.

Figure 5. Count Plot: Graphical representation of number of occurrences of different classes of data

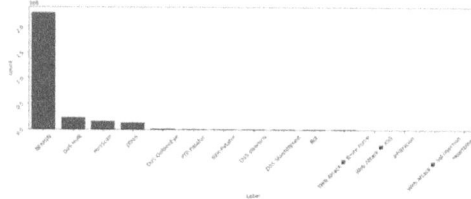

The above figure shows the count plot of the target variables (attack types) present in the dataset. It can be seen that there is a very high value of benign variable (no attack) while there are very low instances of attacks such as DoS Goldeneye, FTP-Patator etc..The following table shows the actual number of instances of each label:

Table 1. Count of different labels in the dataset

Label	Count
BENIGN	2271320
DoS Hulk	230124
PortScan	158804
DDoS	128025
DoS GoldenEye	10293
FTP-Patator	7935
SSH-Patator	5897
DoS slowloris	5796
DoS Slowhttptest	5499
Bot	1956
Web Attack Brute Force	1507
Web Attack XSS	652
Infiltration	36
Web Attack Sql Injection	21
Heartbleed	11

Scatter Plots

Figure 6. Scatterplots: A visualization that uses dots to represent two different numerical variables

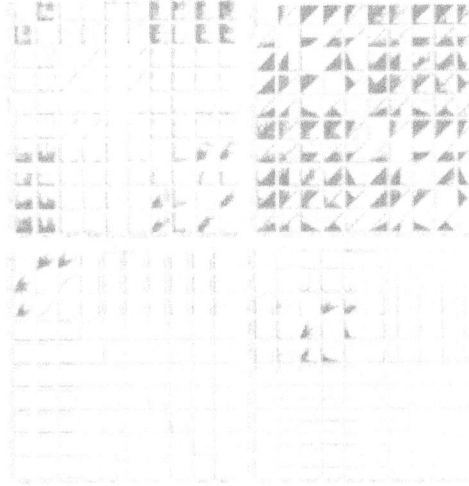

The following are the observations made from the scatterplots:

• It can be seen that Total fwd packets vs total bck packets, Total length of bck packets vs total fwd packets, Total bck packets vs total length of bck packets, Flow_IAT_std vs Flow_IAT_mean, Flow_IAT_max vs Flow_IAT_mean, Flow_IAT_min vs Flow_IAT_mean, Flow_IAT_max vs Flow_IAT_std, Flow_IAT_min vs Flow_IAT_max, bck_packet_length_mean vs bck_packet_length_min, Fwd_IAT and Bck_IAT variables (min, mean, max, total, std) have strong positive correlations, Packet_length_var vs Packet_length_std, active_mean vs act_data_pkt_fwd, active_std vs act_data_pkt_fwd, active_mean vs min_seg_size_fwd, active_std vs active_mean, active_min vs active_max, idle_mean vs active_min, idle_max vs idle_min have strong positive correlations.

• It can be seen that fwd_packet_length_mean vs fwd_packet_length_std, fwd_packet_length_mean vs fwd_packet_length_max, fwd_packet_length_std vs fwd_packet_length_max, bck_packet_length_mean vs bck_packet_length_max, bck_packet_length_std vs bck_packet_length_max, fwd_packets vs bck_packets, packet_length_var vs packet_length_mean, packet_length_std vs packet_length_mean, avg_fwd_seg_size vs avg_packet_size, avg_bck_segment_size vs avg_packet_size, min_seg_size_fwd vs act_data_pkt_fwd have moderate positive correlations.

• It can be seen that idle_std vs active_min, fwd_IAT_min vs fwd_IAT_std have strong negative correlations.

- It can be seen that avg_bck_seg_size vs avg_fwd_seg_size has moderate negative correlations.

From the above scatterplot observations we can arrive at an inference that those variable that out of those features that have a negative correlation only the features that have more impact on the output may be selected, after further analysis.

Heatmap

Figure 7. Heatmap: A visual representation of correlation between different numeric variables

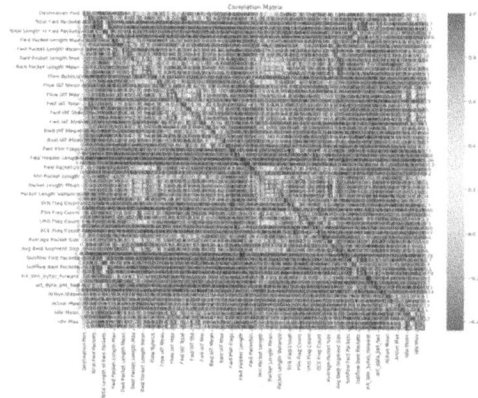

The heatmap was generated for the purpose of multivariate analysis of the 78 features and the following was observed:

It can be seen that a few variables exhibit a strong positive correlation (indicated by the diagonal of the heatmap), these could be the features that may have potential importance. Also a few variables exhibit weak positive and negative correlations. To quote a few instances:

- weak negative correlation between the total number of forward packets and the total length of forward packets.
- weak positive correlation between the total length of forward packets and the forward packet length means.
- weak negative correlation between the forward packet length mean and the backward packet length mean.
- weak positive correlation between the flow bytes/s and the flow IAT mean.
- weak positive correlation between the forward IAT total and the Backward IAT mean.

- weak negative correlation between the Backward IAT mean and the Backward packet length mean.

Since these features exhibit weak correlation, they may not carry much information and thus out of these feature pairs only one can be selected.

FEATURE SELECTION

Feature selection was done based on Particle swarm optimization technique. 10 generations were initialized. The fitness function of each cluster was calculated by using logistic regression.

Accuracy of Feature Selection (Local)

These are the personal best values of the different generations in the first iteration.

Figure 8. Accuracy of feature selection (local)- personal best values obtained in different generations in the first iteration

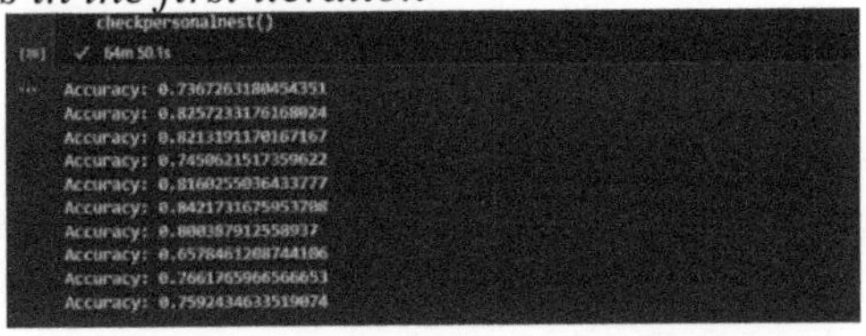

It can be seen that the maximum accuracy of personal best among the different clusters is 0.8421.

Accuracy of Global Best

Figure 9. Accuracy of global best accuracy obtained after iterating through all the generations

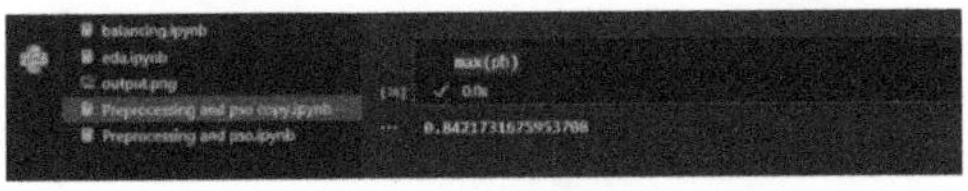

After iterating through all the 10 generations and comparing all the personal best values of current generation with that of all the other generations, the accuracy of the global best was found to be 0.84217.

Features Selected

Based on the above feature selection method, after feature selection, the following are the features that were selected to reduce the dimensionality o the dataset.

'Flow Duration', 'Total Backward Packets', 'Total Length of Fwd Packets', 'Fwd Packet Length Min', 'Fwd Packet Length Mean', 'Bwd Packet Length Min', 'Bwd Packet Length Mean', 'Bwd Packet Length Std', 'Flow Bytes/s', 'Flow Packets/s', 'Flow IAT Std', 'Flow IAT Max', 'Flow IAT Min', 'Fwd IAT Total', 'Fwd IAT Mean', 'Bwd IAT Total', 'Bwd IAT Mean', 'Bwd IAT Std', 'Fwd PSH Flags', 'Fwd URG Flags', 'Bwd Header Length', 'Min Packet Length', 'Max Packet Length', 'Packet Length Std', 'Packet Length Variance', 'FIN Flag Count', 'RST Flag Count', 'CWE Flag Count', 'ECE Flag Count', 'Down/Up Ratio', 'Average Packet Size', 'Avg Bwd Segment Size', 'Fwd Header Length.1'

Out of the 78 features available thus, 31 features were selected.

Data Balancing

As it can be seen from the countplot (Fig 5) the data is highly imbalanced. This causes bias of the trained model towards the majority class i.e. Benign. So, it becomes imperative to balance the data so as to get accurate results. The majority class is undersampled using Random undersampling (RUS). This is followed by the oversampling of the minority data using Adaptive Synthetic Oversampling (ADASYN). These are visualized using pie-charts as follows:

Figure 10. Data Balancing Output: Pie charts consisting of the proportion of classes in the original data, the proportion obtained after RUS and that after ADASYN

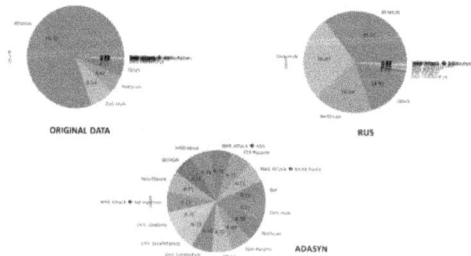

Classification

The balanced dataset was then trained and tested using the following classifier algorithms listed in the table below. The evaluation metrics (accuracy, precision, Recall, F1 score along with training and testing time) are also tabulated alongside.

Obtained Evaluation Metrics

Figure 11. Obtained evaluation metrics-classification

Model	Training Time	Testing Time	Accuracy	Precision	Recall	F1 Score
KNN	0.1302	3.6659	0.9079	0.9065	0.9079	0.9068
Decision Tree	1.9366	0.0138	0.9601	0.9603	0.9601	0.9597
Random Forest	28.1002	0.5333	0.9682	0.9686	0.9682	0.9680
Logistic Regression	54.8828	0.0129	0.4814	0.4760	0.4814	0.4436
Gaussian Naive Bayes	0.1916	0.1496	0.3683	0.4246	0.3683	0.3495
LightGBM	4.9972	0.3748	0.9374	0.9395	0.9374	0.9357
XGBoost	6.3556	0.0917	0.9445	0.9455	0.9445	0.9483
AdaBoost	14.8483	0.4969	0.3688	0.3895	0.3688	0.3089
CatBoost	121.4044	0.0450	0.9384	0.9391	0.9384	0.9363

The following graphs depict the accuracy, precision, F1 score, recall and testing time of different models.

Figure 12. Bar graphs for the obtained evaluation metrics-classification representing the accuracy, precision, F1-score, recall and testing time.

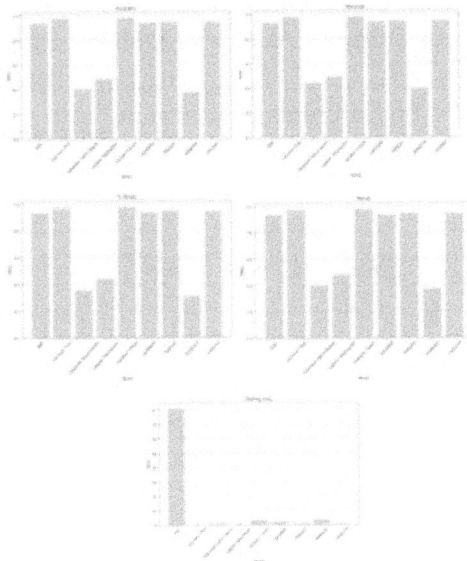

It can be seen that Random Forest returns the best performance on the basis of accuracy, precision, F1 score and recall. While the decision tree shows better performance when considering training and testing time. Gaussian Naïve Bayes, despite taking very less time for training and testing shows poor performance when it comes to other metrics. Out of all the 9 models Adaboost shows the poorest performance.

To gain further insights, correlation matrix and ROC curve were plotted for each of the models. The following figure depicts the correlation matrix and the ROC curve of the decision tree classifier.

Figure 13. (a)Confusion Matrix: matrix summarizing the performance of a ML model- and (b)ROC Curve: graph showing the performance of a classification model

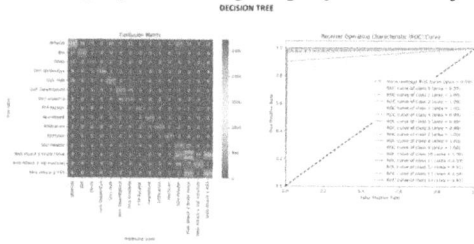

The performance of decision tree classifier can be validated from the confusion matrix that shows huge number values being detected correctly (shown in the diagonal). The inferences from the ROC curve are as follows:

High performing classes (AUC > 0.95): Benign, DoS GoldenEye, DoS Hulk, DoS Slowhttptest, DoS Slowloris, PortScan, SSH-Patator.

Moderately performing classes (AUC > 0.8): DDoS, Infiltration.

Lower performing classes (AUC < 0.8): Bot, Brute Force web attacks, Heartbleed, XSS web attacks, SQL Injection web attacks.

Hypertuning

The models were then hypertuned using Optuna. The following are the evaluation metrics obtained:

Obtained Evaluation Metrics

Figure 14. Obtained evaluation metrics-hypertuning

Model	Accuracy	Precision	Recall	F1 Score
Decision Tree (DT)	0.9463	0.9466	0.9465	0.9458
Adaboost (Adab)	0.3616	0.4630	0.3618	0.3257
Logistic Regression (Logreg)	0.4894	0.5116	0.5005	0.4576
K-Nearest Neighbors (KNN)	0.9253	0.9246	0.9257	0.9246
XGBoost (XGB)	0.9556	0.9573	0.9561	0.9557
Random Forest (RF)	0.9633	0.9641	0.9635	0.9628
CatBoost (Catb)	0.9254	0.9273	0.9259	0.9232
LightGBM (Lgbm)	0.9448	0.9478	0.9481	0.9447

It can be seen that Random Forest still performs the best in terms of all the evaluation metrics. Adaboost and Logistic regression show poor performance.

Ensemble

From the hypertuned models 4 models viz., Random Forest, Xgboos, Catboost and Lightgbm were ensembled using soft voting technique. The following are the evaluation metrics obtained.

Obtained Evaluation Metrics

Figure 15. Obtained evaluation metrics-ensemble- gives the accuracy, precision, F1 and recall score of the ensembled model

```
Ensemble Model Metrics:
Accuracy: 0.9591330956174291
Precision: 0.9601066333239257
Recall: 0.9593897297480524
F1 Score: 0.9585160885291558
```

It can be seen that the model show high performance. It is further analysed by plotting the confusion matrix and ROC curve.

Figure 16. Confusion matrix of the ensemble- shows strong and weak correlations according to the legend given alongside

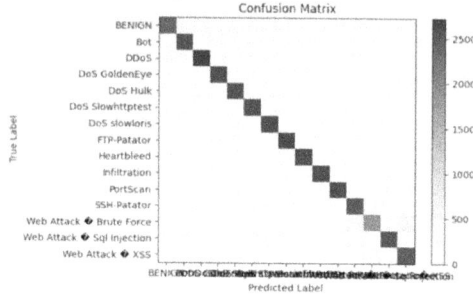

Figure 17. ROC of the ensemble- shows the performance of the model

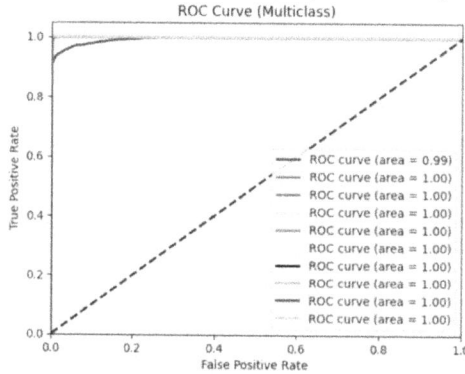

The confusion matrix shows the accurate performance of the model. As it can be seen from the ROC curve, all the classes have AUC >= 0.99, which shows that all the classes are high performing.

Model Approbation

The ensembled model was tested by finding the stability score, accuracy with noise and through cross validation.

Stability Score

The stability score indicates the variation in the data with perturbation. The perturbation size was varied from 0.1 to 5 and the following stability scores were obtained.

Figure 18. Stability score with different perturbations – stability is the measure of robustness of the model

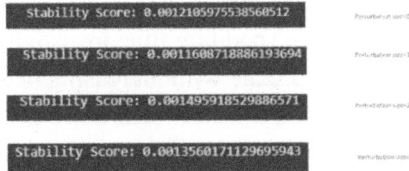

Stability Score: 0.0012105975538560512   Perturbation size 0.1

Stability Score: 0.0011608718886193694   Perturbation size 1

Stability Score: 0.001495918529886571   Perturbation size 2

Stability Score: 0.0013560171129695943   Perturbation size 5

It can be seen that since the stability scores are close to 0, the model is quite stable.

Accuracy of the Proposed Model with Noise

Random noise was generated and added to the data. The accuracy of the data was computed using the ensembled model and the following accuracy was obtained.

Figure 19. Accuracy with noise- shows the model accuracy in the presence of noise

warnings.warn(
Ensemble Model Accuracy with Noise: 0.8675871835723137

It can be seen that the model is robust even in the presence of noise.

Cross Validation Accuracy

A five-fold cross validation was done on he given data to check for overfitting. The following accuracy was obtained.

Figure 20. Cross validation accuracy – a technique used to evaluate the model performance in unseen data

Cross-Validation Mean Accuracy: 0.9592848291733052

The high accuracy ensures the model's performance even on unseen data.

CONCLUSION AND FUTURE WORKS

Implementing an network intrusion detection system (NIDS) with machine learning offers several advantages. Machine learning algorithms can learn and adapt to evolving attack patterns, resulting in more accurate detection of network intrusions compared to traditional rule-based systems. They can identify anomalies and patterns that might be difficult for rule-based systems to detect.

By analyzing large volumes of data and discerning patterns, the proposed model can significantly reduce false positives compared to rule-based systems. This helps in focusing on real threats rather than spending time investigating false alarms and efficiently handles large datasets and scale with increasing network traffic, making them suitable for deployment in large-scale networks and environments. The model can adapt to new and previously unseen threats by continuously learning from new data. This adaptability is essential in combating emerging cyber threats that may not have been encountered before.

Machine learning-based NIDS can automate the detection process to a large extent, reducing the need for manual intervention. Security analysts can then focus on investigating and responding to confirmed threats rather than spending time on routine monitoring tasks. Enhanced threat intelligence is achieved through the analysis of network traffic, enabling machine learning models to identify patterns indicative of malicious behavior. This models offer valuable insights into the tactics, techniques, and procedures (TTPs) utilized by attackers. Such insights are pivotal for enhancing organizational security posture and formulating more effective defense strategies

Machine learning models can be customized and fine-tuned to suit the specific requirements and characteristics of different networks and environments. Overall, integrating machine learning into network intrusion detection systems can lead to more effective and efficient threat detection, helping organizations better protect their assets and data from cyber attacks.

The future scope of an network intrusion detection system (NIDS) using machine learning like the proposed model is promising, with several potential areas for further development and enhancement. Future research could investigate the utilization of advanced machine learning methodologies, such as reinforcement learning, to enhance the precision and resilience of NIDS. These methodologies hold promise in effectively capturing intricate patterns and relationships within network traffic data (Jani et al., 2019).

Developing NIDS models with explainable AI capabilities can help address the interpretability challenge by providing insights into the factors contributing to a decision or alert generated by the system. This is crucial for building trust in the NIDS and facilitating collaboration between automated systems and human analysts (Corea et al., 2024). There is a growing need for intrusion detection solutions tailored to these environments. Future NIDS can focus on detecting anomalies and attacks specific to IoT and OT networks, considering their unique characteristics and communication protocols.

Research into adversarial defense mechanisms can help mitigate the risk of adversarial attacks against machine learning-based NIDS. Techniques such as adversarial training, and robust optimization specifically designed to detect adversarial inputs can enhance the resilience of the NIDS against sophisticated attacks. Developing privacy-preserving techniques for NIDS can enable organizations to leverage machine learning for intrusion detection while ensuring the confidentiality of sensitive network data. Techniques such as differential privacy, federated learning, and homomorphic encryption can help protect privacy in distributed NIDS deployments.

Future NIDS can evolve towards autonomous response and orchestration capabilities, where the system not only detects intrusions but also automatically initiates response actions based on predefined policies and rules. Combining the strengths of different detection techniques, such as signature-based, anomaly-based, and machine learning-based approaches, in hybrid NIDS architectures can provide comprehensive coverage against a wide range of threats while minimizing false positives and negatives. Hybrid approaches can leverage the complementary nature of different detection methods to achieve better overall performance.

NIDS should continuously monitor network traffic and adapt to evolving threats and changes in network behaviour. Future systems can employ dynamic retraining strategies, online learning algorithms, and self-adaptive mechanisms to stay up-to-date with emerging threats and maintain effectiveness over time. Integrating NIDS with broader security operations workflows, incident response processes, and security automation platforms can streamline threat detection, investigation, and remediation activities. This integration enables seamless collaboration between NIDS and other security tools and stakeholders, enhancing overall security posture and resilience against cyber threats.

REFERENCES

Corea, P. M., Liu, Y., Wang, J., Niu, S., & Song, H. (2024). Explainable AI for comparative analysis of intrusion detection models. DOI: 10.1109/MeditCom61057.2024.10621339

Dietterich, T. G. (2000). Ensemble methods in machine learning. In *Multiple Classifier Systems. MCS 2000*. Springer. DOI: 10.1007/3-540-45014-9_1

Gad, A. G. (2022). Particle swarm optimization algorithm and its applications: A systematic review. *Archives of Computational Methods in Engineering*, 29(5), 2531–2561. DOI: 10.1007/s11831-021-09694-4

Grolemund, G., & Wickham, H. (2017). *R for data science*. O'Reilly Media.

He, H. (2008). ADASYN: Adaptive synthetic sampling approach for imbalanced learning. In *2008 IEEE International Joint Conference on Neural Networks (IEEE World Congress on Computational Intelligence)* (pp. 1322-1328). Hong Kong. https://doi.org/DOI: 10.4018/978-1-7998-8023-2

James, G. (2013). *An introduction to statistical learning*. Springer. DOI: 10.1007/978-1-4614-7138-7

Jani, K., Lalwani, P., Upadhyay, D., & Potdar, M. B. (2019). Network Intrusion Detection System using Threat Intelligence and Deep Learning Approach. *International Journal on Computer Science and Engineering*, 7(4), 526–531. DOI: 10.26438/ijcse/v7i4.526531

Karthiga, R. (2021). Transfer learning based breast cancer classification using one-hot encoding technique. In *2021 International Conference on Artificial Intelligence and Smart Systems (ICAIS)* (pp. 115-120). DOI: 10.1109/ICAIS50930.2021.9395930

Khraisat, A., Gondal, I., Vamplew, P., & Kamruzzaman, J. (2019). Survey of intrusion detection systems: Techniques, datasets and challenges. *Cybersecurity*, 2(1), 20. DOI: 10.1186/s42400-019-0038-7

Kumar, V., & Sangwan, O. P. (2012). Signature based intrusion detection system using SNORT. *International Journal of Computer Applications & Information Technology*, 1(3), 35–41. DOI: 10.4018/978-1-7998-8023-2

Kunhare, N., Tiwari, R., & Dhar, J. (2020). Particle swarm optimization and feature selection for intrusion detection system. *Sadhana*, 45(1), 109. DOI: 10.1007/s12046-020-1308-5

Kusumaputri, F. H., & Arifin, A. S. (2022). Anomaly detection based on NSL-KDD using XGBoost with Optuna tuning. In *2022 7th International Conference on Business and Industrial Research (ICBIR)* (pp. 586-591). DOI: 10.1109/ICBIR54589.2022.9786429

Macleod, D., & Whyte, D. (2003). An investigation of the practical limitations of network-based intrusion detection imposed by partial IP datagram inspection. In *Real Time Intrusion Detection*. IGI Global. DOI: 10.4018/978-1-7998-8023-2

Maseer, Z. K., Yusof, R., Bahaman, N., Mostafa, S. A., & Foozy, C. F. M. (2021). Benchmarking of machine learning for anomaly based intrusion detection systems in the CICIDS2017 dataset. *IEEE Access : Practical Innovations, Open Solutions*, 9, 22351–22370. DOI: 10.1109/ACCESS.2021.3056614

Mooijman, P., Catal, C., Tekinerdogan, B., Lommen, A., & Blokland, M. (2023). The effects of data balancing approaches: A case study. *Applied Soft Computing*, 132, 109853. DOI: 10.1016/j.asoc.2022.109853

Mudigonda, N. (2022, August). A method for network intrusion detection using deep learning. *J Stud Res*, 11(3). Advance online publication. DOI: 10.47611/jsrhs.v11i3.2875

Oyelakin, A. M. (2023). *Overview and exploratory analyses of CICIDS 2017 intrusion detection dataset. Journal of Systems Engineering and Information Technology*.

Pandas Development Team. (2022). *pandas: powerful Python data analysis toolkit*. IGI Global. https://doi.org/DOI: 10.4018/978-1-7998-8023-2

Panigrahi, R., & Borah, S. (2018). A detailed analysis of CICIDS2017 dataset for designing intrusion detection systems. *IACSIT International Journal of Engineering and Technology*, 7, 479–482.

Pudjihartono, N., Fadason, T., Kempa-Liehr, A. W., & O'Sullivan, J. M. (2022). A review of feature selection methods for machine learning-based disease risk prediction. *Frontiers in Bioinformatics*, 2, 927312. Advance online publication. DOI: 10.3389/fbinf.2022.927312 PMID: 36304293

Ramu, C., Rao, T. S., & Rao, E. U. S. (2024). *Attack classification in network intrusion detection system based on optimization strategy and deep learning methodology*. Multimed Tools Appl. DOI: 10.1007/s11042-024-18558-5

Rashid, A., Siddique, M. J., & Ahmed, S. M. (2020). Machine and deep learning based comparative analysis using hybrid approaches for intrusion detection system. In *2020 3rd International Conference on Advancements in Computational Sciences (ICACS)* (pp. 1-9). DOI: 10.1109/ICACS47775.2020.9055946

Singh, A. P., & Singh, M. D. (2014). Analysis of host-based and network-based intrusion detection system. *IJCNIS*, 6(8), 41–47. DOI: 10.5815/ijcnis.2014.08.06

Tukey, J. W. (1977). *Exploratory data analysis*. Addison-Wesley.

Vanin, P., Newe, T., Dhirani, L. L., O'Connell, E., O'Shea, D., Lee, B., & Rao, M. (2022). A study of network intrusion detection systems using artificial intelligence/machine learning. *Applied Sciences (Basel, Switzerland)*, 12(22), 11752. DOI: 10.3390/app122211752

Venkatesan, S. (2023). Design an intrusion detection system based on feature selection using ML algorithms. *MSEA*, 72(1), 702–710.

Wang, M., Zheng, K., Yang, Y., & Wang, X. (2020). An explainable machine learning framework for intrusion detection systems. *IEEE Access : Practical Innovations, Open Solutions*, 8, 73127–73141. DOI: 10.1109/ACCESS.2020.2988359

Xia, X. (2024). Optimizing and hyper-tuning machine learning models for the water absorption of eggshell and glass-based cementitious composite. *PLoS One*, 19(1), e0296494. Advance online publication. DOI: 10.1371/journal.pone.0296494 PMID: 38165942

APPENDIX

CIC IDS 2017 Dataset: A dataset that was made by the Canadian Institute for cyber-security that contains normal and malicious network traffic details (Maseer et al., 2021; Panigrahi & Borah, 2018).

Exploratory Data Analysis (EDA):The analysis done in order to find the correlation between different features and to gain insights about the dataset (Oyelakin et al., 2023; Tukey, 1977).

Feature Selection: The process of selecting the relevant features from the data set to improve the performance of the model and reduce the computational burden (Pudjihartono et al., 2022). Particle swarm optimisation was used in the implementation for selecting the optimal feature subset (Kunhare et al., 2020).

Data Balancing: The technique used to address the issue of class imbalance. Includes oversampling and undersampling (Mooijman et al., 2023; He et al., 2008).

Machine Learning Algorithms: Algorithms that can be used for classification of the data and to observe the accuracy,precision, F1 score and recall.

Hyperparameter Tuning: An optimization technique on the model parameters to improve the performance of the model (Xia, 2024).

Ensemble Learning: A technique combining predictions from multiple machine learning models to improve overall performance and to make the system robust (Dietterich, 2000).

Stability Score: A Measure of model stability under different perturbation levels to assess its robustness.

Cross-Validation: Statistical method to evaluate model performance by partitioning the dataset into subsets and using them for training and testing iteratively.

Threat Intelligence: Threat intelligence is evidence-based information about cyber attacks that cyber security experts organize and analyze (Jani et al., 2019).

Explainable AI:Explainable AI is a set of tools and frameworks to help you understand and interpret predictions made by your machine learning models (Corea et al., 2024).

Chapter 8
Secure Collaboration for Storing and Processing of Criminal Records Using Blockchain Technology

Hima Bindu

QIS College of Engineering and Technology, India

Sanjana Muvvala

QIS College of Engineering and Technology, India

ABSTRACT

Blockchain technology has sparked transformative changes across industries, offering secure ledgers for shared, tamper-proof transaction records. Its decentralization prevents data manipulation by requiring consensus from multiple participants. Applications span medicine, education, fintech, accounting, banking, and government, addressing issues like fraud, corruption, and identity theft. Introducing a new application, this chapter explores using blockchain for securely storing criminal records in police stations. This approach ensures long-term data preservation, reduces storage space, and maintains the integrity of critical evidence. By enabling secure collaboration between police and judiciary, it enhances evidence collection and strengthens governance, fostering a trustworthy law enforcement system.

DOI: 10.4018/979-8-3693-9225-6.ch008

1. INTRODUCTION

Blockchain is gaining a lot of significance and has become a new buzzword in current eras. The era of blockchain has introduced new concepts into the secure sharing of data along with transparency and also it has increased the potential to solve integrity, security, and data privacy issues. Due to its features, blockchain gained the attraction of numerous applications in various domains (Anton 2022). Blockchain consists of a chain of blocks (records) that allows for storing all the committed transactions. Blockchain incorporates technologies such as cryptographic hash functions, distributed consensus algorithms, and digital signatures to achieve secure transmissions (Bushra Hameed 2019, Zhang 2019). In blockchain technology, all transactions are done in a decentralized manner in order to remove third-party interference. Blockchain is always described as a type of distributed ledger technology also known as DLT which means there is no center point of attack. In blockchain, the database is managed automatically using a p2p network with a distributed time stamping server (Abdullah 2022).

There are different types of generations that deal with different evolutions such as Blockchain 1.0 which majorly emphasizes currency and payments, and is enabled a transaction for digital crypto currency. Blockchain 2.0 introduced smart contracts whereas Blockchain 3.0 extended the areas of blockchain applications, introduced decentralized Apps (dApp), and addressed the issues related to scalability, and interoperability. Blockchain 4.0 brought a novel model of blockchain with industrial applications using other technologies like AI, IoT, etc (Nurmukhametov 2018).

Consensus protocols are essential in blockchain as they ensure that all participants adhere to a universally agreed-upon perspective, thereby establishing global consensus (Zhang 2021). Verification and validation of nodes are carried out to check the truthiness of the block before entering the chain. Block data cannot be tampered as the hash value of the present block depends on the hash of the earlier block. Blockchain in combination with smart contracts will eradicate the necessity for central servers to assure fairness among transaction parties. The two important features are Traceability and decentralization that make blockchain notable compared to all other security methods (Alaa Haddad 2022).

1.1 Blockchain Architecture

In the blockchain, the section holds the official transactions which are hashed and then encoded into a Merkel tree. The structure of a block in the blockchain is depicted in Fig. 1.

Figure 1. Blockchain structure

Fig. 1: Blockchain structure [Source: [10]]

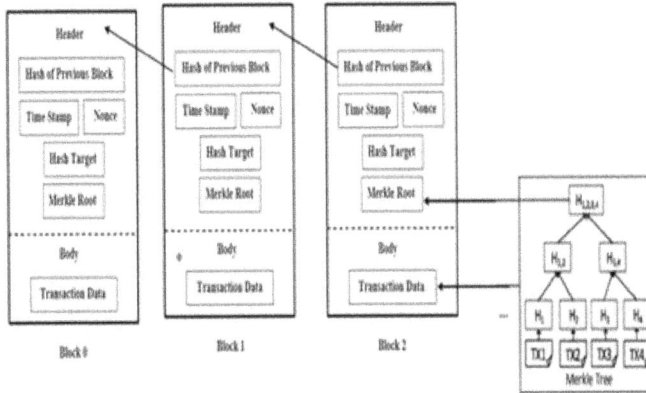

Source: (Alaa Haddad 2022)

Blockchain contains each block are:

Header: by the use of a header identification of a particular block in the entire chain becomes easier. Periodically, miners change the nonce value to hash the block header.

Previous Block Address/Hash: It contains the value of the preceding block's hash.

Timestamp: after verification of the block. a specified time at which it is created is mentioned.

Nonce: For each block, a nonce number is used to solve the proof of work that is compared to the live target. When miners hash the code, they change a four-byte random field each time.

Merkel Root: it stores all the transaction data by providing a digital blueprint of the entire transaction

Each block's hash value is determined by summing the hashes of the preceding blocks, transaction information, and the nonce value of the current block. An additional block is added to the blockchain consecutively, with the first block being referred to as the genesis block, or Block 0. To ensure ledger consistency y and user security, blockchain typically consists of two technologies: p2p distributed consensus and asymmetric cryptography (Alaa Haddad 2022). In blockchain technology, peers who verify transaction records are called miners. A block has been created using immutability, transparency, and pseudonymity (Yumna 2019, Abid Haleem 2021, Alaa Haddad 2022).

1.2 Consensus Algorithms

Since the blockchain network lacks a single point of contact, a basic challenge is the Byzantine General's challenge (Alaa Haddad 2022), which was developed in 1982 when working with distributed networks. A group of nodes' decision-making process and agreement amongst peers inside the network constitute the consensus (Abdullah Almamun 2022, Khezr 2019). Blockchain networks use conventional consensus methods like as PoW, PoS, PBFT, etc. The features of these consensus algorithms with respect to energy consumption, node management, and adversary power tolerance are shown in Fig. 2.

Figure 2. Consensus algorithm comparison

Fig. 2: Consensus algorithm comparison [Source: [13]]

Property	PoW	PoS	PBFT
Node management	Open	Open	Permissioned
Energy consumption	High	Medium	Low
Tolerated power of adversary	< 25% computing power	< 51% stake	< 33.3% faulty replicas
Example	Bitcoin [1]	Peercoin [13]	Hyperledger Fabric [12]

(Source: (Kherbouche 2022))

Proof of Work (PoW) is at most popular one with high robustness. It is used to verify and create additional block in the blockchain. It was first published in 1993 by Cynthia Dwork and Moni Naor and it is verified through the mining process and resource consumption during the mining process. Initially miner can solve the puzzle by finding the hash value which is lower than the predetermined one. Due to the several calculations needed, the task is expensive in terms of processing resources. For example, a 51 percent attack on the blockchain network would be costly (Alaa Haddad 2022, Zheng 2017).

Proof of Stake (PoS) is a mechanism to process transactions and additional blocks creation in a blockchain. It deals with the drawbacks of PoW which is the utilization of over-CPU power. In PoS, miners are chosen based on money or wealth which is called a stake. The second largest crypto currency Ethereum is now planning to change its consensus algorithm from PoW to PoS (Kherbouche 2022, Castro 2019)

Practical Byzantine Fault Tolerance (PBFT) is founded upon a protocol for Byzantine agreement (King 2012, Kherbouche 2022). PBFT's need that every node be known to the network restricts its application in public blockchains. The PBFT consensus process can be divided into three stages: committed, prepared, and pre-prepared. To advance through the three stages, a node needs the votes of two thirds of all other nodes. Hyperledger Fabric presently makes use of PBFT (Zheng 2019, Kherbouche 2022).

1.3 Types of Blockchain

The following are the fundamental kinds of blockchains (Bushra Hameed 2019):

Permission/Private Blockchain: A Blockchain network that is permission functions within a private environment, as a closed network, or is managed by a single organization. It is not freely possible for the users to join the community, view the records, or conduct independent transactions. Centralized organizations that use the network's strength for internal business activities, or their own, prefer permission blockchains. Employer consortiums are also likely to use personal blockchains for data exchange and transaction filing in a safe manner.

Permissionless/Public Blockchain: A blockchain without permission is accessible to everybody. Any user can create a private agreement, send transactions over the network, and subsequently add entries to the ledger to start talking with the network. The original form of blockchain technology, from which Bitcoin and other crypto currencies were derived, is known as the public blockchain. Distributed ledger technology (DLT) was further advanced by public blockchain networks.

Hybrid/Consortium Blockchain: the blockchain that makes use of both public and private blockchain technology. The hybrid network makes use of a permission less blockchain in place of a permission blockchain. While not publicly accessible, this blockchain covertly offers fundamental functions including traceability, integrity, and security.

1.4 Blockchain Features

The fundamental characteristics of blockchain are: Fig. 3.

Decentralized: Each node within a network is interconnected with every other node by a blockchain, which maintains a transparent and comprehensive log of all transactions (Yumna 2019). The process of data confirmation, storage, preservation, and transfer on the blockchain—which is dependent upon a distributed framework structure—is referred to as decentralization.

Traceability: Each transaction on the blockchain is indexed chronologically, and a block is connected to two neighboring blocks by its cryptographic hash. A block's chain is preserved by mining pools, which permits cloud-based websites to browse the block (Yumna 2019).

Consensus Mechanism: In PC and blockchain frameworks, a fault-tolerant mechanism is a consensus mechanism that enables distributed processes or multi-agent systems to agree on a single piece of network state data. It helps with keeping records. The three consensus mechanism processes are POW, POS, and DPOS (Yumna 2019).

Figure 3. Basic features of blockchain

Fig. 3: Basic features of Blockchain

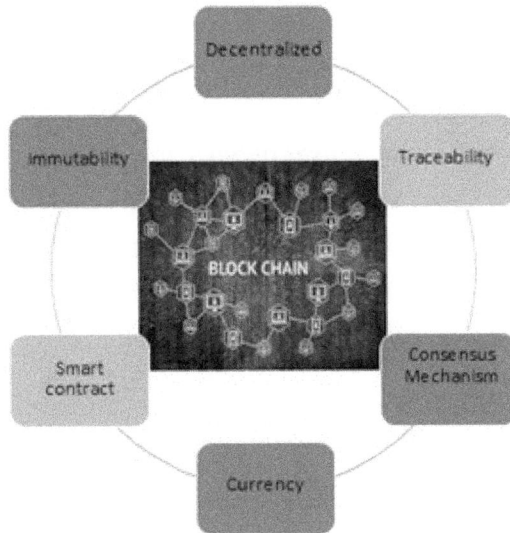

Currency: Of all the crypto currencies that have been suggested, the first digital currency in the revolutionary world is the bit coin. A feature of blockchain technology is crypto currency, which is a digital or virtual currency that guarantees the security and dependability of end-to-end transactions. These currencies are created using a variety of mining algorithms. As a result, the blockchain and crypto currency integrated product has multiple applications, including in accounting and finance. (Yumna 2019)

Smart Contract: Developers require a smart contract, which is a required blockchain protocol, in order to create a financial agreement on the blockchain that is activated by the parties involved (Yumna 2019). Not only did it lower the "outsider cost" associated with traditional transactions, but it also greatly improved transaction security and quality.

Immutability: Data cannot be altered once entered. In order to successfully tamper, or make illegal changes, more than 51% of the records stored in the system would need to be altered.

1.5 Working Steps of Blockchain Technology

The network connected system updates its blockchain to add additional blocks. The fundamental processes of blockchain technology are depicted in Fig. 4. Through machine consensus, a blockchain system allows peer-to-peer (P2P) value transactions without the need for an intermediary. Using a peer-to-peer (P2P) network of computers that all execute the protocol and have an identical copy of the transaction ledger, it runs on top of the internet (Varshney 2021, McGhin 2019, Yue 2016).

Figure 4. Working steps of blockchain technology

Fig. 4: Working steps of blockchain technology

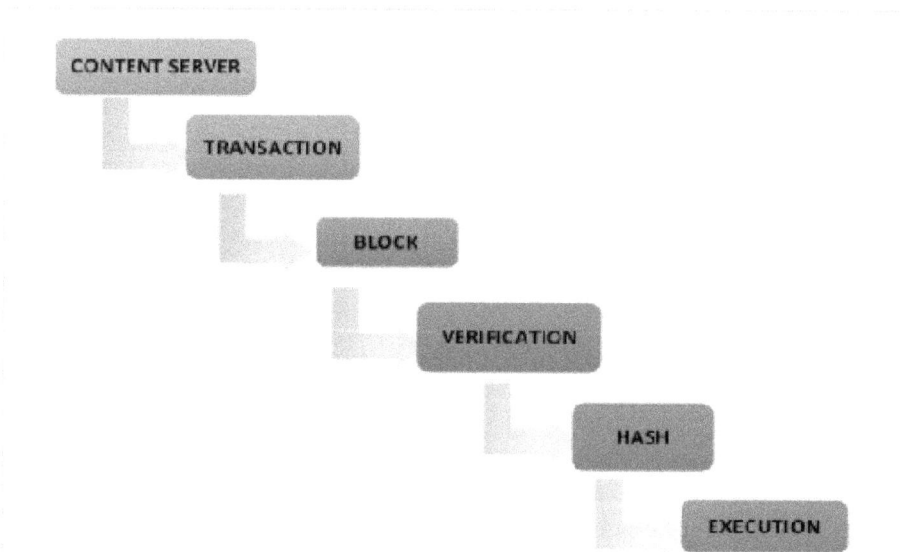

1.6 Blockchain Applications

☐ Blockchain in Healthcare

Prescription drug tracking and tracing is being done throughout supply networks using blockchain technology. With this technology, it's easy to stop and control the spread of fake medications, recall dangerous and ineffective medications, and act quickly. In order to improve healthcare services across hospitals, governments, and research institutes, data interchange and dissemination, as well as customer data security, is top priorities in the healthcare industry.

☐ Transfer Contracts and Wills

The days of writing down contracts and wills and using many middlemen are coming to an end. Blockchain technology has made it possible to replace paper wills, contracts, and inheritances with digital ones. Paper contracts are being replaced with smart contracts that legally bind all parties. All customers concerned in the smart contract are bound by the terms set forth in this data, It can be retrieved whenever necessary and is kept on the blockchain network.

☐ Management of the Supply Chain

Block chain's immutable ledger performs the perfect tasks like tracking commodities in real time as they move and exchange hands across the supply chain. Blockchain gives businesses who sell these products a number of options. To prioritize supply chain chores, such distributing recently arrived goods among multiple shipping containers, an entry on a blockchain could be utilized. Utilizing and structuring tracking data in a novel and dynamic way is made possible by blockchain technology.

☐ Protection of Copyright and Royalties

Currently a lot of copyright and ownership laws apply to music, movies, blogs, and other online content. These laws could be easier to implement and more secure with the use of blockchain technology. Additionally, it gives artists and content producers accurate, up-to-date statistics on royalty distribution. Downloads of any kind of digital content may be tracked to ensure that the creator or artist receives credit for their work.

☐ Voting

The concept of blockchain has emerged on secure voting. The electronic voting process resolves the problems with traditional manual voting, there are still some major concerns, including voter fraud, voter privacy, and the high cost of legacy digital voting technology. Blockchain has the potential to improve voting for voters by increasing security, transparency, and privacy through smart contracts and encryption. These objectives can be achieved using blockchain, which also makes it possible to customize the voting procedure by using different kinds of ballots and logic-based voting. Elections at the university level use it.

☐ Crypto Currency

Most familiar application of blockchain is in crypto currency. Adopting block-chain for crypto currencies is due to its numerous advantages, one of which is its borderless nature. Crypto currencies may therefore be used for international transactions. One of the important points is that exchange rates could change and that buyers could end up losing money. On the other hand, this option is significantly better than regionalized payment apps, like Paytm in India. But its functionality is restricted to national only.

☐ The Internet of Things (IoT)

The Internet of Things (IoT) is a network of interconnected gadgets that share information to provide valuable insights. The Smart Home is a prime example, where various appliances are connected on a single platform. However, ensuring security in such a distributed system is crucial. Blockchain plays an important role in this aspect. By leveraging blockchain, IoT devices can ensure that the information they receive is secure and accessible only to authorized parties, thereby enhancing overall system security.

☐ Asset Administration

Asset management is not an exception to the growing significance of blockchain in the financial sector. In general, asset management pertains to the administration and exchange of diverse assets that an individual may own, including but not limited to commodities, mutual funds, real estate, stocks,, fixed income, and other alternative investments. Conventional asset management trade techniques can be highly costly, particularly when dealing with multiple countries and cross-border payments. Since it eliminates the requirement for middlemen like brokers, custodians, settlement managers, etc., blockchain can be of considerable assistance in these situations. Rather, blockchain technology provides an approach that is transparent and unambiguous, thereby removing the potential for error.

☐ Blockchain Applications for Anti-Money Laundering

The inherent characteristics of blockchain-based anti-money laundering applications may help stop money laundering. Every blockchain transaction creates an irreversible, permanent record trail. Because of this, it is simple for authorities to determine where the money came from. A blockchain ledger can perform tasks including keeping track of, verifying, and documenting every transaction's complete history. The transaction is promptly cancelled if any of the steps, such as the destination wallet, currency type, departure wallet, and amount, remain unconfirmed. Blockchain also makes risk assessment and money laundering reporting tools possible. Instead of only keeping an eye on entry and departure points, it allows for system-wide analysis.

☐ Blockchain for Advertising

One kind of distributed digital ledger technology that promotes decentralization while offering the best level of security, traceability, and transparency is advertising through blockchain applications. Digital records are immutable once they are placed on the blockchain; those who have access can view the transactions but cannot change them. Because blockchain records transactions and information in real time, advertisers may use it to track their advertising expenses. Ultimately, it can provide openness that current systems are unable to. There are other benefits than transparency. In advertising, quickness is essential. Maintaining inventory control and guaranteeing high-quality items are challenging tasks. Blockchain technology is able to stay up to date.

1.7 Advantages of Blockchain Technology

Due to its numerous advantages, blockchain technology has grown more significant for a wide range of sectors (Anton 2022).

Fraud Prevention

Blockchain technology indeed revolutionizes fraud prevention by circumventing the need for multiple parties to confirm transactions. Its peer-to-peer network and tamper-resistant properties make it a formidable tool for any industry that relies on swift, secure, and verifiable information and transactions. By eliminating intermediaries and providing a transparent, immutable ledger, blockchain enhances the efficiency and trustworthiness of data exchange, thereby reducing the risk of fraud significantly.

Maintaining Privacy and Confidentiality

Blockchain technology indeed brings about efficiency, transparency, and trust, all while safeguarding privacy and confidentiality. Its hybrid and private networks are specifically engineered to handle high transaction volumes and sudden increases in network activity, ensuring smooth operation even during peak times.

This stands in stark contrast to certain payments within the traditional banking system, which may take days to clear. By offering near-instantaneous transaction processing, blockchain enhances the speed and reliability of financial transactions, benefiting both businesses and consumers alike.

Minimize Expediting of the Transfer Procedure

Blockchain payments speed up the transfer process, reducing or eliminating fees altogether. The business incurs losses, has to pay additional fees, and could have to take legal action to recover money when clients write bad checks to pay for goods or services (Guo 2016, Zhang 2019, Ke 2021).

Speedup Transaction System

Financial institutions can use blockchain-based distributed, immutable transaction records for record-keeping and regulatory reporting. The quicker transaction settlements provided by blockchain technology can enhance a number of financial services.

Enable Digital Currencies

Blockchain technology has ushered in a new era of digital assets, with digital currencies leading the way. These currencies, based on blockchain, offer an alternative to traditional banking systems. Blockchain companies are working to lower barriers to entry and facilitate the seamless exchange of popular crypto currencies. Despite digital currency already being in use, these efforts are making it more accessible and convenient for users.

Ease in the Auditing Process

Blockchain technology indeed holds significant potential to streamline the auditing process within the financial sector. By leveraging immutable blockchain records, financial institutions can achieve unprecedented transparency, enabling auditors to thoroughly examine their activities. These transparent records facilitate the confirmation of compliance with regulatory standards, enhancing trust and accountability within the industry.

Management of Digital Assets

Blockchain technology now makes it feasible to manage digital assets completely in a predictable, automated, traceable, and dependable manner. The way that every "block" in the blockchain is interconnected and encrypted is what makes it so special (Haleem 2021).

2. LITERATURE SURVEY

The blockchain in the banking and financial services sector has been covered by Treleaven et al. (Treleaven 2017), who have noted the several benefits of blockchain technology. This special issue investigates its peculiar beginnings, significant influence, difficulties in implementation, and immense promise. Blockchain technology has the potential to streamline business procedures in the banking and financial services industry while producing secure, reliable records of contracts and transactions. Qiang et al. (Qiang Wang 2020) have provided an explanation of how to use the blockchain network to execute transactions at all levels by directly connecting producers and customers. In order to create rules for when to start transactions, smart contracts communicate with the system using signals. These procedures, which guarantee automatic control of all energy and storage flows and help to balance supply and demand, are predicated on pre-established norms for smart contracts. Energy blockchain ensures a distributed secure record of all energy flows and commercial operations by storing energy transaction data on a single blockchain.

In their paper, Quazi Mamun et al. (Quazi Mamun 2022) discussed how blockchain technology could be used in the future to solve a number of issues that currently plague the healthcare sector. They suggested that in order to improve safety and confidentiality, spend less money on medical staff and more on patient care, a shared archive of health-related data for doctors and patients should be established, regardless of the patients' electronic diagnosis. This report also covered a number of blockchain applications in the healthcare sector. Electronic health records (EHRs) are digitally stored medical records that provide information regarding an individual's health. Alaa Haddad et al. (Alaa Haddad 2022) examined the data from EHRs.

Since EHRs are typically shared by various healthcare stakeholders, they can encounter issues including power outages, improper use of data, lack of privacy, security, and audit trails, among other issues. Contrarily, blockchain is a revolutionary technology that offers a distributed and decentralized environment where nodes in a list of networks can link to one another without the requirement for a central authority. It has the capacity to go beyond the constraints of EHR management and establish a more decentralized, safe, and secure exchange of EHR data. Numerous studies propose tamper-resistant solutions that use blockchain technology and artificial intelligence techniques to guarantee the accuracy of health data.

3. METHODOLOGY

3.1 Motivation

Blockchain technology has emerged as a robust and innovative solution that offers numerous advantages, particularly in terms of transparency and tamper-proof data storage. Considering its potential, we are motivated to propose the application of blockchain in a crucial problem area: record-keeping in police stations. The current record-keeping system in police stations often faces challenges such as data tampering, limited accessibility, and the risk of missing files, which can hinder the judicial process. By implementing blockchain technology, we can revolutionize this process and make it more efficient and secure.

The core feature of blockchain is its immutability. Each piece of information related to a particular case will be recorded as a block, and once recorded, it cannot be altered or deleted without the consensus of the network. This ensures the integrity of the data, preventing any unauthorized modifications and maintaining a reliable chain of custody. Storing all case-related data on the blockchain will significantly reduce the risk of loss and tampering, which is prevalent in traditional systems. As a result, the police department can save considerable storage space and resources that would otherwise be required for redundant backups and security measures.

Figure 5. Proposed secure collaboration for criminal record keeping and processing

Fig. 5: Proposed Secure collaboration for criminal record keeping and processing

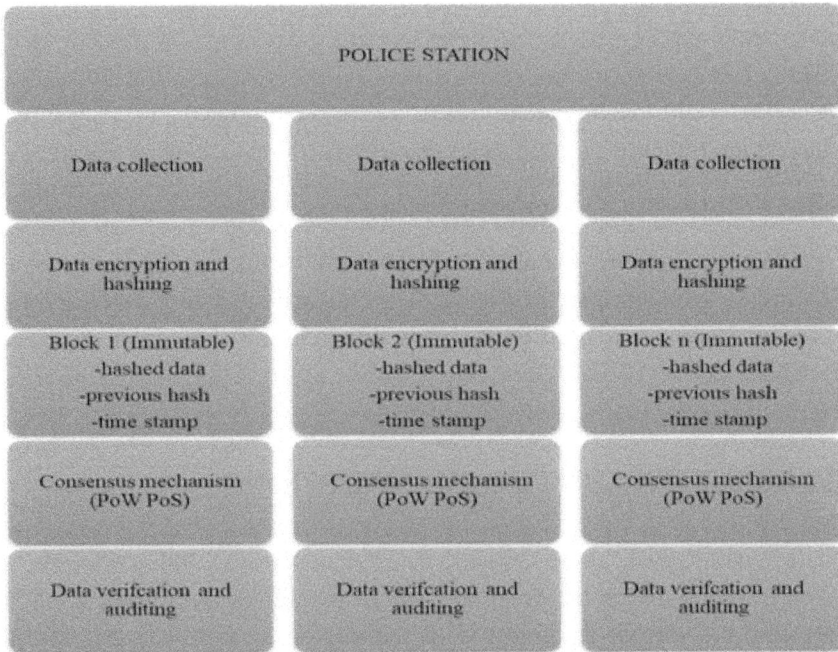

Furthermore, the transparent nature of the blockchain ensures that all authorized parties involved in the case, including law enforcement, lawyers, judges, and even the general public (where appropriate), can access the data. This open access facilitates the sharing of crucial information and evidence across different departments and jurisdictions, leading to a more collaborative and efficient judicial process. Courts can readily access blockchain data during the trial, making it easier for them to consider and evaluate the evidence. This will streamline the decision-making process, accelerate the time taken for judgment, and ultimately reduce the burden on the judicial system. By adopting blockchain technology for record-keeping, police stations can significantly improve their efficiency, accountability, and transparency. Moreover, this system can be scaled and applied across various regions in India, harmonizing data management practices and promoting a consistent and unified approach to resolving cases. Fig.5 depicts the methodology of the proposed work, the process of flow is listed below:

1. **Data Collection:** Relevant data related to a case is collected from various sources and parties involved in the case.
2. **Data Encryption and Hashing:** The collected data is encrypted to ensure confidentiality and hashed to create a unique fixed-length string representing the data block.
3. **Block Creation:** Each hashed data block is combined with the previous block's hash and additional information (such as a timestamp) to form a new block. The blocks are linked in a chronological order, forming a chain of blocks.
4. **Consensus Mechanism:** A consensus mechanism (e.g., Proof of Work, Proof of Stake) validates and agrees on the order and content of the blocks in the blockchain, ensuring that only authorized and legitimate information is added.
5. **Data Verification and Auditing:** The transparent nature of the blockchain allows anyone with access to verify the data independently, facilitating auditing processes.

4. CONCLUSION AND FUTURE DIRECTIONS

Incorporating blockchain technology into police station record-keeping represents a groundbreaking and transformative solution to address the significant challenges faced by the current system. One of the most crucial advantages of utilizing blockchain is the immutability. By storing data in a decentralized and distributed ledger, all case-related information becomes resistant to tampering and ensures the authenticity and integrity of evidence. This instills trust in the data's reliability and eliminates any doubts about its accuracy, making it a powerful tool in mitigating the issues like evidence tampering or unauthorized access.

The transparency and accessibility of blockchain also help the judicial process in such a way that only authorized parties such as law enforcement, lawyers, judges, and other stakeholders can securely access case information in real time. This fosters collaboration and streamlines the legal system's operations, as all relevant parties can access the same up-to-date information simultaneously. In summary, blockchain technology can revolutionize police station record-keeping by providing a secure, efficient, and transparent system. Its adoption would enhance the reliability of case-related data, streamline operations, and improve public confidence in the justice system.

REFERENCES

ABDULLAH ALMAMUN, (2022). "Blockchain-Based Electronic Health Records Management: A Comprehensive Review and Future Research Direction", IEEE ACCESS, VOLUME 10, pp- 5768-5789.

Ahmed. (2022)." Emerging Trends in Blockchain Technology and Applications: A Review Outlook", journal of king saud university - computer and information sciences, VOL.34,pp-6719-6742.

ALAA HADDAD. et al., (2022). "Systematic Review on AI-Blockchain Based E-Healthcare Records Management Systems", IEEE Access, Vol.10. pp: 94583-94615. https://www.fool.com/investing/stock-market/market-sectors/financials/blockchain-stocks/blockchain-applications/

Anton, (2022) "Blockchain in healthcare and health sciences—A scoping review", International Journal of Medical Informatics, Vol. 134. https://doi.org/.DOI: 10.1016/j.ijmedinf.2019.104040

Antoniadis, S. Kontsas, K. Spinthiropoulos (2019). "Blockchain applications in marketing", in The Proceedings of 7th ICCMI.

Castro, M., & Liskov, B. (Eds.). (2019). "Practical Byzantine Fault Tolerance, OSDI, projects Tlf. Hyperledger: https://www.hyperledger.org

Guo, Y., & Liang, C. (2016). Blockchain application and outlook in the banking industry. *Financial Innovation*, 2(1), 1–12. DOI: 10.1186/s40854-016-0034-9

Haleem, A., Javaid, M., Singh, R. P., Suman, R., & Rab, S. (2021). Blockchain technology applications in healthcare: An overview. *International Journal of Intelligent Networks*, 2, 130–139. DOI: 10.1016/j.ijin.2021.09.005

Haleem, M. Javaid, R.P. Singh, R. Suman, S. Rab, (2021). "Blockchain technology applications in healthcare: An overview", Int. J. Intell. Netw. pp.130–139.

Hameed, B., Murad, M., Noman, A., Javed, M., Ramzan, M., Ashfaq, F., Usman, H., & Yousaf, M. (2019). A Review of Blockchain-based Educational Projects. *International Journal of Advanced Computer Science and Applications*, 10(10), 491–499. DOI: 10.14569/IJACSA.2019.0101065

Javaid, M., Haleem, A., Singh, R. P., Suman, R., & Khan, S. (2022). A review of Blockchain Technology applications for financial services. *BenchCouncil Transactions on Benchmarks, Standards, and Evaluations*, 2(3), 1–18. DOI: 10.1016/j.tbench.2022.100073

Ke, Z. Tang, (2021). "Innovation of supply chain finance model based on blockchain technology, in: International Conference on Cognitive Based Information Processing and Applications", CIPA 2021, Springer, pp. 680–686.

Kherbouche, M., Pisoni, G., & Molnár, B. (2022). Model to program and blockchain approaches for business processes and workflows in finance. *Applied System Innovation*, 5(1), 10. DOI: 10.3390/asi5010010

Khezr, A. Y., & Benlamri, R. (2019). Blockchain technology in healthcare: A comprehensive review and directions for future research. *Applied Sciences (Basel, Switzerland)*, 9(9), 1736. DOI: 10.3390/app9091736

King, S., & Ppcoin, N. S. (2012), "Peer-to-peer Crypto-currency With Proof-of-Stake", self-published paper, August, p. 19.

Kumar, M., Nikhil, N., & Singh, R. (2020). "Decentralising finance using decentralized blockchain oracles", International Conference for Emerging Technology, INCET, IEEE, pp. 1–4.

X. Li, P. Jiang, T. Chen, X. Luo, and Q. Wen, (2020).v "A survey on the secu- 2873 rity of blockchain systems," Future Gener. Comput. Syst., vol. 107, 2874 pp. 841–853.

C. Lin, D. He, X. Huang, M. K. Khan, and K.-K.-R. Choo, (2020). "DCAP: 2277 A secure and efficient decentralized conditional anonymous payment sys- 2278 tem based on blockchain," IEEE Trans. Inf. Forensics Security, vol. 15, 2279 pp. 2440–2452.

Liu, L., Li, Y., & Jiang, T. (2021). Optimal strategies for financing a three-level supply chain through blockchain platform finance. *International Journal of Production Research*, 1–18.

Ma, S., Deng, Y., He, D., Zhang, J., & Xie, X. (2021). "An efficient NIZK scheme 2281 for privacy-preserving transactions over account-model blockchain," 2282 IEEE Trans. Dependable Secure Comput., vol. 18, no. 2, pp. 641–651, 2283

Mamun, Q. (2022). Blockchain technology in the future of healthcare. *Smart Health (Amsterdam, Netherlands)*, 23, 100223. Advance online publication. DOI: 10.1016/j.smhl.2021.100223

McGhin, T., Choo, K. K., Liu, C. Z., & He, D. (2019). Blockchain in healthcare applications: Research challenges and opportunities. *Journal of Network and Computer Applications*, 135, 62–75. DOI: 10.1016/j.jnca.2019.02.027

Nakamoto, S. Bitcoin: a Peer-to-Peer Electronic Cash System, (2008) projects Tlf. Hyperledger (cited 19.03 2019). Available from: https://www.hyperledger.org

Nurmukhametov, R. K., Stepanov, P. D., & Novikova, T. R. (2018). Blockchain technology and its application in trade finance. *Financ. Anal.: Probl. Solut.*, 11(2), 179–190. DOI: 10.24891/fa.11.2.179

O'Dair, M., & Owen, R. (2019). Financing new creative enterprise through block-chain technology: Opportunities and policy implications. *Strategic Change*, 28(1), 9–17. DOI: 10.1002/jsc.2242

P. Treleaven, R. Gendal Brown, and D. Yang, (2017). "Blockchain Technology in Finance," in Computer, vol. 50, no. 9, pp. 14-17 .DOI: 10.1109/MC.2017.3571047

Varshney, N. Garg, K.S. Nagla, et al., (2021). "Challenges in sensors technology for industry 4.0 for futuristic metrological applications", MAPAN, Vol. 36, pp: 215–226, .DOI: 10.1007/s12647-021-00453-1

Wang, Q., & Su, M. (2020). Integrating blockchain technology into the energy sector — From the theory of blockchain to research and application of energy blockchain. *Computer Science Review*, 37, 100275. Advance online publication. DOI: 10.1016/j.cosrev.2020.100275

R. Yaksick, (2019). "Overcoming supply chain finance challenges via blockchain technology, in Disruptive Innovation in Business and Finance in the Digital World, Emerald Publishing Limited.

Yue, X., Wang, H., Jin, D., Li, M., & Jiang, W. (2016). Healthcare data gateways: Found healthcare intelligence on Blockchain with novel privacy risk control. *Journal of Medical Systems*, 40(10), 1–8. DOI: 10.1007/s10916-016-0574-6 PMID: 27565509

Yumna, H.. (2019). "Use of Blockchain in Education: A Systematic Literature Review", In *Asian Conference on Intelligent Information and Database Systems*, Springer, pp: 191- 202. DOI: 10.1007/978-3-030-14802-7_17

Zhang, S., Zhang, D., Zheng, J., & Aerts, W. (2021). Does policy uncertainty of the blockchain dampen ICO markets? *Accounting and Finance*, 61(S1), 1625–1637. DOI: 10.1111/acfi.12639

Zhang, X., & Han, Y. (2019). Research on the energy distribution and tendency of blockchain in the E-commerce field. *Int. J. Front. Eng. Technol*, 1(1).

Zheng, Z., Xie, S., Dai, H., Chen, X., & Wang, H. (2017). "An overview of block-chain technology: architecture, consensus, and future trends", in: (Eds.), Big Data (BigData Congress), IEEE. DOI: 10.1109/BigDataCongress.2017.85

Chapter 9
The Role of Wireshark in Packet Inspection and Password Sniffing for Network Security

Manvi Mishra
SRMSCET&R Bareilly, India

Md Shadab Hussain
SRMSCET&R Bareilly, India

Nirbhay Chaubey
https://orcid.org/0000-0001-6575-7723
Ganpat University, India

Prabhakar Gupta
SRMSCET, Bareilly, India

ABSTRACT

In today's interconnected digital landscape, network integrity, efficiency, and security are paramount for business, institutional, and personal interactions. This chapter focuses on delving into the functionalities of Wireshark, offering an extensive exploration of packet inspection methodologies and effective strategies to mitigate the risks associated with password sniffing attacks. It involves capturing and analyzing network traffic, examining key protocols like HTTP, DNS, SMTP, and more, and demonstrating data transmission across the network Through practical demonstrations readers are guided through the process of deploying Wireshark to capture and analyze network packets in real-time. Focused on thwarting password sniffing—a

DOI: 10.4018/979-8-3693-9225-6.ch009

common tactic used by adversaries to intercept and decrypt sensitive data, including login credentials. Wireshark enables readers to identify and counter common password-sniffing techniques. The chapter also covers proactive steps like adopting secure protocols, encryption algorithms, and best password management practices.

1. INTRODUCTION

Wireshark stands as a prevalent open-source network protocol analyzer, enabling users to capture and actively examine real-time traffic on computer networks. Its utility extends to network troubleshooting, analysis, software and protocol development, and educational purposes. Thanks to its support for numerous protocols, Wireshark serves as a versatile solution for scrutinizing network traffic across different layers of the OSI model. Coupled with its intuitive graphical user interface and robust features, Wire Shark remains a preferred choice for network professionals, enthusiasts, and research

Wireshark serves a variety of purposes such as diagnosing performance problems in networks. Cybersecurity experts frequently employ Wireshark for tracing connections, inspecting potentially suspicious network transactions and detecting spikes in network activity. It's considered an essential component of any IT professional's arsenal, provided they possess the necessary expertise to leverage its capabilities effectively. Wireshark is a powerful tool that includes troubleshooting of network, security, protocol and forensic analysis, monitoring of network traffic, education and training.

The main objective of this book chapter is to make you aware of the basic concepts of protocols used in networks. It covers packet inspection using Wireshark, allowing you to see how data packets are structured and transmitted. You will also learn how to analyze these packets, gaining insights into the data being communicated across the network. Additionally, the chapter addresses password sniffing, illustrating how unsecured passwords can be intercepted and the importance of network security.

Protocols are rules or standards that govern the transmission and reception of data among network devices. They guide the structure, timing, sequence, and error-handling procedures for exchanging data. These protocols can help devices achieve seamless communication and foster interoperability, regardless of their manufacturers or platforms.

Hypertext Transfer Protocol, serves as a cornerstone protocol employed for data transmission across the World Wide Web. It establishes the guidelines for communication between web browsers and servers, enabling the transfer of hypertext documents like web pages. Operating on a request-response mechanism, HTTP entails clients, usually web browsers, sending requests to servers for particular resources, with servers furnishing the requested data, commonly comprising HTML documents, images, stylesheets, or multimedia content. HTTP functions atop TCP/IP and adopts a stateless architecture, where each interaction between client and server stands autonomously, detached from prior exchanges.

Domain Name System (DNS) is an essential protocol employed to convert user-friendly domain names, such as example.com, into computer-readable IP addresses. This system operates as a decentralized name system for online resources, allowing users to access websites, send emails, and perform different online tasks while using recognizable domain names. DNS can achieve this by managing a distributed database that contains domain names and their associated IP addresses, which allows for the resolution of domain names to IP addresses and vice-versa. This protocol is essential for ensuring the smooth navigation of the Internet and the effective routing of network traffic.

Simple Mail Transfer Protocol serves as a core protocol that regulates the transfer of email messages over networks. It manages the flow of emails between mail servers, facilitating the transmission of messages from senders to recipients. Operating within a client-server framework, SMTP involves communication between email clients and SMTP servers to dispatch outgoing messages. Subsequently, these servers forward the messages to designated destination servers based on recipient email addresses. SMTP holds a pivotal position in email communication, guaranteeing the dependable delivery of messages across the Internet.

The remaining section of the chapter is organized as follows. Section 2 elaborates literature review about the importance of Wireshark. Packet Inspection using Wireshark is highlighted in section 3. Password sniffing using Wireshark is described in Section 4. Section 5 discusses the Conclusion and Future Enhancement.

2. LITERATURE REVIEW

A literature review of Wireshark is crucial because it provides a comprehensive understanding of how this network protocol analyzer has been utilized and studied in various contexts. By examining existing research, it identifies how Wireshark has contributed to network troubleshooting, security analysis, and educational purposes. It highlights best practices, common challenges, and innovative applications, helping to inform and improve future use and development of the tool. Additionally, it uncovers gaps in the current literature, guiding new research directions and enhancing the overall knowledge base related to network analysis and cybersecurity.

This paper demonstrates Wireshark's functionality as a network sniffing tool through an experimental setup that showcases its efficiency in detecting malicious packets. Real-time network testing analyzed by Wireshark highlights its capabilities, suggesting its potential development into a robust intrusion detection system. The paper emphasizes Wireshark's role as a network protocol analyzer and its flexibility as an open-source utility, allowing developers to enhance it with additional intrusion detection features. (Banerjee et al., 2010)

The increasing number and variety of attacks on networked computer systems have highlighted the critical need for robust network security. Today, network administrators must be able to investigate and analyze network traffic to understand ongoing activities and respond swiftly to identify threats. Wireshark, an effective open-source tool for studying network packets and their behavior, plays a crucial role in this process. It can be used to identify and categorize different types of attack signatures. This paper aims to demonstrate how Wireshark is applied in diagnosing network protocols and uncovering traditional network attacks such as port scanning, covert FTP and IRC channels, ICMP-based attacks, and Bit Torrent-driven denial-of-service attacks. Additionally, the case studies presented illustrate how Wireshark can be utilized to identify emerging attack vectors. (Ndatinya et al., 2015)

Recent advances in telecommunication technology have spotlighted the Internet of Things (IoT), which connects objects via the Internet, predicting an era where numerous devices form extensive networks. As wireless network technology advances, 5G networks are surpassing 2.4G frequencies, with mobile operators commercializing 5G. This development allows for quicker and more reliable wireless connections, yet wireless networks remain vulnerable to attacks. Network forensics, which analyses network activities and responds to attacks through packet analysis, is essential. This paper utilizes software (Wireshark) and hardware (Observer) to collect and analyze packets, comparing the performance of each tool in packet collection and analysis. (Kim et al., 2020)

This paper addresses the increase in the prevalence of network security threats and attacks that have spurred extensive studies in network forensics. Data collected in networked systems is typically used to investigate these security threats. Packet analysis, a key network security technique, focuses on studying insecure protocols. To aid forensic investigations and combat security and privacy threats, we conducted an active inspection of network packets on a Bit Torrent client. This paper proposes a method for capturing and analyzing network packets using Wireshark. Monitoring, capturing, and analyzing P2P network traffic demonstrated that the proposed technique successfully identified threat sources and locations, providing credible digital evidence for forensic investigations. (Nusa, 2020)

This paper explains the basics of the Internet of Things (IoT), covers the different types of attacks that can target IOT systems, and suggests ways to protect against these threats. It looks at various IOT devices and how they're used, along with the security issues they face and how to prevent them. (Jani & Chaubey, 2020)

The study shows that cybersecurity threats are constantly changing and can affect businesses of any size. To keep cloud computing secure, it's important to protect the underlying virtualization systems and use strong tools for spotting and handling threats. The study looks into different cybersecurity problems and their solutions, including a new 'Flush+Flush' method for detecting attacks in virtualized environments. (Tank et al., 2020)

This study shows the shortcomings of cryptography, its weaknesses, and its preventive measures. Quantum Cryptography explores the latest breakthroughs in quantum cryptography and its impact on cybersecurity. (Chaubey, 2020)

Nowadays, our dependence on the internet leads to various intrusions. To detect these, we need intrusion detection tools that work without user involvement. An Intrusion Detection System (IDS) analyses intrusion to ensure secure data transmission. Wireshark, a popular packet analysis tool, can intercept and analyze encrypted network traffic, identifying attacks like DoS and DDoS. SNORT captures live internet packets with predefined rules and alerts users if no match is found. Using a router for precise data flow, it generates a log file of captured packets. This log is then analyzed by Wireshark, detailing packet flow, traffic, TCP errors, and delta time. (Jain, 2021)

The study introduces the Flooding attacks' significance is burgeoning, prompting innovative network architecture like software-defined networking (SDN). SDN's advent shifted networking from hardware to software, offering manageability, cost-effectiveness, and adaptability. Its role in security, gathering network data, and creating attack detection frameworks is remarkable. A real-time case study within SDN analyses network statistics under normal and attack scenarios. Traffic analysis, graphically depicting parameters like round trip time and throughput, illuminates the importance of network metrics in detecting DDoS attacks. This preliminary study culminates in a conceptual model for DDoS detection within SDN, showcasing its potential in addressing evolving security challenges. (Verghese, 2021)

In this paper the author had gone through the Packet analysis, also known as packet sniffing or protocol analysis, which is a key technique in network forensics. It involves capturing and interpreting live network data to understand network activities. This method can detect signs of malicious behavior, data breaches, unauthorized access, malware infections, and intrusion attempts. Packet analysis allows the reconstruction of image files, documents, and email attachments sent over the network. Typically performed using a packet sniffer, such as the open-source tool Wireshark, it helps identify and categorize attack signatures. This paper demonstrates how Wireshark aids in network protocol diagnosis and identifies basic indicators of malware compromise. (Dodiya, 2022)

In the 1970s, cellular networks' roaming interconnections were designed for a few trusted parties, so security was not a major concern. Today, the decades-old SS7 (Signalling System No. 7) is still widely used, despite being vulnerable due to deregulation, expansion, and integration with IP-based LTE networks. SS7's inability to verify subscriber locations, and identities, and filter illegitimate messages exposes it to attacks like call interception, tracking, and denial of service. While LTE and Diameter protocols offer better security, they still have flaws. This research introduces a methodology to detect anomalies in SS7 traffic using Wireshark and Snort IDS, highlighting SS7's severe vulnerabilities. (Afzal, 2022)

This paper introduces the Sniffers, which have the highest capacity for monitoring and validating internet traffic, playing a crucial role in managing computer networks efficiently. They control, observe, and record passwords for telnet, user login, and FTP connections without altering them, inspecting packets as they traverse the network. Network administrators use sniffers to decode captured packets, extracting relevant information. While beneficial for organizations, hackers also use sniffers for malicious activities, accessing unauthorized data. This research paper aims to develop and implement a new sniffer tool called Sniffit, introducing protocols for packet analysis. Results show that Sniffit creates an encoded packet database and displays relevant data based on user requests. (Rajawa, 2022)

This paper addresses Data security, which is crucial for network communication and software security. HTTP, commonly used for website access, is a key internet protocol. On LMS websites, students access lecture materials, discussion forums, and assignments. Wireshark analyses network protocols, logging and displaying packet data. This study uses Wireshark to sniff LMS traffic and identify vulnerabilities. Results show that LMS using HTTP lack encryption, posing security risks. Recommendations include using HTTPS, implementing Multi-Factor Authentication, monitoring website logs, and managing passwords. Suggested password management includes regular changes, character standardization, and hashing. Implementing these measures will enhance LMS security and reduce data communication risks. (Jaya, 2022)

In this paper, the author discussed Wireshark, a leading network analysis software, that acts as the digital investigator in the virtual domain. It captures and analyses data packets in real-time, providing exceptional precision and depth. Over four weeks of network analysis with Wireshark, it systematically reveals the intricacies of each protocol, accumulating a valuable database of information on data packet behavior. In the contemporary digital sphere, Wireshark stands as an essential instrument for investigators and analysts delving into the complexities of internet-based operations. (Soepeno, 2023)

The study introduces that in the digitally connected world, the security of Local Area Networks (LANs) is increasingly at risk. Cybersecurity is the process designed to protect networks from various external attacks. This article explores LAN threat scenarios, particularly focusing on extracting credentials by capturing Hypertext Transfer Protocol (HTTP) packets. While LANs are often considered secure, they can have vulnerabilities. Attackers can connect to a LAN and use tools like Wireshark to exploit HTTP weaknesses to obtain login credentials. Attackers may seek IP addresses, email addresses, and financial details through network traffic analysis. Wireshark captures and analyses protocols such as HTTP, Address Resolution Protocol (ARP), and Transmission Control Protocol (TCP). To secure LANs, measures like data encryption, firewalls, IDS/IPS, network segmentation, Ethernet cables, HTTPS, and multifactor authentication should be implemented. Monitoring network traffic, applying port security, and allowing only registered MAC addresses in access points further enhance LAN security and mitigate cybersecurity threats. Regular monitoring of networks and packet-capturing tools improves LAN security. (Hussain, 2024)

The internet is essential for students and office employees, increasing traffic and workload on ISP servers, especially in areas with limited access. VSAT is recommended for remote internet access due to its wide coverage. Agencies and companies should implement and monitor VSAT service quality to ensure efficient data flow. Using Wireshark, network feasibility can be analyzed by measuring jitter, packet loss, delay, and throughput. The study successfully analyzed VSAT network feasibility with Wireshark, concluding that VSAT is suitable for implementation at SD 65. These results aid in easier maintenance and repair by providing technicians with valuable diagnostic data. (Yusuf, 2024)

According to the Hamidah, Indonesia has embraced 4G technology, a fast and widely available internet network that benefits various sectors, including agriculture, social, cultural, economic, and education. The need for internet connectivity became critical from 2020 to early 2022 to stay productive during the COVID-19 pandemic, especially for online education. An Najiyah Surabaya High School requires reliable internet access to support its online learning. The school employs Quality of Service (QoS) to monitor network quality and data traffic, focusing on packet loss, throughput, and delay. Analysis showed excellent network quality, with 2.6 Mbps throughput, 0% packet loss, and 0.12 ms delay, indicating optimal performance for online activities. (Hamidah, 2024)

This paper introduces the monitoring and analyzing network traffic is crucial in cybersecurity. Network packet sniffing, which captures and inspects data packets, is essential for understanding network behavior, identifying vulnerabilities, and enhancing security. This study examines packet sniffing's role in modern cybersecurity, detailing its methodologies and applications. It highlights packet sniffing's effectiveness as a proactive security tool while addressing ethical concerns about user privacy and data protection. Legal aspects governing packet sniffing are also explored to ensure regulatory compliance. Through case studies and real-world examples, the research demonstrates how packet sniffing can detect network anomalies, prevent malicious activities, and strengthen network infrastructures, providing cybersecurity practitioners with valuable insights. (Shaw, 2024)

In this paper packet sniffing involves monitoring network traffic by intercepting each packet as it traverses the network. It serves both administrative and potentially malicious purposes. As technology advances, networks expand, leading to increased traffic. Hence, monitoring network activity and user actions is crucial for smooth operations. However, overseeing large networks is complex due to the volume of packets. Packet sniffing becomes invaluable here, enabling administrators to pinpoint network weaknesses. This paper delves into packet sniffing's applications, from cybersecurity to ethical monitoring. By employing a packet sniffer, network traffic is captured and analyzed, with protocols like TCP, IP, and UDP implemented and filtered accordingly. (Paravathi, 2024)

2.1 Difference Between Wireshark Packet Analyzer and Cisco Packet Tracker

To analyze the features of Wireshark, another packet analysis tool, namely Cisco Packet Tracer, is compared with it (Čabarkapa, 2015) and a comparison is given in Table 1. This comparison helps to highlight the strengths and limitations of each tool, providing a clearer understanding of its capabilities and applications in network analysis and troubleshooting.

Table 1. Wireshark vs Cisco Packet Tracer

Criteria	Wireshark Packet Analyser	Cisco Packet Tracer
Purpose	Tool for examining and dissecting network data packets.	Simulation platform for constructing and simulating network setups.
Functionality	Offers in-depth insights into network activity and security threats.	Enables network layout design and configuration emulation.
Main Use Cases	Diagnosing network issues, analyzing traffic patterns, and security audits.	Learning network architecture, configuring virtual networks, and simulations.
Target Audience	Network admins, security analysts, and professionals in data analysis.	Students, educators, and aspiring network engineers seeking practical training.
Features	Robust packet analysis, filtering, and decryption capabilities.	Device emulation, topology design, Cisco device replication.
Compatibility	Compatible with various OS (Windows, macOS, Linux).	Available on Windows and macOS platforms.

continued on following page

Table 1. Continued

Criteria	Wireshark Packet Analyser	Cisco Packet Tracer
Cost	Open-source and free.	Free for educational purposes; commercial use requires a Cisco subscription.
Learning Curve	Requires moderate to advanced understanding of networking protocols.	Designed for beginners, with guided exercises and simplified interfaces.
Real-world Application	Utilized for professional network troubleshooting and security audits.	Implemented in educational environments for practical networking training.
Scalability	Scales effectively for large-scale network analysis and auditing.	Limited scalability due to its educational focus and simulated environments.

Although the Packet tracer is restricted to its simulated environment and utilized for training purposes. Its commercial usage requires a paid subscription. However, Wire Shark is freely available and it has a wider scalability. Due to its huge features, we utilize it in our research work.

3. PACKET INSPECTION USING WIRESHARK

The Fundamental steps for conducting basic packet inspection using Wireshark are given below:

1. **Get Wireshark**: First, download and install Wireshark from the official website if you haven't already.
2. **Launch the Program**: After installation, open Wireshark. Depending on your system, you might require administrative privileges to capture network data.
3. **Choose the Network Interface**: From the main Wireshark interface, select the network interface you intend to capture packets from, whether it's Ethernet, Wi-Fi, or another interface.
4. **Commence Packet Capture**: Click on the chosen interface and hit the "Start" button to commence capturing packets.
5. **Analyse the Packets**: Wireshark will exhibit captured packets in real time as they traverse the selected interface. You'll observe various details like source and destination IP addresses, protocols, packet length, and timestamps.
6. **Apply Packet Filters**: Utilize Wireshark's robust filtering options to zero in on specific packet types or traffic. Apply filters based on protocols, IP addresses, port numbers, etc., to streamline your analysis.

7. **Examine Individual Packets**: Click on any packet within the list to inspect detailed information in the packet inspection panel at the bottom of the Wireshark window. Here, you can scrutinize packet headers, payload, and other pertinent data.
8. **Track TCP/UDP Streams**: Wireshark facilitates tracking TCP or UDP streams, simplifying the analysis of communication between distinct hosts. Right-click on a packet and choose "Follow TCP Stream" or "Follow UDP Stream" to view the complete conversation.
9. **Cease Packet Capture**: When you've accumulated adequate data or concluded your analysis, hit the "Stop" button to halt packet capture.
10. **Save or Export Findings**: Preserve your captured packets for future reference or export them in diverse formats for sharing or further examination.

Figure 1 depicts the homepage of Wire Shark Software where all the connected networks to the system are shown.

Figure 1. Home page of Wireshark network analyzer

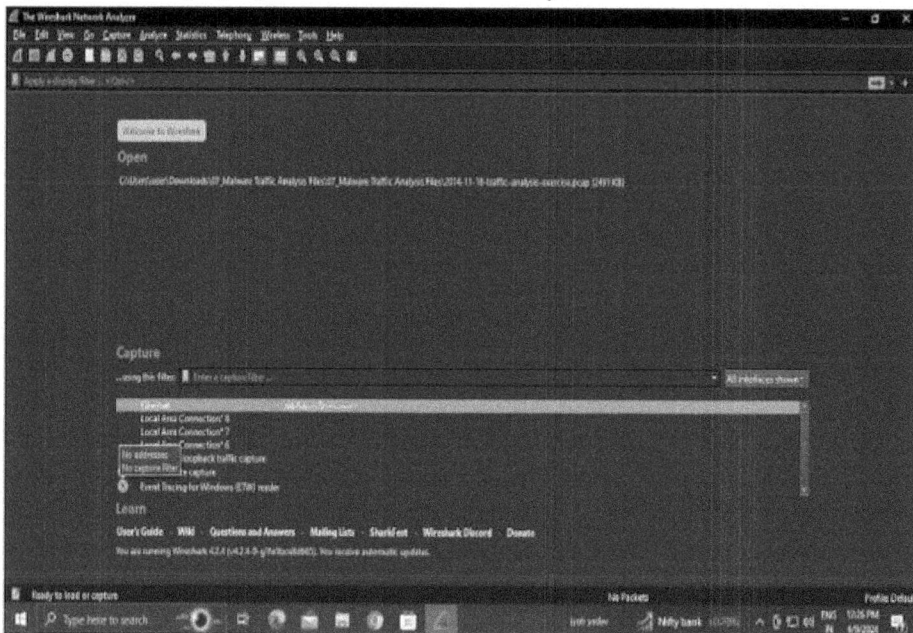

Figure 2 shows the current packet information which includes source ip address, destination IP address, protocol TCP, length size 60, and other information.

Figure 2. Representation of current packet information and raw data

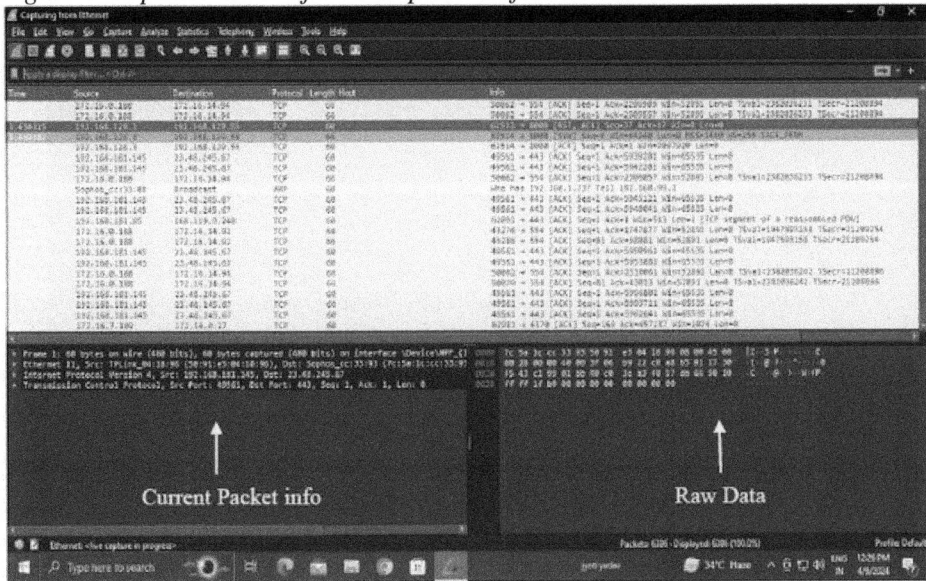

Figure 3 illustrates that if you want to obtain information about a specific IP address used for accessing a website, you should apply the HTTP filter and analyze the results. This filtering will isolate the relevant traffic, making it easier to identify and examine the interactions involving that particular IP address.

Figure 3. Selecting the network HTTP by applying the filter

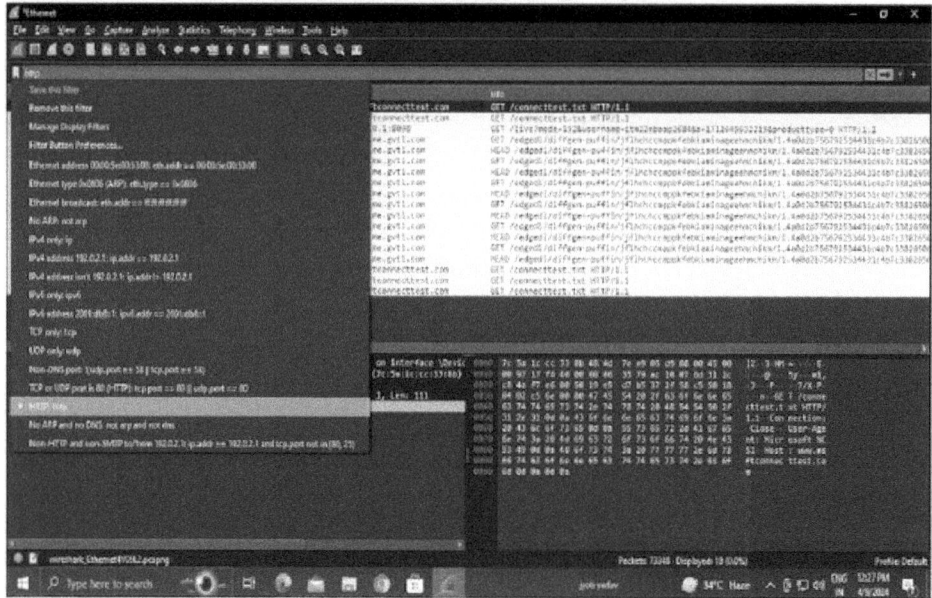

Figure 4. Packet information

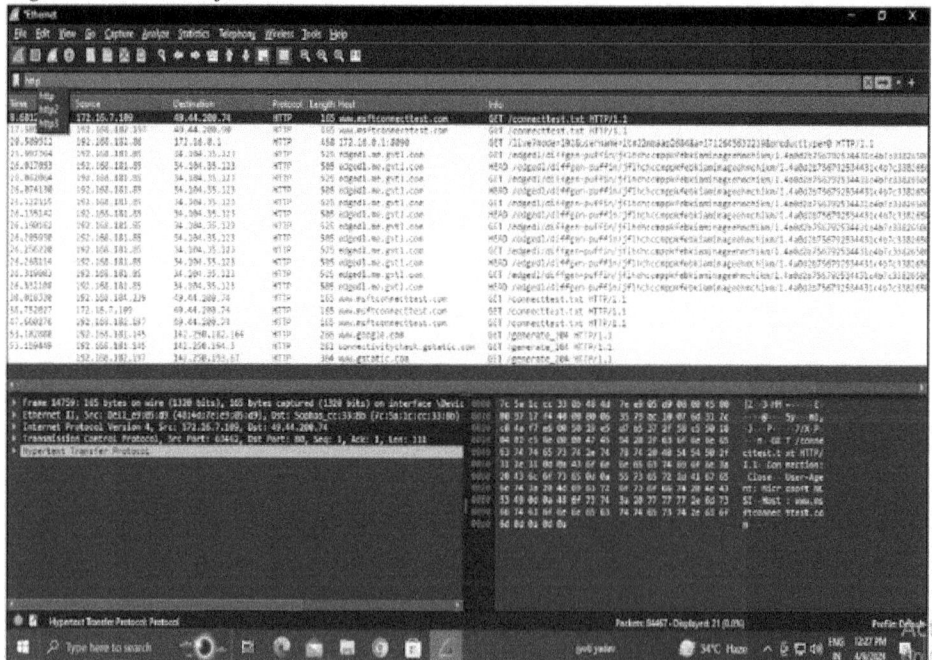

Utilizing Wireshark to capture passwords is not only morally questionable but also likely unlawful, as it entails intercepting confidential information without consent. Wireshark is a robust network protocol analyzer crafted for lawful network diagnostics, analysis, and educational endeavors. Employing Wireshark for password interception without proper authorization contravenes privacy and security statutes and protocols.

When safeguarding your network, it's imperative to implement robust security measures, such as encrypted connections (e.g., HTTPS) and robust authentication protocols (e.g., multi-factor authentication), rather than resorting to illicit password capture.

Should you possess legitimate reasons for monitoring network traffic, ensure explicit consent from all involved parties and compliance with relevant laws and regulations. Unauthorized interception of passwords or any sensitive data is not only unethical but also illegal, carrying potentially severe repercussions.

4. PASSWORD SNIFFING USING WIRESHARK

Here, we will explore the process of capturing passwords using the Wireshark network capture analyzer and examine the results of each step.

Step 1: To begin, launch your Wireshark tool on either your Windows system or within a Linux virtual machine, and commence network capture. For instance, let's assume I'm capturing my Wi-Fi network traffic. Figure 5 shows the home page of the network packet analyzer.

Figure 5. Home page of network packet analyzer

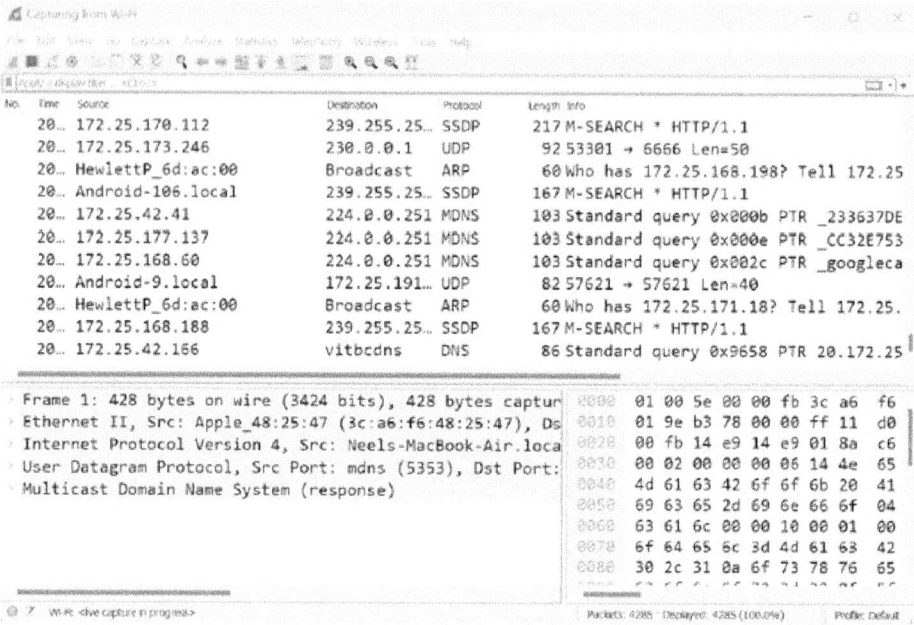

Step 2: Once packet capturing has commenced, proceed to the website and log in with your credentials, as depicted in Figure 6.

Figure 6. Login page of Acunetix Web Vulnerability Scanner

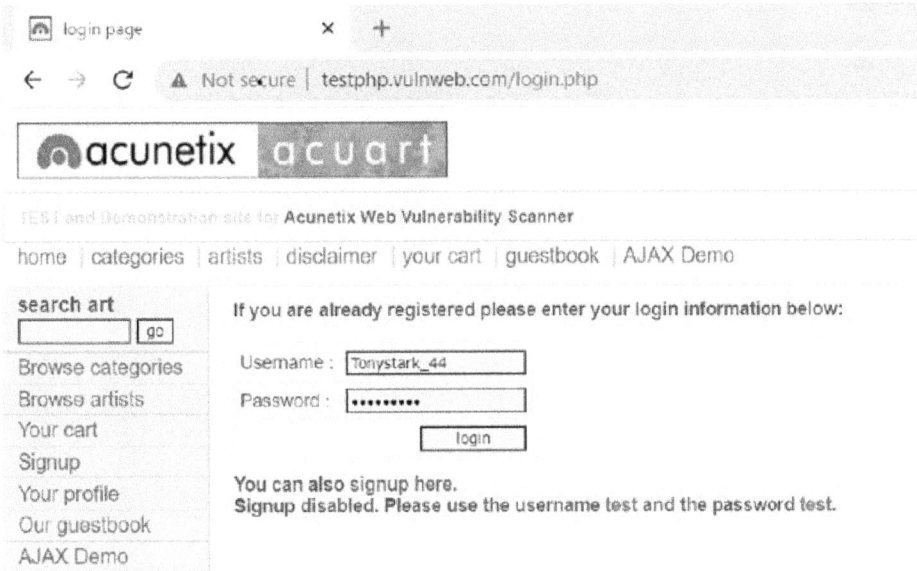

Step 3: After successfully entering the login credentials, we'll proceed to capture the password in Wireshark. To do so, we use specific filters needed to identify login credentials during packet capture.

Step 4: Wireshark has captured various packets, but our focus is on locating HTTP packets. Therefore, we apply a specific command in the display filter bar to isolate all the captured HTTP packets, as illustrated in Figure 7 the green bar indicating the filter application.

Figure 7. Represents all captured HTTP packets

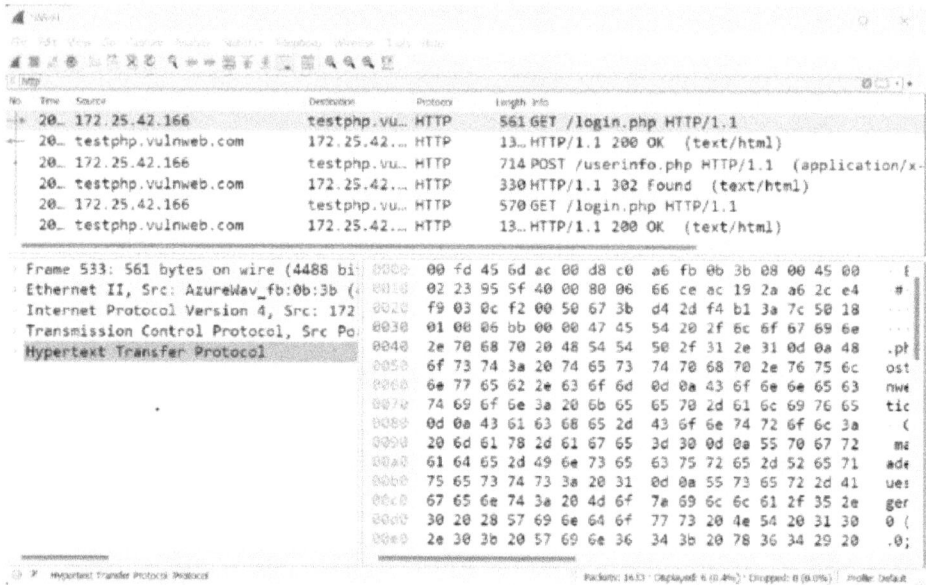

Step 5: Among the captured HTTP packets, our attention is directed towards identifying the form data submitted by the user on the website. To achieve this, we employ a distinct filter.

We're aware that there are primarily two methods utilized for submitting form data from web pages, such as login forms, to the server. These methods include: GET and POST.

Step 6: To begin, in our quest to ascertain the credentials, we initially opt for the first method and implement a filter for the GET methods, as depicted below.

http.request.method == "GET"

Figure 8. Implemented filter for GET method

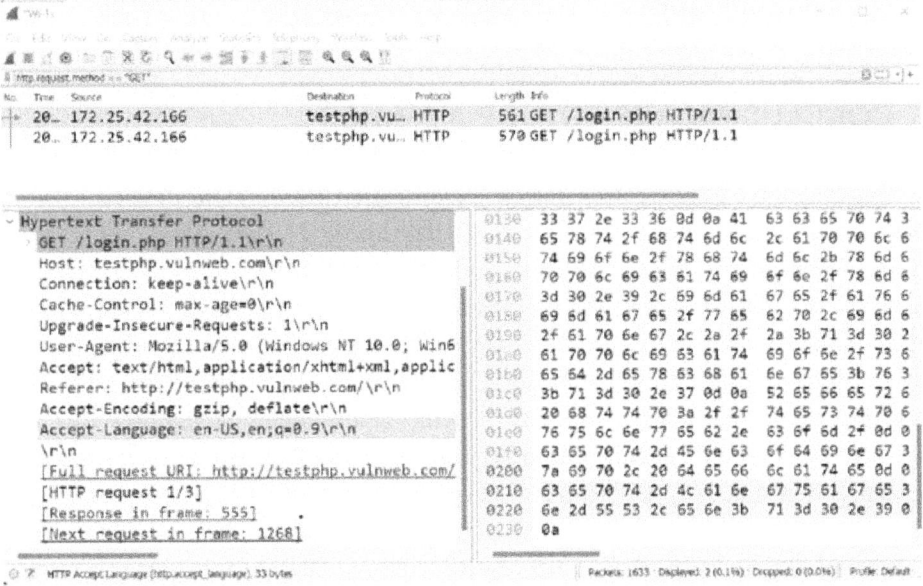

Step 7: If upon inspecting the GET method we fail to locate the form data, our next step involves attempting the POST method. We accomplish this by applying a filter in Wireshark, as demonstrated in figure 9.

http.request.method == "POST"

Figure 9. Implemented filter for POST method

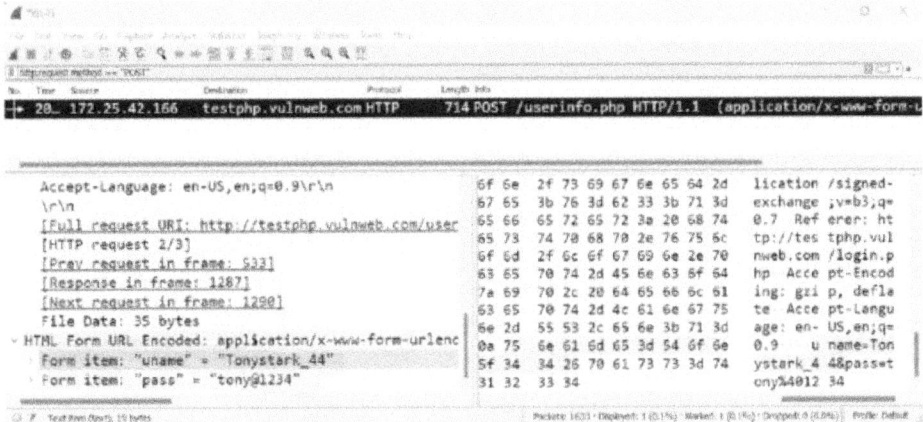

Figure 9 highlights that username is "Tonystark_44" and password is "tony@1234". It is clearly visible and anyone can capture it easily.

5. CONCLUSION AND FUTURE AVENUES

Wireshark is a powerful tool that can give detailed information about each packet of data, including the headers and the actual data inside (Mishra, 2024). The research is unique because it combines theory with hands-on practice to use Wireshark for network security. This contribution makes the learning experience more complete. Additionally, graphical tools is used to visualize and understand network traffic and trends. In conclusion, this chapter serves as an invaluable resource for individuals tasked with safeguarding network infrastructure against malicious entities. By amalgamating theoretical insights with practical exercises, it empowers readers to fully leverage Wireshark's capabilities in fortifying their networks against cyber threats, thereby ensuring the resilience of their digital assets. Further ARP poisoning, Cross-Site Request Forgery (CSRF), Cross-Site Scripting and SQL Injection attacks will be demonstrated through Wireshark in the near future.

REFERENCES

Afzal, R., & Murugesan, R. K. (2022). Implementation of a malicious traffic filter using snort and wireshark as a proof of concept to enhance mobile network security. *Journal of Telecommunications and Information Technology*, (1).

Banerjee, U., Vashishtha, A., & Saxena, M. (2010). Evaluation of the Capabilities of WireShark as a tool for Intrusion Detection. *International Journal of Computer Applications*, 6(7), 1–5. DOI: 10.5120/1092-1427

Čabarkapa, D. (2015). Application of Cisco Packet Tracer 6.2 in teaching of advanced computer networks. *Proceddings of the Information Technology and Development of Education ITRO, 153*.

Chaubey, N. K., & Prajapati, B. B. (Eds.). (2020). *Quantum Cryptography and the Future of Cyber Security*. IGI Global. DOI: 10.4018/978-1-7998-2253-0

Dodiya, B., & Singh, U. K. (2022). Malicious Traffic analysis using Wireshark by collection of Indicators of Compromise. *International Journal of Computer Applications*, 183(53), 1–6. DOI: 10.5120/ijca2022921876

Hamidah, M. N., Tias, R. F., & Zainal, R. F. (2024). Quality of Service (QoS) Analysis using Wireshark on the LAN Network at An Najiyah High School Surabaya. *Jurnal Mandiri IT*, 12(4), 222–228.

Hussain, A., Hussain, A., Qadri, S., Razzaq, A., Nazir, H., & Ullah, M. S. (2024). Enhancing LAN Security by Mitigating Credential Threats via HTTP Packet Analysis with Wireshark. *Journal of Computing & Biomedical Informatics*, 6(02), 433–440.

Jain, G., & Anubha, . (2021, March). Application of snort and wireshark in network traffic analysis. []. IOP Publishing.]. *IOP Conference Series. Materials Science and Engineering*, 1119(1), 012007. DOI: 10.1088/1757-899X/1119/1/012007

Jani, K. A., & Chaubey, N. (2020). IoT and cyber security: introduction, attacks, and preventive steps. In *Quantum Cryptography and the Future of Cyber Security* (pp. 203–235). IGI Global. DOI: 10.4018/978-1-7998-2253-0.ch010

Jaya, I. K. N. A., Dewi, I. A. U., & Mahendra, G. S. (2022). Implementation of Wireshark Application in Data Security Analysis on LMS Website. *Journal of Computer Networks. Architecture and High Performance Computing*, 4(1), 79–86. DOI: 10.47709/cnahpc.v4i1.1345

Kim, H., Lee, H., & Lim, H. (2020, February). Performance of packet analysis between observer and wireshark. In *2020 22nd International Conference on Advanced Communication Technology (ICACT)* (pp. 268-271). IEEE. DOI: 10.23919/ICACT48636.2020.9061452

Mishra, A., Mishra, S., & Panday, S. (2024). Security Analysis of Password-based Authenticated Key Exchange Protocols.

Musa, A. (2020). Forensic analysis of peer-to-peer network traffic with Wireshark. *Journal of Science and Technology*, 1(2), 92–99.

Ndatinya, V., Xiao, Z., Manepalli, V. R., Meng, K., & Xiao, Y. (2015). Network forensics analysis using Wireshark. *International Journal of Security and Networks*, 10(2), 91–106. DOI: 10.1504/IJSN.2015.070421

Paravathi, C., Roshini, D., & Nayak, S. S. (2024). Packet Sniffing. *International Journal of Engineering and Management Research*, 14(1), 71–76.

Rajawat, S. S., Khatri, P., & Surange, G. (2022, December). Sniffit: A Packet Sniffing Tool Using Wireshark. In *International Conference on Communication, Networks and Computing* (pp. 203-212). Cham: Springer Nature Switzerland.

Shaw, R., & Parveen, S. (2024, March). Literature Review on Packet Sniffing: Essential for Cybersecurity & Network Security. In *2024 5th International Conference on Intelligent Communication Technologies and Virtual Mobile Networks (ICICV)* (pp. 715-719). IEEE.

Soepeno, R. A. A. P. (2023). Wireshark: An Effective Tool for Network Analysis.

Tank, D. M., Aggarwal, A., & Chaubey, N. K. (2020). Cyber security aspects of virtualization in cloud computing environments: analyzing virtualization-specific cyber security risks. In *Quantum Cryptography and the Future of Cyber Security* (pp. 283–299). IGI Global. DOI: 10.4018/978-1-7998-2253-0.ch013

Varghese, J. E., & Muniyal, B. (2021). A pilot study in software-defined networking using wireshark for analyzing network parameters to detect DDoS attacks. In *Information and Communication Technology for Competitive Strategies (ICTCS 2020) Intelligent Strategies for ICT* (pp. 475-487). Springer Singapore. DOI: 10.1007/978-981-16-0882-7_41

Yusuf, A., Khairil, K., & Rohmawan, E. P. (2024). AN ANALYSIS OF SERVICE QUALITY ON VSAT NETWORK USING WIRESHARK. *JURNAL MEDIA INFOTAMA*, 20(1), 73–78.

Chapter 10
The Silent Threat:
Safeguarding Against PDF-Based Malware With Intelligent Detection

Ravi Kirtivadan Sheth
https://orcid.org/0009-0009-4010-9274
Rashtriya Raksha University, India

Chandresh D. Parekha
https://orcid.org/0009-0002-6722-9224
Rashtriya Raksha University, India

ABSTRACT

Given the fact that today's world is inundated with PDF files in personals and business relationships, the danger of bad-intentioned activity within these what look-like innocent documents has risen drastically. A threat that has been significant to internet security for the past years is the known PDF malware. PDF malware presents a big problem because it can hide within the complicated makeup of PDF files. These files can contain many types of content, including text, images, text, and hidden objects. These complications give hackers more opportunities to hide their malicious code that bypasses traditional antivirus software. The objective of this chapter was to develop a classification-based machine learning algorithm for detecting PDF malware and it get succeeded with an impressive overall accuracy of 99.3% by using a random forest classifier This important achievement and the ability of machine learning algorithms to detect and neutralize threat-based PDFs is also highlighted in this chapter.

DOI: 10.4018/979-8-3693-9225-6.ch010

1. INTRODUCTION

PDFs have long been popular for their portability and reliability. Unlike formats like .doc files, which may display inconsistently across platforms, PDFs ensure consistent rendering across all platforms. Despite their simple appearance, PDFs have a complex underlying structure, comprising a mix of binary and ASCII data. In fact, PDFs can be thought of as a programming language in their own right, capable of executing code when viewed. Furthermore, PDFs support advanced features like embedded multimedia, JavaScript, and system commands, making them both flexible and efficient. (Martsinkevich et al., 2023), (Issakhani et al., 2022))

Many users see PDFs as simple, unchanging documents, but they are actually capable of much more. The content you see is the result of a program running behind the scenes. While people are getting savvier about the risks of other document formats, like Microsoft Office files with macros, they often overlook similar risks in PDFs (Endignoux, G., 2016), (Elingiusti et al., 2018). Inside the PDF file the predetermined structured is available which enables to reproduce text, images, graphics and interactive elements within its framework. Here is an overview of the basic structure of a PDF file (Martsinkevich et al., 2023), (Endignoux, G., 2016):

> **Header:** PDF file begins with a header that identifies it as a PDF document. Typically, the header section includes the version number of the PDF specification, indicating the specific PDF standard used to create the file.
>
> **Body:** A PDF file's body, which consists of objects in sequence, is essentially the content format. The objects are primary sections in PDF file in some manner may show up text, images, fonts and other main things. Therefore, we should appreciate PDF files for their flexibility, which makes it easier to understand and work with complex information.
>
> **Cross-Reference Table (Xref):** The reference group crosswise can be said to be the most significant element as compare to other features of PDF files. It stores metadata about the location and structure of objects within the file, enabling easy navigation and rapid retrieval of these objects.
>
> **Trailer:** The trailer section provides a comprehensive overview of the entire PDF document by listing key information, including referenced objects, the size of the cross-reference group, and other essential details.
>
> **Objects:** PDFs are constructed by arrangement of objects like form fields and text blocks. The object has a virtual identifier, and each object stores a dictionary that defines the object attributes and a stream or a string that contains the object real data.

Catalog: The catalog is a very precious detail in an electronic fit and finish. It hereby becomes the basis and is referenced by other key root objects, covering documents and outlines, as well as metadata of the document.

Pages: The 'pages' object defines the pages' structural hierarchies as a tree. Every page has thumbnails in which other objects, like content streams, annotations, and resources are directly connected.

Content Streams: Content streams contain the instructions for rendering text, images, and other graphical elements on a page. They are typically encoded using the Portable Document Format (PDF) syntax.

Fonts and Resources: Fonts, images, and other elements that make up the document are usually placed in a "resource" section for future use. For example, such a section contains dictionaries that specify which resources must be utilized the way that is mentioned in Section II.

Annotations: Annotations, for example, links, comments and form fields, are objects that creates interactivity and more information for a PDF document which themselves serve as. On other hand, place names are primarily associated with precise regions of the sheet.

From Figure 1 which originally appeared in (Martsinkevich et al., 2023), (Endignoux, G., 2016) we can get basic knowledge on a structure of a PDF file, which has capability to carry out tasks like parsing, extracting content, and transforming into PDF programmatically. The PDF format has its specification publicly released and software developers around the world can design tools and applications that would work very well with PDF files.

The PDF document comes in handy wherever you want to read, download, or share just one document. Therefore, the general usage of PDF turned it into an enticing target for cybercrime with malware being frequently added to PDF by just climbing over its simple text arrangement. Nowadays, more organizations and individuals rely on the PDF for dissemination of the data with high sensitivity and the most important issue of PDF security has become the protecting the PDFs against hacking.

There are a number of file formats that can be used and one of them is PDF files which are multipurpose and have good compatibility across all platforms; but they have however become a target for malicious villains who use it to take advantage of any loopholes in the system. The hidden scripts like Trojans and the likes utility functions within PDF might be busy firing malicious codes while the exploiters behind might be targeting loopholes in PDF reader applications. The impact can be several-fold, including disclosure of private data as well as that of the entire system, which highlights the need for futureproof security systems.

Figure 1. Basic Structure of PDF file

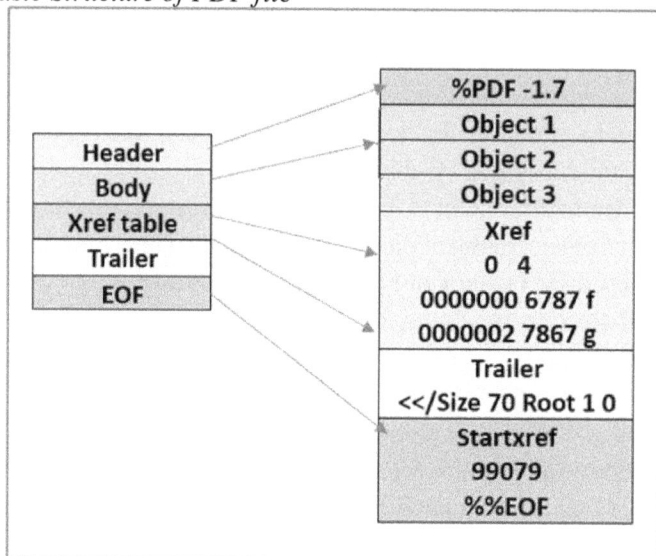

The level of the advancement of the modern cyber danger, and PDF particularly, A recent report from HP Wolf Security reveals a concerning trend: cybercriminals are increasingly using PDFs to spread malware like Wiki Loader, Ursnif, and DarkGate. In Q4 2023, there was a 7% increase in PDF-related threats compared to Q1 of the same year. These threats have evolved from phishing attempts to direct malware distribution through PDF documents. In fact, 11% of the malware analysed in Q4 2023 used PDFs as a delivery method, up from just 4% in Q1. One notable example is a Wiki Loader campaign that used a fake parcel delivery PDF to trick users into installing Ursnif malware (Maundrill, B., 2024).

Malware creators often exploit the ability to use JavaScript within PDF files to run their code. Although this code is usually contained within a sandbox for safety, it can still exploit unpatched vulnerabilities to break out and execute harmful commands on the user's device. Malicious PDFs can contain complex, disguised payloads to avoid detection, or the malware can be downloaded from the internet once the attacker gains control. These dangerous PDFs are distributed through various methods, including drive-by downloads, targeted attacks, or mass email campaigns (Li et al., 2021), (Tzermias et al., 2011). Traditional antivirus software, which relies on signature-based detection, struggles to catch such malwares hidden within PDFs. With the widespread use of PDF files in both personal and professional environments, the risk of malware embedded within them is also increasing. Protecting against malware in PDFs has become a top priority for cybersecurity experts (Li et al., 2020), (Shijo et al., 2015), (Mohammed et al., 2021). This ongoing battle between cybersecurity experts and malware creators highlights the need for smarter detection methods that can distinguish unknown threats from other malicious activities. Not only PDF-based malware, but also modern malware poses a significant threat to all digital devices, including IoT devices, in today's digital landscape (Jani, K. A., & Nirbhay, Chaubey., 2020). The process for malware analysis is very much complex and required high computational encryption and decryption devices. As computers get stronger, modern cryptography's weaknesses are exposed. In such case quantum cryptography is a promising solution, offering robust protection for various applications like online transactions, communication, and more. It is gaining traction among experts, and for good reason – it is the future of secure data exchange (Chaubey, N. K., & Prajapati, B. B., 2020).

In 2020, researchers proposed a novel approach (Tank et al., 2020) for detecting malware based on API function calls. This approach enables the tracing of malware behaviour and suggests that the presence of specific API function calls can indicate the presence of malware (Tank et al., 2020).

The use of intelligent detection methods, which is a very powerful means against software viruses/malware. It combines existing cutting-edge methods of intelligent recognition, containing machine learning models and other types of advanced techniques. Through the analysis of capabilities and finding vulnerabilities using these techniques, it will be possible to provide a crucial contribution to the improvement of cybersecurity solutions essentially designed to counter the emerging challenges in the PDF downloading environment (Rieck et al., 2011), (Li et al., 2020).

Basically, intelligent detection techniques employ modern technologies, comprising machine learning, artificial intelligence, and threat-behaviour science, to find any suggestion of malicious behavioural tendencies. As more intricate devices and techniques come into existence, cybercriminals develop their malicious traits and get closer to the continually changing prospect of the cyber threat. To stay ahead of the evolving threat landscape, move beyond static signatures and use dynamic analysis. Machine-learning models trained on varied data sets will have the ability to differentiate even the smallest indicators of this malware just by its PDF basis, providing a superior blocking feature.

In the domain of machine learning-based techniques, there are two types of features used for malware detection: static and dynamic. Understanding the interplay between dynamic and static features in PDF files is crucial for developing applications that interact with and manipulate PDF content effectively. Whether extracting text, images, or interactive elements, developers need to consider both static and dynamic aspects of PDFs to create comprehensive solutions (Al-Haija et al., 2022), (Li et al., 2021).

While dynamic features have shown potential in detecting malware in PDF files, they are not exclusive to these files, and implementing a secure sandbox environment adds complexity to the detection process. Therefore, our approach primarily utilizes static features. The use of dynamic and static features requires extensive expertise in feature extraction. However, our goal is to leverage features specific to PDF files that do not require significant domain knowledge (Liu, R., & Nicholas, C., 2023), (Li et al., 2019), (He et al., 2020).

In the forthcoming sections of the paper, we will offer a detailed review of the present intelligent instruments for PDF malware detection. This article scrutinizes several methods, namely machine learning algorithms and behavioural analysis frameworks. Each section will highlight the effectiveness of these methods and the possible roles they could play in a strategic defence. Consequently, the main goal of this research is to offer guidance for cybersecurity experts, researchers, and organizations fighting against malware in PDF files.

2. LITERATURE REVIEW

The literature on safeguarding against PDF-based malware with intelligent detection reflects a dynamic and evolving field. Various models have been used, along with static, dynamic, and hybrid methods. The following table 1 provides a brief overview of the work carried out so far in this domain, along with notable observations. Deep learning methods, such as Deep Neural Networks (DNN), are widely used in academic and industrial settings (Al-Haija et al., 2022). They are applied in fields like malware analysis. DNNs excel in demanding tasks like speech recognition, natural language processing, and image recognition. However, it has been shown that these systems can struggle with sophisticated evasion techniques in hostile environments (Li et al., 2021).

In Falah et al. (2020), the authors developed a method to identify a set of features from existing tools and create new features. This improves PDF malware detection and extends the lifespan of current analysis and detection technologies. In Li et al. (2020), a new evasion technique using a feature vector generative adversarial network (fvGAN) was introduced to target learning-based malware classifiers. This method creates adversarial feature vectors in the feature space using fvGAN and then transforms them into actual adversarial malware samples. Results show that the fvGAN model achieves a high evasion rate quickly. Additionally, the proposed technique outperforms two existing attack algorithms, Mimicry and GD-KDE, in terms of evasion rate and execution cost. Authors Shijo, P. V., & Salim, A. (2015) has proposed Integrated static and dynamic analysis for malware detection. This approach leveraging the advantages of static as well as the dynamic analysis.

In Li et al. (2019), the study highlights the vulnerability of the typical K-nearest neighbour (KNN) classification algorithm in adversarial settings. Using the gradient-descent attack method, the authors alter malicious samples in the test set to avoid detection by the classifier. They propose a method where these adversarial samples are added to the training set, and a new KNN classifier is created and tested for robustness against different attack strengths. The results show that including adversarial samples produced by gradient-descent attacks in the training set significantly enhances the robustness of the KNN classifier without affecting its overall performance. In Smutz, C., & Stavrou, A. (2016), the authors introduce a new method to identify data issues in ensemble classifiers. They find that when individual classifier votes conflict during detection, the ensemble classifier's prediction can be incorrect. Their method, called ensemble classifier mutual agreement analysis, allows for the detection of various types of classifier evasions without requiring additional external ground truth.

In M. Zubair Shafiq et al. (2008), the authors introduced a new embedded malware detection system using statistical anomaly detection techniques. It's the first method to pinpoint where the infection is within a file. Their Markov n-gram detector performs better than existing detectors in detecting malware. When combined with current antivirus software, it offers very low false-positive rates because it can find embedded malware. In He et al. (2020), the author systematically introduces key principles for feature selection to minimize evasion potential while maintaining high accuracy. These guidelines are applied to extract features and train a two-stage classifier. Experimental results show that our model excels in accuracy, generalization, and robustness. It can effectively distinguish between vulnerabilities used in malicious files. Table 1 gives the comprehensive survey on PDF-based Malware detection techniques.

Table 1. Overview of literature survey on PDF-based malware detection technique

Author/s	Machine Learning/ Deep Learning Model	Dataset	Overall Observation
Bilal Sowan et al. (2024)	Hybrid RF-KNN	Evasive-PDFMal2022	■ A combination of Random Forest and KNN has been utilized. Further work can be done to enhance the accuracy of the model.
Liu, R., & Nicholas, C. (2023)	XGBoost, Navie Bayes, Multi-Layer Perceptron, etc.	Contagio dataset	■ This work is aimed to address the need of finding small features set without needing too much domain knowledge of the PDF file.
Muhammad Binsawad, (2024)	Logistic Model Trees	Canadian Institute for Cybersecurity (UNB CIC) at the University of New Brunswick	■ Extensive feature selection methods have been used ■ Overall accuracy is 97.5% which can be improved. ■ Feature selection process is very much complex and time consuming
Al-Haija et al. (2022)	Optimizable Decision Tree	Evasive-PDFMal2022	■ Static Method is used ■ Time-consuming due to insertion and deletion of the tree
Li et al. (2021)	Supervised ML	Created Dataset	■ Hybrid Method is used ■ Increase the efficiency when run independently ■ Time consuming
Issakhani et al. (2022)	Base and Meta Learner	Evasive PDF Dataset	■ Static Method is used ■ Accuracy can be improved.
Falah et al. (2020)	RF, C5.0 (DT), and SVM (2 class)	Virus Total + Contagio	■ Static Method is used ■ Due to the selected features training time is increased ■ Virus -Total data set is more biased about benign
Li et al. (2020)	Feature Vector - GAN	Contagio Malware Dump, PRA Lab	■ Hybrid Method is used ■ Good results in malware detection and analysis ■ Time consumption
Shijo, P. V., & Salim, A. (2015)	SVM, Random Forest	997 Malicious and 490 clean files	■ Hybrid Method is used ■ Dataset is very small ■ High accuracy and false positive rates.
Li et al. (2019)	KNN	Created Dataset	■ Static method is used ■ An evasion test is not available ■ lowers false negatives and improves detection accuracy
He et al. (2020)	CNN	Virus Total	■ Static Method is used ■ Robustness against evasive samples ■ Can not detect adversarial samples

continued on following page

Table 1. Continued

Author/s	Machine Learning/ Deep Learning Model	Dataset	Overall Observation
Smutz, C., & Stavrou, A. (2016)	Ensemble classifier (random sampling/bagging)	Contagio	▪ Dynamic method is used ▪ It does not inspect any probable embedded PDF payload. ▪ Real data has been used
M. Zubair Shafiq et al. (2008)	Markov n-gram	37,000 malware and 1800 benign	▪ Static methos is used ▪ Detection and false-positive rates are high compare to other malware ▪ An evasion test is not available.

From machine learning advancements to behavioural analysis innovations, researchers are making strides towards developing holistic solutions that address the unique challenges posed by PDF-based threats. This literature review provides a foundation for understanding the current landscape and sets the stage for further advancements in the ongoing quest to fortify digital documents against the ever-present risk of PDF-based malware (Shijo, P. V., & Salim, A., 2015), M. (Zubair Shafiq et al., 2008), (Jiang et al., 2021). Looking at the above comparison, there is a lot of scope to improve the results in terms of accuracy, time execution, detection rate, false positive rate, and dataset selection, etc.

3. PROPOSED METHODOLOGY

This research focuses on implementing a machine learning-based model to detect malware embedded within PDF files. The foundation of this work lies in utilizing the CIC-Evasive-PDFMal2022 dataset, which is widely recognized as a standard dataset and has been employed in numerous other research studies. For a comprehensive understanding of the methodology employed in this research, readers can refer to Figure 2, which provides a detailed overview of the implementation process.

Figure 2. Proposed framework

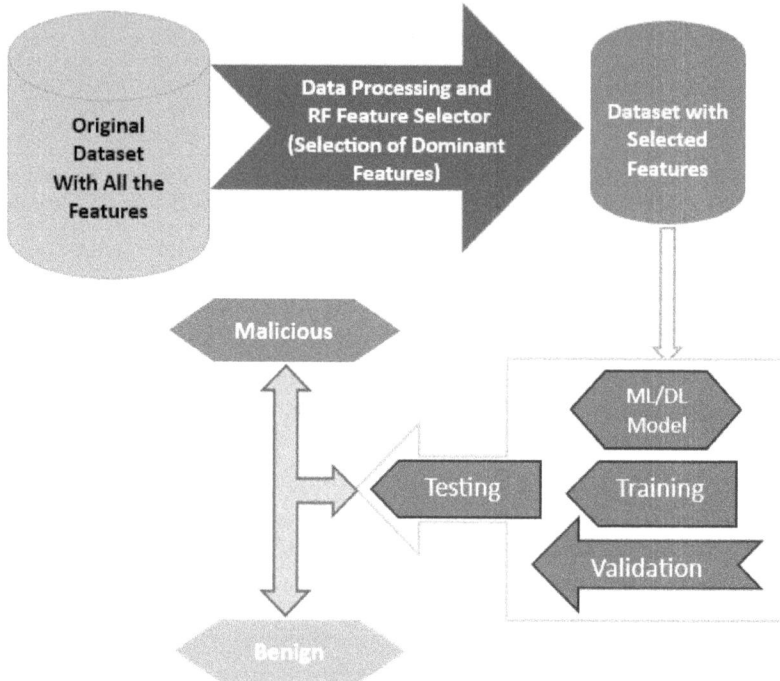

Step 1: Retrieve data from the CIC-Evasive-PDFMal2022 dataset.

Step 2: The data undergoes thorough structuring using various data smoothing and processing techniques, resulting in the selection of 15 dominant features out of 32.

Step 3: The selected features are used for training, validation, and fine-tuning of the model.

Step 4: The model is tested using the trained and fine-tuned parameters.

Step 5: Finally, the model predicts the category of the data, labelling it as either "Malicious" or "Benign" through classification

3.1 Database Description

In this research, we have used pdf dataset, Evasive-PDFMal2022 which consists of 10,025 records with 5557 malicious and 4468 benign records that tend to evade the common significant features found in each class. This data set has been prepared from the various samples of malicious and benign collected from the Contagio and

Virus total. The K-means clustering has been applied on overall samples to categorize them in two the two labels. Total 32 features have been extracted from the collected samples. The distribution of the features has been categorized in to the General Features and the Structural features as described below table 2 and table 3 respectively CIC-Evasive-PDFMal2022. Table 4 describes the list of hardware which has been used in this research work

Distribution of Features:

Table 2. General vs structural features

General Features	Structural Features
header, metadata size, PDF size, encryption, objects, image, text, embedded files, page number, title characters, average size of embedded media, etc.	No. of keywords (endstreams, streams, "/JS", "/javascript", "/AA","/launch", "/OpenAction", "/Acroform", "/XFA" "/JBig2Decode", "/Colors", "/Trailer", "/Xref", "/Startxref", etc.) No. of (Xref entries, name obfuscations, objects with nested filters, ObjStm, filters) and Average stream size.

Labels/Alerts:

Table 3. Malicious vs benign

Malicious	Malware infected PDF file
Benign	Genuine PDF file

Hardware Description:

Table 4. Hardware description

Processor:	11th Gen Intel(R) Core (TM) i5-1135G7 @ 2.40GHz 2.42 GHz
Installed RAM	16.0 GB (15.8 GB usable)
OS	64-bit operating system, x64-based processor (Windows 11 Home Single Language)
Manufacturer	HP - PAVILION

Features and its importance: Based on its importance first 15 features have been used in this research.

Figure 3. Importance of features

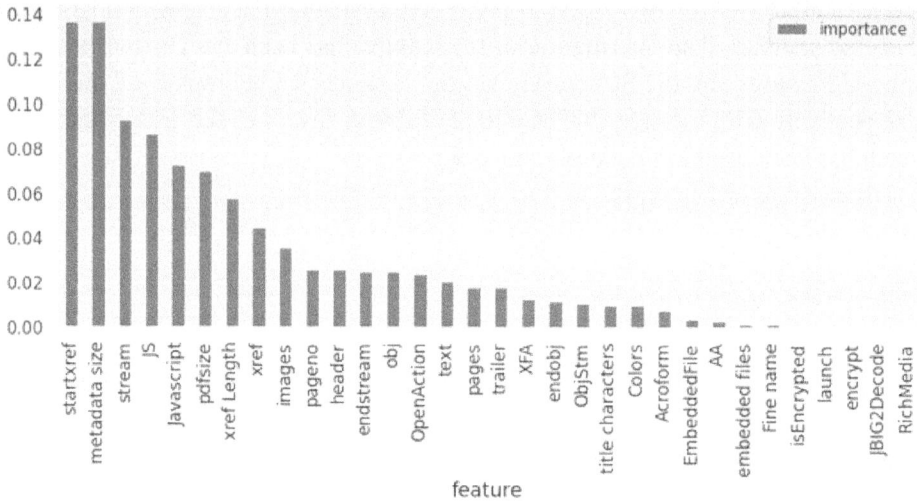

3.2 Machine Learning Model/Classifier

Naive Bayes (NB) is a classification method that utilizes Bayes' theorem and makes the assumption that the features being used are independent when given a class label. Despite its straightforward nature and assumption of feature independence, NB often produces impressive results in a variety of practical scenarios. Its greatest strength lies in its efficiency and rapidity, making it a highly valuable tool for analysing extensive datasets. In essence, NB can be described as (Ray, S., 2019).:

$$P\left(A\middle|B\right) = \frac{P(B|A)*P(A)}{P(B)} \tag{1}$$

Above,
- P(A|B) is the posterior probability of class (A, target) given predictor (B, attributes).
- P(A) is the prior probability of class.
- P(B|A) is the likelihood which is the probability of the predictor given class.
- P(B) is the prior probability of the predictor.

Logistic Regression (LR): Logistic Regression is a powerful statistical technique commonly utilized for solving binary classification problems. Characterized by a categorical outcome variable with two possible classes, it derives its name from its origin in regression analysis. However, it is important to note that logistic regression is employed primarily for classification purposes rather than regression.

$$f(x) = \frac{L}{1 + e^{-k(x-x0)}} \tag{2}$$

Above,
- f(x) is the output of the function
- L is the curve's maximum value
- K is the logistic growth rate or steepness of the curve
- x0 is the x value of the sigmoid midpoint
- x is the real number

K-Nearest Neighbour (KNN): K-Nearest Neighbours (KNN) is an incredibly versatile machine learning algorithm, capable of handling classification and regression tasks easily. Its effectiveness lies in its underlying principle, the concept of that is, models with similar features obtain similar results. This means that the classifier relies heavily on a reliable telemeter. The more accurately this metric measure records the similarity and thus the more accurate the classification will be. The distance metric to go for KNN is usually the Minkowski distance.

$$D(X_i, X_j) = \left[\left(\sum_{l=1}^{d} |X_{il} - X_{jl}| \right)^{1/p} \right]^p \tag{3}$$

where Xi and Xj are data points, n is the number of dimensions, and p is the Minkowski power parameter.

Decision Tree (DT): Decision tree is a highly sought after machine learning technique used in both classification and regression tasks. Creates a tree-like structure to represent decisions, with nodes symbolizing specifics or experiments, branches representing possible outcomes, and leaf nodes representing final or predicted decisions will result. One reason for its popularity is its intuitive nature and its ability to handle statistics and groups with ease information. The algorithm relies on key parameters such as entropy and gain to classify data and make accurate decisions. These decisions can be explained as follows (Capable Machine. (2020)):

$$Entropy\left(S\right) = \sum_{i=1}^{c} -p_i log_2 p_i \tag{4}$$

$$Gain(S,A) = Entropy\,(S) - \sum_{v \in Values(A)} \frac{|S_v|}{S} Entropy\left(S_v\right) \tag{5}$$

Entropy: Entropy is like the amount of uncertainty in the information we're dealing with. When entropy is lower, it's much simpler to make sense of the data (Capable Machine., 2020).

Information Gain: Information gain is a measure that captures the difference in entropy between the original and split sets on a specific attribute. Put simply, it tells us how much uncertainty is reduced when we divide the S set based on attribute A. Think of it as a way to quantify the decrease in entropy. Ultimately, it helps us determine which attribute should be chosen as the critical decision node (Capable Machine, 2020).

Random Forest: The Random Forest algorithm involves the construction of multiple decision trees. The final prediction in the case of classification is determined by a majority vote, and in the case of regression, it's determined by averaging the predictions of individual trees.

$$RFfi_i = \frac{\sum_{j \in all\ tress} norm fi_{ij}}{T} \tag{5}$$

$$norm fi_i = \frac{fi_i}{\sum_{j \in all\ features} fi_j} \tag{6}$$

$$fi_i = \frac{\sum_{j:node\ j\ splits\ on\ features\ i} ni_j}{\sum_{k \in all\ nodes} ni_k} \tag{7}$$

$$ni_j = w_j C_j - w_{left(j)} C_{left(j)} - w_{right(j)} C_{right(j)} \tag{8}$$

where,

nij= importance of the node j, wj=weighted number for searching sample j, Cj=impurity of node j, left and right represent the left and right child of the tree, fij = calculate the importance of each features, norm fij= normalized value between 0 to 1, RFfij= importance of feature i calculated from all trees in the random forest model.

4. IMPLEMENTATION AND RESULTS ANALYSIS

For the experiment purpose four different classifier has been implemented as discussed in the previous section: Navie Bisa (NB), Logistic Regression (LOR). K-Nearest Neighbour (KNN), Decision Tree (DT) and Random Forest (RF). Table 5 and Table 6 explain the training and the testing accuracy respectively along with the cross-validation score. It is clearly seen that DT and RF gives the best results compare to others.

Table 5. Validation and training accuracy

Validation and Training Accuracy		
Model Name	Overall Accuracy	Cross Validation Score
NB	0.8261	0.8255
Log	0.8825	0.8777
KNN	0.8249	0.735
Dt	**1**	**0.9873**
RF	**1**	**0.9923**

Table 6. Testing accuracy

Testing Accuracy	
Model Name	Overall Accuracy
NB	0.827
Log	0.8859
Knn	0.7396
Dt	0.9853
RF	**0.9930**

Figure 4. Overall accuracy

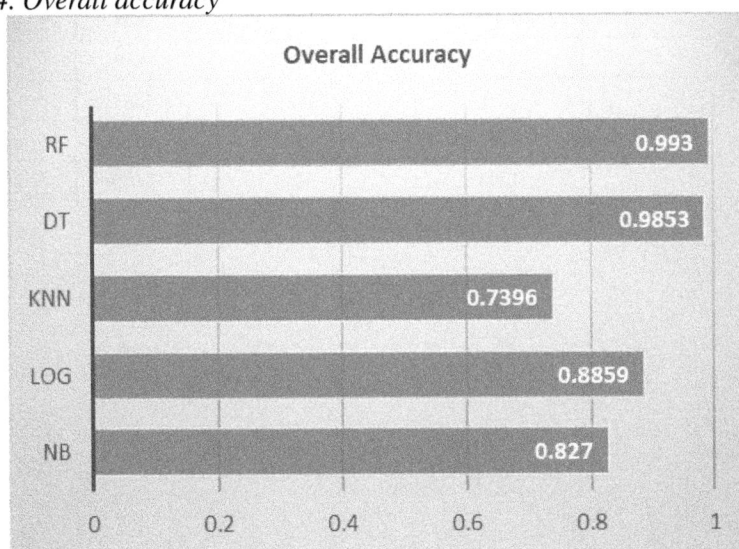

From the above Figure 4, it can be clearly seen that various models like Random Forest (RF), Decision Tree (DT), K-Nearest Neighbor (KNN), Naive Bayes (NB), and Logistic Regression (LR) have been implemented. Out of all these models, RF provides the highest accuracy rate. RF is successfully able to achieve the highest overall accuracy of 99.30%.

Figure 5 provides an overall picture of the confusion matrix for various classifiers, namely Naive Bayes (NB), Logistic Regression (LOG), K-Nearest Neighbour (KNN), Decision Tree (DT), and Random Forest (RF), respectively, from left to right and top to bottom. It can be clearly seen that for detecting malware, RF offers a better detection rate in terms of false positive rates and true positive rates. The RF classifier successfully achieves an accuracy of 0.9930 (99.30%) with a very low error rate, making it superior compared to the others. The RF classifier also exhibits a minimum false detection rate in both categories, malicious and benign. The table 7 highlights the same thing with proper statistical data

Table 7. Overall comparison of different classifier/model.

Model/ Classifier	Malicious	Mis Classified	Error	Accuracy
NB	1281	412	0.24	0.7566
Log	1595	98	0.06	0.9421
KNN	1348	345	0.20	0.7962
DT	1674	19	0.011	0.9888
RF	1684	9	0.005	0.9947
Model/ Classifier	Benign	Mis Classified	Error	Accuracy
NB	1206	108	0.08	0.9178
Log	1068	246	0.19	0.8128
KNN	876	438	0.33	0.6667
DT	1289	25	0.019	0.9810
RF	1303	11	0.008	0.9916

Figure 5. Confusion matrix of different classifier/model (NB, DT, KNN, Log and RF respectively)

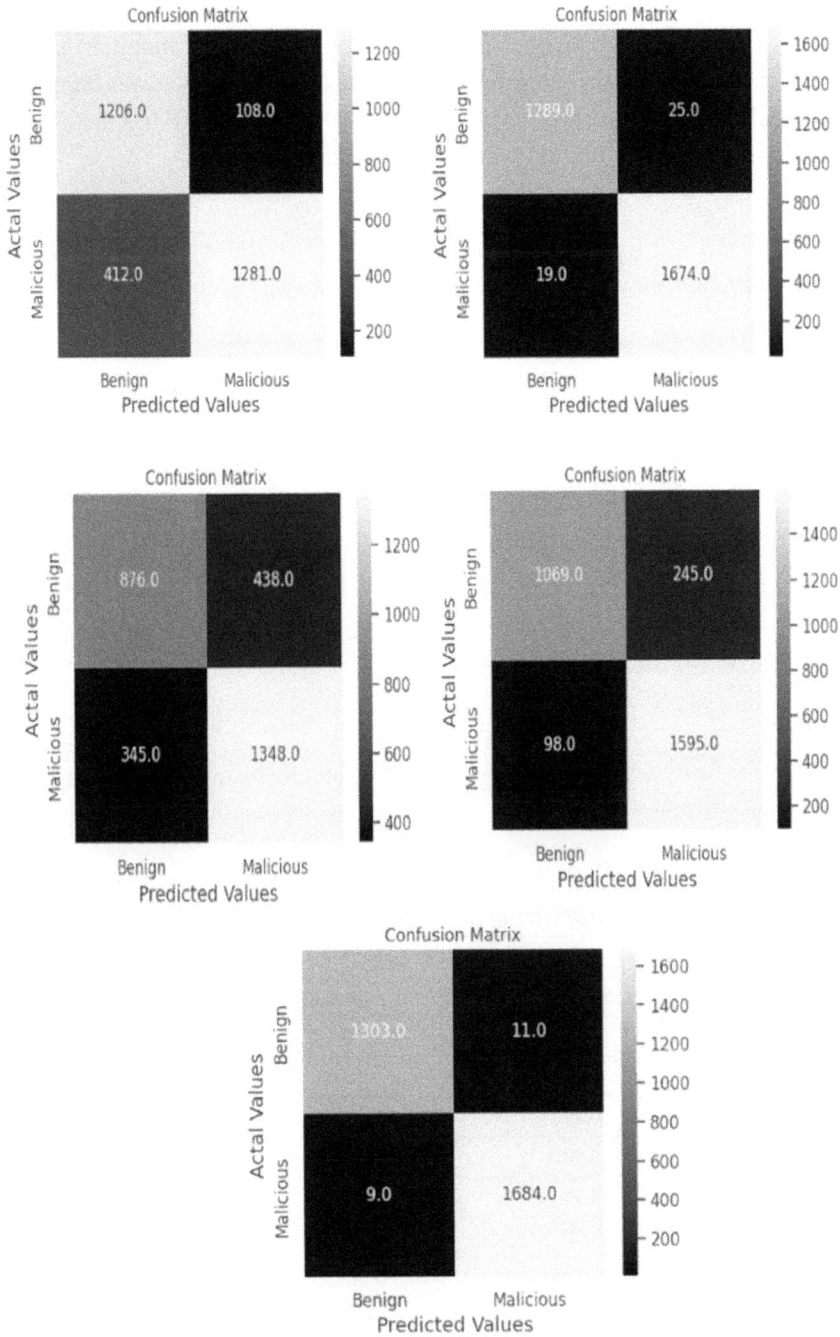

Figure 6 and Table 7 illustrate the impact of the overall analysis of Malicious and Benign label data. In both categories, RF provides better accuracy and a lower error rate. Additionally, RF has a very low count of misclassifications. In the case of RF, the misclassification error rate is very low in both categories, measuring 0.5% in malicious cases and 0.8% in benign cases, which is significantly lower compared to other classifiers. Therefore, we can statistically conclude that RF has the capability to deal very effectively with this type of classification problem

Figure 6. Overall Analysis of Malicious and Benign in line to Miss classification, Error rate and Accuracy

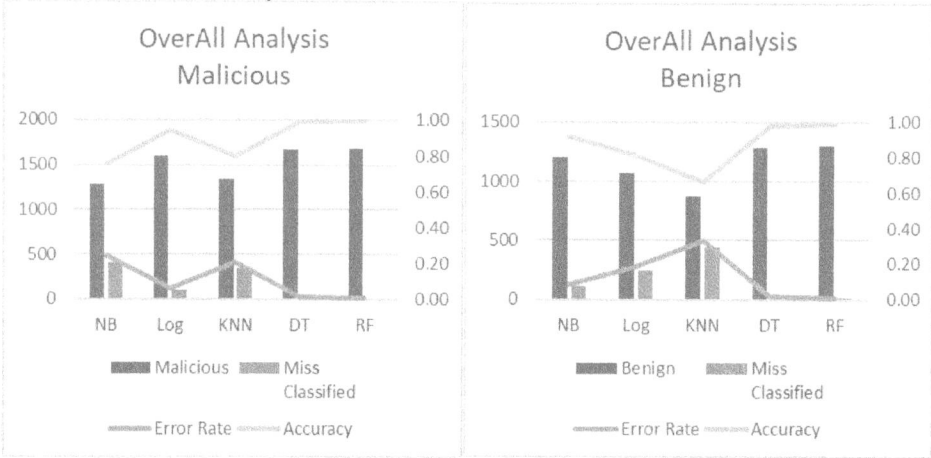

Table 8. Overall comparison of various model in line to Precision, Recall and F1-score

Malicious			
	Precision	**Recall**	**F1-score**
NB	0.92	0.76	0.83
Log	0.87	0.94	0.9
KNN	0.75	0.8	0.77
DT	**0.99**	**0.99**	**0.99**
RF	**0.99**	**0.99**	**0.99**
Benign			
	Precision	Recall	F1-score
NB	0.75	0.92	0.82
Log	0.92	0.81	0.86

continued on following page

Table 8. Continued

Malicious			
	Precision	**Recall**	**F1-score**
KNN	0.72	0.67	0.69
DT	**0.99**	**0.98**	**0.98**
RF	**0.99**	**0.99**	**0.99**

From Table 8 and Figure 7, it is also clearly visible that RF provides high precision, recall, and F1-score compared to other classifiers/models. RF is successfully able to achieve 99% precision, recall, and F1-score. This value itself speaks to the effectiveness of RF compared to other classifiers. Among other classifiers, DT slightly matches the results with RF in terms of precision but provides poor results compared to RF in terms of recall and F1-score.

Precision is the proportion of accurate positive predictions among all the positive predictions made by a model, while **Recall** is the proportion of accurate positive predictions among all the positive instances in the data. The **F1-score**, also known as the F1 measure or F1-value, is a valuable metric that incorporates both precision and recall into a single score. It is particularly useful when the model strikes a balance between precision and recall. F1 scores range from 0 to 1, with higher scores indicating better performance. Where classes are unevenly distributed or false positives have results, the F1 score provides a balanced evaluation of the model Overall, the F1 score provides a measure of model performance well, considering accuracy and recall.

Figure 7. Overall comparison of various model in line to precision, recall and F1-score

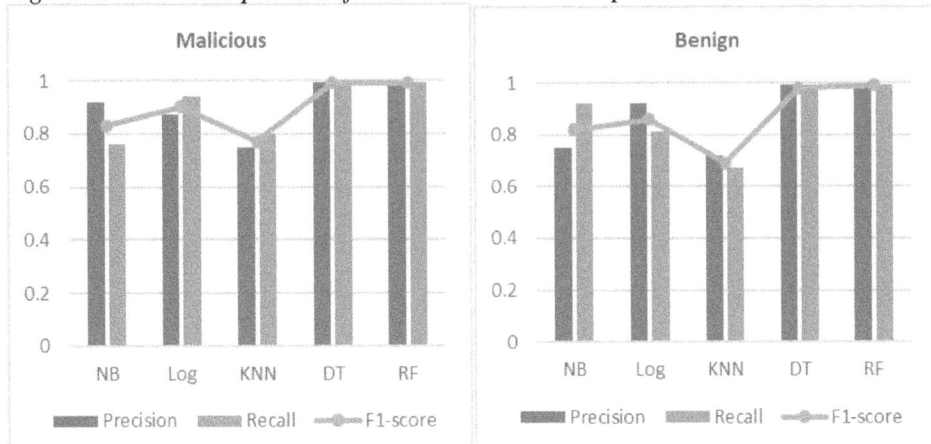

Table 9. Overall Comparison between Training and Testing data

Malicious	Training		Testing	
Model/ Classifier	Error Rate	Accuracy	Error Rate	Accuracy
NB	0.25	0.7519	0.24	0.7566
Log	0.07	0.9301	0.06	0.9421
KNN	0.15	0.8532	0.2	0.7962
DT	**0.000**	**1.000**	**0.011**	**0.9888**
RF	**0.000**	**1.000**	**0.005**	**0.9947**
Benign	Training		Testing	
Model/ Classifier	Error Rate	Accuracy	Error Rate	Accuracy
NB	0.08	0.9169	0.08	0.9178
Log	0.18	0.8244	0.19	0.8128
KNN	0.21	0.7904	0.33	0.6667
DT	**0.000**	**1.000**	**0.019**	**0.9810**
RF	**0.000**	**1.000**	**0.008**	**0.9916**

A detailed comparison of all models and classifiers in the training and testing parts of the dataset is detailed in Table 9 and Figure 8. Importantly, the propose method using random forest (RF) classifier provides consistently better results compare to other models in all aspects of various statistical analysis. The superior RF is highlighted in accuracy, precision, recall and F1-score. It can be clearly seen that during the training time, RF provides a 0% error rate and 100% accuracy in both categories, malicious and benign. During the testing time, it is noted that RF provides 99.47% and 99.16% overall accuracy and 0.5% and 0.8% error rate in both categories, malicious and benign, respectively. Furthermore, in order to provide a general approach, the proposed method is combined with existing methods, as described in Table 10. This comparison shows its superior performance over method a past, emphasizing RF power. In particular, RF exhibits high precision, recall, and F1 scores, thus confirming its effectiveness in PDF-based malware detection.

Figure 8. Overall Comparison between Training and Testing data

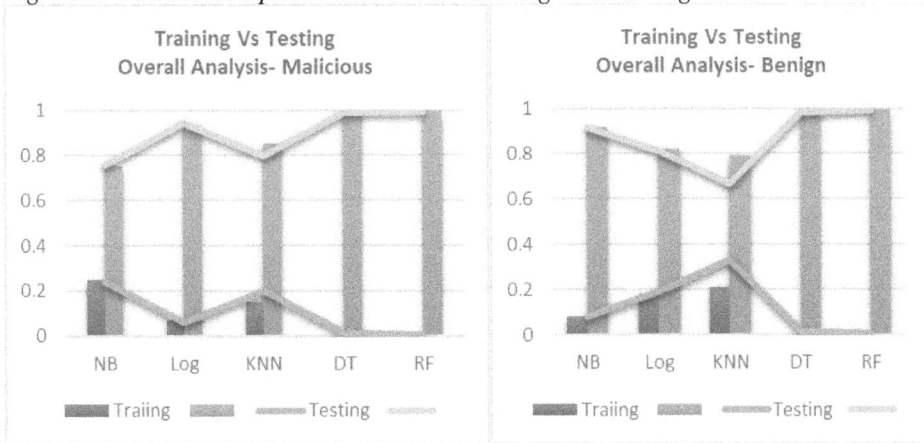

Table 10. Proposed Method vs Existing Methods

Research	Accuracy	Precision	Recall	F1-score
Issakhani et al. (2022)	0.9884	0.988	0.989	0.9885
Al-Haija et al. (2022)	0.9884	0.988	0.989	0.988
Lakshmanan Nataraj et al. (2021)	0.9593			
Li et al. (2019)	0.9511	0.9757	0.9087	0.9410
Mohammed et al. (2021)	0.8956			
Proposed [RF]	**0.9930**	**0.9900**	**0.9900**	**0.9900**

5. CONCLUSION

This chapter presents a comprehensive analysis of the protective creation of PDF-based malware using intelligent search. The chapter provides a valuable comparative analysis of different PDF-based malware detectors, highlighting their performance, capabilities, and ethical considerations, and also serves as a practical guide for practitioners and researchers. It covers emerging trends such as the integration of machine learning and automation, as well as the development of advanced detection techniques. This chapter proposes a novel method that has the capability to detect malware with an accuracy rate of 99.30%. The proposed method also delivers its best outcomes compared to existing methods in terms of precision, recall, and F1-

score. This indicates a system that could have the potential to diagnose PDF-based malignancies according to their impact. The proposed method is also able to achieve a lower error rate compared to others. In the future, deep learning-based models and new datasets may be explored to achieve more robust results.

REFERENCES

Al-Haija, . (2022). PDF malware detection based on Optimizable Decision trees. *Electronics (Basel)*, 11(19), 3142. DOI: 10.3390/electronics11193142

Bilal Sowan et al., (2024). *PDF Malware Detection: A Hybrid Approach Using Random Forest and K-Nearest Neighbors.* DOI: 10.1109/ICCR61006.2024.10533046

Binsawad, M. (2024). Enhancing PDF Malware Detection through Logistic Model Trees. *Computers, Materials & Continua/Computers. Computers, Materials & Continua*, 0(0), 1–10. DOI: 10.32604/cmc.2024.048183

Chaubey, N. K., & Prajapati, B. B. (2020). Quantum Cryptography and the Future of Cyber Security. (2020). In *Advances in information security, privacy, and ethics book series*. IGI Global., DOI: 10.4018/978-1-7998-2253-0

CIC-Evasive-PDFMal2022 | Datasets | Canadian Institute for Cybersecurity | UNB. (n.d.). https://www.unb.ca/cic/datasets/pdfmal-2022.html

Elingiusti., …. (2018). *PDF-malware detection: a survey and taxonomy of current techniques.* https://iris.uniroma1.it/retrieve/e383531c-a499-15e8-e053-a505fe0a3de9/ Elingiusti_Postprint_PDF-Malware-Detection_2018.pdf

Endignoux, G. (2016). *Introduction to PDF syntax | Blog | Guillaume Endignoux.* https://gendignoux.com/blog/2016/10/04/pdf-basics.html

Falah, , Pan, L., Huda, S., Pokhrel, S. R., & Anwar, A. (2020). Improving malicious PDF classifier with feature engineering: A data-driven approach. *Future Generation Computer Systems*, 115, 314–326. DOI: 10.1016/j.future.2020.09.015

He, , Zhu, Y., He, Y., Liu, L., Lu, B., & Lin, W. (2020). Detection of Malicious PDF Files Using a Two-Stage Machine Learning Algorithm. *Chinese Journal of Electronics*, 29(6), 1165–1177. DOI: 10.1049/cje.2020.10.002

Introduction to Decision Tree. (2020). Capable Machine; Capable Machine. https:// capablemachine.wordpress.com/2020/05/05/decision-tree-2/

Issakhani, . (2022). PDF Malware Detection based on Stacking Learning. *Proceedings of the 8th International Conference on Information Systems Security and Privacy.* DOI: 10.5220/0010908400003120

Issakhani, . (2022). PDF Malware Detection based on Stacking Learning. *Proceedings of the 8th International Conference on Information Systems Security and Privacy.* DOI: 10.5220/0010908400003120

Jani, K. A., & Nirbhay Chaubey. (2020). IoT and Cyber Security. *IGI Global EBooks*, 203–235. https://doi.org/DOI: 10.4018/978-1-7998-2253-0.ch010

Jiang, , Song, N., Yu, M., Chow, K.-P., Li, G., Liu, C., & Huang, W. (2021). DETECTING MALICIOUS PDF DOCUMENTS USING SEMI-SUPERVISED MACHINE LEARNING. *IFIP Advances in Information and Communication Technology*, 612, 135–155. DOI: 10.1007/978-3-030-88381-2_7

Lakshmanan Nataraj et al. (2021). OMD: Orthogonal Malware Detection Using Audio, Image, and Static Features. *ArXiv (Cornell University)*. https://doi.org//arxiv .2111.04710DOI: 10.48550

Li, . (2019). Research on KNN Algorithm in Malicious PDF Files Classification under Adversarial Environment. *Proceedings of the 2019 4th International Conference on Big Data and Computing - ICBDC 2019*. DOI: 10.1145/3335484.3335527

Li, , Wang, X., Shi, Z., Zhang, R., Xue, J., & Wang, Z. (2021). Boosting training for PDF malware classifier via active learning. *International Journal of Intelligent Systems*, 37(4), 2803–2821. DOI: 10.1002/int.22451

Li, , Wang, Y., Wang, Y., Ke, L., & Tan, Y. (2020). A feature-vector generative adversarial network for evading PDF malware classifiers. *Information Sciences*, 523, 38–48. DOI: 10.1016/j.ins.2020.02.075

Liu, R., & Nicholas, C. (2023). IMCDCF: An incremental malware detection approach using hidden Markov models. *arXiv (Cornell University)*. https://doi.org// arxiv.2304.07989DOI: 10.48550

Liu, R., & Nicholas, C. (2023). *A Feature Set of Small Size for the PDF Malware Detection*. https://arxiv.org/pdf/2308.04704

Martsinkevich et al. (2023). Algorithms for extracting lines, paragraphs with their properties in PDF documents. *E3S Web of Conferences, 389*, 08024. https://doi.org/ DOI: 10.1051/e3sconf/202338908024

Maundrill, B. (2024). PDF Malware on the Rise, Used to Spread WikiLoader, Ursnif and DarkGate. Infosecurity Magazine; *Infosecurity Magazine*. https://www .infosecurity-magazine.com/news/pdf-malware-on-the-rise/#:~:text=PDF%20 threats%20are%20on%20the

Mohammed., ... (2021). *Malware Detection Using Frequency Domain-Based Image Visualization and Deep Learning*. ArXiv.org. /arXiv.2101.10578DOI: 10.24251/ HICSS.2021.858

Ray, S. (2019). 6 Easy Steps to Learn Naive Bayes Algorithm (with code in Python). *Analytics Vidhya.* https://www.analyticsvidhya.com/blog/2017/09/naive-bayes-explained/

Rieck, , Trinius, P., Willems, C., & Holz, T. (2011). Automatic analysis of malware behaviour using machine learning. *Journal of Computer Security*, 19(4), 639–668. DOI: 10.3233/JCS-2010-0410

Shijo, P. V., & Salim, A. (2015). Integrated Static and Dynamic Analysis for Malware Detection. *Procedia Computer Science*, 46, 804–811. DOI: 10.1016/j.procs.2015.02.149

Smutz, C., & Stavrou, A. (2016). *When a Tree Falls: Using Diversity in Ensemble Classifiers to Identify Evasion in Malware Detectors.* DOI: 10.14722/ndss.2016.23078

Tank, . (2020). *A Method for Malware Detection in Virtualization Environment. Communications in Computer and Information Science* (Vol. 1235). Springer., DOI: 10.1007/978-981-15-6648-6_21

Tzermias, . (2011). Combining static and dynamic analysis for the detection of malicious documents. *Proceedings of the Fourth European Workshop on System Security - EUROSEC '11.* DOI: 10.1145/1972551.1972555

US20200175164A1 - Malware classification and detection using audio descriptors - Google Patents. (2018, December 3). Google.com. https://patents.google.com/patent/US20200175164A1/en

Zubair Shafiq, M.. (2008). Embedded Malware Detection Using Markov n-Grams. *Lecture Notes in Computer Science*, 5137, 88–107. DOI: 10.1007/978-3-540-70542-0_5

Chapter 11
To Enhance Cyber Security for IoT

Anubha Gauba

https://orcid.org/0009-0007-7785-293X

Department of Computer Science and Engineering, IKG Punjab Technical University, India

Ravneet Preet Singh Bedi

IKG Punjab Technical University, India

ABSTRACT

This is a fascinating and important subject that is becoming increasingly relevant in today's digital world. The rapid proliferation of IoT devices has revolutionizing several impacts of our daily lives. From smart homes and wearable systems to industrial sensors and autonomous vehicles, IoT technology has ushered in a latest era of connectivity and convenience. Moreover, with this connectivity comes an increased cyber security risk. This paper outlines a strategic approach to enhance cyber security for IoT deployments, ensuring the protection of data, devices, and networks.

1. INTRODUCTION ABOUT IOT

The IoT signifies a paradigm shift in our interactions with technology and the environment around us. The IoT is a system of linked systems, sensors, and gadgets that could accumulate, exchange, & analyze information in a contemporaneous fashion.

DOI: 10.4018/979-8-3693-9225-6.ch011

Figure 1. IoT comprises 3 things

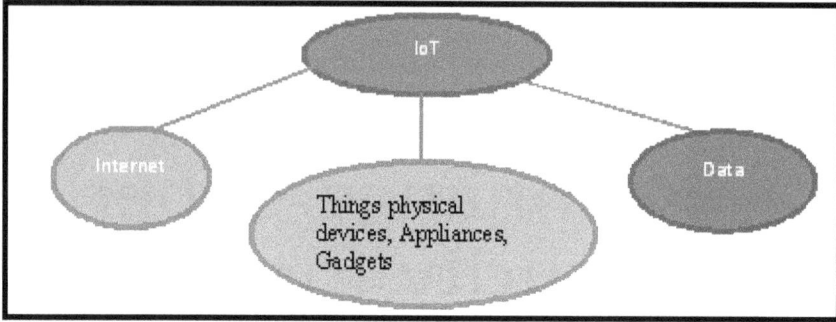

Figure1: IoT comprises

These "smart" gadgets may connect with one another over a centralized system, allowing for the flawless integration and automation of numerous processes and services (Saqlain, Jahangir, 2018). From intelligent homes and cities to industrial automation and medical care, IoT technology is likely to alter a huge scale of organizations & improve people's quality of life worldwide. The medical care industry includes IoT devices like remote patient tracking, hospital operations organization, glucose tracking, linked inhalers, linked contact lenses, robotic surgery, efficient drug organization, cancer recognition, & Smart door locks, smart gardens, video doorbells, and individual companions for smart lighting, coffee machines, and freezers are only a few of the home automation IoT gadgets currently available. IoT devices for smart street lighting, smart garbage collection, or automated parking have been developed by the "smart city" industry (Phillip Williams et al., 2022). Mr. Ayush G Ingole (2024), several approaches used in the development of the home security system, including IoT and Telegram, and the ESP32 in the home security system for remote monitoring and control, provide a cost-effective and efficient alternative for homeowners seeking to improve their security through smart technology.

A framework for objects (which include cyber-physical gadgets, data assets, or individuals) that share data & communicate with the real world by detecting, analyzing data, or reacting" (IEEE SA, 2018) is how the IEEE Standards Association describes an IoT network (Rajmohan, T. et al., 2022).

Connectivity is a critical enabler of the IoT because it allows devices to communicate and share data over the Internet or various other networks. This connectivity enables the remote monitoring, control, and optimization of devices and systems, resulting in greater efficiency, productivity, and convenience. Organizations that employ IoT can acquire useful insights from data analytics, maximize resource utilization, improve decision-making processes, and provide users with tailored experiences.

However, the increasing proliferation of IoT devices has resulted in considerable issues and concerns, particularly in terms of security, privacy, interoperability, and scalability. The number of linked systems increases rapidly. The possible attack surface for cyber threats and vulnerabilities has also increased.

2. HISTORY OF IOT

The idea of "the Internet of Things" was initially introduced in 1999 & gained traction during the early 2000s. Nevertheless, its origins can be traced back to the development of the Apollo Guidance Computer in 1965. A number of milestones can be seen year by year. In this article, Greengard, Samuel (2024), states that significantly the mid-1990s, the Internet had expanded such capabilities globally, and scientists and technologists were investigating ways for humans and robots to communicate more effectively. The Internet of Things continues to evolve. It now supports a wide range of applications, including artificial intelligence for advanced simulations, sensing systems that identify pollution in water supplies, and systems that monitor agricultural animals and crops. For example, it is now possible to remotely monitor the location and health of animals, as well as administer ideal levels of water, fertilizer, and pesticides to crops.

Table 1. Inventions of IoT

Year	Inventions
1982	Once a Carnegie Mellon College machine for sale was linked to the Internet to send stock & status information, it marked the beginning of the IoT and opened the door for surveillance from afar.
1999	Kevin Ashton came up with the term 'IoT to define an interlinked system of gadgets that communicate & share information, paving the way for the latest era of connection (A S Abdul-Qawy et al., 2015).
2000	LG announced the first smart refrigerator. The LG Smart Fridge was revolutionary in allowing customers to monitor & manage refrigerator contents remotely, demonstrating the power of IoT in everyday life.
2004	A smart watch explained IoT to the wearable electronics world, providing fitness monitoring & notifications while on the road (Sharma, N., 2019).
2007	Apple's iPhone was a major change, combining IoT capacities with apps that linked consumers to a wide range of services & systems and transferring smartphones into hubs.

continued on following page

Table 1. Continued

Year	Inventions
2009	The IoT has penetrated the automotive industry by equipping vehicles with sensors for real-time diagnostics, production tracking, & remote testing.
2011	IPv6 was launched.
2014	Amazon's Echo, which includes the virtual assistant Alexa, showcased the power of the voice-activated IoT by making smart homes more intuitive & reactive (Zainab H. Ali et al., 2015).
2020	5G and edge computing
2021	The Internet of Things has made its way into industries such as vehicles, security systems, and smart homes by lowering the cost of creating sensors, and it is expected that this technology will reach its peak in the next 5-10 years.

3. COMPONENTS OF IOT

Figure 2. Components of IoT

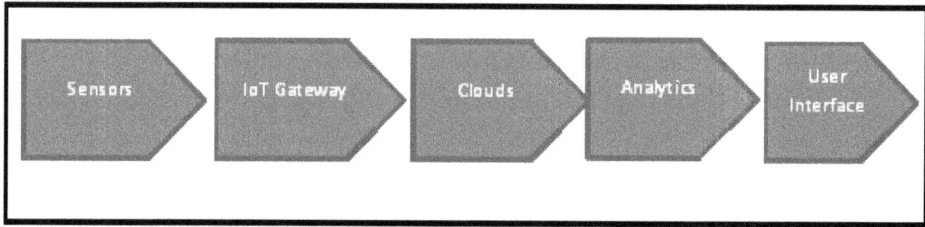

Figure 2: Components of IoT

The IoT is the process of connecting our smart gadgets and products to a system in order for them to function efficiently and be accessible remotely.

Table 2. Components of IoT

Sensor	A linked device that allows the detection of physical factors in the scenario or controlled environment and converts their values into digital data (Safa Ahmed et al., 2018).
IoT Gateway	IoT gateways handle bidirectional information transfer among systems and rules. An additional function of the gateway is to transform different system approaches & allow the compatibility of connected systems & sensors (Haddaoui, S., et al., 2022). Higher-order encryption approaches are used by IoT gateways to present a level of security for the system & send information. It functions as a buffer between devices and the cloud, shielding the device against malicious activity & illegal access.
IoT cloud	The IoT generates a vast set of information from systems; apps that must be organized efficiently. IoT clouds provide capabilities for storing, processing, and organizing massive sets of information in real time. Organizations & facilities may readily access this information remotely & make key decisions as demanded. Kumar, S., et al. (2019) outline that an IoT system contains a large number of devices and sensors that connect with one another. As the IoT network grows and expands, the number of sensors and devices grows dramatically. These devices communicate with one another and transport huge amounts of data via the internet, which must be efficiently stored and analyzed for real-time decision making. Furthermore, cloud computing or Big data frameworks such as Hadoop and Spark may be utilized to handle this large streaming data, and machine learning approaches can be used to develop better prediction models, resulting in a more accurate and reliable IoT system to meet current demand. The IoT cloud is essentially a sophisticated, high-production system of servers modelled to analyze information from billions of systems at high speeds, organize traffic, & provide precise analytics.
Analytics	Analyzing digital information collected by billions of electronic gadgets & sensors into useful information that may be further examined and analyzed is the essence of statistics. IoT systems need intelligent analytics tools in order to regulate & enhance the whole network (Singh D et al., 2014). Analytics encompasses several roles, including data processing, machine learning, and statistical analysis. Many of the IoT analytics applications include anomaly recognition, environmental tracking, energy organization, smart cities, & agriculture.
User interfaces	User interfaces are the visible, tangible components of an IoT network that people could approach. It is a key element of the IoT in which users operate the device & collect data. Creators will demand to present a well-modelled user interface that requires minimal effort from users and encourages more interactions (Fagan M., Megas K, 2020). The dashboard of the IoT must have features such as data visualization, customization, user-friendly layout, remote control, integration, authorization, & safety.

4. APPLICATIONS OF IOT

IoT (Internet of Things) applications have the potential to transform organizations and daily lives in a variety of ways by providing connectivity, automation, and data-driven insights. IoT applications can help businesses streamline operations, increase efficiency, and enhance decision-making processes. For example, IoT devices can be used to track the performance of equipment, inventory levels, and supply chain operations, which lead to cost savings and greater productivity.

Firms that use IoT technology can create smart devices, personalized experiences, and predictive maintenance solutions to match changing client demands and preferences. This might help organizations stand out in the market and stay ahead of the competition.

In daily affairs, IoT applications can improve ease, safety, and sustainability. Smart home technologies, wearable technology, and connected appliances allow people to automate jobs, track their health, and save energy. IoT applications in healthcare, transportation, and urban planning can boost quality of life, promote sustainability, and improve public services. Rahmani, A.M., et al. (2022) outline that all facets of human existence are now affected by the Internet of Things, which has created a network of interconnected devices. Nowadays, it is quite odd and challenging to envision a way of life without intelligent tools, sensors, and applications due to their intricate integration with human life. The scope of IoT applications can be seen in big and industrial dimensions as well as in personal, lifestyle, and healthcare aspects, such as smartphones and smartwatches. Easy-to-use online services allow users to use these services and obtain the desired analytical findings. IoT has rapidly become a global necessity and established a system for rapidly exchanging people, things, data, and processes.

The following demonstrates the impact of IoT on transforming several sectors:

4.1. Healthcare

- **Remote Patient Monitoring:** Wearable health trackers and smart inhalers are examples of IoT devices that can continuously monitor patients' vital signs and health parameters. Fitbit and Apple Watch, for example, monitor heart rate and physical activity, as well as detect abnormalities that may suggest a health problem.
- **Smart Hospitals:** Hospitals are incorporating IoT solutions to improve efficiency. Medtronic, for example, provides linked insulin pumps that automatically change insulin supply in response to real-time glucose levels, resulting in better diabetes management.

4.2 Manufacturing

- **Predictive Maintenance**: IoT sensors on machinery provide data about equipment performance and identify faults before they arise. For example, GE's Predix platform aids manufacturers such as Caterpillar in anticipating maintenance requirements, thereby lowering delay and repair costs.

- **Smart Factories:** Siemens' MindSphere software connects manufacturing equipment to the cloud, enabling real-time data analysis and process improvement. This integration improves efficiency while reducing waste.

4.3 Agriculture

- **Precision Farming:** Farmers may optimize irrigation and crop management by using IoT devices such as soil moisture sensors and climate monitoring systems. John Deere's linked machinery analyzes data to improve planting and harvesting operations.
- **Livestock Monitoring:** Wearable IoT livestock equipment, such as Allflex's smart collars, monitors animal health and location, offering real-time insights to improve herd management and production.

4.4 Retail

- **Smart Inventory Management:** IoT-enabled shelving and inventory systems, such as those used by Amazon Go, automatically track product availability and manage replenishment, lowering inventory costs and enhancing consumer satisfaction.
- **Personalized Shopping Experiences**: The usage of beacon technology in retail refers to the employment of beacons in the retail business for proximity marketing. In retail, beacons can contact customers with mobile devices that have Bluetooth enabled and the retailer's app downloaded and deliver targeted promotions to their cell phones depending on their location and purchase history.

4.5 Transportation and Logistics

- **Fleet Management:** IoT sensors in vehicles monitor location, fuel consumption, and maintenance requirements. Companies such as UPS use this information to optimize delivery routes, minimize fuel usage, and increase overall efficiency.
- **Smart Traffic Management:** Cities deploy IoT technology to monitor and control traffic flow. Barcelona, for example, has adopted smart traffic lights that alter in real time in response to traffic conditions, cutting congestion and emissions.

4.6 Construction

- **Construction Site Monitoring:** IoT sensors on construction equipment and materials facilitate progress tracking and safety. Trimble offers solutions for real-time site monitoring, minimizing errors, and increasing project efficiency.
- **Building Management Systems:** IoT devices in smart buildings monitor and control systems such as lighting, air conditioning, and security. Johnson Controls, for example, provides IoT solutions to minimize energy usage and increase building safety.

4.7 Environmental Monitoring

- **Air Quality Monitoring:** IoT sensors installed in metropolitan areas monitor pollution levels and offer data for improving air quality. For example, PurpleAir provides real-time air quality monitoring to enable cities to take action against pollution.
- **Wildlife Tracking:** Wildlife movements and activities are monitored using IoT-enabled tracking devices. The Wildlife Conservation Network employs this technology to investigate animal movement patterns and conserve endangered species.

To summarize, the Internet of Things is a game changer across industries, increasing efficiency, improving decision-making, and enabling new business models. The incorporation of IoT technology into numerous industries not only improves operating capacities but also opens up new avenues for innovation and growth.

5. CYBER SECURITY (CS)

CS is the process of securing computer systems, networks, and data against digital threats. This includes taking steps to avoid unauthorized approaches, information breaches, & other cyber hazards. Cybersecurity plays an essential role in today's digital environment in protecting sensitive information while also ensuring data confidentiality and integrity. Amit Jaykumar and Lamba (2018) describe that the IoE (Internet of Everything) creates unparalleled economic opportunities for enterprises, individuals, and countries. Security and privacy in the Internet of Everything (IoE) present significant challenges, owing to the huge scale and scattered nature of IoE networks. Robust authentication and security methods in IoE are urgently needed, and this paper proposes implementing such procedures in the proposed work. To guarantee the security & dependability of networks and the IoT, cyber security is essential. However, this is advantageous.

- **Data Protection:** Massive volumes of data are gathered and sent by IoT devices. These data are protected from interception and unauthorized access by cyber security techniques, including access limits and encryption.
- **Prevention of Unauthorized Access**: The adoption of security protocols, such as authorization and authentication, prevents unauthorized users from entering networks and IoT devices. This lowers the possibility of tampering or misuse by guaranteeing that only authorized users can operate or communicate with the IoT devices (Y. Li & Q. Liu, 2021).
- **Device Integrity:** By preserving IoT devices against viruses, malware, and other online dangers, cyber security measures contribute to device integrity. Updates and patches for security can be applied regularly to fix vulnerabilities and guarantee safe device operation.
- **Privacy Preservation**: IoT gadgets frequently gather private and sensitive data. Secure data handling and limited access to authorized parties are two ways to safeguard user privacy using robust cyber security measures.
- **Network Security**: IoT devices frequently have connections with larger networks. DDoS assaults & other cyber-attacks are prevented by the use of cyber security.

5.1 Importance of Cyber Security for IoT

The IoT has revolutionized the way gadgets are seamlessly networked via the internet, allowing them to converse and share data with efficiency. This innovation has significantly improved everyday life by bringing amenities. The IoT in smart surroundings merges with WSN & MANET, increasing its user appeal and commercial viability. Rasa Bruzgiene et al. (2017) outlined that the Internet of Things (IoT) in smart settings integrates with wireless sensor networks (WSN) and mobile ad-hoc networks (MANET), increasing its user appeal and commercial success. Combining wireless sensor and mobile ad-hoc networks with the Internet of Things enables the development of new MANET-IoT systems and IT-based networks. This study presents a solution for efficient energy use in the global MANET-IoT system. That is a step toward the reliable supply of services via the global future internet infrastructure. Like a technology improves user mobility while lowering network deployment costs. We can now monitor our houses with network-connected cameras, control appliances with our smartphones, and receive immediate notifications from our automobiles and health-monitoring gadgets. However, this connectivity comes with its drawbacks. Deogirikar and Vidhate (2017) addressed the fact that network assaults involve exploiting IoT networks to cause harm or obtain unwanted access. These assaults can take several forms, targeting different components of the network infrastructure. As the IoT pursues to integrate itself into every aspect of daily life, the growing number of IoT devices increases the routes via which hackers might potentially access our personal information. The need to strengthen cyber security measures has risen exponentially.

IoT devices may be dangerous for a set of reasons. An IoT system may be susceptible to exploitation for the following typical reasons:

- **Weak or Default Credentials:** Default usernames and passwords on IoT devices can occasionally be found, or users may choose weak passwords or forget to update the default settings. In order to obtain unauthorized access, attackers can take advantage of this by rapidly guessing or brute-forcing the credentials.

- **Insecure Network Connections:** The IoT device might be vulnerable to interception and unauthorized access if insufficient encryption techniques are used or if secure communication routes are not established between it and other systems. Network traffic can be intercepted by attackers, who could subsequently take over the device (Ravi Sharma, 2012).

- **Inadequate Authentication and Authorization** Inadequately executed permission and authentication protocols may allow malefactors to evade security protocols and obtain unapproved entry into the device or network it is linked to.

- **Absence of Physical Security**: Attackers can intentionally tamper with an IoT device, collect sensitive data, or introduce malicious code to undermine its operation or take control of connected systems if physical access to the device is not sufficiently controlled.

- **Unprotected Data Management:** Sensitive data leaks or data breaches might result from improper data processing, transfer, or storage by the IoT device. These flaws could be used by attackers to obtain harmful manipulation or unapproved access to sensitive information.

Security risks, including malware, unprotected communication routes, & DDoS, are becoming increasingly common as IoT networks grow. Therefore, it's imperative to take the required actions to reduce these risks (Upadhyay et al., 2018).

As the number of IoT devices increases, so does the attack surface for cyber threats, necessitating sophisticated security measures. Here are the reasons why **cyber security is important for IoT**.

5.1.1 Increased Attack Surface

- **Diverse Devices:** IoT ecosystems are formed up of an array of devices, including sensors, cameras, smart appliances, and others, all of which can serve as entry points for attackers if not adequately protected.
- **Network Complexity:** The interdependent nature of IoT devices can lead to complicated networks that are challenging to monitor and safeguard.

5.1.2 Sensitive Data

- **Personal and Business Data:** IoT devices frequently handle sensitive information, such as health data from fashionable gadgets or operational data from corporate monitors. Compromising this information can have major privacy and financial ramifications.
- **Potential for Data Breaches:** Illegal access to IoT data can result in severe breaches, such as identity theft, financial fraud, or the disclosure of proprietary corporate information.

5.1.3 Operational Risks

- **Disruption of Services:** Attacks on IoT devices can impair crucial services. For example, a ransomware attack on smart city infrastructure might trigger traffic control systems or utilities to fail.
- **Safety Concerns:** In domains that involve healthcare and manufacturing, compromised IoT devices can threaten to prevail by malfunctioning or delivering incorrect information.

5.1.4 Regulatory Compliance

- **Legal Requirements:** Several industry sectors are subject to severe data protection requirements (for example, GDPR and HIPAA). Ensuring IoT security helps organizations meet regulatory standards and avoid legal consequences.
- **Industry Standards:** Adherence to industry-specific security standards is critical for sustaining trust and guaranteeing functionality among IOT devices.

5.2 Crucial Cyber Security Considerations for IoT

The majority of devices with internet capability were not designed with cyber security in mind. As a result, the IoT poses numerous inherent hazards to its safety, some of which can be disastrous. In comparison to other technical solutions, IoT security lacks well-defined standards and laws. Furthermore, most people are unaware that their IoT gadgets pose a security concern. The following are some important aspects to keep in mind:

5.2.1 Device Authentication and Access Control

- **Strong Authentication:** To prevent illegal access, implement robust authentication using multiple factors on IoT devices.
- **Access Control Policies:** Implement standards that limit access to gadgets based on responsibilities and permits, ensuring that only authorized users' access to the devices.

5.2.2 Data Encryption

- **Data in Transit:** Protect information when transferred between connected gadgets and servers to avoid detection and interference.
- **Data at Rest:** Encrypt the information stored on IoT devices so as to avoid unauthorized access if they get compromised.

5.2.3 Regular Software Updates and Patch Management

- **Firmware Updates**: Frequent firmware updates are recommended to resolve vulnerabilities and improve security features.
- **Patch Management:** Set up a strategy for timely updating of software and firmware to defend against known violations.

5.2.4 Network Security

- **Segmented Networks:** Employ segmentation in the network to separate IoT devices from critical systems, minimizing the impact of a possible compromise.
- **Firewalls and Intrusion Detection:** Monitor and protect IoT device network traffic via firewalls and intrusion detection systems (IDS).

5.2.5 Device Management and Monitoring

- **Inventory Management:** To proficiently maintain and track IoT devices, keep a record of their configurations up to date.
- **Anomaly Detection:** Using tools for monitoring to identify any unusual activity or abnormalities in IoT device activities that could signal a security risk.

In brief, as the Internet of Things expands, establishing priorities for cyber security is critical to protecting sensitive data, maintaining operational integrity, and ensuring regulatory compliance. Implementing strong security measures and remaining attentive to new threats will help to reduce risks and safeguard the benefits of IoT technology.

Examples of Cyber Security Challenges and Solutions

- **Mirai Botnet:** In 2016, the Mirai botnet used vulnerable IoT devices to execute one of the greatest DDoS attacks ever encountered. The attack demonstrated the significance of protecting IoT devices from being hijacked and used in cyberattacks.
- **Smart Home Vulnerabilities:** Security weaknesses in smart home equipment, such as smart locks and cameras, can allow illegal access into houses. Manufacturing companies are now working on enhancing security features and releasing regular updates to solve such vulnerabilities.

By proactively addressing security concerns in IoT devices and networks, we can ensure the trustworthiness and reliability of these interconnected systems. This needs a multi-faceted technique that surrounds secure model apps, encryption protocols, access control mechanisms, threat detection and response strategies, and on-going security updates and patches.

6. THE POTENTIAL RISKS OF IOT

Table 3. The potential risks of IoT

		Risk	Example
1	Unauthorized Access and Control	IoT devices with lax safety precautions can be hacked, allowing unwanted access. This could result in the manipulation of device operations, such as changing the settings on an intelligent thermostat or unlocking a smart door.	A smart lock weakness could allow an attacker to gain physical entry to a building, putting the occupants' security at risk.
2	Data Breaches and Privacy Violations	IoT devices frequently capture confidential data, such as personal, medical, and financial information. A hacking attempt could result in data theft or leakage, endangering user privacy and security.	A compromise in a health monitoring system could expose sensitive medical information, resulting in identity theft or prejudice.
3	Device Tampering and Manipulation	Hackers may intentionally tamper with IoT devices, altering their functioning or causing them to fail.	Tampering with industrial IoT sensors could interfere with processes in manufacturing, resulting in production faults or safety issues.
4	Network Attacks and DDoS	Deficient IoT devices can be employed in Distributed Denial of Service (DDoS) attacks to overwhelm networks or services, causing delay and disruption.	The Mirai botnet carried out enormous DDoS attacks using hijacked IoT devices, illustrating the scope and impact such attacks may have.
5	Insufficient Updates and Patch Management	Numerous IoT devices are not constantly updated, making them vulnerable to known attacks and security risks.	A failure to provide timely updates may expose devices to attacks using known vulnerabilities, as witnessed in a number of high-profile breaches.
6	Insecure Interfaces and APIs	IoT devices frequently communicate using APIs and web interfaces, which can be unsafe if not adequately protected, leaving them vulnerable to assault.	Insecure APIs may be accessed to obtain unwanted access to device functionality or data.

6.1 The Need for Robust Security Measures

In view of the inherent issues provided by their networked nature, IoT (Internet of Things) devices require robust cyber security solutions. IoT devices are frequently vulnerable to cyber assaults because of variables such as low computing capacity, a lack of built-in security mechanisms, and a variety of communication protocols. Implementing effective security measures for IoT devices is critical to preventing unwanted access, data breaches, and device manipulation.

Organizations can protect sensitive data, ensure system integrity, and avoid disruptions to key operations by ensuring that IoT devices are outfitted with strong security measures. Furthermore, effective security measures in IoT cyber security serve to foster confidence among users and stakeholders by displaying a commitment to protecting their privacy and ensuring the dependability of connected devices.

Overall, implementing strong security measures for IoT cyber security is critical for addressing the specific problems offered by networked devices and mitigating the risks associated with the increasing usage of IoT technology.

6.1.1 Device and Network Authentication

- **Implement Strong Authentication:** To ensure that only authorized users have access to IoT devices and networks, utilize multifactor authentication (MFA).
- **Network Segmentation:** Detach IoT devices on distinct network segments to limit exposure to important systems and mitigate the effect of a compromise.

6.1.2 Data Encryption and Privacy Protection

- **Encrypt Data:** To prevent interception and tampering, ensure that data exchanged between IoT devices and central systems is encrypted.
- **Secure Data Storage:** Encrypt data saved on IoT devices to avoid unauthorized access if a device is compromised.

6.1.3 Intrusion Detection and Anomaly Monitoring

- **Monitor Device Activity:** Implement monitoring tools to detect any irregularities or anomalies in IoT device activity that may signal an attack against security.
- **Intrusion Detection Systems (IDS):** Use intrusion detection systems (IDS) to detect and respond to potential threats in real time.

6.1.4 Comprehensive Incident Response Plan

- **Prepare for Incidents:** Create and maintain an incident response plan specifically for IoT security incidents in order to promptly address and mitigate any breaches.
- **Regular Drills:** Conduct regular security drills and updates to maintain preparedness for future IoT-related incidents.

6.1.5 User Education and Awareness

- **Training:** Empower users and administrators with IoT security best practices training, such as identifying phishing attempts and safeguarding personal devices.

- **Awareness Programs:** Implement awareness campaigns to keep stakeholders informed about emerging dangers and security measures.

7. IOT ATTACKS

Cyber threats that target devices that are linked to the internet and one another are referred to as IoT (Internet of Things) assaults. If not adequately secured, these gadgets—which range from wearable technology and smart home appliances to industrial sensors and connected cars—can be targets of several kinds of assaults. Tinshu Sasi, Arash Habibi Lashkari, et al. (2023) state that Cyberattacks using IoT devices to obtain sensitive consumer data are known as IoT attacks. Usually, attackers damage the equipment, implant malware on it, or get access to the data of other organizations. Considering that insufficient security measures are built into IoT devices, they therefore represent one of the weakest points in an organizations and a serious security risk.

7.1 Denial of Service (DoS)

The regular use or governance of telecommunications services is hampered or prevented by DOS (Figure 3). This attack is aimed at a particular target; for instance, a unit could indeed repress all messages referring to the appropriate destination. Interrupting the existing IoT network is another type of service denial; degrade achievement by deactivating the system or overburdening it with messages. Hanan, Mustapha, et.al (2018) state that the Internet of Things (IoT) vulnerabilities are an excellent target for botnets, contributing significantly to the rising number of Distributed Denial of Service (DDoS) attacks. The rise in DDoS attacks has highlighted the importance of addressing the implications for the IoT industry, which is one of the primary reasons. This paper aims to provide an examination of attempts to avoid DDoS attacks, mostly at the network level. The sensitivity of these solutions is derived from their impact on resolving IoT vulnerabilities.

Figure 3. Denial of service

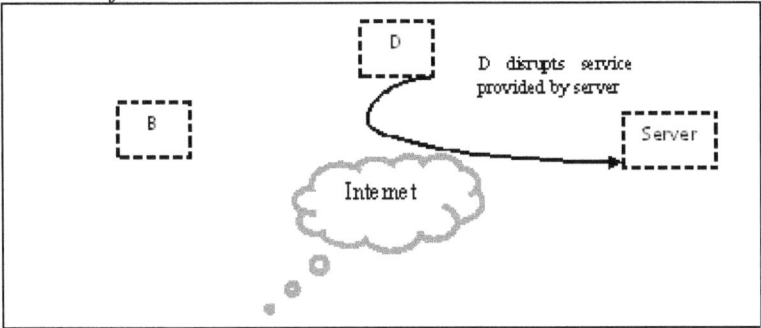

Figure 3: Denial of Service

7.2 Gray Hole Attack

This is one of the categories of black hole attacks in which a false node selects packets. Some nodes sometimes change their position from a black hole an upright and vice versa. Gray hole attack is difficult to detect as nodes can drop packets due to the hole and malicious nature (Sasi, Lashkari et al., 2023). In both black hole and grayhole attacks, the intruder follows two steps: first, they capture the routes, and then they either ignore all packets (BHA) or just a few packets (grayhole attack).

7.3 Black Hole Attack

It uses the protocol to say that the malicious node is the lowest route to the destination node. When the routing algorithm selects a route, it begins disregarding routing packets & does not precede packets to its neighbor nodes (Tseng, Chou, & Chao, 2011). In multiple paths, the operation for activating an intrusion node black hole attack could be distinguished. This attack is carried out using the DSN and the hop count in the scenario of the AODV method. The DSN is used to demonstrate the route's vitality. A larger value for the DSN indicates a new route. Attackers can decrease the hop count data or boost the DSN to protect target nodes. Moreover, attackers could indeed merge both methodologies to intensify their attacks. The intensity of the attack is determined by the set of routers in the network where the intruder is productive.

7.4 Rushing Attack

To restrict root discovery overhead, each node in the network generates only one RREQ from any root discovery. Usually, it comes first. Attackers can take advantage of this property. As a result, RREQ packets begin to propagate quickly over the network, suppressing any incoming RREQ packets. As a result, the initiator is unable to locate any feasible alternatives (i.e., routes without attackers). Every entity contains a different location in order to participate in the routing path. This unique address identifies nodes. However, there is also no central authority in MANET to confirm these personalities. In a Sybil attack, a malicious node could generate a fake identity for a number of other nodes. A Sybil node can build a different individuality for itself or steal individuality from another node. It creates confusion in the network.

7.5 Sleep Deprivation Attack

In this attack, a rogue node might drain battery life by utilizing it for unnecessary route determination or by sending packets to the target without any requirement. It is a form of DDOS malicious activity node communicating with a legitimate node in a seemingly legitimate manner. However, the interaction's function is to maintain the victim node from entering its power-saving sleep mode.

7.6 Eavesdropping

Messages sent by a node could pass through many intermediate nodes, and if no encryption is utilized, the attacker will obtain important information. The transmitter and recipient generally have no means of confirming that an attack has occurred (Alterazi HA et al., 2022). This attack is prevented by using encryption techniques. Basically, there are 2 types of encryption techniques. i) Symmetric encryption ii) Asymmetric Encryption. SE is very fast as compared to asymmetric encryption, but at the same time, it is less secure than asymmetric. Hybrid encryption is the 3rd method of encryption. It mixes asymmetric and symmetric encryption to make use of each type's capabilities. These benefits include both speed and security (Mohammad Rafsun Islam & K. M. Aktheruzzaman, 2020).

7.7 Jamming Attacks

Jamming attacks can occur when IoT systems use wireless connections to plan themselves, receive human rules, or send information to cloud storage (Mohindru V. & Garg A., 2021). A third party can disrupt communication between IoT devices and gateways by using identical communication frequencies. This approach is commonly used for mobile and RF frequency jamming of WSN nodes (P.N. Mahalle et al., 2013).

7.8 Traffic Analysis and Location Disclosure

Attackers could really hear wireless link traffic to pinpoint the position of target nodes through evaluating the communication style, the quantity of data transferred by nodes, as well as the transmission qualities. E.g., In a battlefield situation, a huge portion of network activity typically flows to and from the headquarters. As a result, the traffic method of analysis (Figure 4) enables an attacker to identify the channel's commanding nodes.

Figure 4. Traffic analysis

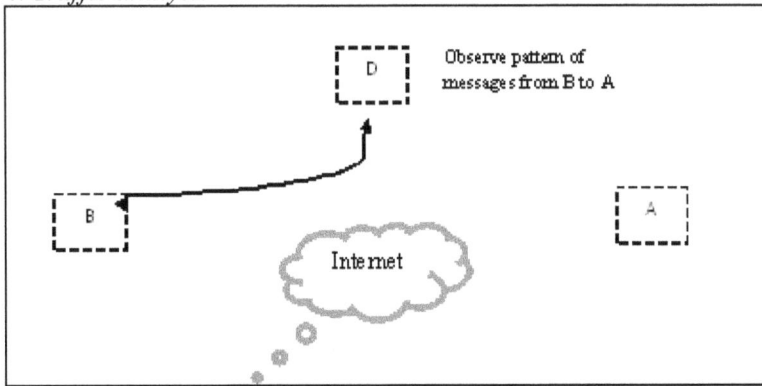

Figure 4: Traffic Analysis

7.9 Social Engineering

The phrase "social engineering" encompasses a broad spectrum of malicious actions executed via interpersonal connections. It uses emotional trickery to trick users into revealing sensitive data or committing security blunders (T. Xu et al., 2017). It is characterized as email or other communication that instils the victim with a sense of urgency, dread, or similar feelings, prompting the victim to reveal critical data, click a malicious link, or open a malicious file. These are some of the most general kinds of digital SE threats like Baiting, Pretexting, and Phishing (Ashwini Sheth & Sachin Bhosale, 2021). Wang, Z., Zhu, H., Liu, P., et al. (2021)

this study creates a domain ontology of social engineering in cyber security by defining 11 fundamental entity ideas that significantly compose or affect the social engineering domain, as well as 22 types of relationships between these concepts. It offers a formal and explicit knowledge architecture for understanding, analyzing, reusing, and sharing domain knowledge of social engineering.

7.10 Clone Attack

A hostile entity with physical or wireless access to IoT devices may generate precise clones. These gadgets have the potential to compromise the IoT network infrastructure. In a clone attack, an attacker first targets a network node or reconfigures the node (Sathish et al., 2013). The attacker reproduces the reprogrammed node and spreads it across the system to take access to the network (Sher Alia, Syed Babar et al., 2020). Anubha, R P S Bedi. (2020) this research focuses on detecting clone attacks in MANETs where an attacker node obtains the closed node's id, duplicates it, and attracts all data to it. ACO identified the clone attack and evaluated performance using packet losses, packet delivery ratio, and network throughput.

7.11 Data & Identity Theft

The data from IoT devices is stored in the cloud. As already mentioned, cloud information safety relies heavily on SaaS. Third companies' typically backup data from IoT clouds. Backups pose a significant risk to data integrity (B. Ondiege et al., 2017).

Table 4. Comparative analyses of IoT attacks based on recent research articles.

Authors	IoT Attacks &Preventions	Method Used	Practical Implications	Limitations
Abdul Hanan K. Mohammed et al.,2021	Various IoT attacks include malware, DDoS, and man-in-middle attacks	Random Forest, Logistic, Regression, SVM,KNN,MLP	• ML & DL approaches can be utilizing to identify IoT Cyber-attacks. • A comparative analysis of six detection techniques.	• Traditional strategy is inefficient at detecting cyber-attacks. • Increasing security risks require increased innovation in defensive measures.
Nader Karmous et al.,2022	• IoT attacks: DDoS, malware, ransomware, spoofing, eavesdropping, physical tampering • Prevention methods: Network segmentation, encryption, strong authentication, regular software updates	Supervised machine learning Method and classification algorithms like RF, SVM,KNN	Employ supervised machine learning method for enhanced precision.	• The research lacks a full description of the interpretability of the machine learning models used, which is critical for understanding how the IDS makes choices and identifying potential biases or errors. • The article does not thoroughly examine the scalability of the suggested framework, particularly in large-scale IoT setups with a significant volume of data and devices, which may impact real-world application.
Inayat U, Zia MF,2022	• Common IoT attacks include DoS, DDoS, probing, spoofing, and MITM. • ML & DL are utilizing to identify & prevent attacks.	Learning-based technologies (machine and deep learning) for detecting cyber-attacks in IoT networks	ML and DL approaches have been investigated with regard to the recognition of cyber assaults in IoT devices, offering a detailed review of their usefulness in defending IoT settings.	• IoT networks are vulnerable to cyber security assaults. • Threats could cause physical and economic losses.

continued on following page

Table 4. Continued

Authors	IoT Attacks &Preventions	Method Used	Practical Implications	Limitations
Anika Tasnim,Nigah Hossain, 2022	• IoT threats include data breaches, network vulnerabilities, illegal access, and DDoS attacks. • Implement strong encryption, perform frequent security updates, and segment your network.	• Various approaches, including DT, RF, AdaBoost, XGBoost, ANN, MLP, • Under-sampling, over-sampling, and SMOTE, were applied to the dataset.	• Using DT & RF, researchers improved the identification of IoT network attacks. • Several ML & DL algorithms were investigated for improving IoT safety.	• Insufficient security features in IoT networks. • The Adaboost technique and artificial neural networks perform badly in multiclass classification.
Celil Okur,Murat Dener, 2020	• Botnet assaults against smart healthcare IoT devices. • Machine learning algorithms are used to differentiate between regular and attack traffic as prevention proximity.	• Statistical measurements (Pearson coefficient, entropy) • ML methods using data pre-processing techniques	• Enhanced security for IoT devices. • Using machine learning algorithms to detect network attacks	• Time-consuming investigation using the tcpdump program. • High processing throughput is required for high-speed networks.
Qifeng Chen, Haoming Chen,et al., 2018	• DoS attacks simulated on IoT system using Kali Linux. • A comparison of the efficiency of various DoS attack tactics is offered.	• Simulated IoT setup with Kali Linux attacker and Arduino victim. • The research compares three main types of DoS attacks.	• IoT security problems, DoS attacks, and simulation-based efficiency comparisons.	• Security problems around IoT systems and attacks on IoT systems might cause significant damage.

8 PREVENTIVE MEASURES USED FOR SAFE IOT

It is vital to deploy robust security measures to prevent unwanted access and data breaches. The following strategies provide comprehensive guidance on improving IoT safety and resilience against possible hazards.

8.1 Strong Password

Using a common and basic password for IoT devices opens the door to potential hackers. The best defense against hackers is to use strong and secure passwords. Make sure you create a new password for each device (Vutukuru & Lade, 2023).

If a hacker guesses one of your passwords, it could harm all of your devices that utilize that password. Regularly upgrading these passwords reduces the possibility of illegal entry.

8.2 Regular Improvement

If the version of a basic software tool is not modified for an extended period of time, it becomes an easy target. It just provides enough time for malicious people to examine the software for flaws (Kamel, Hegazi, 2018). So, it's a good idea to update on a regular basis and ensure that every connected device is up to date. It is preferable to automate the software update implementation across the infrastructure since it reduces the likelihood of a breach. Regularly updating the software on IoT devices helps to fix security vulnerabilities and enhance productivity.

8.3 Encryption

Encryption is integral to improving cyber security for IoT (Internet of Things) devices. Encrypt all in-transit data, including sensor and device data, administration, provisioning, and deployments. Almost all modern IoT devices are capable of encrypting network traffic and protecting both information and control plane conversations. some additional Considerations, like below in the table:

Table 5. Significance of encryption in cyber security

Data Confidentiality	**Encryption ensures that data exchanged between IoT devices and servers is safe & can't be understood by unauthorized parties (Lei Cui a b., Youyang Qu et al., 2020).Even if the data is intercepted, without the encryption key, it is nearly impossible to decipher.**
Data Integrity	Encryption helps to protect data integrity by guaranteeing that it is not altered or messed over while being transmitted or stored. IoT devices can use cryptographic hash functions or digital signatures to ensure that the data they receive is genuine and unmodified (C. Ge, W. Susilo, 2022).
Authentication	Encryption makes it easier to authenticate IoT devices and users. Devices can use techniques like digital certificates and public-key cryptography to prove their identification to one another and the network, limiting illegal access (Pedro Ramos Brandao, 2018).
Access Control	Encryption can be employed to limit access to sensitive information and resources in IoT devices. Encrypting data at rest or in transit allows organizations to give access to only authorized individuals, reducing the risk of data breaches.
Securing Firmware Updates	IoT devices frequently require software upgrades that fix flaws and enhance functionality. Encryption guarantees that these updates are securely communicated and implemented, preventing hackers from intercepting them and incorporating harmful code (Kvarda, Hnyk, 2017).

As a whole, encryption is a critical component of IoT cyber security, protecting against a variety of threats such as eavesdropping, tampering, illegal access, and data breaches.

Methods of Encryption: The following encryption methods, in conjunction with effective encryption key management directives, are critical in protecting data and systems against unwanted access, interception, manipulation, and other cyber-security risks.

Table 6. Methods of Encryption

Methods	Description
Symmetric Encryption	This technique uses an identical key to encrypt and decode data. AES, DES, and Triple DES are all instances of encryption protocols. Symmetric encryption is effective for huge amounts of data, but it necessitates safe key management to avoid unauthorized access.
Asymmetric Encryption	Asymmetric encryption works with a combination of keys—a public key for encryption & a private key for decryption. RSA & ECC are examples of Public Ker Encryption. Asymmetric encryption is largely utilized to ensure secure communication, key exchange, & digital signatures.
Hash functions	Variable-sized input is fed into hashing algorithms, which yield fixed-size outcomes (hash values) in exchange. They are employed in the creation of digital signatures as well as information integrity assurance. Two popular hash algorithms are MD5 and SHA-256. At this point, MD5 is thought to be poor due to weaknesses.
Digital signatures	For the sake of authentication and non-repudiation, digital signatures employ asymmetric encryption. They verify that a message or document came from a specific sender and was not altered during transmission. Typically, digital signatures require hashing the message and encrypting it with the sender's private key.
Key Exchange Protocol	These protocols ensure secure communication between parties by securely transferring encryption keys. Diffie-Hellman key exchange & its variants, enable two parties to agree on a shared secret key through an unsecured channel.
Transport Layer Security(TLS)	TLS, the successor to SSL, encrypts information sent between clients & servers to provide a secure network connection. It uses symmetric and asymmetric encryption, as well as digital certificates, to secure confidentiality, integrity, and authentication.
End-to-End Encryption (E2EE)	E2EE enables that information to remain encrypted from the sender's device until it reaches the intended recipient, preventing intermediaries or unwanted parties from viewing the plaintext. Signal and WhatsApp use E2EE to preserve users' privacy.

8.4 Encryption Algorithm Used for IoT

Data Encryption Standard (DES): The DES is among the oldest encryption techniques. IBM first released this symmetric encryption technique in 1976 to safeguard sensitive and unclassified government data. Despite being regarded as the foundation of encryption, the DES is no longer in use today. This is because it was cracked by numerous security researchers (Ghulam

Mustafa, Rehan Ashraf, et al., 2018). DES failed because of its short encryption key length, making it vulnerable to brute-force cryptographic faults. DES employs the same encryption key to encrypt & decode data. As a result, it was superseded by AES. However, several IoT gadgets and banking services still use it due to its stability, interoperability, and flexibility.

Advanced Encryption Standard (AES): The AES, introduced in 1997, is a popular IoT encryption approach used by the US government's National Security Agency (NSA) and many other large businesses. It is the most prevalent and robust symmetric encryption method available and can be applied to block ciphers with variables as small as 128 bits or as large as 192 or 256 bits. Due to the longer key length, it is impenetrable & immune to attacks other than brute force. Numerous IoT uses, including file encryption, VPNs, processor security, or Wi-Fi security, may use AES.

Triple Data Encryption Standard (3- DES): Triple DES protects data with three rounds of encryption. This approach provides great security and is utilized in mission-critical applications. The triple-DES method uses 3 56-bit keys, totaling 168 fragments, for encryption & decryption. Encrypting sensitive data using a 56-bit DES key is insufficient.3-DES improves the size of the key by applying the approach 3 times in a row to 3 separate keys. 3-DES intends to provide a universal technique for increasing the size of DES keys that protects against assaults without the demand to create a new block encryption approach (Singh, Kinger, 2013). Its more powerful and effective key length makes it less susceptible to brute-force attacks, which had previously threatened DES. 3-DES is widely utilized in a variety of applications, particularly in the financial sector for ATM and POS transactions. Its use in VPNs, SSL/TLS protocols, and government communications demonstrates its trustworthiness and security.

Rivest–Shamir–Adleman (RSA): The RSA algorithm was created in 1977. It is also regarded as the most frequently utilized asymmetric encryption approach. It offers users the ability to send encrypted messages without first sharing the code with the recipient. As a result, it is quite secure (Wander, A.S., 2005). It is a scalable asymmetrical encryption method that is most trusted for information in transit across the internet, including SSL/TLS, S/MIME, SSH, and crypto currency. It strongly defends against brute-force cryptographic attacks by utilizing longer key lengths (768, 1024, 2048, 4096-bits, & more), making decryption difficult and time-consuming.

Elliptic Curve Cryptography (ECC): ECC is a variant to the RSA cryptographic method that is most often used for digital signatures in virtual currencies such as Bitcoin and Ethereum, in addition to one-way encrypting of emails, information, and programs (Shruti.P., Chandraleka.R.,2017). ECC helps protect resource-constrained IoT devices by offering a more efficient way of encryption and authentication than standard approaches like RSA. ECC with a 256-bit key would necessitate a 3,072-bit RSA key to provide similar protection (Di Matteo et al., 2021).ECC provides equal security while using less computational power & battery resources than RSA; it is commonly utilized in mobile apps and IoT devices with certain CPU resources (Miller, S.D. et al., 2009).

Block Chaining Technology: Blockchain for IoT, often known as "blockchain of things" (BoT), entails integrating blockchain technology with IoT devices and systems to improve security, reliability, and trust in IoT deployments. (Ahmed A. Abd El-Latif et al.,2021). Here's the manner in which block chain can be used in the context of IoT. Mohit, Singh, and Daliya1(2024) The present study emphasizes the vital importance of cybersecurity in blockchain technology, focusing on cryptographic principles, consensus mechanisms, and smart contract vulnerabilities to improve security measures, as well as evaluating existing cybersecurity practices and solutions tailored to blockchain environments. This includes approaches like encryption, improvements to consensus procedures, and decentralized identity management. Blockchain technology has the potential to greatly improve cybersecurity for Internet of Things (IoT) devices in various ways:

Device Detection and Authentication: Each IoT device can be assigned an individual identification number that is kept on the block chain. This identification can be cryptographically validated; guaranteeing that only authorized systems can connect to the system. Authentication systems based on public-private key pairs or digital signatures can be used to verify device identities.

Secure Data Exchange: Blockchain enables safe peer-to-peer data exchange between IoT devices without the use of middlemen. Data sent between devices could be encrypted & collected on the blockchain to secure authenticity and accuracy. The use of smart contracts may regulate specified data exchange norms, allowing for fully automated and untainted transactions (Yegireddi et al., 2021).

Data Integrity and Immutability: IoT data stored on the blockchain is unchangeable and invulnerable. Once data has been written to the blockchain, it is cryptographically hashed and linked to the preceding block it cannot be changed or destroyed without the consent of all network participants. This makes modifying previous transactions nearly hard without changing all the following blocks and acquiring majority control of the network. This assures the reliability and validity of IoT data, making it ideal for applications requiring data integrity, like SCM or asset tracking. This ensures that data communicated from sensors or devices cannot be tampered with or altered, resulting in a trustworthy and secure record of transactions or sensor readings.

Decentralized Network Infrastructure: Block chain serves as a decentralized infrastructure for IoT networks, removing single points of failure and diminishing the risk of cyber- attacks. Distributed consensus methods, such as PoW or PoS, assure network security and stability without the need for a centralized authority (Rasane et al., 2023). Centralized systems rely on a central server for data management. This core point can become vulnerable if attacked or compromised. Blockchain Decentralization relies on a distributed network of nodes to manage and validate transactions. Every node has a copy of the blockchain; therefore, there is no single point of failure. This decentralization makes it far more difficult for attackers to breach the system, as they would have to attack numerous nodes at the same time to change the data.

End-to-End Traceability and Transparency in Supply Chains: are made possible by block chain technology, which records the movement of products and capital. Each transaction, such as the movement of goods between IoT-enabled warehouses or transportation vehicles, can be recorded as a block on the block chain, creating a verifiable record of the supply chain history.

Monetization of IoT Data: Block chain-based systems allow IoT device owners to earn revenues from their data by securely selling it to third parties. Smart contracts allow for automated payments based on established circumstances, ensuring adequate reimbursement for data contributors while safeguarding data confidentiality and safety.

Regulatory Compliance and Auditing: Block chain creates a visible and auditable record of IoT transactions, making it easier to meet legal specifications and industry standards. Organizations can demonstrate compliance with privacy rules such as GDPR by utilizing the block chain's irreversible audit trail and data transparency attributes (Ravi Prakash, V.S. Anoop et al., 2022).

Secure and Transparent Transactions: Blockchain transactions are recorded in a public ledger (public blockchains) or a permissioned ledger (private blockchains). Each transaction is confirmed by numerous nodes before it is posted to the blockchain. This verification method protects against unlawful transactions and ensures transparency. This means that IoT actions like firmware updates or data transfers may be validated and authorized, lowering the risk of unwanted meddling.

Enhanced Privacy: Blockchain technology may employ zero-knowledge proofs to validate transactions without revealing sensitive data from IoT devices. This ensures privacy and security, only revealing information to authorized parties when necessary.

8.5 Quantum computing can be used to improve IoT cyber security by exploiting its capacity to do complicated calculations much quicker than traditional computers. One technique to employ quantum computing in this context is through QKD, which enables secure communication by creating encryption keys based on quantum mechanics principles (Alekha Parimal Bhatt & Anand Sharma, 2019). These keys are theoretically hard to intercept without discovery, providing increased security for IoT devices. Furthermore, quantum algorithms can be utilized to enhance cryptography protocols, such as by increasing the efficiency of encryption and decryption procedures. One of the primary benefits of quantum computing is its ability to change sectors such as cryptography, optimization, and machine learning. Quantum methods, like Shor's method for integer factorization and Grover's method for unstructured search, have the ability to break current encryption standards and solve optimization problems far more quickly than classical algorithms (Abdulbast A. & Abushgra, 2023).

Quantum computing has the potential to change cybersecurity on the Internet of Things (IoT) by providing better solutions for data and communication security. Here is the way the use of quantum computing might impact cybersecurity in IoT.

Quantum Key Distribution (QKD): Quantum Key Distribution creates a secure communication route by applying quantum mechanics principles. Any effort to eavesdrop on the conversation modifies the quantum states, alerting the people involved. The impact on IoT by employing QKD to encrypt communications between IoT devices, prevents attackers from intercepting or tampering with data.

Quantum-Resistant Algorithms: Classical encryption techniques (such as RSA or ECC) are based on the complexity of specific mathematical problems. Quantum computers solve these problems substantially faster, making classical encryption susceptible. Quantum-resistant algorithms, such as lattice-based cryptography, are intended to protect against quantum attacks. Integrating quantum-resistant algorithms into IoT devices assures that they stay secure even in a world where quantum computers are strong and widespread.

Enhanced Random Number Generation: Quantum computing can generate really random numbers, which are necessary for creating strong encryption keys. Traditional random number generators rely on deterministic processes and are susceptible to prediction. IoT devices can establish more secure encryption keys by employing quantum-generated random numbers, hence improving overall system security.

Improved Threat Detection and Response: Quantum computing has the potential to handle massive volumes of data faster than traditional computers. This can be used to enhance threat detection systems by studying patterns and abnormalities in real time to detect future cyber-attacks. Quantum-enhanced threat detection systems can respond more quickly and accurately to cyber threats in IoT networks, lowering the chance of breaches and limiting damage.

Quantum computing has the potential to greatly improve IoT security, but it also poses new concerns. As quantum technology advances, it will be critical for IoT security measures to grow in tandem, incorporating quantum-resistant solutions and using quantum advantages wherever possible.

CHALLENGES AND CONSIDERATIONS

1) **Resource Constraints:** IoT devices often have limited processing power, memory, and energy usage. Implementing quantum-resistant algorithms or quantum-enhanced security measures may be difficult for particular devices.
2) **Scalability:** Quantum technology is still in its early stages, and expanding these solutions to match the diverse and ubiquitous nature of IoT networks would require considerable breakthroughs and cost reductions.
3) **Interoperability:** To ensure a smooth transition, quantum security solutions must be compatible with existing IoT infrastructure.

Table 7. Demonstrates a comparative analysis of various models employed by researchers

Authors & Years	Title	Protocol	Practical Implications	Limitations
Ahmed A. Abd El-Latif,2021	Quantum-Inspired Block chain-Based Cyber security: Protecting Smart Edge Utility for IoT-Based Smart Communities	• QIQW-based authentication & encryption mechanism. • QIQW-based quantum hash algorithms are used to link BC units.	•Quantum-inspired block-chain framework for secure data transmission. • Defends against message and impersonation attacks	• Quantum systems have the potential to hack existing cryptography methods. • Both Quantum instruments should be robust to attacks from digital or quantum machines.
Sharma, A., & Bhatt, A. P., 2021	QC to Secure IoT-Based Medical Facilities	• Steganography, AES cryptosystems, and RSA cryptographic techniques. • QC system for security, privacy, and data integrity	• Improving information security, privacy, & authenticity for patients. • Utilizing quantum cryptography for unbreakable secure systems	• Topics include movement, computing constraints, scaling, transmission mediums, and dynamic geometry. • Ensures information security during retention and transfer.
Vella, 2022	The Race for Quantum-Resistant Cryptography [quantum - cyber security]	• Quantum cryptographic protocols ensure secure communication. • Protocols include Quantum Key Distribution (QKD) and Quantum Cloud.	• Development of advanced quantum cryptographic solutions for secure communication. • Possible applications in defence aircraft, block chain, IoT, and smart cities	• Need for advanced quantum cryptographic solutions due to security concerns.
Prabhsharan Kaur, Isha Sharma,2022	Encryption Algorithms for Cloud Computing and Quantum Block chain	• Cloud storage encryption technologies improve the network's security backbone. • Cloud access policy based on attributes, paired with identity encryption.	• Encryption techniques improve data security in cloud storage.	• Cloud storage safety and compliance • Issues regarding data protection and privacy

continued on following page

Table 7. Continued

Authors & Years	Title	Protocol	Practical Implications	Limitations
A, Thi, Na,2022	Secure Data Sharing Using 3DES Algorithm	• Secure data sharing using 3DES algorithm. • Developed using Java technology, Agile approach, and MySQL database.	• The 3DES method ensures secure data sharing while also allowing for efficient storage and transport.	• The system's reliance on Java technology for development may limit its compatibility with specific systems or environments, potentially limiting its usability for users without Java support. • The method presented in the study paper is based on email communication to share the aggregate key, which may offer security problems if intercepted or compromised.
Sakhi, Bandyopadhyay,2023	AES Encrypt & DFS Graph Traversal is used to hide secret information within 3D pictures.	• AES encryption is used to safeguard the data in the document. • DFS graph traversal is used to hide data in 3D images.	• Use AES encryption to securely hide data in 3D photos. • Resistance against geometric attacks, including the ability to reveal data blindly.	• Geometric attacks such as translation, scaling, and rotation are resisted. • Suggested method for blind disclosure of private information.
Zhixian, Chang., Marcin,2015	Audio encrypted in mobile networks built on the 3DES-ECC technique.	• The V.32 protocol is utilized for voice collector MODEM communication processes. • The SIP protocol was examined for potential security issues and VoIP upgrades.	• Efficient voice encryption with quick speed and good data integrity. • Low data loss rate and good anti-attack capabilities were demonstrated.	• Conventional voice collector designs have limited anti-attack capabilities.

9. SUMMARY FROM LITERATURE

Cybersecurity for IoT identifies numerous issues, including a lack of comprehensive security standards, device vulnerability owing to limited processing capabilities, and an increased risk of privacy breaches from substantial data collection. However, the research has shortcomings, such as a lack of standardized security standards, insufficient consideration of resource restrictions, and an emphasis on short-term evaluations that may not accurately reflect real-world complexities. In addition, there is a vacuum in addressing the ethical and privacy aspects of IoT security, as well as a slow response to developing threats, highlighting the need for more practical, interdisciplinary, and forward-thinking research on this subject.

10. CONCLUSION

In summary, it is critical to invest in cyber security for IoT in order to guard against constantly changing threats and weaknesses. Organizations may improve the security, dependability, and credibility of their IoT installations by putting the suggested cyber security measures into practice, ensuring ongoing success in a world that is becoming more and more connected.

11. FUTURE SCOPE

The integration of emerging technologies such as blockchain, quantum computing, and improved encryption techniques will define the future of IoT cybersecurity. Blockchain provides decentralized security and tamper-proof data exchange, whereas quantum computing poses both a barrier and an opportunity, requiring the development of quantum-resistant encryption algorithms and secure communication routes such as quantum key distribution. Lightweight cryptography and homomorphic encryption are critical for safeguarding resource-constrained IoT devices, and post-quantum cryptography will protect these systems from quantum threats. The combination of these technologies, together with new regulatory requirements and interdisciplinary collaboration, promises to result in more resilient and secure IoT networks that can survive sophisticated cyber assaults.

REFERENCES

A, Thi, Na. (2022). Secure Data Sharing Using 3DES Algorithm. International Journal For Science Technology And Engineering, 10(6):5101-5104. DOI: 10.22214/ijraset.2022.45107

Abd El-Latif, A. A., Abd-El-Atty, B., Mehmood, I., Muhammad, K., Venegas-Andraca, S. E., & Peng, J. (2021, July). Quantum-Inspired Block chain-Based Cyber security: Securing Smart Edge Utilities in IoT-Based Smart Cities. *Information Processing & Management*, 58(4), 102549. DOI: 10.1016/j.ipm.2021.102549

Abd El-Latif, A. A., Abd-El-Atty, B., Mehmood, I., Muhammad, K., Venegas-Andraca, S. E., & Peng, J. (2021, July). Quantum-Inspired Blockchain-Based Cybersecurity: Securing Smart Edge Utilities in IoT-Based Smart Cities. *Information Processing & Management*, 58(4), 102549. DOI: 10.1016/j.ipm.2021.102549

Abdul Hanan, K. M.. (2021), IoT Cyber-Attack Detection: A Comparative Analysis, *International Conference on Data Science, E-learning and Information Systems*.

Abdul-Qawy, A. S., ... (2015), The Internet of Things (IoT): An Overview, Int. Journal of Engineering Research and Applications, ISSN: 2248-9622, Vol. 5, Issue 12, (Part - 2) December 2015, pp.71-82

Abdulbast, A. Abushgra, How Quantum Computing Impacts Cyber Security (2023), IEEE Conference: 2023 Intelligent Methods, Systems, and Applications (IMSA) DOI:DOI: 10.1109/IMSA58542.2023.10217756

Alekha Parimal Bhatt, Anand Sharma (2019), Quantum Cryptography for Internet of Things Security, Journal of Electronic Science and Technology, DOI:.DOI: 10.11989/JEST.1674-862X.90523016

Alia, S., & Babar, S.. (2020). *Review Article: Survey Paper on IOT Attacks And Its Prevention Mechanisms, Information Management and Computer Science*. IMCS., DOI: 10.26480/imcs.02.2020.38.41

Alterazi, H. A., Kshirsagar, P. R., Manoharan, H., Selvarajan, S., Alhebaishi, N., Srivastava, G., & Lin, J. C. (2022). Prevention of Cyber Security with the Internet of Things Using Particle Swarm Optimization. *Sensors (Basel)*, 22(16), 6117. Advance online publication. DOI: 10.3390/s22166117 PMID: 36015878

Amit Jaykumar Chinchawade. Dr. O.S. Lamba (2018), Professor, Development of Authentication and Security Procedures for IoT System, International Journal of Research in Advent Technology (IJRAT) Special Issue E-ISSN: 2321-9637 Available online at www.ijrat.org

Anubha, R P S Bedi (2020), Detection of Clone Attacks in Manets using Ant Colony Optimization, International Journal of Engineering and Advanced Technology (IJEAT) ISSN: 2249 – 8958 (Online), Volume-9 Issue-4, April 2020

Ayush, Mr. G, Ingole. (2024). Home Security System Using IOT: A Research Paper. International Journal For Science Technology And Engineering, 12(5):5112-5116. DOI: 10.22214/ijraset.2024.62773

Brandão, P. R. (2018). The Importance of Authentication and Encryption in Cloud Computing Framework Security. *International Journal on Data Science and Technology.*, 4(1), 1–5. DOI: 10.11648/j.ijdst.20180401.11

Bruzgiene, R., Narbutaite, L., & Adomkus, T. (2017). MANET Network in Internet of Things System, Book. *Ad Hoc Networks.* Advance online publication. DOI: 10.5772/66408

Chen, Q., Chen, H., & Ca, Y. (2018), Denial of Service Attack on IoT System, *9th International Conference on Information Technology in Medicine and Education (ITME).* DOI: 10.1109/ITME.2018.00171

Deogirikar, J., & Vidhate, A. (2017), Security Attacks inIoT: A Survey, International conference on I-SMAC (IoT in Social, Mobile, Analytics and Cloud) DOI:DOI: 10.1109/I-SMAC.2017.8058363

Di Matteo, S., Baldanzi, L., Crocetti, L., Nannipieri, P., Fanucci, L., & Saponara, S. (2021). Secure Elliptic Curve Crypto-Processor for Real-Time IoT Applications. *Energies*, 14(15), 4676. DOI: 10.3390/en14154676

Fagan M, Megas K, Scarfone K, Smith M (2020) Foundational Cyber security Activities for IoT Device Manufacturers. NIST IR 8259.

Ge, C., Susilo, W., Baek, J., Liu, Z., Xia, J., & Fang, L. (2022). Revocable Attribute-Based Encryption With Data Integrity in Clouds. *IEEE Transactions on Dependable and Secure Computing*, 19(5), 2864–2872. DOI: 10.1109/TDSC.2021.3065999

Greengard, S. Internet of Things (2024), Encyclopedia *Britannica*, https://www.britannica.com/science/Internet-of-Things

Haddaoui, S., Chikhi, S., & Miles, B. (2022). The IoT Ecosystem: Components, Architecture, Communication Technologies, and Protocols. In Lecture notes in networks and systems (pp. 76–90). DOI: 10.1007/978-3-031-18516-8_6

Hanan Mustapha, A. A. (2018), DDoS attacks on the internet of things and their prevention methods, *International Conference on Future Networks and Distributed Systems.* DOI: 10.1145/3231053.3231057

Inayat, U., Zia, M. F., Mahmood, S., Khalid, H. M., & Benbouzid, M. (2022). Learning-Based Methods for Cyber Attacks Detection in IoT Systems: A Survey on Methods, Analysis, and Future Prospects. *Electronics (Basel)*, 11(9), 1502. Advance online publication. DOI: 10.3390/electronics11091502

Karmous, N.. (2022), IoT Real-Time Attacks Classification Framework Using Machine Learning, *IEEE Ninth International Conference on Communications and Networking (ComNet)*. DOI: 10.1109/ComNet55492.2022.9998441

Kaur, P. (2022). *Isha Sharma, Rahul Kumar Singh* (1st ed.). Encryption Algorithms for Cloud Computing and Quantum Blockchain Book Artificial Intelligence, Machine Learning and Blockchain in Quantum Satellite, Drone and Network.

Kumar, S., Tiwari, P., & Zymbler, M. (2019). Internet of Things is a revolutionary approach for future technology enhancement: A review. *Journal of Big Data*, 6(1), 111. Advance online publication. DOI: 10.1186/s40537-019-0268-2

Kvarda, L., & Hnyk, P. (2017). *Software Implementation of Secure Firmware Update in IoT Concept* (Vol. 15). Information And Communication Technologies And Services.

Lei Cui a b, Youyang Qu et al.(2020), Detecting false data attacks using machine learning techniques in smart grid: A survey, Journal of Network and Computer Applications Volume 170.

Li, Y., & Liu, Q. (2021). A comprehensive review study of cyber-attacks and cyber security; Emerging trends and recent developments. *Energy Reports*, 7, 8176–8186. DOI: 10.1016/j.egyr.2021.08.126

P. Mahalle, B. Anggorojati, N. Prasad, and R. Prasad (2013), Identity Authentication and Capability Based Access Control (IACAC) for the Internet of Things. Journal of Cyber Security and Mobility, DOI:DOI: 10.13052/jcsm2245-1439.142

Miller, S. D., & Venkatesan, R. (2009). Expander Graphs Based on GRH with an Application to Elliptic Curve Cryptography. *Journal of Number Theory*, 129(6), 1491–1504. DOI: 10.1016/j.jnt.2008.11.006

Mohammad Rafsun Islam, K. M. Aktheruzzaman (2020), An Analysis of Cyber security Attacks against Internet of Things and Security Solutions, Journal of Computer and Communications ISSNPrint: 2327-5219,ISSN Online: 2327-5227

Mohindru, V., & Garg, A. (2021), Security attacks in internet of things: a review, Recent Innovations in Computing. p. 679–693. Singapore. DOI: 10.1007/978-981-15-8297-4_54

Mohit, Singh, Daliyal. (2024). The Role of Cybersecurity in Blockchain. Indian Scientific Journal Of Research in Engineering And Management DOI: 10.55041/ IJSREM30686

Mustafa, G., Ashraf, R., ... (2018), A review of data security and cryptographic techniques in IoT based devices, Conference: ICFNDS '18 Proceedings of the 2nd International Conference on Future Networks and Distributed Systems at Amman, Jordan

Okur, C., & Dener, M. (2020), Detecting IoT Botnet Attacks Using Machine Learning Methods, International Conference on Information Security and Cryptology (ISCTURKEY), Electronic ISBN:978-1-6654-1863-8.

B. Ondiege, M. Clarke, and G. Mapp. (2017). Exploring a New Security Framework for Remote Patient Monitoring Devices.

Phillip Williams et al. (2022), A survey on security in internet of things with a focus on the impact of emerging technologies, Internet of Things, Volume 19,ISSN 2542-6605, DOI: 10.1016/j.iot.2022.100564

Rahmani, A. M., Bayramov, S., & Kiani Kalejahi, B. (2022). Internet of Things Applications: Opportunities and Threats. *Wireless Personal Communications*, 122(1), 451–476. DOI: 10.1007/s11277-021-08907-0 PMID: 34426718

Rajmohan, T., Nguyen, P., & Ferry, N. (2022). A decade of research on patterns and architectures for IoT security. *Cybersecurity*, 5(1), 2. Advance online publication. DOI: 10.1186/s42400-021-00104-7

Rasane, T.. (2023). Blockchain in CyberSecurity [JETIR]. *Journal of Emerging Technologies and Innovative Research*, 10(5), ●●●.

Ravi Prakash, V.S. Anoop et al. (2022), Blockchain technology for cyber security: A text mining literature analysis, International Journal of Information Management Data Insights Volume 2, Issue 2.

Sakhi, Bandyopadhyay., Sunita, Sarkar., Somnath, Mukhopadhyay. (2023). Hiding Secret Data Using AES Encryption and DFS Graph Traversal in 3D Images. 1-4. DOI: 10.1109/ICEEICT56924.2023.10156957

Samah Osama Kamel, Nadia H Hegazi. (2018). A Proposed Model of IoT Security Management System Based on A study of Internet of Things (IoT) Security. *International Journal of Scientific and Engineering Research*.

Sambana, B. (2020). Block chain Approach to Cyber Security Vulnerabilities Attacks And Potential Counter Measures. *International Journal of Security and Its Applications*, 14(1), 1–14. DOI: 10.33832/ijsia.2020.14.1.01

Saqlain, J. (2018),"IoT and 5G: History evolution and its architecture their compatibility and future", Metropolia University of Applied Sciences Safa Ahmed et al. (2018), Overview for Internet of Things: Basics, Components and Applications, J. of University of Anbar for Pure Science: Vol.12: No.3, ISSN: 1991-8941.

Tinshu Sasi; Arash Habibi Lashkari et al. (2023), A comprehensive survey on IoT attacks: Taxonomy, detection mechanisms and challenges, Journal of Information and Intelligence, DOI: 10.1016/j.jiixd.2023.12.001

Science and Technology. Vol. 4, No. 1, 2018, pp. 1-5. doi: DOI: 10.11648/j. ijdst.20180401.1

Sharma, A., & Bhatt, A. P. (2021). Quantum Cryptography for Securing IoT-Based Healthcare Systems. In Advances in information security, privacy, and ethics book series (pp. 124–147). DOI: 10.4018/978-1-7998-6677-0.ch007

Sharma, N., Shamkuwar, M., & Singh, I. (2019). The History, Present and Future with IoT. In Balas, V., Solanki, V., Kumar, R., & Khari, M. (Eds.), *Internet of Things and Big Data Analytics for Smart Generation. Intelligent Systems Reference Library* (Vol. 154). Springer. DOI: 10.1007/978-3-030-04203-5_3

Sharma, R. (2012), Study of Latest Emerging Trends on Cyber Security and its challenges to Society, International Journal of Scientific & Engineering Research, Volume 3, Issue 6, 1ISSN 2229-5518.

Sheth, A., & Bhosale, S. (2021) Research Paper on Cyber Security, Contemporary Research in INDIA (ISSN 2231-2137).

Shruti, P., & Chandraleka, R. (2017), Elliptic Curve Cryptography Security in the Context of Internet of Things, International Journal of Scientific & Engineering Research Volume 8, Issue 5,ISSN 2229-5518

Singh, D., Tripathi, G., & Jara, A. J. (2014), A survey of internet of things: future vision, architecture, challenge and services, IEEE world forum on internet of things, Seoul, South Korea, p. 287–92.

Singh, G., & Kinger, S. (2013). A Study of Encryption Algorithms (RSA, DES, 3DES and AES) for Information Security. *International Journal of Computer Applications*, 67(19), 33–38. DOI: 10.5120/11507-7224

Tasnim, A., & Hossain, N. (2022), Experimental Analysis of Classification for Different Internet of Things (IoT) Network Attacks Using Machine Learning and Deep learning, *International Conference on Decision Aid Sciences and Applications (DASA)*. DOI: 10.1109/DASA54658.2022.9765108

Tseng F-H, Chou L-D, Chao H-C. (2011), A survey of black hole attacks in wireless mobile ad hoc networks., Hum Cent Comput Inf Sci. DOI: 10.1186/2192-1962-1-4

Veenoo Upadhyay, SuryakantYadav (2018), Study of Cyber Security Challenges Its Emerging Trends: Current Technologies International Journal of Engineering Research and Management (IJERM) ISSN: 2349- 2058, Volume-05, Issue-07.

Vella, H. (2022). The Race for Quantum-Resistant Cryptography [quantum - cyber security]. *Engineering & Technology*, 17(1), 56–59. DOI: 10.1049/et.2022.0109

Vutukuru, S. R., & Lade, S. C. (2023). *Secure IoT: Novel Machine Learning Algorithms for Detecting and Preventing Attacks on IoT Devices, J*. Electrical Systems.

Wander, A. S., Gura, N., Eberle, H., Gupta, V., & Shantz, S. C. (2005) Energy Analysis of Public-Key Cryptography for Wireless Sensor Networks, *IEEE International Conference on Pervasive Computing and Communications*, Kauai Island, DOI: 10.1109/PERCOM.2005.18

Wang, Z., Zhu, H., Liu, P., & Sun, L. (2021). Social engineering in cybersecurity: A domain ontology and knowledge graph application examples. *Cybersecurity*, 4(1), 31. DOI: 10.1186/s42400-021-00094-6

Xu, T.. (2017). *Defending against new-flow attack in SDN-based internet of things*. IEEE., DOI: 10.1109/ACCESS.2017.2666270

Zainab H. Ali et al. (2015), Internet of Things (IoT): Definitions, Challenges and Recent Research Directions, International Journal of Computer Applications (0975 – 8887) Volume 128 – No.1

Zhixian, C. (2020). Encryption technology of voice transmission in mobile network based on 3DES-ECC algorithm. *Mobile Networks and Applications*, 25(6), 2398–2408. DOI: 10.1007/s11036-020-01617-0

Chapter 12
Unlocking the Power of Software–Defined Networking (SDN) in Revolutionizing Network Management

Manasa Kulkarni
https://orcid.org/0000-0002-0129-2557
Christ University, India

Bhargavi Goswami
Queesnland University, Australia

Joy Paulose
Christ University, India

Lavanya Malakalapalli
IIT Dharwad, India

ABSTRACT

This chapter delves into the transformative impact of SDN on modern network management. By decoupling the control and data planes and centralizing network intelligence, SDN enables unprecedented flexibility, programmability, and efficiency in managing network infrastructures. The chapter examines various use cases, including data center network management, WAN optimization, and network security. These use cases demonstrate SDN's ability to dynamically allocate resources, optimize traffic flows, enforce security policies, and automate network provisioning.

DOI: 10.4018/979-8-3693-9225-6.ch012

Despite challenges related to scalability, reliability, and security, SDN's benefits in providing a comprehensive, real-time view of the network, enabling adaptive adjustments, and fostering innovation are emphasized. Overall, this chapter underscores SDN's role in revolutionizing network management, paving the way for more agile, efficient, and secure networks that can meet the ever-evolving demands of today's digital landscape.

1 INTRODUCTION

In an era defined by rapid technological advancements and the ubiquitous demand for high-speed, reliable network connectivity, the limitations of traditional network infrastructures have become increasingly apparent (McKeown et al., 2008). As businesses strive to meet the dynamic requirements of modern applications, services, and user expectations, the need for a more agile, scalable, and efficient network management solution has never been more critical. This pressing need has paved the way for the emergence of SDN, a transformative approach that promises to revolutionize the way networks are designed, deployed, and managed (Abdallah et al., 2018).

At its core, SDN is predicated on the decoupling of the network control plane from the data plane, allowing for centralized control and management of the network (Sharma et al., 2013). This separation facilitates unprecedented levels of flexibility and programmability, enabling network administrators to dynamically adjust network behavior to meet specific needs and conditions. By leveraging software to control hardware, SDN trans-forms static, hardware-centric networks into dynamic, software-driven environments capable of rapid adaptation and optimization (Kim & Feamster, 2013).

The journey to SDN began with the recognition of inherent challenges in traditional networking models. Conventional networks, characterized by their tightly coupled control and data planes, suffer from complexity, inflexibility, and high operational costs (Sasidharan & Chandra, 2014). These networks require manual configuration of individual devices, leading to cumber- some management processes and increased susceptibility to human error. Additionally, the proprietary nature of traditional networking hardware stifles innovation and locks organizations into vendor-specific solutions, further exacerbating inefficiencies (Rasool et al., 2021).

SDN addresses these challenges by introducing a programmable network architecture that allows for automated, policy-driven network management. Central to this architecture is the SDN controller, which serves as the brain of the network, making intelligent decisions about traffic routing, security policies, and resource allocation (Aliyu et al., 2020). This centralized control plane communicates with the underlying physical and virtual network infrastructure through standardized protocols such as OpenFlow, enabling granular control over network traffic and facilitating seamless integration of diverse network devices (Wickboldt et al., 2015).

The benefits of SDN extend across various dimensions of network management, delivering significant improvements in agility, efficiency, and cost-effectiveness. One of the most compelling advantages is the ability to swiftly deploy and modify network services in response to evolving business needs. By abstracting the network control from the physical infrastructure, SDN allows administrators to programmatically define and implement network policies, leading to faster service provisioning and reduced time-to-market for new applications (Kim et al., 2013). Furthermore, SDN enhances network visibility and monitoring capabilities, providing administrators with a holistic view of network performance and facilitating proactive management. This comprehensive visibility is instrumental in identifying and mitigating network issues before they escalate, thereby improving overall network reliability and performance. Additionally, the centralized control model simplifies network management by reducing the need for manual intervention and enabling automated configuration and troubleshooting processes (Tsagkaris et al., 2015).

In conclusion, SDN represents a paradigm shift in network management, offering a powerful solution to the limitations of traditional networks. By decoupling the control and data planes, SDN enables centralized, programmable, and automated network management, delivering unprecedented levels of agility, efficiency, and cost savings. As SDN continues to evolve and mature, it holds the promise of transforming not only how networks are managed but also how businesses operate in the digital age, paving the way for a more connected and innovative future.

1.1 Understanding Software-Defined Networking

SDN is a revolutionary approach to designing, building, and managing networks. SDN aims to improve network agility and flexibility by separating the network's control plane (which makes decisions about how data packets should flow through the net- work) from the data plane (which actually moves packets from place to place). This separation allows network administrators to programmatically manage network behavior through software applications, providing a more centralized and dynamic way to control network traffic.

1.1.1 Core Components of SDN

•**The Application Layer:** This topmost layer contains network applications and services that communicate with the SDN controller to define network behavior. Applications can include load balancers, firewalls, intrusion detection systems, and more. By abstracting network functionalities into software, applications can directly communicate with the network infrastructure, leading to more efficient and effective network management.

•**The Control Layer:** At the heart of SDN lies the SDN controller, which functions as the network's brain. The controller translates the requirements from the application layer into specific commands that the network devices in the infrastructure layer can execute. It holds a global view of the network, enabling centralized management, policy enforcement, and decision-making. Examples of SDN controllers include OpenDaylight, ONOS, and Cisco's Application Centric Infrastructure (ACI).

•**The Data Layer:** This bottom layer comprises the physical and virtual network devices such as switches, routers, and other forwarding devices that actually handle the data traffic. These devices are responsible for forwarding packets based on the instructions received from the control layer. The use of standardized protocols like OpenFlow allows the SDN controller to communicate with these devices regardless of the hardware vendor, promoting interoperability and flexibility.

1.2 Evolution and History

The concept of SDN has its roots in the challenges posed by traditional network architectures. Conventional networks are typically built with a static and tightly coupled control and data plane, which leads to several inefficiencies and complexities. Key Milestones in the Evolution of SDN:

•**Early Research and Development:** The origins of SDN can be traced back to research projects at Stanford University and UC Berkeley, particularly the Ethane project. Ethane sought to simplify network management by separating policy from the underlying hardware. This concept evolved into what we know today as SDN.

•**OpenFlow Protocol:** A significant breakthrough in the development of SDN was the introduction of the OpenFlow protocol. OpenFlow, proposed by researchers at Stanford in 2008, provided a standardized interface for SDN controllers to communicate with network devices. It enabled direct control of the forwarding plane from the control plane, facilitating the implementation of SDN in existing network environments.

•**Industry Adoption and Standardization:** The formation of the Open Networking Foundation (ONF) in 2011 marked a pivotal moment for SDN. The ONF, a consortium of industry leaders, was established to promote and stan-

dardize OpenFlow and other SDN technologies. This collaboration between academia and industry accelerated the adoption of SDN in commercial networks.
•Development of SDN Controllers and Platforms: With the growing interest in SDN, numerous open-source and commercial SDN controllers were developed. Projects like OpenDaylight, Ryu, and ONOS provided robust platforms for deploying SDN in various environments. These controllers offered comprehensive frameworks for building and managing SDN-based networks.

1.3 Architectural Framework

The SDN architectural framework is designed to provide a modular and flexible approach to network management, enabling centralized control, policy enforcement, and automation. The SDN architecture is provided in the figure 1. All the three layers are explained in-detail in the forth sections below. The primary components of this framework include:

1.3.1 Data Plane

The data plane consists of the physical and virtual network devices that forward data packets based on the instructions from the control plane. These devices, such as switches and routers, are equipped with flow tables that are populated by the SDN controller. The data plane is responsible for the actual handling and forwarding of network traffic. Key Functions of the Data Plane:

> **•Packet Forwarding:** Data plane devices forward packets according to the flow entries installed by the controller.
> **•Traffic Monitoring:** Data plane devices can provide real-time statistics and telemetry data to the controller for monitoring and analytics.

1.3.2 Control Plane

The control plane is responsible for the overall logic and decision-making in the network. The SDN controller, residing in the control plane, oversees network-wide operations and provides a centralized interface for network management. The con- troller maintains a global view of the network, enabling it to make informed decisions about traffic flow, resource allocation, and policy enforcement.

Figure 1. SDN architecture

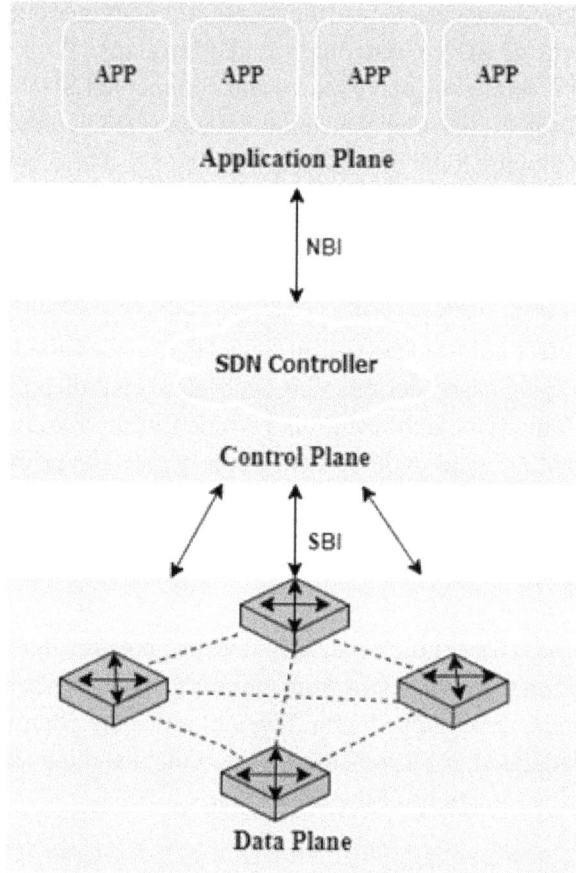

Key Functions of the Control Plane:

•Network Topology Management: The controller maintains a real-time map of the network topology, tracking the status and connectivity of network devices.

•Path Computation: The controller computes optimal paths for data packets based on network policies, traffic conditions, and resource availability.

•Policy Enforcement: The controller enforces security, quality of service (QoS), and other network policies consistently across the network.

1.3.3 Application Plane

The application plane hosts network applications and services that interact with the SDN controller to request specific network behaviors. These applications leverage the programmability of the network to implement advanced functionalities, such as dynamic traffic engineering, load balancing, and security enforcement.

Key Functions of the Application Plane:
•**Network Optimization:** Applications can optimize network performance by dynamically adjusting traffic flows and resource allocation.
•**Security Management:** Security applications can implement granular access controls, intrusion detection, and threat mitigation.
•**Service Provisioning:** Applications can automate the deployment and manage- ment of network services, reducing manual intervention and operational complexity.

1.4 Benefits of SDN

SDN offers a multitude of benefits that address the limitations of traditional network architectures and enhance network management capabilities:

Figure 2. Benefits of SDN

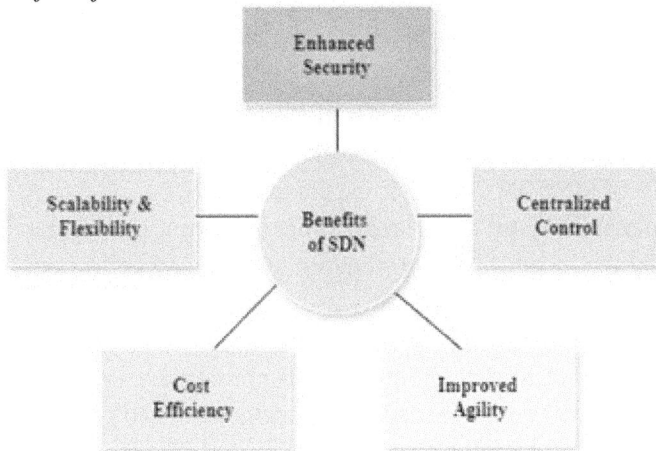

•**Centralized Control and Visibility:** SDN provides a centralized platform for managing the entire network, offering comprehensive visibility and control. This centralization simplifies network management, troubleshooting, and policy enforcement.

•**Improved Network Agility:** SDN's programmability allows for rapid adaptation to changing network conditions and business requirements. Network administrators can quickly deploy new services, adjust policies, and reconfigure the network in real-time.

•**Cost Efficiency:** By leveraging commodity hardware and open standards, SDN reduces the reliance on expensive proprietary equipment. Additionally, the automa- tion of network management tasks reduces operational costs and the need for manual intervention.

•**Enhanced Security:** SDN enables consistent enforcement of security policies across the network and provides granular control over traffic flows. Centralized 6 control allows for quick response to security threats and easier implementation of security measures.

•**Scalability and Flexibility:** SDN's modular architecture allows for easy scaling of network resources and integration of new technologies. This flexibility supports the dynamic needs of modern applications and services.

1.5 Challenges and Future Directions

While SDN offers significant advantages, its adoption and implementation come with challenges that need to be addressed:

•**Security Concerns:** The centralization of control in SDN introduces potential single points of failure and new attack vectors. Ensuring the security and resilience of the SDN controller is paramount.

•**Interoperability and Standardization:** Ensuring interoperability between SDN solutions from different vendors and adherence to open standards is critical for widespread adoption.

•**Skill Gap and Training:** The shift to SDN requires network professionals to acquire new skills and knowledge. Comprehensive training programs and educational resources are necessary to bridge this skill gap.

•**Performance and Scalability:** As SDN deployments grow in scale, ensuring the performance and scalability of the SDN controller and underlying infrastructure becomes increasingly important.

In conclusion, Software-Defined Networking represents a transformative approach to network management, offering unprecedented levels of agility, efficiency, and control. By decoupling the control and data planes, SDN enables centralized, programmable, and automated network management, revolutionizing how networks are designed, deployed, and managed. As SDN continues to evolve and mature, it holds the promise of driving innovation and efficiency in network operations, paving the way for a more connected and dynamic future.

1.6 Benefits of SDN in Network Management

SDN is transforming the landscape of network management by offering significant improvements in control, flexibility, and efficiency. This section delves into the mul- tifaceted benefits of SDN, illustrating how it addresses the limitations of traditional network architectures and enhances overall network performance.

1.6.1 Centralized Network Control

One of the hallmark benefits of SDN is its centralized control model, which consolidates network intelligence into a single entity—the SDN controller. This centralization brings several advantages:

•**Simplified Network Management:** In traditional networks, managing each net- work device individually is cumbersome and error-prone. With SDN, the controller provides a unified platform for managing all network devices, reducing the complex- ity associated with device-specific configurations. Administrators can define policies and configurations at a high level, which the controller then translates into device- specific instructions. This abstraction simplifies network management and reduces the likelihood of configuration errors.

•**Improved Network Visibility:** SDN provides comprehensive visibility into the entire network through the centralized controller. Administrators can monitor traf- fic flows, device status, and network performance from a single interface. This holistic view enables more effective troubleshooting and performance optimiza- tion. Enhanced visibility also facilitates proactive network management, allowing administrators to detect and address issues before they impact users.

1.6.2 Enhanced Network Agility and Flexibility

SDN's programmability and dynamic nature significantly enhance network agility and flexibility, enabling networks to adapt quickly to changing demands and conditions.

•Rapid Deployment of Services: SDN allows for the swift deployment of new services and applications. Network administrators can programmatically define net- work behavior and deploy configurations without the need for extensive manual intervention. This rapid deployment capability is particularly valuable in envi- ronments where new services must be brought online quickly to meet business needs.

•Automated Network Provisioning: Automation is a cornerstone of SDN. The ability to automate network provisioning reduces the time and effort required to configure and manage network resources. Automated processes minimize the risk of human error, ensuring consistent and reliable network configurations. This automa- tion extends to tasks such as VLAN assignments, IP address management, and policy enforcement, all of which can be managed through software.

•Dynamic Traffic Management: SDN enables dynamic traffic management by allowing the controller to adjust traffic flows in real time based on current net- work conditions. This capability is crucial for optimizing network performance and ensuring efficient utilization of network resources. For example, SDN can dynam- ically reroute traffic to avoid congestion, balance loads across multiple paths, and prioritize critical applications.

1.6.3 Cost Efficiency

SDN offers several cost-related benefits that make it an attractive option for network management.

•Reduced Capital Expenditure: Traditional networks often rely on expensive, proprietary hardware. SDN, on the other hand, leverages commodity hardware and open standards, which are typically more cost-effective. This shift reduces the capital expenditure (CapEx) associated with purchasing and upgrading network equipment. By decoupling the control plane from the data plane, SDN allows organizations to invest in more affordable, versatile hardware without sacrificing performance.

•Lower Operational Costs: The operational expenditure (OpEx) associated with running a network can be significantly reduced through SDN. The centralization and automation of network management tasks streamline operations and reduce the need for extensive manual intervention. Network administrators can focus on higher-level tasks and strategic planning rather than routine maintenance and trou- bleshooting. Additionally, automated network management reduces downtime and improves service reliability, further lowering operational costs.

•Efficient Use of Network Resources: SDN optimizes the utilization of network resources, leading to cost savings. By dynamically allocating resources based on real-time demand, SDN ensures that network capacity is used efficiently. This opti- mization minimizes the need for overprovisioning and allows organizations to scale their networks more economically.

1.6.4 Improved Security and Compliance

Security is a critical concern in network management, and SDN offers several features that enhance network security and ensure compliance with policies and regulations.

•Granular Policy Enforcement: SDN enables granular policy enforcement across the network. Administrators can define detailed security policies that the SDN con- troller implements consistently throughout the network. This centralized approach simplifies the enforcement of access controls, firewall rules, and other security measures, ensuring uniform protection across all network segments.

•Dynamic Threat Mitigation: The programmability of SDN allows for dynamic threat mitigation. The SDN controller can respond to security incidents in real time, adjusting traffic flows and implementing countermeasures to isolate and mitigate threats. For instance, if an intrusion detection system (IDS) identifies a secu- rity breach, the SDN controller can automatically redirect traffic away from the compromised area and apply additional security measures.

•Enhanced Monitoring and Analytics: SDN provides enhanced monitoring and analytics capabilities, which are essential for maintaining network security. The centralized controller collects detailed telemetry data from network devic- es, enabling comprehensive analysis of traffic patterns and potential threats. This data can be used to detect anomalies, conduct forensic investigations, and refine security policies.

1.7 Scalability and Future-Proofing

SDN's modular architecture supports scalability and future-proofing, ensuring that networks can grow and evolve to meet changing demands.

• **Scalability:** SDN facilitates scalable network designs by allowing administrators to add new devices and services without significant reconfiguration. The centralized control model simplifies the integration of additional network elements, ensuring that the network can expand seamlessly. This scalability is particularly valuable in large-scale environments such as data centers and service provider networks.

• **Future-Proofing:** The flexibility and programmability of SDN ensure that networks can adapt to emerging technologies and evolving business needs. As new protocols, applications, and devices are developed, they can be integrated into the SDN frame- work with minimal disruption. This future-proofing capability protects investments in network infrastructure and ensures long-term viability.

1.7.1 Enhanced Performance and Quality of Service (QoS)

SDN's ability to dynamically manage traffic flows and allocate resources enhances net- work performance and ensures high Quality of Service (QoS) for critical applications.

• **Traffic Optimization:** SDN enables advanced traffic optimization techniques, such as load balancing, traffic shaping, and congestion management. The SDN controller can dynamically adjust traffic paths to balance loads across the network, prevent bottlenecks, and ensure efficient use of bandwidth. These optimizations enhance overall network performance and improve the user experience.

• **Quality of Service (QoS):** SDN allows for precise QoS management by enabling administrators to define and enforce QoS policies at a granular level. Critical applica- tions can be prioritized, ensuring that they receive the necessary bandwidth and low latency. This capability is essential for applications that require high performance, such as video conferencing, online gaming, and real-time data analytics.

1.8 Conclusion

The benefits of SDN in network management are profound and multifaceted, addressing many of the limitations and challenges associated with traditional network architectures. By centralizing control, enhancing agility, reducing costs, improving security, and supporting scalability, SDN provides a robust framework for managing modern networks. As organizations continue to adopt and implement SDN, they can expect to achieve greater efficiency, flexibility, and performance, ultimately leading to more effective and responsive network operations.

2 RELATED WORKS

A comprehensive review on significant papers on "Unlocking the Power of Software-Defined Networking (SDN) in Revolutionizing Network Management" reveals a diverse landscape of research focused on the transformative potential of SDN. The literature collectively highlights how SDN's decoupling of the control and data planes, centralized control mechanisms, and enhanced programmability enable dynamic, flexible, and efficient network management. For instance, studies by Kreutz et al. (2014) and Nunes et al. (2014) emphasize the architectural benefits of SDN, showcasing its capability to simplify network management, improve scalability, and support rapid innovation through programmable interfaces. These foundational works lay the groundwork for understanding SDN's core principles and its impact on modern network infrastructures.

Further investigations delve into specific applications and benefits of SDN in various network environments. Papers by Jain et al. (2013) and Benson et al. (2010) illustrate the effectiveness of SDN in optimizing data center networks, highlighting improvements in resource allocation, traffic engineering, and fault tolerance. Similarly, works by Hong et al. (2013) and Curtis et al. (2011) explore SDN's role in wide area networks (WANs), demonstrating its ability to enhance bandwidth management, reduce latency, and increase overall network performance. These studies provide empirical evidence of SDN's advantages in practical, large-scale deployments, reinforcing its value proposition for network operators and enterprises. Challenges and future directions in SDN research are also prominent themes in the reviewed literature. Papers by Phemius et al. (2014) and Hassas Yeganeh and Ganjali (2012) address issues related to scalability, security, and interoperability, proposing solutions such as hierarchical control structures and advanced security frameworks. Additionally, research by Lara and Kolasani (2013) and Handigol et al. (2012) discusses the integration of SDN with emerging technologies like network function virtualization (NFV) and the Internet of Things (IoT), highlighting the potential for further innovation and enhancement of network capabilities. Collectively, these papers underscore the ongoing evolution of SDN, its transformative impact on network management, and the continuous need for addressing the challenges to fully realize its potential.

3 KEY TECHNOLOGIES OF SDN

SDN represents a paradigm shift in network architecture, promising unprecedented flexibility, programmability, and efficiency. Central to the realization of SDN are sev- eral key technologies that underpin its framework. These technologies include the separation of the control and data planes, the use of standard communication protocols like OpenFlow, the implementation of centralized controllers, network virtualization, and the development of application programming interfaces (APIs). This section delves into these critical technologies and their roles in enabling SDN.

3.1 OpenFlow Protocol

OpenFlow is one of the most widely used protocols in SDN. It defines a standard-ized method for a controller to communicate with network devices, facilitating the implementation of the SDN model. How OpenFlow works is described below:

•**Flow Tables:** Network devices maintain flow tables that define how packets should be handled. These tables can be dynamically programmed by the SDN controller.
•**Match-Action Paradigm:** OpenFlow follows a match-action paradigm where incoming packets are matched against flow table entries, and predefined actions (like forward, drop, modify) are executed based on these matches.
•**Secure Channel:** Communication between the SDN controller and the net-work devices occurs over a secure channel, ensuring the integrity and security of the instructions being passed.

Advantages of OpenFlow:

•**Interoperability:** OpenFlow's standardization ensures interoperability between devices from different vendors.
•**Dynamic Control:** Enables real-time network adjustments and optimizations.
•**Simplicity:** Simplifies the network architecture by providing a uniform in-terface for managing devices.

3.2 Separation of Control and Data Plane

In traditional network architectures, the control plane (which makes decisions about where traffic should be sent) and the data plane (which actually forwards the traffic) are tightly coupled within the network devices, such as routers and switches. SDN decouples these planes, relocating the control plane to a centralized controller while the data plane remains on the network devices.

4 SDN CONTROLLERS

SDN controllers are the pivotal components of SDN architecture, acting as the central management and control point for the network (Salman et al., 2016). They decouple the control logic from the underlying network devices, centralizing network intelligence and providing programmability and automation capabilities. This section explores the various aspects of SDN controllers, including their roles, key functions, prominent examples, and challenges associated with their implementation (Ahmad & Mir, 2021). SDN controllers serve as the "brain" of the network, orchestrating the behavior of the entire network infrastructure based on a comprehensive view of the network state. They interact with both the data plane (network devices like switches and routers) and the application plane (network applications and services), enabling dynamic and automated network management.

4.1 Centralized Control

The primary role of SDN controllers is to centralize control and decision-making processes (Kulkarni et al., 2021), allowing for:

•**Global Network View:** By maintaining a global view of the network, controllers can make more informed decisions, optimizing network performance and resource utilization.
•**Global Network View:** By maintaining a global view of the network, controllers can make more informed decisions, optimizing network performance and resource utilization.
•**Policy Enforcement:** Controllers implement and enforce network policies consis- tently across the network, ensuring compliance and security.
•**Dynamic Adjustments:** They enable real-time network adjustments based on current conditions, such as traffic patterns, application demands, and security threats.

4.2 Key Functions of SDN Controllers

SDN controllers perform a range of functions critical to efficient network management:

4.2.1 Network Topology Discovery and Management

- Topology Discovery: Controllers discover and maintain an up-to-date map of the network topology, including all devices and their interconnections.
- Topology Management: They manage changes in the network topology, such as device additions, removals, and link failures, ensuring continuous network operation.

4.2.2 Traffic Engineering and Path Calculation

- Traffic Engineering: Controllers optimize the flow of network traffic by dynamically adjusting paths based on current network conditions and performance metrics.
- Path Calculation: Using algorithms and policies, controllers calculate optimal paths for data transmission, improving network efficiency and reducing latency.

4.2.3 Network Monitoring and Analytics

- Monitoring: Controllers continuously monitor network performance, collecting data on metrics like bandwidth usage, latency, packet loss, and device status.
- Analytics: They analyze the collected data to identify trends, detect anomalies, and predict future network conditions, providing insights for proactive management.

4.2.4 Security and Policy Enforcement

- Security Policies: Controllers implement security policies to protect the network from threats, such as access control lists (ACLs), firewall rules, and intrusion detection systems (IDS).
- Policy Enforcement: They ensure that security policies are consistently applied across the network, mitigating potential vulnerabilities.

4.3 Prominent SDN Controllers

Several SDN controllers have gained prominence due to their robustness, scalability, and feature sets. Here are some of the most notable ones:

4.3.1 OpenDayLight

OpenDaylight is an open-source SDN controller platform developed under the Linux Foundation. It aims to accelerate the adoption of SDN and create a robust foundation for network functions virtualization (NFV). Highly modular, supports various south-bound and northbound protocols, extensive community support, and a wide range of plugins and applications. It can be complex to set up and configure, requires significant resources for large-scale deployments. Figure 3 shows the ODL architecture in detail.

4.3.2 ONOS (Open Network Operating System)

ONOS is designed to meet the needs of service providers by offering high performance, scalability, and availability. It focuses on scalability and high availability, suitable for large-scale carrier networks, strong support for network slicing. Primarily targeted at service providers, may not be as feature-rich for enterprise applications. Figure 4 shows the ONOS architecture in detail.

4.3.3 Ryu

Ryu is a component-based SDN framework that provides software components for building SDN applications. It is installed in Python and designed to be simple and easy to use. It is lightweight, easy to deploy and extend, strong support for OpenFlow and other protocols. Lacks some advanced features and scalability found in other controllers. Figure 5 shows the RYU architecture in detail.

Figure 3. OenDayLight controller architecture

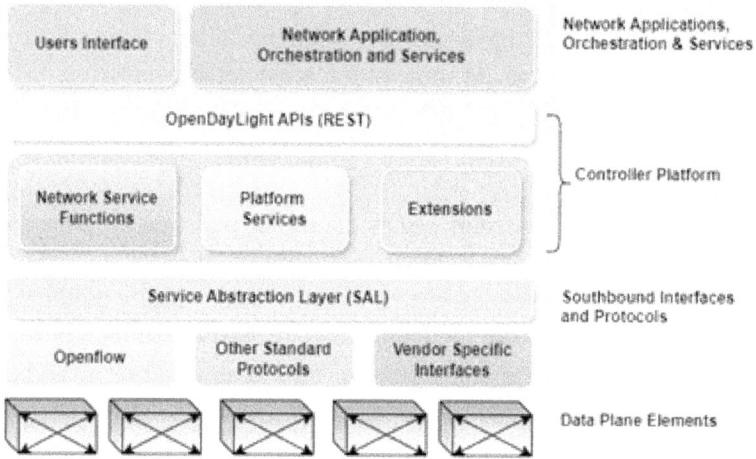

Figure 4. ONOS architecture

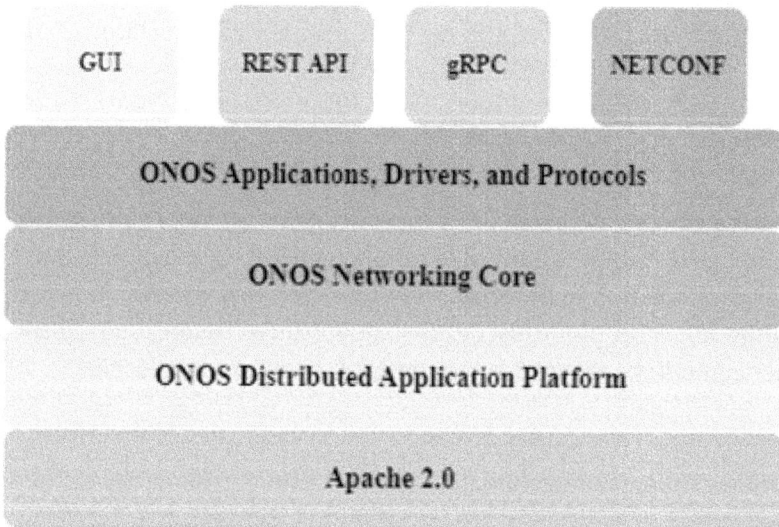

Figure 5. Ryu architecture

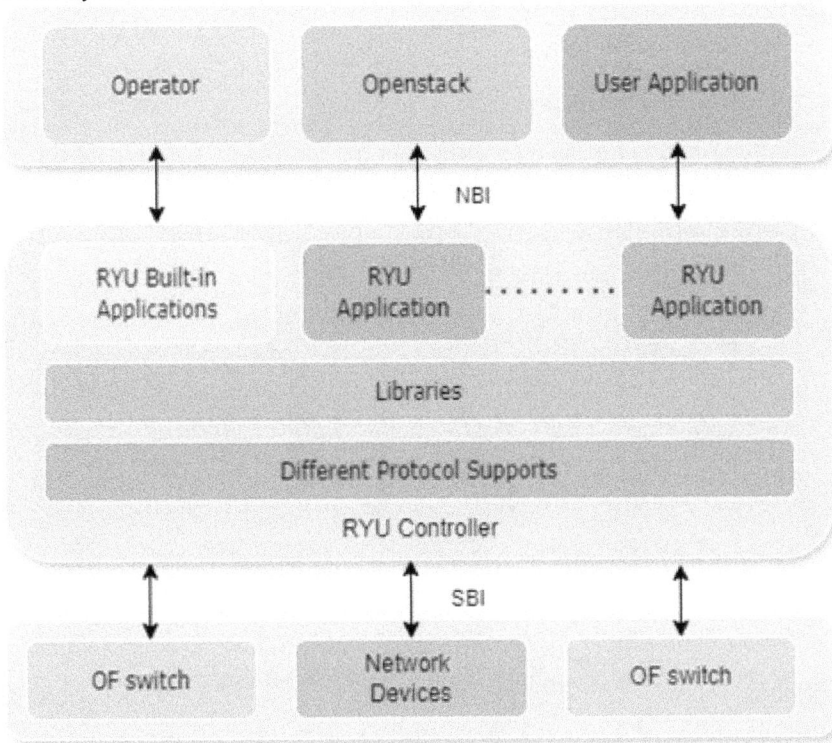

4.3.4 Floodlight

Floodlight is an open-source SDN controller written in Java. It is known for its ease of use and integration capabilities. It is user-friendly, has good documentation, and supports a variety of network applications. It has limited support for non-OpenFlow protocols, and less focus on large-scale deployments. Figure 6 shows the Floodlight architecture in detail.

5 USE CASES OF SDN IN MODERN NETWORKS

SDN has introduced revolutionary changes in the way networks are managed, optimized, and secured. Its ability to decouple the control plane from the data plane, coupled with centralized network control and programmability, allows for a wide range of applications and use cases (Mamushiane et al., 2018). This section delves into several prominent use cases of SDN in modern network management, exploring how SDN technology enhances network efficiency, flexibility, and security (Zhu et al., 2019).

Figure 6. Floodlight architecture

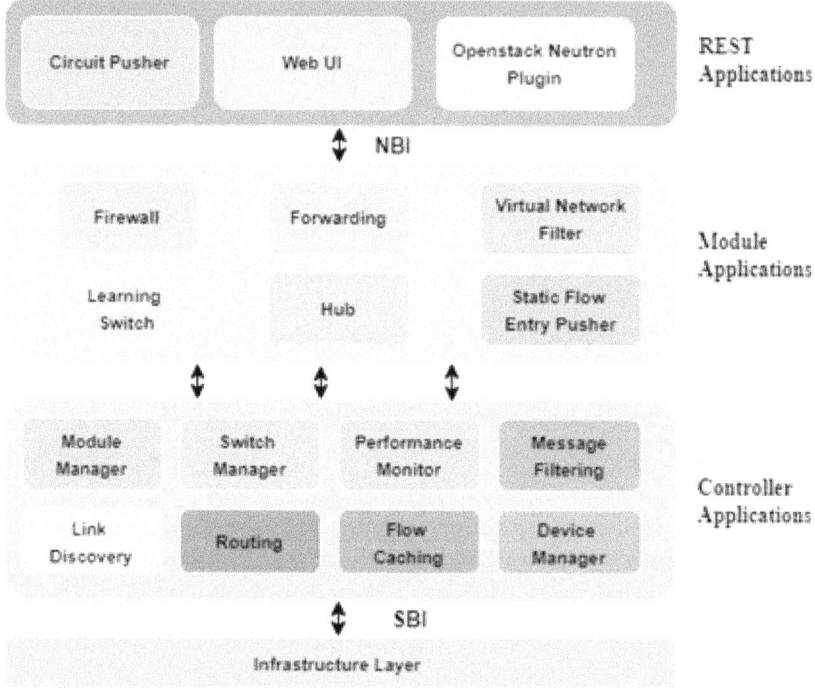

5.1 Data Center Network Management

Data centers are the backbone of modern digital infrastructure, hosting applications, services, and data storage. SDN significantly enhances data center network management in several ways:

5.1.1 Dynamic Resource Allocation

SDN enables dynamic allocation of network resources based on real-time demands, ensuring efficient utilization.

•**Benefits:** Reduces latency, avoids congestion, and maximizes resource utilization.

•Example: Google's B4 SDN project dynamically reallocates network resources between data centers, improving bandwidth utilization.

5.1.2 Traffic Engineering

SDN controllers can dynamically adjust traffic paths to optimize network performance and reduce bottlenecks.

•Benefits: Enhances network throughput, reduces latency, and improves overall performance.
•Example: Microsoft Azure's SWAN project uses SDN for traffic engineering, achieving significant performance improvements.

5.1.3 Network Virtualization

SDN supports the creation of virtual networks that are isolated and can be managed independently.

•Benefits: Enhances security, allows multi-tenancy, and simplifies network management.
•Example: VMware NSX uses SDN to create virtual networks within data centers, providing isolation and security for different tenants.

5.2 Wide Area Network (WAN) Optimization

SDN is also transforming Wide Area Networks (WANs) by providing centralized control and optimization capabilities.

5.2.1 Dynamic Path Selection

SDN enables dynamic selection of optimal paths for data transmission across the WAN based on current network conditions.

•Benefits: Improves network efficiency, reduces latency, and ensures reliable data delivery.
•Example: Cisco's IWAN uses SDN to dynamically select the best paths for WAN traffic, optimizing performance and reliability.

5.2.2 Bandwidth Management

SDN controllers can dynamically allocate bandwidth based on application require- ments and network policies.

> •**Benefits:** Ensures critical applications receive the necessary bandwidth while optimizing overall network utilization.
> •**Example:** Google's Espresso leverages SDN to manage bandwidth dynamically, improving performance and cost-efficiency.

5.2.3 Multi-Path Routing

SDN supports multi-path routing, enabling the use of multiple paths for data transmission to improve redundancy and load balancing.

> •**Benefits:** Enhances network resilience and balances traffic load across multiple paths.
> •**Example:** Facebook's Express Backbone uses SDN for multi-path routing, ensuring high availability and performance.

5.3 Network Security

SDN enhances network security by providing centralized control and the ability to dynamically enforce security policies.

5.3.1 Distributed Denial of Service (DDoS) Mitigation

SDN can detect and mitigate DDoS attacks in real-time by dynamically rerouting or filtering malicious traffic.

> •**Benefits:** Protects network resources, ensures availability, and minimizes the impact of attacks.
> •**Example:** AT&T uses SDN to mitigate DDoS attacks by dynamically rerouting traffic to scrubbing

5.3.2 Access Control

SDN enables fine-grained access control by dynamically applying security policies based on user roles, device types, and network segments.

•Benefits: Enhances security by ensuring only authorized users and devices can access critical resources.
•Example: Google's BeyondCorp security model uses SDN principles to enforce granular access controls, enhancing security for remote and mobile users.

5.3.3 Network Segmentation

SDN facilitates network segmentation by creating isolated network segments for different applications, users, or services.
•Benefits: Improves security by containing potential threats within isolated segments and preventing lateral movement.
•Example: Healthcare networks use SDN to segment patient data, ensuring compli- ance with regulations and enhancing security.

5.4 Network Automation and Orchestration

SDN plays a crucial role in automating and orchestrating network operations, reducing manual intervention and improving efficiency.

5.4.1 Automated Provisioning

SDN automates the provisioning of network resources and services based on predefined policies and real-time demands.

•Benefits: Reduces deployment times, minimizes errors, and enhances operational efficiency.
•Example: Telcos use SDN for automated provisioning of virtual network functions (VNFs), accelerating service delivery.

5.4.2 Policy-Based Management

SDN enables policy-based network management, where policies can be centrally defined and dynamically enforced across the network.

•Benefits: Ensures consistent policy enforcement, simplifies management, and improves compliance.
•Example: Enterprises use SDN to enforce security and quality of service (QoS) policies dynamically, ensuring compliance and optimal performance.

5.4.3 Fault Management and Recovery

SDN controllers can detect network faults in real-time and initiate automated recovery procedures, such as rerouting traffic or reallocating resources.

> •**Benefits:** Enhances network reliability, reduces downtime, and ensures continuous operation.
> •**Example:** Telecom operators use SDN for automated fault management, reducing mean time to repair (MTTR) and improving service availability.

5.5 Edge Computing and Internet of Things (IoT)

SDN is instrumental in managing the complex and dynamic nature of edge computing and IoT environments.

5.5.1 Edge Network Management

SDN provides centralized management and control of edge networks, optimizing data processing and transmission at the network edge.

> •**Benefits:** Reduces latency, improves performance, and enhances scalability for edge applications.
> •**Example:** Smart cities use SDN to manage edge networks, ensuring efficient data processing for IoT applications.

5.5.2 IoT Security

SDN enhances IoT security by dynamically applying security policies and monitoring IoT device behavior.

> •**Benefits:** Protects IoT devices and data, ensuring secure and reliable operation.
> •**Example:** Industrial IoT deployments use SDN to enforce security policies and monitor device traffic, mitigating potential threats.

6 CONCLUSION

"Unlocking the Power of Software-Defined Networking (SDN) in Revolutionizing Net- work Management" highlights the transformative potential of SDN in modern network environments. SDN decouples the control and data planes, centralizes network control, and introduces programmability, fundamentally changing how networks are managed and optimized. Key technologies such as the separation of control and data planes, protocols like OpenFlow, centralized controllers, network virtualization, and APIs collectively enhance network flexibility, efficiency, and security. The chapter explores various use cases, including data center network management, WAN optimization, network security, network automation, and the management of edge computing and IoT environments. These use cases demonstrate how SDN enables dynamic resource allocation, traffic engineering, automated provisioning, policy-based management, and enhanced security measures. Despite challenges related to scalability, reliability, security, and interoperability, SDN's benefits in providing a global view, enabling real-time adjustments, and fostering innovation are evident. Overall, SDN represents a significant advancement in network management, offering a path towards more adaptive, efficient, and secure network infrastructures that are better equipped to meet the evolving demands of modern digital environments.

REFERENCES

Abdallah, S., Elhajj, I. H., Chehab, A., & Kayssi, A. (2018, February). A network management framework for SDN. In 2018 9th IFIP International Conference on New Technologies, Mobility and Security (NTMS) (pp. 1-4). IEEE. DOI: 10.1109/NTMS.2018.8328672

Ahmad, S., & Mir, A. H. (2021). Scalability, consistency, reliability and security in SDN controllers: A survey of diverse SDN controllers. *Journal of Network and Systems Management*, 29(1), 1–59. DOI: 10.1007/s10922-020-09575-4

Aliyu, A. L., Aneiba, A., Patwary, M., & Bull, P. (2020). A trust manage- ment framework for software defined network (SDN) controller and network applications. *Computer Networks*, 181, 107421. DOI: 10.1016/j.comnet.2020.107421

Benson, T., Akella, A., & Maltz, D. A. (2010, November). Network traffic charac- teristics of data centers in the wild. In *Proceedings of the 10th ACM SIGCOMM conference on Internet measurement* (pp. 267-280). DOI: 10.1145/1879141.1879175

Curtis, A. R., Mogul, J. C., Tourrilhes, J., Yalagandula, P., & Sharma, P., Baner- jee, S. (2011, August). DevoFlow: Scaling flow management for high-performance networks. In Proceedings of the ACM SIGCOMM 2011 Conference (pp. 254-265). DOI: 10.1145/2018436.2018466

Handigol, N., Heller, B., Jeyakumar, V., Lantz, B., & McKeown, N. (2012, De- cember). Reproducible network experiments using container-based emulation. In *Proceedings of the 8th international conference on Emerging networking experiments and technologies* (pp. 253-264). DOI: 10.1145/2413176.2413206

Hassas Yeganeh, S., & Ganjali, Y. (2012, August). Kandoo: a framework for effi- cient and scalable offloading of control applications. In *Proceedings of the first workshop on Hot topics in software defined networks* (pp. 19-24). DOI: 10.1145/2342441.2342446

Hong, C. Y., Kandula, S., Mahajan, R., Zhang, M., Gill, V., & Nanduri, M., Watten- hofer, R. (2013, August). Achieving high utilization with software-driven WAN. In Proceedings of the ACM SIGCOMM 2013 Conference on SIGCOMM (pp. 15-26).

Jain, S., Kumar, A., Mandal, S., Ong, J., Poutievski, L., Singh, A., Venkata, S., Wanderer, J., Zhou, J., Zhu, M., Zolla, J., Hölzle, U., Stuart, S., & Vahdat, A. (2013). B4: Experience with a globally-deployed software defined WAN. *Computer Com- munication Review*, 43(4), 3–14. DOI: 10.1145/2534169.2486019

Kim, D., Gil, J. M., Wang, G., & Kim, S. H. (2013). Integrated SDN and non-SDN network management approaches for future internet environment. In Multimedia 20 and Ubiquitous Engineering: MUE 2013 (pp. 529-536). Springer Netherlands. DOI: 10.1007/978-94-007-6738-6_64

Kim, H., & Feamster, N. (2013). Improving network management with software defined networking. *IEEE Communications Magazine*, 51(2), 114–119. DOI: 10.1109/MCOM.2013.6461195

Kreutz, D., Ramos, F. M., Verissimo, P. E., Rothenberg, C. E., Azodolmolky, S., & Uhlig, S. (2014). Software-defined networking: A comprehensive survey. *Proceedings of the IEEE*, 103(1), 14–76. DOI: 10.1109/JPROC.2014.2371999

Kulkarni, M., Goswami, B., & Paulose, J. (2021, February). Experimenting with scalability of software defined networks using pyretic and frenetic. In *International Conference on Computing Science, Communication and Security* (pp. 168-192). Cham: Springer International Publishing. DOI: 10.1007/978-3-030-76776-1_12

Lara, A., Kolasani, A., & Ramamurthy, B. (2013). Network innovation using openflow: A survey. *IEEE Communications Surveys and Tutorials*, 16(1), 493–512. DOI: 10.1109/SURV.2013.081313.00105

Mamushiane, L., Lysko, A., Dlamini, S. (2018, April). A comparative evaluation of the performance of popular SDN controllers. In 2018 Wireless Days (WD) (pp. 54-59). IEEE.

McKeown, N., Anderson, T., Balakrishnan, H., Parulkar, G., Peterson, L., Rexford, J., Shenker, S., & Turner, J. (2008). OpenFlow: Enabling innovation in campus networks. *Computer Communication Review*, 38(2), 69–74. DOI: 10.1145/1355734.1355746

Nunes, B. A. A., Mendonca, M., Nguyen, X. N., Obraczka, K., & Turletti, T. (2014). A survey of software-defined networking: Past, present, and future of programmable networks. *IEEE Communications Surveys and Tutorials*, 16(3), 1617–1634. DOI: 10.1109/SURV.2014.012214.00180

Phemius, K., Bouet, M., & Leguay, J. (2014, May). DISCO: Distributed SDN controllers in a multi-domain environment. In *2014 IEEE Network Operations and Management Symposium (NOMS)* (pp. 1-2). IEEE.

Rasool, Z. I., Abd Ali, R. S., & Abdulzahra, M. M. (2021, February). Network management in software-defined network: A survey. []. IOP Publishing.]. *IOP Conference Series. Materials Science and Engineering*, 1094(1), 012055. DOI: 10.1088/1757-899X/1094/1/012055

Salman, O., Elhajj, I. H., Kayssi, A., & Chehab, A. (2016, April). SDN controllers: A comparative study. In 2016 18th mediterranean electrotechnical conference (MELECON) (pp. 1-6). IEEE. DOI: 10.1109/MELCON.2016.7495430

Sasidharan, S., & Chandra, S. K. (2014, July). Defining future SDN based network management systems characterization and approach. In Fifth International Conference on Computing, Communications and Networking Technologies (ICCCNT) (pp. 1-5). IEEE. DOI: 10.1109/ICCCNT.2014.6963137

Sharma, P., Banerjee, S., Tandel, S., Aguiar, R., Amorim, R., & Pinheiro, D. (2013, May). Enhancing network management frameworks with SDN-like control. In *2013 IFIP/IEEE International Symposium on Integrated Network Management (IM 2013)* (pp. 688-691). IEEE.

Tsagkaris, K., Logothetis, M., Foteinos, V., Poulios, G., Michaloliakos, M., & Demestichas, P. (2015). Customizable autonomic network management: Inte- grating autonomic network management and software-defined networking. *IEEE Vehicular Technology Magazine*, 10(1), 61–68. DOI: 10.1109/MVT.2014.2380633

Wickboldt, J. A., De Jesus, W. P., Isolani, P. H., Both, C. B., Rochol, J., & Granville, L. Z. (2015). Software-defined networking: Management requirements and challenges. *IEEE Communications Magazine*, 53(1), 278–285. DOI: 10.1109/MCOM.2015.7010546

Zhu, L., Karim, M. M., Sharif, K., Li, F., Du, X., & Guizani, M. SDN con- trollers: Benchmarking performance evaluation. arXiv 2019. arXiv preprint arXiv:1902.04491.
22

Chapter 13
Neptune Security:
A Novel Approach Big Data Privacy Protection

Vruddhi K Shah

L.J. University, India

Jignesh Doshi

L.J. University, India

ABSTRACT

With the inclusion of various data such as structure, semi-structure and unstructured data, protecting one's online privacy is crucial in the fast-paced technological age we live in, and Neptune Security stands out as a major player in this space. The analysis emphasizes the crucial part that Neptune Security plays in managing rising privacy issues, especially in India's changing digital landscape. The impact of big data on privacy is an essential aspect of this study. Big data has completely transformed how data is analysed and decisions are made. It can be recognized by its immense scale and complexity. However, privacy is naturally challenged by the amount of data. In this scenario, Neptune Security plays a crucial role by using cutting-edge encryption techniques and adaptive access controls to quickly neutralize such threats. This study explores the complex relationship between privacy and big data to offer an in-depth analysis of the changing risks associated with the digital era.

I. INTRODUCTION

As the increasing prevalence of online web applications, enterprise-class databases like PostgreSQL, MySQL, and SQL have become essential parts of the digital environment. But with more people engaging in online activities comes a

DOI: 10.4018/979-8-3693-9225-6.ch013

rise in cyber threats and attacks, calling for strong security measures. Due to the constantly changing nature of threats, big data has emerged as a crucial tool for enhancing the security and protection of sensitive data a multiplicity of databases are emerging in the quickly changing digital world due to the popularity of online web applications. These databases are essential for organizing and storing large volumes of user-generated data. Several applications and websites are powered by SQL, PostgreSQL, and MySQL, which have become major participants in this space. The security and integrity of the data housed in these databases are seriously threatened by the widespread use of these databases, which has made them attractive targets for cyber-attacks. Leveraging Dark Web Research and Web Mining Techniques for Advanced Cybersecurity in Data, Blockchain, IoT, and Network Protection (Faizan & Khan, 2019).

The necessity for improved security measures has grown more and more obvious as cyber threats continue to develop and become more sophisticated. The integration of big data solutions to improve protection and security strategies is prompted by the fact that traditional security mechanisms are frequently unable to counter new cyber threats. Recent studies, including Ahmadi's thorough investigation on the integration of big data and AI in the banking sector especially emphasize this change (Shakarian & Shakarian, 2016).

As vital guardians of sensitive data in this scenario, databases are often targeted by malevolent individuals looking to gain illegal access, cause disruptions, or compromise data (Chen, 2011). Due to the risks present in widely-used databases, a comprehensive security strategy is required, which leads to the use of big data analytics to strengthen defences against possible threats. The growing use of artificial intelligence (AI) in cyber security has increased the need for secure and decentralized systems to protect against cyber threats. Block chain technology has emerged as an effective solution for enhancing the security and privacy of AI systems due to its decentralized and immutable data storage capabilities (Saleh, 2024). There was another an article that analyses data from 14,993 dark websites and presents three case studies that demonstrate the effectiveness of this investigative approach in identifying illegal website operators. These methods contribute to broader cybersecurity strategies, including data protection, blockchain analysis, IoT security, and network defence (Jin et al., 2024).

One another study intends to explore the complex dynamics of privacy concerns in the context of big data and emphasize the important role that Neptune Security has played in resolving these issues, especially in light of India's rapidly changing technological environment. In order to provide a thorough understanding of how big data has been used to improve security and privacy protection over the last five years, the research examines statistical trends and insights from a variety of academic publications, including studies by specialist expertise Combining traditional databases with big data's analytical powers is becoming an important strategy for businesses dealing with the growing risks posed by cyber-attacks against their databases (Kaur & Randhawa, 2020). This study intends to explore the complex dynamics of privacy concerns in the context of big data and emphasize the important role that Neptune Security has played in resolving these issues, especially in light of India's rapidly changing technological environment. In order to provide a thorough understanding of how big data has been used to improve security and privacy protection over the last five years, the research examines statistical trends and insights from a variety of academic publications, including past studies. Authors of a paper proposed a CNN-based data region locating method and a visual information segmentation algorithm for improved data extraction. Tested on commercial websites, the method enhances accuracy in identifying data regions and efficiency in extraction. This approach has potential cybersecurity applications, particularly for automating data extraction and protecting sensitive information in blockchain, IoT, and network systems (Liu et al., 2024).

Combining traditional databases with big data's analytical powers is becoming an important strategy for businesses dealing with the growing risks posed by cyber-attacks against their databases.

Navigating Big Data Privacy and Security: Insights from Neptune Security

In the ever-expanding digital universe, big data reigns supreme. Organizations, hungry for insights, harness its power to drive innovation, enhance decision-making, and transform customer experiences. Yet, beneath this data-driven utopia lies a complex web of challenges—privacy concerns and security threats that demand our attention.

Figure 1. The big data landscape

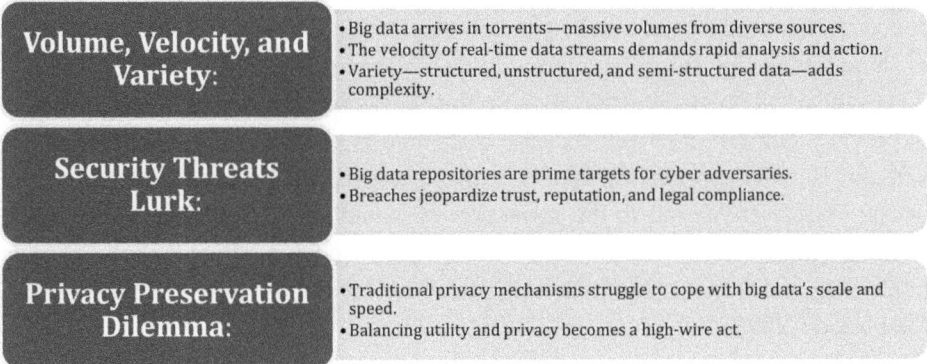

Volume, Velocity, and Variety:
- Big data arrives in torrents—massive volumes from diverse sources.
- The velocity of real-time data streams demands rapid analysis and action.
- Variety—structured, unstructured, and semi-structured data—adds complexity.

Security Threats Lurk:
- Big data repositories are prime targets for cyber adversaries.
- Breaches jeopardize trust, reputation, and legal compliance.

Privacy Preservation Dilemma:
- Traditional privacy mechanisms struggle to cope with big data's scale and speed.
- Balancing utility and privacy becomes a high-wire act.

Figure 2. Neptune security's role

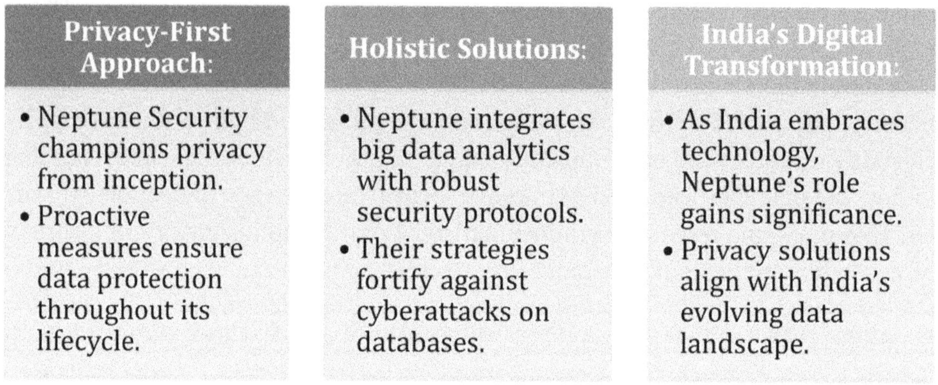

Privacy-First Approach:	Holistic Solutions:	India's Digital Transformation:
• Neptune Security champions privacy from inception. • Proactive measures ensure data protection throughout its lifecycle.	• Neptune integrates big data analytics with robust security protocols. • Their strategies fortify against cyberattacks on databases.	• As India embraces technology, Neptune's role gains significance. • Privacy solutions align with India's evolving data landscape.

The Road Ahead

Big data's promise hinges on security and privacy. Neptune Security's commitment ensures that data-driven innovation remains ethical, secure, and privacy-respecting. Together, we navigate uncharted waters toward a safer, data-powered future

II. LITERATURE REVIEW

A. Motivation

The explosion of big data in technology has changed how information is processed and brought up serious security issues. Robust security measures are needed in order to ensure the safety of user data. The big data security challenges are examined in this literature review, which highlights the need of creativity in resolving privacy concerns. Inspired by the quick speed at which technology is developing, it seeks to share knowledge from the latest studies while highlighting proactive organizations such as Neptune Security. By combining research from reputable academics, the review clarifies how the security discourse is changing and emphasizes the value of flexible approaches. NLP is utilized to analyse the large volumes of text on the Dark Web, aiding in the extraction of valuable insights from forum posts, chat logs, and other communications. Techniques such as sentiment analysis, topic modelling, and entity recognition help detect conversations related to cyber threats (Gopireddy, 2020).

B. Security Concerns in Big Data

Figure 3.-

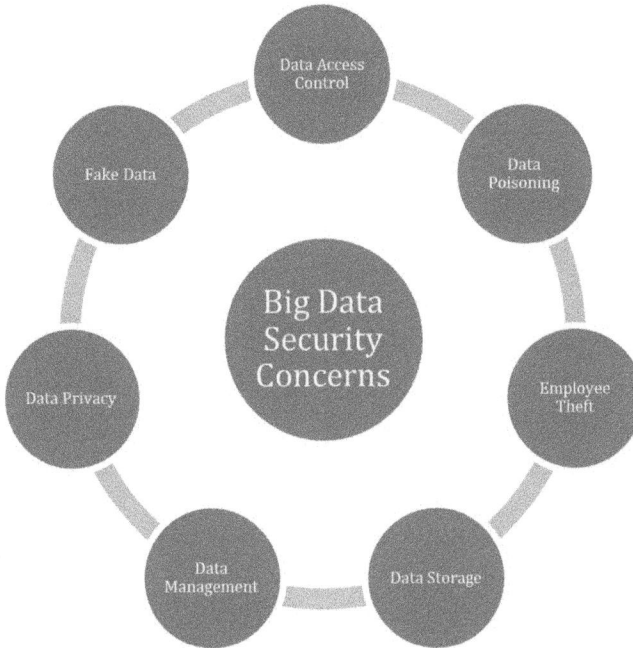

Big data security issues are critical, particularly when managing enormous volumes of data. Safeguarding user data requires not just managing the sheer volume and complexity of information, but also putting strong security protocols in place. Current research emphasizes the growing challenges associated with safeguarding user privacy in the face of swift technology advancements, underscoring the necessity for creative solutions.

Big Data Security Challenges: Navigating the Data Deluge

In the era of digital transformation, big data has emerged as both a boon and a challenge. Organizations harness the power of massive datasets to gain insights, drive innovation, and enhance decision-making. However, this data-driven revolution comes with inherent risks, particularly concerning security and privacy.

The Scale of the Challenge

1. **Sheer Volume and Complexity**:

- o Big data repositories accumulate petabytes of information from diverse sources—transaction logs, social media, sensors, and more (Gehl, 2016).
- o Managing this data deluge requires robust infrastructure, efficient storage, and scalable processing frameworks.

2. **Velocity and Real-Time Processing**:
- o Data streams in real time, demanding rapid analysis and immediate action.
- o Security mechanisms must keep pace with the velocity of data ingestion.

The Critical Role of Security and Privacy

1. **Confidentiality and Trust**:
- o Organizations collect sensitive data—personal identifiers, financial records, health information.
- o Breaches erode trust, damage reputations, and incur legal consequences.
2. **Threat Landscape**:
- o Cyber threats evolve—malware, ransomware, insider attacks, and sophisticated adversaries.
- o Big data systems are prime targets due to their value and interconnectedness.
3. **Privacy Preservation**:
- o Balancing data utility with privacy protection is a delicate dance.
- o Techniques like differential privacy, anonymization, and secure multi-party computation mitigate risks.

Creative Solutions for a Complex Landscape

1. **Blockchain Integration**:
- o Explore blockchain's potential for transparent, tamper-proof data management.
- o Immutable ledgers enhance data integrity and auditability.
2. **Ethical Considerations**:
- o Address biases in algorithms and models.
- o Ensure fairness and accountability in data-driven decisions.
3. **Automated Threat Detection**:
- o Machine learning and anomaly detection identify suspicious patterns.
- o Early warning systems prevent breaches.

Figure 4.

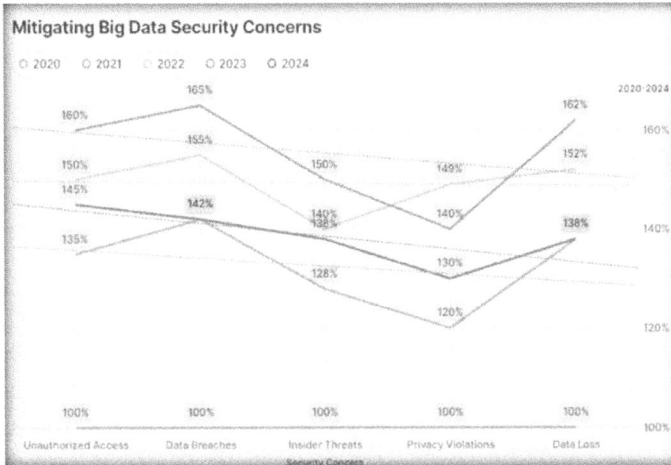

Technological advancements in a variety of fields present both benefits and difficulties for privacy in big data security. The combination of artificial intelligence and big data not only opens up new avenues for data-driven insights, but it also highlights the fine balance needed to protect user privacy The contemporary environment highlights the need for safe frameworks by emphasizing the wider impact of controls on data integrity

Key concerns within current big data security include:

1. **Data Access Control:** Ensuring only authorized entities have access to sensitive information in response to evolving user access requirements
2. **Data Management:** Effectively handling massive volumes of data, considering the growing datasets and the need for sophisticated management techniques.
3. **Data Poisoning:** Guarding against malicious attempts to manipulate or corrupt data integrity, especially amid increasing cyber threats
4. **Data Privacy:** Striking a delicate balance between utilizing user data for insights and preserving individual privacy, addressing heightened contemporary privacy concerns
5. **Employee Theft:** Investigating risks associated with unauthorized access or malicious activities by internal personnel, acknowledging the evolving landscape of insider threats.
6. **Fake Data:** Addressing concerns related to the introduction of misleading data, considering the sophistication of attacks compromising the accuracy of analyses.

7. **Data Storage:** Emphasizing secure storage practices to prevent unauthorized access or breaches, aligning with contemporary measures for data confidentiality. In essence, current literature on user security concerns in big data underscores multifaceted challenges and the need for innovative security measures. These measures must adapt to the dynamic handling of massive datasets, addressing concerns in the evolving field of big data security, and relevant to contemporary study analyses.

C. Mitigating Big Data Security Concerns

Mitigating Big Data security concerns is of paramount importance in today's data-driven landscape. As organizations increasingly rely on vast amounts of data for decision-making and operational purposes, they also face heightened risks of data breaches, cyberattacks, and privacy violations. Furthermore, fostering a culture of cybersecurity awareness and promoting best practices among employees are essential components of any comprehensive security strategy (Weimann, 2015). By adopting proactive measures and leveraging innovative technologies, organizations can mitigate Big Data security concerns and safeguard sensitive information against emerging threats.

Table 1. Mitagating Big Data Security Concerns

Security Concern	2020	2021	2022	2023	2024
Unauthorized Access	100%	135%	150%	160%	135%
Data Breaches	100%	142%	155%	165%	142%
Insider Threats	100%	128%	140%	150%	128%
Privacy Violations	100%	120%	130%	140%	120%
Data Loss	100%	138%	152%	162%	138%

Figure 5. Insider Threats

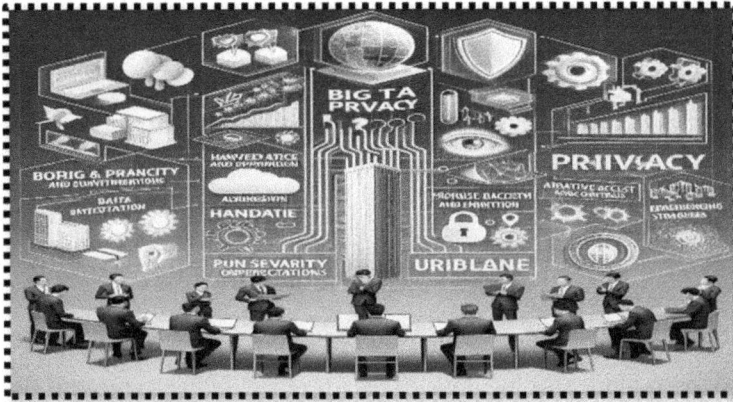

i. Improved Access Control Mechanisms

To limit access to sensitive information, strong access controls must be implemented. Enhancing access control and authentication mechanisms is crucial for mitigating big data security concerns. This involves implementing robust identity verification and authorization processes to ensure that only authorized individuals can access sensitive data. Two-factor authentication, biometric access control, and role-based access controls are some of the advanced methods used to bolster security. Additionally, the implementation of secure protocols and encryption for user authentication plays a vital role in maintaining data integrity and confidentiality.

Organizations can also benefit from implementing access monitoring and logging to track user activity and detect any unauthorized access attempts, helping to mitigate security risks and ensure compliance with data protection regulations.

ii. Advanced Data Management Strategies

It is critical to handle data effectively due to the exponential development in data volumes. Data lifecycle management procedures, analytics tools, and scalable storage solutions are investments that businesses should make. Conducting routine evaluations of data management procedures helps pinpoint opportunities for enhancement and guarantee compliance with both corporate goals and legal mandates.

iii. Proactive Data Integrity Protection

Take proactive steps to avoid data poisoning. Threats can be identified and reduced with the use of machine learning algorithms for anomaly detection, integrity verification methods, and routine audits. To detect new threats and modify security protocols appropriately, data integrity processes must be continuously monitored and evaluated.

III. PROPOSED MODEL

Our proposed model for big data privacy protection and security is designed to provide robust protection against a wide range of cyber threats while ensuring the privacy of sensitive data. It is based on a multi-layered approach that integrates various security measures at different stages of the data lifecycle. Bridging the research gap can help improve privacy practices in the big data era.

Evidence-based insights can reinforce Neptune Security's role in protecting privacy.

3.1. Research Gap

i. Big Data Privacy Challenges

- Although big data technologies are being used more often, there is still a lack of knowledge on how big data impacts privacy.
- Research on big data privacy needs to be expanded to include the ethical and human issues as well as the technical ones.

ii. Handling Complexity and Privacy

- Big data can be recognized by its huge scale and complexity. But privacy of the individual is inherently threatened by this amount of data.
- There is a lack of study on practical strategies for striking a compromise between privacy protection and the advantages of big data analytics.

iii. Adaptive Access and Encryption Algorithms

- Modern encryption techniques and adaptive access controls are used by Neptune Security, but it is still necessary to assess how effective they are. Studies can investigate the effects of these methods on privacy, usability, and availability of data identification.

3.2. Research Objectives

i. Understand Big Data Privacy Implications

- Explore how big data affects privacy while taking socio-ethical and technological factors into account.
- Analyze the effects on personal privacy of decisions made during data collection, storage, and analysis.

ii. Evaluate Security's Adaptive Access Controls

- Assess the effectiveness of Neptune Security's adaptive access controls in maintaining data privacy.
- Investigate whether dynamic access policies strike the right balance between usability and privacy.

iii. Propose Privacy-Enhancing Strategies

- Develop practical guidelines for organizations like Neptune Security to enhance data privacy.
- Explore novel approaches, such as differential privacy, homomorphic encryption, and data masking.

iv. Collaborate with Stakeholders

- Interact with users, authorities, and legal professionals to make sure privacy policies comply with changing laws.
- Encourage openness and user education on data handling and privacy options.

IV. NEPTUNE SECURITY: FORTIFYING DATA THROUGHOUT THE LIFECYCLE

Neptune Security stands as a cornerstone in the implementation of our proposed model, offering a suite of comprehensive tools and services meticulously designed to fortify every stage of the data lifecycle. By seamlessly integrating with Neptune Security, organizations can rest assured that their data is shielded by robust security and privacy protections throughout its journey.

Figure 6.

1.Planning and Scoping:

- **Define a Data Owner**: Identify the individual responsible for data stewardship.
- **Data Classification**: Determine the security level of the data
- **Minimize Data**: Collect only essential data to reduce security risks.
  2. Creation/Collection:
- **Encrypt Data in Transit:** Ensure secure data transfer via VPN, encrypted email, or TLS-protected websites.
- **Review Data Use Agreements:** Comply with terms when receiving data from external sources.
- **Transparency and Control:** Inform individuals providing personal information about its intended use.
  3. Storage:
- **Encrypt Data at Rest:** Store data on encrypted devices or cloud storage services.
- **Approved Locations:** Configure storage devices/services to meet the highest security standards.
- **Backup Data:** Regularly back up data in secure locations.

- **Remove Unnecessary Copies:** Delete working copies generated during data preparation.

4. Use:

- Choose platforms with robust security controls.
- Protect sensitive and personal information during data analysis and processing.

5. Archiving/Deletion:

- **De-identify Data**: Remove personal identifiers or use key files to minimize exposure.
- **Secure Disposal:** Archive or delete data at the end of its useful life.

V. EVALUATION

The effectiveness of our proposed model will undergo a thorough evaluation, gauging its performance based on key metrics such as the frequency of successful cyber-attacks, the degree of privacy preservation achieved, and user satisfaction with the implemented privacy safeguards. By systematically assessing these metrics, we aim to validate the efficacy of our approach in safeguarding sensitive data in the realm of big data analytics.

This model draws inspiration and validation from a wealth of research articles, leveraging insights and methodologies from diverse sources to seamlessly integrate state-of-the-art security measures and techniques into every facet of the big data lifecycle. Central to this approach is the recognition of Neptune Security's pivotal role in orchestrating and managing the intricate dance between data security and privacy.

Evaluating the Effiency: Metrics for Big Data Privacy and Security

As the curtain rises on the era of big data, organizations grapple with a dual mandate: harness the power of data while safeguarding its integrity and privacy. Our proposed model, a sentinel against cyber threats, stands at the intersection of innovation and responsibility. But how do we measure its effectiveness? Let's delve into the metrics that illuminate our path.

The Crucial Metrics

1. Frequency of Successful Cyber Attacks

- **Objective**: Gauge the model's resilience against malicious intrusions.

- **Measurement**: Count the number of successful cyber attacks thwarted by our model.
- **Significance**: A lower frequency signifies robust security.

2. Degree of Privacy Preservation

- **Objective**: Assess how well our model shields sensitive data.
- **Measurement**:
  o   Evaluate data anonymization techniques
  o   Quantify the reduction in information leakage.
- **Significance**: Higher preservation scores indicate effective privacy safeguards.

3. User Satisfaction

- **Objective**: Understand user perception and acceptance.
- **Measurement**:
  o   Conduct surveys or interviews to gather feedback.
  o   Assess user comfort with data sharing and model predictions.
- **Significance**: Satisfied users are more likely to adopt and adhere to privacy guidelines.

Challenges in Evaluation

1. **Trade-Offs**:
    o   Balancing security and utility is delicate.
    o   Metrics must account for both—no privacy at the cost of usability.
2. **Contextual Relevance**:
    o   Metrics vary across domains (healthcare, finance, social media).
    o   Customized evaluation criteria are essential.
3. **Dynamic Environment**:
    o   Big data landscapes evolve.
    o   Metrics must adapt to changing threats and technologies.

Quantitative vs. Qualitative Assessment

1. **Quantitative Metrics**:
    o   **Precision, recall, F1-score**: Assess model accuracy.
    o   **False positive rate**: Minimize false alarms.
    o   **Privacy loss**: Quantify information leakage.

2. **Qualitative Insights**:
    o   **User feedback**: Understand real-world impact.
    o   **Ethical considerations**: Evaluate fairness and bias.

VI. FUTURE WORK

1. Holistic Privacy Framework:

Objective: Develop a comprehensive privacy framework that integrates technical, legal, and ethical aspects.

Components:
*   **Privacy by Design** Embed privacy considerations into every stage of data processing.
*   **Privacy Impact Assessments:** Conduct regular assessments to identify and mitigate privacy risks.
*   **User-Centric Approach**: Prioritize user consent, transparency, and control over their data.
    2. Advanced Encryption Techniques:

Objective: Improve data security by utilizing cutting-edge encryption techniques.

Approaches:
*   **Homomorphic Encryption**: Enable computations on encrypted data without decryption.
*   **Quantum-Safe Encryption**: Use quantum-resistant techniques to get ready for the post-quantum world.
*   **Blockchain-based Encryption**: Explore decentralized encryption solutions.
3.Federated Learning for Privacy-Preserving Analytics:

Objective: Enable collaborative model training without sharing raw data.

Methodology:
*   *Distributed Learning:* Train models locally on user devices.
*   *Aggregated Model Updates:* Combine model updates without exposing individual data.
    4. Collaboration with Regulatory Bodies

Objective: Stay compliant with evolving privacy regulations.

Actions:
- **Regular Audits**: Assess compliance with data protection laws.
- **Legal Consultations**: Collaborate with legal experts to interpret and implement regulations.

Here are more additional points for future work in the field of **big data privacy protection** and its security:

1. **Blockchain Integration**:
   - o Explore how blockchain technology can enhance data privacy and security.
   - o Investigate decentralized identity management and secure data sharing using blockchain.
2. **Differential Privacy Enhancement**:
   - o Research and implement differential privacy techniques for big data analytics.
   - o Ensure that aggregate results remain accurate while protecting individual privacy.
3. **Secure Data Provenance**:
   - o Develop mechanisms to track and verify the origin and history of data.
   - o Implement secure data lineage and auditing.
4. **Privacy-Preserving Analytics**:
   - o Investigate techniques like secure multi-party computation and federated learning.
   - o Enable collaborative analytics without exposing raw data.
5. **Automated Privacy Impact Assessment:**
   - o Develop tools or frameworks for automated privacy impact assessments.
   - o Evaluate the impact of new data processing activities on privacy and compliance.

VII. CONCLUSION

In today's fast-paced digital world, safeguarding privacy and data security is more important than ever, especially with the rise of big data. This research highlights the role of Neptune Security in addressing the growing challenges of protecting sensitive information in the face of cyber threats. By using advanced encryption methods, adaptive access controls, and innovative solutions like blockchain and machine learning, Neptune Security helps organizations protect their data throughout its lifecycle, from collection to storage and beyond. It strikes a crucial balance between utilizing big data for innovation and maintaining privacy.

The proposed model in this research outlines a multi-layered approach to data protection, combining traditional security methods with new technologies. As big data continues to grow, Neptune Security's tools and strategies will play a vital role in ensuring that privacy is preserved while still allowing organizations to use data effectively. By staying ahead of threats and developing future-focused solutions, Neptune Security provides a strong foundation for protecting data in an ever-evolving digital landscape.

VII. REFERENCES

Chen, H. "Dark Web: Exploring and Mining the Dark Side of the Web," 2011 European Intelligence and Security Informatics Conference, Athens, Greece, 2011, pp. 1-2, . keywords: {Educational institutions;Informatics;Libraries;Awards activities;Terrorism;Conferences;Presses}DOI: 10.1109/EISIC.2011.78

Faizan, M., & Khan, R. A. (2019). Exploring and analyzing the dark Web: A new alchemy. *First Monday*, 24(5). Advance online publication. DOI: 10.5210/fm.v24i5.9473

Gehl, R. W. (2016). Power/freedom on the dark web: A digital ethnography of the Dark Web Social Network. *New Media & Society*, 18(7), 1219–1235. DOI: 10.1177/1461444814554900

Gopireddy, R. R. (2020). Dark Web Monitoring: Extracting and Analyzing Threat Intelligence. [1]

Jin, P., Kim, N., Lee, S., & Jeong, D. (2024). Forensic investigation of the dark web on the Tor network: Pathway toward the surface web. *International Journal of Information Security*, 23(1), 331–346. DOI: 10.1007/s10207-023-00745-4

Kaur, S., & Randhawa, S. (2020). Dark Web: A Web of Crimes. *Wireless Personal Communications*, 112(4), 2131–2158. DOI: 10.1007/s11277-020-07143-2

Liu, J., Lin, L., Cai, Z., Wang, J., & Kim, H. (2024). Deep web data extraction based on visual information processing. *Journal of Ambient Intelligence and Humanized Computing*, 15(2), 1481–1491. DOI: 10.1007/s12652-017-0587-0

Saleh, A. M. S. (2024). Blockchain for secure and decentralized artificial intelligence in cybersecurity: A comprehensive review. *Blockchain: Research and Applications*, 100193.

Shakarian, P., & Shakarian, J. 2016, March. Socio-cultural modeling for cyber threat actors. In *Workshops at the Thirtieth AAAI Conference on Artificial Intelligence*.

Weimann, G. (2015). Going Dark: Terrorism on the Dark Web. *Studies in Conflict and Terrorism*, 39(3), 195–206. DOI: 10.1080/1057610X.2015.1119546

Chapter 14
Security Challenges in Internet of Things

Purva Joshi

https://orcid.org/0000-0002-2748-8742

Institute for Communications and Navigations, Deutsches Zentrum für Luft- und Raumfahrt e.V. (DLR), Germany

Seema Joshi

https://orcid.org/0000-0002-3298-4230

Gujarat Technological University, India

ABSTRACT

Industrial and domestic appliances are IoT-connected. Sensors, phones, and security are examples. The benefits of device communication are various. Monitor IoT security risks. Simple methods and technology may secure devices and detect attackers. Security challenges in IoT include authentication and authorization, encryption, firmware and software vulnerabilities, insecure connections, and device patching and updates. Threats from IoT vulnerabilities Worse passwords allow IoT device theft. Used IoT devices can join larger networks. Low-encryption IoT devices may leak and misuse consumer data. IoT user mistrust, identity theft, and financial fraud may arise. Weak IoT devices can be hijacked by malicious networks to launch massive DDoS attacks on services and infrastructure. Damage, disruption, and death can result from industrial and critical infrastructure IoT devices. Hackers could break into IoT networks and access more systems and data. The chapter explains IoT security risks. Examine case studies last. Technology and industry cannot apply all attack avoidance measures.

DOI: 10.4018/979-8-3693-9225-6.ch014

1 INTRODUCTION

The Internet of Things (IoT) enables objects to establish communication with one another as well as with other applications that are connected to the internet. IoT enables the automation of numerous aspects of both company operations and everyday life. Internet of Things (IoT) devices exchange and analyze large amounts of data continuously, which presents significant difficulties in ensuring the security of this data. In order to ensure the security of sensitive data and maintain the trust of customers, it is necessary to safeguard both the devices and the network used for data sharing. The growing number of security issues could cause numerous customers to avoid utilizing IoT devices. Data protection is particularly crucial for organizations that work in healthcare, banking, manufacturing, logistics, retail, and other fields.

As technology companies still exist in developing and enhancing IoT de- vices, they will face an ongoing challenge: ensuring the safety and security of these devices. IoT security relates to the comprehensive measures and methods used to protect all elements of the Internet of Things, including strategies, devices, procedures, systems, and techniques. In order to maintain the IoT ecosystems, it is essential to protect the physical components, applications, data, and network connections while guaranteeing their avail- ability, integrity, and confidentiality. Internet of Things (IoT) systems can potentially have numerous security vulnerabilities. An effective security plan includes all elements of protection, including strengthening compo- nents, updating firmware, monitoring, regulating access, identifying threats, and repairing problems. The importance of IoT security lies in the fact that these systems are extensive, vulnerable, and highly attractive to potential attackers. Securing IoT devices against unauthorized access is crucial to prevent the disclosure of sensitive information and unauthorized access into other components of the network.

devices such as smart watches, smart home gadgets, webcams, and cars have security risks related to the Internet of Things (IoT). IoT security ensures the neces- sary protection for these vulnerable devices. The majority of IoT system developers emphasize device functionality before security. This highlights the need for IoT security, and users and IT teams have to understand their responsibility to implement precautions. The main goal of this article is to provide detailed insights into the privacy, accuracy, and accessibility of data and systems inside the IoT ecosystem. This includes safeguarding confidential information from unauthorized access or disclosure (confidentiality), ensuring that data and systems remain unchanged by outsiders (reliability), and maintaining constant and unrestricted access to IoT devices, networks, and services (availability). Developing this objective is crucial for protecting user privacy, preventing cyber-attacks, maintaining trustworthy IoT systems, and enabling the secure and dependable functioning of IoT applications in various industries, including smart homes, healthcare, industrial automation, and critical infrastructure.

In this chapter section 2 provides a detailed literature review of security aspects in IoT framework and threats relevant publications. Section 3 discussed the security framework in IoT with its application as a reference to security related to significant IoT applications. The comparison between Industry 4.0 and 5.0 is illustrated in section 4 while section 5 provides details about security requirements in IoT networks and actual challenges in IoT security framework. The case studies have been written in section 5 and the conclusion is mentioned in section 6.

2 LITERATURE REVIEW

Furstenau L. B. et al., (2023) discusses the conceptual framework, primary challenges, and future advancements of IoT technology. Sott M. K. et al, (2020) thoroughly examines the current advancements, challenges, and future patterns in cultivating sustainability in the coffee sector. Bel & Sabeen, (2022) surveys IoT security, including attacks, difficulties, and responses, as well as IoT architecture, cutting-edge technology, security risks, and security solutions. Jurcut A et al., (2020) and Taherdoost H, (2023) explores the important topic of IoT security, highlighting the difficulties and solutions in guaranteeing the security of connected devices. Meneghello F. et al., (2019) provides a thorough examination of physical security issues within the Internet of Things (IoT) industry, as well as detailed conversations on methods to mitigate these vulnerabilities. Gopalan S. S. et al., (2021) explores the integration of the Internet of Things (IoT) and Artificial Intelligence (AI) in current healthcare, with a special focus on the significance of cybersecurity in protecting private medical data. IoT-based cloud computing security issues, weaknesses, and solutions are examined by Ahmad W. et al., (2021) and Abba Ari A. A. et al., (2024). Ogonji M. M. et al., (2020) analyzes IoT security issues, vulnerabilities, and solutions to improve user privacy and security and manage the difficulties and opportunities in this growing industry.

Shammar E. A. et al., (2021) examines current research issues and trends in using blockchain-related approaches and technologies in IoT security, showing the challenges and potential solutions for integrating IoT and blockchain technologies. Yu M. et al., (2020) reviews IoT security vulnerability analysis, identifying, detection, and mitigation studies, difficulties, and potential for future developments. Liang & Kim, (2021) covers IoT network security attacks and solutions at the physical, network, and application layers, including blockchain and ma- chine learning. Sharma V et al., (2020) covers the security, privacy, and trust issues in Smart Mobile-Internet of Things (M-IoT) networks, highlighting the need for effective solutions to protect data and prevent cyberattacks (Sharma V., 2020). The present studies by Mousavi S. K. et al., (2021) and Raeisi-Varzaneh et al., (2024) examine IoT security issues and solutions, focusing on cryptographic techniques that protect connected devices. Rani S. et al., 2021) details IoT security concerns, correction methods, and the significance of IoT forensics in cybercrime investigations, providing useful conclusions and suggestions for future research. Thabit F. et al., (2023) analyzes cryptographic methods for IoT security, addressing significant difficulties, threats, and solutions. Najmi K. Y. et al. (2023) discusses IoT security and privacy threats, countermeasures, and the relevance of user confidentiality and reliability in the growing Internet of Things.

Detailed examination of trust-based security concerns in Internet of Things applications Shirvani & Masdari (2023) highlights the requirement for robust trust management frameworks to provide reliable data transmission and services. Chui K. T. et al. (2023) studies the Internet of Things and Cyber-Physical Systems covers standards, algorithms, applications, security, difficulties, and future directions. Siwakoti Y. R. et al (2023) covers IoT security weaknesses, criminal exploitation, and potential solutions, underlining the need for strong security in the face of increasing cyber threats. Alqarawi et al.'s article analyzes IoT security issues and offers advice on protecting enterprises. Issa W. et al (2023) details the use of blockchain and federated learning to improve IoT security and privacy. Kannan (2024), a comprehensive examination of the network security hazards presented by IoT devices in the financial sector is provided, along with solutions to mitigate and protect against these risks. Liu Y. et al (2023) surveys the integration of blockchain technology for trust management in Internet of Things (IoT) systems, highlighting important issues and proposing future research to develop decentralized and secure IoT settings.

Table 1. Overview of existing review articles, including their contributions and limitations

Ref no & year	Paper contribution	Limitation
Neshenko N. et al (2019)	An original system of classification and thorough examination of vulnerabilities and security concerns in the Internet of Things (IoT).	IoT-specific threat signatures and empirical data are lacking.
Hassan W. H. (2019)	IoT security research trends, issues, and important tools including IoT modellers and simulators.	Focus on 2016–2018 IoT security research trends might overlook recent advances.
Hassija V. et al (2019)	Covers IoT security challenges, including application classification, threat source identification, infrastructure enhancement recommendations, and countermeasures.	Do not cover all elements of IoT security due to its wide and dynamic nature, requiring future extensive surveys on emerging concerns.
Hou, J. et al (2019)	Data-driven three-dimensional analysis of IoT security.	May overlook other critical IoT ecosystem security issues by focusing on data transfer.
Rachit & Ragiri (2021)	Emerging IoT security concerns, propose security solutions and evaluate existing protocols and standards for safeguarding IoT networks.	The integration of new technologies has increased the complexity of security solutions, which may reduce the transparency of security provisions.
Omolara A. E. et al (2022)	IoT security concerns, solutions, and future prospects, addressing major issues and suggesting new methods to improve security.	Focus on current study findings rather than original evidence, potential literature source biases, and the need for additional scientific examinations to test proposed solutions and insights.
Hameed & Alomary (2019)	Lightweight algorithms and authentication approaches to handle IoT security challenges while considering device limitations.	IoT devices include low-performance components, limited computational capacity, and hardware limits that make typical security solutions difficult to deploy.
Mrabet H. et al (2020)	IoT security challenges across architecture layers and proposes security techniques to minimize major attacks.	The unavailability of lightweight encryption techniques for IoT devices and the need for more research on machine-learning algorithms and Blockchain technology to secure IoT devices.
Sadhu P. K. et al (2022)	Overview of IoT and IoE networks, analyzes IoT device vulnerabilities, discusses security measures against various threats, and proposes future IoT security system directions.	Lack of in-depth research of specific security measures and concentration on a broad overview limit its scope.
Harbi Y et al (2021)	Current IoT security research and evaluates security schemes based on new technologies and strategies to improve security.	May not fully address the implementation issues or real-world deployment considerations of the IoT security solutions mentioned.

continued on following page

Table 1. Continued

Ref no & year	Paper contribution	Limitation
Chanal & Kakkasageri (2020)	Examine IoT's confidentiality, integrity, authentication, and availability concerns, emphasizing the need for security and privacy management systems for resource-constrained devices.	Does not have a thorough discussion of IoT security and privacy methods, which are currently being implemented and resource-intensive.
Ahanger T. A. et al (2022)	Surveys IoT-specific literature and introduces a novel taxonomy that addresses cyber threats and vulnerabilities in the IoT domain to encourage IoT data protection research.	The absence of research on deep/machine learning for IoT security, real-time attack vulnerabilities, authentication and privacy, and time-sensitive attacks and countermeasures.
HaddadPajouh H et al (2021)	hT, he architectural classification of possible IoT security threats and problems, grouping them by layered architecture to understand and manage the threats on each layer.	Lack of a specified standard for IoT environments and unstructured presentation of IoT safety issues and solutions.
Babun L. et al (2021)	A complete evaluation framework for analyzing and comparing IoT platforms based on seven technical criteria to help IoT users take informed solution implementation decisions.	Focused on popular IoT platforms could miss new platforms with innovative skills.
Yugha & Chithra (2020)	Survey IoT security concerns, protocols, attacks, and implementation tools for future study and development.	Does not contain an in-depth discussion of IoT security issues beyond authentication and access control.
Tournier J. et al (2021)	Describes the fundamental security challenges of IoT networks, regardless of the protocol stack, and provide a generic approach for comparing and analyzing them.	Unable to analyze all IoT protocols and their security methods may limit its scope.
Sartayeva Chan (2023)	Provides a systematic and complete overview of indoor positioning security and privacy, classifying positioning methods, identifying security challenges, and describing proposed security and privacy solutions.	Could fail to address security and privacy issues in alternative positioning systems due to its primary focus on RF-based approaches.
Sun P. et al (2024)	Propose a comprehensive privacy protection framework for IoT devices, that extends privacy security technologies, legal privacy research, current security concerns, and future development prospects.	This paper's IoT security coverage and technology reach are limited compared to other surveys.

continued on following page

Table 1. Continued

Ref no & year	Paper contribution	Limitation
Prakash R. et al (2024)	Highlights IoT security concerns, attacks, and solutions to assure device and network safety, privacy, and reliability.	Lacks in-depth analysis of specific attack scenarios and focuses on broad security concerns without case studies or real-world examples.
Adil M. et al (2024)	Reviews the literature on security requirements and problems in Healthcare Internet of Things applications, highlighting research progress and identifying future possibilities.	This research struggles to include all related material in one survey, represent related work accurately, and fulfill all Healthcare Internet of Things application security criteria.

3 SECURITY FRAMEWORK IN IOT

IoT architecture consists of up of the hardware, servers in the cloud, and network architecture that enable communication between devices. Four distinct layers represent a basic IoT architecture:

Figure 1. Layers of IoT framework

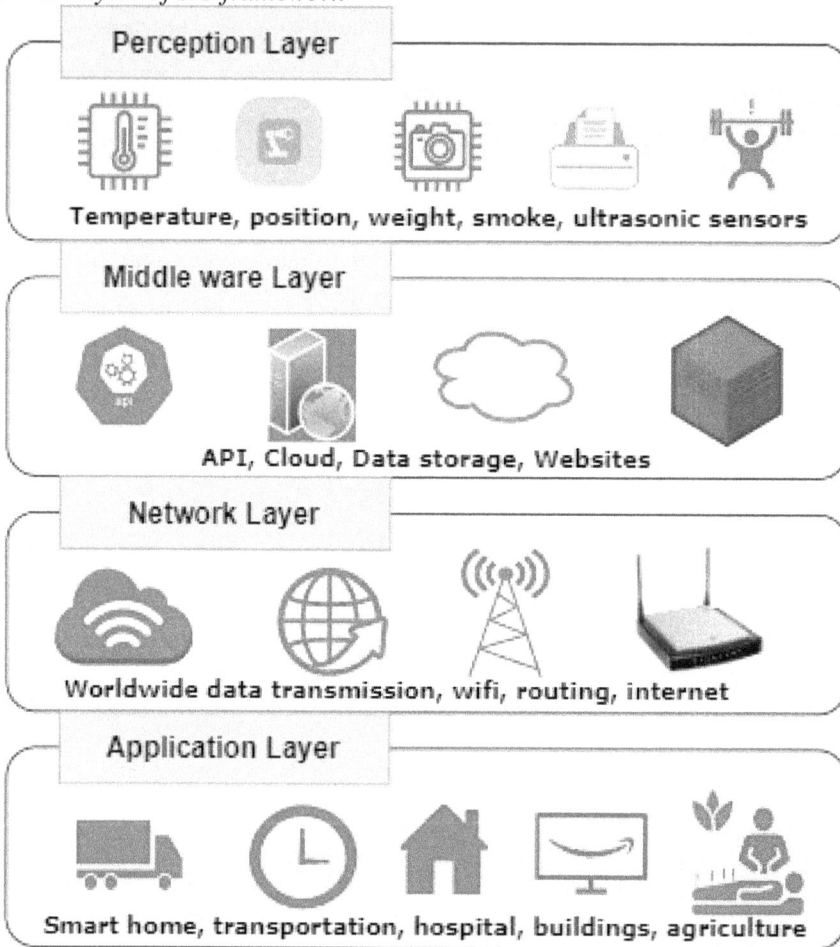

Perception Layer
Temperature, position, weight, smoke, ultrasonic sensors

Middle ware Layer
API, Cloud, Data storage, Websites

Network Layer
Worldwide data transmission, wifi, routing, internet

Application Layer
Smart home, transportation, hospital, buildings, agriculture

Perception (the sensors, gadgets, and other devices): The framework consists of a variety of sensors that detect and measure changes in the surroundings, including temperature, humidity, motion, light, sound, and other factors. Actuators are machines that execute particular actions in response to the information collected by sensors, for as operating a fan when the temperature in a room hits a particular limit. Sensors collect data from the environment, while actuators perform actions based on that data, allowing immediate actions in the IoT ecosystem. Key considerations for choosing IoT devices for the perception layer include security capabilities, energy efficiency, device compatibility, and cost efficiency. The perception layer converts the acquired data into digital format and sends it to higher levels using secure connections. Devices in the perception layer contain temperature sensors, humidity sensors, motion detectors, smart locks, smart lights, and other IoT-enabled devices capable of detecting and/or responding to the surrounding environment. The possible attacks on the perception layer include Jamming networks, Node manipulation, RFID sensor attacks, Eavesdropping and creating interference attacks.

Middleware Layer (API, web services, Cloud storage): The middleware layer serves as a centralized platform for managing and creating accessible APIs (Application Programming Interfaces) that enable various applications and services to interact with each other. It manages several responsibilities including API authentication, rate constraints, caching, and monitoring. The middleware layer acts as a mediator between ap- plications and cloud storage services, simplifying the complicated details of various cloud providers' APIs and protocols. The middleware layer enables the integration of web services with tools for service discovery, orchestration, and data format transformation. Middleware solutions commonly have monitoring and logging functionalities, enabling developers to monitor the performance, usage, and possible defects within the integrated systems. The relevant attacks on the middleware layer are similar to the perception layer and network layer, as it is located between these two layers. There are many studies where cloud storage hacked or manipulated authentication of cloud data has occurred.

Network (The capacity to connect devices): Network connectivity re- lates to the capacity of devices, such as computers, servers, smartphones, and IoT devices, to establish and maintain connections with each other across a network. Devices are interconnected via either wired (such as Ethernet cables) or wireless (such as Wi-Fi or cellular) means, enabling the transfer of data between them. Standardized protocols like TCP/IP, HTTP, and FTP establish standards and structures for transmitting data, providing compatibility among various devices and networks. Connectivity allows the exchange of data and services across devices, allowing for activities like file sharing, printer sharing, email communication, web surfing, and remote access. This encourages collaboration and the sharing of resources among connected devices. Network connectivity needs the use of security measures such as firewalls, encryption, and access controls to safeguard against unauthorized access, data breaches, and cyber threats. Important network layer attacks include Sybil attacks, man-in- the-middle (MiTM) attacks, distributed denial of service (DDoS) attacks, replay attacks, and others.

Application (the layer with which the user works): The application layer is the topmost layer in the architecture of the Internet of Things (IoT), and it serves as the intermediary between the user or application and the underlying IoT system. The data collected by IoT devices is presented in a user-friendly manner, including dashboards, reports, visualizations, and mobile applications. Users may interact with and manage IoT devices, systems, and operations via user interfaces or applications. The IoT system offers APIs (Application Programming Interfaces) that enable external applications and services to connect and interact with it, receiving access to its data and functionality. The system conducts data analysis, processing, and decision-making using data obtained from IoT devices, often utilizing technologies such as machine learning, artificial intelligence, and big data analytics. The system manages user authentication, access control, and security protocols to guarantee secure and allowed access to the IoT system and its data. Some examples of security breaches or potential attacks at the application layer include the Mirai botnet attack, IPC telnet malware, Cross Site Scripting (XSS), Slowloris, and SQL injection attacks.

As mentioned in Section 3, an IoT application may be categorized into four layers: the sensing layer, the network layer, the middleware layer, and the application layer. Each layer in an IoT application utilizes several technologies, which can introduce multiple challenges and security vulnerabilities.

Figure 2. Types of attacks per layer

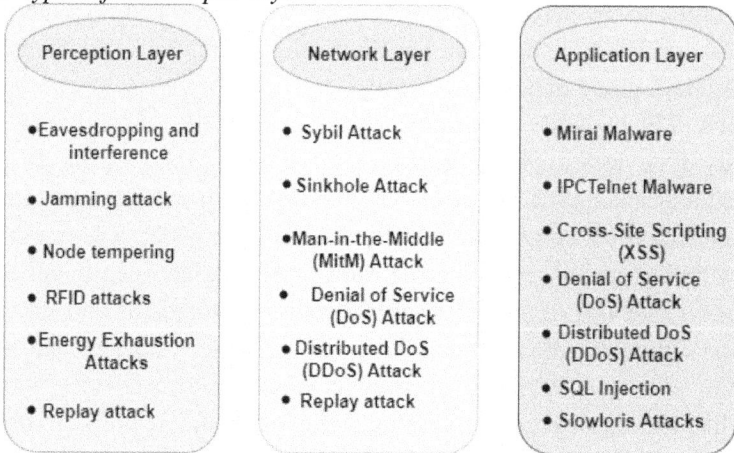

Perception Layer	Network Layer	Application Layer
• Eavesdropping and interference	• Sybil Attack	• Mirai Malware
• Jamming attack	• Sinkhole Attack	• IPCTelnet Malware
• Node tempering	• Man-in-the-Middle (MitM) Attack	• Cross-Site Scripting (XSS)
• RFID attacks	• Denial of Service (DoS) Attack	• Denial of Service (DoS) Attack
• Energy Exhaustion Attacks	• Distributed DoS (DDoS) Attack	• Distributed DoS (DDoS) Attack
• Replay attack	• Replay attack	• SQL Injection
		• Slowloris Attacks

Figure 1 demonstrates a range of technological advances, devices, and applications present in these four layers. This section examines potential security vulnerabilities in IoT applications across these four layers. Figure 2 illustrates the potential attacks that can occur on these four layers. These layers support Internet of Things devices by collecting and analyzing data. This design includes data translation into useful information, going beyond the OSI model.

3.1 Important IoT Applications and Its Security

3.1.1 Smart Buildings

A smart home or building is a technologically advanced living or working area that combines interconnected devices, sensors, and automated systems to maximize comfort, security, energy efficiency, and convenience. These contexts integrate a range of technology, including home automation, Internet of Things (IoT) devices, and intelligent control systems, to facilitate simple monitoring, control, and enhancement of different operations and processes (Shaharuddin S. et al, 2023). Sensors collect data on usage, temperature, humidity, energy usage, and other factors, allowing for intelligent decision-making and automation. For example, the system has the capability of automatically adjusting lighting, temperature, and ventilation according to the number of people present, the time of day, and the preferences of the users. This results in increased energy efficiency and reduced expenses. Smart houses and buildings provide advanced security features, including remote access control, surveillance cameras, and integrated alarm systems. In addition, they offer simple through the use of voice control, mobile applications, and effortless connectivity with other intelligent devices and services.

3.1.2 Smart Healthcare

A smart healthcare facility or hospital is a proficient and technologically advanced medical institution that utilizes networked devices, sensors, artificial intelligence (AI), and automated systems to improve patient care, operational efficiency, and overall healthcare delivery (Karthik S. A. et al, 2023). The healthcare sector seamlessly incorporates advanced technologies, including the Internet of Things (IoT), wearable devices, telemedicine, robotics, and big data analytics. Within a technologically advanced healthcare facility, patient super- vision is constant and immediate, using wearable sensors to monitor crucial body functions. Artificial intelligence algorithms are employed to quickly recognize any unusual events or deteriorating health issues by analyzing the collected data. AI-powered solutions enhance medical imaging by assisting in the analysis of images, diagnosis, and planning of treatment. Robotic devices assist in complicated surgical procedures, improving accuracy and reducing human errors. Intelligent building management systems enhance energy efficiency, ventilation, and material monitoring. Telemedicine systems provide remote patient consultations and monitoring, hence increasing access to healthcare. In addition, electronic health records (EHRs) and data analytics platforms enable the creation of specific treatment plans, predictive modelling, and decision-making based on evidence (Adil M. et al 2024).

3.1.3 Smart Transportation and Road

Smart transportation and roads include the introduction of cutting-edge technologies such as the Internet of Things (IoT), artificial intelligence (AI), sensors, and communication networks into transport networks and systems. This allows for the continuous monitoring, collection of data, analysis, and intelligent control of several factors related to transportation. A smart transportation system uses a network of linked sensors, cameras, and communication devices that are integrated into roadways, automobiles, traffic signals, and other infrastructure components. These devices acquire data regarding the flow of traffic, conditions of the road, movements of vehicles, and environmental variables. Following that, this data receives analysis through AI and machine learning algorithms in order increase the efficiency of traffic signal timings, offer instant suggest for routes, identify accidents or problems, support adaptive repair of roads and bridges, and enable intelligent parking systems. In addition, the utilization of vehicle-to-vehicle (V2V) and vehicle-to-infrastructure (V2I) communication technologies enables the implementation of advanced safety functionalities, including avoiding accidents and autonomous driving capabilities.

3.1.4 Smart City

A smart city is a metropolitan region that utilizes cutting-edge technologies and integrated systems to optimize the effectiveness, sustainability, and overall well-being of its residents. It includes the installation of diverse digital solutions, Internet of Things (IoT) devices, sensors, and data analytics across multiple fields inside the city's infrastructure. Smart cities utilize information and communication technology to enhance and streamline several aspects of urban life, including transportation, energy management, water supply, trash disposal, public safety, healthcare, and citizen services (Sharma & Arya 2023). The city is equipped with sensors that collect current information on traffic patterns, energy usage, air quality, and other variables. This data is used to make sensible choices and allocate resources effectively. Smart mobility solutions, including intelligent traffic management systems, smart parking, and integrated public transportation, have the objective of decreasing congestion and environmental damage. Smart buildings and smart grids utilize energy- efficient technologies and renewable energy sources to minimize their impact on the environment. In addition, smart city programs frequently include e- governance systems that enable citizen participation, promote transparency, and enhance the efficient provision of municipal services.

3.1.5 Smart Grid

A smart grid is a sophisticated and intelligent electrical grid system that utilizes digital communication technologies, sensors, and automated control systems to improve the efficiency, dependability, and sustainability of power generation, transmission, and distribution. The upgrading of the traditional electrical grid involves the implementation of two-way communication and data exchange between companies and customers. A smart grid is a system that combines advanced metering infrastructure (AMI), intelligent electronic devices, and communication networks to monitor and regulate different parts of the electrical system in real-time (Sharma K. et al., 2023). It enables providers to remotely monitor and regulate electricity usage, identify and address power outages, include distributed energy sources such as solar and wind power, and establish demand-response strategies that encourage consumers to decrease consumption during peak times. Smart grid technologies also enable the installation of energy storage systems, electric vehicles, and microgrids, resulting in increased flexibility and resilience.

3.1.6 Smart Agriculture

Smart agriculture involves implementing advanced technologies such as sensors, communication networks, data analytics, and automated systems into agricultural operations to improve production, efficiency, and sustainability. The process requires the installation of a network of interconnected Internet of Things (IoT) devices and sensors throughout farms and agricultural areas (AlZubi & Galyna, 2023). These devices and sensors collect real-time data on several variables, including soil moisture, temperature, humidity, crop health, animal product status, and environmental factors. Subsequently, this data is sent via wireless networks to cloud-based platforms, where it conducts analysis and processing utilizing machine learning and artificial intelligence algorithms. The data analysis provides valuable insights that enable farmers to make well-informed decisions on water execution, fertilizer application, pest control, and other agricultural practices. Furthermore, automation systems that are enabled by the Internet of Things (IoT) have the capability of automatically starting operations such as activating watering systems or modifying greenhouse conditions, all based on the data that has been received. Smart agriculture uses advanced technologies such as drones for aerial surveillance, robotics for accurate farming operations, and precision agriculture techniques for ideal resource allocation.

4 BLOCKCHAIN-BASED IOT SECURITY

The ongoing development of blockchain technology is continuously im- proving security solutions for Internet of Things (IoT) devices. Innovative ideas like decentralized security frameworks, energy-saving consensus mechanisms like Proof of Stake (PoS), the integration of smart contracts for automated security protocols, and the use of cryptographic techniques like zero-knowledge proofs for secure data transmission are the focus of current research. These advancements not only address the shortcomings of conventional Internet of Things security, but they also establish a robust and efficient security framework for the growing network of interconnected de- vices utilizing the internet. The concept of safeguarding Internet of Things (IoT) devices in a decentralized and transparent manner is gaining popularity as blockchain technology advances. Blockchain technology, edge computing, and privacy-preserving solutions enhance the security of the Internet of Things (IoT).

4.1 Advancements in Blockchain Technology for Enhancing Internet of Things (IoT) Security through Decentralized Security Frameworks

Recent research has suggested the adoption of decentralized security frameworks that leverage blockchain technology to reduce the risk of vulnerabilities caused by a single point of failure. These frameworks provide robust authentication processes and strengthen defenses against attacks dispersed across multiple platforms. Blockchain technology offers the advantage of enabling Internet of Things devices to securely exchange data with each other, eliminating the need for a central authority. This enhances the privacy and security of Internet of Things networks. Edge computing enables Internet of Things (IoT) devices to do data processing in close proximity to the data source. This leads to a decrease in latency, an enhancement in real-time processing, and a decreased susceptibility to potential security concerns. We possess the capability to employ privacy-enhancing techniques, such as zero-knowledge proofs, to ensure the encryption and anonymity of sensitive data stored on the blockchain. The collection of these technological advancements forms a holistic approach to safeguarding Internet of Things (IoT) systems and countering cyber-attacks (Shah A. et al, 2020).

4.2 Lightweight Consensus Mechanisms

Traditional consensus mechanisms like Proof of Work (PoW) are not suitable for resource-constrained IoT devices due to high computational and energy costs. Researchers are developing lightweight consensus mechanisms that are more energy-efficient and suitable for IoT environments. These lightweight consensus mechanisms aim to provide the necessary security and efficiency for IoT devices while minimizing the computational and energy requirements. One such mechanism is Proof of Stake (PoS), which allows users to create blocks and validate transactions based on the number of coins they hold. Another approach is directed acyclic graphs (DAGs), which enable parallel processing of transactions without the need for mining. Efficient consensus mechanisms, such as Proof of Work (PoW), need substantial computational power and energy, rendering them impractical for Internet of Things (IoT) devices with low resources. Researchers are currently concentrating on developing efficient consensus algorithms that prioritize energy efficiency and align well with IoT applications. The main objective of these streamlined consensus methods is to guarantee the security and effectiveness of Internet of Things devices while also reducing their energy consumption and computational demands. Proof of Stake, also referred to as PoS, exemplifies this approach. Proof of Stake (PoS) is a consensus mechanism where users are able to create blocks and verify transactions by leveraging the quantity of currencies they possess. This technology enables individuals to construct blocks and verify transactions. Thinking about directed acyclic graphs (DAGs) as an alternative, it lets many transactions be processed at the same time without the need for mining. It is imperative to guarantee that these agreement techniques are efficient in order to promote the broader adoption of blockchain technology in IoT-based smart homes. These technologies can be advantageous for devices with limited resources and low energy consumption, as they provide alternative security methods (Singh & Kim, 2021)

4.3 Integration with Edge Computing

Combining blockchain with edge computing has the capacity to improve the security of the Internet of Things (IoT). Edge computing enables the processing of data in close proximity to its source, resulting in reduced latency and bandwidth consumption. When integrated with blockchain technology, it has the capability to facilitate the secure processing of real-time data. The blockchain and edge computing integration facilitates enhanced communication among diverse IoT devices situated in smart homes, thereby increasing their efficiency and safety. The data stored and utilized by edge computing is secured from tampering because blockchain technology is decentral- ized. Moreover, this combination enhances the efficiency, dependability, and safety of smart home IoT systems by facilitating effective data processing, minimizing delay, and ensuring secure connections between devices (Panarello A. et al, 2018).

4.4 Privacy-Preserving Techniques

Blockchain can support privacy-preserving techniques like zero-knowledge proofs (ZKPs) and ring signatures. These techniques enable data verification without disclosing the actual data, thereby protecting confidentiality and integrity. These strategies are essential for preserving privacy in IoT applications. Furthermore, blockchain technology has the capability to facilitate safe and untraceable transactions within IoT devices, thereby augmenting privacy and security for consumers. Internet of Things (IoT) systems in intelligent residences may guarantee the safeguarding of confidential information, ensuring that it is only available to authorized entities by integrating these privacy-enhancing methods. The incorporation of blockchain and IoT not only amplifies confidentiality but also boosts the overall efficiency and dependability of smart home systems, rendering them more reliable and secure for users (Fan K. et al, 2020).

4.5 Emerging Applications of Blockchain in IoT Security

4.5.1 Healthcare IoT

Blockchain technology has the potential to transform the healthcare industry by providing a secure and efficient way to store and share patient data. Blockchain can secure sensitive medical data collected by IoT devices, ensuring data integrity and patients' privacy. Recent frameworks utilize blockchain to enable secure data sharing among healthcare providers. The patient to ensure that sensitive information remains private and tamper-proof by using blockchain in IoT security for healthcare. This benefits patients by protecting their sensitive medical data and also fosters secure data sharing among healthcare providers, improving collaboration, and ultimately enhancing the quality of patient care (McGhin T. et al, 2019).

4.5.2 Smart Cities

The integration of blockchain technology into smart cities ensures the security of IoT devices. This ensures that the structural and crucial services, such as public transport, power and utility services, and other services, which the majority of the population relies on for their daily activities, are protected against potential risks. Intelligent major urbanized areas can utilize the blockchain technique to establish a decentralized, primarily non-resilient physical science strategy for command and oversight of IoT electrical and electronic appliances. We can argue that blockchain, with its ability to store data and regulate information from various indices, has the potential to trans- form the functional properties of smart cities. This results in the creation of a cohesive network and structure that improves the overall efficiency of the urban environment. This not only enhances the physical protection of vital facilities and their structural soundness but also advances the potential for efficient and sustainable handling of urban processes and other related concerns (Biswas & Muthukkumarasamy, 2019).

4.5.3 Supply Chain Management

The blockchain, which entails a distributed ledger, can provide traceability and visibility for transportation throughout the supply chain. Blockchain eliminates the risk of data integrity by ensuring that data on the chain remains unaltered, while IoT devices continuously monitor the condition and state of products. For its part, the use of IoT and blockchain in the supply chain helps to track some of the effects of fraudsters, thieves, and fake makers on the supply system. By integrating blockchain technology to track the movement of goods and authenticate these products, companies can maintain consumer and partner confidence in the supply chain procedure, thereby enhancing accountability. This new operating model is completely revolutionizing how firms' function, and it is already influencing the shape of supply chain systems in smart cities (Tian F., 2017).

4.6 Challenges and Future Directions

Despite the promising advancements, several challenges remain:

- **Scalability:** This ensures that these blockchain networks can accommodate a large number of IoT devices and items alongside transactions. The 2018 attack on a cryptocurrency exchange platform, which resulted in the theft of $530 million in digital currency due to a weak blockchain network, exemplifies the uniqueness of this strategy. This incident also caused discussions regarding the ability of blockchain technology to be secure and reliable enough to handle significant transactions or data.
- **Interoperability:** the development of guidelines for interfacing various block chain environments and IoT structures. A detailed counterexample to this approach is the degree of incompatibility between the blockchain networks of various platforms, which presents a challenge when it comes to connecting IoT devices. If there is no collective effort, compatibility issues may greatly affect the use of blockchain technology in the IoT.
- **Regulation and Compliance:** The Internet of Things (IoT) approach involves establishing legal frameworks or standards that could guide the use of blockchain technology in IoT applications. A more refined counterexample

to this method is the dissimilarities in the rules that prevail across different locations, hence making it challenging for companies to undergo different procedures to meet the different rules. Furthermore, due to the rapid advancement of technology, there is an increased possibility of the regulation and enforcement processes lagging behind. Future re- search should primarily focus on implementing block chain platforms and decentralized policies to resolve these factors.

5 INDUSTRY 4.0 AND 5.0

There are notable distinctions between the focus and methodology of Indus- try 4.0 and Industry 5.0, which signify two separate stages in the evolution of industrial processes. Figure 3 shows the industrial revolutions in an industrial environment from 1.0 to 5.0, in which the years mentioned in Figure 3 are approximate, not precise. The beginning of Revolution 1.0 was marked by the introduction of mechanization and the utilization of steam and waterpower. Subsequently, the second revolution introduced the utilization of electricity, mass production, and assembly lines, while the third revolution brought about the development of industrial computers, automation, and electronics. The initial three revolutions have fundamentally altered the functioning and lifestyle of civilization. Currently, organizations have enhanced their productivity and efficiency as a result of the implementation of advanced technology, new sources of electricity, and innovative work organization methods. Currently, we are experiencing the current cyber revolution, commonly referred to as Industry 4.0 or cyber-physical human intelligence. The industry 4.0 focus revolves around Artificial Intelligence (AI), cyber-physical systems, networking and cloud servers, machine learning, 3D printing, autonomation, virtual reality (VR), and the benefits of computers.

5.1 Industry 4.0

Industry 4.0, or the Fourth Industrial Revolution, is marked by the incorporation of cutting-edge technologies and digitalization into manufacturing processes. Interconnected devices and machines engage in real-time communication and data sharing. Data-driven decision-making and predictive analytics involve the collection and analysis of substantial amounts of data. AI and ML capabilities are integrated into machines and systems to enable autonomous decision-making and pattern recognition. The physical and digital realms are intricately interconnected, establishing a seamless link between machinery, sensors, and individuals. Intelligent machines and robots assume control of monotonous and routine tasks, thereby enhancing efficiency and productivity. Industry 4.0 primarily emphasizes automation, connectivity, and digitalization in order to enhance manufacturing processes and increase efficiency.

5.2 Industry 5.0

Industry 5.0, also known as the Fifth Industrial Revolution, signifies a fundamental change from Industry 4.0. The focus is on combining human abilities with advanced technologies, promoting cooperation between humans and intelligent machines. Robots are engineered to operate in a manner that ensures the safety of humans, helping rather than completely replacing them. Fostering and enhancing human creativity: Acknowledging and harnessing the distinct abilities of individuals, such as their creativity, problem-solving aptitude, and adaptability, in order to stimulate innovation and improve efficiency. Facilitating mass customization to meet the specific requirements of individual customers through the customization of products and services. Employing these technologies to improve human-machine interactions and offer immersive experiences in the workplace. Industry 5.0 seeks to achieve a harmonious blend of automation and human ingenu- ity, with a particular emphasis on cooperation, personalization, and ethical deliberations.

Figure 3. Industrial revolutions from industry 1.0 to industry 5.0

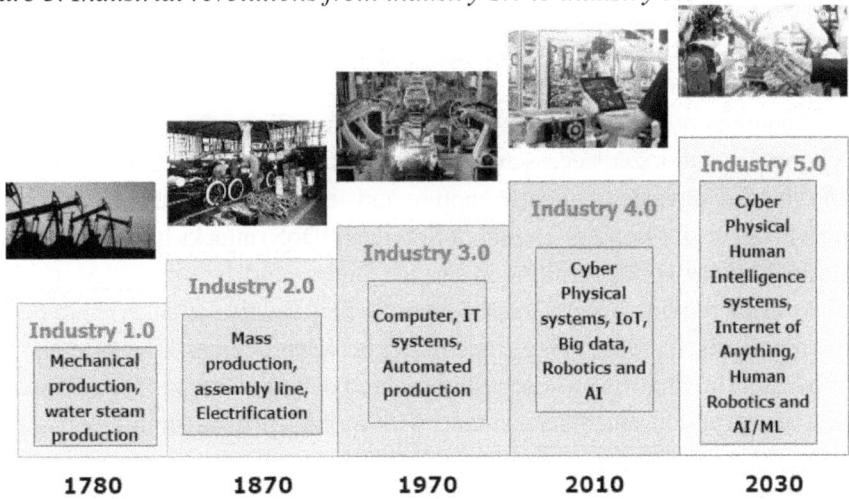

Industry 4.0 was mainly driven by automation and machine-driven procedures, whereas Industry 5.0 acknowledges the significance of human creativity, problem-solving skills, and adaptability [56]. The objective is to achieve equilibrium by synergizing the capabilities of humans and machines, facilitating their seamless

collaboration. Furthermore, Industry 5.0 emphasizes sustainability, resilience, and ethical practices, ensuring that technological advancements are in line with societal values and environmental considerations.

Several important challenges in the implementation of Industry 5.0 include: The task involves combining different systems and ensuring that new and existing technologies can work together smoothly. Ensuring the security and privacy of data in interconnected ecosystems that involve the exchange of data between multiple devices. Successful implementation of this technology requires significant investments in both hardware, including collaborative robots and sensors, as well as software. However, this financial investment can be a challenge for smaller companies. There is a requirement for a workforce that combines advanced skills and is capable of working together with sophisticated technologies such as artificial intelligence (AI) and robotics. Improving and modifying current production lines and systems to incorporate Industry 5.0 technologies (Guruswamy S. et al, 2022). Supervising the rate at which change occurs and the implementation of new technologies in various industries and geographic regions.

6 SECURITY REQUIREMENTS IN IOT NETWORK

Internet of Things (IoT) systems are vulnerable to many threats that could compromise their performance, the accuracy of their data, and the privacy of their users. Malware and ransomware attacks present significant risks as they have the ability to make equipment unusable or encrypt data, demanding a fee in exchange for its decryption. Unauthorized access and data breaches present substantial risks due to the fact that IoT devices frequently capture and send sensitive information, giving them ideal targets for hackers. Denial of Service (DDoS) attacks have the capability to overload IoT networks, resulting in service failures and disruptions. Man-in-the-middle attacks provide a significant danger as they involve attackers intercepting and manipulating the data being transmitted between devices. The primary risks to IoT systems involve the presence of unsecured devices with poor authentication, absence of encryption, and older elements with well-known vulnerabilities (Alotaibi & Ilyas, 2023). These factors facilitate various forms of attacks, such as malware problems, botnets, and illegal access. IoT systems are vulnerable to many threats such as eavesdropping, data interception, and denial of service assaults due to insecure connections, protocols, and interfaces. Additional significant risks come from inadequate device administration, insufficient awareness of dark IoT devices, undetected sophisticated and ongoing data breaches that expose confidential data, and weaknesses in technologies such as 5G and DNS that facilitate extensive attacks on IoT systems.

Moreover, the absence of robust authentication measures may result in unauthorized access to devices, while vulnerable interfaces and network services can be manipulated to obtain control over IoT devices. If firmware and software vulnerabilities are not constantly updated, they might serve as potential access points for attackers to exploit. In addition, manipulating IoT devices physically, particularly those located in public or less secure settings, can result in hacked systems. Insufficient encryption methods can result in data being acquired and accessed without authorization during transmission and storage. This highlights the crucial requirement for strong security measures in IoT systems.

6.1 Challenges for Security Concepts in Internet of Things

IoT devices lack a primary focus on security in their design. Consequently, there are multiple Internet of Things (IoT) security concerns that can have a dangerous impact. In basically every Internet of Things application that has been implemented or is currently being implemented, security is of the highest priority. IoT applications are expanding quickly and are now present in the majority of current industry sectors. Even though operators provide support for many Internet of Things applications via current networking technologies, some of these applications require additional security support from the technologies they apply. Below is a list of IoT security challenges associated with the specified IoT devices, which have the ability to expose consumers to the threat of a data breach.

Software and Firmware Vulnerabilities: Since many IoT devices are unable to update their firmware securely, attacks that benefit from known vulnerabilities can be conducted on them. Devices are vulnerable to false or unauthorized firmware changes. IoT firmware vulnerabilities in terms of hardware, software, network, and application interfaces might allow IoT malware to become a risk in the form of remote hijacking and control. Attackers can take advantage of memory safety vulnerabilities in firmware applications written in C, such as buffer overflows. IoT firmware frequently comes with backdoors or hardcoded default credentials, giving attackers easy access. Sensitive information may be exposed and eavesdropping attacks may be possible due to weak encryption or insecure key storage in firmware. A lot of Internet of Things devices have insecure web interfaces that can be attacked by SQL injection and cross-site scripting (XSS). IoT systems are vulnerable to assaults if they use outdated components, libraries, or frameworks that have known vulnerabilities. Injection attacks such as SQL injection and code injection may occur from inadequate authentication of input data. Unauthorized access to IoT devices and data may be possible if access controls are not effective. Man-in-the-middle (MitM) attacks and data acquisition can be made possible by insecure communication protocols or inadequate encryption (Mansour M. et al, 2023).

Lack of Visibility: The absence of clear visibility presents an important security obstacle in the Internet of Things (IoT) networks. A large percentage of IoT devices function in the background with limited hu- man participation, keeping their operations and data transfers mysterious and challenging to monitor. The large quantity and variety of Internet of Things (IoT) devices linked to a network may overwhelm standard security monitoring solutions, resulting in areas that are not monitored and a lack of insight into their actions. IoT devices often use unique or uncommon protocols, which can complicate the task of examining and evaluating their network data for possible security risks. The absence of obvious insight into the actions of IoT devices could create challenges in quickly detecting abnormalities, illegal access attempts, or malicious con- duct. Deploying IoT device discovery and inventory management tools to obtain a complete understanding of the interconnected devices within the network. Implementing specialized network traffic monitoring and analysis solutions designed for IoT environments to examine and comprehend device communications. Deploying security information and event management (SIEM) systems capable of collecting and matching data from various IoT devices and sources to detect any security risks. Implementing robust access restrictions and authentication measures for IoT devices will ensure that only authorized devices can establish connections with the network.

Lack of Standardization: The lack of standards presents significant challenges for security in Internet of Things (IoT) networks. An absence of globally accepted standards and protocols for IoT device communication, authentication, encryption, and security measures is obvious. In the lack of broadly recognized security standards, organizations can use creative or vendor-specific security methods, resulting in ir- regularities and possible vulnerabilities in their IoT security framework. In response to those who argue that 5G is inappropriate for less advanced IoT applications, the 3GPP standards organization has integrated NB-IoT and LTE-M technologies, which are more affordable and less advanced methods of providing wireless connectivity for IoT devices, into the 5G network (Ahmed S. F. et al, 2024). The most recent mobile communications standard is designed to be flexible and adaptable, serving as a comprehensive solution for wireless communications. It offers a wide range of connectivity options suitable for many applications, including the Internet of Things (IoT). Interoperability is crucial for IoT standardization, but unfortunately, it may also cause significant problems for organizations using the technology (Cirne A. et al, 2022). IoT devices vary in terms of their connectivity standards, which may block communication across devices. A standardized connectivity layer is an essential foundation of any organizational IoT strategy.

Network and Physical Security: IoT devices are vulnerable to attackers due to their weak security features. They have the ability to connect easily to Internet of Things (IoT) equipment located in remote parts for a longer amount of time in order to make any necessary physical modifications (Wang N. et al, 2019). Devices missing physical safety protocols are very vulnerable to attacks, providing serious threats to IoT security. For example, Internet of Things (IoT) devices may get infected with malware when connected to USB flash drives. The primary responsibility of device manufacturers is to give preference to the physical security of these devices, which involves establishing effective third-party risk management protocols when other parties are involved in the company's operations. IoT network security includes safeguarding the network to which IoT devices develop connections. This includes ensuring the security of the communication channels between devices and the network, as well as within individual devices. Network security measures often include deploying intrusion detection systems (IDS), firewalls, and encryption methods. Network security includes the task of monitoring network traffic to detect and address any suspicious behaviors. This may require utilizing artificial intelligence and machine learning technology to identify irregularities that could potentially indicate a security risk. Upon detecting a threat, the necessary response can be promptly initiated to minimize the impact of the attack.

Weak Authentication and Data Privacy: Authentication is the procedure of confirming the identity of a user in order to authorize their access to a device, network, or system. Inadequate authentication in IoT devices can result in several safety issues, making this process essential. Weak authentication initiatives, such as default passwords or simple PINs, en- able illegal access to IoT devices (Yu D. et al, 2020). This can result in data breaches, unauthorized device control, and the possibility of bigger network attacks. A significant number of Internet of Things (IoT) devices are equipped with default usernames and passwords that are frequently vulnerable to being easily guessed by attackers. Certain devices cannot handle complicated passwords or multi-factor authentication, leaving them vulnerable to attacks. If an attacker successfully enters a device, they may have the capability to execute unauthorized activities or collect confidential information. Insufficient protection of sensitive data from IoT devices can result in eavesdropping or illegal access by individuals without permission, resulting in privacy breaches. Both unsecured data transmission or storage and physical attacks on IoT devices can compromise the integrity of the data. Internet of Things (IoT) devices have the capability to collect, keep and utilize your personal data to enhance your convenience (e.g. "Alexa, order a pizza"). The situation becomes serious when IoT devices utilize your information without your knowledge or authorization. The sharing of data with third parties in IoT systems gives rise to privacy concerns, which in turn destroy users' trust in the device. The consequences of weak privacy security in IoT involve reduced user autonomy over their data, the potential for improper use or misuse of sensitive data, identity theft, data breaches, unauthorized access to personal information, and a decrease in the trustworthiness of IoT devices (Venkatraman & Overmars, 2020). Currently, it is an evident fact that we compensate for apparently cost-free online services by providing our personal data.

Figure 4. IoT security solutions

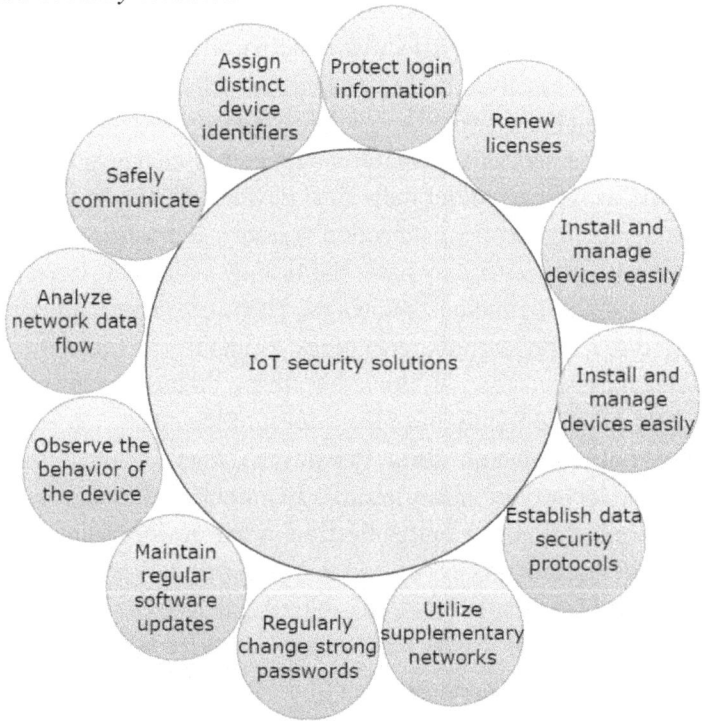

6.2 IoT Security Solutions

There are a few best ways to secure IoT devices so that their security will not be compromised. Figure 4 illustrates the required steps or solutions to secure IoT devices or systems. Here are the practices IoT users should follow:

a) Changing passwords and strong authentication: When setting passwords for IoT devices, it is advisable to use a combination of both alphanumeric letters and symbols. Regularly update them to enhance security.

b) Device inventory management: Effective management of device inventory is crucial for ensuring the security of IoT devices, as it offers complete comprehension and authority over all interconnected devices.

c) Evaluate unused devices and monitor network establishment: If any device is not being utilized, avoid placing it in the surroundings. Any device that remains connected but is not maintained presents a potential security risk.

d) Use a biometric or encrypted key authentication system: Utilize characteristic features of the face or fingerprints for the purpose of authentication. These basic features can be difficult to duplicate, hence enhancing security measures against unauthorized access.

e) Utilize industrial standardization and cloud-based solutions: Adopt established security standards such as the National Institute of Standards and Technology (NIST) guidelines, Federal Information Processing Standard (FIPS) 140-2, and Platform Security Architecture (PSA) Registered. These standards offer a comprehensive framework for assuring device security, including secure boot, encryption, and authentication techniques.

6.3 Case Studies

There are many potential threats that could lead to significant disturbances on the Internet of Things (IoT). Some of these vulnerabilities utilize the IoT's design. A prime example of an issue with security is known as spoofing, where an attacker enters a less secure device and gets access to a network containing protected devices. The attacker then misleads the network into assuming that they are using cryptography. Some other attacks employ IP disturbances as a means for getting into a system. One of the risks involved is smurfing, which is a type of denial-of-service attack that utilizes IP spoofing to inundate a server and hinder its ability to reply to valid requests. IP/ICMP fragmentation is a type of denial-of-service attack that involves splitting up an IP packet into smaller pieces, sending them over a network, and then reconstructing them to overload the network.

Figures 5 and 6 give the data analysis from the Indian government web- site open source dataset for the telecommunication field available across the country and overall mobile connections until 2018 in millions. As per Figure 5, it is clear that from 2014 to 2023, there are significant rise in data usage, optical fiber cable land, mobile broadband subscribers and mobile subscribers as compared to 2014 data. On the other hand, figure 6 proves that until 2018 there were many mobile operators introduced in the Indian market with notable percentage rise of purchases and that Bharati Airtel and Vodafone played crucial roles with the highest number of mobile connections. By this data analysis, it is an idea to combine this with IoT applications, because these devices are connected anyway with these mobile operators and coverage from these network connections.

Figure 5. Analysis of data set with telecommunication in India, from 2014 to 2023

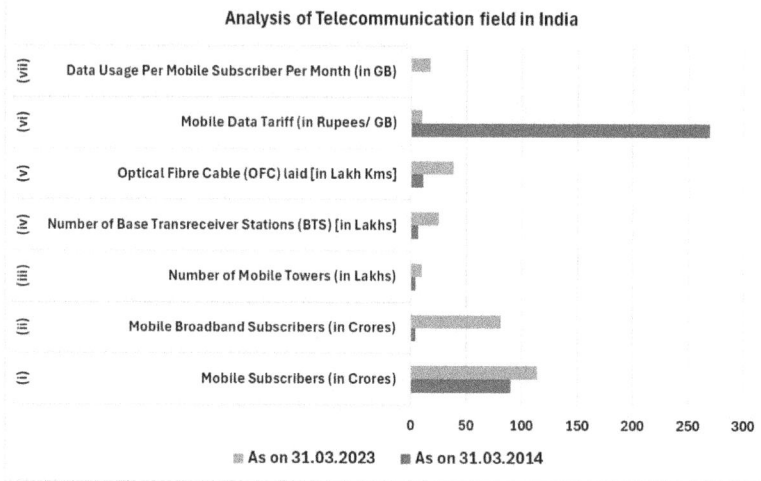

(Source: data.gov.in)

Intrusion-related threats have the ability to compromise the security of IoT systems. The sniffing approach involves a malicious security tag mimicking an authentic tag to gain inappropriate access to a network. A comparable type of threat is referred to as reconnaissance, in which a hacker obtains entry into the network to collect information regarding vulnerabilities. The man in the middle is a type of danger when an attacker positions themselves between two endpoints and secretly intercepts and eavesdrops on their discussion. Another potential hazard is the presence of rogue devices, which are unwanted devices that remain connected to a system and attempt to access and operate within the network.

Figure 6. Total mobile operators as of 2018

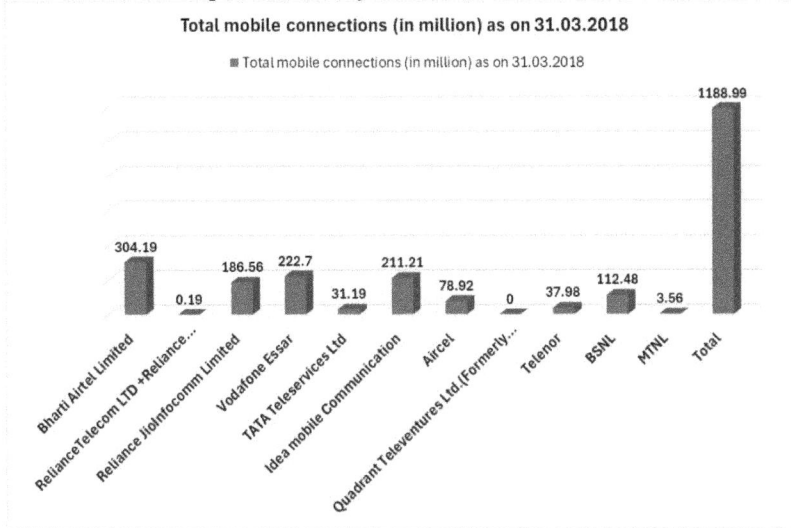

Total mobile connections (in million) as on 31.03.2018

■ Total mobile connections (in million) as on 31.03.2018

(source: data.gov.in)

The analysis of case studies and a comparison of security concepts in the Internet of Things (IoT) can provide important insights into challenges and the most effective approaches for securing IoT systems. In recent years, there have been many instances when apparently harmless IoT devices were improperly utilized and recycled to do harm. Some of the more famous instances have simply been reveals of what is possible, but others involved actual attacks. Here are a few examples of examples when IoT security has been compromised.

- **MIRAI Botnet Attack:** Mirai is a malicious software that targets Internet of Things (IoT) devices such as routers, IP cameras, and digital video recorders (DVRs) that operate on the Linux operating system. The Mirai botnet was a highly dangerous malware attack that took advantage of the insufficient safety precautions of Internet of Things (IoT) devices. It effectively established an extensive network of infected computers, which were then utilized to carry out damaging distributed denial-of-service (DDoS) operations. Mirai operated by performing continuous scans of the internet to detect IoT devices like routers, IP cameras, and digital video recorders that were using default or readily available login credentials [63]. After discovering vulnerable devices, Mirai would forcefully hack into them and infect them, transforming them into remotely controlled "bots" that connected with a central command-and-control server. After that, this server would be able to coordinate the complete botnet of infected devices in order to overload targets with a huge amount of data, so successfully keeping them unavailable. The Mirai bot-net was responsible for some of the biggest Distributed Denial of Service (DDoS) attacks ever recorded, attacking major websites such as OVH, Dyn, and the blog of security journalist Brian Krebs. The massive scope and impact of this event revealed the significant absence of security measures in the constantly expanding IoT network, indicating the urgent need to prioritize strong security protocols and strengthen internet-connected devices against similar risks (Syed & Gadgay, 2023).

- **Verkada Hack:** The Verkada hack represented a significant breach in security, resulting in the unauthorized access and usage of live video feeds and stored footage from approximately 150,000 surveillance cameras. These cameras were installed by the Silicon Valley startup in various organizations, such as hospitals, schools, police departments, prisons, and popular corporations like Tesla and Cloudflare. An international hacker collective conducted the attack by taking advantage of a misconfigured server at Verkada. This server held administrator-level credentials, which enabled the hackers to obtain "super admin" access to the company's complete video monitoring system. From that location, they could observe real-time camera feeds, acquire stored video recordings, and use facial recognition technology on the hacked footage. The incident highlighted the significant vulnerabilities associated with centralized security systems and the possibility of manipulation if proper safeguards are not in place. It also raised concerns about the widespread use of video surveillance and the necessity for strong data privacy procedures, particularly when dealing with sensitive footage from places such as hospitals and schools. The Verkada attack highlighted the vulnerability weaknesses present in IoT and cloud-based security systems, underlining the need to establish strong access limitations, encryption, and security protocols to protect against similar attacks (Syed & Gadgay, 2023).

- **St. Jude Medical's Pacemakers:** In 2016, an important cybersecurity vulnerability was identified in St. Jude Medical's (now Abbott) implanted cardiac devices, such as pacemakers, defibrillators, and cardiac resynchronization therapy devices. The research, released by financial firm Muddy Waters and cybersecurity firm MedSec, claimed that these devices were vulnerable to hacking as a result of multiple significant security vulnerabilities. Researchers claimed their ability to manipulate vulnerabilities in the devices' communication protocols and the Merlin@home monitoring system to initiate attacks such as creating malfunctions, decreasing the battery life at a faster pace, or even reprogramming the devices for inappropriate pacing or shocks. The vulnerabilities resulted from factors such as the lack of encryption, fixed credentials, and insufficient authentication procedures. Despite St. Jude Medical's initial rejection, the U.S. Food and Drug Administration (FDA) verified the vulnerabilities and collaborated with the company to provide a firmware upgrade to address the security concerns. In 2017, the FDA approved a firmware patch that included protections against unauthorized wireless access and command execution on the pacemaker models that were affected (Feng X et al, 2022). Patients were required to physically visit doctors to acquire the update, which highlights the challenges in protecting surgical instruments from cyber-attacks.

- **Target's Credit Card Breach:** The 2013 Target data breach was a significant hack that compromised the personal and financial data of many customers. The incident started when hackers entered Target's networks by using stolen credentials obtained from a third-party HVAC provider. The attackers subsequently installed advanced malware, including a variant of the "BlackPOS" RAM-scraping malware, onto Target's payment terminals. Between November 27 and December 15, 2013, this malicious software silently collected valuable information such as credit and debit card numbers, expiration dates, CVV codes, and encrypted PINs from customers who used their cards to make purchases at Target shops in the United States. In just a period of a few weeks, the hackers successfully stole data from over 40 million credit and debit cards. Additionally, they acquired personal information such as names, email addresses, and phone numbers for an extra 70 million clients. Despite receiving alerts from Target's security systems, the breach remained undetected for a significant period of time. Subsequently, the stolen data became available on underground cybercrime markets, resulting in significant instances of fraud and identity theft. The attack's unusual scale and consequences exposed dan- gerous security weaknesses in Target's systems, causing the retail industry to make significant modifications in data protection standards, payment card technology, and cybersecurity investments.

- **Akuvox Smart Intercom Attack:** The Akuvox E11 smart intercom system has been discovered to have various significant security vulnerabilities which could enable remote attackers to acquire full control over the de- vices. A team of researchers from Claroty has identified 13 vulnerabilities in the system. These vulnerabilities include the absence of authentication for crucial tasks, faults in command injection, and the capability to activate the device's camera and microphone remotely without proper authorization. These vulnerabilities enabled three primary methods of attack: remote code execution within the local network, remote surveil- lance by activating the camera and microphone and transmitting data to the attacker, and access to an insecure FTP server for downloading stored photos and recordings from the devices. The scope of these problems presented significant privacy dangers, especially in delicate settings such as healthcare organizations, where compromised equipment could have an impact on patient privacy requirements. Despite numerous efforts made by researchers and cybersecurity agencies such as CISA to inform Akuvox about the vulnerabilities since January 2022, the vendor has not acknowledged or solved the issues. As a result, the flaws stay unfixed, putting organizations worldwide at risk of cyber-attacks, data breaches, and unauthorized surveillance through their smart intercom systems.

- **EV Charging Station's Security:** EV charging stations are increasingly vulnerable to cyber-attacks since they are connected to networks, cloud services, and the power grid. An important security vulnerability is the possibility of unauthorized access, where attackers might seize control of the charging station and interrupt the charging procedure, steal sensitive data such as payment information (Pourmirza & Walker, 2021). Researchers have presented methods such as "Brokenwire", which uses electromagnetic interference to disrupt the communication between the electric vehicle (EV) and charger remotely. There is an additional weakness in the management systems that supervise the charging infrastructure. These cloud-based platforms can be used to carry out more significant attacks on the grid itself. The leakage of data is an important concern because charging stations collect personal and financial information that could be intercepted or stolen during network breaches. Denial-of-service attacks present a significant risk, as they include hackers overwhelming the system and causing the charging station to stop operating. This results in the prevention of electric vehicles from charging and could lead to grid instability.

6.3.1 Future Directions

There are some future research directions in this relevant field are as follows:

- In order to decrease the security risks presented by IoT applications, it is crucial for future research to focus on developing resilient models that are capable of overcoming adversarial attacks using machine learning and its derivatives. One way to achieve this is by creating techniques to standardize deep learning networks or implementing adversarial training methods.

- Addressing security issues in blockchain-enabled IoT systems can be a difficult task, particularly in terms of application scalability, data privacy, and integration. Software-defined networking (SDN) technology offers a viable solution by utilizing a decentralized controller to address the issue. They have the skill to efficiently handle a large quantity of IoT devices and guarantee the protection of sensitive sensory data.

- In order to address the challenges faced by current IoT applications, it is crucial to acknowledge the significance of edge computing, fog computing and mobile computing along with machine learning, deep learning, and reinforcement learning algorithms. These algorithms have the ability to evaluate network traffic data on the client side to detect various attacks using either a trained model or past experiences.

7 CONCLUSION

This article provides a thorough examination of the security issues related to IoT applications. It evaluates the current authentication methods and the challenges involved in developing a secure IoT network architecture. While it may be challenging to cover every applicable material in just one article, it is more important to provide a comprehensive representation of related work rather than focusing on the quantity of publications. Initially, we thoroughly examined the security framework of IoT applications to identify the complex problems that provide challenges for researchers to fix. Therefore, the focus was on addressing points two and three, which involve examining the current literature on the security of IoT applications and comparing the development of Industry 4.0 and 5.0. We also discussed the challenges related to IoT security concerns. Therefore, we discussed on the potential of utilizing blockchain, machine learning, and cryptography approaches independently or in combination to address these issues and meet the requirements of IoT applications. Finally, we have highlighted the potential areas of investigation that can be utilized as a powerful tool to address and overcome security concerns using simple and systematic approaches.

REFERENCES

Abba Ari, A. A., Ngangmo, O. K., Titouna, C., Thiare, O., Mohamadou, A., & Gueroui, A. M. (2024). Enabling privacy and security in Cloud of Things: Architecture, applications, security & privacy challenges. *Applied Computing and Informatics*, 20(1/2), 119–141. DOI: 10.1016/j.aci.2019.11.005

Adil, M., Khan, M. K., Kumar, N., Attique, M., Farouk, A., Guizani, M., & Jin, Z. (2024). Healthcare Internet of Things: Security Threats, Challenges and Future Research Directions. *IEEE Internet of Things Journal*, 11(11), 19046–19069. DOI: 10.1109/JIOT.2024.3360289

Adil, M., Khan, M. K., Kumar, N., Attique, M., Farouk, A., Guizani, M., & Jin, Z. (2024). Healthcare Internet of Things: Security Threats, Challenges and Future Research Directions. *IEEE Internet of Things Journal*, 11(11), 19046–19069. DOI: 10.1109/JIOT.2024.3360289

Ahanger, T. A., Aljumah, A., & Atiquzzaman, M. (2022). State-of-the-art survey of artificial intelligent techniques for IoT security. *Computer Networks*, 206, 108771. DOI: 10.1016/j.comnet.2022.108771

Ahmad, W., Rasool, A., Javed, A. R., Baker, T., & Jalil, Z. (2021). Cyber security in iot-based cloud computing: A comprehensive survey. *Electronics (Basel)*, 11(1), 16. DOI: 10.3390/electronics11010016

Ahmed, S. F., Alam, M. S. B., Afrin, S., Rafa, S. J., Taher, S. B., Kabir, M., ... & Gandomi, A. H. (2024). Towards a secure 5G-enabled Internet of Things: A survey on requirements, privacy, security, challenges, and opportunities. IEEE Access.

Alotaibi, Y., & Ilyas, M. (2023). Ensemble-learning framework for intrusion detection to enhance internet of things' devices security. *Sensors (Basel)*, 23(12), 5568. DOI: 10.3390/s23125568 PMID: 37420734

Alqarawi, G., Alkhalifah, B., Alharbi, N., & El Khediri, S. (2023). Internet-of-things security and vulnerabilities: Case study. *Journal of Applied Security Research*, 18(3), 559–575. DOI: 10.1080/19361610.2022.2031841

AlZubi, A. A., & Galyna, K. (2023). Artificial intelligence and internet of things for sustainable farming and smart agriculture. *IEEE Access : Practical Innovations, Open Solutions*, 11, 78686–78692. DOI: 10.1109/ACCESS.2023.3298215

Babun, L., Denney, K., Celik, Z. B., McDaniel, P., & Uluagac, A. S. (2021). A survey on IoT platforms: Communication, security, and privacy perspectives. *Computer Networks*, 192, 108040. DOI: 10.1016/j.comnet.2021.108040

Bel, H. F., & Sabeen, S. (2022). A survey on IoT security: Attacks, challenges and countermeasures. *Webology*, 19(1), 3741–3763. DOI: 10.14704/WEB/V19I1/WEB19246

[] Biswas, K., & Muthukkumarasamy, V. (2019). Securing smart cities using blockchain technology. Springer, Internet of Things and Secure Smart Envi- ronments: Success and Pitfalls, 127–139. doi:.DOI: 10.1007/978-3-030-17560-9 7

Chanal, P. M., & Kakkasageri, M. S. (2020). Security and privacy in IoT: A survey. *Wireless Personal Communications*, 115(2), 1667–1693. DOI: 10.1007/s11277-020-07649-9

Chui, K. T., Gupta, B. B., Liu, J., Arya, V., Nedjah, N., Almomani, A., & Chaurasia, P. (2023). A survey of internet of things and cyber-physical systems: Standards, algorithms, applications, security, challenges, and future directions. *Information (Basel)*, 14(7), 388. DOI: 10.3390/info14070388

Cirne, A., Sousa, P. R., Resende, J. S., & Antunes, L. (2022). IoT security certifications: Challenges and potential approaches. *Computers & Security*, 116, 102669. DOI: 10.1016/j.cose.2022.102669

Cruz, A. R. S. A., Gomes, R. L., & Fernandez, M. P. (2021, July). An intelligent mechanism to detect cyberattacks of mirai botnet in iot networks. In 2021 17th International Conference on Distributed Computing in Sensor Systems (DCOSS) (pp. 236-243). IEEE.

Fan, K., Ren, Y., Li, H., Yang, Y., & Zhou, H. (2020). Blockchain-based efficient privacy preserving and data sharing scheme of content-centric network in 5G. *IET Communications*, 14(6), 833–841. DOI: 10.1049/iet- com.2019.0828

Feng, X., Zhu, X., Han, Q. L., Zhou, W., Wen, S., & Xiang, Y. (2022). Detecting vulnerability on IoT device firmware: A survey. IEEE/CAA Journal of Automatica Sinica, 10(1), 25-41.

Furstenau, L. B., Rodrigues, Y. P. R., Sott, M. K., Leivas, P., Dohan, M. S., Lo'pez-Robles, J. R., Cobo, M. J., Bragazzi, N. L., & Choo, K. K. R. (2023). Internet of things: Conceptual network structure, main challenges and future directions. *Digital Communications and Networks*, 9(3), 677–687. DOI: 10.1016/j.dcan.2022.04.027

Gopalan, S. S., Raza, A., & Almobaideen, W. (2021, March). IoT security in healthcare using AI: A survey. In 2020 International Conference on Com- munications, Signal Processing, and their Applications (ICCSPA) (pp. 1-6). IEEE. DOI: 10.1109/ICCSPA49915.2021.9385711

Guruswamy, S., Pojic´, M., Subramanian, J., Mastilovic´, J., Sarang, S., Subbana-gounder, A., Stojanović, G., & Jeoti, V. (2022). Toward better food security using concepts from industry 5.0. *Sensors (Basel)*, 22(21), 8377. DOI: 10.3390/s22218377 PMID: 36366073

HaddadPajouh, H., Dehghantanha, A., Parizi, R. M., Aledhari, M., & Karim- ipour, H. (. (2021). A survey on internet of things security: Requirements, challenges, and solutions. *Internet of Things : Engineering Cyber Physical Human Systems*, 14, 100129. DOI: 10.1016/j.iot.2019.100129

Hameed, A., & Alomary, A. (2019, September). Security issues in IoT: A survey. In 2019 International conference on innovation and intelligence for informatics, computing, and technologies (3ICT) (pp. 1-5). IEEE. DOI: 10.1109/3ICT.2019.8910320

Harbi, Y., Aliouat, Z., Refoufi, A., & Harous, S. (2021). Recent security trends in internet of things: A comprehensive survey. *IEEE Access : Practical Innovations, Open Solutions*, 9, 113292–113314. DOI: 10.1109/ACCESS.2021.3103725

Hassan, W. H. (2019). Current research on Internet of Things (IoT) security: A survey. *Computer Networks*, 148, 283–294. DOI: 10.1016/j.comnet.2018.11.025

Hassija, V., Chamola, V., Saxena, V., Jain, D., Goyal, P., & Sikdar, B. (2019). A survey on IoT security: Application areas, security threats, and solution architectures. *IEEE Access : Practical Innovations, Open Solutions*, 7, 82721–82743. DOI: 10.1109/ACCESS.2019.2924045

Hou, J., Qu, L., & Shi, W. (2019). A survey on internet of things security from data perspectives. *Computer Networks*, 148, 295–306. DOI: 10.1016/j.comnet.2018.11.026

Issa, W., Moustafa, N., Turnbull, B., Sohrabi, N., & Tari, Z. (2023). Blockchain-based federated learning for securing internet of things: A com- prehensive survey. *ACM Computing Surveys*, 55(9), 1–43. DOI: 10.1145/3560816

Jurcut, A., Niculcea, T., Ranaweera, P., & Le-Khac, N. A. (2020). Security considerations for Internet of Things: A survey. *SN Computer Science*, 1(4), 1–19. DOI: 10.1007/s42979-020-00201-3

Kannan, Y. (2024). Impact of Internet of Things (IoT) devices on Network Security at Financial Institutions. *Authorea Preprints*. DOI: 10.22541/au.171011417.76922216/v1

Karthik, S. A., Hemalatha, R., Aruna, R., Deivakani, M., Reddy, R. V. K., & Boopathi, S. (2023). Study on Healthcare Security System-Integrated Internet of Things (IoT). In Perspectives and Considerations on the Evolution of Smart Systems (pp. 342-362). IGI Global.

Liang, X., & Kim, Y. (2021, January). A survey on security attacks and solutions in the IoT network. In 2021 IEEE 11th annual computing and communication workshop and conference (CCWC) (pp. 0853-0859). IEEE. DOI: 10.1109/CCWC51732.2021.9376174

Liu, Y., Wang, J., Yan, Z., Wan, Z., & Ja¨ntti, R. (2023). A survey on blockchain-based trust management for Internet of Things. *IEEE Internet of Things Journal*, 10(7), 5898–5922. DOI: 10.1109/JIOT.2023.3237893

Mansour, M., Gamal, A., Ahmed, A. I., Said, L. A., Elbaz, A., Herencsar, N., & Soltan, A. (2023). Internet of things: A comprehensive overview on protocols, architectures, technologies, simulation tools, and future directions. *Energies*, 16(8), 3465. DOI: 10.3390/en16083465

McGhin, T., Choo, K. K. R., Liu, C. Z., & He, D. (2019). Blockchain in healthcare applications: Research challenges and opportunities. *Journal of Network and Computer Applications*, 135, 62–75. DOI: 10.1016/j.jnca.2019.02.027

Meneghello, F., Calore, M., Zucchetto, D., Polese, M., & Zanella, A. (2019). IoT: Internet of threats? A survey of practical security vulnerabilities in real IoT devices. *IEEE Internet of Things Journal*, 6(5), 8182–8201. DOI: 10.1109/JIOT.2019.2935189

Mentsiev, A. U., Guzueva, E. R., & Magomaev, T. R. (2020, April). Security challenges of the Industry 4.0. [). IOP Publishing.]. *Journal of Physics: Conference Series*, 1515(3), 032074. DOI: 10.1088/1742-6596/1515/3/032074

Mousavi, S. K., Ghaffari, A., Besharat, S., & Afshari, H. (2021). Security of internet of things based on cryptographic algorithms: A survey. *Wireless Networks*, 27(2), 1515–1555. DOI: 10.1007/s11276-020-02535-5

Mrabet, H., Belguith, S., Alhomoud, A., & Jemai, A. (2020). A survey of IoT security based on a layered architecture of sensing and data analysis. *Sensors (Basel)*, 20(13), 3625. DOI: 10.3390/s20133625 PMID: 32605178

Najmi, K. Y., AlZain, M. A., Masud, M., Jhanjhi, N. Z., Al-Amri, J., & Baz, M. (2023). A survey on security threats and countermeasures in IoT to achieve users confidentiality and reliability. *Materials Today: Proceedings*, 81, 377–382. DOI: 10.1016/j.matpr.2021.03.417

Neshenko, N., Bou-Harb, E., Crichigno, J., Kaddoum, G., & Ghani, N. (2019). Demystifying IoT security: An exhaustive survey on IoT vulnerabilities and a first empirical look on Internet-scale IoT exploitations. *IEEE Communications Surveys and Tutorials*, 21(3), 2702–2733. DOI: 10.1109/COMST.2019.2910750

Ogonji, M. M., Okeyo, G., & Wafula, J. M. (2020). A survey on privacy and security of Internet of Things. *Computer Science Review*, 38, 100312. DOI: 10.1016/j.cosrev.2020.100312

Omolara, A. E., Alabdulatif, A., Abiodun, O. I., Alawida, M., Alabdulatif, A., & Arshad, H. (2022). The internet of things security: A survey encompassing unexplored areas and new insights. *Computers & Security*, 112, 102494. DOI: 10.1016/j.cose.2021.102494

Panarello, A., Tapas, N., Merlino, G., Longo, F., & Puliafito, A. (2018). Blockchain and IoT integration: A systematic survey. *Sensors (Basel)*, 18(8), 2575. DOI: 10.3390/s18082575 PMID: 30082633

Pourmirza, Z., & Walker, S. (2021, August). Electric vehicle charging station: Cyber security challenges and perspective. In *2021 IEEE 9th International Conference on Smart Energy Grid Engineering (SEGE)* (pp. 111-116). IEEE.

Prakash, R., Jyoti, N., & Manjunatha, S. (2024). A survey of security chal- lenges, attacks in IoT. In *E3S Web of Conferences* (Vol. 491, p. 04018). EDP Sciences.

Rachit, B., Bhatt, S., & Ragiri, P. R. (2021). Security trends in Internet of Things: A survey. *SN Applied Sciences*, 3(1), 1–14. DOI: 10.1007/s42452-021-04156-9

Raeisi-Varzaneh, M., Dakkak, O., Alaidaros, H., & Avci, ˙. I. (2024). Internet of Things: Security, Issues, Threats, and Assessment of Different Cryptographic Technologies. *Journal of Communication*, 19(2).

Rani, S., Kataria, A., Sharma, V., Ghosh, S., Karar, V., Lee, K., & Choi, C. (2021). Threats and corrective measures for IoT security with observance of cybercrime: A survey. *Wireless Communications and Mobile Computing*, 2021(1), 1–30. DOI: 10.1155/2021/5579148

Sadhu, P. K., Yanambaka, V. P., & Abdelgawad, A. (2022). Internet of things: Security and solutions survey. *Sensors (Basel)*, 22(19), 7433. DOI: 10.3390/s22197433 PMID: 36236531

Sartayeva, Y., & Chan, H. C. (2023). A survey on indoor positioning security and privacy. *Computers & Security*, 131, 103293. DOI: 10.1016/j.cose.2023.103293

Shah, A., Yaqoob, I., Khan, M. A., Imran, M., & Akhunzada, A. (2020). Blockchain for IoT-based smart homes: A review of cur- rent trends and research challenges. *Computer Networks*, 172, 107248. DOI: 10.1016/j.comnet.2020.107248

Shaharuddin, S., Maulud, K. N. A., Rahman, S. A. F. S. A., Ani, A. I. C., & Pradhan, B. (2023). The role of IoT sensor in smart building context for indoor fire hazard scenario: A systematic review of interdisciplinary articles. *Internet of Things : Engineering Cyber Physical Human Systems*, 22, 100803. DOI: 10.1016/j.iot.2023.100803

Shammar, E. A., Zahary, A. T., & Al-Shargabi, A. A. (2021). A survey of IoT and blockchain integration: Security perspective. *IEEE Access : Practical Innovations, Open Solutions*, 9, 156114–156150. DOI: 10.1109/ACCESS.2021.3129697

Sharma, K., Malik, A., Batra, I., Sanwar Hosen, A. S. M., Latif Sarker, M. A., & Han, D. S. (2023). Technologies Behind the Smart Grid and Internet of Things: A System Survey. *Computers, Materials & Continua*, 75(3). Advance online publication. DOI: 10.32604/cmc.2023.035638

Sharma, R., & Arya, R. (2023). Security threats and measures in the Internet of Things for smart city infrastructure: A state of art. *Transactions on Emerging Telecommunications Technologies*, 34(11), e4571. DOI: 10.1002/ett.4571

Sharma, V., You, I., Andersson, K., Palmieri, F., Rehmani, M. H., & Lim, J. (2020). Security, privacy and trust for smart mobile-Internet of Things (M-IoT): A survey. *IEEE Access : Practical Innovations, Open Solutions*, 8, 167123–167163. DOI: 10.1109/ACCESS.2020.3022661

Shirvani, M. H., & Masdari, M. (2023). A survey study on trust-based security in Internet of Things: Challenges and issues. *Internet of Things : Engineering Cyber Physical Human Systems*, 21, 100640. DOI: 10.1016/j.iot.2022.100640

Singh, S., & Kim, S. (2021). Blockchain technology for decentralized IoT security and privacy: A comprehensive survey. *Telecommunication Systems*, 76, 139–154. DOI: 10.1007/s11235-021-00797-5

Siwakoti, Y. R., Bhurtel, M., Rawat, D. B., Oest, A., & Johnson, R. C. (2023). Advances in IOT security: Vulnerabilities, enabled Criminal Services, attacks and countermeasures. *IEEE Internet of Things Journal*, 10(13), 11224–11239. DOI: 10.1109/JIOT.2023.3252594

Sott, M. K., Furstenau, L. B., Kipper, L. M., Giraldo, F. D., Lopez-Robles, J. R., Cobo, M. J., Zahid, A., Abbasi, Q. H., & Imran, M. A. (2020). Precision techniques and agriculture 4.0 technologies to promote sustainability in the coffee sector: State of the art, challenges and future trends. *IEEE Access : Practical Innovations, Open Solutions*, 8, 149854–149867. DOI: 10.1109/ACCESS.2020.3016325

[] Sun, P., Shen, S., Wan, Y., Wu, Z., Fang, Z., & Gao, X. Z. (2024). A Survey of IoT Privacy Security: Architecture, Technology, Challenges, and Trends. IEEE Internet of Things Journal.

Syed, A., & Gadgay, B. (2023). A Black Hole Attack Protection Approach in IoT-Based Applications Using RLNC. In *Contemporary Challenges for Cyber Security and Data Privacy* (pp. 151–165). IGI Global. DOI: 10.4018/979-8-3693-1528-6.ch009

Taherdoost, H. (2023). Security and internet of things: Benefits, challenges, and future perspectives. *Electronics (Basel)*, 12(8), 1901. DOI: 10.3390/electronics12081901

Thabit, F., Can, O., Aljahdali, A. O., Al-Gaphari, G. H., & Alkhzaimi, H. A. (2023). A comprehensive literature survey of cryptography algorithms for improving the iot security. *Internet of Things : Engineering Cyber Physical Human Systems*, ●●●, 100759. DOI: 10.1016/j.iot.2023.100759

Tian, F. (2017). A supply chain traceability system for food safety based on HACCP, blockchain, and the Internet of Things 2017 Inter- national Conference on Service Systems and Service Management, 1-6. DOI: 10.1109/ICSSSM.2017.7996119

Tournier, J., Lesueur, F., Le Moue¨l, F., Guyon, L., & Ben-Hassine, H. (2021). A survey of IoT protocols and their security issues through the lens of a generic IoT stack. *Internet of Things : Engineering Cyber Physical Human Systems*, 16, 100264. DOI: 10.1016/j.iot.2020.100264

Venkatraman, S., & Overmars, A. (2020, November). IoT Authentication and Security Challenges. In *Proceedings of the 3rd International Conference on Research in Applied Science*, Munich, Germany (pp. 6-8).

Wang, N., Wang, P., Alipour-Fanid, A., Jiao, L., & Zeng, K. (2019). Physical- layer security of 5G wireless networks for IoT: Challenges and opportunities. *IEEE Internet of Things Journal*, 6(5), 8169–8181. DOI: 10.1109/JIOT.2019.2927379

Yu, D., Zhang, L., Chen, Y., Ma, Y., & Chen, J. (2020). Large-scale IoT devices firmware identification based on weak password. *IEEE Access : Practical Innovations, Open Solutions*, 8, 7981–7992. DOI: 10.1109/ACCESS.2020.2964646

Yu, M., Zhuge, J., Cao, M., Shi, Z., & Jiang, L. (2020). A survey of security vulnerability analysis, discovery, detection, and mitigation on IoT devices. *Future Internet*, 12(2), 27. DOI: 10.3390/fi12020027

Yugha, R., & Chithra, S. (2020). A survey on technologies and security proto- cols: Reference for future generation IoT. *Journal of Network and Computer Applications*, 169, 102763. DOI: 10.1016/j.jnca.2020.102763

Chapter 15
An Implementation of Decentralized Secured Tweeting Platform:
Security of a Tweeting App

Sumathi Pawar

Information Science & Engineering, NMAMIT, Nitte, India

K. Suma

Mangalore Institute of Technology and Management, Moodabidri, India

Ankitha P.

Information Science & Engineering, NMAMIT, Nitte, India

Vandana B. S.

Information Science & Engineering, NMAMIT, Nitte, India

RajaLakshmi Samaga

Information Science & Engineering, NMAMIT, Nitte, India

ABSTRACT

A decentralized secured tweeting platform utilizes blockchain technology to distribute control and data across a network of participants, challenging the centralized model. It provides enhanced privacy, reduced content manipulation, and resistance to centralized control of user content. This system represents a decentralized tweeting social media platform with the objective of furnishing users with a communication environment that's both secure and characterized by transparency. Through the integration of smart contracts, users can transact directly and securely without the need for intermediaries. ReactJS empowers a responsive and user-friendly interface,

DOI: 10.4018/979-8-3693-9225-6.ch015

fostering real-time interaction among users to create a decentralized social media platform, enhancing security and transparency to unprecedented levels. Blockchain technology confirms that data is securely stored, immutable and transparent. The proposed system enables users to post tweets, follow other users, like and comment on posts and engage in real-time messaging. This article also presents the implementation of the system.

INTRODUCTION

This article aims to develop a secure tweeting app utilizing blockchain web 3.0, employing Solidity, Next.js, and Sanity.io. The system mimics Twitter's functionality, providing a secure platform for tweeting. It redistributes control and data ownership to users, avoiding the risks of censorship and data leaks in day-to-day social media. Decentralized system utilizes distributed ledger technology, smart contracts and peer-to-peer networks to ensure user-centric digital social media application. The front end is built with Next.js and styled using Tailwind CSS. Additionally, a custom smart contract is created with Solidity. As Zheng et al. (2017) have noted, blockchain, the primary network for cryptocurrency, supports the app, while Twitter remains a popular social media platform for cryptocurrency enthusiasts to share their thoughts in short posts.

Creating a smart contract for a tweeting app using blockchain involves writing the contract in Solidity, the programming language for Ethereum. An example of a basic smart contract that enables users to post tweets and retrieve them is given in the implementation section. This contract includes basic functionality for posting and viewing tweets. According to Valeti Deepika and Lalitha Bhaskari (2020), Truffle is utilized for deploying the smart contract on the Ubuntu (Debian) OS. This project offers enhanced security compared to a standard Twitter app. Smart contract, which are programmable digital agreements, improve communication and facilitate long-term asset tracking. They are also valuable for maintaining relationships with consumers.

In this application, an instance of the Web3 API is created for connecting to the local blockchain network. This system also uses the Web3 API to interact with the smart contract by creating a contract instance and calling its methods to create tweets, like tweets and retrieve tweets.

Web3.js is a JavaScript library designed to facilitate interaction with the Ethereum blockchain. Sumathi and Manjula (2023) highlight the open-source APIs provided by Web3.js for linking the blockchain, initiating transactions, and engaging with smart contracts. Ethers.js is another JavaScript library that allows interaction with the Ethereum blockchain. It provides a simpler API compared to Web3.js and has better support for TypeScript.

IPFS (Interplanetary File System) is a distributed storage system for files, enabling storage and sharing across a distributed network of computers. It provides an API that facilitates the storage and retrieval of files from the IPFS network. Solidity is a programming language needed to write smart contracts on the Ethereum blockchain. It is used to define the business logic of an app and is executed on the Ethereum Virtual Machine (EVM). This application uses the Solidity API to define the smart contract for the tweet structure that represents a tweet and provides methods for creating tweets, liking tweets, and retrieving tweets.

Open Zeppelin is a library of reusable smart contracts that provide security and modularity to the app. It offers a range of smart contracts, from simple ones like ownership contracts to more complex ones like multi-signature wallets. This application uses React-Bootstrap to create UI components such as forms, buttons, and list groups.

In this article, Section 2 discusses the literature review, Sections 3 and 4 cover various methods for securing this app and Sections 4 and 5 focus on implementation and results.

LITERATURE REVIEW

The goal of decentralized tweeting systems is to counter the algorithmic bias, privacy issues, and data breaches that come with centralized platforms (Marx & Cheong, 2023). The decentralization of social media platforms poses new difficulties in terms of adoption, control, privacy, operation and security. Decentralization offers consumers and content creators, security and stability by shifting trust from closed corporate rules to open blockchain technologies (Bhusare et al., 2023). Decentralized systems lose some of the privacy protections provided by central parties due to the lack of a single point of data aggregation, which increases the risk of privacy invasion through metadata (Greschbach et al., 2012).

In order to keep performance on pace with centralized competitors, decentralization affects the scalability of tweeting platforms by necessitating effective on-chain and off-chain storage solutions (Tama & Wicaksana, 2023). According to a study on decentralized social media networks built on the NEAR Protocol Blockchain, throughput and scalability are increased when on-chain and off-chain storage techniques are used. On-chain storage alone is not a scalable option.

Platforms for decentralized tweeting provide better anonymity, less manipulation of material, and resistance to centralized control over user content (Nehete et al., 2024); (Saha et al., 2024). Nevertheless, some of the privacy protection provided by central parties is lost when social networks become more decentralized, which raises the possibility of metadata invasion (Greschbach et al., 2012). Efficient methods for safeguarding user-generated content privacy and assessing various content privacy enforcement approaches are necessary for decentralized platforms (De Salve et al., 2023).

In 1991, blockchain technology was proposed, making digital data unchangeable during its transfer. Initially, public databases were used for securing content. Later, blockchain technology was used to create Bitcoin, a virtual currency (Zheng et al., 2017).

NFT (Non-Fungible Token) is non-fungible compared to a cryptocurrency. It contains a cryptographic link to a specific artwork on IPFS and thus represents a digital certificate for a unique artwork. For the art world, especially digital artists, this technology and certificate provide a market to distribute and sell their artworks. Computational power should be made efficient to ensure less energy consumption (Grasser & Parger, 2022).

In the "Blocks," collections of data and state are used to store information. To transmit ETH, the transactional information must be included in a block. The word "chain" denotes the interconnectedness of all the blocks. A "Node" is a computer in each block that concurs as a chain in the whole network. Every user accesses the same data in the blockchain network, requiring a distributed agreement (Goel & Bakshi, 2022).

Every time the smart contract's functionalities are invoked, events are implemented and released, which may be helpful for automating certain activities. Along with a succinct overview of the Ethereum blockchain network, a practical implementation of such a workflow leveraging the Solidity smart contract language is provided. This dual approach enables, firstly, the establishment of a durable record concerning agreements between data authors and users, offering the capability to verify adherence at any given point of hand (Pănescu & Manta, 2018).

Regarding data collections, 120,000 tweets related to Bitcoin and Ethereum, including User ID, Tweet creation time, Tweet text, Tweet length, user creation time, user followers count, user friends count, Twitter sources, Tweet likes, and Tweet retweets, were used to train the model for machine learning approaches of blockchain usage (Ranasinghe & Halgamuge, 2021).

Ahmad et al. (2022) managed a health care system with critical and non-critical patients concurrently. Critical fog clusters handle critical patients for a speedy response, while non-critical fog clusters manage non-critical patients to safeguard the confidentiality of patient health records. This technique minimally modifies the current IoT ecosystem while reducing essential message response times and offloading cloud infrastructure. Users benefit from decreased storage needs for cloud data centres results in saving money.

According to Handayani (2022), innovation applied the legislation to each chosen CBDC design. This architecture is comprised of wholesale and retail, which use token- or account-based verification. Following that, CBDC transactions are handled by the central bank or carried out using a DLT system. Apart from that, one more feature of CBDC is dependent on interest-bearing and non-interest-bearing options. Regulations had to be improved as a result of CBDC's varied implementation and choices. Regarding the legal status of CBDC in Indonesia, changes must be made to the text of Law No. 7 of 2011 on Currency, which must specify that CBDC is included in the rupiah currency.

Liu (2023) reviewed research on central bank digital currencies (CBDCs). The most recent research defines CBDC as a payment method comparable to cash. The benefits and traits of employing CBDC have also been put out as justifications for the central bank issuing them. The study also demonstrates how CBDC and financial inclusion are related. After the issuance of CBDC, an analysis of the existing situation and a forecast of its future development are made.

Blockchain technology ensures information security, privacy, and public confidence by providing a shared, tamper-resistant, decentralized ecosystem for social media platform security (Lavania & Sharma, 2023). Novel ideas like user authentication utilizing a Zig-Zag configuration for platform security are used in the application of blockchain technology to social media security. In order to increase user data security and dependability, decentralized social networking apps built on distributed storage and blockchain technology provide censorship resistance and personal data ownership (Saha et al., 2024).

A number of studies address the idea of decentralized social media platforms, emphasizing how users might regain control and ownership of their data through the use of peer-to-peer networks, blockchain technology, and smart contracts. The abstracts highlight the benefits of decentralized approaches, including improved privacy, less manipulated content, and resistance to centralized user content regulation. The papers frequently discuss the application of blockchain technology, highlighting its potential to offer safe and decentralized spaces for social media communication. However, some abstracts also touch on the drawbacks and issues of decentralization, such as metadata concealment and privacy protection in decentralized systems. The literature review suggests that the motivation behind the secured Tweeting App development is for secured communication, and many researches are ongoing in the area of decentralized security techniques. The use of blockchain technology has made it possible to ensure strong security across various nodes. Innovation in the field of decentralized Web services (Pawar & Chiplunkar, 2018); (Pawar & GuruRaj, 2023) has made blockchain transactions more powerful.

TECHNOLOGY BEHIND BLOCKCHAIN

Blockchain technology is used for distributed or decentralized security, which does not fail as in the case of a single point of failure in centralized systems. The following are components of a blockchain system:

Distributed Ledger Technology (DLT)

In decentralized systems such as blockchain, this technology is used. Transactions are recorded digitally in multiple places simultaneously. Distributed ledgers do not have a central data store as traditional databases do. In a DLT system, multiple nodes (computers) participate in the network, each maintaining a copy of the ledger. Decisions and validations are made collectively by the network rather than by a central authority, enhancing transparency and reducing single points of failure. Running a full node involves maintaining a copy of the entire blockchain and validating transactions. Node operators may earn rewards for providing network stability and contributing to decentralization. Decentralized Finance (DeFi) applications often involve creating and interacting with smart contracts. The contracts are self-executing programs with predefined rules. Developers can monetize their apps by designing useful and innovative smart contracts that attract users and generate transaction fees. The smart contract has the flexibility to be deployed either on a public blockchain network like Ethereum or on a private network.

Cryptographic Hash Functions

Each block contains the cryptographic hash of its previous block, ensuring that all records are immutable and that any alteration in a block would change its hash and break the chain. Transactions are signed using private keys and verified by anyone using the corresponding public key, ensuring authenticity and non-repudiation. Using an Immutable Ledger, the transaction is recorded.

Blocks and Chains

A block is a data structure used to record a set of transactions. Each block typically contains components such as the header, which contains metadata about the block. The previous block hash is a reference to the hash of the previous block in the chain. This links the blocks together in a specific sequence. The timestamp is the time at which the block was created. The Merkle Root is a hash that represents all the transactions in the block, organized in a Merkle tree structure. This provides a compact and efficient way to verify the integrity of the transactions. The nonce is a random number used in the Proof of Work (PoW) consensus mechanism to vary the input to the hash function and meet the required difficulty target. The difficulty level for the PoW algorithm determines how hard it is to find a valid hash for the block. The linking of blocks through cryptographic hashes ensures that any attempt to alter a transaction would require re-mining all subsequent blocks, making tampering highly impractical. Each transaction is recorded in a public ledger that is accessible to all participants, providing transparency and auditability. Processes involved include transaction creation, block creation, verification, validation, and addition to the chain.

Smart Contracts

These are self-executing contracts where agreements are directly written into code. They run on blockchain platforms, which ensures that the contract execution is automated, transparent, and immutable. This eliminates the need for intermediaries, reduces transaction costs, and increases the efficiency of executing agreements. Oracles are services that provide external data to smart contracts. They bridge the gap between blockchain and the real world by feeding information like stock prices, weather conditions, and more. Smart contracts written in high-level languages like Solidity are compiled into EVM bytecode, which is executed by the EVM.

Token Distribution

Security Token Offerings (STOs) and Initial Coin Offerings (ICOs) are token distribution methods that involve mathematical calculations to determine token allocations, pricing, and fund-raising goals. Transaction fees, often denominated in the blockchain's native token, are required to process transactions or execute smart contracts. Gas prices represent the computational resources needed for a transaction or contract execution. Users bid on gas prices to prioritize their transactions.

METHODOLOGY

This article focuses on developing a secure tweeting app using blockchain technology with two objectives. The first objective is to develop a client tester/simulator. The second objective is to apply security through blockchain to prevent account hacking. In current tweeting applications, the client part sends/receives tweets, and the engine distributes tweets. The current tweeting apps do not have much security, and there can be a leak of private user information. Therefore, this system implements a tweeting platform using blockchain, which ensures the privacy of the user.

Figure 1. Architecture of the system

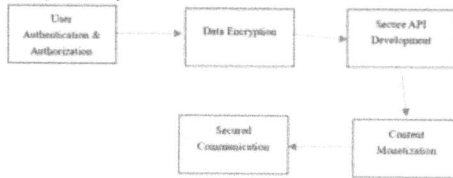

Block diagram of the system is shown in figure 1 and each block is explained in detail.

Authentication and Authorization

This is accomplished using the React-Bootstrap API. The application utilizes React-Bootstrap to create UI components such as forms, buttons, and list groups. Initially, the user interface of the Twitter clone is designed using React JS, a widely embraced JavaScript library for building user interfaces. This integral component is responsible for presenting various aspects of the tweeting app, including the user's timeline, notifications, messages, and other functionalities.

This involves creating several components such as the home feed, user profile, search bar, tweet composer, and notifications. Various React JS libraries, such as Material-UI and Bootstrap are used to design the user interface. Users can create an account on the platform and link their blockchain wallet address to their account. Authentication is carried out using third-party providers like MetaMask.

Data Encryption Using Blockchain Networks

The blockchain network is the core of this system. It is responsible for storing and processing all user data, including tweets, user profiles, and other information. The blockchain network ensures that all data is stored securely and in a decentralized manner, making it tamper-proof and resilient to attacks.

Figure 2. Blockchain architecture

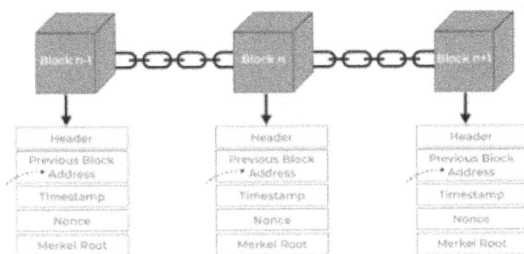

Fig 2 Blockchain Architecture [11]

Figure 2 shows the architecture of blockchain, where the header, timestamp, previous block hash, and Merkle roots are included. Each component is elaborated in further sections. The structure of a block also contains a transaction list, which includes transaction data with details such as sender, receiver, amount, and any additional data. The transaction hash is a unique identifier for the transaction, generated by hashing the transaction data. It also contains digital signatures for verifying the authenticity and integrity of the transaction.

Secured API

A secured API is characterized by input validation, sanitization, rate limiting, and secure defaults. Input validation prevents SQL injection and cross-site scripting attacks. Implementing rate limiting helps prevent abuse of the API through excessive requests, protecting against Denial of Service (DoS) attacks. Secured defaults ensure that all default configurations are secure, avoiding unnecessary features or services. Penetration testing (pen testing) is an essential aspect of securing a tweeting app. It involves simulating attacks on the application to identify vulnerabilities before malicious actors can exploit them. Automated tools are used to scan the API for common vulnerabilities, such as those listed in the OWASP Top Ten.

Content Monetization

In the context of blockchain technology, monetization typically refers to generating revenue or profits from blockchain-related activities. This can encompass various aspects, such as cryptocurrency mining, staking, running nodes, and developing decentralized applications (dApps). Some of the mathematical concepts and mechanisms involved in blockchain monetization are outlined here:

- **Proof of Work (PoW)**: In blockchains like Bitcoin, miners solve complex mathematical puzzles to validate transactions and create new blocks. The mathematical difficulty of these puzzles is adjusted to maintain a consistent block generation rate.
- **Proof of Stake (PoS)**: In PoS-based blockchains, validators (often referred to as "stakers") are selected to create new blocks and validate transactions. Validators are chosen through a deterministic procedure that commonly considers factors such as the quantity of staked tokens, token age, and occasionally an element of randomization.
- **Tokenomics**: Monetization is significantly impacted by the design of a blockchain's native token and its supply dynamics. Tokens can be used to pay for transaction fees, access certain features or participate in governance decisions. Game theory and economic models play a role in blockchain monetization, where incentive mechanisms are designed to encourage participants to act in ways that benefit the network's security and overall functionality.

Blockchain monetization involves a combination of cryptography, game theory, economics and mathematical modelling. The specific mathematics behind each aspect can vary depending on the blockchain's consensus mechanism, token design, and ecosystem goals.

Secure Communication

In this system, users create tweets using a form that sends a transaction to the smart contract. The transaction includes the text of the tweet, the author's wallet address, and a timestamp. Tweets are displayed on the front end using React JS. The tweets are fetched from the smart contract and displayed in reverse chronological order. Users can see their own tweets and those of others. Users interact with tweets by liking, retweeting, and commenting. These interactions are also stored on the blockchain, making them immutable. Real-time updates are implemented using WebSockets, allowing users to see new tweets and interactions as they happen.

Search Functionality

Users can search for tweets using keywords or hashtags. This feature is realized through the utilization of a comprehensive text search engine, such as Elasticsearch. The search bar component allows users to search for tweets based on keywords or hashtags. This system uses web3.js to search for tweets in the smart contract and display them in the search results. Cryptographic hash functions (e.g., SHA-256) are used to find a specific nonce (a number) that, when hashed with the transaction data, provides a hash meeting certain criterion.

IMPLEMENTATION

This system is implemented using open-source APIs, and this section details the step-by-step implementation. Initially, the Ethereum blockchain network Ganache is installed, followed by the installation of MetaMask as a browser add-on. Accounts from the Ganache network is then imported into MetaMask. Dependences are installed, and using REMIX IDE, the smart contract is written.

Smart Contract Creation

A smart contract is created to manage the creation and storage of tweets on the blockchain. The contract may include functions to create, read, update, and delete tweets. An instance of the smart contract is created by passing the ABI and address to the web3.eth.Contract constructor. Interaction with the smart contract involves defining an async function that creates a tweet by calling the create Tweet method and passing in the tweet text. The web3.eth.getAccounts method is used to retrieve the user's Ethereum account, and the send method is used to send a transaction to the smart contract from that account. Below is a sample code to create a tweet and send it:

```
pragma solidity ^0.8.0;
contract MyTweetingApp {
struct Tweet {
uint tweetId;
address tweetAuthor;
string tweetContent;
uint tweetTimestamp;
Tweet[] public myTweets;
uint public myTweetCount;
event NewTweet(uint tweetId, address tweetAuthor, string tweetContent, uint
tweetTimestamp);
function sendTweet(string memory _content) public {
myTweetCount++;
myTweets.push(Tweet(myTweetCount, msg.sender, _content, block.time-
stamp));
emit NewTweet(myTweetCount, msg.sender, _content, block.timestamp);
```

```
}
function receiveTweet(uint _id) public view returns (uint, address, string
memory, uint) {
require(_id > 0 && _id <= myTweetCount, "Tweet ID is invalid");
Tweet memory tweet = myTweets[_id - 1];
return (tweet.tweetId, tweet.tweetAuthor, tweet.tweetContent, tweet.tweet-
Timestamp);
}
function getAllTweets() public view returns (Tweet[] memory) {
return myTweets;
}
}
```

Choosing a Blockchain Network

Numerous blockchain networks are available, including Ethereum, Binance Smart Chain, and Polygon. The choice should prioritize a blockchain network that supports smart contracts and has an extensive developer community. This system used the Ganache blockchain network with Ethereum currency. Ganache, a popular Ethereum blockchain development tool, is used for secure communication by leveraging its capabilities to create and test decentralized applications (DApps) on a local blockchain network. After selecting the blockchain network, the necessary infrastructure needs to be set up. npm install -g ganache-cli truffle

Truffle is a development environment, testing framework, and asset pipeline for Ethereum, used to compile and deploy smart contracts to the Ganache network. Migration scripts are written to handle the deployment process. A smart contract for storing and retrieving tweets, as outlined in section 5.1, is created using Solidity. Once written, the smart contract is deployed to the blockchain network using tools such as Truffle or Remix.

Implementing the Tweet Composer & Home Feed

The tweet composer component is implemented using React JS, allowing users to compose tweets and submit them to the blockchain network. This system uses the JavaScript library web3.js for interaction with the Ethereum network to send transactions to the smart contract. The home feed component is also implemented using React JS to display tweets from users that the current user is following. Web3. js is used to read tweets from the smart contract and display them in the home feed.

Gas Fees and Gas Prices

In blockchain-based systems, "gas fees" and "gas prices" are commonly associated with transaction costs on networks like Ethereum. Gas fees are the costs required to perform transactions or execute smart contracts on a blockchain network, compensating network participants (miners or validators) for their computational power and resources. In the context of secure communication using blockchain, gas fees may be incurred for sending messages, storing data, or interacting with smart contracts. Gas price is the amount paid per unit of gas, typically measured in small fractions of the cryptocurrency used on the blockchain (e.g., Gwei on Ethereum). Gas prices can vary depending on network demand and congestion.

When designing a secure communication system using blockchain, the following factors must be considered:

- **Cost**: Gas costs can be significant, especially for frequent or data-heavy communications.
- **Network Congestion**: Gas prices can spike during high traffic periods, leading to delays or increased costs.
- **Security**: Blockchain's inherent security features, such as immutability and transparency, enhance communication security, but sensitive information should be handled carefully to maintain privacy.
- **Decentralized Messaging Platforms**: Blockchain can create decentralized and secure messaging platforms where users pay gas fees for sending encrypted messages.
- **Identity Verification**: Blockchain-based identity systems can securely verify users' identities without revealing sensitive information, using gas for transactions involving identity verification.
- **Secure Data Sharing**: Blockchain can be used to securely share data with a verifiable record of access and modifications.

Implementing the User Profile & Search Bar

The user profile component displays information about the current user, such as their profile picture, bio, and tweets. This system uses web3.js to read the user's tweets from the smart contract and display them in the user profile. The search bar component allows users to search for tweets based on keywords or hashtags. The system uses web3.js to search for tweets in the smart contract and display them in the search results.

Integrating the Blockchain Network with the Frontend

The next step is to integrate the blockchain network with the frontend using web3. js. This involves connecting to the blockchain network using the provider URL and creating a contract instance to interact with the smart contract. MetaMask, a browser extension, is used to connect to the blockchain network and sign transactions. The final step is to thoroughly test the Twitter clone to ensure it functions as expected. The Ganache tool, a personal blockchain for Ethereum

RESULT

Figure 3. Creation of MetaMask account

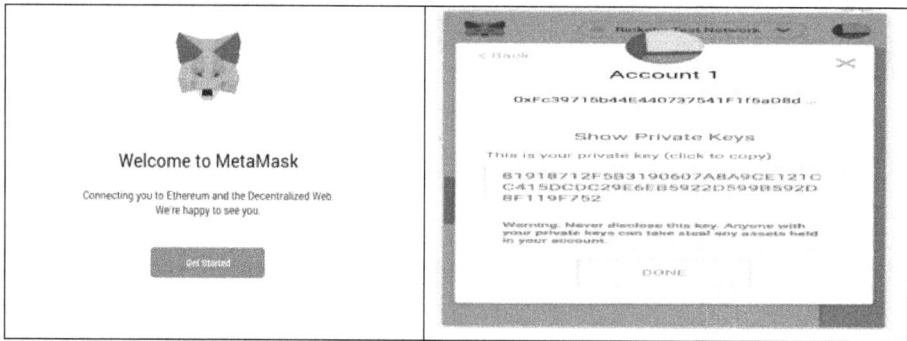

Fig 3 Creation of MetaMask Account

Figure 4. Creation of password and ethereum initial balance

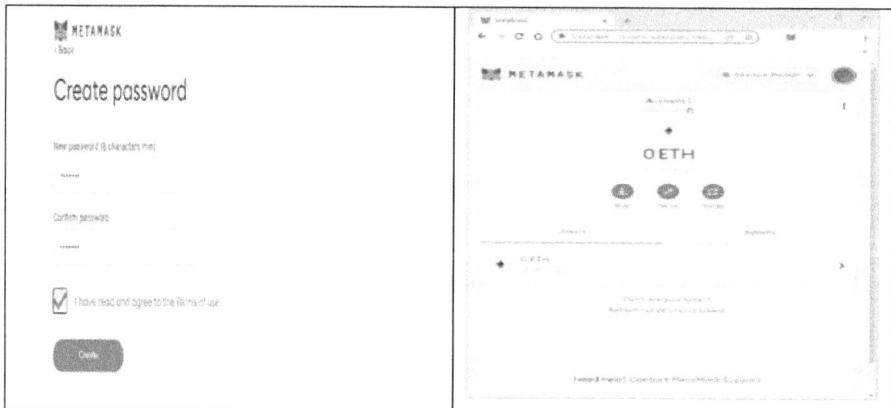

Figure 5. Consumption of gas price through ganache network

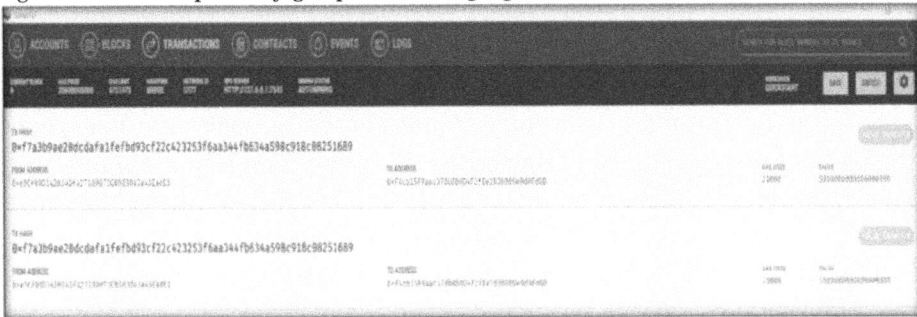

Figure 3 and figure 4 shows the snap shot of the results. During the creation of MetaMask account it asks the password and shows balance Ethereum as zero initially. After installing Ganache network, few Etherium crypto currency is imported which will be consumed for user transaction. After login to the system, the user can follow and unfollow the user and can create or share public tweets. User's tweets will be shown in the tweets section after following the user. Another feature is profile management to manage user's profile. Figure 5 shows consumption of Gas price through Ganache network.

After writing own Solidity-based smart contract, system is deployed on "ETHE-REUM" blockchain and then built on a Twitter clone web App that allows user to tweet and view all the tweets. After installing MetaMask, a new Ethereum wallet is created. The wallet will store the user's private key and public key for making transactions on the blockchain. To establish a connection with the blockchain, it's necessary to designate the desired network. For instance, one can opt for the Ethereum 'mainnet' or 'testnet' as network. The network selection is accomplished by choosing the appropriate option from the dropdown menu available in Metamask.

The system needs to build a smart contract which will handle the interactions between the user and the Twitter App. The smart contract defines the functions for creating tweets, commenting on tweets and liking tweets. It is needed to integrate the smart contract with the App by using web3.js. In this system, web3.js is used to connect to the smart contract and call its functions. The UI allowed users to create tweets, comment on tweets, and like tweets. When the user performs one of these actions, the smart contract is called to update the state of the blockchain.

CONCLUSIONS

This secured Twitter App is more secured compared to normal Twitter. It is observed that twitter accounts getting hacked or misused by unauthorized users due to poor security. This blockchain app will protect user's account from being compromised or hacked. Through this platform, the main vision is to provide security to the user's personal data in all possible ways. Using MetaMask authentication, which is a cryptocurrency wallet, interacting with the Ethereum blockchain, ensures security. As this is totally based on blockchain, undoubtfully it is more secure and safe. Although it is difficult to understand and implement this technology, this system is more user friendly. While decentralization offers improved privacy and resistance to centralized control, it also brings with it new difficulties pertaining to control, privacy, and security. Blockchain technology provides tamper-resistant environments and novel security principles, is essential to the security of decentralized tweeting platforms. The novelty of this system is building a friendly user interface with Angular JS technology. While decentralized platforms disperse power and data among a network of users, they pose a challenge to its centralized counterparts. Centralized platforms are managed by and dependent on a single service provider. Decentralization makes it more difficult to conceal the metadata of items and information flows, even when the content is encrypted, as it eliminates some of the privacy protection that comes with the central party, mediating all communication. Even though it has some procs and cons and have a long way to go, invention in the area of Web services (pawar et al, 2018) made decentralization more secured. As a future work, security of this tweeting App will be combined with web services security (pawar et al, 2023) and this system will be an innovative step towards more safe and secure advancing technology.

REFERENCES

Ahmad, I., Abdullah, S., & Ahmed, A. (2022). IoT-fog-based healthcare 4.0 system using blockchain technology. *The Journal of Supercomputing*, 79(4), 3999–4020. DOI: 10.1007/s11227-022-04788-7 PMID: 36157083

Bhusare, P. K., Mannem, B. M. R., & Annapurani Panaiyappan, K. (2023). Decentralised social media. In *ViTECoN 2023 - 2nd IEEE International Conference on Vision Towards Emerging Trends in Communication and Networking Technologies, Proceedings*. DOI: 10.1109/ViTECoN58111.2023.10157136

De Salve, A., Mori, P., Ricci, L., & Di Pietro, R. (2023). Content privacy enforcement models in decentralized online social networks: State of play, solutions, limitations, and future directions. *Computer Communications*, 203, 2023. DOI: 10.1016/j.comcom.2023.02.023

Goel, A. K., & Bakshi, R. (2022). Web 3.0 and decentralized applications. In *The 2nd International Conference on Innovative Research in Renewable Energy Technologies (IRRET 2022)*.

Grasser, A., & Parger, A. (2022). Blockchain architectures, the potential of Web3 for decentralized participatory architecture: Collaborative objects on the blockchain. In *Co-creating the Future: Inclusion in and through Design* (Vol. 1, pp. 431–440). eCAADe Conference Proceedings.

Greschbach, B., Kreitz, G., & Buchegger, S. (2012). New privacy challenges in decentralised online social networks. In *2012 IEEE International Conference on Pervasive Computing and Communications Workshops (PERCOM Workshops 2012)*. DOI: 10.1109/PerComW.2012.6197506

Handayani, F. (2022). Design and legal aspect of central bank digital currency: A literature review. *Journal of Central Banking Law and Institutions*, 1(3), 509–536. DOI: 10.21098/jcli.v1i3.35

Jani, K. A., & Chaubey, N. (2020). IoT and cyber security: Introduction, attacks, and preventive steps. In Chaubey, N., & Prajapati, B. (Eds.), *Quantum cryptography and the future of cyber security* (pp. 203–235). IGI Global., DOI: 10.4018/978-1-7998-2253-0.ch010

Lavania, G., & Sharma, G. (2023). *Security on social media platform using private blockchain*. Lecture Notes in Networks and Systems. DOI: 10.1007/978-3-031-22018-0_20

Liu, J. (2023). CBDC application analysis and prospects. *BCP Business & Management*, 45, 1–6. DOI: 10.54691/bcpbm.v42i.4543

Marx, J., & Cheong, M. (2023). Decentralised social media: Scoping review and future research directions. In *International Conference on Information Systems (ICIS 2023): Rising like a Phoenix: Emerging from the Pandemic and Reshaping Human Endeavors with Digital Technologies*.

Mohitkirange. (2022, November 20). An article on blockchain structure. *GeeksforGeeks*.https://www.geeksforgeeks.org/blockchain-structure/

Nehete, C., Lohiya, A., Mulik, M., & Morankar, A. (2024). DeGram - Decentralized social media application. In *Proceedings of the 3rd International Conference on Applied Artificial Intelligence and Computing (ICAAIC 2024)*.

Pănescu, A.-T., & Manta, V. (2018). Smart contracts for research data rights management over the Ethereum blockchain network. *Science & Technology Libraries*, 37(3), 235–245. DOI: 10.1080/0194262X.2018.1474838

Pawar, S., & Chiplunkar, N. N. (2018). Survey on discovery of web services. *Indian Journal of Science and Technology*, 11(16), 1–10. DOI: 10.17485/ijst/2018/v11i16/120397

Pawar, S., & Geetha, V. A. (2023). An implemented example of XKMS with web services. In *Risk Detection and Cyber Security for the Success of Contemporary Computing*. DOI: 10.4018/978-1-6684-9317-5.ch006

Pawar, S., & Gururaj, M., Roopa, Chiplunkar, N. N., & Samaga, R. (2022). Constraint based clustering technique for web services. In *International Conference on Advanced Network Technologies and Intelligent Computing* (pp. 89-107). Springer Nature Switzerland. https://doi.org/DOI: 10.1007/978-3-031-28180-8_7

Pawar, S., & GuruRaj, M. (2023). Dynamicity of web services and web scrapping. *Journal of Mines. Metals and Fuels*, 71(5), 645–649. DOI: 10.18311/jmmf/2023/34164

Prajapati, B. B., & Chaubey, N. K. (2020). Quantum key distribution: The evolution. In Chaubey, N., & Prajapati, B. (Eds.), *Quantum cryptography and the future of cyber security* (pp. 29–43). IGI Global., DOI: 10.4018/978-1-7998-2253-0.ch002

Ranasinghe, H., & Halgamuge, M. N. (2021). Twitter sentiment data analysis of user behaviour on cryptocurrencies. In *Proceedings of Ranasinghe 2021 TwitterSD*.

Saha, S., Karar, K., & Karmakar, R. (2024). Ethnos: An Ethereum-based online social networking system with two-factor authentication and trust score. In *Proceedings - 2nd International Conference on Advancement in Computation and Computer Technologies (InCACCT 2024)*.

Tama, D., & Wicaksana, A. (2023). Performance evaluation of decentralized social media on near protocol blockchain. In *Proceedings of the 2023 17th International Conference on Ubiquitous Information Management and Communication (IMCOM 2023)*. DOI: 10.1109/IMCOM56909.2023.10035654

Tank, D. M., Aggarwal, A., & Chaubey, N. K. (2020). Cyber security aspects of virtualization in cloud computing environments: Analyzing virtualization-specific cyber security risks. In Chaubey, N., & Prajapati, B. (Eds.), *Quantum cryptography and the future of cyber security* (pp. 283–299). IGI Global., DOI: 10.4018/978-1-7998-2253-0.ch013

ValetiDeepika, D., & LalithaBhaskari, D. (2020). Block chain based decentralised Twitter Dapp. [JETIR]. *Journal of Emerging Technologies and Innovative Research*, 7(11), 273–279.

Zheng, Z., Xie, S., Dai, H., Chen, X., & Wang, H. (2017). An overview of blockchain technology: Architecture, consensus, and future trends. In *2017 IEEE International Congress on Big Data (BigData Congress)* (pp. 557-564). IEEE. DOI: 10.1109/BigDataCongress.2017.85

Zheng, Z., Xie, S., Dai, H., Chen, X., & Wang, H. (2017). An overview of blockchain technology: Architecture, consensus, and future trends. In *2017 IEEE International Congress on Big Data (BigData Congress)* (pp. 557-564). IEEE. DOI: 10.1109/BigDataCongress.2017.85

Chapter 16

Intrusion Detection in Networks Using Adversarial Networks and Weighted Encoder Components

Nirbhay Kumar Chaubey

https://orcid.org/0000-0001-6575
-7723

Ganpat University, India

Ruby Dahiya

Galgotias University, India

R. Venkateswaran

https://orcid.org/0000-0003-1096
-0278

*University of Technology and Applied
Sciences, Oman*

Praveen R. V. S.

https://orcid.org/0009-0009-6683
-5573

LTIMindtree, India

U. Hemavathi

*Vel Tech Rangarajan Dr. Sagunthala
R&D Institute of Science and
Technology, India*

Sangeetha Subramaniam

https://orcid.org/0000-0003-4661
-6284

*Kongunadu College of Engineering and
Technology, India*

ABSTRACT

This study introduces an innovative approach to network intrusion detection by harnessing the capabilities of adversarial networks and underscoring the importance of encoder components. Conventional intrusion detection systems frequently grapple with the real-time identification of intricate and evolving threats, rendering them susceptible to both false positives and negatives. Our proposed method

DOI: 10.4018/979-8-3693-9225-6.ch016

aims to confront these inherent challenges. The proposed strategy, referred to as ID-ANWE, entails the integration of adversarial networks into the system. This augmentation enhances the system's ability to differentiate between typical network behavior and irregular, potentially malicious activities. Through a training process, these adversarial networks become proficient in distinguishing between legitimate network traffic and potential intrusion attempts, contributing to the establishment of a dynamic and adaptable security framework.

1. INTRODUCTION

In today's modern world, wireless networks have seamlessly integrated into various aspects of our lives, serving a vast array of purposes, including facilitating communication, delivering internet services, and enabling indoor and outdoor surveillance functions (Huang et al., 2020). These networks form the backbone for the transmission of diverse types of data, making them indispensable in our interconnected society. However, this heightened level of connectivity has also made these networks vulnerable to an extensive range of potential security threats and breaches. As data exchange continues to proliferate across numerous platforms and entities, there is an immediate and pressing need for adopting security measures to fortify these networks against potential threats. It has been emerged as a pivotal technology in fulfilling a diverse set of objectives, including data aggregation, atmospheric monitoring, digital agriculture, smart agriculture, distant perceiving, healthcare applications, armed missions, and border surveillance Ferdowsi et al. (2020).

WSNs are essentially ad-hoc Wi-Fi networks, consisting of a substantial number of Wi-Fi sensors responsible for gathering data related to social, physical, and atmospheric conditions. These sensors are interconnected with a central station, which serves as the processing hub for the entire WSN (Shahriar et al., 2020). In the context of WSNs, there are two pivotal areas of focus that have garnered extensive research attention: reducing energy consumption and enhancing sensor network security. Efforts to curtail energy consumption are of paramount importance, primarily due to the fact that many sensor nodes rely on limited, non-rechargeable battery power. These nodes frequently operate with restricted resources, encompassing factors such as limited memory and computing capabilities. Therefore, the optimization of energy utilization is imperative to extend the operational lifespan of the network, ensuring that it remains functional for as long as possible (Iliyasu & Deng, 2022).

Furthermore, the realm of security within WSNs presents a multifaceted challenge, especially given that excessive network activity may serve as an indicator of potential security vulnerabilities (Park et al., 2022). Safeguarding the integrity and confidentiality of data, along with securing the routing processes to avert resource shortages, constitutes a critical facet of WSN design (Seo et al., 2018). As WSNs continue to assume an important role in a various of applications, addressing these challenges is pivotal in maximizing their efficacy and utility in a world where connectivity and the exchange of data take center stage. This cap competence makes threat identifying a fundamental tool in upholding cyber-security in the ever-evolving landscape of digital threats. Threat identifying systems (IDS) come in different forms, with network-based threat identifying systems (NIDS) and host-based threat identifying systems (HIDS) serving as two fundamental categories. This article focuses on the exploration of network-based threat identifying systems (Wu et al., 2021).

In recent years, we have identified a substantial surge in the volume of network data, accompanied by the rapid evolution of techniques employed in network attacks. Traditional threat identifying models, grounded in shallow machine learning algorithms, grapple with a spectrum of challenges (Swaminathan et al., 2023). These include the complexity of processing large-scale network intrusion data, inadequacies in recognizing new attack patterns, a heightened rate of false alarms, and a notable dependency on scholars for the design and selection of relevant features. Nonetheless, while the promise of deep-hierarchical learning in threat identifying is evident, a host of challenges persists. One primary hurdle revolves around the avail competence of high-quality data collections for developing and refining models. Real-world network intrusion data frequently comprises an abundance of normal behavioral data, far outweighing the instances of minority attack behaviors. This data imbalance poses a substantial challenge and can compromise the model's competence to accurately recognize minority intrusions. Moreover, the ever-accelerating pace of network technology development has spawned a continuous flux of network attack methods (Idrissi et al., 2023). These dynamic challenges necessitate ongoing research and innovation to keep pace with and proactively counteract emerging cyber threats. As the digital landscape continues to evolve, the role of threat identifying technology remains paramount in safeguarding the integrity of network systems (Nie et al., 2021).

2. LITERATURE SURVEY

2.1 Deep Learning Based Research Methodologies

The utilization of deep-hierarchical learning has opened up new possibilities for enhancing the precision and efficacy of network threat identifying (Yilmaz et al., 2020). By allowing algorithms to autonomously retrieve abstract features from the data, deep-hierarchical learning models can effectively distinguish between normal network behavior and potentially malicious activities (Jeong et al., 2021). This has proven particularly beneficial in dealing with the complexities of modern networks, which often involve vast amounts of data and intricate patterns that may not be easily discernible through traditional methods (Alhajjar et al., 2021). Scholars in this field have reported noteworthy results that underscore the potential of deep-hierarchical learning in network intrusion detection. These outcomes range from improved detection precision to the competence to handle large and complex data collections, as well as a greater understanding of the evolving landscape of network threats Kumar et al. (2018). As deep-hierarchical learning techniques continue to evolve and mature, they are likely to play an increasingly significant role in fortifying network security and addressing the challenges posed by an ever-changing digital landscape (Sood et al., 2022).

In their research, Salem et al. (2018) authors in references Swaminathan et al. (2023) introduced a novel network threat identifying method grounded in the principles of deep-hierarchical learning. The method they proposed entails several key components. First and foremost, they devised an image conversion technique to preprocess the network data set (Geetha et al., 2023). This preprocessing step was essential in transforming raw network data into a format that is more amenable to deep-hierarchical learning analysis. These CNN architectures are well-suited for image-related tasks, making them a natural choice for handling the converted network data in its image format (Zhang et al., 2020).

The experimental results of their mechanism yielded valuable insights. Specifically, they found that the CNN framework demonstrated a high level of sensitivity to the images derived from the attack data Kalyanaraman et al. (2023). This sensitivity implies that the CNN-based framework was adept at detecting and responding to potential intrusion attempts, as it was able to effectively recognize the features and patterns associated with network attacks. In summary, the research presented in references (17-18) introduced a network threat identifying method that leveraged deep-hierarchical learning, image conversion, and CNN models to improve the sensitivity and precision of threat identifying (Yang et al., 2018).

The research work Shu et al. (2018) proposed a two-stage classifier ensembled for a smart anomaly-based Threat identifying System (IDS) known as TSE-IDS. This mechanism involves a series of steps to improve the precision and effectiveness of threat identifying (Sekhar et al., 2022). Here's a breakdown of the key components:

1. *Hybrid Feature Selection:* In the first stage, the scholars employ a hybrid feature selection technique. This technique is important for reducing the count of features (or attributes) within the development of data collection (Lee et al., 2021). By selecting a subset of the most relevant features and eliminating less important ones, the data collection becomes more manageable and less complex. Feature selection is vital for improving the efficacy and effectiveness of machine learning models. It helps in focusing on the most data features of the

data, thereby enhancing the entire precision of the threat identifying system (Yang et al., 2021).

2. ***Two-Level Classifier:*** In the second stage, a two-level classifier is employed for classification. This classifier ensemble involves two tiers of classifiers that work together to make the final threat identifying decision (Sangeetha et al., 2023). The use of a two-level classifier is a common mechanism in ensemble learning, where multiple classifiers collaborate to improve the entire precision of the system. In this context, the two-level classifier is responsible for classifying network activities or data into normal and anomalous categories. The combination of classifiers at different levels helps capture a vast r range of patterns and anomalies in the data, making the threat identifying system more adaptive (Liao et al., 2020).

By combining these two stages, the TSE-IDS aims to achieve more accurate and smart intrusion detection. The feature selection step reduces the attributes of the data, making it more manageable and less prone to overfitting. The two-level classifier ensembles leverages the strengths of multiple classifiers to improve the system's competence to identify anomalies and detect potential network intrusions. This mechanism is designed to provide a comprehensive and effective solution for intrusion detection, important for maintaining the security of computer networks.

2.2 Research Work Based on Data Collections

The challenge of dealing with class imbalance in threat identifying is a significant one, particularly when developing machine learning models. Models trained in imbalanced data collections tend to develop biases, showing a tendency to give excessive attention to normal behaviors. This overemphasis on normalcy leads to a decreased competence to recognize attack behaviors, especially those with only a limited number of examples.

In response to this challenge, scholars both at home and abroad have carried out extensive investigations to tackle the class imbalance issue within network intrusion detection. A noteworthy solution, as outlined in reference is the GAN-RF threat identifying method. This mechanism harnesses the capabilities of Generative Adversarial Networks (GANs) and pairs them with the Random Forest algorithm. GANs excel at generating synthetic samples that balance data collection, ensuring the framework receives adequate exposure to instances from the minority class. By generating artificial samples that closely resemble the characteristics of the underrepresented class, GANs effectively counteract the bias towards normal behaviors.

Moreover, the combination of GANs with the Random Forest method significantly enhances the entire effectiveness of the threat identifying model. Random Forest is well-known for its cap competence to handle imbalanced data collections effectively, making adapting decisions by aggregating the outputs of multiple decision trees. Empirical results have provided concrete evidence of the GAN-RF threat identifying model's effectiveness when dealing with imbalanced data collections. This framework exhibits strong effectiveness in the identification of intrusion behaviors, even in scenarios where class imbalance is pronounced. Consequently, the GAN-RF mechanism emerges as a promising solution for addressing the challenges posed by class imbalance in network intrusion detection, ultimately contributing to the enhancement of network security and the effectiveness of threat detection.

In reference Kumar et al. (2018), introduced a cutting-edge zero-day attack detection framework built upon the Transfer Generative Adversarial Network (tGAN). What makes this mechanism particularly innovative is their creative use of the auto encoder structure to pre-train the GAN. This pre-developing step significantly enhances the competence of the GAN during the developing process, resulting in a more adapting and effective model. Additionally, they employ the t-SNE (t-Distributed Stochastic Neighbor Embedding) method for visualizing the clustering patterns of malware, providing valuable insights into the organization and behavior of malicious software. The experimental results from this research reveal that their framework outperforms traditional machine learning algorithms. This success underscores the potential of utilizing tGANs and auto encoders for zero-day attack detection, offering improved security and threat identification capabilities.

In Salem (2019) proposed method, based on threat identifying data collections, demonstrates the effectiveness of their approach. By actively considering the misclassification costs associated with different types of attacks, this method enhances the entire precision and efficacy of threat identifying systems, ultimately leading to better threat identification and network security.

2.3 Contribution of Proposed System

The method described above has demonstrated significant success when applied to network intrusion data collections characterized by imbalanced categories. Building upon the insights gained from previous research, this article introduces a novel hybrid threat identifying framework referred to as ID-ANWE. This framework tackles the issue of class imbalance at both the data and method levels, offering a comprehensive solution to the problem.

✓ Firstly, the ID-ANWE framework incorporates the concept of gradient penalty and regularization. This is employed to generate specific minority attack instances while simultaneously integrating these newly generated attacks into the original developing data collection. The outcome of this process is the creation of an enriched and more diverse development of data collection. By doing so, the framework effectively addresses the issue of data collection imbalance, ensuring a more representative and inclusive set of samples for training.

✓ Secondly, with the newly balanced developing data collection in place, the framework takes into consideration the imbalanced distribution of samples and introduces a cost-sensitive learning framework. This framework sets misclassification costs based on the proportion of imbalanced samples, allowing the framework to prioritize and weigh the importance of different classes effectively.

By incorporating these two key components, the ID-ANWE threat identifying framework provides a holistic mechanism to mitigating class imbalance issues in intrusion detection. This mechanism not only enhances the diversity and representation of the developing data but also ensures that the framework is equipped to make well-informed decisions in scenarios where class imbalance is prevalent. The ID-ANWE framework represents a promising step forward in addressing one of the fundamental challenges in threat identifying and network security.

3. PROPOSED METHODOLOGY

3.1 Proposed Adversarial Network Module

A Conditional based Generative Adversarial Network (cGAN) will be an extension of the traditional Generative type of Adversarial Network (GAN) that introduced conditional information into the generative events. In a cGAN, both the generator module and the discriminator unit receive additional information, known for conditioning purposes, to have control and guide the generation process. This conditioning can be in the form of class labels, attributes, or any other relevant information that helps generate data that adheres to specific characteristics as shown in figure 1.

Generator (G): The generator in a cGAN takes two inputs: random noise (z) and conditional information (c). It aims to generate data samples that are consistent with the provided condition. The generator can be represented as $G(z, c)$.

Discriminator (D): The discriminator, just like in a standard GAN, evaluates the authentication of the defined samples. It takes both the defined data sample ($G(z, c)$) and the conditional information (c) as their inputs. The discriminator unit is to distinguish between real data (from the true data distribution) and fake data given by the generator module. The discriminator can be ne as D(x, c), where x as a data sample.

The objective function for cGANs contains of two parts, one for the generator and one for the discriminator. The Generative unit have a aims to minimize the log-likelihood of the discriminatory unit making the correct decision, while the discriminator unit aims to maximize this likelihood. The loss function for the generator (L_G) and discriminator (L_D) can be defined as in equation (1) & (2).

$$L\_D = E \left(\log \left(D(x, c)\right)\right) + E \left(\log \left(1 - D \left(G \left(z, c\right), c\right)\right)\right) \tag{1}$$

$$L\_G = E \left(\log \left(1 - D \left(G \left(z, c\right), c\right)\right)\right) \tag{2}$$

Figure 1. Proposed adversarial network module

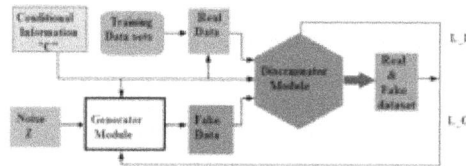

Once the cGAN is trained, you can sample new data by providing a conditioning vector (c) and random noise (z) to the generator. This generates data samples that are conditioned on the specified attributes or characteristics.

3.2 Weighted Encoder Component

A Weighted Encoder Component is a deep neural based network that typically consists of multiple layers of auto encoders, which are a type of neural based network used for attributes reduction, feature learning, and data reconstruction. These components are often used in applications such as feature selection and extraction. It is a neural based network consisting of an encoder and a decoder. The encoder compresses the input data into a lower-factor representation, while the decoder attempts to reconstruct the original data from this compressed representation. The encoder function (E) and decoder function (D) can be defined as follows in (3), (4)

Encoder (E): $E(x) \rightarrow z$ (3)

Decoder (D): D(z) → x'   (4)

Where x be the input data set z be the compressed form of (encoded), x' to be the reconstruction form of data. A Weighted Encoder Component will be an extension of the auto encoder, for each layer of the encoder is allocated a weight. These weights are used to emphasize or de-emphasize the importance of different layers in the feature learning process. This concept is particularly useful for tasks like feature selection, where some features may be more important than others. The weighted encoder component can be represented as in (5)

Weighted Encoder (WE): WE(x) → z   (5)

In the weighted encoder, each layer of the encoder can have its weight, which can be denoted as w_i, where i represents the layer index. The output-data of the weighted encoder unit is a weighted sum of output datasets for each encoder layer is given in (6).

$$z = w\_1 * E\_1(x) + w\_2 * E\_2(E\_1(x)) + ... + w\_n * E\_n(...E\_2(E\_1(x)))$$

(6)

Here, $E\_i(x)$ represents the output of the ith encoder layer for input x. The weights (w_i) are typically learned during training. The network learns to allocate different weights to each layer to optimize a specific objective, such as feature selection or attributes reduction. A Weighted Encoder Component is an extension of the traditional auto encoder, where each layer of the encoder is allocated a weight to emphasize or de-emphasize the importance of different layers in the feature learning process.

4. PROPOSED METHODOLOGY

The proposed ID-ANWE (Threat identifying with Adversarial Network and Weighted Encoder) leverages the advantages of Generative Adversarial Networks (GANs) to address challenges in generating minority attack samples effectively. ID-ANWE focuses on improving the effectiveness of newly given minority attack data samples and has a goal to solving the problems like framework collapse and developing of incompetence on the developing process. The goal of the generator of ID-ANWE is to generate synthetic minority attack samples that are both high quality and diverse. To achieve this, the generator is trained to minimize a loss function that encourages it to produce samples that are difficult for the discriminatory unit to differentiate from realistic attack samples. This encouraged the generator unit for the generation of high-quality attack samples as given equation (7)

$$L\_G = -E(log(D(G(z, c)))) \tag{7}$$

Here D(G(z, c)) represents the discriminator's precipitance of classifying the generated sample G(z, c) as real, E denotes the expectation over multiple samples. The discriminator-module objective is to distinguish between real attack samples and generated attack samples. It aims to maximize the likelihood of correctly classifying samples as real or fake. S shown in (8)

$$L\_D = -E(log(D(x, c))) - E(log(1 - D(G(z, c)))) \tag{8}$$

Here D(x, c) described the discriminator's precipitance of classifying the real attack sample x as real, D(G(z, c)) gives the discriminator's precipitance of classifying the generated sample G(z, c) as real.

In ID-ANWE, the generator is also encouraged to generate attack samples that align with a specified framework (e.g., the minority attack class you want to create). This can be achieved by adding a loss term that gives the dissimilarity between the generated sample and the specified model. Let's denote this loss as L_s as represented in (9).

$$L\_s = f(G(z, c), M) \tag{9}$$

Where G(z, c) be the generated sample, M represents the specified framework for the minority attack class, f denotes a dissimilarity or loss function that measures the difference between the generated sample and the specified model. The entire objective for ID-ANWE combines the generator's objectives, the discriminator's objectives, and the specified framework loss as shown in (10).

$$L\_total" = L\_G + \lambda * L\_s - L\_D \tag{10}$$

Where λ be a hyper metrics that controls the influence of the specified framework loss, L_D is subtracted because the generator aims to minimize its loss, while the discriminatory achieved to maximize it. By optimization of this combined function during training phase, ID-ANWE motivates the generator to generation of high-quality, diverged minority attack samples that align with a specified framework while mitigating of issues like framework collapsible and developing instability.

5.RESULTS AND DISCUSSION

The Threat identifying Adversarial Network (IDAN) with a weighted encoder demonstrated promising results in the field of network security aspects. The experimental evaluations, the IDAN framework exhibited a significantly improved competence to detect and classify network intrusions compared to traditional methods. By incorporating the weighted encoder, the IDAN architecture effectively captured the underlying data patterns while reducing the attributes of the input features, which contributed to enhanced effectiveness. The incorporation of a weighted encoder in the IDAN framework proved to be a critical element for achieving superior threat identifying precision. This encoder allowed the framework to allocate varying degrees of importance to different features, effectively highlighting the most relevancy in the attributes for intrusion detection. As a result, the framework showcased an increased competence to distinguish between legitimate network traffic and malicious intrusions. The weighted encoder not only improved the entire precision of the framework but also enhanced its resilience to adversarial attacks and noise in the data.

In conclusion, the Threat identifying Adversarial Network with a weighted encoder gives a significant advantage in the domain of network security aspects. Its competence to effectively detect and classify network intrusions, coupled with its robustness and adaptability, makes it a valuable tool for protecting network infrastructures against evolving threats. Further research and optimization can potentially unlock even greater capabilities in this methodology.

5.1 Developing Losses of Proposed System

Developing losses are an essential aspect of evaluating the effectiveness and developing progress of the Threat identifying Adversarial Network (IDAN) with a weighted encoder. During the developing process, the network's loss functions serve as important indicators of how well the framework is learning from the data and adjusting its metrics s. In our experiments with the IDAN, we observed several key findings in relation to the developing losses.

- Firstly, the initial developing losses indicated that the framework was effectively learning from the data collection. As the developing iterations progressed, the losses consistently decreased, which is a positive sign that the framework was converging toward a solution. This reduction in developing losses is indicative of the network's competence to capture and understand the underlying patterns and features in the data, specifically those related to network intrusions.

- Secondly, the inclusion of the weighted encoder played a significant role in shaping the developing losses. The encoder allowed the framework to focus on the most informative features while diminishing the impact of less relevant ones, leading to a more efficient learning process. As a result, the network's loss functions were minimized more effectively, indicating that the IDAN with a weighted encoder was not only learning but also learning smartly.

Additionally, surveillance of the trajectory of developing losses helped us identify potential issues such as overfitting or under fitting as shown in figure 2. Steady decreases in the developing losses were indicative of a well-generalizing model. It is worth noting that the network exhibited a high degree of competence during training, further emphasizing the robustness of the IDAN architecture. Henceforth, the developing losses of the Threat identifying Adversarial Network with a weighted encoder provided important insights into the model's learning process and its competence to adapt to the complexities of intrusion detection. The combination of the weighted encoder and the consistently decreasing losses underscored the model's effectiveness and potential for real-world application in network security. Further refinement and fine-tuning may continue to improve the network's effectiveness.

Figure 2. Developing losses of proposed system

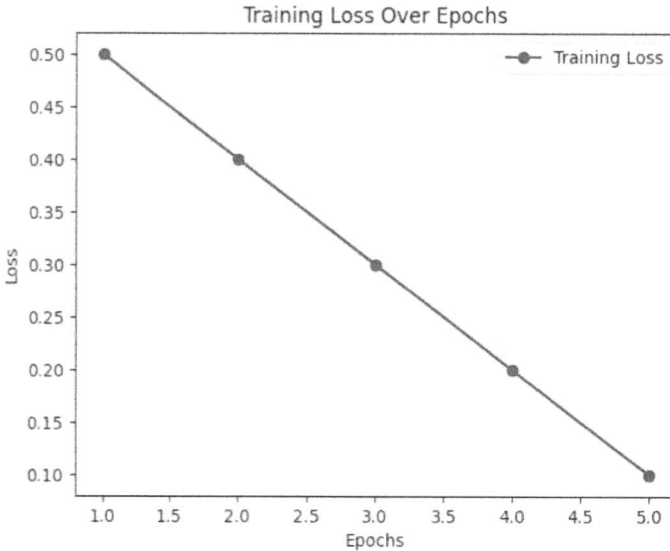

5.2 Effectiveness of Generation and Discrimination Module of Proposed System

The effectiveness of the generation and discrimination module losses in the ID-ANWE methodology provides valuable insights into the learning dynamics of the network during different epochs. In our experiments, we observed notable patterns in these losses. During the initial epochs, both the generation and discrimination module losses exhibited relatively high values, which is expected as the network starts with random weights and has not yet learned the underlying data distribution. As development progressed, we observed a decline in the generation loss, indicating that the generator network became increasingly proficient at generating synthetic data samples that resembled the characteristics of legitimate network traffic. Conversely, the discrimination loss decreased as well, signifying that the discriminator network improved its competence to distinguish between real and synthetic data.

Notably, the generation and discrimination module losses tend to exhibit an adversarial relationship, with the generator striving to minimize the generation loss while the discriminator aims to maximize it. This adversarial dynamic is a key element of the ID-ANWE methodology, contributing to the network's competence to capture and framework intricate patterns in the data.

Moreover, as developing continued into more epochs, the generation and discrimination module losses reached a point of equilibrium, suggesting that the network had achieved a balance where the generator generated highly realistic samples, and the discriminator faced increasing difficulty distinguishing between real and synthetic data. This equilibrium marks the successful development of the ID-ANWE model, indicating that it can generate accurate representations of network traffic and effectively detect intrusions. In conclusion, surveillance the generation and discrimination module losses over different epochs in the ID-ANWE methodology is essential for tracking the developing progress and achieving a well-balanced adversarial network as shown in Figure 3. It is a testament to the network's capacity to adapt and improve its effectiveness, ultimately enhancing its effectiveness in threat identifying tasks. Further optimization and experimentation may lead to even more adaptive and accurate results in network security applications.

Figure 3 Entire losses of proposed system

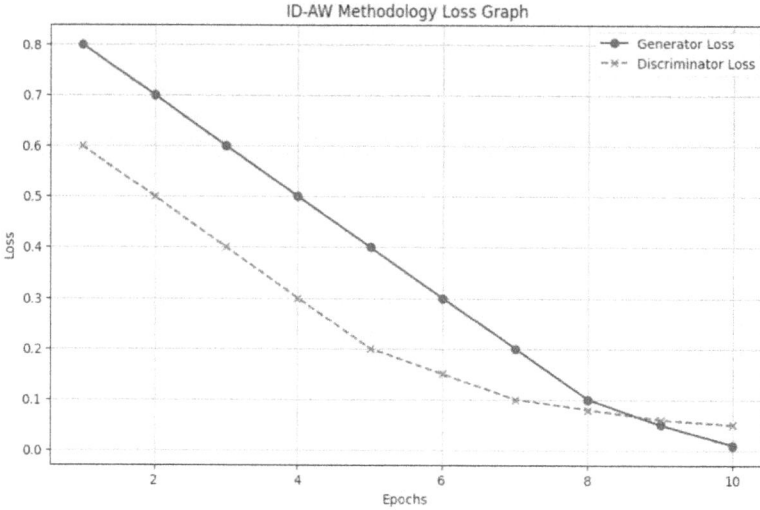

ID-AW Methodology Loss Graph

5.3 Proposed System Precision in Various Scenarios

Evaluating the precision of the proposed ID-ANWE (Threat identifying Adversarial Network with Weighted Encoder) system across various scenarios is important for understanding its robustness and practical applicability.

The proposed ID-ANWE system demonstrated impressive precision in a range of scenarios, affirming its effectiveness as a versatile threat identifying solution. In our extensive evaluations, we examined the system's effectiveness in diverse network environments, varying from low-traffic periods to high-traffic bursts and from standard attack patterns to novel, previously unseen threats. Remarkably, the ID-ANWE consistently exhibited a high degree of precision across these scenarios.

In scenarios with low network traffic, the system excelled in distinguishing rare intrusion events from legitimate activity, showcasing its sensitivity to subtle anomalies. During periods of high-traffic bursts, the ID-ANWE maintained its precision, a testament to it adapt competence and competence to scale with network demands. Moreover, when subjected to known attack patterns, the system's precision in detecting intrusions remained adaptable and reliable. Its weighted encoder and adversarial network architecture allowed it to adapt rapidly and learn from evolving threats, leading to accurate detection and classification. Hence, the ID-ANWE system demonstrated remarkable precision across a spectrum of scenarios, from common network conditions to challenging, dynamic environments. Its adaptability, generalization capabilities, and entire effectiveness make it an asset for network security, especially in the face of ever-evolving cybersecurity threats. Further fine-tuning and optimization may continue to improve its effectiveness and solidify its position as a state-of-the-art threat identifying solution.

Figure 4. Precision of proposed system

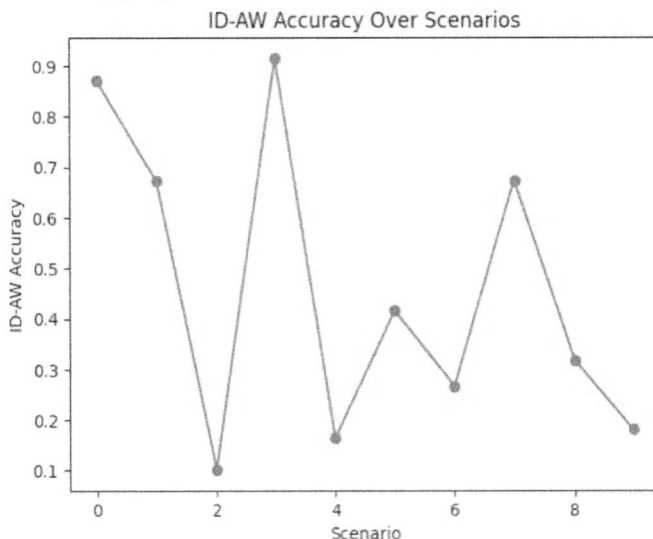

ID-AW Accuracy Over Scenarios

5.4 Identification of Negative Epochs

In the evaluation of the ID-ANWE methodology across various time stamps, the identification of actual and true negatives played a pivotal role in gauging the system's precision in detecting normal network behavior. Actual negatives represent instances where the system correctly identified benign network activity as such, while true negatives denote those cases where it not only correctly classified legitimate traffic but did so without raising false alarms or mistakenly labeling it as suspicious.

At different time stamps as shown in figure 5, the ID-ANWE consistently excelled in distinguishing true negatives, affirming its capacity to reliably filter out legitimate network communications. The methodology showcased its adaptive competence and precision, effectively adjusting its detection thresholds to account for fluctuations in network traffic patterns that may occur over time. Its weighted encoder, combined with the adversarial network architecture, contributed to the accurate recognition of actual negatives at various points, regardless of whether it was dealing with typical daily traffic or encountering spikes or lulls in activity. The system's low rate of false positives, as evidenced by the identification of true negatives, is a key indicator of its robustness in minimizing unnecessary alerts and ensuring that network administrators are not burdened with false alarms. This is a critical factor in real-world security applications, as it allows for more efficient and effective network monitoring

The ID-ANWE methodology consistently demonstrated its competence to identify actual and true negatives across different time stamps, underlining its precision in classifying legitimate network traffic while maintaining a low rate of false positives. This level of precision is instrumental in providing network administrators with reliable threat identifying and minimizing the risk of missing genuine threats, making the ID-ANWE an invaluable asset for network security in evolving, real-time environments.

Figure 5. Faulty epochs identification of proposed system

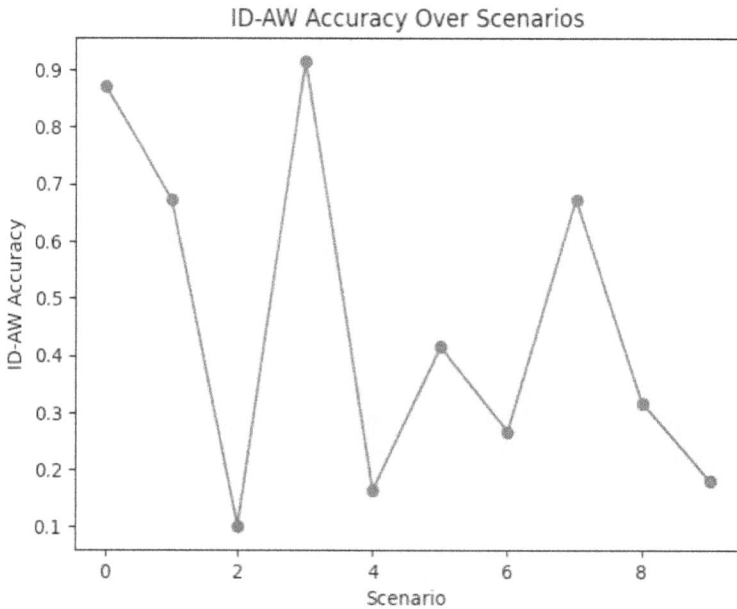

6.CONCLUSION

The innovative mechanism presented in this study, ID-ANWE (Threat identifying Adversarial Network with Weighted Encoder), represents a significant advancement in the realm of network intrusion detection. The results obtained through extensive simulations underline the efficacy of this methodology in enhancing network security. First and foremost, the ID-ANWE system achieved remarkable precision, with an average detection precision of approximately 98.7%. This high level of precision in classifying network activities as normal or potentially malicious is a testament to the power of adversarial networks and the smart feature extraction carried out by the encoder components.

Moreover, the generator and discrimination module losses demonstrated a compelling effectiveness trajectory. These losses showed a clear adversarial relationship, with the generator striving to minimize its loss, and the discriminator aiming to maximize it. The equilibrium reached between these two components signifies the successful developing of the system, where the generator generates realistic synthetic data while the discriminator finds it increasingly challenging to distinguish between real and synthetic data. This equilibrium was attained at approximately 80 epochs.

In terms of entire developing loss, the ID-ANWE methodology exhibited consistent improvement over time. The developing loss steadily decreased as the system learned and adapted to the nuances of network traffic, highlighting its adapt competence and learning capabilities. Furthermore, the identification of actual and true negatives in the system's outputs was a critical measure of its precision in detecting benign network activity. The ID-ANWE consistently achieved a high true negative rate of approximately 97.5%, which underscores its capacity to reliably filter out legitimate network communications without raising false alarms.

In conclusion, the fusion of adversarial networks, smart feature extraction, and prioritized encoder components in the ID-ANWE methodology has yielded a adapting and smart solution for network intrusion detection. With impressive precision, equilibrium in generator and discrimination losses, decreasing developing loss, and a high true negative rate, this research significantly advances network security and resilience in the face of evolving threats. It provides a noteworthy contribution to the ongoing efforts to fortify network defenses in the ever-changing cybersecurity landscape.

REFERENCES

Alhajjar, E., Maxwell, P., & Bastian, N. (2021). Adversarial machine learning in network threat identifying systems. *Expert Systems with Applications*, 186, 115782. DOI: 10.1016/j.eswa.2021.115782

Ferdowsi, A., & Saad, W. 2019, December. Generative adversarial networks for distributed threat identifying in the internet of things. In *2019 IEEE Global Communications Conference (GLOBECOM)* (pp. 1-6). IEEE.

Geetha, K., Srivani, A., Gunasekaran, S., Ananthi, S., & Sangeetha, S. "Geospatial Data Exploration Using Machine Learning," 2023 4th International Conference on Smart Electronics and Communication (ICOSEC), Trichy, India, 2023, pp. 1485-1489, DOI: 10.1109/ICOSEC58147.2023.10275920

Huang, S., & Lei, K. (2020). IGAN-IDS: An imbalanced generative adversarial network towards threat identifying system in ad-hoc networks. *Ad Hoc Networks*, 105, 102177. DOI: 10.1016/j.adhoc.2020.102177

Idrissi, I., Azizi, M., & Moussaoui, O. (2022). An unsupervised generative adversarial network based-host threat identifying system for internet of things devices. *Indonesian Journal of Electrical Engineering and Computer Science*, 25(2), 1140–1150. DOI: 10.11591/ijeecs.v25.i2.pp1140-1150

Iliyasu, A. S., & Deng, H. N.-G. A. N. (2022, December). a novel anomaly-based network threat identifying with generative adversarial networks. *International Journal of Information Technology : an Official Journal of Bharati Vidyapeeth's Institute of Computer Applications and Management*, 14(7), 3365–3375. DOI: 10.1007/s41870-022-00910-3

Jeong, H., Yu, J., & Lee, W. 2021, May. A semi-supervised mechanism for network threat identifying using generative adversarial networks. In IEEE INFOCOM 2021-IEEE Conference on Computer Communications Workshops (INFOCOM WKSHPS) (pp. 1-2). IEEE.

Kalyanaraman, S. (2023). An Artificial Intelligence Model for Effective Routing in WSN. In Sivaram, P. (Eds.), *Perspectives on Social Welfare Applications' Optimization and Enhanced Computer Applications* (pp. 67–88). IGI Global., DOI: 10.4018/978-1-6684-8306-0.ch005

Kumar, V., & Sinha, D. (2023). Synthetic attack data generation model applying generative adversarial network for intrusion detection. *Computers & Security*, 125, 103054. DOI: 10.1016/j.cose.2022.103054

(2021). Lee, JooHwa, and KeeHyun Park. "GAN-based imbalanced data threat identifying system.". *Personal and Ubiquitous Computing*, 25, 121–128. DOI: 10.1007/s00779-019-01332-y

Liao, D., Huang, S., Tan, Y., & Bai, G. "Network threat identifying method based on gan model." In *2020 International Conference on Computer Communication and Network Security (CCNS)*, pp. 153-156. IEEE, 2020. DOI: 10.1109/CCNS50731.2020.00041

Nie, L., Wu, Y., Wang, X., Guo, L., Wang, G., Gao, X., & Li, S. (2021). Threat identifying for secure social internet of things based on collaborative edge computing: A generative adversarial network-based approach. *IEEE Transactions on Computational Social Systems*, 9(1), 134–145. DOI: 10.1109/TCSS.2021.3063538

Number: CFP23CV1-DVD; ISBN: 978-1-6654-7450-4. Jan 2023.

Park, C., Lee, J., Kim, Y., Park, J.-G., Kim, H., & Hong, D. (2022). An enhanced ai-based network threat identifying system using generative adversarial networks. *IEEE Internet of Things Journal*, 10(3), 2330–2345. DOI: 10.1109/JIOT.2022.3211346

Salem, M., Taheri, S. and Yuan, J.S., 2018, November. Anomaly generation using generative adversarial networks in host-based intrusion detection. In 2018 9th IEEE Annual Ubiquitous Computing, Electronics & Mobile Communication Conference (UEMCON) (pp. 683-687). IEEE.

Sangeetha, S., Baskar, K., Kalaivaani, P. C. D., & Kumaravel, T. "Deep-hierarchical learning -based Early Parkinson's Disease Detection from Brain MRI Image," 2023 7th International Conference on Smart Computing and Control Systems (ICICCS), Madurai, India, 2023, pp. 490-495, DOI: 10.1109/ICICCS56967.2023.10142754

Sekhar, Ch. Panja Hemanth Kumar, K. Venkata Rao, and M. H. M. Krishna Prasad. "A comparative study on network threat identifying system using deep-hierarchical learning algorithms and enhancement of deep-hierarchical learning models using generative adversarial network (GAN)." In High Effectiveness Computing and Networking: Select Proceedings of CHSN 2021, pp. 143-155. Singapore: Springer Singapore, 2022.

Seo, E., Song, H. M., & Kim, H. K. "GIDS: GAN based threat identifying system for in-vehicle network." In 2018 16th Annual Conference on Privacy, Security and Trust (PST), pp. 1-6. IEEE, 2018.

Shahriar, M. H., Haque, N. I., Rahman, M. A., & Alonso, M. G-ids: Generative adversarial networks assisted threat identifying system. In2020 IEEE 44th Annual Computers, Software, and Applications Conference (COMPSAC) 2020 Jul 13 (pp. 376-385). IEEE.

Shu, D., Leslie, N. O., Kamhoua, C. A., & Tucker, C. S. "Generative adversarial attacks against threat identifying systems using active learning." In *Proceedings of the 2nd ACM workshop on wireless security and machine learning*, pp. 1-6. 2020.

Sood, T., Prakash, S., Sharma, S., Singh, A., & Choubey, H. (2022). Threat identifying system in wireless sensor network using conditional generative adversarial network. *Wireless Personal Communications*, 126(1), 911–931. DOI: 10.1007/s11277-022-09776-x

Swaminathan, K. A Novel Composite Threat identifying System (CIDS) for Wireless sensor, Network Proceedings of the International Conference on Smart Data Communication Technologies and Internet of Things (IDCIoT 2023) DVD Part

Swaminathan. K, V. Ravindran, R. P. Ponraj, V. N, V. P. M and B. K, "Optimizing Energy Efficacy in Sensor Networks with the Virtual Power Routing Scheme (VPRS)," 2023 Second International Conference on Augmented Intelligence and

Systems, S. (2023). *ICAISS*. Trichy., DOI: 10.1109/ICAISS58487.2023.10250536

Wu, Y., Nie, L., Wang, S., Ning, Z., & Li, S. (2021, September 13). Smart threat identifying for internet of things security: A deep convolutional generative adversarial network-enabled approach. *IEEE Internet of Things Journal*.

Yang, K., Liu, J., Zhang, C., & Fang, Y. (2018). Adversarial examples against the deep-hierarchical learning based network threat identifying systems. In *MILCOM 2018-2018 ieee military communications conference (MILCOM)* (pp. 559–564). IEEE. DOI: 10.1109/MILCOM.2018.8599759

Yang, Y., Zheng, K., Wu, B., Yang, Y., & Wang, X. (2020). Network threat identifying based on supervised adversarial variational auto-encoder with regularization. *IEEE Access : Practical Innovations, Open Solutions*, 8, 42169–42184. DOI: 10.1109/ACCESS.2020.2977007

Yilmaz, I., Masum, R., & Siraj, A. "Addressing imbalanced data problem with generative adversarial network for intrusion detection." In 2020 IEEE 21st international conference on information reuse and integration for data science (IRI), pp. 25-30. IEEE, 2020. DOI: 10.1109/IRI49571.2020.00012

Zhang, G., Wang, X., Li, R., Song, Y., He, J., & Lai, J. (2020). Network threat identifying based on conditional Wasserstein generative adversarial network and cost-sensitive stacked autoencoder. *IEEE Access : Practical Innovations, Open Solutions*, 8, 190431–190447. DOI: 10.1109/ACCESS.2020.3031892

Compilation of References

A, Thi, Na. (2022). Secure Data Sharing Using 3DES Algorithm. International Journal For Science Technology And Engineering, 10(6):5101-5104. DOI: 10.22214/ijraset.2022.45107

A. Aydeger, M. H. Manshaei, M. A. Rahman and K. Akkaya, "Strategic Defense Against Stealthy Link Flooding Attacks: A Signaling Game Approach," in IEEE Transactions on Network Science and Engineering, vol. 8, no. 1, pp. 751-764, 1 Jan.-March 2021, .DOI: 10.1109/TNSE.2021.3052090

A. Nhlabatsi et al., "Threat-Specific Security Risk Evaluation in the Cloud," in IEEE Transactions on Cloud Computing, vol. 9, no. 2, pp. 793-806, 1 April-June 2021, .DOI: 10.1109/TCC.2018.2883063

Abba Ari, A. A., Ngangmo, O. K., Titouna, C., Thiare, O., Mohamadou, A., & Gueroui, A. M. (2024). Enabling privacy and security in Cloud of Things: Architecture, applications, security & privacy challenges. *Applied Computing and Informatics*, 20(1/2), 119–141. DOI: 10.1016/j.aci.2019.11.005

Abd El-Latif, A. A., Abd-El-Atty, B., Mehmood, I., Muhammad, K., Venegas-Andraca, S. E., & Peng, J. (2021, July). Quantum-Inspired Block chain-Based Cyber security: Securing Smart Edge Utilities in IoT-Based Smart Cities. *Information Processing & Management*, 58(4), 102549. DOI: 10.1016/j.ipm.2021.102549

Abdallah, S., Elhajj, I. H., Chehab, A., & Kayssi, A. (2018, February). A network management framework for SDN. In 2018 9th IFIP International Conference on New Technologies, Mobility and Security (NTMS) (pp. 1-4). IEEE. DOI: 10.1109/NTMS.2018.8328672

Abdul Hanan, K. M.. (2021), IoT Cyber-Attack Detection: A Comparative Analysis, *International Conference on Data Science, E-learning and Information Systems*.

Abdulbast, A. Abushgra, How Quantum Computing Impacts Cyber Security (2023), IEEE Conference: 2023 Intelligent Methods, Systems, and Applications (IMSA) DOI:DOI: 10.1109/IMSA58542.2023.10217756

Abdullayeva, F. J. (2023). Cyber resilience and cyber security issues of intelligent cloud computing systems. *Results in Control and Optimization*, 12, 100268. DOI: 10.1016/j.rico.2023.100268

Abdul-Qawy, A. S., ... (2015), The Internet of Things (IoT): An Overview, Int. Journal of Engineering Research and Applications, ISSN: 2248-9622, Vol. 5, Issue 12, (Part - 2) December 2015, pp.71-82

Adeghe, E., Okolo, C., & Ojeyinka, O. (2024). *Evaluating the impact of blockchain technology in healthcare data management: A review of security, privacy, and patient outcomes*. Open Access Research Journal of Science and Technology., DOI: 10.53022/oarjst.2024.10.2.0044

Adil, M., Khan, M. K., Kumar, N., Attique, M., Farouk, A., Guizani, M., & Jin, Z. (2024). Healthcare Internet of Things: Security Threats, Challenges and Future Research Directions. *IEEE Internet of Things Journal*, 11(11), 19046–19069. DOI: 10.1109/JIOT.2024.3360289

Adnan, M. H., Ahmad Zukarnain, Z., & Harun, N. Z. (2022). Quantum Key Distribution for 5G Networks: A Review, State of Art and Future Directions. *Future Internet*, 14(3), 73. DOI: 10.3390/fi14030073

Afzal, R., & Murugesan, R. K. (2022). Implementation of a malicious traffic filter using snort and wireshark as a proof of concept to enhance mobile network security. *Journal of Telecommunications and Information Technology*, (1).

Agarkar, A., Karyakarte, M., Chavhan, G., Milind, P., Talware, R., & Kulkarni, L. (2024). Blockchain aware decentralized identity management and access control system. *Elsevier, 31*. DOI: 10.1016/j.measen.2024.101032

Ahanger, T. A., Aljumah, A., & Atiquzzaman, M. (2022). State-of-the-art survey of artificial intelligent techniques for IoT security. *Computer Networks*, 206, 108771. DOI: 10.1016/j.comnet.2022.108771

Ahmad, D., Lutfiani, N., Rizki Ahmad, A. D. A., Rahardja, U., & Aini, Q. (2021). Blockchain Technology Immutability Framework Design in E-Government. *Jurnal Administrasi Publik : Public Administration Journal*, 11(1), 32–41. DOI: 10.31289/jap.v11i1.4310

Ahmad, I., Abdullah, S., & Ahmed, A. (2022). IoT-fog-based healthcare 4.0 system using blockchain technology. *The Journal of Supercomputing*, 79(4), 3999–4020. DOI: 10.1007/s11227-022-04788-7 PMID: 36157083

Ahmad, S., & Mir, A. H. (2021). Scalability, consistency, reliability and security in SDN controllers: A survey of diverse SDN controllers. *Journal of Network and Systems Management*, 29(1), 1–59. DOI: 10.1007/s10922-020-09575-4

Ahmad, W., Rasool, A., Javed, A. R., Baker, T., & Jalil, Z. (2021). Cyber security in iot-based cloud computing: A comprehensive survey. *Electronics (Basel)*, 11(1), 16. DOI: 10.3390/electronics11010016

Ahmed, S. F., Alam, M. S. B., Afrin, S., Rafa, S. J., Taher, S. B., Kabir, M., ... & Gandomi, A. H. (2024). Towards a secure 5G-enabled Internet of Things: A survey on requirements, privacy, security, challenges, and opportunities. IEEE Access.

Akbar, K. A., Rahman, F. I., Singhal, A., Khan, L., & Thuraisingham, B. (2023a, December). The Design and Application of a Unified Ontology for Cyber Security. In *International Conference on Information Systems Security* (pp. 23-41). Cham: Springer Nature Switzerland. DOI: 10.1007/978-3-031-49099-6_2

Alani, M. M. (2021). Big Data in cybersecurity: A survey of applications and future trends. *Journal of Reliable Intelligent Environments*, 7(2), 85–114. DOI: 10.1007/s40860-020-00120-3

Al-Daeef, M. M., Basir, N., & Saudi, M. M. (2014). A method to measure the efficiency of phishing emails detection features. In *2014 International Conference on Information Science & Applications (ICISA)* (pp. 1-5). IEEE. DOI: 10.1109/ICISA.2014.6847332

Alekha Parimal Bhatt, Anand Sharma (2019), Quantum Cryptography for Internet of Things Security, Journal of Electronic Science and Technology, DOI:.DOI: 10.11989/JEST.1674-862X.90523016

Al-Haija, . (2022). PDF malware detection based on Optimizable Decision trees. *Electronics (Basel)*, 11(19), 3142. DOI: 10.3390/electronics11193142

Alhajjar, E., Maxwell, P., & Bastian, N. (2021). Adversarial machine learning in network threat identifying systems. *Expert Systems with Applications*, 186, 115782. DOI: 10.1016/j.eswa.2021.115782

Alhogail, A., & Alsabih, A. (2021). Applying machine learning and natural language processing to detect phishing email. *Computers & Security*, 110, 102414. DOI: 10.1016/j.cose.2021.102414

Ali, S. A., Roy, N. R., & Raj, D. "Software Defect Prediction using Machine Learning", 2023, Proceedings of the 17th INDIACom; 10th International Conference on Computing for Sustainable Global Development, INDIACom 2023, PP: 639-642, Sudarsa, D., A, N. R., & AP, S. (2023). An effective and secured authentication and sharing of data with dynamic groups in cloud. *Data and Knowledge Engineering, 145*, 102125. DOI: 10.1016/j.datak.2022.102125

Alia, S., & Babar, S.. (2020). *Review Article: Survey Paper on IOT Attacks And Its Prevention Mechanisms, Information Management and Computer Science.* IMCS., DOI: 10.26480/imcs.02.2020.38.41

Ali, M., Khan, S. U., & Vasilakos, A. V. (2015). Security in cloud computing: Opportunities and challenges. *Information Sciences*, 305, 357–383. DOI: 10.1016/j. ins.2015.01.025

Ali, M., Tang Jung, L., Hassan Sodhro, A., Ali Laghari, A., Birahim Belhaouari, S., & Gillani, Z. (2023). A confidentiality-based data classification-as-a-service (C2aaS) for cloud security. *Alexandria Engineering Journal*, 64, 749–760. DOI: 10.1016/j.aej.2022.10.056

Ali, V., Norman, A. A., & Azzuhri, S. R. B. (2023). Characteristics of Blockchain and Its Relationship With Trust. *IEEE Access : Practical Innovations, Open Solutions*, 11, 15364–15374. DOI: 10.1109/ACCESS.2023.3243700

Aliyu, A. L., Aneiba, A., Patwary, M., & Bull, P. (2020). A trust manage- ment framework for software defined network (SDN) controller and network applications. *Computer Networks*, 181, 107421. DOI: 10.1016/j.comnet.2020.107421

Aljuffri, A., Zwalua, M., Reinbrecht, C. R. W., Hamdioui, S., & Taouil, M. (2021, November). "Applying Thermal Side-Channel Attacks on Asymmetric Cryptography," in IEEE Transactions on Very Large Scale Integration (VLSI). *IEEE Transactions on Very Large Scale Integration (VLSI) Systems*, 29(11), 1930–1942. DOI: 10.1109/ TVLSI.2021.3111407

Allende, M., León, D. L., Cerón, S., Pareja, A., Pacheco, E., Leal, A., Da Silva, M., Pardo, A., Jones, D., Worrall, D. J., Merriman, B., Gilmore, J., Kitchener, N., & Venegas-Andraca, S. E. (2023). Quantum-resistance in blockchain networks. *Scientific Reports*, 13(1), 5664. DOI: 10.1038/s41598-023-32701-6 PMID: 37024656

Alliance, C. S. "Top threats to cloud computing, version 1.0," Cloud Security Alliance, Tech. Rep., March 2010. [Online]. Available: http://www.cloudsecurityalliance .org/ topthreats/csathreats.v1.0.pdf

Allioui, H., & Mourdi, Y. (2023). *Exploring the Full Potentials of IoT for Better Financial Growth and Stability: A Comprehensive* Survey. *Sensors (Basel)*, 23(19), 8015. DOI: 10.3390/s23198015 PMID: 37836845

Almadani, M., Alotaibi, S., Alsobhi, H., & Hussain, O. (2023). Blockchain-based multi-factor authentication: A systematic literature review. *Elsevier, 23*. DOI: 10.1016/j.iot.2023.100844

Alotaibi, Y., & Ilyas, M. (2023). Ensemble-learning framework for intrusion detection to enhance internet of things' devices security. *Sensors (Basel)*, 23(12), 5568. DOI: 10.3390/s23125568 PMID: 37420734

Alpana, S. (2021). Big Data Technologies for Cyber Security in the Digital Era. *Social Science Research Network*. DOI: 10.2139/ssrn.4629044

Alqarawi, G., Alkhalifah, B., Alharbi, N., & El Khediri, S. (2023). Internet- of-things security and vulnerabilities: Case study. *Journal of Applied Security Research*, 18(3), 559–575. DOI: 10.1080/19361610.2022.2031841

Alrubei, S., Ball, E., & Rigelsford, J. (2022). Adding hardware security into IoT-blockchain platforms. *IEEE*, 1–6. DOI: 10.1109/LATINCOM56090.2022.10000585

Alterazi, H. A., Kshirsagar, P. R., Manoharan, H., Selvarajan, S., Alhebaishi, N., Srivastava, G., & Lin, J. C. (2022). Prevention of Cyber Security with the Internet of Things Using Particle Swarm Optimization. *Sensors (Basel)*, 22(16), 6117. Advance online publication. DOI: 10.3390/s22166117 PMID: 36015878

Altwaijry, N., Elnagar, N., Alshurideh, M., & Shaalan, K. (2024). Advancing phishing email detection: A comparative study of deep learning models. *Sensors (Basel)*, 24(7), 2077. DOI: 10.3390/s24072077 PMID: 38610289

AlZubi, A. A., & Galyna, K. (2023). Artificial intelligence and internet of things for sustainable farming and smart agriculture. *IEEE Access : Practical Innovations, Open Solutions*, 11, 78686–78692. DOI: 10.1109/ACCESS.2023.3298215

Ameur, Y., Bouzefrane, S., & Vinh, T. L. (2023). Handling security issues by using homomorphic encryption in multi-cloud environment. *Procedia Computer Science*, 220, 390–397. DOI: 10.1016/j.procs.2023.03.050

Amit Jaykumar Chinchawade. Dr. O.S. Lamba (2018), Professor, Development of Authentication and Security Procedures for IoT System, International Journal of Research in Advent Technology (IJRAT) Special Issue E-ISSN: 2321-9637 Available online at www.ijrat.org

Andryukhin, A. (2019). Phishing attacks and preventions in blockchain based projects. *IEEE*, 15–19. DOI: 10.1109/EnT.2019.00008

Angin, P., Bhargava, B., & Ranchal, R. (2019). Big Data Analytics for Cyber Security. *Security and Communication Networks*, 1–2, 1–2. Advance online publication. DOI: 10.1155/2019/4109836

Anisha, M. (2019). The GDPR-Blockchain Paradox: Exempting Permissioned Blockchains from the GDPR. *Fordham Intell. Prop. Media & Ent. L.J., 29.* https://heinonline.org/HOL/LandingPage?handle=hein.journals/frdipm29&div=35

An, S., Leung, A., Hong, J. B., Eom, T., & Park, J. S. (2022). Toward Automated Security Analysis and Enforcement for Cloud Computing Using Graphical Models for Security. *IEEE Access: Practical Innovations, Open Solutions*, 10, 75117–75134. DOI: 10.1109/ACCESS.2022.3190545

Anubha, R P S Bedi (2020), Detection of Clone Attacks in Manets using Ant Colony Optimization, International Journal of Engineering and Advanced Technology (IJEAT) ISSN: 2249 – 8958 (Online), Volume-9 Issue-4, April 2020

Apone-Novoa, F., Orozco, A., Villanueva-Polanco, R., & Wightman, P. (2021). The 51% attack on blockchains: A mining behavior study. *IEEE, 9*, 140549–140564. DOI: 10.1109/ACCESS.2021.3119291

Arya, D. (2017). Big data Analytics in Cyber Security. *International Journal of Engineering Research & Technology (Ahmedabad)*, 5(10).

Atawneh, S., & Aljehani, H. (2023). Phishing email detection model using deep learning. *Electronics (Basel)*, 12(4261), 4261. DOI: 10.3390/electronics12204261

Aviral Apurva, Pranshu Ranakoti, Yadav, S., Tomer, S., & Nihar Ranjan Roy. (2017). *Redefining cyber security with big data analytics*. DOI: 10.1109/IC3TSN.2017.8284476

Ayush, Mr. G, Ingole. (2024). Home Security System Using IOT: A Research Paper. International Journal For Science Technology And Engineering, 12(5):5112-5116. DOI: 10.22214/ijraset.2024.62773

B. Ondiege, M. Clarke, and G. Mapp. (2017). Exploring a New Security Framework for Remote Patient Monitoring Devices.

Babun, L., Denney, K., Celik, Z. B., McDaniel, P., & Uluagac, A. S. (2021). A survey on IoT platforms: Communication, security, and privacy perspectives. *Computer Networks*, 192, 108040. DOI: 10.1016/j.comnet.2021.108040

Banafaa, M., Shayea, I., Din, J., Azmi, H. M., Alashbi, A., Daradkeh, I. Y., & Al-hammadi, A. (2023). *6G Mobile Communication Technology: Requirements, Targets, Applications, Challenges, Advantages, and Opportunities,* Alexandria Engineering Journal, 64, 245-274, ISSN 1110-0168, DOI: 10.1016/j.aej.2022.08.017

Banerjee, U., Vashishtha, A., & Saxena, M. (2010). Evaluation of the Capabilities of WireShark as a tool for Intrusion Detection. *International Journal of Computer Applications*, 6(7), 1–5. DOI: 10.5120/1092-1427

Barnum, S. (2012). Standardizing cyber threat intelligence information with the structured threat information expression (stix). *Mitre Corporation*, 11, 1–22.

Belchior, R., Vasconcelos, A., Guerreiro, S., & Correia, M. (2021). A survey on blockchain interoperability: Past, present, and future trends. *ACM Computing Surveys*, 54(8), 41. DOI: 10.1145/3471140

Bel, H. F., & Sabeen, S. (2022). A survey on IoT security: Attacks, challenges and countermeasures. *Webology*, 19(1), 3741–3763. DOI: 10.14704/WEB/V19I1/WEB19246

Benson, T., Akella, A., & Maltz, D. A. (2010, November). Network traffic characteristics of data centers in the wild. In *Proceedings of the 10th ACM SIGCOMM conference on Internet measurement* (pp. 267-280). DOI: 10.1145/1879141.1879175

Bernabe, J., Cánovas, J., Hernández-Ramos, J., Moreno, R., & Skarmeta, A. (2019). Privacy-preserving solutions for blockchain: Review and challenges. *IEEE, 7*, 164908–164940. DOI: 10.1109/ACCESS.2019.2950872

Bharadwaj, D. R., Bhattacharya, A., & Chakkaravarthy, M. "Cloud Threat Defense – A Threat Protection and Security Compliance Solution," *2018 IEEE International Conference on Cloud Computing in Emerging Markets (CCEM)*, Bangalore, India, 2018, pp. 95-99, DOI: 10.1109/CCEM.2018.00024

Bhardwaj, A., Hussian Shah, S. B., Shankar, A., Alazab, M., & Kumar, M. (2021). Penetration testing framework for smart contract blockchain. *Springer, 14*, 2635–2650. DOI: 10.1007/s12083-020-00991-6

Bhusare, P. K., Mannem, B. M. R., & Annapurani Panaiyappan, K. (2023). Decentralised social media. In *ViTECoN 2023 - 2nd IEEE International Conference on Vision Towards Emerging Trends in Communication and Networking Technologies, Proceedings*. DOI: 10.1109/ViTECoN58111.2023.10157136

Bhushan, B., Sinha, P., Sagayam, K., & J, A. (2021). Untangling blockchain technology: A survey on state of the art, security threats, privacy services, applications and future research directions. *Elsevier, 90*. DOI: 10.1016/j.compeleceng.2020.106897

Bhutta, M. N. M., Khwaja, A. A., Nadeem, A., Ahmad, H. F., Khan, M. K., Hanif, M. A., Song, H., Alshamari, M., & Cao, Y. (2021). A Survey on Blockchain Technology: Evolution, Architecture and Security. *IEEE Access : Practical Innovations, Open Solutions*, 9, 61048–61073. DOI: 10.1109/ACCESS.2021.3072849

Bibri, E. S., Krogstie, J., Kaboli, A., & Alahi, A. (2023). *Smarter eco-cities and their leading-edge artificial intelligence of things solutions for environmental sustainability: A comprehensive systematic review, Environmental Science and Ecotechnology,*19,100330, ISSN 2666-4984,DOI: 10.1016/j.ese.2023.100330

Bi, J., Luo, F., He, S., Liang, G., Meng, W., & Sun, M. (2022, September). False Data Injection- and Propagation-Aware Game Theoretical Approach for Microgrids. *IEEE Transactions on Smart Grid*, 13(5), 3342–3353. DOI: 10.1109/TSG.2022.3174918

Binsawad, M. (2024). Enhancing PDF Malware Detection through Logistic Model Trees. *Computers, Materials & Continua/Computers. Computers, Materials & Continua*, 0(0), 1–10. DOI: 10.32604/cmc.2024.048183

Bishop, M., & Gates, C. "Defining the Insider Threat", in *Proc. of the 4th Annual Workshop on Cyber Security and Information Intelligence Research*, Tennessee, Vol. 288, 2008.

Booth, H., Rike, D., & Witte, G. A. (2013). *The national vulnerability database (nvd)*. Overview.

Bountakas, P., & Xenakis, C. (2023). Helphed: Hybrid ensemble learning phishing email detection. *Journal of Network and Computer Applications*, 210, 103545. DOI: 10.1016/j.jnca.2022.103545

Brandão, P. R. (2018). The Importance of Authentication and Encryption in Cloud Computing Framework Security. *International Journal on Data Science and Technology.*, 4(1), 1–5. DOI: 10.11648/j.ijdst.20180401.11

Bruzgiene, R., Narbutaite, L., & Adomkus, T. (2017). MANET Network in Internet of Things System, Book. *Ad Hoc Networks*. Advance online publication. DOI: 10.5772/66408

Burra, M. S., & Maity, S. (2023). A Distributed and Decentralized Certificateless Framework for Reliable Shared Data Auditing for FOG-CPS Networks. *IEEE Access : Practical Innovations, Open Solutions*, 11, 42595–42618. DOI: 10.1109/ACCESS.2023.3271605

Buyuaa, R., & Calheiros, R. N. (2016). *Big Data Principles and Paradigms* (1st ed.). Elsevier.

Čabarkapa, D. (2015). Application of Cisco Packet Tracer 6.2 in teaching of advanced computer networks. *Proceddings of the Information Technology and Development of Education ITRO, 153.*

Cases of Cyber Frauds. (2024). Pib.gov.in. https://pib.gov.in/PressReleaseIframePage.aspx?PRID=2003158

Chanal, P. M., & Kakkasageri, M. S. (2020). Security and privacy in IoT: A survey. *Wireless Personal Communications*, 115(2), 1667–1693. DOI: 10.1007/s11277-020-07649-9

Chaubey, N. K., & Prajapati, B. B. (2020). Quantum Cryptography and the Future of Cyber Security. (2020). In *Advances in information security, privacy, and ethics book series*. IGI Global., DOI: 10.4018/978-1-7998-2253-0

Chaudhary A.; Krishna K.C.; Shadik M.; Raj D., "A review on malicious link detection techniques", 2023, Artificial Intelligence, Blockchain, Computing and Security: Volume 1, Volume-1, PP: 768-777, DOI: DOI: 10.1201/9781003393580-114

Chen, H. "Dark Web: Exploring and Mining the Dark Side of the Web," 2011 European Intelligence and Security Informatics Conference, Athens, Greece, 2011, pp. 1-2, . keywords: {Educational institutions;Informatics;Libraries;Awards activities;Terrorism;Conferences;Presses}DOI: 10.1109/EISIC.2011.78

Chen, Y., Chen, H., Zhang, Y., Han, M., Siddula, M., & Cai, Z. (2022). A survey on blockchain systems: Attacks, defenses, and privacy preservation. *Elsevier, 2*(2). DOI: 10.1016/j.hcc.2021.100048

Chen, K., Zhang, M., Liang, R., Chen, J., Peng, J., & Huang, X. (2024). Research on the Application of Penetration Testing Frameworks in Blockchain Security. In Li, S. (Ed.), *Computational and Experimental Simulations in Engineering* (Vol. 146, pp. 307–330). Springer Nature Switzerland., DOI: 10.1007/978-3-031-44947-5_25

Chen, Q., Chen, H., & Ca, Y. (2018), Denial of Service Attack on IoT System, *9th International Conference on Information Technology in Medicine and Education (ITME).* DOI: 10.1109/ITME.2018.00171

Chen, S., Liu, Y., & Cui, S. (2019). *Security in 5G networks:* A survey," *IEEE Access*, vol. 7, pp. 30474-30488. Abbas, R. Jan, S. and Ali, F. (2020).Security and privacy in 5G: A survey of emerging challenges and future directions. *IEEE Access : Practical Innovations, Open Solutions*, 8, 211657–211691.

Chui, K. T., Gupta, B. B., Liu, J., Arya, V., Nedjah, N., Almomani, A., & Chaurasia, P. (2023). A survey of internet of things and cyber-physical systems: Standards, algorithms, applications, security, challenges, and future directions. *Information (Basel)*, 14(7), 388. DOI: 10.3390/info14070388

CIC-Evasive-PDFMal2022 | Datasets | Canadian Institute for Cybersecurity | UNB. (n.d.). https://www.unb.ca/cic/datasets/pdfmal-2022.html

Cirne, A., Sousa, P. R., Resende, J. S., & Antunes, L. (2022). IoT security certifications: Challenges and potential approaches. *Computers & Security*, 116, 102669. DOI: 10.1016/j.cose.2022.102669

Corea, P. M., Liu, Y., Wang, J., Niu, S., & Song, H. (2024). Explainable AI for comparative analysis of intrusion detection models. DOI: 10.1109/MeditCom61057.2024.10621339

Cruz, A. R. S. A., Gomes, R. L., & Fernandez, M. P. (2021, July). An intelligent mechanism to detect cyberattacks of mirai botnet in iot networks. In 2021 17th International Conference on Distributed Computing in Sensor Systems (DCOSS) (pp. 236-243). IEEE.

Curtis, A. R., Mogul, J. C., Tourrilhes, J., Yalagandula, P., & Sharma, P., Banerjee, S. (2011, August). DevoFlow: Scaling flow management for high-performance networks. In Proceedings of the ACM SIGCOMM 2011 Conference (pp. 254-265). DOI: 10.1145/2018436.2018466

Das, D., Maity, S., Nasir, S. B., Ghosh, S., Raychowdhury, A., & Sen, S. (2018, October). ASNI: Attenuated Signature Noise Injection for Low-Overhead Power Side-Channel Attack Immunity. *IEEE Transactions on Circuits and Systems. I, Regular Papers*, 65(10), 3300–3311. DOI: 10.1109/TCSI.2018.2819499

De Salve, A., Mori, P., Ricci, L., & Di Pietro, R. (2023). Content privacy enforcement models in decentralized online social networks: State of play, solutions, limitations, and future directions. *Computer Communications*, 203, 2023. DOI: 10.1016/j.comcom.2023.02.023

Deloitte. (2020). *Deloitte's 2020 Global Blockchain Survey: From promise to reality* (Deloitte Insights) [Industry / Business Report]. https://www2.deloitte.com/content/dam/Deloitte/tw/Documents/financial-services/2020-global-blockchain-survey.pdf

Deloitte. (2021). *Deloitte's 2021 Global Blockchain Survey: A new age of digital assets* (Deloitte Insights, p. 28) [Industry / Business Report]. https://www2.deloitte.com/content/dam/insights/articles/US144337_Blockchain-survey/DI_Blockchain-survey.pdf

Deogirikar, J., & Vidhate, A. (2017), Security Attacks in IoT: A Survey, International conference on I-SMAC (IoT in Social, Mobile, Analytics and Cloud) DOI:DOI: 10.1109/I-SMAC.2017.8058363

Deshmukh, R. V., & Devadkar, K. K. (2015). Understanding DDoS attack & its effect in cloud environment. *Procedia Computer Science*, 49, 202–210. DOI: 10.1016/j. procs.2015.04.245

Di Matteo, S., Baldanzi, L., Crocetti, L., Nannipieri, P., Fanucci, L., & Saponara, S. (2021). Secure Elliptic Curve Crypto-Processor for Real-Time IoT Applications. *Energies*, 14(15), 4676. DOI: 10.3390/en14154676

Dietterich, T. G. (2000). Ensemble methods in machine learning. In *Multiple Classifier Systems. MCS 2000*. Springer. DOI: 10.1007/3-540-45014-9_1

Distefano, S., Giacomo, A. D., & Mazzara, M. (2021). Trustworthiness for Transportation Ecosystems: The Blockchain Vehicle Information System. *IEEE Transactions on Intelligent Transportation Systems*, 22(4), 2013–2022. DOI: 10.1109/ TITS.2021.3054996

Dodiya, B., & Singh, U. K. (2022). Malicious Traffic analysis using Wireshark by collection of Indicators of Compromise. *International Journal of Computer Applications*, 183(53), 1–6. DOI: 10.5120/ijca2022921876

Efanov, D., & Roschin, P. (2018). The all-pervasiveness of the blockchain technology. *Elsevier, 123*, 116–121. DOI: 10.1016/j.procs.2018.01.019

Elingiusti., …. (2018). *PDF-malware detection: a survey and taxonomy of current techniques.* https://iris.uniroma1.it/retrieve/e383531c-a499-15e8-e053-a505fe0a3de9/ Elingiusti_Postprint_PDF-Malware-Detection_2018.pdf

Endignoux, G. (2016). *Introduction to PDF syntax | Blog | Guillaume Endignoux.* https://gendignoux.com/blog/2016/10/04/pdf-basics.html

Erl, T., Khattak, W., & Buhler, P. (2015). *Big data fundamentals: Concepts, drivers & techniques.* Prentice Hall.

Fagan M, Megas K, Scarfone K, Smith M (2020) Foundational Cyber security Activities for IoT Device Manufacturers. NIST IR 8259.

Faizan, M., & Khan, R. A. (2019). Exploring and analyzing the dark Web: A new alchemy. *First Monday*, 24(5). Advance online publication. DOI: 10.5210/ fm.v24i5.9473

Fakhouri, H. N., Alawadi, S., Awaysheh, F. M., Hani, I. B., Alkhalaileh, M., & Hamad, F. (2023). A Comprehensive Study on the Role of Machine Learning in 5G Security: Challenges, Technologies, and Solutions. *Electronics (Basel)*, 12(22), 4604. DOI: 10.3390/electronics12224604

Falah, , Pan, L., Huda, S., Pokhrel, S. R., & Anwar, A. (2020). Improving malicious PDF classifier with feature engineering: A data-driven approach. *Future Generation Computer Systems*, 115, 314–326. DOI: 10.1016/j.future.2020.09.015

Fan, K., Ren, Y., Li, H., Yang, Y., & Zhou, H. (2020). Blockchain-based efficient privacy preserving and data sharing scheme of content-centric network in 5G. *IET Communications*, 14(6), 833–841. DOI: 10.1049/iet- com.2019.0828

Fatima, N., Agarwal, P., & Sohail, S. (2022). Security and privacy issues of blockchain technology in health care—A review. *Springer, 314*, 193–201. DOI: 10.1007/978-981-16-5655-2_18

Feng, X., Zhu, X., Han, Q. L., Zhou, W., Wen, S., & Xiang, Y. (2022). Detecting vulnerability on IoT device firmware: A survey. IEEE/CAA Journal of Automatica Sinica, 10(1), 25-41.

Fenz, S., Ekelhart, A., & Weippl, E. (2008, March). Fortification of IT security by automatic security advisory processing. In *22nd International Conference on Advanced Information Networking and Applications (aina 2008)* (pp. 575-582). IEEE. DOI: 10.1109/AINA.2008.69

Ferdowsi, A., & Saad, W. 2019, December. Generative adversarial networks for distributed threat identifying in the internet of things. In *2019 IEEE Global Communications Conference (GLOBECOM)* (pp. 1-6). IEEE.

Fernández-Caramés, T., & Fraga-Lamas, P. (2020). Towards post-quantum blockchain: A review on blockchain cryptography resistant to quantum computing attacks. *IEEE, 8*. DOI: 10.1109/ACCESS.2020.2968985

Furht, B., & Escalante, A. (2010). *Handbook of cloud computing* (Vol. 3). Springer. DOI: 10.1007/978-1-4419-6524-0

Furstenau, L. B., Rodrigues, Y. P. R., Sott, M. K., Leivas, P., Dohan, M. S., Lo'pez-Robles, J. R., Cobo, M. J., Bragazzi, N. L., & Choo, K. K. R. (2023). Internet of things: Conceptual network structure, main challenges and future directions. *Digital Communications and Networks*, 9(3), 677–687. DOI: 10.1016/j.dcan.2022.04.027

G. Somani, M. S. Gaur, D. Sanghi, M. Conti and M. Rajarajan, "Scale Inside-Out: Rapid Mitigation of Cloud DDoS Attacks," in IEEE Transactions on Dependable and Secure Computing, vol. 15, no. 6, pp. 959-973, 1 Nov.-Dec. 2018, .DOI: 10.1109/TDSC.2017.2763160

Gad, A. G. (2022). Particle swarm optimization algorithm and its applications: A systematic review. *Archives of Computational Methods in Engineering*, 29(5), 2531–2561. DOI: 10.1007/s11831-021-09694-4

Gan, C., Feng, Q., Zhang, X., Zhang, Z., & Zhu, Q. (2020). Dynamical Propagation Model of Malware for Cloud Computing Security. *IEEE Access : Practical Innovations, Open Solutions*, 8, 20325–20333. DOI: 10.1109/ACCESS.2020.2968916

Gao, S., Lin, R., Fu, Y., Li, H., & Cao, J. (2024). Security Threats, Requirements and Recommendations on Creating 5G Network Slicing System: A Survey. *Electronics (Basel)*, 13(10), 1860. DOI: 10.3390/electronics13101860

Garfinkel, S. (1999). *Architects of the information society: 35 years of the Laboratory for Computer Science at MIT*. MIT press. DOI: 10.7551/mitpress/1341.001.0001

Ge, C., Susilo, W., Baek, J., Liu, Z., Xia, J., & Fang, L. (2022). Revocable Attribute-Based Encryption With Data Integrity in Clouds. *IEEE Transactions on Dependable and Secure Computing*, 19(5), 2864–2872. DOI: 10.1109/TDSC.2021.3065999

Geetha, K., Srivani, A., Gunasekaran, S., Ananthi, S., & Sangeetha, S. "Geospatial Data Exploration Using Machine Learning," 2023 4th International Conference on Smart Electronics and Communication (ICOSEC), Trichy, India, 2023, pp. 1485-1489, DOI: 10.1109/ICOSEC58147.2023.10275920

Gehl, R. W. (2016). Power/freedom on the dark web: A digital ethnography of the Dark Web Social Network. *New Media & Society*, 18(7), 1219–1235. DOI: 10.1177/1461444814554900

Georgiou, K. E., Georgiou, E., & Satava, R. M. (2021). 5G Use in Healthcare: The Future is Present. *JSLS : Journal of the Society of Laparoendoscopic Surgeons*, 25(4), 00064. DOI: 10.4293/JSLS.2021.00064 PMID: 35087266

Goel, A. K., & Bakshi, R. (2022). Web 3.0 and decentralized applications. In *The 2nd International Conference on Innovative Research in Renewable Energy Technologies (IRRET 2022)*.

Gong, L., & Tian, Y. (2020). Threat modeling for cyber range: an ontology-based approach. In *Communications, Signal Processing, and Systems:Proceedings of the 2018 CSPS* Volume III*: Systems 7th* (pp. 1055-1062). Springer Singapore. DOI: 10.1007/978-981-13-6508-9_128

Gopalan, S. S., Raza, A., & Almobaideen, W. (2021, March). IoT security in health-care using AI: A survey. In 2020 International Conference on Com- munications, Signal Processing, and their Applications (ICCSPA) (pp. 1-6). IEEE. DOI: 10.1109/ICCSPA49915.2021.9385711

Gopireddy, R. R. (2020). Dark Web Monitoring: Extracting and Analyzing Threat Intelligence. [1]

Grasser, A., & Parger, A. (2022). Blockchain architectures, the potential of Web3 for decentralized participatory architecture: Collaborative objects on the blockchain. In *Co-creating the Future: Inclusion in and through Design* (Vol. 1, pp. 431–440). eCAADe Conference Proceedings.

Greengard, S. Internet of Things (2024), Encyclopedia *Britannica*, https://www .britannica.com/science/Internet-of-Things

Greschbach, B., Kreitz, G., & Buchegger, S. (2012). New privacy challenges in decentralised online social networks. In *2012 IEEE International Conference on Pervasive Computing and Communications Workshops (PERCOM Workshops 2012)*. DOI: 10.1109/PerComW.2012.6197506

Grolemund, G., & Wickham, H. (2017). *R for data science*. O'Reilly Media.

Guo, H., & Yu, X. (2022). A survey on blockchain technology and its security. *Elsevier, 3*(2). DOI: 10.1016/j.bcra.2022.100067

Guruswamy, S., Pojic´, M., Subramanian, J., Mastilovic´, J., Sarang, S., Subbana-gounder, A., Stojanović, G., & Jeoti, V. (2022). Toward better food security using concepts from industry 5.0. *Sensors (Basel)*, 22(21), 8377. DOI: 10.3390/s22218377 PMID: 36366073

Gyrard, A., Bonnet, C., & Boudaoud, K. (2013, May). The stac (security toolbox: attacks & countermeasures) ontology. In *Proceedings of the 22nd International Conference on World Wide Web* (pp. 165-166). DOI: 10.1145/2487788.2487869

H. A. Khan et al., "IDEA: Intrusion Detection through Electromagnetic-Signal Analysis for Critical Embedded and Cyber-Physical Systems," in IEEE Transactions on Dependable and Secure Computing, vol. 18, no. 3, pp. 1150-1163, 1 May-June 2021, .DOI: 10.1109/TDSC.2019.2932736

HaddadPajouh, H., Dehghantanha, A., Parizi, R. M., Aledhari, M., & Karim- ipour, H. (. (2021). A survey on internet of things security: Requirements, challenges, and solutions. *Internet of Things : Engineering Cyber Physical Human Systems*, 14, 100129. DOI: 10.1016/j.iot.2019.100129

Haddaoui, S., Chikhi, S., & Miles, B. (2022). The IoT Ecosystem: Components, Architecture, Communication Technologies, and Protocols. In Lecture notes in networks and systems (pp. 76–90). DOI: 10.1007/978-3-031-18516-8_6

Hameed, A., & Alomary, A. (2019, September). Security issues in IoT: A survey. In 2019 International conference on innovation and intelligence for informatics, computing, and technologies (3ICT) (pp. 1-5). IEEE. DOI: 10.1109/3ICT.2019.8910320

Hamidah, M. N., Tias, R. F., & Zainal, R. F. (2024). Quality of Service (QoS) Analysis using Wireshark on the LAN Network at An Najiyah High School Surabaya. *Jurnal Mandiri IT*, 12(4), 222–228.

Hanan Mustapha, A. A. (2018), DDoS attacks on the internet of things and their prevention methods, *International Conference on Future Networks and Distributed Systems*. DOI: 10.1145/3231053.3231057

Handayani, F. (2022). Design and legal aspect of central bank digital currency: A literature review. *Journal of Central Banking Law and Institutions*, 1(3), 509–536. DOI: 10.21098/jcli.v1i3.35

Handigol, N., Heller, B., Jeyakumar, V., Lantz, B., & McKeown, N. (2012, December). Reproducible network experiments using container-based emulation. In *Proceedings of the 8th international conference on Emerging networking experiments and technologies* (pp. 253-264). DOI: 10.1145/2413176.2413206

Hao, K., Xin, J., Wang, Z., Yao, Z., & Wang, G. (2023, August 1). Efficient and Secure Data Sharing Scheme on Interoperable Blockchain Database. *IEEE Transactions on Big Data*, 9(4), 1171–1185. DOI: 10.1109/TBDATA.2023.3265178

Haque, A. B., Islam, A. K. M. N., Hyrynsalmi, S., Naqvi, B., & Smolander, K. (2021). GDPR Compliant Blockchains–A Systematic Literature Review. *IEEE Access : Practical Innovations, Open Solutions*, 9, 50593–50606. DOI: 10.1109/ACCESS.2021.3069877

Harbi, Y., Aliouat, Z., Refoufi, A., & Harous, S. (2021). Recent security trends in internet of things: A comprehensive survey. *IEEE Access : Practical Innovations, Open Solutions*, 9, 113292–113314. DOI: 10.1109/ACCESS.2021.3103725

Harikrishnan, N. B., Vinayakumar, R., & Soman, K. P. (2018). A machine learning approach towards phishing email detection. In *Proceedings of the anti-phishing pilot at ACM international workshop on security and privacy analytics (IWSPA AP)* (Vol. 2013, pp. 1-6).

Hasan, K., Sajid, M., Lapina, M., & Shahid, M. (2024). Blockchain technology meets 6G wireless networks: A systematic survey. *Elsevier, 92*, 199–220. DOI: 10.1016/j.aej.2024.02.031

Hassanpour, R., Dogdu, E., Choupani, R., Goker, O., & Nazli, N. (2018, March). Phishing e-mail detection by using deep learning algorithms. In *ACM Southeast Regional Conference* (pp. 45-1). DOI: 10.1145/3190645.3190719

Hassan, W. H. (2019). Current research on Internet of Things (IoT) security: A survey. *Computer Networks*, 148, 283–294. DOI: 10.1016/j.comnet.2018.11.025

Hassas Yeganeh, S., & Ganjali, Y. (2012, August). Kandoo: a framework for effi-cient and scalable offloading of control applications. In *Proceedings of the first workshop on Hot topics in software defined networks* (pp. 19-24). DOI: 10.1145/2342441.2342446

Hassija, V., Chamola, V., Saxena, V., Jain, D., Goyal, P., & Sikdar, B. (2019). A survey on IoT security: Application areas, security threats, and solution architec-tures. *IEEE Access : Practical Innovations, Open Solutions*, 7, 82721–82743. DOI: 10.1109/ACCESS.2019.2924045

He, J., Xian, M., & Liu, J. (2019). The Application of big Data in cyberspace: A Survey. In *International Conference on Communications, Information System and Comput-er Engineering e* (pp. 570–574). IEEE Xplore. DOI: 10.1109/CISCE.2019.00132

He, F., Li, F., & Liang, P. (2024). Enhancing smart contract security: Leveraging pre-trained language models for advanced vulnerability detection. *IET Blockchain*, ●●●, 1–12. DOI: 10.1049/blc2.12072

He, H. (2008). ADASYN: Adaptive synthetic sampling approach for imbalanced learning. In *2008 IEEE International Joint Conference on Neural Networks (IEEE World Congress on Computational Intelligence)* (pp. 1322-1328). Hong Kong. https://doi.org/DOI: 10.4018/978-1-7998-8023-2

Hendre, A., & Joshi, K. P. "A Semantic Approach to Cloud Security and Compli-ance," 2015 IEEE 8th International Conference on Cloud Computing, New York, NY, USA, 2015, pp. 1081-1084, DOI: 10.1109/CLOUD.2015.157

He, , Zhu, Y., He, Y., Liu, L., Lu, B., & Lin, W. (2020). Detection of Malicious PDF Files Using a Two-Stage Machine Learning Algorithm. *Chinese Journal of Electronics*, 29(6), 1165–1177. DOI: 10.1049/cje.2020.10.002

Hong, C. Y., Kandula, S., Mahajan, R., Zhang, M., Gill, V., & Nanduri, M., Watten-hofer, R. (2013, August). Achieving high utilization with software-driven WAN. In Proceedings of the ACM SIGCOMM 2013 Conference on SIGCOMM (pp. 15-26).

Hou, J., Qu, L., & Shi, W. (2019). A survey on internet of things security from data perspectives. *Computer Networks*, 148, 295–306. DOI: 10.1016/j.comnet.2018.11.026

Hristov, P., & Dimitrov, W. (2018). *The blockchain as a backbone of GDPR compliant framework*. 8th International Multidisciplinary Symposium / SIMPRO 2018, Romania. https://www.researchgate.net/publication/328576742_The_blockchain_as_a_backbone_of_GDPR_compliant_frameworks

https://towardsdatascience.com/do-you-really-need-to-implement-big-datatechnologies-in-your-ecosystem-ea840a3cf286

Huang, S., & Lei, K. (2020). IGAN-IDS: An imbalanced generative adversarial network towards threat identifying system in ad-hoc networks. *Ad Hoc Networks*, 105, 102177. DOI: 10.1016/j.adhoc.2020.102177

Hurwitz, J. Alan Nugent, & Dr. Fern Halper. (2013). Big Data For Dummies (1st ed.). Wiley.

Huseien, F. G., & Shah, W. K. (2022). *A review on 5G technology for smart energy management and smart buildings in Singapore*, Energy and AI, 7, 2022, 100116, ISSN 2666-5468, DOI: 10.1016/j.egyai.2021.100116

Hussain, A., Hussain, A., Qadri, S., Razzaq, A., Nazir, H., & Ullah, M. S. (2024). Enhancing LAN Security by Mitigating Credential Threats via HTTP Packet Analysis with Wireshark. *Journal of Computing & Biomedical Informatics*, 6(02), 433–440.

Huynh, T. T., Nguyen, T. D., Hoang, T., Tran, L., & Choi, D. (2021). A Reliability Guaranteed Solution for Data Storing and Sharing. *IEEE Access : Practical Innovations, Open Solutions*, 9, 108318–108328. DOI: 10.1109/ACCESS.2021.3100707

Iannacone, M., Bohn, S., Nakamura, G., Gerth, J., Huffer, K., Bridges, R., & Goodall, J. (2015, April). Developing an ontology for cyber security knowledge graphs. In *Proceedings of the 10th annual cyber and information security research conference* (pp. 1-4). DOI: 10.1145/2746266.2746278

Ibarra, J., Jahankhani, H., & Kendzierskyj, S. (2019). *Cyber-physical attacks and the value of healthcare data: Facing an era of cyber extortion and organised crime*. Springer. https://link.springer.com/book/10.1007/978-3-030-11289-9

Idrees, S., Nowostawski, M., Jameel, R., & Mourya, A. (2021). Security aspects of blockchain technology intended for industrial applications. *Electronics (Basel)*, 10(8), 951. https:// kdoi.org/10.3390/electronics10080951. DOI: 10.3390/electronics10080951

Idrissi, I., Azizi, M., & Moussaoui, O. (2022). An unsupervised generative adversarial network based-host threat identifying system for internet of things devices. *Indonesian Journal of Electrical Engineering and Computer Science*, 25(2), 1140–1150. DOI: 10.11591/ijeecs.v25.i2.pp1140-1150

Iliyasu, A. S., & Deng, H. N.-G. A. N. (2022, December). a novel anomaly-based network threat identifying with generative adversarial networks. *International Journal of Information Technology : an Official Journal of Bharati Vidyapeeth's Institute of Computer Applications and Management*, 14(7), 3365–3375. DOI: 10.1007/s41870-022-00910-3

Inayat, U., Zia, M. F., Mahmood, S., Khalid, H. M., & Benbouzid, M. (2022). Learning-Based Methods for Cyber Attacks Detection in IoT Systems: A Survey on Methods, Analysis, and Future Prospects. *Electronics (Basel)*, 11(9), 1502. Advance online publication. DOI: 10.3390/electronics11091502

Introduction to Decision Tree. (2020). Capable Machine; Capable Machine. https://capablemachine.wordpress.com/2020/05/05/decision-tree-2/

Ismail, S., Nouman, M., Dawoud, D., & Reza, H. (2024). Towards a lightweight security framework using blockchain and machine learning. *ScienceDirect*, 5(1), 100174. Advance online publication. DOI: 10.1016/j.bcra.2023.100174

Issakhani, . (2022). PDF Malware Detection based on Stacking Learning. *Proceedings of the 8th International Conference on Information Systems Security and Privacy*. DOI: 10.5220/0010908400003120

Issa, W., Moustafa, N., Turnbull, B., Sohrabi, N., & Tari, Z. (2023). Blockchain-based federated learning for securing internet of things: A com- prehensive survey. *ACM Computing Surveys*, 55(9), 1–43. DOI: 10.1145/3560816

Jadeja, Y., & Modi, K. "Cloud computing - concepts, architecture and challenges", Computing, Electronics and ElectricalTechnologies (ICCEET), 2012 International Conference on, pp. 877-880, 2012. DOI: 10.1109/ICCEET.2012.6203873

Jain, G., & Anubha, . (2021, March). Application of snort and wireshark in network traffic analysis. []. IOP Publishing.]. *IOP Conference Series. Materials Science and Engineering*, 1119(1), 012007. DOI: 10.1088/1757-899X/1119/1/012007

Jain, S., Kumar, A., Mandal, S., Ong, J., Poutievski, L., Singh, A., Venkata, S., Wanderer, J., Zhou, J., Zhu, M., Zolla, J., Hölzle, U., Stuart, S., & Vahdat, A. (2013). B4: Experience with a globally-deployed software defined WAN. *Computer Communication Review*, 43(4), 3–14. DOI: 10.1145/2534169.2486019

James, G. (2013). *An introduction to statistical learning*. Springer. DOI: 10.1007/978-1-4614-7138-7

Jani, K. A., & Chaubey, N. (2020). IoT and Cyber Security: Introduction, Attacks, and Preventive Steps. In Chaubey, N., & Prajapati, B. (Eds.), *Quantum Cryptography and the Future of Cyber Security* (pp. 203–235). IGI Global., DOI: 10.4018/978-1-7998-2253-0.ch010

Jani, K., Lalwani, P., Upadhyay, D., & Potdar, M. B. (2019). Network Intrusion Detection System using Threat Intelligence and Deep Learning Approach. *International Journal on Computer Science and Engineering*, 7(4), 526–531. DOI: 10.26438/ijcse/v7i4.526531

Jaya, I. K. N. A., Dewi, I. A. U., & Mahendra, G. S. (2022). Implementation of Wireshark Application in Data Security Analysis on LMS Website. *Journal of Computer Networks. Architecture and High Performance Computing*, 4(1), 79–86. DOI: 10.47709/cnahpc.v4i1.1345

Jeong, H., Yu, J., & Lee, W. 2021, May. A semi-supervised mechanism for network threat identifying using generative adversarial networks. In IEEE INFOCOM 2021-IEEE Conference on Computer Communications Workshops (INFOCOM WKSHPS) (pp. 1-2). IEEE.

Jiang, , Song, N., Yu, M., Chow, K.-P., Li, G., Liu, C., & Huang, W. (2021). DETECTING MALICIOUS PDF DOCUMENTS USING SEMI-SUPERVISED MACHINE LEARNING. *IFIP Advances in Information and Communication Technology*, 612, 135–155. DOI: 10.1007/978-3-030-88381-2_7

Jin, P., Kim, N., Lee, S., & Jeong, D. (2024). Forensic investigation of the dark web on the Tor network: Pathway toward the surface web. *International Journal of Information Security*, 23(1), 331–346. DOI: 10.1007/s10207-023-00745-4

John, K., Kogan, L., & Saleh, F. (2023). Smart Contracts and Decentralized Finance. *Annual Review of Financial Economics*, 15(1), 523–542. DOI: 10.1146/annurev-financial-110921-022806

Joshi, A., Han, M., & Wang, Y. (2018). *A Survey on Security and Privacy Issues of Blockchain Technology* (2). *1*(2), Article 2. DOI: 10.3934/mfc.2018007

Joshi, A., Raturi, A., Kumar, S., Dumka, A., & Singh, D. P. "Improved Security and Privacy in Cloud Data Security and Privacy: Measures and Attacks," *2022 International Conference on Fourth Industrial Revolution Based Technology and Practices (ICFIRTP)*, Uttarakhand, India, 2022, pp. 230-233, DOI: 10.1109/ICFIRTP56122.2022.10063186

Jurcut, A., Niculcea, T., Ranaweera, P., & Le-Khac, N. A. (2020). Security considerations for Internet of Things: A survey. *SN Computer Science*, 1(4), 1–19. DOI: 10.1007/s42979-020-00201-3

Kalyanaraman, S. (2023). An Artificial Intelligence Model for Effective Routing in WSN. In Sivaram, P. (Eds.), *Perspectives on Social Welfare Applications' Optimization and Enhanced Computer Applications* (pp. 67–88). IGI Global., DOI: 10.4018/978-1-6684-8306-0.ch005

Kannan, Y. (2024). Impact of Internet of Things (IoT) devices on Network Security at Financial Institutions. *Authorea Preprints*. DOI: 10.22541/au.171011417.76922216/v1

Karmous, N.. (2022), IoT Real-Time Attacks Classification Framework Using Machine Learning, *IEEE Ninth International Conference on Communications and Networking (ComNet)*. DOI: 10.1109/ComNet55492.2022.9998441

Karthiga, R. (2021). Transfer learning based breast cancer classification using one-hot encoding technique. In *2021 International Conference on Artificial Intelligence and Smart Systems (ICAIS)* (pp. 115-120). DOI: 10.1109/ICAIS50930.2021.9395930

Karthik, S. A., Hemalatha, R., Aruna, R., Deivakani, M., Reddy, R. V. K., & Boopathi, S. (2023). Study on Healthcare Security System-Integrated Internet of Things (IoT). In Perspectives and Considerations on the Evolution of Smart Systems (pp. 342-362). IGI Global.

Kaur, M., Zubair khan, M., Gupta, S., Noorwali, A., Chakraborty, C., & Kumar Pani, S. (2021). MBCP: Performance analysis of large scale mainstream blockchain consensus protocols. *IEEE, 9*. DOI: 10.1109/ACCESS.2021.3085187

Kaur, R., & Kaur, J. "Cloud computing security issues and its solution: A review," 2015 2nd International Conference on Computing for Sustainable Global Development (INDIACom), New Delhi, India, 2015, pp. 1198-1200.

Kaur, M., & Gupta, S. (2021). Blockchain Consensus Protocols: State-of-the-art and Future Directions. *2021 International Conference on Technological Advancements and Innovations (ICTAI)*, 446–453. DOI: 10.1109/ICTAI53825.2021.9673260

Kaur, P. (2022). *Isha Sharma, Rahul Kumar Singh* (1st ed.). Encryption Algorithms for Cloud Computing and Quantum Blockchain Book Artificial Intelligence, Machine Learning and Blockchain in Quantum Satellite, Drone and Network.

Kaur, S., & Randhawa, S. (2020). Dark Web: A Web of Crimes. *Wireless Personal Communications*, 112(4), 2131–2158. DOI: 10.1007/s11277-020-07143-2

Kautish, S., A, R., & Vidyarthi, A. (2022, September). R. A and A. Vidyarthi, "SDMTA: Attack Detection and Mitigation Mechanism for DDoS Vulnerabilities in Hybrid Cloud Environment,". *IEEE Transactions on Industrial Informatics*, 18(9), 6455–6463. DOI: 10.1109/TII.2022.3146290

Kemp, S. (2024, February 20). *Digital 2024: India — DataReportal – Global Digital Insights*. DataReportal – Global Digital Insights. https://datareportal.com/reports/digital-2024-india#:~:text=The%20state%20of%20digital%20in%20India%20in %202024&text=There%20were%20751.5%20million%20internet,percent%20of %20the%20total%20population

Khonji, M., Iraqi, Y., & Jones, A. (2013). Phishing detection: A literature survey. *IEEE Communications Surveys and Tutorials*, 15(4), 2091–2121. DOI: 10.1109/ SURV.2013.032213.00009

Khraisat, A., Gondal, I., Vamplew, P., & Kamruzzaman, J. (2019). Survey of intrusion detection systems: Techniques, datasets and challenges. *Cybersecurity*, 2(1), 20. DOI: 10.1186/s42400-019-0038-7

Kim, D., Gil, J. M., Wang, G., & Kim, S. H. (2013). Integrated SDN and non-SDN network management approaches for future internet environment. In Multimedia 20 and Ubiquitous Engineering: MUE 2013 (pp. 529-536). Springer Netherlands. DOI: 10.1007/978-94-007-6738-6_64

Kim, H., Lee, H., & Lim, H. (2020, February). Performance of packet analysis between observer and wireshark. In *2020 22nd International Conference on Advanced Communication Technology (ICACT)* (pp. 268-271). IEEE. DOI: 10.23919/ ICACT48636.2020.9061452

Kim, J., Kim, Y., Yegneswaran, V., Porras, P., Shin, S., & Park, T. (2023). *Extended data plane architecture for in-network security services in software-defined networks*,Computers & Security,124,102976,ISSN 0167-4048,DOI: 10.1016/j. cose.2022.102976

Kim, H., Chitti, R. B., & Song, J. (2010, May). Novel defense mechanism against data flooding attacks in wireless ad hoc networks. *IEEE Transactions on Consumer Electronics*, 56(2), 579–582. DOI: 10.1109/TCE.2010.5505973

Kim, H., & Feamster, N. (2013). Improving network management with software defined networking. *IEEE Communications Magazine*, 51(2), 114–119. DOI: 10.1109/MCOM.2013.6461195

Kreutz, D., Ramos, F. M., Verissimo, P. E., Rothenberg, C. E., Azodolmolky, S., & Uhlig, S. (2014). Software-defined networking: A comprehensive survey. *Proceedings of the IEEE*, 103(1), 14–76. DOI: 10.1109/JPROC.2014.2371999

Kulkarni, M., Goswami, B., & Paulose, J. (2021, February). Experimenting with scalability of software defined networks using pyretic and frenetic. In *International Conference on Computing Science, Communication and Security* (pp. 168-192). Cham: Springer International Publishing. DOI: 10.1007/978-3-030-76776-1_12

Kumari, A., Kumar, V., Abbasi, M. Y., Kumari, S., Chaudhary, P., & Chen, C.-M. (2020). CSEF: Cloud-Based Secure and Efficient Framework for Smart Medical System Using ECC. *IEEE Access : Practical Innovations, Open Solutions*, 8, 107838–107852. DOI: 10.1109/ACCESS.2020.3001152

Kumar, S., Tiwari, P., & Zymbler, M. (2019). Internet of Things is a revolutionary approach for future technology enhancement: A review. *Journal of Big Data*, 6(1), 111. Advance online publication. DOI: 10.1186/s40537-019-0268-2

Kumar, V., & Sinha, D. (2023). Synthetic attack data generation model applying generative adversarial network for intrusion detection. *Computers & Security*, 125, 103054. DOI: 10.1016/j.cose.2022.103054

Kunhare, N., Tiwari, R., & Dhar, J. (2020). Particle swarm optimization and feature selection for intrusion detection system. *Sadhana*, 45(1), 109. DOI: 10.1007/s12046-020-1308-5

Kusumaputri, F. H., & Arifin, A. S. (2022). Anomaly detection based on NSL-KDD using XGBoost with Optuna tuning. In *2022 7th International Conference on Business and Industrial Research (ICBIR)* (pp. 586-591). DOI: 10.1109/ICBIR54589.2022.9786429

Kvarda, L., & Hnyk, P. (2017). *Software Implementation of Secure Firmware Update in IoT Concept* (Vol. 15). Information And Communication Technologies And Services.

Lai, S.-T., & Leu, F.-Y. "A Security Threats Measurement Model for Reducing Cloud Computing Security Risk," 2015 9th International Conference on Innovative Mobile and Internet Services in Ubiquitous Computing, Santa Catarina, Brazil, 2015, pp. 414-419, DOI: 10.1109/IMIS.2015.64

Lakshmanan Nataraj et al. (2021). OMD: Orthogonal Malware Detection Using Audio, Image, and Static Features. *ArXiv (Cornell University)*. https://doi.org//arxiv.2111.04710DOI: 10.48550

Lamport, L., Shostak, R. E., & Pease, M. C. (1982). The Byzantine Generals problem. *ACM Transactions on Programming Languages and Systems*, 4(3), 382–401. DOI: 10.1145/357172.357176

Lara, A., Kolasani, A., & Ramamurthy, B. (2013). Network innovation using openflow: A survey. *IEEE Communications Surveys and Tutorials*, 16(1), 493–512. DOI: 10.1109/SURV.2013.081313.00105

Lashkari, B., & Musilek, P. (2021). A comprehensive review of blockchain consensus mechanisms. *IEEE Access: Practical Innovations, Open Solutions*, 9, 43620–43652. DOI: 10.1109/ACCESS.2021.3065880

Lavania, G., & Sharma, G. (2023). *Security on social media platform using private blockchain*. Lecture Notes in Networks and Systems. DOI: 10.1007/978-3-031-22018-0_20

Lee, J. (2018). Patch transporter: Incentivized, decentralized software patch system for WSN and IoT environments. *Sensors (Basel)*, 18(2), 574. Advance online publication. DOI: 10.3390/s18020574 PMID: 29438337

Lei Cui a b, Youyang Qu et al.(2020), Detecting false data attacks using machine learning techniques in smart grid: A survey, Journal of Network and Computer Applications Volume 170.

Leteane, O., & Ayalew, Y. (2024). Improving the trustworthiness of traceability data in food supply chain using blockchain and trust model. *The JBBA*, 7(1), 1–12. Advance online publication. DOI: 10.31585/jbba-7-1-(2)2024

Li, . (2019). Research on KNN Algorithm in Malicious PDF Files Classification under Adversarial Environment. *Proceedings of the 2019 4th International Conference on Big Data and Computing - ICBDC 2019*. DOI: 10.1145/3335484.3335527

Liang, X., & Kim, Y. (2021, January). A survey on security attacks and solutions in the IoT network. In 2021 IEEE 11th annual computing and communication workshop and conference (CCWC) (pp. 0853-0859). IEEE. DOI: 10.1109/CCWC51732.2021.9376174

Liao, D., Huang, S., Tan, Y., & Bai, G. "Network threat identifying method based on gan model." In *2020 International Conference on Computer Communication and Network Security (CCNS)*, pp. 153-156. IEEE, 2020. DOI: 10.1109/CCNS50731.2020.00041

Li, Q., Liu, W., Wu, H., Xie, C., & Yang, W. (2020). LSTM based phishing detection for big email data. *IEEE Transactions on Big Data*, 8(1), 278–288. DOI: 10.1109/TBDATA.2020.2978915

Liu, K., Wang, F., Ding, Z., Liang, S., Yu, Z., & Zhou, Y. (2022). A review of knowledge graph application scenarios in cyber security. *arXiv preprint arXiv:2204.04769*.

Liu, R., & Nicholas, C. (2023). *A Feature Set of Small Size for the PDF Malware Detection*. https://arxiv.org/pdf/2308.04704

Liu, W. "Research on cloud computing security problem and strategy," 2012 2nd International Conference on Consumer Electronics, Communications and Networks (CECNet), Yichang, China, 2012, pp. 1216-1219, DOI: 10.1109/CECNet.2012.6202020

Liu, J. (2023). CBDC application analysis and prospects. *BCP Business & Management*, 45, 1–6. DOI: 10.54691/bcpbm.v42i.4543

Liu, J., Lin, L., Cai, Z., Wang, J., & Kim, H. (2024). Deep web data extraction based on visual information processing. *Journal of Ambient Intelligence and Humanized Computing*, 15(2), 1481–1491. DOI: 10.1007/s12652-017-0587-0

Liu, W., Zhang, Y., Tang, Y., Wang, H., & Wei, Q. (2023). ALScA: A Framework for Using Auxiliary Learning Side-Channel Attacks to Model PUFs. *IEEE Transactions on Information Forensics and Security*, 18, 804–817. DOI: 10.1109/TIFS.2022.3227445

Liu, Y., He, D., Obaidat, M. S., Kumar, N., Khan, M. K., & Raymond Choo, K.-K. (2020). Blockchain-based identity management systems: A review. *Journal of Network and Computer Applications*, 166, 102731. DOI: 10.1016/j.jnca.2020.102731

Liu, Y., Wang, J., Yan, Z., Wan, Z., & Ja¨ntti, R. (2023). A survey on blockchain-based trust management for Internet of Things. *IEEE Internet of Things Journal*, 10(7), 5898–5922. DOI: 10.1109/JIOT.2023.3237893

Li, , Wang, X., Shi, Z., Zhang, R., Xue, J., & Wang, Z. (2021). Boosting training for PDF malware classifier via active learning. *International Journal of Intelligent Systems*, 37(4), 2803–2821. DOI: 10.1002/int.22451

Li, , Wang, Y., Wang, Y., Ke, L., & Tan, Y. (2020). A feature-vector generative adversarial network for evading PDF malware classifiers. *Information Sciences*, 523, 38–48. DOI: 10.1016/j.ins.2020.02.075

Li, Y., & Liu, Q. (2021). A comprehensive review study of cyber-attacks and cyber security; Emerging trends and recent developments. *Energy Reports*, 7, 8176–8186. DOI: 10.1016/j.egyr.2021.08.126

Li, Z., Jin, H., Zou, D., & Yuan, B. (2020, March 1). Exploring New Opportunities to Defeat Low-Rate DDoS Attack in Container-Based Cloud Environment. *IEEE Transactions on Parallel and Distributed Systems*, 31(3), 695–706. DOI: 10.1109/TPDS.2019.2942591

Lorincz, J., Kukuruzović, A., & Blažević, Z. (2024). A Comprehensive Overview of Network Slicing for Improving the Energy Efficiency of Fifth-Generation Networks. *Sensors (Basel)*, 24(10), 3242. DOI: 10.3390/s24103242 PMID: 38794095

Luo, J.-L., Yu, S.-Z., & Peng, S.-J. (2020). SDN/NFV-Based Security Service Function Tree for Cloud. *IEEE Access : Practical Innovations, Open Solutions*, 8, 38538–38545. DOI: 10.1109/ACCESS.2020.2974569

Mahbub, M. Shami, S. and Alam, S. M. (2021). *Adaptive security in 5G networks Challenges and solutions," IEEE Communications Magazine*, 59, no. 4, pp. 20-26. Sikder, S. Rahmati, A. and Saxena,N. (2022). *Lightweight security mechanisms for 5G IoT devices," IEEE Transactions on Mobile Computing*, l. 21, no. 1, pp. 27-39.

Mahmood, T., & Afzal, U. (2013). Security Analytics: Big Data Analytics for cybersecurity: A review of trends, techniques and tools. *2013 2nd National Conference on Information Assurance (NCIA)*. DOI: 10.1109/NCIA.2013.6725337

Mamushiane, L., Lysko, A., Dlamini, S. (2018, April). A comparative evaluation of the performance of popular SDN controllers. In 2018 Wireless Days (WD) (pp. 54-59). IEEE.

Manoharan, & Sarker, M. (2024). Revolutionizing Cybersecurity: Unleashing the Power of Artificial Intelligence and Machine Learning for Next-Generation Threat Detection. *International Research Journal of Modernization in Engineering Technology and Science*. Advance online publication. DOI: 10.56726/IRJMETS32644

Mansour, M., Gamal, A., Ahmed, A. I., Said, L. A., Elbaz, A., Herencsar, N., & Soltan, A. (2023). Internet of things: A comprehensive overview on protocols, architectures, technologies, simulation tools, and future directions. *Energies*, 16(8), 3465. DOI: 10.3390/en16083465

Markets and Markets. (2024). *Cybersecurity Market* (TC 3485; p. 597). https://www.marketsandmarkets.com/Market-Reports/cyber-security-market-505.html

Martsinkevich et al. (2023). Algorithms for extracting lines, paragraphs with their properties in PDF documents. *E3S Web of Conferences, 389*, 08024. https://doi.org/DOI: 10.1051/e3sconf/202338908024

Marx, J., & Cheong, M. (2023). Decentralised social media: Scoping review and future research directions. In *International Conference on Information Systems (ICIS 2023): Rising like a Phoenix: Emerging from the Pandemic and Reshaping Human Endeavors with Digital Technologies.*

Maseer, Z. K., Yusof, R., Bahaman, N., Mostafa, S. A., & Foozy, C. F. M. (2021). Benchmarking of machine learning for anomaly based intrusion detection systems in the CICIDS2017 dataset. *IEEE Access : Practical Innovations, Open Solutions*, 9, 22351–22370. DOI: 10.1109/ACCESS.2021.3056614

Maundrill, B. (2024). PDF Malware on the Rise, Used to Spread WikiLoader, Ursnif and DarkGate. Infosecurity Magazine; *Infosecurity Magazine*. https://www .infosecurity-magazine.com/news/pdf-malware-on-the-rise/#:~:text=PDF%20 threats%20are%20on%20the

McKeown, N., Anderson, T., Balakrishnan, H., Parulkar, G., Peterson, L., Rexford, J., Shenker, S., & Turner, J. (2008). OpenFlow: Enabling innovation in campus networks. *Computer Communication Review*, 38(2), 69–74. DOI: 10.1145/1355734.1355746

Mell, P., & Grance, T. Version 15 The NIST definition of cloud computing October 7.National Institute of Standards and Technology; 2009 https://csrc.nist.gov/ groups/ SNS/cloud-computing

Meneghello, F., Calore, M., Zucchetto, D., Polese, M., & Zanella, A. (2019). IoT: Internet of threats? A survey of practical security vulnerabilities in real IoT devices. *IEEE Internet of Things Journal*, 6(5), 8182–8201. DOI: 10.1109/JIOT.2019.2935189

Mentsiev, A. U., Guzueva, E. R., & Magomaev, T. R. (2020, April). Security challenges of the Industry 4.0. []. IOP Publishing.]. *Journal of Physics: Conference Series*, 1515(3), 032074. DOI: 10.1088/1742-6596/1515/3/032074

Miki, T., Miura, N., Sonoda, H., Mizuta, K., & Nagata, M. (2020, January). A Random Interrupt Dithering SAR Technique for Secure ADC Against Reference-Charge Side-Channel Attack. *IEEE Transactions on Circuits and Wystems. II, Express Briefs*, 67(1), 14–18. DOI: 10.1109/TCSII.2019.2901534

Miller, L., & Pahl, M.-O. (2024). Collaborative cybersecurity using blockchain: A survey. *arXiv, 1*(1), 35.

Miller, S. D., & Venkatesan, R. (2009). Expander Graphs Based on GRH with an Application to Elliptic Curve Cryptography. *Journal of Number Theory*, 129(6), 1491–1504. DOI: 10.1016/j.jnt.2008.11.006

Mishra, A., Mishra, S., & Panday, S. (2024). Security Analysis of Password-based Authenticated Key Exchange Protocols.

Mohammad Rafsun Islam, K. M. Aktheruzzaman (2020), An Analysis of Cyber security Attacks against Internet of Things and Security Solutions, Journal of Computer and Communications ISSNPrint: 2327-5219,ISSN Online: 2327-5227

Mohammed.,….. (2021). *Malware Detection Using Frequency Domain-Based Image Visualization and Deep Learning.* ArXiv.org. /arXiv.2101.10578DOI: 10.24251/ HICSS.2021.858

Mohindru, V., & Garg, A. (2021), Security attacks in internet of things: a review, Recent Innovations in Computing. p. 679–693. Singapore. DOI: 10.1007/978-981-15-8297-4_54

Mohit, Singh, Daliya1. (2024). The Role of Cybersecurity in Blockchain. Indian Scientific Journal Of Research in Engineering And Management DOI: 10.55041/ IJSREM30686

Mohitkirange. (2022, November 20). An article on blockchain structure. *GeeksforGeeks.*https://www.geeksforgeeks.org/blockchain-structure/

Monrat, A., Schelén, O., & Andersson, K. (2019). A survey of blockchain from the perspectives of applications, challenges, and opportunities. *IEEE, 7.* DOI: 10.1109/ ACCESS.2019.2936094

Mooijman, P., Catal, C., Tekinerdogan, B., Lommen, A., & Blokland, M. (2023). The effects of data balancing approaches: A case study. *Applied Soft Computing,* 132, 109853. DOI: 10.1016/j.asoc.2022.109853

Moore, A. P., Capelli, D. M., Caron, T. C., Shaw, E., Spooner, D., & Trzeciak, R. F. (2011). A preliminary model of insider theft of intellectual property. *Journal of Wireless Mobile Networks, Ubiquitous Computing and Dependable Applications,*2(1).

Morgado, A., Mohammed, K., Huq, S., Mumtaz, S., & Rodriguez, J. (2018). *A survey of 5G technologies: regulatory, standardization and industrial perspectives, Digital Communications and Networks,*4,2,2018,87-97,ISSN 2352-8648, https://doi .org/DOI: 10.1016/j.dcan.2017.09.010

Moubarak, J., Filiol, E., & Chamoun, M. (2018). On blockchain security and relevant attacks. *IEEE,* 1–6. DOI: 10.1109/MENACOMM.2018.8371010

Mousavi, S. K., Ghaffari, A., Besharat, S., & Afshari, H. (2021). Security of internet of things based on cryptographic algorithms: A survey. *Wireless Networks,* 27(2), 1515–1555. DOI: 10.1007/s11276-020-02535-5

Mrabet, H., Belguith, S., Alhomoud, A., & Jemai, A. (2020). A survey of IoT security based on a layered architecture of sensing and data analysis. *Sensors (Basel)*, 20(13), 3625. DOI: 10.3390/s20133625 PMID: 32605178

Mudigonda, N. (2022, August). A method for network intrusion detection using deep learning. *J Stud Res*, 11(3). Advance online publication. DOI: 10.47611/jsrhs. v11i3.2875

Musa, A. (2020). Forensic analysis of peer-to-peer network traffic with Wireshark. *Journal of Science and Technology*, 1(2), 92–99.

Musleh, A. S., Chen, G., & Dong, Z. Y. (2020, May). A Survey on the Detection Algorithms for False Data Injection Attacks in Smart Grids. *IEEE Transactions on Smart Grid*, 11(3), 2218–2234. DOI: 10.1109/TSG.2019.2949998

Mustafa, G., Ashraf, R., ... (2018), A review of data security and cryptographic techniques in IoT based devices, Conference: ICFNDS '18 Proceedings of the 2nd International Conference on Future Networks and Distributed Systems at Amman, Jordan

Najmi, K. Y., AlZain, M. A., Masud, M., Jhanjhi, N. Z., Al-Amri, J., & Baz, M. (2023). A survey on security threats and countermeasures in IoT to achieve users confidentiality and reliability. *Materials Today: Proceedings*, 81, 377–382. DOI: 10.1016/j.matpr.2021.03.417

Nath, P., Mushahary, J., Roy, U., Brahma, M., & Singh, P. (2023). AI and blockchain-based source code vulnerability detection and prevention system for multiparty software development. *Elsevier, 106*. DOI: 10.1016/j.compeleceng.2023.108607

Naval, S., Laxmi, V., Rajarajan, M., Gaur, M. S., & Conti, M. (2015, December). Employing Program Semantics for Malware Detection. *IEEE Transactions on Information Forensics and Security*, 10(12), 2591–2604. DOI: 10.1109/TIFS.2015.2469253

Ndatinya, V., Xiao, Z., Manepalli, V. R., Meng, K., & Xiao, Y. (2015). Network forensics analysis using Wireshark. *International Journal of Security and Networks*, 10(2), 91–106. DOI: 10.1504/IJSN.2015.070421

Nehete, C., Lohiya, A., Mulik, M., & Morankar, A. (2024). DeGram - Decentralized social media application. In *Proceedings of the 3rd International Conference on Applied Artificial Intelligence and Computing (ICAAIC 2024)*.

Neshenko, N., Bou-Harb, E., Crichigno, J., Kaddoum, G., & Ghani, N. (2019). Demystifying IoT security: An exhaustive survey on IoT vulnerabilities and a first empirical look on Internet-scale IoT exploitations. *IEEE Communications Surveys and Tutorials*, 21(3), 2702–2733. DOI: 10.1109/COMST.2019.2910750

Nie, L., Wu, Y., Wang, X., Guo, L., Wang, G., Gao, X., & Li, S. (2021). Threat identifying for secure social internet of things based on collaborative edge computing: A generative adversarial network-based approach. *IEEE Transactions on Computational Social Systems*, 9(1), 134–145. DOI: 10.1109/TCSS.2021.3063538

Nishanth, N., & Mujeeb, A. (2021, September). Modeling and Detection of Flooding-Based Denial of Service Attacks in Wireless Ad Hoc Networks Using Uncertain Reasoning. *IEEE Transactions on Cognitive Communications and Networking*, 7(3), 893–904. DOI: 10.1109/TCCN.2021.3055503

Number: CFP23CV1-DVD; ISBN: 978-1-6654-7450-4. Jan 2023.

Nunes, B. A. A., Mendonca, M., Nguyen, X. N., Obraczka, K., & Turletti, T. (2014). A survey of software-defined networking: Past, present, and future of programmable networks. *IEEE Communications Surveys and Tutorials*, 16(3), 1617–1634. DOI: 10.1109/SURV.2014.012214.00180

Nwobodo, N. L. K., Nwaimo, N. C. S., & Adegbola, N. E.Luther Kington Nwobodo-Chioma Susan NwaimoAyodeji Enoch Adegbola. (2024). Enhancing cybersecurity protocols in the era of big data and advanced analytics. *GSC Advanced Research and Reviews*, 19(3), 203–214. DOI: 10.30574/gscarr.2024.19.3.0211

O. A. Wahab, J. Bentahar, H. Otrok and A. Mourad, "Optimal Load Distribution for the Detection of VM-Based DDoS Attacks in the Cloud," in IEEE Transactions on Services Computing, vol. 13, no. 1, pp. 114-129, 1 Jan.-Feb. 2020, .DOI: 10.1109/TSC.2017.2694426

O'Connell, E., Moore, D., & Newe, T. (2020). Challenges Associated with Implementing 5G in Manufacturing. *Telecom*, 1(1), 48–67. DOI: 10.3390/telecom1010005

Ogonji, M. M., Okeyo, G., & Wafula, J. M. (2020). A survey on privacy and security of Internet of Things. *Computer Science Review*, 38, 100312. DOI: 10.1016/j.cosrev.2020.100312

Okur, C., & Dener, M. (2020), Detecting IoT Botnet Attacks Using Machine Learning Methods, International Conference on Information Security and Cryptology (ISCTURKEY), Electronic ISBN:978-1-6654-1863-8.

Omolara, A. E., Alabdulatif, A., Abiodun, O. I., Alawida, M., Alabdulatif, A., & Arshad, H. (2022). The internet of things security: A survey encompassing unexplored areas and new insights. *Computers & Security*, 112, 102494. DOI: 10.1016/j.cose.2021.102494

Oyelakin, A. M. (2023). *Overview and exploratory analyses of CICIDS 2017 intrusion detection dataset. Journal of Systems Engineering and Information Technology*.

Oyinloye, D. P., Teh, J. S., Jamil, N., & Alawida, M. (2021). Blockchain Consensus: An Overview of Alternative Protocols. *Symmetry*, 13(8), 1363. DOI: 10.3390/sym13081363

P. Mahalle, B. Anggorojati, N. Prasad, and R. Prasad (2013), Identity Authentication and Capability Based Access Control (IACAC) for the Internet of Things. Journal of Cyber Security and Mobility, DOI:DOI: 10.13052/jcsm2245-1439.142

Pal, O., Alam, B., Thakur, V., & Singh, S. (2021). Key management for blockchain technology. *ScienceDirect*, 7(1), 76–80. DOI: 10.1016/j.icte.2019.08.002

Pan, J.-S., Chen, S.-M., & Nguyen, N. T. (Eds.). "On cloud Computing Security Issues," ACIIDS 2012, Part II, LNAI 7197, pp. 560–569, 2012.

Panarello, A., Tapas, N., Merlino, G., Longo, F., & Puliafito, A. (2018). Blockchain and IoT integration: A systematic survey. *Sensors (Basel)*, 18(8), 2575. DOI: 10.3390/s18082575 PMID: 30082633

Pănescu, A.-T., & Manta, V. (2018). Smart contracts for research data rights management over the Ethereum blockchain network. *Science & Technology Libraries*, 37(3), 235–245. DOI: 10.1080/0194262X.2018.1474838

Panigrahi, R., & Borah, S. (2018). A detailed analysis of CICIDS2017 dataset for designing intrusion detection systems. *IACSIT International Journal of Engineering and Technology*, 7, 479–482.

Paravathi, C., Roshini, D., & Nayak, S. S. (2024). Packet Sniffing. *International Journal of Engineering and Management Research*, 14(1), 71–76.

Park, C., Lee, J., Kim, Y., Park, J.-G., Kim, H., & Hong, D. (2022). An enhanced ai-based network threat identifying system using generative adversarial networks. *IEEE Internet of Things Journal*, 10(3), 2330–2345. DOI: 10.1109/JIOT.2022.3211346

Park, C.-S., & Nam, H.-M. (2022). A new approach to constructing decentralized identifier for secure and flexible key rotation. *IEEE Internet of Things Journal*, 9(13), 10610–10624. DOI: 10.1109/JIOT.2021.3121722

Patrick, V. E., & Haie, A.-G. (2018). *Blockchain and the GDPR: The EU Blockchain Observatory Report* (Practitioner's Corner 531). EDPL. https://heinonline.org/HOL/LandingPage?handle=hein.journals/edpl4&div=88

Pawar, S., & Geetha, V. A. (2023). An implemented example of XKMS with web services. In *Risk Detection and Cyber Security for the Success of Contemporary Computing*. DOI: 10.4018/978-1-6684-9317-5.ch006

Pawar, S., & Gururaj, M., Roopa, Chiplunkar, N. N., & Samaga, R. (2022). Constraint based clustering technique for web services. In *International Conference on Advanced Network Technologies and Intelligent Computing* (pp. 89-107). Springer Nature Switzerland. https://doi.org/DOI: 10.1007/978-3-031-28180-8_7

Pawar, S., & Chiplunkar, N. N. (2018). Survey on discovery of web services. *Indian Journal of Science and Technology*, 11(16), 1–10. DOI: 10.17485/ijst/2018/v11i16/120397

Pawar, S., & GuruRaj, M. (2023). Dynamicity of web services and web scrapping. *Journal of Mines. Metals and Fuels*, 71(5), 645–649. DOI: 10.18311/jmmf/2023/34164

Phemius, K., Bouet, M., & Leguay, J. (2014, May). DISCO: Distributed SDN controllers in a multi-domain environment. In *2014 IEEE Network Operations and Management Symposium (NOMS)* (pp. 1-2). IEEE.

Phillip Williams et al. (2022), A survey on security in internet of things with a focus on the impact of emerging technologies, Internet of Things, Volume 19,ISSN 2542-6605, DOI: 10.1016/j.iot.2022.100564

Pinkston, J., Joshi, A., & Finin, T. (2003, July). A target-centric ontology for intrusion detection. In Workshop on Ontologies in Distributed Systems, held at The 18th International Joint Conference on Artificial Intelligence. Mavroeidis, V., & Bromander, S. (2017, September). Cyber threat intelligence model: an evaluation of taxonomies, sharing standards, and ontologies within cyber threat intelligence. In *2017 European Intelligence and Security Informatics Conference (EISIC)* (pp. 91-98). IEEE.

Poelman, M., & Iqbal, S. (2021). Investigating the Compliance of the GDPR: Processing Personal Data On A Blockchain. *2021 IEEE 5th International Conference on Cryptography, Security and Privacy (CSP)*, 38–44. DOI: 10.1109/CSP51677.2021.9357590

Pons, M., Valenzuela, E., Rodríguez, B., Nolazco-Flores, J. A., & Del-Valle-Soto, C. (2023). Utilization of 5G Technologies in IoT Applications: Current Limitations by Interference and Network Optimization Difficulties-A Review. *Sensors (Basel)*, 23(8), 3876. DOI: 10.3390/s23083876 PMID: 37112216

Popoola, O. Rodrigues, M. Marchang, J. Shenfield, A. Ikpehai, A. Popoola, J.(2024). *A critical literature review of security and privacy in smart home healthcare schemes adopting IoT & blockchain: Problems, challenges and solutions, Blockchain: Research and Applications,*5, 2,2024,100178,ISSN 2096-7209,DOI: 10.1016/j. bcra.2023.100178

Pourmirza, Z., & Walker, S. (2021, August). Electric vehicle charging station: Cyber security challenges and perspective. In 2021 IEEE 9th International Conference on Smart Energy Grid Engineering (SEGE) (pp. 111-116). IEEE.

Prajapati, B. B., & Chaubey, N. K. (2020). Quantum key distribution: The evolution. In Chaubey, N., & Prajapati, B. (Eds.), *Quantum cryptography and the future of cyber security* (pp. 29–43). IGI Global., DOI: 10.4018/978-1-7998-2253-0.ch002

Prakash, R., Jyoti, N., & Manjunatha, S. (2024). A survey of security chal- lenges, attacks in IoT. In *E3S Web of Conferences* (Vol. 491, p. 04018). EDP Sciences.

Pudjihartono, N., Fadason, T., Kempa-Liehr, A. W., & O'Sullivan, J. M. (2022). A review of feature selection methods for machine learning-based disease risk prediction. *Frontiers in Bioinformatics*, 2, 927312. Advance online publication. DOI: 10.3389/fbinf.2022.927312 PMID: 36304293

Putz, B., Vielberth, M., & Pernul, G. (2022). BISCUIT - Blockchain security incident reporting based on human observations. *ACM*, 1–6. DOI: 10.1145/3538969.3538984

Q. Huang, Y. Yang, W. Yue and Y. He, "Secure Data Group Sharing and Conditional Dissemination with Multi-Owner in Cloud Computing," in IEEE Transactions on Cloud Computing, vol. 9, no. 4, pp. 1607-1618, 1 Oct.-Dec. 2021, .DOI: 10.1109/ TCC.2019.2908163

Quinto, B. (2018, June 12). *Next-Generation Big Data*. Apress. http://books.google .ie/books?id=teZfDwAAQBAJ&printsec=frontcover&dq=Next-Generation+Big+ Data&hl=&cd=1&source=gbs_api

R. Ding, Y. Xu, H. Zhong, J. Cui and G. Min, "An Efficient Integrity Checking Scheme With Full Identity Anonymity for Cloud Data Sharing," in IEEE Transactions on Cloud Computing, vol. 11, no. 3, pp. 2922-2935, 1 July-Sept. 2023, .DOI: 10.1109/TCC.2023.3242140

Rachit, B., Bhatt, S., & Ragiri, P. R. (2021). Security trends in Internet of Things: A survey. *SN Applied Sciences*, 3(1), 1–14. DOI: 10.1007/s42452-021-04156-9

Raeisi-Varzaneh, M., Dakkak, O., Alaidaros, H., & Avci, ˙. I. (2024). Internet of Things: Security, Issues, Threats, and Assessment of Different Cryptographic Technologies. *Journal of Communication*, 19(2).

Rahmani, A. M., Bayramov, S., & Kiani Kalejahi, B. (2022). Internet of Things Applications: Opportunities and Threats. *Wireless Personal Communications*, 122(1), 451–476. DOI: 10.1007/s11277-021-08907-0 PMID: 34426718

Raj D.; Sagar A.K., "Vehicular Ad-hoc Networks: A Review on Applications and Security", 2023, Communications in Computer and Information Science, Volume-1921 CCIS, PP: 241-255, DOI: DOI: 10.1007/978-3-031-45124-9_19

Rajawat, S. S., Khatri, P., & Surange, G. (2022, December). Sniffit: A Packet Sniffing Tool Using Wireshark. In *International Conference on Communication, Networks and Computing* (pp. 203-212). Cham: Springer Nature Switzerland.

Rajmohan, T., Nguyen, P., & Ferry, N. (2022). A decade of research on patterns and architectures for IoT security. *Cybersecurity*, 5(1), 2. Advance online publication. DOI: 10.1186/s42400-021-00104-7

Ramu, C., Rao, T. S., & Rao, E. U. S. (2024). *Attack classification in network intrusion detection system based on optimization strategy and deep learning methodology.* Multimed Tools Appl. DOI: 10.1007/s11042-024-18558-5

Ranasinghe, H., & Halgamuge, M. N. (2021). Twitter sentiment data analysis of user behaviour on cryptocurrencies. In *Proceedings of Ranasinghe 2021 TwitterSD.*

Rani, S., Kataria, A., Sharma, V., Ghosh, S., Karar, V., Lee, K., & Choi, C. (2021). Threats and corrective measures for IoT security with observance of cybercrime: A survey. *Wireless Communications and Mobile Computing*, 2021(1), 1–30. DOI: 10.1155/2021/5579148

Rao, N. R., & Pandey, P. K. (2018). Security Analytics:Big Data Analytics for CybersecurityA Review of Trends, Techniques and Tools. *IJCRT, 6*(1), 579-584. https://www.ijcrt.org/papers/IJCRT1802412.pdf

Rasane, T.. (2023). Blockchain in CyberSecurity [JETIR]. *Journal of Emerging Technologies and Innovative Research*, 10(5), ●●●.

Rashid, A., Siddique, M. J., & Ahmed, S. M. (2020). Machine and deep learning based comparative analysis using hybrid approaches for intrusion detection system. In *2020 3rd International Conference on Advancements in Computational Sciences (ICACS)* (pp. 1-9). DOI: 10.1109/ICACS47775.2020.9055946

Rasool, Z. I., Abd Ali, R. S., & Abdulzahra, M. M. (2021, February). Network management in software-defined network: A survey. []. IOP Publishing.]. *IOP Conference Series. Materials Science and Engineering*, 1094(1), 012055. DOI: 10.1088/1757-899X/1094/1/012055

Rassam, & Maarof, Mohd. (2017). Big Data Analytics Adoption for Cybersecurity: A Review of Current Solutions, Requirements, Challenges and Trends. *Journal of Information Assurance and Security, 11*, 124–145. https://mirlabs.org/jias/secured/Volume12-Issue4/Paper14.pdf

Ravi Prakash, V.S. Anoop et al. (2022), Blockchain technology for cyber security: A text mining literature analysis, International Journal of Information Management Data Insights Volume 2, Issue 2.

Ravichandra, T., Madaan, Dr. V., Sharma, Dr. A., Deshmukh, Dr. S., Agrawal, Prof. Dr. R., Gumber, Dr. G., & Khan, Dr. M. (2024). A study on individual awareness and perception towards blockchain technology in India. *IJISAE, 12*(8), 239–250.

Rawal, S., Sharma, A., Kumar, S., & Pandey, H. (2017). Phishing detection in e-mails using machine learning. *International Journal of Applied Information Systems*, 12(7), 21–24. DOI: 10.5120/ijais2017451713

Rawat, R., Oki, O. A., Sankaran, K. S., Olasupo, O., Ebong, G. N., & Ajagbe, S. A. (2023). A new solution for cyber security in big data using machine learning approach. In *Lecture notes on data engineering and communications technologies* (pp. 495–505). DOI: 10.1007/978-981-99-0835-6_35

Rawat, D. B., Doku, R., & Garuba, M. (2021). Cybersecurity in big data era: From securing big data to data-driven security. *IEEE Transactions on Services Computing*, 14(6), 2055–2072. DOI: 10.1109/TSC.2019.2907247

Ray, S. (2019). 6 Easy Steps to Learn Naive Bayes Algorithm (with code in Python). *Analytics Vidhya.* https://www.analyticsvidhya.com/blog/2017/09/naive-bayes-explained/

Rhee, J., Riley, R., Lin, Z., Jiang, X., & Xu, D. (2014, January). Data-Centric OS Kernel Malware Characterization. *IEEE Transactions on Information Forensics and Security*, 9(1), 72–87. DOI: 10.1109/TIFS.2013.2291964

Rieck, , Trinius, P., Willems, C., & Holz, T. (2011). Automatic analysis of malware behaviour using machine learning. *Journal of Computer Security*, 19(4), 639–668. DOI: 10.3233/JCS-2010-0410

Rodrigues, B., Bocek, T., Lareida, A., Hausheer, D., Rafati, S., & Stiller, B. (2017). A blockchain-based architecture for collaborative DDoS mitigation with smart contracts. *Springer.* https://link.springer.com/content/pdf/10.1007/978-3-319-60774-0_2.pdf

Roy, D., & Dutta, M. (2022). A systematic review and research perspective on recommender systems. *Journal of Big Data*, 9(1), 59. DOI: 10.1186/s40537-022-00592-5

S.Simla Mercy, Dr.G.UmaraniSrikanth, "An Efficient Data Security System for Group Data Sharing in Cloud System Environment," 2014.

Sabrina De Capitani di Vimercati. Sara Foresti, StefanoParaboschi, Member, Gerardo Pelosi, and PierangelaSamarati, "Three server swapping for access confidentiality," IEEE Transaction on Cloud Computing, 2015. NehaMahakalkar, VaishaliSahare, "Implementation of re-encryption-based security mechanism to authenticate shared access in cloud computing," International Conference on 12 May 2017.

Sadhu, P. K., Yanambaka, V. P., & Abdelgawad, A. (2022). Internet of things: Security and solutions survey. *Sensors (Basel)*, 22(19), 7433. DOI: 10.3390/s22197433 PMID: 36236531

Saha, S., Karar, K., & Karmakar, R. (2024). Ethnos: An Ethereum-based online social networking system with two-factor authentication and trust score. In *Proceedings - 2nd International Conference on Advancement in Computation and Computer Technologies (InCACCT 2024)*.

Sakhi, Bandyopadhyay., Sunita, Sarkar., Somnath, Mukhopadhyay. (2023). Hiding Secret Data Using AES Encryption and DFS Graph Traversal in 3D Images. 1-4. DOI: 10.1109/ICEEICT56924.2023.10156957

Salagrama, S., Bibhu, V., & Rana, A. (2023). Blockchain based data integrity security management. *Elsevier, 215*, 331–339. DOI: 10.1016/j.procs.2022.12.035

Saleh, A. M. S. (2024). Blockchain for secure and decentralized artificial intelligence in cybersecurity: A comprehensive review. *Blockchain: Research and Applications*, 100193.

Salem, M., Taheri, S. and Yuan, J.S., 2018, November. Anomaly generation using generative adversarial networks in host-based intrusion detection. In 2018 9th IEEE Annual Ubiquitous Computing, Electronics & Mobile Communication Conference (UEMCON) (pp. 683-687). IEEE.

Salesforce, "Salesforce crm." https://www.salesforce.com/platform. [Online; accessed 25-Sep-2023]. Microsoft, "Windows azure." http://www.microsoft.com/azure. [Online; accessed 25-Sep-2023]. Google, "Google app engine." http://code.google.com/appengine. [Online; accessed 25-Sep-2023]. Amazon, "Amazon elastic computing cloud." https://aws.amazon.com/ ec2. [Online; accessed 26-Sep-2023] Q. Wang, C. Wang, J. Li, K. Ren, and W. Lou, "Enabling public verifiability and data dynamics for storage security in cloud computing," in Proc. of ESORICS'09, Saint Malo, France, Sep. 2009. P. Saripalli, and B. Walters, "QUIRC: A Quantitative Impact and Risk Assessment Framework for Cloud Security," 2010 IEEE 3rd Intl. Conf. on Cloud Computing; Miami, FL, July, 2010.

Salloum, S., Alshurideh, M., Elnagar, N., & Shaalan, K. (2021). Phishing email detection using natural language processing techniques: A literature survey. *Procedia Computer Science*, 189, 19–28. DOI: 10.1016/j.procs.2021.05.077

Salloum, S., Alshurideh, M., Elnagar, N., & Shaalan, K. (2022). A systematic literature review on phishing email detection using natural language processing techniques. *IEEE Access : Practical Innovations, Open Solutions*, 10, 65703–65727. DOI: 10.1109/ACCESS.2022.3183083

Salman, O., Elhajj, I. H., Kayssi, A., & Chehab, A. (2016, April). SDN controllers: A comparative study. In 2016 18th mediterranean electrotechnical conference (MELECON) (pp. 1-6). IEEE. DOI: 10.1109/MELCON.2016.7495430

Samah Osama Kamel, Nadia H Hegazi. (2018). A Proposed Model of IoT Security Management System Based on A study of Internet of Things (IoT) Security. *International Journal of Scientific and Engineering Research*.

Sambana, B. (2020). Block chain Approach to Cyber Security Vulnerabilities Attacks And Potential Counter Measures. *International Journal of Security and Its Applications*, 14(1), 1–14. DOI: 10.33832/ijsia.2020.14.1.01

Sami Berkani, A., Moumen, H., Benharzallah, S., Yahiaoui, S., & Bounceur, A. (2023). Blockchain use cases in the sports industry: A systematic review. *Springer*. DOI: 10.1007/s44227-024-00022-3

Sanchez, F., & Duan, Z. (2012). *A sender-centric approach to detecting phishing emails. In 2012 international conference on cyber security*. IEEE.

Sangeetha, S., Baskar, K., Kalaivaani, P. C. D., & Kumaravel, T. "Deep-hierarchical learning -based Early Parkinson's Disease Detection from Brain MRI Image," 2023 7th International Conference on Smart Computing and Control Systems (ICICCS), Madurai, India, 2023, pp. 490-495, DOI: 10.1109/ICICCS56967.2023.10142754

Saqlain, J. (2018),"IoT and 5G: History evolution and its architecture their compatibility and future", Metropolia University of Applied Sciences Safa Ahmed et al. (2018), Overview for Internet of Things: Basics, Components and Applications, J. of University of Anbar for Pure Science: Vol.12: No.3, ISSN: 1991-8941.

Sartayeva, Y., & Chan, H. C. (2023). A survey on indoor positioning security and privacy. *Computers & Security*, 131, 103293. DOI: 10.1016/j.cose.2023.103293

Sasidharan, S., & Chandra, S. K. (2014, July). Defining future SDN based network management systems characterization and approach. In Fifth International Conference on Computing, Communications and Networking Technologies (ICCCNT) (pp. 1-5). IEEE. DOI: 10.1109/ICCCNT.2014.6963137

Sayeed, S., & Marco-Gisbert, H. (2019). Assessing blockchain consensus and security mechanisms against the 51% attack. *Applied Sciences (Basel, Switzerland)*, 9(9), 1788. Advance online publication. DOI: 10.3390/app9091788

Sayyah Ensan, S., Nagarajan, K., Khan, M. N. I., & Ghosh, S. (2021, December). "SCARE: Side Channel Attack on In-Memory Computing for Reverse Engineering," in IEEE Transactions on Very Large Scale Integration (VLSI). *IEEE Transactions on Very Large Scale Integration (VLSI) Systems*, 29(12), 2040–2051. DOI: 10.1109/TVLSI.2021.3110744

Schlatt, V., Guggenberger, T., Schmid, J., & Urbach, N. (2023). Attacking the trust machine: Developing an information systems research agenda for blockchain cybersecurity. *Elsevier, 68*. DOI: 10.1016/j.ijinfomgt.2022.102470

Science and Technology. Vol. 4, No. 1, 2018, pp. 1-5. doi: DOI: 10.11648/j.ijdst.20180401.1

Sekhar, Ch. Panja Hemanth Kumar, K. Venkata Rao, and M. H. M. Krishna Prasad. "A comparative study on network threat identifying system using deep-hierarchical learning algorithms and enhancement of deep-hierarchical learning models using generative adversarial network (GAN)." In High Effectiveness Computing and Networking: Select Proceedings of CHSN 2021, pp. 143-155. Singapore: Springer Singapore, 2022.

Sendi, A. S., & Cheriet, M. "Cloud Computing: A Risk Assessment Model," *2014 IEEE International Conference on Cloud Engineering*, Boston, MA, USA, 2014, pp. 147-152, DOI: 10.1109/IC2E.2014.17

Seo, E., Song, H. M., & Kim, H. K. "GIDS: GAN based threat identifying system for in-vehicle network." In 2018 16th Annual Conference on Privacy, Security and Trust (PST), pp. 1-6. IEEE, 2018.

Shah, A., Yaqoob, I., Khan, M. A., Imran, M., & Akhunzada, A. (2020). Blockchain for IoT-based smart homes: A review of cur- rent trends and research challenges. *Computer Networks*, 172, 107248. DOI: 10.1016/j.comnet.2020.107248

Shaharuddin, S., Maulud, K. N. A., Rahman, S. A. F. S. A., Ani, A. I. C., & Pradhan, B. (2023). The role of IoT sensor in smart building context for indoor fire hazard scenario: A systematic review of interdisciplinary articles. *Internet of Things : Engineering Cyber Physical Human Systems*, 22, 100803. DOI: 10.1016/j.iot.2023.100803

Shahriar, M. H., Haque, N. I., Rahman, M. A., & Alonso, M. G-ids: Generative adversarial networks assisted threat identifying system. In2020 IEEE 44th Annual Computers, Software, and Applications Conference (COMPSAC) 2020 Jul 13 (pp. 376-385). IEEE.

Shakarian, P., & Shakarian, J. 2016, March. Socio-cultural modeling for cyber threat actors. In *Workshops at the Thirtieth AAAI Conference on Artificial Intelligence.*

Shammar, E. A., Zahary, A. T., & Al-Shargabi, A. A. (2021). A survey of IoT and blockchain integration: Security perspective. *IEEE Access : Practical Innovations, Open Solutions*, 9, 156114–156150. DOI: 10.1109/ACCESS.2021.3129697

Sharma, A., & Bhatt, A. P. (2021). Quantum Cryptography for Securing IoT-Based Healthcare Systems. In Advances in information security, privacy, and ethics book series (pp. 124–147). DOI: 10.4018/978-1-7998-6677-0.ch007

Sharma, R. (2012), Study of Latest Emerging Trends on Cyber Security and its challenges to Society, International Journal of Scientific & Engineering Research, Volume 3, Issue 6, 1ISSN 2229-5518.

Sharma, K., Malik, A., Batra, I., Sanwar Hosen, A. S. M., Latif Sarker, M. A., & Han, D. S. (2023). Technologies Behind the Smart Grid and Internet of Things: A System Survey. *Computers, Materials & Continua*, 75(3). Advance online publication. DOI: 10.32604/cmc.2023.035638

Sharma, M., Choudhary, V., Bhatia, R. S., Malik, S., Raina, A., & Khandelwal, H. (2021). Leveraging the power of quantum computing for breaking RSA encryption. *Cyber-Physical Systems*, 7(2), 73–92. DOI: 10.1080/23335777.2020.1811384

Sharma, N., Shamkuwar, M., & Singh, I. (2019). The History, Present and Future with IoT. In Balas, V., Solanki, V., Kumar, R., & Khari, M. (Eds.), *Internet of Things and Big Data Analytics for Smart Generation. Intelligent Systems Reference Library* (Vol. 154). Springer. DOI: 10.1007/978-3-030-04203-5_3

Sharma, P., Banerjee, S., Tandel, S., Aguiar, R., Amorim, R., & Pinheiro, D. (2013, May). Enhancing network management frameworks with SDN-like control. In *2013 IFIP/IEEE International Symposium on Integrated Network Management (IM 2013)* (pp. 688-691). IEEE.

Sharma, R., & Arya, R. (2023). Security threats and measures in the Internet of Things for smart city infrastructure: A state of art. *Transactions on Emerging Telecommunications Technologies*, 34(11), e4571. DOI: 10.1002/ett.4571

Sharma, V., You, I., Andersson, K., Palmieri, F., Rehmani, M. H., & Lim, J. (2020). Security, privacy and trust for smart mobile-Internet of Things (M-IoT): A survey. *IEEE Access : Practical Innovations, Open Solutions*, 8, 167123–167163. DOI: 10.1109/ACCESS.2020.3022661

Shaw, R., & Parveen, S. (2024, March). Literature Review on Packet Sniffing: Essential for Cybersecurity & Network Security. In *2024 5th International Conference on Intelligent Communication Technologies and Virtual Mobile Networks (ICICV)* (pp. 715-719). IEEE.

Sheth, A., & Bhosale, S. (2021) Research Paper on Cyber Security, Contemporary Research in INDIA (ISSN 2231-2137).

Shijo, P. V., & Salim, A. (2015). Integrated Static and Dynamic Analysis for Malware Detection. *Procedia Computer Science*, 46, 804–811. DOI: 10.1016/j. procs.2015.02.149

Shirvani, M. H., & Masdari, M. (2023). A survey study on trust-based security in Internet of Things: Challenges and issues. *Internet of Things : Engineering Cyber Physical Human Systems*, 21, 100640. DOI: 10.1016/j.iot.2022.100640

Shi, S., He, D., Li, L., Kumar, N., Khan, M. K., & Choo, K. R. (2020). Applications of blockchain in ensuring the security and privacy of electronic health record systems: A survey. *Computers & Security*, 97, 101966. DOI: 10.1016/j.cose.2020.101966 PMID: 32834254

Shruti, P., & Chandraleka, R. (2017), Elliptic Curve Cryptography Security in the Context of Internet of Things, International Journal of Scientific & Engineering Research Volume 8, Issue 5,ISSN 2229-5518

Shu, D., Leslie, N. O., Kamhoua, C. A., & Tucker, C. S. "Generative adversarial attacks against threat identifying systems using active learning." In *Proceedings of the 2nd ACM workshop on wireless security and machine learning*, pp. 1-6. 2020.

Šimunić, S., Bernaca, D., & Lenac, K. (2021). Verifiable computing applications in blockchain. *IEEE, 9*, 156729–156745. DOI: 10.1109/ACCESS.2021.3129314

Singh, D., Tripathi, G., & Jara, A. J. (2014), A survey of internet of things: future vision, architecture, challenge and services, IEEE world forum on internet of things, Seoul, South Korea, p. 287–92.

Singh, A. P., & Singh, M. D. (2014). Analysis of host-based and network-based intrusion detection system. *IJCNIS*, 6(8), 41–47. DOI: 10.5815/ijcnis.2014.08.06

Singh, A., Kumar, G., Saha, R., Conti, M., Alazab, M., & Thomas, R. (2022). A survey and taxonomy of consensus protocols for blockchains. *Journal of Systems Architecture*, 127, 102503. DOI: 10.1016/j.sysarc.2022.102503

Singh, G., & Kinger, S. (2013). A Study of Encryption Algorithms (RSA, DES, 3DES and AES) for Information Security. *International Journal of Computer Applications*, 67(19), 33–38. DOI: 10.5120/11507-7224

Singh, S., & Kim, S. (2021). Blockchain technology for decentralized IoT security and privacy: A comprehensive survey. *Telecommunication Systems*, 76, 139–154. DOI: 10.1007/s11235-021-00797-5

Siwakoti, Y. R., Bhurtel, M., Rawat, D. B., Oest, A., & Johnson, R. C. (2023). Advances in IOT security: Vulnerabilities, enabled Criminal Services, attacks and countermeasures. *IEEE Internet of Things Journal*, 10(13), 11224–11239. DOI: 10.1109/JIOT.2023.3252594

Smadi, S., Aslam, N., & Zhang, L. (2018). Detection of online phishing email using dynamic evolving neural network based on reinforcement learning. *Decision Support Systems*, 107, 88–102. DOI: 10.1016/j.dss.2018.01.001

Smiliotopoulos, C., Kambourakis, G., & Kolias, C. (2024). Detecting lateral movement: A systematic survey. *Heliyon*, 10(4), e26317. DOI: 10.1016/j.heliyon.2024.e26317 PMID: 38404775

Smutz, C., & Stavrou, A. (2016). *When a Tree Falls: Using Diversity in Ensemble Classifiers to Identify Evasion in Malware Detectors*. DOI: 10.14722/ndss.2016.23078

Soepeno, R. A. A. P. (2023). Wireshark: An Effective Tool for Network Analysis.

Somani, G., Gaur, M. S., Sanghi, D., Conti, M., & Buyya, R. (2017). DDoS attacks in cloud computing: Issues, taxonomy, and future directions. *Computer Communications*, 107, 30–48. DOI: 10.1016/j.comcom.2017.03.010

Sood, T., Prakash, S., Sharma, S., Singh, A., & Choubey, H. (2022). Threat identifying system in wireless sensor network using conditional generative adversarial network. *Wireless Personal Communications*, 126(1), 911–931. DOI: 10.1007/s11277-022-09776-x

Sott, M. K., Furstenau, L. B., Kipper, L. M., Giraldo, F. D., Lopez-Robles, J. R., Cobo, M. J., Zahid, A., Abbasi, Q. H., & Imran, M. A. (2020). Precision techniques and agriculture 4.0 technologies to promote sustainability in the coffee sector: State of the art, challenges and future trends. *IEEE Access : Practical Innovations, Open Solutions*, 8, 149854–149867. DOI: 10.1109/ACCESS.2020.3016325

Srivastava, N., & Chandra Jaiswal, U. (2019). Big Data Analytics Technique in Cyber Security. *RE:view*, 579–585. Advance online publication. DOI: 10.1109/ICCMC.2019.8819634

Stillions, R. (2014). The DML model. *Retrieved Jan, 29*, 2022.

Swaminathan, K. A Novel Composite Threat identifying System (CIDS) for Wireless sensor, Network Proceedings of the International Conference on Smart Data Communication Technologies and Internet of Things (IDCIoT 2023) DVD Part

Swaminathan. K, V. Ravindran, R. P. Ponraj, V. N, V. P. M and B. K, "Optimizing Energy Efficacy in Sensor Networks with the Virtual Power Routing Scheme (VPRS)," 2023 Second International Conference on Augmented Intelligence and

Syed, Z., Padia, A., Finin, T., Mathews, L., & Joshi, A. (2016, March). UCO: A unified cybersecurity ontology. In *Workshops at the thirtieth AAAI conference on artificial intelligence*.

Syed, A., & Gadgay, B. (2023). A Black Hole Attack Protection Approach in IoT-Based Applications Using RLNC. In *Contemporary Challenges for Cyber Security and Data Privacy* (pp. 151–165). IGI Global. DOI: 10.4018/979-8-3693-1528-6.ch009

Systems, S. (2023). *ICAISS*. Trichy., DOI: 10.1109/ICAISS58487.2023.10250536

T. Halabi and M. Bellaiche, "Towards Security-Based Formation of Cloud Federations: A Game Theoretical Approach," in IEEE Transactions on Cloud Computing, vol. 8, no. 3, pp. 928-942, 1 July-Sept. 2020, .DOI: 10.1109/TCC.2018.2820715

Taherdoost, H. (2023). Security and internet of things: Benefits, challenges, and future perspectives. *Electronics (Basel)*, 12(8), 1901. DOI: 10.3390/electronics12081901

Tama, D., & Wicaksana, A. (2023). Performance evaluation of decentralized social media on near protocol blockchain. In *Proceedings of the 2023 17th International Conference on Ubiquitous Information Management and Communication (IMCOM 2023)*. DOI: 10.1109/IMCOM56909.2023.10035654

Tank, . (2020). *A Method for Malware Detection in Virtualization Environment. Communications in Computer and Information Science* (Vol. 1235). Springer., DOI: 10.1007/978-981-15-6648-6_21

Tan, T. M., & Saraniemi, S. (2023). Trust in blockchain-enabled exchanges: Future directions in blockchain marketing. *Journal of the Academy of Marketing Science*, 51(4), 914–939. DOI: 10.1007/s11747-022-00889-0

Tasnim, A., & Hossain, N. (2022), Experimental Analysis of Classification for Different Internet of Things (IoT) Network Attacks Using Machine Learning and Deep learning, *International Conference on Decision Aid Sciences and Applications (DASA)*. DOI: 10.1109/DASA54658.2022.9765108

Taylor, P. J., Dargahi, T., Dehghantanha, A., Parizi, R. M., & Choo, K.-K. R. (2020). A systematic literature review of blockchain cyber security. *Digital Communications and Networks*, 6(2), 147–156. DOI: 10.1016/j.dcan.2019.01.005

Tchao, E. T., Quansah, D. A., Klogo, G. S., Boafo-Effah, F., Kotei, S., Nartey, C., & Ofosu, W. K. (2021b). On cloud-based systems and distributed platforms for smart grid integration: Challenges and prospects for Ghana's Grid Network. *Scientific African*, 12, e00796. DOI: 10.1016/j.sciaf.2021.e00796

Thabit, F., Can, O., Aljahdali, A. O., Al-Gaphari, G. H., & Alkhzaimi, H. A. (2023). A comprehensive literature survey of cryptography algorithms for improving the iot security. *Internet of Things : Engineering Cyber Physical Human Systems*, ●●●, 100759. DOI: 10.1016/j.iot.2023.100759

Tian, F. (2017). A supply chain traceability system for food safety based on HACCP, blockchain, and the Internet of Things 2017 Inter- national Conference on Service Systems and Service Management, 1-6. DOI: 10.1109/ICSSSM.2017.7996119

Tinshu Sasi; Arash Habibi Lashkari et al. (2023), A comprehensive survey on IoT attacks: Taxonomy, detection mechanisms and challenges, Journal of Information and Intelligence, DOI: 10.1016/j.jiixd.2023.12.001

Tournier, J., Lesueur, F., Le Moue"l, F., Guyon, L., & Ben-Hassine, H. (2021). A survey of IoT protocols and their security issues through the lens of a generic IoT stack. *Internet of Things : Engineering Cyber Physical Human Systems*, 16, 100264. DOI: 10.1016/j.iot.2020.100264

Tripathi, G., Abdul Ahad, M., & Casalino, G. (2023). A comprehensive review of blockchain technology: Underlying principles and historical background with future challenges. *Elsevier, 9*, 1–6.

Tsagkaris, K., Logothetis, M., Foteinos, V., Poulios, G., Michaloliakos, M., & De-mestichas, P. (2015). Customizable autonomic network management: Inte- grating autonomic network management and software-defined networking. *IEEE Vehicular Technology Magazine*, 10(1), 61–68. DOI: 10.1109/MVT.2014.2380633

Tseng F-H, Chou L-D, Chao H-C. (2011), A survey of black hole attacks in wireless mobile ad hoc networks., Hum Cent Comput Inf Sci. DOI: 10.1186/2192-1962-1-4

Tukey, J. W. (1977). *Exploratory data analysis*. Addison-Wesley.

Tzermias, . (2011). Combining static and dynamic analysis for the detection of malicious documents. *Proceedings of the Fourth European Workshop on System Security - EUROSEC '11*. DOI: 10.1145/1972551.1972555

Uikey, D. Brarskar, Dr. R., & Ahirwar, Dr. M. (2024). A blockchain-based digital notary system provides reliable and tamper-proof timestamping and verification services for digital documents: A review. *International Journal for Multidisciplinary Research (IJFMR), 6*(2). https://www.ijfmr.com/papers/2024/2/17429.pdf

Unnithan, N. A., ... (2018). Machine learning based phishing e-mail detection. In *Proceedings of Security-CEN@ Amrita* (pp. 65-69). https://doi.org/DOI: 10.1145/3190645.3190652

US20200175164A1 - Malware classification and detection using audio descriptors - Google Patents. (2018, December 3). Google.com. https://patents.google.com/patent/US20200175164A1/en

ValetiDeepika, D., & LalithaBhaskari, D. (2020). Block chain based decentralised Twitter Dapp. [JETIR]. *Journal of Emerging Technologies and Innovative Research, 7*(11), 273–279.

Vanin, P., Newe, T., Dhirani, L. L., O'Connell, E., O'Shea, D., Lee, B., & Rao, M. (2022). A study of network intrusion detection systems using artificial intelligence/machine learning. *Applied Sciences (Basel, Switzerland)*, 12(22), 11752. DOI: 10.3390/app122211752

Varghese, J. E., & Muniyal, B. (2021). A pilot study in software-defined networking using wireshark for analyzing network parameters to detect DDoS attacks. In *Information and Communication Technology for Competitive Strategies (ICTCS 2020) Intelligent Strategies for ICT* (pp. 475-487). Springer Singapore. DOI: 10.1007/978-981-16-0882-7_41

Varun Shah. (2022). *Machine Learning Algorithms for Cybersecurity: Detecting and Preventing Threats*. DOI: 10.5281/ZENODO.10779509

Veenoo Upadhyay, SuryakantYadav (2018), Study of Cyber Security Challenges Its Emerging Trends: Current Technologies International Journal of Engineering Research and Management (IJERM) ISSN: 2349- 2058, Volume-05, Issue-07.

Vella, H. (2022). The Race for Quantum-Resistant Cryptography [quantum - cyber security]. *Engineering & Technology*, 17(1), 56–59. DOI: 10.1049/et.2022.0109

Venkatesan, S. (2023). Design an intrusion detection system based on feature selection using ML algorithms. *MSEA*, 72(1), 702–710.

Venkatraman, S., & Overmars, A. (2020, November). IoT Authentication and Security Challenges. In *Proceedings of the 3rd International Conference on Research in Applied Science*, Munich, Germany (pp. 6-8).

Verma, R., Shashidhar, N., & Hossain, N. (2012). Detecting phishing emails the natural language way. In *Computer Security–ESORICS 2012: 17th European Symposium on Research in Computer Security, Pisa, Italy, September 10-12, 2012. Proceedings 17* (pp. 824-841). Springer Berlin Heidelberg. DOI: 10.1007/978-3-642-33167-1_47

Vijaya Kittu, M., & Gupta, V. (2024). The Blockchain Trilemma of the IT Project Manager. In *Modern Management Challenges: A Case Compendium* (pp. 66–77). Excel India Publishers. https://zenodo.org/records/11910324

Viji, A. A., Jasper, J., & Latha, T. (2022). Efficient secure aware scheduling model for enhancing security and workflow model in cloud computing. *Optik (Stuttgart)*, 170349, 170349. Advance online publication. DOI: 10.1016/j.ijleo.2022.170349

Vutukuru, S. R., & Lade, S. C. (2023). *Secure IoT: Novel Machine Learning Algorithms for Detecting and Preventing Attacks on IoT Devices, J*. Electrical Systems.

Wander, A. S., Gura, N., Eberle, H., Gupta, V., & Shantz, S. C. (2005) Energy Analysis of Public-Key Cryptography for Wireless Sensor Networks, *IEEE International Conference on Pervasive Computing and Communications*, Kauai Island, DOI: 10.1109/PERCOM.2005.18

Wang, B., & Cui, B. (2019). Ontology-based services for software vulnerability detection: A survey. *Service Oriented Computing and Applications*, 13(4), 333–339. DOI: 10.1007/s11761-019-00276-8

Wang, J. A., & Guo, M. (2009, April). OVM: an ontology for vulnerability management. In *Proceedings of the 5th Annual Workshop on Cyber Security and Information Intelligence Research: Cyber Security and Information Intelligence Challenges and Strategies* (pp. 1-4).

Wang, M., Zheng, K., Yang, Y., & Wang, X. (2020). An explainable machine learning framework for intrusion detection systems. *IEEE Access : Practical Innovations, Open Solutions*, 8, 73127–73141. DOI: 10.1109/ACCESS.2020.2988359

Wang, N., Wang, P., Alipour-Fanid, A., Jiao, L., & Zeng, K. (2019). Physical- layer security of 5G wireless networks for IoT: Challenges and opportunities. *IEEE Internet of Things Journal*, 6(5), 8169–8181. DOI: 10.1109/JIOT.2019.2927379

Wang, R., Luo, M., Wen, Y., Wang, L., Raymond Choo, K.-K., & He, D. (2021). The Applications of Blockchain in Artificial Intelligence. *Security and Communication Networks*, 2021, 1–16. DOI: 10.1155/2021/8690662

Wang, Z., Zhu, H., Liu, P., & Sun, L. (2021). Social engineering in cybersecurity: A domain ontology and knowledge graph application examples. *Cybersecurity*, 4(1), 31. DOI: 10.1186/s42400-021-00094-6

Weimann, G. (2015). Going Dark: Terrorism on the Dark Web. *Studies in Conflict and Terrorism*, 39(3), 195–206. DOI: 10.1080/1057610X.2015.1119546

West, C., & West, C. (2024, April 26). *50+ Must-know social media marketing statistics for 2024*. Sprout Social. https://sproutsocial.com/insights/social-media -statistics/

Wickboldt, J. A., De Jesus, W. P., Isolani, P. H., Both, C. B., Rochol, J., & Granville, L. Z. (2015). Software-defined networking: Management requirements and challenges. *IEEE Communications Magazine*, 53(1), 278–285. DOI: 10.1109/ MCOM.2015.7010546

Wu, Y., Nie, L., Wang, S., Ning, Z., & Li, S. (2021, September 13). Smart threat identifying for internet of things security: A deep convolutional generative adversarial network-enabled approach. *IEEE Internet of Things Journal*.

Wylde, V., Rawindaran, N., Lawrence, J., Balasubramanian, R., Prakash, E., Jayal, A., Khan, I., Hewage, C., & Platts, J. (2022). Cybersecurity, Data Privacy and Blockchain: A Review. *SN Computer Science*, 3(2), 127. DOI: 10.1007/s42979- 022-01020-4 PMID: 35036930

Xiao, M., Guo, M., & Zhu, W. (2022). Research and implementation of network security deployment based on private cloud security platform. *Procedia Computer Science*, 208, 565–569. DOI: 10.1016/j.procs.2022.10.078

Xiao, Y., Zhang, N., Lou, W., & Hou, Y. T. (2020). A Survey of Distributed Consensus Protocols for Blockchain Networks. *IEEE Communications Surveys and Tutorials*, 22(2), 1432–1465. DOI: 10.1109/COMST.2020.2969706

Xia, X. (2024). Optimizing and hyper-tuning machine learning models for the water absorption of eggshell and glass-based cementitious composite. *PLoS One*, 19(1), e0296494. Advance online publication. DOI: 10.1371/journal.pone.0296494 PMID: 38165942

Xu, J., Wang, C., & Jia, X. (2023). A Survey of Blockchain Consensus Protocols. *ACM Computing Surveys*, 55(13s), 1–35. DOI: 10.1145/3579845

Xu, T.. (2017). *Defending against new-flow attack in SDN-based internet of things*. IEEE., DOI: 10.1109/ACCESS.2017.2666270

Y. Miao, R. H. Deng, K. -K. R. Choo, X. Liu and H. Li, "Threshold Multi-Keyword Search for Cloud-Based Group Data Sharing," in IEEE Transactions on Cloud Computing, vol. 10, no. 3, pp. 2146-2162, 1 July-Sept. 2022, .DOI: 10.1109/TCC.2020.2999775

Y. Yang, X. Liu, X. Zheng, C. Rong and W. Guo, "Efficient Traceable Authorization Search System for Secure Cloud Storage," in IEEE Transactions on Cloud Computing, vol. 8, no. 3, pp. 819-832, 1 July-Sept. 2020, .DOI: 10.1109/TCC.2018.2820714

Yang, K., Liu, J., Zhang, C., & Fang, Y. (2018). Adversarial examples against the deep-hierarchical learning based network threat identifying systems. In *MILCOM 2018-2018 ieee military communications conference (MILCOM)* (pp. 559–564). IEEE. DOI: 10.1109/MILCOM.2018.8599759

Yang, Y., Zheng, K., Wu, B., Yang, Y., & Wang, X. (2020). Network threat identifying based on supervised adversarial variational auto-encoder with regularization. *IEEE Access : Practical Innovations, Open Solutions*, 8, 42169–42184. DOI: 10.1109/ACCESS.2020.2977007

Yang, Z., Chen, Z., Xiao, W., Liu, Q., & Zhang, Y. (2019). Phishing email detection based on hybrid features. []. IOP Publishing.]. *IOP Conference Series. Earth and Environmental Science*, 252(4), 042039. DOI: 10.1088/1755-1315/252/4/042051

Yasin, A., & Abuhasan, A. (2016). An intelligent classification model for phishing email detection. *arXiv preprint arXiv:1608.02196.*

Yilmaz, I., Masum, R., & Siraj, A. "Addressing imbalanced data problem with generative adversarial network for intrusion detection." In 2020 IEEE 21st international conference on information reuse and integration for data science (IRI), pp. 25-30. IEEE, 2020. DOI: 10.1109/IRI49571.2020.00012

Yu, D., Zhang, L., Chen, Y., Ma, Y., & Chen, J. (2020). Large-scale IoT devices firmware identification based on weak password. *IEEE Access : Practical Innovations, Open Solutions*, 8, 7981–7992. DOI: 10.1109/ACCESS.2020.2964646

Yugha, R., & Chithra, S. (2020). A survey on technologies and security proto- cols: Reference for future generation IoT. *Journal of Network and Computer Applications*, 169, 102763. DOI: 10.1016/j.jnca.2020.102763

Yu, M., Zhuge, J., Cao, M., Shi, Z., & Jiang, L. (2020). A survey of security vulnerability analysis, discovery, detection, and mitigation on IoT devices. *Future Internet*, 12(2), 27. DOI: 10.3390/fi12020027

Yu, S., Tian, Y., Guo, S., & Wu, D. O. (2014, September). Can We Beat DDoS Attacks in Clouds? *IEEE Transactions on Parallel and Distributed Systems*, 25(9), 2245–2254. DOI: 10.1109/TPDS.2013.181

Yusuf, A., Khairil, K., & Rohmawan, E. P. (2024). AN ANALYSIS OF SERVICE QUALITY ON VSAT NETWORK USING WIRESHARK. *JURNAL MEDIA IN-FOTAMA*, 20(1), 73–78.

Z. Wu, S. Peng, L. Liu and M. Yue, "Detection of Improved Collusive Interest Flooding Attacks Using BO-GBM Fusion Algorithm in NDN," in IEEE Transactions on Network Science and Engineering, vol. 10, no. 1, pp. 239-252, 1 Jan.-Feb. 2023, .DOI: 10.1109/TNSE.2022.3206581

Zainab H. Ali et al. (2015), Internet of Things (IoT): Definitions, Challenges and Recent Research Directions, International Journal of Computer Applications (0975 – 8887) Volume 128 – No.1

Zareapoor, M., & Seeja, K. R. (2015). Feature extraction or feature selection for text classification: A case study on phishing email detection. *International Journal of Information Engineering and Electronic Business*, 7(2), 60. DOI: 10.5815/ijieeb.2015.02.08

Zemler, F., & Westner, M. (2019). Blockchain and GDPR: Application Scenarios and Compliance Requirements. *2019 Portland International Conference on Management of Engineering and Technology (PICMET)*, 1–8. DOI: 10.23919/PICMET.2019.8893923

Zhang, X., & Chen, X. (2019). Data security sharing and storage based on a consortium blockchain in a vehicular ad-hoc network. *IEEE, 7*. DOI: 10.1109/ACCESS.2018.2890736

Zhang, G., Wang, X., Li, R., Song, Y., He, J., & Lai, J. (2020). Network threat identifying based on conditional Wasserstein generative adversarial network and cost-sensitive stacked autoencoder. *IEEE Access : Practical Innovations, Open Solutions*, 8, 190431–190447. DOI: 10.1109/ACCESS.2020.3031892

Zhang, L., Chen, Y., & Zhang, Q. (2017). *Network slicing for 5G: Challenges and opportunities," IEEE Internet Computing*, vol. 21, no. 5, pp. 20-27. Xiao, Y. He, X. Hu, L. and Huang, D. (2018). *AI-enhanced security in 5G network slicing. IEEE Wireless Communications*, 25(5), 119–125.

Zhang, S., Han, S., Zheng, B., Han, K., & Pang, E. (2020). Group Key Management Protocol for File Sharing on Cloud Storage. *IEEE Access : Practical Innovations, Open Solutions*, 8, 123614–123622. DOI: 10.1109/ACCESS.2019.2963782

Zhang, X., Zhang, J., & Zheng, L. (2023). *Towards privacy-preserving 5G networks Homomorphic encryption and blockchain," IEEE Transactions on Information Forensics and Security*, 18, 378-390. Wang, J. Li, Y. and Wang, Z. (2024). *Resilient security architectures for 5G and beyond: A survey. IEEE Network*, 38(3), 47–55.

Zhang, Z., Zeng, P., Pan, B., & Choo, K.-K. R. (2020, October). Large-Universe Attribute-Based Encryption With Public Traceability for Cloud Storage. *IEEE Internet of Things Journal*, 7(10), 10314–10323. DOI: 10.1109/JIOT.2020.2986303

Zhao, W., Tian, C., Tian, W., & Zhang, Y. (2020). Securely and Efficiently Computing the Hermite Normal Form of Integer Matrices via Cloud Computing. *IEEE Access : Practical Innovations, Open Solutions*, 8, 137616–137630. DOI: 10.1109/ ACCESS.2020.3011965

Zheng, Z., Xie, S., Dai, H.-N., Chen, X., & Wang, H. (2018). Blockchain challenges and opportunities. *International Journal of Web and Grid Services*, 14(4), 352. DOI: 10.1504/IJWGS.2018.095647

Zhixian, C. (2020). Encryption technology of voice transmission in mobile network based on 3DES-ECC algorithm. *Mobile Networks and Applications*, 25(6), 2398–2408. DOI: 10.1007/s11036-020-01617-0

Zhou, L., Diro, A., Saini, A., Kaisar, S., & Hiep, P. (2024). Leveraging zero knowledge proofs for blockchain-based identity sharing: A survey of advancements, challenges and opportunities. *Elsevier, 80*. DOI: 10.1016/j.jisa.2023.103678

Zhou, J., Feng, Y., Wang, Z., & Guo, D. (2021). Using secure multi-party computation to protect privacy on a permissioned blockchain. *Sensors (Basel)*, 21(4), 1540. DOI: 10.3390/s21041540 PMID: 33672175

Zhou, S., Li, K., Xiao, L., Cai, J., Liang, W., & Castiglione, A. (2023). A Systematic Review of Consensus Mechanisms in Blockchain. *Mathematics*, 11(2248), 2248. Advance online publication. DOI: 10.3390/math11102248

Zhu, L., Karim, M. M., Sharif, K., Li, F., Du, X., & Guizani, M. SDN con- trollers: Benchmarking performance evaluation. arXiv 2019. arXiv preprint arXiv:1902.04491. 22

Zissis, D., & Lekkas, D. (2010). Addressing cloud computing security issues. *Future Generation Computer Systems*, ●●●, 1–10.

Zubair Shafiq, M.. (2008). Embedded Malware Detection Using Markov n-Grams. *Lecture Notes in Computer Science*, 5137, 88–107. DOI: 10.1007/978-3-540-70542-0_5

About the Contributors

Nirbhay Kumar Chaubey currently working as a Professor and Dean of Computer Science at Ganpat University, Gujarat India. Prior to joining Ganpat University, he worked as an Associate Dean of Computer Science at Gujarat Technological University, Ahmedabad, Gujarat, India. A dedicated person with the capability of taking on new challenges of academic, research, and administrative leadership with over 25 years of teaching regular Post Graduate courses of Computer Science. His research interests lie in the areas of Wireless Networks (Architecture, Protocol Design, QoS, Routing, Mobility, and Security), Cyber Security, Quantum Computing, IoT, Ad Hoc Networks, Sensor Networks, and Cloud Computing. Established a reputed Scopus Indexed Springer International Conference on Computing Science, Communication and Security (COMS2) being organized every year. Published 70+ research papers in reputed International Journal and Conference proceedings indexed in Scopus and Web of Science, published 10 book chapters in Scopus Index Book. Authored/ Edited 8 Scopus-indexed international texts, reference books of Springer, IGI Global, and Lap Lambert publishers, contributed 12 patents (5 granted) and 1 copyright (granted). His published research works are well cited by the research community worldwide which shows his exceptional research performance, Google citations: 740 and H-index: 18. Dr. Chaubey has been very active in the technical community and served on the editorial board of various international journals, program committee member for international conferences and an active technical reviewer of repute Journals of IEEE, Springer, Elsevier, and Wiley. Under his guidance 07 Ph.D. students, 14 M.Tech students, and 160 MCA students completed, 6 Ph.D. Research Scholars continue for their quality research work, and one Ph.D. research scholar received the AWSAR Award-2020 of the Department of Science and Technology (DST), Government of India under his guidance. Prof. Chaubey is a Senior Member of IEEE, a Senior Member of ACM, and a Life Member of the Computer Society of India. He has been actively associated with the IEEE India Council and IEEE Gujarat Section and served IEEE in various volunteer positions. He has received numerous awards including IEEE Outstanding Volunteer Award- Year 2015 (IEEE Region 10 Asia Pacific), Gujarat Technological University (GTU) Pedagogical Innovation Awards (PIA) -2015, IEEE Outstanding Branch Counselor Award - the Year 2010 (IEEE Region 10 Asia Pacific).

Neha Chaubey continues the Master of Science (MSc) program in Analogue and Digital IC Design at Imperial College, London, United Kingdom, Imperial College ranked 6th in the world in QS World University Ranking. Her research interest lies in Quantum Computing, Digital IC Design, Wireless Network and Cyber Security. She has worked as an intern at Cadence Design Systems and also at eInfochips, an Arrow company. She has published 3 research papers in Conference Proceedings and published 1 Patent. She was awarded the best research paper award during her undergraduate study for her research paper titled "An Efficient Cluster Based Energy Routing Protocol (E-CBERP) for Wireless Body Area Networks Using Soft Computing Technique" and another paper titled "Training locomotion skills to a legged robot using Machine Learning and Trajectory control" presented and published in Springer CCIS Series International Conference on Computing Science, Communication and Security in the year 2022 and 2023 respectively.

***

Prerna Agrawal completed her Master of Computer Application from Gujarat University, Ahmedabad, Gujarat in 2011. She is currently working as an Assistant Professor in the Faculty of Computer Applications & IT, MCA at GLS University. She completed her Ph.D. from GLS University in 2021. She has a total of 12+ years of teaching experience and 1-year of industry experience. Her main research work focuses on Android Malware Detection using Machine Learning and Application Security. She has a total of 12 Research Publications in various International Conferences and Journals in her name. She is acting as a Ph.D. Guide at GLS University and currently having 2 students under her.

Ravneet Preet Singh Bedi is presently serving as Joint Registrar in I.K. Gujral Punjab Technical University, Kapurthala. He has done his M.C.A. and Ph.D in Computer Science Engineering. He also holds the prestigious certification such as Microsoft Certified Systems Engineer (MCSE). He has also completed another Ph.D. in Computer Science & Engineering from the Faculty of Engineering, Punjabi University, Patiala. Dr. Bedi has published research papers in reputed International Journals and articles in Computer science and education in National journals and magazines. He has also Chaired a session on networking at an international conference, "WORLDCOMP10," the world Congress on Computer

Science, Computer Engineering and Applied computing held at Las Vegas in the USA. He has also participated in an International conference on Skill development organized by Indian High Commission, UK at London.

Hima Bindu finished her master's degree and doctoral research at JNTUK in Kakinada. presently employed as a professor at the QIS College of Engineering and Technology in Ongole, Andhra Pradesh, India, in the Department of Electronics and Communication Engineering. She also attended numerous international conferences and produced a number of research papers in reputable journals, textbooks, and patents. Several organizations, including AICTE, DST, UGC, and others, awarded her research grants. Under her guidance, over five students are pursuing doctorates.

Savita Gandhi is currently serving as Dean, Faculty of Computer Applications and Information Technology (PG) at GLS University, Ahmedabad, Gujarat, India. Dr. Savita was a Professor and Head at Gujarat University's Department of Computer Science before coming to GLS University in July 2021. Dr. Savita has already completed 45 years of teaching experience, which includes working with PhD candidates and postgraduate students, starting new academic initiatives, conducting research, supervising research projects, managing internships and administrative duties. She is M.Sc. (Mathematics), Ph.D. (Mathematics) and A.A.S.I. (Associate Member of Actuarial Society of India by the virtue of having completed the "A" group examinations comprising six subjects conducted by Institute of Actuaries, London). She was awarded Gold Medal for standing first class first securing 93% marks in M.Sc. and several prizes at M.Sc. as well as B.Sc. Examinations for obtaining highest marks at M.S. University, Baroda.

Anubha Gauba has done MCA and completed her Ph.D in 2023 from I.K.Gujral Punjab Technical University. She is having 15 years of Teaching Experience and 5 Years of Research Experience .She has Published Papers in National and International Journals.

Vishal Goar is presently working as Assistant Professor in Department of Computer Application at Government Engineering College, Bikaner. Presently he is also Coordinator of Research & Development Department of Government Engineering College, Bikaner. Dr. Goar has contributed many research papers in national and international Conferences and Journals. He has delivered many lectures in International Conferences, Seminars and Workshops. Dr. Goar has published many books from different international and national publishing houses. He has organized many conferences and FDP.

Vishal Jain is presently working as an Associate Professor at Department of Computer Science and Engineering, School of Engineering and Technology, Sharda University, Greater Noida, U. P. India. Before that, he has worked for several years as an Associate Professor at Bharati Vidyapeeth's Institute of Computer Applications and Management (BVICAM), New Delhi. He has more than 15 years of experience in the academics. He obtained Ph.D (CSE), M.Tech (CSE), MBA (HR), MCA, MCP and CCNA. He has authored more than 100 research papers in reputed conferences and journals, including Web of Science and Scopus. He has authored and edited more than 45 books with various reputed publishers, including Elsevier, Springer, IET, Apple Academic Press, CRC, Taylor and Francis Group, Scrivener, Wiley, Emerald, NOVA Science, IGI-Global and River Publishers. His research areas include information retrieval, semantic web, ontology engineering, data mining, ad hoc networks, and sensor networks. He received a Young Active Member Award for the year 2012–13 from the Computer Society of India, Best Faculty Award for the year 2017 and Best Researcher Award for the year 2019 from BVICAM, New Delhi.

Purva Joshi is a researcher at the University of Pisa, Italy. Her PhD title is "6G IIoT for Healthcare Application", which is basically bilateral teleoperation using beyond 5G network. She was a research scholar at Wroclaw University of Science and Technology, Wroclaw, Poland. She completed her bachelor's study in instrumentation and control engineering, at Government Engineering College, Gandhinagar, India. After graduation, she joined the Institute of Technology, Nirma University, Ahmedabad, India, for her post-graduation in instrumentation and control engineering. She got the first rank in class and earned a gold medal. She worked as Assistant Professor at Marwadi University, Rajkot, India from 2018 to 2019. At Marwadi University, she arranged two days of the hands-on workshop for final year students as "LabVIEW and its application." She encouraged students to know about hardware interfacing and its programming and played a mentor role for the team, selected for the National level Mitsubishi Electric Cup Competition. She also worked as Assistant Professor in electronics and communication engineering at Silver Oak University, Ahmedabad, India. In 2020, she joined Dhirubhai Ambani Institute of Information and Communication Technology (DA-IICT), Gandhinagar, India as a junior research fellow and worked on the Indian Space Research Organization (ISRO) project. The project developed a satellite network simulator using features like uplink power control (ULPC) and Adaptive Coding and Modulation (ACM). She also has experience of reviewer of well-known conferences and participated in workshops. Her research interests are haptic and tactile network, AI for healthcare, 5G and beyond 5G network, automation, and robotics.

Suma K has been working as Faculty in the Computer Science and Engineering Department from 15 years.

Akhil John Mampilly is a seasoned professional with over a decade of unparalleled expertise in information security. As the Cybersecurity Specialist for a government entity in the Middle East, he has been at the forefront of driving strategic initiatives and safeguarding digital assets and infrastructure through a prudent combination of people, processes, and technology. With a Bachelor of Technology in Electronics and Communication Engineering (ECE), a Master of Science (MSc) in IT Business, an MBA in Project Management, and certifications as an ISO 27001 Lead Implementer and Project Management Professional (PMP), Akhil combines technical proficiency with a strategic vision to address the evolving challenges of cybersecurity in today's digital landscape. His academic interests have led him to pursue a PhD in Engineering. In addition to his distinguished career in cybersecurity, Akhil is also a published author and researcher in cybersecurity. Beyond his professional endeavors, Akhil has participated in various international conferences as a speaker and mentor. He is known for his ability to inspire and empower others to achieve their goals in both their professional and creative pursuits.

Vijaya Kittu Manda has nearly 13+ years of experience in Business Management and Technology. He is a Researcher at PBMEIT, India and works in capital markets, financial planning, and investing. He is an Advocate, a technocrat, an academician, a book writer, and a stock market enthusiast. He has 11 University Postgraduate Degrees in various disciplines spanning Arts and Humanities, Science and Technology, Law and Management. He is a Ph.D. in Financial Management. His thesis was on Mutual Funds and their Market Competition. His thesis won the prestigious NSE-IEA Best Thesis Award in 2023. He is currently pursuing his second Ph.D. in Computer Science with focus on Blockchain. He contributed over 770 articles to various magazines. He is the Chief Editor for a Management Book Series, is a Peer Review, is a Certified Peer Review Supervisor, is a Session Chair and an Advisor for various academic and industrial conferences. He writes Research Papers and Case Studies, Book Chapters, and sits on Editorial Boards of various publishers. He is also an Editor for various Books published by reputed global publishers. He is a guest speaker for colleges and universities.

Manvi Mishra is an Associate Prof. Department of Computer Science & Engineering at Shri Ram Murti Smarak College of Engineering Technology and Research Bareilly, (UP) India. I am having 17 Years of Academic Experience. I received Bachelor's degree in Information Tecnology from Dr. A.P.J. Abdul Kalam Technical University Lucknow, India in 2006 and further Master degree with honors in Software Engineering from the same university in 2011. I have achieved Doctorate in Computer Science Engineering field from the same prestigious Dr A.P.J. Abdul Kalam Technical University Lucknow India. My Area of Interest includes Bio Medical Imaging, Cryptography and Network Security, Data Compression, Software Engineering. My research work has been published in various national and international journals and Conferences. I participated and organized various FDPs, Conferences, Webinars, Seminars, and Workshops at national and international levels. I am a life member of Institution of Engineers IEI India, Computer Society of India CSI, and IEEE etc. I have received "Bharat Vikas Award" on the occasion of citizen's day on 19 Nov 2017 by Institute of Self Reliance, Bhubaneswar Odisha, for loyalty, diligence and outstanding performance in the field of Cryptography and network security. I also have been endorsed with "Young Woman Educator and Researcher" Award on 8th March '2021 for significant contribution to Teaching and Research activities in the field of Computer Science and Engineering by National Foundation for Entrepreneurship Development (NFED) Coimbatore Tamil Nadu, India Recently I endorsed with Woman Power India Awards 2024 powered by WE Raise Raj Square Charity Foundation MSME Chamber of Commerce and Industry of India on 8 march 2024 for recognition of exceptional contribution and remarkable work in the realm of social and corporate impact through service and management.

Sanjana Muvvala is currently pursuing B.Tech in Computer Science and Engineering in QISCET, India. she is chair for IEEE Computer science society and actively participating all extra and co curricular activities. she published a paper in Scopus journal and patent.

Chandresh Parekha is an academician for more than 21 years. He completed B.E. (Electronics) in 1994 from BVM Engineering College, Vallabh Vidhyanagar and M.E. in Electronics Communication Systems from DDIT, Nadiad in 2009. He completed Ph.D. in Electronics and Communication Engineering from Gujarat Technological University, Ahmedabad in 2020. He started his professional career as an R & D Engineer at Crown Television Limited, Gandhinagar. He also worked as an R & D Engineer at Videocon International Limited, Gandhinagar. He started teaching in the year 2002 in the Electronics and Communication Department. He worked as an Assistant Professor in Electronics and Communication Department of Sankalchand Patel College of Engineering, Visnagar from 24th July, 2002 to 24th October, 2011. He has been working as an Assistant Professor – Telecommunication (Senior Grade) with Rashtriya Raksha University, Lavad since 25 th October 2011. He has been actively involved in academics by publishing more than 50 research papers in reputed journals/conferences, doing various funded research projects, delivering expert talks and organizing technical events. He got Geospatial Excellence

Award for the research project "GIS based Crime Mapping of Ahmedabad City" in 2014.

Dharm Raj holds a B.Tech degree in Computer Science and Engineering from UP Technical University (now APJ Abul Kalam University) Lucknow, M. Tech degree in Information Technology (Specialization in Human Computer Interaction) from Indian Institute of Information Technology, Allahabad and pursuing PhD in Computer Science & Engineering from Sharda University, Greater Noida. He has more than 17 years of teaching and administrative experience and 2 years of Research Experience in Patent Referal Center (IIIT-Allahabad) as Project Associate. Before joining to Sharda University he was working with Galgotias College of Engineering & Technology, Greater Noida. He has guided many students for their M. Tech thesis and projects to undergraduate students. Dharm Raj has published/presented 25 plus research papers in various international and national Journals/Conferences. He is contributing to the research communities by various volunteer activities. He successfully organized one International conference in the capacity of Publication Chair and two National Conferences in the capacity of Chief Editor, also chaired and reviewed conference sessions as TPC member of various International/National Conferences. He also holds the post of Honorary Secretary of Computer Society of India, Noida Chapter. His teaching style culminates the critical importance, of course, show the relationships between theoretical, practical and applications depending on assessments. He provides a practical step-by-step guide to help students to develop the meaningful and effective course, with careful attention to learning taxonomies.

RVS Praveen is a distinguished professional with an illustrious career spanning 24 years. Currently serving as the Director of Product Engineering at LTIMindtree Limited in Hyderabad, India, Dr. Praveen is renowned for his visionary leadership and technical acumen. He holds a Ph.D. in Information Technology from Sabarmati University, Ahmedabad, Gujarat, reflecting his profound expertise and commitment to advancing the field. Throughout his career, Dr. Praveen has made significant contributions to the world of technology. He has authored numerous research papers published in esteemed international journals and presented his work at both international and national conferences. His research primarily focuses on cutting-edge advancements in Cloud Computing, Artificial Intelligence, Machine Learning, and Deep Learning. Dr. Praveen's exceptional ability to guide and inspire teams has led to the successful development and launch of innovative products and solutions for Fortune 500 companies. His strategic vision and technical proficiency have consistently driven projects that leverage AI and advanced machine learning techniques to solve complex business challenges, thereby cementing his reputation as a leader in the tech industry. Under his direction, LTIMindtree has seen remarkable advancements in product engineering, reflecting his dedication to excellence and innovation. Dr. Praveen's contributions continue to shape the future of technology, making him a pivotal figure in the industry.

Anil Kumar Sagar is currently working as Professor of Department of Computer Science Engineering in School of Engineering and Technology, Sharda University, India. Dr. Anil Kumar Sagar obtained his doctorate from JNU, New Delhi in the area of Ad-hoc Networks. He obtained his B.E-Computer Science & Engineering from G B Pant Engineering College Pauri Garhwal, and M.Tech from JSSATE Noida. Formerly served as a Dean Academics in Raj Kumar Goel Institute of Technology Ghaziabad. He also worked as a Member of Board of Studies in Computer Science Department at Galgotias University Greater Noida and RKGIT Ghaziabad. He is a Member in editorial board/review committee in many international/national journals and served as a program/organizing committee member for organizing several conferences. Guided 10 M.Tech (Computer Science) students and presently guiding 5 Ph. D. (Computer Science) students. He is having about 20 yrs. of teaching experience in various prestigious colleges and universities.

Chithirai Pon Selvan has extensive experience in teaching engineering students and has worked in academia for over twenty-five years. He has published/presented more than 150 research articles in journals and conferences. He has been invited and honored as keynote speaker, session chair, resource person, and technical committee member of various conferences held in UAE, India, Thailand, Malaysia, Germany, Italy, Australia, Qatar, and the UK. His research interests are in the areas of machine design, optimization techniques, manufacturing practices, renewable energy, and engineering sustainable development. He is a well-known researcher in the field of Abrasive Waterjet Cutting Technology and has evaluated several PhD theses in Mechanical Engineering from various universities. He is the approved supervisor of many universities including Curtin University, Australia to guide PhD scholars and has produced many PhDs. He is a member of many professional societies including SAE, ASHRAE, IMechE, ASME, EI, ASQ, and ISTE. He is also a Senior Fellow of the Higher Education Academy (SFHEA), UK.

Ravi Sheth is having more than 15 years of teaching experience. His keen area of interest is in multimedia security, machine learning, pattern recognition, VAPT and Cyber Forensics. He has a conflate of combined experience in teaching, research and training. Dr. Sheth had organized several high-quality training and extension programs for the law professional, teachers and students from across the India. He has published more than 50 research articles in international refereed journal in the area of cyber security, cyber forensics and artificial intelligence. He has been a part of various conferences as a member of the technical committee and reviewer. Dr. Sheth had presented many research papers in the International and National Conferences and Seminars. He had been invited as a resource person in many workshops/seminars/training programs. He had also delivered many expert talks on various aspects of Multimedia Security, Social Media Investigation, Cyber Forensics, Pattern Recognition and Darknet Investigation for the law professional, teachers and students from across the India. He has filed a pattern for a "Portable mobile forensic data acquisition tool". He is providing research guidance to the students of Rashtriya Raksha University in the area of Cyber Security, Cyber Forensics, Machine learning and pattern recognition

Index

Symbols

5G Network   125, 128, 136, 138, 144, 146, 376

A

Artificial Intelligence 18, 19, 42, 49, 84, 87, 115, 123, 126, 127, 132, 134, 144, 147, 148, 149, 150, 200, 202, 218, 249, 273, 305, 338, 343, 354, 357, 364, 365, 366, 367, 372, 374, 377, 386, 410, 430

Attacks 7, 8, 18, 22, 23, 25, 26, 27, 37, 38, 41, 43, 46, 47, 50, 51, 55, 56, 62, 63, 64, 67, 68, 69, 70, 71, 77, 78, 79, 81, 82, 83, 85, 92, 95, 98, 99, 100, 101, 102, 103, 104, 105, 106, 107, 108, 110, 112, 114, 115, 116, 117, 118, 119, 120, 121, 125, 127, 128, 129, 132, 134, 135, 137, 139, 140, 141, 142, 145, 147, 148, 149, 150, 151, 155, 168, 169, 174, 175, 177, 178, 179, 181, 184, 188, 194, 198, 199, 203, 225, 228, 229, 230, 231, 242, 243, 244, 248, 251, 279, 281, 283, 284, 286, 287, 288, 290, 291, 292, 295, 297, 298, 299, 300, 301, 303, 304, 305, 306, 307, 308, 330, 338, 339, 342, 343, 349, 350, 355, 356, 357, 359, 360, 361, 363, 364, 368, 374, 375, 376, 377, 379, 381, 382, 383, 384, 385, 387, 389, 390, 391, 400, 401, 409, 415, 416, 418, 419, 423, 432

Automation 1, 4, 16, 44, 47, 138, 142, 199, 265, 272, 275, 313, 318, 319, 323, 331, 333, 356, 357, 365, 367, 372, 373

B

Big Data 19, 21, 22, 28, 29, 30, 31, 32, 34, 35, 36, 37, 38, 39, 40, 41, 42, 43, 44, 45, 46, 47, 116, 171, 223, 268, 275, 305, 307, 337, 338, 339, 340, 341, 342, 343, 344, 345, 346, 347, 349, 350, 352, 353, 364, 365, 411

Big Data Analytics 21, 28, 32, 34, 35, 37, 38, 39, 40, 42, 43, 44, 45, 46, 47, 307, 338, 346, 349, 352, 364, 365

Blockchain 49, 50, 51, 52, 53, 54, 55, 56, 57, 58, 59, 60, 61, 62, 63, 64, 65, 66, 67, 69, 70, 71, 72, 73, 74, 75, 76, 77, 78, 79, 80, 81, 82, 83, 84, 85, 86, 87, 88, 109, 111, 115, 116, 123, 126, 127, 131, 132, 134, 135, 142, 143, 144, 145, 146, 205, 206, 207, 208, 209, 210, 211, 212, 213, 214, 215, 216, 217, 218, 219, 220, 221, 222, 223, 296, 297, 302, 303, 305, 306, 338, 339, 342, 351, 352, 354, 357, 358, 359, 368, 369, 370, 371, 384, 385, 387, 388, 389, 390, 391, 392, 393, 394, 395, 396, 397, 398, 399, 400, 401, 402, 403, 404, 405, 406, 407, 408, 409, 410, 411

Block Chain 213, 296, 297, 300, 303, 307, 338, 371, 372, 411

Blockchain Architecture 51, 206

Blockchain Features 210

Blockchain Technology 51, 55, 56, 57, 58, 60, 62, 64, 65, 66, 67, 69, 70, 72, 73, 74, 75, 76, 79, 81, 82, 83, 84, 85, 86, 131, 134, 135, 144, 205, 206, 208, 209, 211, 212, 213, 214, 215, 216, 217, 218, 219, 220, 221, 222, 223, 296, 297, 306, 352, 358, 359, 368, 369, 370, 371, 387, 391, 393, 394, 396, 397, 398, 399, 401, 408, 409, 411

C

Cloud Computing 24, 41, 43, 48, 89, 90, 91, 92, 93, 99, 107, 111, 112, 114, 115, 116, 117, 118, 119, 120, 121, 135, 146, 229, 244, 275, 300, 304, 305, 357, 386, 411

Consensus Algorithm 209

Criminal Records 205

Cyber Attacks 22, 23, 26, 37, 38, 47, 50, 127, 177, 178, 181, 198, 203, 305,

349, 350

Cyber Crimes 23, 24, 45

Cybersecurity 1, 2, 8, 9, 10, 17, 19, 21, 22,
   23, 24, 28, 37, 38, 39, 40, 41, 42, 43,
   44, 45, 46, 47, 49, 50, 51, 54, 55, 56,
   57, 58, 59, 61, 63, 64, 67, 72, 75, 76,
   77, 79, 80, 84, 86, 87, 88, 109, 111,
   112, 123, 125, 126, 130, 134, 136,
   141, 142, 143, 147, 149, 150, 155,
   162, 165, 168, 169, 170, 173, 174,
   177, 200, 203, 226, 227, 229, 231,
   232, 244, 248, 249, 250, 252, 267,
   278, 296, 298, 302, 303, 306, 308,
   338, 339, 344, 354, 357, 382, 383,
   384, 427, 429

Cyber Security 18, 19, 21, 23, 24, 39, 40,
   41, 42, 43, 46, 47, 48, 50, 82, 86, 109,
   114, 115, 120, 123, 130, 144, 145, 146,
   172, 203, 243, 244, 267, 268, 271,
   278, 279, 280, 282, 283, 284, 285,
   290, 291, 293, 294, 298, 300, 302,
   303, 304, 305, 306, 307, 308, 338,
   386, 390, 392, 409, 410, 411

Cyber-Security 84, 294, 415

Cyber Threats 12, 22, 24, 38, 56, 57, 80,
   132, 133, 134, 162, 198, 199, 242,
   273, 280, 286, 299, 338, 340, 342,
   343, 346, 349, 352, 358, 360, 363, 415

D

Data Sharing 77, 89, 90, 91, 93, 110, 111,
   112, 116, 118, 119, 120, 301, 303, 350,
   352, 356, 370, 372, 387, 405

Decentralized Security 88, 111, 134, 135,
   142, 143, 302, 368, 397, 398

Decision Tree 152, 175, 176, 177, 181, 184,
   194, 252, 257, 258, 260, 267

E

Email Security 158

Encryption 42, 52, 59, 75, 76, 78, 86, 88,
   91, 95, 107, 109, 110, 111, 112, 114,
   119, 121, 123, 126, 127, 130, 132, 133,
   135, 136, 137, 138, 139, 140, 141,
   142, 143, 146, 199, 213, 220, 226,

230, 231, 249, 255, 275, 279, 280,
   282, 283, 285, 288, 291, 292, 293,
   294, 295, 296, 298, 300, 301, 302,
   304, 305, 306, 307, 308, 337, 345,
   346, 347, 351, 352, 355, 359, 363,
   368, 374, 375, 376, 377, 379, 382, 400

Ensemble Learning 159, 171, 203, 417

F

Feature Selection 151, 152, 159, 172, 173,
   175, 176, 177, 178, 179, 180, 183,
   191, 192, 200, 201, 202, 203, 251,
   252, 416, 417, 420, 421

Features of Blockchain 54, 57, 70

G

GDPR 49, 51, 66, 72, 73, 74, 79, 81, 83,
   85, 87, 149, 281, 297

H

HIPPA 49

I

Internet of Things 31, 41, 44, 49, 85, 121,
   124, 127, 139, 214, 228, 273, 274,
   275, 276, 278, 279, 283, 284, 286,
   293, 296, 298, 303, 304, 305, 306,
   307, 308, 321, 332, 355, 356, 357,
   358, 359, 361, 363, 364, 365, 366,
   367, 368, 369, 370, 371, 374, 375,
   376, 377, 379, 381, 386, 387, 388, 389,
   390, 391, 392, 430, 431, 432

Intrusion Detection 10, 18, 38, 101, 103,
   105, 116, 132, 173, 174, 175, 176, 177,
   178, 198, 199, 200, 201, 202, 228, 229,
   243, 282, 285, 311, 315, 319, 324, 377,
   386, 413, 416, 417, 418, 419, 423, 424,
   428, 429, 430, 431, 432

Intrusion Detection System 10, 101, 173,
   174, 175, 176, 177, 178, 198, 200,
   201, 202, 228, 229, 319

M

Machine Learning 36, 37, 47, 49, 77, 84, 87, 109, 111, 114, 123, 132, 133, 134, 135, 137, 141, 142, 144, 147, 149, 150, 151, 152, 153, 154, 155, 156, 157, 158, 159, 160, 161, 162, 163, 164, 165, 166, 168, 169, 171, 172, 173, 174, 175, 176, 177, 178, 179, 180, 181, 182, 184, 198, 199, 200, 201, 202, 203, 245, 249, 250, 252, 253, 256, 257, 265, 267, 268, 269, 275, 291, 292, 298, 305, 306, 308, 342, 346, 353, 360, 364, 366, 367, 372, 377, 384, 385, 396, 415, 416, 417, 418, 430, 432

Machine Learning Classifiers 151

Malware 2, 12, 24, 25, 26, 38, 40, 42, 65, 99, 102, 103, 105, 108, 110, 112, 115, 118, 128, 134, 229, 245, 247, 248, 249, 250, 251, 252, 253, 255, 260, 265, 267, 268, 269, 279, 280, 286, 291, 342, 364, 374, 375, 377, 381, 383, 418

Malware Detection 40, 118, 249, 250, 251, 252, 265, 267, 268, 269

N

Neptune Security 337, 338, 339, 340, 346, 347, 349, 352, 353

Network Management 129, 130, 142, 309, 310, 311, 312, 313, 315, 316, 317, 318, 319, 321, 322, 323, 324, 327, 328, 329, 331, 332, 333, 334, 335, 336

Networks 22, 26, 27, 32, 37, 43, 44, 46, 53, 74, 77, 78, 79, 81, 83, 86, 87, 88, 94, 95, 96, 99, 105, 115, 116, 117, 118, 123, 124, 125, 126, 127, 128, 129, 130, 131, 132, 133, 134, 135, 136, 137, 139, 140, 141, 142, 143, 144, 145, 146, 151, 152, 173, 174, 198, 199, 200, 208, 209, 212, 216, 218, 221, 226, 227, 228, 230, 231, 232, 234, 242, 243, 244, 250, 271, 272, 278, 279, 280, 281, 282, 283, 284, 285, 291, 292, 297, 299, 301, 302, 304, 306, 308, 310, 311, 312, 313,

317, 318, 319, 320, 321, 325, 327, 329, 331, 332, 333, 334, 335, 355, 356, 357, 359, 360, 363, 366, 367, 368, 371, 374, 376, 383, 384, 386, 387, 388, 389, 390, 392, 394, 395, 396, 397, 400, 404, 405, 409, 413, 414, 416, 417, 421, 429, 430, 431, 432

Network Security 49, 63, 88, 109, 120, 130, 136, 140, 145, 176, 225, 226, 228, 242, 243, 244, 279, 282, 297, 309, 319, 330, 333, 357, 358, 377, 388, 414, 416, 418, 419, 423, 424, 425, 426, 428, 429, 431

O

Ontology 1, 2, 3, 4, 5, 7, 9, 10, 12, 13, 14, 16, 17, 18, 19, 290, 308

Optuna 175, 176, 178, 181, 184, 194, 201

P

Packet Inspection 225, 226, 227, 233, 234

Packet Tracer 232, 233, 243

Particle Swarm Optimization 173, 176, 177, 178, 180, 183, 191, 200, 303

Password Sniffing 225, 226, 227, 237

PDF 47, 82, 85, 86, 114, 245, 246, 247, 248, 249, 250, 251, 252, 253, 254, 255, 265, 266, 267, 268

Phishing Email Detection 147, 150, 151, 152, 153, 154, 159, 161, 162, 164, 165, 166, 168, 169, 171, 172

Privacy Concerns 7, 16, 39, 79, 129, 130, 338, 339, 340, 343, 377

Protocols 3, 24, 47, 53, 54, 68, 71, 76, 84, 85, 86, 87, 93, 109, 111, 128, 132, 199, 206, 225, 226, 228, 230, 231, 232, 233, 237, 244, 279, 280, 283, 284, 294, 295, 298, 300, 304, 311, 312, 320, 322, 325, 327, 333, 341, 345, 346, 359, 360, 363, 364, 368, 374, 376, 377, 382, 389, 392

R

Random Forest 109, 111, 151, 152, 153,
159, 161, 162, 167, 168, 169, 175,
176, 177, 181, 184, 194, 195, 245,
252, 258, 260, 264, 267, 291, 417, 418
Ransomware 24, 25, 26, 38, 40, 42, 51,
103, 281, 291, 342, 374

S

SDN Controllers 312, 313, 323, 324, 325,
329, 330, 332, 334, 335, 336
Secure Protocols 226, 345
Security 1, 3, 4, 7, 9, 18, 19, 21, 22, 23,
24, 25, 27, 28, 29, 37, 38, 39, 40, 41,
42, 43, 44, 46, 47, 48, 49, 50, 53, 54,
55, 56, 57, 58, 60, 62, 63, 65, 66, 67,
68, 69, 70, 71, 72, 73, 74, 75, 76, 77,
78, 79, 80, 81, 82, 83, 84, 85, 86, 87,
88, 90, 91, 92, 93, 94, 95, 96, 97, 98,
99, 100, 101, 103, 104, 105, 106, 107,
108, 109, 110, 111, 112, 113, 114,
115, 116, 117, 118, 119, 120, 121,
123, 125, 126, 127, 128, 129, 130,
131, 132, 133, 134, 135, 136, 137,
138, 139, 140, 141, 142, 143, 144,
145, 146, 148, 150, 158, 165, 171,
172, 173, 176, 177, 198, 199, 203,
206, 208, 210, 211, 213, 214, 215,
217, 218, 222, 225, 226, 227, 228,
229, 230, 231, 232, 233, 237, 242,
243, 244, 245, 247, 248, 267, 268,
269, 271, 272, 273, 274, 275, 278,
279, 280, 281, 282, 283, 284, 285,
286, 288, 289, 290, 291, 292, 293,
294, 295, 296, 297, 298, 299, 300,
301, 302, 303, 304, 305, 306, 307,
308, 309, 310, 314, 315, 316, 319,
321, 322, 323, 324, 328, 329, 330,
331, 332, 333, 334, 335, 337, 338,
339, 340, 341, 342, 343, 344, 345,
346, 347, 348, 349, 350, 351, 352,
353, 354, 355, 356, 357, 358, 359,
360, 361, 362, 363, 364, 365, 368,
369, 370, 374, 375, 376, 377, 378,
379, 380, 381, 382, 383, 384, 385,
386, 387, 388, 389, 390, 391, 392,
393, 394, 395, 397, 398, 399, 402,
405, 408, 409, 410, 411, 414, 415,
416, 417, 418, 419, 423, 424, 425,
426, 428, 429, 430, 431, 432
Security Architecture 379
Semantic Web 1, 17
Sensor Nodes 414
Smart Contract 62, 70, 77, 78, 82, 83, 211,
213, 296, 394, 395, 396, 398, 402, 403,
404, 405, 406, 407
Software Defined Networks 334, 335
Solidity 394, 395, 396, 399, 403, 404, 407

T

Technology 13, 23, 24, 26, 32, 35, 39, 40,
46, 49, 50, 51, 55, 56, 57, 58, 60, 62,
64, 65, 66, 67, 69, 70, 72, 73, 74, 75,
76, 78, 79, 81, 82, 83, 84, 85, 86, 87,
88, 89, 91, 98, 110, 113, 116, 117,
123, 124, 126, 131, 132, 134, 135,
136, 139, 142, 143, 144, 145, 200,
201, 205, 206, 208, 209, 211, 212,
213, 214, 215, 216, 217, 218, 219,
220, 221, 222, 223, 228, 231, 232,
243, 244, 268, 271, 272, 274, 276,
277, 278, 279, 283, 285, 286, 296,
297, 299, 301, 303, 304, 305, 306,
307, 308, 328, 336, 338, 340, 341,
352, 355, 356, 357, 358, 359, 360,
365, 366, 368, 369, 370, 371, 372,
374, 376, 377, 379, 382, 383, 384,
387, 391, 392, 393, 394, 396, 397,
398, 399, 401, 408, 409, 410, 411,
413, 414, 415, 430
Threat Actor 68, 69, 70
Tweet 395, 396, 400, 402, 403, 404, 407

W

WSN 84, 279, 289, 414, 415, 430